THE GHOST IN THE LITTLE HOUSE

Missouri Biography Series

William E. Foley, Editor

THE GHOST IN THE LITTLE HOUSE

A Life of
Rose Wilder Lane

WILLIAM HOLTZ

University of Missouri Press
Columbia   London

5 4 3 2   97 96 95 94 93

Library of Congress Cataloging-in-Publication Data

Holtz, William V.
    The ghost in the little house : a life of Rose Wilder Lane /
William Holtz.
        p.   cm.
    Includes bibliographical references and index.
    ISBN 0–8262–0887–8
    1. Lane, Rose Wilder, 1886-1968. 2. Authors, American—20th
century—Biography. I. Title.
    PS3523.A553Z69   1993
    813'.52—dc20
    [B]   92–46883
                                                            CIP

∞™ This paper meets the minimum requirements of
the American National Standard for Permanence of Paper
for Printed Library Materials, Z39.48, 1984.

Designer: Danah Coester
Typesetter: Connell Zeko Type and Graphics
Printer and binder: Thomson-Shore, Inc.
Typefaces: Aldous Vertical, Gill Sans, Old Fashion Script, Palatino

for Lora,

who has with patience

and good humor

long tolerated my interest

in this other woman

*The myth of the Wandering Jew
is really the expression of
the human heart's desire.
Immortality is a poor compromise. . . .*

Rose Wilder Lane

ONTENTS

$\mathscr{A}$CKNOWLEDGMENTS

y primary obligation is to Roger MacBride, heir of Rose Wilder Lane, who first preserved her papers, then collected her letters wherever he could, and then gave me access to this material and aided my work in many ways. William T. Anderson, who knows more about the Wilder-Lane family than anyone, has been generous in answering my questions and sharing his experience. Norma Lee Browning has offered her recollections of Lane and has advised me in my writing, as have John Turner, Susan Ford Hammaker, and Ruth Levine. Each of these has read substantial portions or versions of my manuscript, as have Tom Quirk and Antonia Young. Time to write was provided by a research leave supported by the Research Council of the University of Missouri–Columbia and by a fellowship from the National Endowment for the Humanities.

Researchers are at the mercy of librarians, and among the many who have helped me I must mention particularly Dwight M. Miller of the Herbert Hoover Presidential Library; Carolyn A. Davis of the George Arents Research Library of Syracuse University; Rudolph A. Clemen, Jr., of the American Red Cross Archives; Kenneth W. Duckett of the University of Oregon Library; and Diana Haskell of the Newberry Library.

The following have helped me in ways large and small: H. Porter Abbott, Douglas A. Bakken, Martha Banta, Edzard Baumann, Millicent Bell, Daniel P. Bierman, Virginia P. Boyd, Helen Dore Boylston, Elaine Bradford, Harold F. Breimyer, Mary G. Cappiello, Ethel Cooley, Paul Cooley, Sister Doretta Cornell, James Curtis, Susan Denny, Joseph M. Ditta, Delmer J. Dooley, Ellen S. Dunlap, Sheryl Edgerly, Mr. and Mrs. Sidney Feld, Anita Claire Fellman, Chester Elmore, Nora Fennell, Ruth Freeman, Vivian Glover, Susan Guerrero, Richard Hocks, Mary Paxton Keeley, Marilynn Keil, Linda Kerber, Alice Lambertson, Jackson Lears, Irene Lichty LeCount, Don Levine, Isaac Don Levine, Cynthia Lowry, Doris Lyman, Fern McClanahan, Dorothy B. McNeely, Paula L. Mac-Neill, Ellen Gray Massey, Rosa Ann Moore, George H. Nash, Jane Northshield, Catherine N. Parke, Catherine N. Parke, Sr., Joye Patterson, Carolyn Perry, Connie Reece, Sarah Riddick, Carrie Rogers, Walter B. Rideout, Bruce Rosenberg, Robert Sattlemeyer, Marci Schramm, Aubrey Sherwood, Donald Soucy, Greg Stratman, Lynne Stuart, Kathleen Sullivan, Lowell Thomas, Al Turner, Lucille Morris Upton, Carl Watner, and Donald Zochert.

Special thanks are owed to the staff of the Laura Ingalls Wilder Home and Museum in Mansfield, Missouri; to the staff of the Laura Ingalls Wilder Memorial Society of De Smet, South Dakota; and to the staff of the University of Missouri Press—particularly to Clair Willcox for his skill in converting my manuscript into a book.

Quotations from the letters of Charmian London and Eliza Shepard are used with the permission of I. Milo Shepard.

The photographs in this volume appear courtesy of the following organizations:

Herbert Hoover Presidential Library, West Branch, Iowa: pages 204; 205; 206; 208; 209; 211, bottom; 212; 213, bottom left and right; 214, top

Laura Ingalls Wilder Memorial Society, De Smet, South Dakota, and South Dakota State Historical Society, Pierre, South Dakota: page 207, top

Laura Ingalls Wilder–Rose Wilder Lane Museum and Home, Mansfield, Missouri: pages 203; 207, bottom; 210, bottom; 214, bottom; 215, bottom

Special Collections, Syracuse University Library, and Estate of Dorothy Thompson: page 211, top

BIBLIOGRAPHICAL NOTE

My narrative of Lane's life draws on many documents, and to reduce the clutter of note numbers upon the page I have often collected all references into one note for a paragraph or series of paragraphs. In the text, my ellipses are represented by spaced periods. Ellipses in the original material are represented by unspaced periods. I have silently corrected misspellings and lapses in punctuation in a few occasions.

For the location of my sources, see the remarks preceding the notes at the back of this volume.

THE
GHOST IN
THE LITTLE
HOUSE

PROLOGUE
MOTHER AND DAUGHTER

For we think back through our mothers if we are women.
Virginia Woolf, *A Room of One's Own*

Virginia Woolf, who furnishes me the introductory epigraph, offers also my initial justification for a biography of a woman whose name few readers will recognize. "Is not anyone," Woolf wrote of the genre, "Is not anyone who has lived a life, and left a record of that life, worthy of biography—the failures as well as the successes, the humble as well as the illustrious?" Her answer, clearly, is yes. And perhaps even more apropos, she continues, "And what is greatness? And what smallness?"[1]

What indeed? For to begin the life of the obscure Rose Wilder Lane is to confront immediately the problem that her more famous mother presents. In the books that bear her name, Laura Ingalls Wilder has left a widely known account of her early life; the daughter has left her own record of a life lived, but mainly in private diaries and letters and in ephemeral publications. In the public realm, she stands as a good writer but not a great one, an impassioned thinker but not profound; and for much of her life she adopted a posture of determined ordinariness. "I'm a plump, Middle-western, middle-class, middle-aged woman," she once declared, wondering why anyone wanted to interview writers of fiction; and her later years were spent in assiduously promoting her mother's reputation while fending off inquiries into her own life.[2] Thus the daughter's claim to our attention is mediated, if not obliterated, by her mother's renown; she appears only marginally and late in her mother's last novel; and the accomplishments of her own career have largely failed to outlive her. The problem of the biographer is to retrieve from obscurity the outlines and then the substance of that buried life, which is ultimately to displace the great shadow of the mother's fame and to let the contours of another life shine through. A second task, perhaps more difficult, is to measure the weight of the mother's life on her daughter's career. And equally difficult is a third task that rounds the circle of responsibility: to assess the daughter's share of the mother's renown. The result, I trust, will be a significant realignment of the great to the small in these lives so intertwined.

Although I did not know it at the time, this book had its beginning in 1972, when my wife and I began to read *Little House in the Big Woods* to our daughters. The appeal of the book was immediate, and we went on to other books by Laura Ingalls Wilder. They were that rare accomplishment in children's literature, books for children that could at the same time hold an adult's interest; and we found vivid and persuasive their images of family devotion, disciplined hard work, and optimistic struggle against adversity. We soon learned that the Laura Ingalls Wilder Museum and Home was located near us in Missouri; and a visit to Rocky Ridge Farm with its collection of Wilder memorabilia put us on the meeting ground of history, fiction, and myth: the substantial farm home, where the writer had lived for more than sixty years, seemed a fitting culmination to the series of abandoned homes in her books about her childhood; and the family items, the treasured household gods from the books themselves, cast a presence from the fictionalized past over the whole.

As literary scholar, I found myself more and more interested in the configuration of an entire set of circumstances. The Little House books had found a receptive audience from their beginning in 1932, and each successive volume had increased the number of devoted readers—children and adults. The books had quickly achieved the status of children's classics, and Laura Ingalls Wilder had become something of a celebrity in the small world of children's authors. And something of a curiosity, if not a phenomenon. In her sixties before her books appeared, and with no previous literary distinction before this sudden efflorescence, she struck the imagination as a literary Grandma Moses, an untutored talent springing to life after years of obscurity in the Missouri Ozarks. The books themselves were in form and technique clearly fiction, yet the parallels with the author's life were so explicit and so extensive as to blur the line between history and fiction and to stand on a biographical presumption. The story told, of Laura Ingalls from childhood to marriage, was, however, presented for the most part with such a high degree of literary finish—in pacing, balance, structure, characterization, dialogue, dramatic impact, all within the confines of a deceptively simple style and point-of-view—as to achieve a portrait of a fictional character and a realized world of singular power. The impression of the author Laura Ingalls Wilder as a naive genius was very strong, while the fictional Laura blended with the historical author in an image of mythic dimensions.

This was about the time that "Little House on the Prairie" emerged on the television screens of the nation and lodged a version of Laura Ingalls Wilder and her family in the larger popular consciousness. Piqued by the inauthentic adaptation of the screenwriters, I became concerned with the historical authenticity of the books themselves. In one aspect, this concern led me to visit the locales of the various books, from the wooded hills of Wisconsin to the prairies of Kansas and South Dakota, where in each place I found local memorials, museums, and festivals testifying to the continuing interest in these books. In another aspect, I turned my attention to the history of the westward movement of the American frontier, in which I found the great national saga of which the Wilder stories are an episode.

||

The historical reality that underlay the story of Laura Ingalls Wilder was a series of removes from various marginal or failed farms and homesteads in a meandering, westerly line from Wisconsin across Iowa, Missouri, Kansas, and Minnesota to Dakota Territory before that territory became two states.[3] From the first to the last of these homes—from Lake Pepin, Wisconsin, to De Smet, South Dakota—is about three hundred miles. It is an easy day's journey by automobile if you are a literary tourist seeking shrines; the loop to Kansas and return that the books demand is a separate trip in itself. But to traverse even this easy distance with an eye to the changing landscape is to discover that the line of the Ingalls family's westward progress intersects one of the major natural barriers of our continent.

The route runs along secondary roads for the most part, rising and falling with the lay of the land and curving through town after small town. Here roads still follow the line of least resistance; road and town accommodate themselves to the land; and if you are accustomed to freeway travel you must slow down and watch your way, forcibly reminded of what a great part of our country lies apart from the cities and the four-lane ribbons of concrete that connect them. The rolling farmlands of western Wisconsin are still dotted with small woodlots and shaded farmyards, memorials of the great hardwood stands that once covered much of our Midwest—the Big Woods that would name the first of the Little House books. A few miles back into the countryside from Lake Pepin—a great bulge in the upper Mississippi—is the site of the first Little House; a recent reconstruction of that tiny log cabin marks the spot on a small knoll overlooking mainly cleared land. The lush cultivated fields that have been carved out of the forests support a varied agriculture that testifies to ample rainfall.

Little changes immediately as you cross the Mississippi River and enter Minnesota, but halfway across that state the land gradually flattens into the prairie contours of the western counties. Trees are fewer, and more obviously the result of deliberate cultivation in city streets and farmyards; the natural growth becomes mostly scrub willow and brush along stream and riverbanks. Here you can seek out the site of the dugout home on the banks of Plum Creek and find the grassy depression on that small stream that still remains. But the next book beckons further westward, and by the time you cross the state line into South Dakota, it is clearly a different world. An occasional tree is a landmark; more often it is a grain elevator that rises from the horizon. But what really strikes the eye is the unvaried sameness, as an open land faces up to a great arching sky that drops evenly all around to distant horizons. Sun and wind possess the landscape as by ancient right; in summer a dry heat bakes the earth and in winter the Arctic cold sweeps in unimpeded from across far Canada. It is, for most travelers, a less comforting landscape than Wisconsin's, more challenging to live in.

Sixty miles into South Dakota you come to De Smet. You are here, as the town's welcoming signboard reminds you, because this is the original Little Town on the Prairie, memorialized by Laura Ingalls Wilder in five of her books. You visit the Surveyors' House, and the last home of Pa and Ma Ingalls, and probably you visit the site of Pa's homestead claim, where the cottonwood trees he planted still stand. You can drive out to the little cemetery on the hillside where Pa and Ma rest, and a short distance north of town to the site of Laura and Almanzo's homestead, where nothing remains to hold the eye save a small state historical marker indicating the birthplace of Rose Wilder Lane. Back in the town, which is little larger today than it was at the turn of the century, you might decide to stay for the pageant the townspeople put on in the summer season. And, as many travelers do, you might casually wonder how anyone could ever live here.

Laura Ingalls Wilder tried and failed. In De Smet you can almost straddle the barrier that her story encountered and that finally shifted her life far south to the Missouri Ozarks. It is a barrier none the less real for being occasional and merely statistical. On the eastern side, shading off toward Minnesota and Wisconsin, rainfall will average twenty inches or more over the long measure of time; on the west, the average will be less. The line divides our continent roughly at the ninety-eighth meridian, separating the humid eastern woodlands from the arid Great Plains. Vegetation and wildlife maps follow the curve of this line, marking the adaptive differences in the natural world; it separated the plains Indians from their eastern counterparts; but the Wilders could know it only by the symptomatic disasters along its verge. To view the progress of the young Laura Ingalls and her family from Wisconsin to Dakota from this vantage point is to see their meandering across the transitional zone between the forest and the plains as a failed attempt to farm the plains by methods that had worked for centuries in the more receptive climate of the East and Midwest.[4]

Her family, as well as her husband's, were among those nineteenth-century farmers who migrated from the eastern seaboard into the more fertile lands of the opening Midwest. New York state and Connecticut were the homes of her parents' parents and of her husband's also; but by the 1850s the parents of Laura Ingalls had arrived in southern Wisconsin, where they were married in 1860. The family of Almanzo Wilder left upstate New York a little later, settling in southern Minnesota about 1870. The mode of life that sustained both families was the mixed agriculture of the small family farm. As practiced since the first settlements, such a life depended on a few fields cleared of trees but surrounded by an ample forest. Regular and sufficient rainfall would permit subsistence crops, some livestock, and occasional surpluses for cash sales, while the remaining forests provided game, fuel, and timber for building. On such a land a man with an axe, a gun, and a plow could eke out an existence for his family; and with hard work and good luck another generation might expand a marginal holding into a large and prosperous farm. Certainly this is the way of life in Laura Ingalls Wilder's account of her earliest memories in *Little House in the Big Woods* and her matching account of her husband's childhood in *Farmer Boy*.

What brought Laura Ingalls and Almanzo Wilder together, and brought them to test their inherited way of life against a new and inhospitable land was, first, the Homestead Act of 1861 and, second, the opening of the Dakota Territory by the railroad in the 1880s. The Homestead Act, which promised any settler a free title to 160 acres of government land if he grew crops and lived on it for five years, was conceived largely on the basis of experience in the eastern woodlands; but it came into effect only after those lands had been mostly settled. What remained was the prairie, which had already been passed over as the westward movement had leapfrogged on to the more promising lands of Oregon in the 1840s and 1850s. The last frontier remaining to be settled lay just to the west of the Ingalls and the Wilders, and Laura and Almanzo would be among the first wave of settlers to try their luck in this new land.

Dakota had become a territory in 1861 and would not become the present two states until 1889. Large-scale settlement did not begin until the "Dakota Boom" of 1878–1885. According to Laura Ingalls Wilder's account in *On the Banks of Plum Creek*, her family was drawn from Walnut Grove in southern Minnesota into what is now South Dakota when relatives offered her father a bookkeeper's job with a railroad contractor. The railroad's progress across the territory was, of course, instrumental in opening new lands to homesteading, and the Ingalls family would be among the first to seize the opportunity. The end of one season's work left them at the tiny town of De Smet, where Charles Ingalls filed a claim nearby. Young Almanzo Wilder in the meantime had come of age on his parents' new farm near Spring Valley, Minnesota. In 1879, he was twenty-two years old and in that year he had preceded the Ingalls family to De Smet and had taken up a claim north of the town.

His courtship of Laura Ingalls and their subsequent marriage is told in a charming version in the last two books Laura Ingalls Wilder published in her lifetime, *Little Town on the Prairie* and *These Happy Golden Years*. Almanzo (or Manly, as he was often called) is a skilled, heroic, and laconic young horseman and farmer; Laura is a hard-working, no-nonsense heroine; and together the sturdy and optimistic lovers—married in 1885 when Laura was eighteen—set out full of faith and hope to make their life together on Almanzo's homestead. The romantic narrative, however, promises a fulfillment that the realities of history and geography would not permit. A series of disasters made their early years a chronicle of misery and failure that would finally drive them from the plains.

They began with considerable assets. Almanzo had "proved up" on his original 160-acre claim and had filed on an additional "Tree Claim," which, under a law supplementing the Homestead Act, would become his if he planted it to trees and raised them successfully. He had built a small house for his new bride, and they had horses and a cow. But what they did not realize was that they—and many other settlers—had come too far into the dry zone of the West to farm successfully in the ways they had learned farther east. In the early years of the Dakota Boom, settlers had profited from a series of unusually wet growing seasons; but as the young Wilders began their life together, the statistical reality asserted itself in a series of drought years. Almanzo tried to improve his chances by planting more acres and buying improved equipment, but the interest rates on his borrowed money were ruinous, and more failed crops and low prices for what he could bring to market left him further behind. Problems like his, compounded across the land, would shortly lead to the Panic of 1893, which forced the Wilders and many others out of Dakota for good.[5]

The tracing of personal history through the original series of novels does not proceed this far, however. Rather, the last in the series is a posthumous volume published as *The First Four Years*. It was in considering this posthumous volume that I began to understand the source of the special power of the earlier books. *The First Four Years* is a narrative of unrelieved disaster that marks the failure of an implicit promise of success and security in the earlier volumes. For although a darkening line of pain runs through these earlier books, it is never disabling. On the one hand, the narrative surface is a litany of back-breaking labor, failed hopes, pain, disease, and disaster. On the other, all pain is absorbed and diffused in the glow of family affection and an irrepressible optimism. Only the most determined faith can support a burden so heavy; and the roots must run to the deepest source—as when the grasshopper swarm that destroys the crops becomes a reenactment of the biblical plague of locusts, a trial that must be endured before "the good people" are led to "a land flowing with milk and honey." "Oh, where is that, Ma?" Laura's sister asks. Ma says, "Well, your Pa thinks it will be right here in Minnesota."[6]

Once the human drama of the Wilder books is seen as embedded in a larger drama that repeats itself through history, we are in the realm of myth. Myths cannot survive undisguised in our skeptical age; in our literature, however, we can discover them shrouded beneath an ostensible history; and although the Wilder books are, in style and as individual works, realistic novels, the unifying structure of the series is that of a romance that tends toward myth. What poses as autobiography and history actually becomes an archetypal story with roots deep in American experience and deeper still in ancient anxieties concerning human fecundity and the nourishing land. In its commitment to authenticity, however, it confronts finally some facts too obdurate to be assimilated to its shaping purpose. The autobiography can proceed only as far as the myth will carry it.

The myth is the familiar one that identifies America as a new Eden, the Garden of the World, a version of the Promised Land wherein fallen man will achieve virtue by hard labor, redeeming himself as he redeems the land from the wilderness.[7] Within this framework develops the archetypal romantic story of the young lovers whose union marks the triumphant end of struggle and the establishment of a fruitful order on the land. The Wilder books demonstrate, on the one hand, a radically pure commitment to this optimistic vision and, on the other, a gathering test of its premises against the historical reality that it must assimilate. In these children's books that carry their heroine to the verge of maturity but fail to allow her to enter it, we can find a figurative tracing of a significant strand of American experience.

But in *The First Four Years* the leavening of history by myth fails; the unremitting series of setbacks that actual history provided the Wilders sorts ill with the forced optimism of each fictionalized episode and of the book's concluding vision. It is, in many ways, an adult world, not a child's or adolescent's; the security afforded by parental strength and wisdom has vanished; but vanished also is the sense of a larger order that ratifies their struggle. The problem that the book does not face is to create a credible adult—or mature—version of the mythic vision sustaining the books that bring their heroine to the verge of maturity. Instead, in a strangely flat and undramatic narrative, *The First Four Years* opposes a merely reflexive—and unreflective—optimism to a story that slides inevitably toward crashing disaster. The art of the book, finally, does not persuade. And it does not persuade because it is the only book by Laura

Ingalls Wilder that did not pass under the shaping hand of Rose Wilder Lane.

IV

Into the darkening world of this last novel Rose Wilder Lane was born on December 5, 1886. The radical shift in my interest in the story of her family came when I gained access to the family papers left at her death. My wife and I spent a week in Charlottesville, Virginia, sorting through boxes of letters, diaries, and manuscripts, most of them belonging to daughter Rose.[8] As I picked my way through this collection of papers I began to hear a voice and a story. The voice at its best was vigorous, confident, and winning—and at times miserable and despairing, at others ruthlessly angry. Always it was interesting. The story was a complex one, with many gaps and obscurities, ranging from the Ozarks to Baghdad and from California to Vietnam; but it revealed a life lived energetically and passionately, in pursuit often of ill-defined goals, but repeating a flight from and return to Rocky Ridge Farm and the mother who presided there. The story of the writing of the Little House books would turn out to be but one episode in the larger account of the career of Rose Wilder Lane.

She was, I found, a woman of exceptional talents, and a personality in the deepest sense—a person toward whom no one could remain indifferent. She had above all else the gift of eloquence, followed in almost equal measure by intelligence, wit, and charm. Everyone I have interviewed who knew her testifies that she was a brilliant conversationalist and a compelling raconteur, her fine blue eyes flashing as she pursued an idea or a story to its furthest reaches and beyond. "I have known many good story tellers and sat up all night listening to their tales and telling mine, and of them all I think Rose was the most delightful," noted Floyd Dell, who had known her for fifty years.[9] Some echo of this eloquence is preserved in her letters, which I believe are among the best written in our century. In them, language comes so alive with the force of personality that she is almost incapable of writing a dull line.

She had also a large endowment of energy and ambition. With such gifts there was little she might not have done; and there was much she did achieve; but for many years her abilities were yoked to shifting purposes that she always came to recognize as superficial, never quite in touch with some deeper hunger of the imagination. Helen Boylston, who knew her as well as any of her friends, was deep in senility when I found her, but from the broken music of her recollections emerged a momentary, bell-like note of certainty before confusion claimed her thoughts again: "Rose always wanted *more* than she had. . . ." Suggested here is an aggravated case of simple human desire, which Rose herself recognized clearly, while puzzling over her failure to connect desire with accomplishment. "My trouble," she reflected in her journal, "lies in wanting too many things, but none of them passionately."[10] Or, as I think nearer the truth, wanting all of them passionately, which is to phrase the issue at the peak of desire rather than in the trough of self-doubt, where she often turned to her journals. And so, for much of her life, a career as a professional writer of ephemeral journalism and slick-paper fiction, always in pursuit of the next check, and deviating only occasionally into work serious enough to command her full respect. The money, she always hoped, would eventually free her for . . . what?

For years, the goal was never clear. More clear was what she would be free from. Much of her emotional energy, as well as considerable time and money, were invested in trying to separate herself from a bondage to her mother, to live by values and in a style that in essential ways repudiated her upbringing; but when in middle age she did find herself focusing on an enterprise worthy of her energies, it would be nothing less than an attempt to ratify in metaphysics, history, political theory, and fiction the values that her mother's life had embodied—an adult rendition, that is, of the vision underlying the Little House books. For the moment it is enough to say that this vision was one of radical individualism—a vision deeply and essentially in the American tradition, but of a clarity and intensity seldom asserted in American life. And to the extent that she attempted to live consistently with these values, she became, finally, a genuine American original, out of step with her times but unshakably certain that the drummer she marched to took his beat from history and unchanging human nature. "The question," as she would put it, "is whether personal freedom is worth the terrible effort, the never-lifted burden and risks of self-reliance."[11]

In the pages that follow I have tried wherever possible to let Rose Wilder Lane speak for herself. The voice is distinctive and it enlivens whatever it touches. There was a time, I must confess, when I thought of abandoning the biography for this very reason: the living voice has vanished, leaving only faint echoes in the pages of her writing and in the recollections of those who knew her. With no Boswell to record her talk, this biographer was forced to acknowledge that he could not retrieve what struck most people most forcefully, the blaze of energy that was Rose Wilder Lane in conversation. Conviction, eloquence, and knowledge combined to leave an indelible imprint on those who knew her, and in some a fierce loyalty to her memory. We have noted the testimony of Floyd Dell, who met her early in her career. Roger MacBride, who knew her boy and man during the last twenty-five years of her life, typifies those still able to bear witness: she was, he recalled, full of zest and life, possessed of a range of interests unsurpassed among the people he had known. Educated at Princeton and trained in law at Harvard, MacBride found condensed in hours of talk with her another complete education that marked him for life.[12] Such a presence awaits the dramatist's re-creation (I think of Julie Harris's Emily Dickinson, or Eileen Atkins's Virginia Woolf), but it can only be suggested here.

Connected with the vanished charisma of the living presence was another problem that for a time disabled me. For the charm of her voice, even as it persists in her papers, is often that of the teller of tales, for whom truth may waver in the joy of narrative invention; and often that of the advocate, for whom facts may suffer a subtle distortion under the pressure of heart's desire. Such were her gifts as a writer both of fiction and polemic; and they were curiously suited to her special role in the development of her mother's fiction. Sometimes the record can be corrected, but often there is only one witness, not subject to interrogation. Similarly with her letters, which flowed forth almost daily from her typewriter as she poured her conversation into the keys, her correspondent firmly fixed in her mind's eye; as she herself once recognized, there was in her letters as in her life a shifting adjustment of various phases of herself to different persons, a "quality of adjustment not only in mood but almost in fact, that makes some persons accuse me of posing and lying."[13] Here, no doubt, lies the clue to the charm of the living woman; and in the documents that survive, the posing is, in fact, distinctive, and the carelessness with fact more than occasional. On the other hand, as she listened to her private voice, recording it in her journals, she could be excruciatingly honest and self-analytical. And in between are the more-or-less neutral facts of years of diary entries.

And finally there was the problem of political philosophy, complexly connected to all I have said so far. It was, simply, her consuming interest for over half of her adult life. She was an important figure in the transmission of that persistent strand of libertarian thought in our country, and many of those who respected and loved her were in fact a kind of comradeship of happy warriors against the state. "One of the few great women of our time," free-market economist Hans F. Sennholz has written me, recalling their hours of discussion into the small hours of the night.[14] Largely self-educated, always a voracious and wide-ranging reader, and by temperament an independent thinker, she took little on faith and tested ideas instinctively against her own experience; and in her thought she developed all of the strengths and liabilities of a mind driven simply by its own interests. There is a study yet to be written of Rose Wilder Lane that would follow diligently the theoretical arcana that run through her later publications and letters, but it would not be in any traditional sense a biography. Indeed, the political interest seems largely to have displaced her subjective consciousness, for the introspective journals cease as the gaze out into the world intensifies; and those who knew her in her later years have trouble reconciling the sensitive and troubled diarist with the happy warrior they knew. She herself came to consider her ideas more important than her personal life, again a proposition disabling to the biographer, who would keep alive the connection between the two. Just as the living presence dissolves into memories, personality into shifting adjustments to different correspondents, so does the final consuming interest disappear into finer and finer theoretical distinctions. I have not tried to follow all of these, contenting myself with the broad outlines that would connect her later life with her earlier. And thus a kind of subtle betrayal of my subject, finding as much if not more interest in the early years of wandering and self-doubt—her years of error—as in the years of reiterated certainties discovered on the straight and narrow path she finally attained. It is one of the ironies of this biography that even as the subject leaves the biographer often in doubt, ultimately she is not permitted to be the authority on her life.

Where is truth, where is certainty? the biographer must ask. Approximately just where it is, I finally came to realize, in our knowledge of most of the people in our lives, with whom we establish a tolerable relationship, a degree of trust appropriate to our experience with them, resting more or less short of complete confidence. I took heart from Aristotle's maxim that each subject permits its own standard of certainty; and I came to understand that biography permits not only the truth of certainty but also the truths of probability and approximation, and beyond these, the truth of character that is caught in years of personal witness, however problematical. So that while I accept my role as interpreter of this voice, making judgments where I can, I have been no less a kind of impresario, freeing the voice of my subject from the documents to make its own display of its humanity. At the extremes of left and right, political discourse tends toward caricature of its representative figures, who become deities and demons in a mythology of *ad hominem* arguments. My discourse is of a different order, less simple and more intimate, which seeks at one of these extremes not the ideological mask but the authentic pathos of a life as it was lived. My readers must make their own acquaintance.

V

Until the end she would live in the shadow of her mother's presence. In the later years they had in many ways simply grown old together, mother and daughter, the twenty years' difference between them diminishing gradually to the mere difference between the aged and the aging woman. After her father's death in 1949, Rose had come often to spend the winter months with her mother in the big house at Rocky Ridge Farm that had been home to both of them for most of their lives. But still a daughter, and now again companion and helpmate, she found herself gradually slipping into the role of nurse as well, and learning to cook for a diabetic. And finally one winter came her mother's last illness, the long, clock-ticking hours together as the aged woman grew weaker and weaker, until the February day when Rose occupied a house that was empty in a way it had never been before.

Laura Ingalls Wilder—Mama Bess, Rose had always called her—had lived three days beyond her ninetieth birthday. Rose was alone at last, heir at age seventy to a substantial estate and income from her mother's books. The year was 1957.

Once the funeral was over, Rose returned to the comfortably re-modeled farmhouse outside of Danbury, Connecticut, that had been her other home for two decades. Plans were taking shape back in Missouri for a memorial society to honor her mother's life and works. Rocky Ridge Farm had been sold on a life-lease, and Rose had repurchased the home for the society. In charge of many details were Lewis and Irene Lichty, younger friends of her mother's in her later years; and after a year and more of sorting things through in the home, the Lichtys stopped in Danbury during a vacation trip to deliver a few items that they thought Rose might like to keep. Among these was a box of manuscripts—lined school tablets, most of them, handwritten drafts of some of her mother's books. One was a short novel that had never been published: "The First Three Years and a Year of Grace." And there was a small pocket-sized notebook, an untitled journal that her mother had kept of the family exodus from Dakota Territory to Missouri more than sixty years before.

After looking them over, Rose turned them back to the Lichtys. Perhaps they could be used to make a little money for the memorial home, she suggested. "Use them however you see fit," she said. The manuscripts returned to Missouri with the Lichtys, but before they could consider what might be done with them, a telegram arrived from Rose requesting a return of the manuscripts. The Lichtys complied, and in time Rose sent back all but the two unpublished ones.[15] Clearly she had something on her mind.

It was to be a wholly characteristic enterprise, for she began almost at once to complete a portrait of her mother that had occupied her intermittently during her own lifetime. The vehicle would be an edition of her mother's journal of the trip to Missouri: *On the Way Home,* Rose would call it. In part this project required her to recover some of her own earliest memories, creating as well a selective version of her own childhood in the years before Rocky Ridge Farm.

A PRAIRIE ROSE

1

I hated everything and everybody in my childhood . . .

For seven years," she wrote, thinking back to her childhood and the year 1894, "there had been too little rain."

> The prairies were dust. Day after day, summer after summer, the scorching winds blew the dust and the sun was brassy in a yellow sky. Crop after crop failed. Again and again the barren land must be mortgaged, for taxes and food and next year's seed. The agony of hope ended when there was no harvest and no more credit, no money to pay interest and taxes; the banker took the land. Then the bank failed.

The seven years were the first seven of her own life, but her purpose now was not simply to write an autobiographical reminiscence. Rather, she was recreating herself as a child to make one last act of homage to her mother, Laura Ingalls Wilder. Rose had at hand her mother's earliest manuscript, the journal of the family's removal from South Dakota to Missouri in 1894, which she was about to offer to the world as a posthumous capstone to the series of books that had won her mother fame in her lifetime and continued renown after her death. The manuscript would be published as *On the Way Home,* and to it Rose would add her own recollections in a framing prologue and epilogue.[1]

It was familiar material to her, and a familiar voice she called up for the occasion. Both prologue and epilogue would draw on accounts of her family she had written in the 1930s; and the voice—controlled, confident and vigorous, elegantly simple but faintly declamatory—was the public one she had developed over years as a professional writer. In the prologue she touches only briefly on the events preceding that seventh year, collapsing a series of hardships and several relocations into a few vivid memories. The intent is to situate the family dilemma in the context of a national crisis that in itself appears mainly by vivid allusion.

For not only had the banks failed and the land failed, but the country seemed to have failed as well; and in the broad view, the story of the Wilders in that year was but a footnote to the great national misery following the Panic of 1893. In the years after the Civil War the nation had expanded confidently across the continent and into its new industrial

power, and in the decade of the Wilders' marriage there had been a national surge of railway and business growth that was the equivalent of
the "Dakota Boom" that had brought the Wilders into the new land. But
there was a fateful connection between climate and economics for these
prairie settlers; for just as the period of wet and prosperous farming
years came to an end, so too did the decade of national prosperity. Business everywhere was overextended; debt had grown high as confidence
begot credit; but by 1893 the nation had reached the limits of its ability
to finance expansion and a classic depression ensued. By mid–1894, national unemployment was at 20 percent, a drought was general west of
the Mississippi, and crop prices continued to fall. It would be 1897 before
anything like recovery would be in sight.[2]

Particularly hard hit were the prairie farmers, who found themselves pinched by the need for new machinery to till the new land,
droughts that robbed them of their yield, and monopoly rail-freight rates
and low prices for what they could bring to market. All of these had
combined to break the Wilders, added to the distinctly personal calamities of illness and accident; and the family hardships were felt as one
with the national collapse. "The country was ruined, the whole world
was ruined; nothing like this had ever happened before," Rose had written in an earlier account, recalling those days. The Wilders had hung on
longer than many; already by 1893, half the population of western Kansas
had moved out and 30,000 had left the Wilders' own South Dakota.[3] The
roads were filled north and south, east and west, with anxious people
seeking another start. What was the direction of hope?

From the south came a message to lift the Wilders' hearts. Acquaintances had relocated in the Missouri Ozarks and had sent back reports
and pictures—probably promotional brochures—describing the Land of
the Big Red Apple and a town named Mansfield.[4] Text and pictures apparently limned a new Eden, and on such evidence the Wilders decided
to leave De Smet. Another couple, the Cooleys, would accompany them,
with two boys near Rose's age. The Wilders' major stake in the future was
contained in a hundred-dollar bill hidden in her mother's lap-desk. Everything they owned, including a few chickens, was piled in or onto a small
covered hack; its fresh paint was a measure of their optimism. On July 17,
1894, the Wilders bade goodbye to the relatives and turned the horses
south out of De Smet.

Rose's mother began her daily log of the trip in a small memorandum book, noting the heat, the dust, the condition of the farms, the
burned crops. Six days out they crossed the mile-wide Missouri River at
Yankton. Rose looked back, she recalled, along the road as they waited
for the ferry: "As far as I could see, covered wagons stood one beyond
another in a long, long line. Behind them and over them, high over half
the sky, a yellow wave of dust was curling and coming. My mother said to

me, 'That's your last sight of Dakota.'"[5] "The whole Middle West was shaken loose and moving," Rose had written in a 1935 memoir that would become the basis of this prologue to her mother's work.

> We joined long wagon trains moving south; we met hundreds of wagons going north; the roads east and west were crawling lines of families traveling under canvas, looking for work, for another foothold somewhere on the land. By the fires in the camps I heard talk about Coxey's army, 60,000 men, marching on Washington; Federal troops had been called out. The country was ruined, the whole world was ruined; nothing like this had ever happened before. There was no hope, but everyone felt the courage of despair. Next morning wagons went on to the north, from which we had been driven, and we went on toward the south, where those families had not been able to live.[6]

Six weeks and 650 miles out of De Smet they entered Mansfield, Missouri. By then, Rose's mother had compiled a sober, matter-of-fact record of petty problems, land values, and crop appraisals that contrasts starkly with the vivid drama of Rose's framing narrative. A swelling motif, however, as they turn southeast from the Kansas prairie into the Missouri Ozarks, is the mother's delight in the timbered country and flowing springs:

> We are driving along a lovely road through the woods, we are shaded by oak trees. The farther we go, the more we like this country. Parts of Nebraska and Kansas are well enough but Missouri is simply glorious. There Manly interrupted me to say, "This is beautiful country."
> The road goes up hill and down, and it is rutted and dusty and stony but every turn of the wheels changes our view of the woods and the hills. The sky seems lower here, and it is the softest blue. The distances and the valleys are blue whenever you can see them. It is a drowsy country that makes you feel wide awake and alive but somehow contented.[7]

Her account breaks off with their arrival in Mansfield, as they camp in a shaded grove and prepare to look for a new home.

In an epilogue, Rose resumes the narrative. The prologue had condensed into a few memories seven years of hardship, but the matter-of-fact style implicitly invoked the "courage of despair" that made the exodus from South Dakota a gesture of defiance at fate. The epilogue finds its own weight of pain in a final few days of heartbreak, as though fate were giving them one last shake before letting go. "Here my mother's record ends," Rose wrote. "Fifty years later I began casually to speak of our camp in those vanished woods and she stopped the words in my mouth with a fierce, 'I don't want to *think* of it!'"

Rose could think of it, but only with pain as well, as her reminiscence sinks into a fissure of pain and guilt marked by a hundred-dollar bill at one extreme and fifty cents at the other. While she and the two Cooley boys played day after day in the glory of a September woods, Rose's parents looked for the place that would be their new home. And found it—a property with a flowing spring, timber and rock to build with, and four hundred young apple trees. Rose's writing throbs with the remembered excitement of that afternoon almost seventy years before. Her mother whistles softly when she is happy; she dresses in her best clothes to go to the bank for the signing of the contract; her hair, her jewelry, her shoes and hat all glitter with beauty in the admiring gaze of the seven-year-old daughter.

But the hundred-dollar bill was missing. The child in Rose's memory shares the parents' disbelief as they search the desk item by item, consider thieves, then turn to Rose. "Had I taken it . . . to play with?"

> NO! I felt scalded. She asked, Was I sure? I hadn't just opened the desk sometime, for fun? My throat swelled shut; I shook my head, no. "Don't cry," she said automatically. I wouldn't cry, I never cried, I was angry, insulted, miserable, I was not a baby who'd play with money or open that desk for fun, I was going on eight years old. I was little, alone, and scared. My father and mother sat there, still. In the long stillness I sank slowly into nothing but terror, pure terror without cause or object, a nightmare terror.

The days following she remembered as unreal, filled with her parents' sunken hopes and her own childish hopelessness; she contemplated the day when there would be no food. And then suddenly things were all right again. The hundred-dollar bill had been found, slipped into a crack in the desk. The banker was paid and they traveled directly to the property, just a mile and a half from town, while her parents discussed a transaction so important that it embedded in the child's memory:

> From the talk over my head I learned how lucky it was that the last cent had been just enough to pay for the salt pork and cornmeal. We could make out all right now, selling wood, and do well when the apple trees were in bearing. Paying off the mortgage would be easy then. Three hundred dollars at twelve percent. . . . My mother could do the arithmetic in her head. They ought to be able to carry it if they kept their health.

The rest of Rose's epilogue is a tribute to her parents' prudence and hard work, and a celebration of their future. A life of labor would transform the wooded, rocky land into a successful farm and a comfortable, even elegant, home. But for the moment they had only a rude cabin and no cash. Their first night was interrupted by a visitor, a bony, unkempt man who walked into their circle of firelight with a tale of traveling three days without food, a family destitute and without hope. The child noted a brief, almost wordless struggle between self-interest and sympathy before her parents shared their meager pork and cornmeal with him. Her father offered him the chance to cut firewood on their land on shares. For a month or more he worked with them, a better axeman than her father, repairing his fortunes while helping to clear land and build a log barn, and then he was gone. Rose had seen what lay just the other side of her parents' last few dollars. But she had also seen how even that failure might be redeemed.

Teetering on the brink themselves, the Wilders began their climb toward prosperity with the first load of firewood that her father and the starving stranger cut and sold in the town. But even the triumphant moment when money started to flow in rather than out was marred, and over the span of years Rose recalls that she was the one to mar it. Her heart filled with the anxiety she had absorbed from her parents, she had met her father on his return; he had, he said triumphantly, sold the load for fifty cents. Eager to bear her father's good news, she found herself caught between reprimands from both father and mother:

> I set down the lantern and ran into the house to tell my mother, "Fifty cents! He sold it all for fifty cents!" Her whole face trembled and seemed to melt into softness, she sighed a long sigh. "Aren't you glad?" I exulted.
>
> "Glad? Of course I'm glad!" she snapped at me and to her self, "Oh, thanks be!"
>
> I ran out again, I pranced out, to tell my father how glad she was. And he said, with a sound of crying in his voice, "Oh, why did you tell her? I wanted to surprise her."
>
> You do such things, little things, horrible, cruel, without thinking, not meaning to. You have done it; nothing can undo it. This is a thing you can never forget.[8]

II

It is time to pause to acknowledge that as the aging Rose Wilder Lane drives this epilogue on toward a triumphant celebration of her mother's life, she has discovered a frightened and humiliated little girl as the authoritative witness. Rising up into this occasion is a different note, one from earlier explorations of her childhood—a childhood that, for many years, had been all but inaccessible to her memory. "My own experience for years," she had noted in 1931, "was that I couldn't remember what I felt in my childhood."

> The fact was that I hated everything and everybody in my childhood with such bitterness and resentment that I didn't want to remember anything about it. But . . . I discovered that it was really quite easy to begin quite gently with one little thread of an exterior

happening that I did remember, and disentangle it back to what I
felt about it, and little by little at idle times pretty near the whole
thing has come clear.[9]

A triumphant conclusion to this epilogue would cast a glow back over a
childhood that in some ways had been emotionally crippling. Hindsight
was reshaping history and completing a myth: but as we track this final
account of these years, we can invoke a background of other and sometimes darker voices that have been suppressed in this purposeful and
selective account.

An obscure record of her earliest years comes from the other of
her mother's manuscripts that the Lichtys had delivered and that Rose
had chosen to ignore.[10] *The First Four Years* records Rose's birth,[11] fifteen
months after her parents' marriage and while they still stood within
striking distance—in their own minds, at least—of prosperity and success on their farm just north of De Smet. They had made a poor crop of
wheat their first season and had lost the second year's crop to hail; and to
cover their losses they had mortgaged the homestead and—to satisfy the
lender—had moved out of the little gray home on the tree claim into the
claim shanty on the homestead. But they still had the 320 acres of land,
their youth and their health, and an optimism about the future. In a
narrative that dwells heavily on costs and hardship, the mother duly
notes the difficult pregnancy and birth and the hundred dollars for medical bills. Yet the child is named for the wild rose that dotted the summer
prairie. "A Rose in December was much rarer than a rose in June, and
must be paid for accordingly," the mother wrote years after the event, no
doubt recording a family saying that had caught the mingled joy and
chagrin in an economic metaphor.[12] Laura Ingalls Wilder was not yet
twenty years old when she became a mother.

Rose figures only marginally in the rest of this work, in which concerns other than the economic flicker only briefly. Work, money, danger,
and loss are the main themes, and the problems and joys connected with
a growing child are, like the beauty of the prairie, occasional diversions
from more pressing concerns. The child's first visit to her grandparents
occurs when she travels by horse-drawn sled on a bitter winter evening
with the temperature at fifteen below. This visit would have been to the
homestead east of De Smet memorialized in her mother's books. In the
little shanty would gather all the historical family familiar in the books:
her mother's Pa and Ma; her blind Aunt Mary, slightly older than her
mother; her Aunt Carrie, slightly younger; her Aunt Grace, a big schoolgirl scarcely of age to be an aunt, who kept an intermittent diary. "Laura
has a baby now and it is just beginning to smile, it is eight weeks old. Her
name is Rose." "Laura was over a week ago and put Rose in short dresses.
Rose is a big fat baby now but just as pretty." Shortly, however, Rose
would be taken to the frame house her grandfather had built on a side

street in De Smet. (" . . . not a very large house," Grace observed, "but beter [sic] than the shanty. It has two rooms below and one overhead.")[13] Here Rose would come while her parents fought off diphtheria; scarcely more than a year old, she would toddle from aunt to grandmother to aunt, lisping her first words and asking for her mother and father.

She would write the episode into the prologue, claiming a memory of this early trauma in her life. "For a long time I had been living with Grandpa and Grandma and the aunts in De Smet because nobody knew what would become of my father and mother."

> Only God knew. They had diff-theer-eeah; a hard word and dreadful. I did not know what it was exactly, only that it was big and black and it meant that I might never see my father and mother again.
> Then my father, man-like, would not listen to reason and stay in bed. Grandma almost scolded about that, to the aunts. Bound and determined to get out and take care of the stock, he was. And for working too hard too soon, he was "stricken." Now he would be bed-ridden all his days, and what would Laura do? With me on her hands, besides.[14]

If we search her writings for earliest memories, we come to this, and find it trivialized, the terror deflected into childish prattle and family exasperation. From her aunt's diary entry for the same event (March 5, 1888), we know that Rose was fifteen months old. How early can memory begin? The facts no doubt were learned later; the emotional tone of the recollection is probably more important, grounded in an infant's intuition of adult worry and fear and of the growing child's awareness of her status as a burden. Her mother's fictionalized version tells the details of the grim story. She herself lay gravely ill; her husband suffered less, however; and aided by his ailing brother Royal the adults nursed themselves through the sickness. Almanzo, however, forced himself back to work sooner than he should have, and a slight but debilitating stroke ensued, leaving him with intermittent paralysis of hands and feet and an awkward, shuffling gait. Later accounts reveal that he would never fully recover.

Grace's next diary entries seem to record a return to normalcy. "Rose can walk nicely now she is broad as she is long." "She is the best girl I ever saw. She can now say a good many words such as gramma and grampa and bread and butter and cracker." And diff-theer-eeah, no doubt. As her parents continued their losing struggle to make a home of their own, this crowded little frame house on a side street in De Smet would remain the center of Rose's family life until she left Dakota for good. Her grandfather's claim east of town had been rented; in time it would be sold. Her grandfather, still a hearty man in his fifties, was working mainly as a carpenter, although he had many skills.[15]

Little of this extended family life makes its way into her mother's story, however. As it moves into the summer months, the child is assimilated into the pastoral setting, sleeping in her basket in the fields while her parents work nearby; later, older, she plays innocently among the animals. Her value is acknowledged tacitly when a childless couple offer her parents their best horse in a trade for the infant Rose, while her status as a problem is underlined by her mother's next pregnancy and difficult labor, followed by the sudden death of the new infant son.[16]

Gradually, through the summer, Rose's father regained the use of his hands: new livestock was added, a new crop of wheat was put in. Rose returned from her stay in town a walking child rather than a toddling infant; and a good growing season seemed to bring recovery in sight. The wheat-crop burgeoned toward ripeness, until three days of searing heat shriveled the grains in the milk stage and left the crop worthless. The Wilders had lost their harvest for two of the three years of their marriage.

Somehow another winter was gotten through. Rose, now two, appears in her mother's novel as "an earnest, busy little girl with her picture books and letter blocks and the cat, running around the house, intent on her small affairs." Wolves threatened the livestock but passed on.[17]

Spring brought new hope and seed for a new crop. Then, just after planting, a day of incredible wind—wind strong enough to blow sheep off their feet and the seed out of the freshly plowed ground. New seed to be bought, of course, and planted and watched as spring turned into summer and the young wheat sprang from the soil. And summer brought another drought, weeks with no rain capped by a week of searing wind that left the fields brown and most of the trees on the tree claim dead. The rest of the summer is best told by Grace Ingalls in her diary:

> *August 27, 1889.* A great many things have happened since I last wrote in this book. Laura's little baby boy only a month old died a little while ago, he looked just like Manly. Rose will be three years old next december she is large for her age with golden hair and large blue eyes. Last friday Manly's house caught on fire and burned to the ground. The furniture in the front room and in the bed room and pantry was saved but nothing in the kitchen where the fire started. Laura had just built a fire in their stove went into the other room and shut the door so she could sweep when the noise of the fire startled her and on opening the door she saw the roof and side of the kitchen was on fire. Help came soon but they could not save the house and only some of their old clothing was

saved they stayed down here for a while and then went to keep
house for Mr. Sheldon one of their neighbors taking a hired girl
with them.

The First Four Years covers the same period in essentially the same
detail, although the account of the difficult labor and the baby's birth
were explicit enough to be edited out of the manuscript when it was
published as a children's book. More interesting is the story of the fire. In
the only time she alluded to it, in an autobiographical magazine article,
Rose would assign the blame for the fire to herself, a child not yet three,
trying to help by starting the cookstove. She presents it as a pivotal
instant, when a mantle of guilt for her parents' misfortunes descended
upon her. "I quite well remember watching the house burn, with everything we owned in the world, and knowing I had done it."[18] Can this be
an authentic memory, or are we perhaps one stage beyond her problematical recollection of the diphtheria episode? It is hard to imagine the
child taking such blame to herself without cause, and certainly her
mother might have tried to hide the child's guilt from the rest of the
family. But clearly the young Wilders were at their rope's end, and some
measure of responsibility for the calamity had lodged in the child's consciousness. Her father built a tar-paper shanty near the ruins of the earlier house, and there were some plans to redeem the failed tree claim by a
cash payment to the government. Her mother's fictional version of the
family saga ends here, with an asserted optimism about the future that
nothing in the past four years could justify:

> The incurable optimism of the farmer who throws his seed on the
> ground every spring, betting it and his time against the elements,
> seemed inextricably to blend with the creed of her pioneer fore-
> fathers that "it is better farther on"—only instead of farther on in
> space, it was farther on in time, over the horizon of the years ahead
> instead of the far horizon of the west.[19]

Only in recent years have we been able to grasp how early the
emotional tonality of a family can mark a child; and it is hard to believe
that the problems that the parents had faced, and would continue to face,
could not leave them with an anxiety just short of despair, or that their
child would not take to herself a gnawing sense of disaster from the
gathering series of events that marred their lives. That at some point she
also took to herself a burden of vague guilt also seems clear. Not that the
Wilders ever thought of themselves as defeated or deliberately blamed
their child for their hard times. Indeed, Rose often spoke of her parents'
gaiety in the face of their troubles. Nothing is clearer in *The First Four Years*
than a kind of root optimism that flies in the face of reality. Compounded
of Christian faith and an American sense of manifest destiny, it sustained
the Wilders as it had their parents and as it would Rose herself. But such a

faith is the bedrock that forms and hardens under the pressure of specific and daily anxieties, and to become firm in it is also to have it tested by adversity. The mother's account of these calamitous early years is suffused by a relentless cheer that is the reflex of feelings powerfully repressed. Among those repressed feelings, no doubt, was that ambiguous counter to parental love, the latent resentment of the drag of the child upon energy and resources. Every parent feels it; in the best of circumstances it can emerge in subtle ways; and in times of stress it can run dangerously close to the surface. Doubtless every child senses it at times, and finds a greater or lesser measure of guilt in a normal progress toward maturity and independence. But Rose, precocious in many ways, felt it early and keenly in the complex relationship she developed with her mother. In these years of her infancy Rose was learning from her mother both the pain of broken hopes and the strength to deal with it; but she was also learning, in ways we can only guess at, to carry a burden she would never quite be able to put down. Somewhere in these years was forged an ambiguous filial emotion grounded in love and unspecified guilt, respect and unspecified inadequacy, honor and unspecified obligation. More of this later.

The simple truth of the family's failure by this time, however, is marked by Grace's terse diary entry for November 17, 1889: "Laura was down last Saturday. They expect to go to Spring Valley next spring. I am so sorry." By this time, apparently, the bank had claimed the farm.

IV

Spring Valley lay back in eastern Minnesota, almost as far back east as the Wisconsin cabin where Laura Ingalls had been born. And it was untouched, apparently, by drought. Doubtless it was a sad come-down for Almanzo, to depend again on his father's bounty, but here he and his wife and daughter could recuperate and lay their plans for a new future. Rose was three by the time of this removal, arriving, perhaps, just at the edge of credible continuous memory, as distinct from the discrete recollections, vague impressions, and reconstructions that seem to reach back further.

The trip to Spring Valley was curiously fixed in her mind, in fact, by its association with one of these privileged moments, a dream that she claimed specifically as her earliest clear memory. She dated it from the Christmas following her second birthday—age two years and twenty days. The dream involved a floating entry from on high into a dazzlingly white walled city between green mountains and an intensely blue sea. It was a dream that recurred, she said, many times until she was thirty. Always the details were the same: she walked the city, entering a marketplace filled with strangely dressed, beautiful people. In the market-place was a fountain, a statue of a man, and, at the end of a colonnade, a painting of a beautiful woman enclosing in her arms five children leaning against her legs. And nearby, a huge yellow cat asleep on a chair. By some association, perhaps from overheard conversations between her parents, the splashing water in the fountain had come to say *Minnesota, Minnesota:*

> I remember my eagerness to reach that place again, the place we
> were going to in the covered wagon . . . the place that I thought of
> as Minnesota. . . . I remember riding in the covered wagon, say-
> ing over and over again, endlessly in endless contentment, for-
> ever those lovely syllables, Min-ne-so-ta, Min-ne-so-ta, until my
> mother cried out, "For pity's sake! Be *quiet.*"[20]

The unique significance of this dream will be noted later, but for the moment we might merely observe that it is a vision that assimilates to itself beauty, order, a comely life, and maternal affection—as well as a safe haven and a lavish abundance of water.

They drove a few head of stock in front of them, household goods in a wagon, her mother riding a pony. Her mother's cousin Peter Ingalls accompanied them: he was something of a benefactor, for it was he who had found them the investment in a flock of sheep that yielded almost the only cash they had earned in five years. They had sold out this flock in De Smet for five hundred dollars;[21] doubtless this covered their debts remaining from the years of failed crops and left a little over to stake against the future.

Little record remains of this stay in Spring Valley, which apparently was from May of 1890 to October of the following year.[22] It was, it seems, a period of recuperation—of health and of spirits, if not of money. They were there long enough to make friends that Rose would visit years later as an adult, and there, at age three or four, she posed for her first photo-graph, an event that became a contest of wills. "I remember the picture-taking well, was impressed by the photographer's stupid pretense that there was a little bird in the camera. The photographer also kept putting my right hand on top of the left, and I kept changing them back because I wanted my carnelian ring to show. And in the end I won out."[23]

For a year and a half, Grandfather Wilder's farmhouse was home to the displaced family. The plains had broken them; somewhere they must find another start. In March of 1891 Almanzo Wilder auctioned off eight horses and some harness, perhaps stock remaining from his De Smet farm, or perhaps the result of investments and trading during his stay in Spring Valley. But he was raising cash, it seems. He had always felt the cold of Dakota winters keenly, and he had felt it the more since his illness. A move south seemed in order, and in October the Wilders embarked on a long train ride across the nation for an experiment in living in Florida.

They shipped their household goods and one remaining team of horses. Cousin Peter again accompanied them. Rose was four years old.

Only a few details of this Florida visit can be retrieved. One of Rose's short stories based on this period suggests that her father and Cousin Peter went first by train and established a home and that Rose and her mother followed after. Land records reveal that Peter Ingalls homesteaded 160 acres near Westville in the panhandle area in 1891; he married locally in the same year. The Wilders apparently lived on or near his property for a time. Perhaps they were not ready to try the home-steading gamble again; and later references indicate that her mother found the heat oppressive; but there is more than a hint that the Wilders felt the South to be an uncomfortably alien land. In an autobiographical note, Laura Ingalls Wilder remarked that "we went to live in the piney woods of Florida, where the trees always murmur, where the butterflies are enormous, where plants that eat insects grow in moist places, and alligators inhabit the slowly moving waters of the rivers. But at the time and in that place, a Yankee woman was more of a curiosity than any of these. . . ."[24]

We hear the muffled clash of cultures. Northern in speech and man-ners, the Wilders doubtless found southern ways strange and suspect. Peter Ingalls, however, adapted better, "proving up" on his claim and living on it the rest of his life. Out of this experience, though, Rose retained uncomfortable and disquieting impressions from which would come her finest short story. In "Innocence" a small girl finds herself set down with her parents in a brooding and oppressive Florida landscape. Her uncle has married a local woman, which has strongly disturbed her mother. There are hints of sexual entrapment, of crime, of revulsion at strange folkways and barbarous dialect, of harassment by her uncle's new family, all filtered through the child's consciousness. The family leaves the South for the grandfather's farm up north—as did the Wilders, apparently, some time in 1892.[25]

V

By August 19 of that year they were back in De Smet. "Mr. and Mrs. A. J. Wilder of Westville, Florida, are visiting relatives and old friends," the *De Smet News and Leader* observed.[26] Probably they had stopped at Spring Valley on the way.

It was a time of waiting and pondering the future. They could eke out a living in the town, Rose's father at odd jobs and her mother sewing buttonholes at the local dressmaker's; but such a life led nowhere. To them, success meant owning land, living on it and working it. They had given up on Dakota; farmers still on the land were faring little better than they had. "The crops have failed year after year in this place and are likely to this year," Grace Ingalls noted in her diary for June 23, 1891. The Wilders talked of emigrating to New Zealand.[27]

Almost six now as autumn approached, Rose was rapidly growing out of infancy and into the world, such a world as a tiny town on the prairie afforded. It was in many ways a pleasant life for her, bounded by home, her grandparents' home with three aunts, the ice-cream parlor, and school. The Wilders had arrived with enough money to buy a small house, rather than the rented one Rose remembered, but doubtless authentic was her recollection of it as echoing and empty around their few possessions, most of which crowded the kitchen, the only room they really lived in. We can hear the mother attempting to ameliorate a bad situation, and the child attempting to rise to the occasion: "We were camping, my mother said; wasn't it fun. I knew she wanted me to say yes, so I did."[28] School, however, was the natural arena for her developing talents: late in life, recalling the scraps of formal education she managed to pick up, she was bemused by her own precocity in learning to read "from sheer curiosity when I was three years old" from an alphabet picture book. "So far as memory goes, I have always read." By the time she was five, she remembered, her family was taking books away from her on the theory that she would contract brain fever from too much reading. In that same year she began her formal schooling.

> I learned to write in kindergarten in the De Smet school, when I was five. . . . There was not room on the desktop to spread out the penmanship book, so I learned to write sidewise—not left to right but from me to away from me—and I still do. The Spencerian copy was at the top of each page, to be copied precisely on each of ten lines beneath it. Procrastination is the thief of time. Evil communications corrupt good manners. Sweet are the uses of adversity. . . . I wrote every line, every page, all the way through the kindergarten book and the primer book, and was taken out of school with a malady called "writer's cramp". . . . But I had read the *Primer, First Reader,* and *Second Reader,* anyway; and while convalescing, I read *Robinson Crusoe, Gulliver's Travels,* and the weekly *Inter-Ocean* after the grown-ups had finished it.[29]

When not in school, she was much in the company of her aunts and grandparents while her parents worked to earn a new stake. Here came her initiation into the craft of needlework, which would occupy her odd moments for life, under the guidance of her grandmother and her blind Aunt Mary, who taught her to knit and crochet and sew; and she watched her aunt write Braille so often as to be on the verge of learning to read it, too. Horizons were opening dimly in her mind, the first hints of an eagerness to explore experience and a determination to go her own way. In Spring Valley, she had been willing to test gravity itself, leaning backward into space from a second-floor stairway, holding fast to a doorknob, and experimentally letting go.[30] More daring now, perhaps, was another kind of willingness to experiment:

> When I was five years old, sitting one day in my grandmother's parlor in De Smet on a footstool beside her rocking chair, and helping her sew carpet rags, after a meditative silence I said dreamily, "I wish I had been there when Christ was crucified." My sincerely, deeply pious grandmother was (I now realize) deeply touched by this tender, young piety; I can recall the tone of her voice saying softly, "Why, dear?" I replied, "So I could have cursed him and been the Wandering Jew."

The story of this mythical wanderer, doomed to roam the earth until Christ's return, had long been embedded in Christian culture, and perhaps Eugene Sue's novel of that name had reached De Smet and her mother's family. But whatever its source, it was a story that had already defined something in the child's character at age five. She would understand it clearly only years later, when she could deliberately calculate the curse as a fair price for an infinitude of experience. At the moment, however, it served merely to mark a gulf between the child and the conventionally pious life around her. "I'm sure I recall the incident because of the inexplicable effect, upon my grandmother, of these candidly innocent words. It was like an earthquake, a silent one. She *said* nothing. Somehow the air sort of crashed, terrifically."[31]

There were other hints of this growing gulf, which she associated with the opening up of her mind into the world revealed by books. At the age of six or seven, she recalled, she announced that she was not going to heaven: pressed for an explanation, she said that so far as she could find out there were no books there. The story also marks her growing discomfort with her religious environment. "The hymn-singing at my grandmother's had always made me feel kind of sick," she recalled; "religious people being religious always made me uncomfortable, I always wanted to get away from that, to escape." She experimented with atheism at age six—on the way home from Sunday School with her Aunt Grace, when it began to rain. She prayed for God to hold the rain, which would spoil her dress, and it rained. The atheism she outgrew, but she dated from that incident her rebellion at being forced to go to Sunday School and church.[32]

This was her life for two years. Clearly it was not to be permanent, but the future was obscure. Her mother continued sewing buttonholes at the dressmaker's shop—twelve hours a day, six days a week, at a dollar a day. Her father continued at odd jobs; when he was called for jury duty it was a financial windfall. The young Wilders were diligently accumulating a stake to relaunch themselves into the world. When the time came, they were probably not quite as poverty-stricken as Rose's reminiscence suggests: they had, at least, some small proceeds from the sale of the little house they had been living in.[33] They had likewise some small savings. After equipping themselves for the journey, they set aside for the new home the hundred-dollar bill, the loss of which, however temporary, lay at the bottom of that fissure of remembered pain that had opened up for Rose and her mother as they recalled the end of their trip to Mansfield, Missouri. And deeper still for Rose, writing as an old woman paying tribute to the girl that had been her mother, lay the whole of that childhood that already by age seven she had learned to hate. Only the diff-theer-eeah, the hundred-dollar bill, and the fifty-cent piece rose up to confront her as she drove her reminiscence toward the moment that would justify it all.

VI

And so, finally, as Rose draws her reminiscence to a close, her parents' efforts to establish a new home implicitly become assimilated to the series of new beginnings that defines the Little House books, the writing of which lay—in a charming double perspective—in the future of this struggling family and in the past of the narrator's memory. The rude log cabin needs but a family to make it a home, and the image Rose creates is of a piece with the powerful evocations of emotional security and family warmth in the Little House books:

> Winter evenings were cozy in the cabin. The horses were warm in the little barn, the hens in the new wooden coop. Snow banked against the log walls and long icicles hung from the eaves. A good fire of hickory logs burned in the fireplace. In its heat, over a newspaper spread on the hearth, my father worked oil into the harness-straps between his oily-black hands. I sat on the floor, carefully building a house of corncobs, and my mother sat by the table, knitting needles flashing while she knitted warm woolen socks for my father and read to us from a book propped under the kerosene lamp.[34]

Rose begins school, they acquire a cow, and the new house is planned. Rose brings this exercise in memory to a close with a portrait of her mother on the verge of achieving the enduring home that had eluded her during her childhood and early marriage:

> It was springtime; the hickory trees on the hill were in young green leaves, the oak leaves were pink, and all the flinty ground underneath them was covered with one blue-purple mat of dog's-tooth violets. Along the brook the sarvice trees were blooming a misty white. The ancient white-oak was lively with dozens of young squirrels whisking into and out of their nests in the hollow branches.

My mother stood under it in her brown-sprigged white lawn
dress, her long braid hanging down her back. Below the curled
bangs her eyes were as purple-blue as the violets. It would be a
white house, she said, all built from our farm. Everything we
needed to build it was on the land: good oak beams and boards,
stones for the foundation and the fireplace. The house would have
large windows looking west across the brook, over the gentle little
valley and up the wooded hills that hid the town, to the sunset
colors in the sky. There would be a nice big porch to the north, cool
on hot summer afternoons. The kitchen would be big enough to
hold a wood stove for winter and one of the new kerosene stoves
that wouldn't heat up the place worse in the summer. Every window would be screened with mosquito netting. There would be a
well, with a pump, just outside the kitchen door; no more lugging
water from the spring. And in the parlor there would be a bookcase, no, *two* bookcases, big bookcases full of books, and a hanging lamp to read them by, in winter evenings by the fireplace.[35]

The prophetic vision goes on in more detail, shimmering in mythic
significance. We are present at an epochal moment, as a young heroine
stands at the end of a long struggle and looks confidently forward to the
future in the Promised Land. Beside her stands her daughter, whose
memory will record the moment. The epilogue ends with Laura Ingalls
Wilder whistling happily in the kitchen, looking forward to a bright future. It is with something of a jolt that we disengage ourselves from the
compelling scene in the past and recall that the writer is the remembering
child, now in her seventies as she writes—remembering, yes, but with
the novelist's shaping imagination.

OLD HOME TOWN
GROWING UP IN MANSFIELD 2

Influences: 1 to 16: no affection, poverty, inferiority.

More than a decade lay between that prophetic vision of home on the spring hillside and any kind of realization of the dream. For the moment, the Wilders were dirt poor and almost without resources. Land they had, with timber to harvest, and some apple trees years from bearing; but there was also a mortgage, and existence could only be hand-to-mouth until the land could be made to pay. Their wanderings, though, had brought them to a land they could live on: the ample wood and water of the Missouri Ozarks made possible a life much like that in upstate New York or southern Wisconsin and Minnesota—the kind of simple, mixed agriculture that had sustained their forebears but that had not been possible on the Dakota prairie.

But progress beyond mere subsistence would be painfully slow. The nation continued to linger in the depression that followed the Panic of 1893. Cash was scarce, and a deep populist sense of resentment lay across the agricultural heartland. These were the years of the "battle of the standards," the great national debate over monetary policy. "Sound" money (gold) was favored by owners and lenders, whose assets appreciated as the demand for credit grew. Alternative silver coinage (bimetallism) was favored by those who had to borrow to grow, particularly in the agricultural states, and who resented the scarcity of loans, the high rates, and the injustice of having to repay with dollars dearer than they had borrowed. Silver sentiment grew rapidly in the West and South after 1894 as anger at the depressed economy found its voice in the newly energized Democratic Party, which in 1896 repudiated the sitting president, Grover Cleveland, and nominated William Jennings Bryan as its candidate. His famous "cross of gold" speech raised the economic argument for silver coinage into moral and religious dimensions. Nationally the debate was bitterly framed as a contest between property and people, haves and have-nots, those with wealth and those demanding a fairer share.[1] Bryan's loss calmed the nation, but for some of those still suffering in the depression the calm was that of despair. Rose was old enough to understand something of the national news that filtered into Mansfield and to embrace the populist sentiment of the conversations around

her. Even the summer asters along the front-yard fences in Mansfield had
their economic symbolism:

> Those white and yellow flowers were symbols. In those years of
> hard times that followed The Panic . . . those white and yellow
> flowers became symbols of fanaticism. To me, a yellow aster still
> stands for the hated gold standard; the white aster means William
> Jennings Bryan, whose free coinage of silver would have taken us
> back to prosperity. But Bryan was defeated by the soulless corpo-
> rations and our country was forever ruined.[2]

II

Meanwhile, the first order of business for Rose was to go back to school.
And what greater terror than the sinking feeling of a seven-year-old
starting school in a new community? In De Smet, the Wilders had been
founding citizens, her grandfather a town elder, and when Rose had
started school there she had been on equal footing with any child in the
town. Her two years there, from ages five to seven, had brought her
barely out of infancy, barely to the edge of the broader world where the
certainties of family life might be challenged by a problematical society.
Here in Mansfield she knew no one and no one knew her or her family.
Nothing in the town was familiar. The school was two miles away—a long
walk but not uncommon for schoolchildren of that day. It is perhaps a
mark of her parents' indulgence that they sent her to school that first
autumn on a donkey.[3]

Rose did not record whether arriving by donkey was a social liability or not. Enough students came by horseback that a roofed shelter was
provided for their animals. What she did discover at once was that arriving from the country, barefoot and shabbily dressed, was the deepest
humiliation. "No sensitive child who has gone to school from a poverty-
besieged home, in patched clothes, with second-hand books, fails to
learn that human beings are barbarous," she later wrote.[4] Already by the
third grade Mansfield children distinguished between town girls and
country girls: pretty dresses and ribbons, curled hair, and occasional
nickels for candy made the difference. Rose longed to sit with these para-
gons, but she was condemned to share her desk with "the horrid, snuf-
fling, unwashed, barefooted mountain girls" while admiring her betters
from a social distance that seemed absolute. Small wonder that her closest friend was her donkey Spookendyke—an ungrateful beast who slipped
his saddle regularly and kicked the horses tied next to him. She tried the
trick of dangling an apple before his nose to urge him along the road, but
he simply balked in disgust. As often as not, he and Rose arrived at
school walking side by side, and once in the classroom Rose was likely to
have to leave again to quiet Spookendyke among her classmates' horses.

When she began to study formal grammar, she marked her isolation by inventing her own private language; she called it Fispooko and talked it to Spookendyke as they traveled the road from home to school. Once she detoured to explore a nearby cave and ventured with a torch far back until she found a lake. She waded out until the water was up to her waist before her torch, and her courage, gave out.

The school was probably neither better nor worse than most in rural America in the 1890s. Somewhat more than the one-room country school-house, the Mansfield establishment was a red-brick structure of four rooms and a crowning cupola.[5] Its very existence bespoke the value early settlers placed on education, while its dubious staff and meager resources reflected their general poverty. In 1898, Rose recalled, fifty-five students who used slates because they could not afford tablets contributed a nickel each to buy Prescott's *Conquest of Mexico* on the condition that each of them be allowed to read it.[6] These students were "Sixth Readers," which was to say that they had mastered McGuffey's Readers from Primer through Fifth Reader. When Rose entered in 1894 at age seven, she probably had not yet read Prescott, but she had completed the Second Reader in De Smet and thus was assigned to the room of "Professor" Kay, who presided over the Third to Fifth Readers. Notable chiefly for the long beard that spared him the need of a necktie, Kay was also an auctioneer whose occasional outside duty would provide an extra holiday. In the classroom, his symbol of authority was a long cane, which he used mostly to insert between his skin and soiled shirt for a satisfying scratch. Rose, probably the youngest and smallest of his scholars, had time to watch him from her high bench as her aching legs dangled above the floor, for her lessons came easily. On one wall of the room was a bookcase with almost two shelves of donated books: the class library. In these Rose pursued a random education during her lunch hour, eating alone to conceal the shame of butterless bread.

Equally random was the education gleaned as her mother read to her and her father in the winter evenings. The description of those evenings that she composed late in life to conclude *On the Way Home* is substantially identical to one she wrote in 1920 to cap a brief history of her early years. What is striking in both versions is the glamour suffusing the portrait of her mother as seen through a child's eyes. Rose would bring a book home from those two shelves—Dickens, Jane Austen, even Gibbon's *Decline and Fall of the Roman Empire*, as well as an indiscriminate collection of obscure romances. Her father would pop a big pan of popcorn and, while she and her father ate, her mother would read aloud:

> She sat beside the table with the lamp on it. Her hair was combed back smoothly and braided in a heavy braid, and the lamplight glistened on it. Her mouth was very sensitive and whenever she was amused it twitched at the corners. Her eyelids covered her

eyes and her lashes were very long. . . . It was the cozy, comfortable hour for all of us. We had had supper, the room was warm, we
were alone together, the horses fed and sleeping in the barn, nothing to worry or hurt us till tomorrow.[7]

The two versions are more than forty years apart, but both confirm an
image from childhood of hearth and home, books and love and mother, a
powerful center of value in a painful and uncertain world. It is easy to see
the source of an emotional dependence on the one hand, and the need to
develop the skills to survive on the other.

By eight or nine Rose knew poverty as a state of mind, not simply as a
condition of childhood; and other recollections of those years suggest
that the little girl who stood at her mother's side on that prophetic spring
morning was often sullen, frightened, and silent, suffering adult anxiety
without the emotional strength of maturity. Her parents' problems terrified her:

> I was always very quiet. No one knew what went on in my mind.
> Because I loved my parents I would not let them suspect that I was
> suffering. I concealed from them how much I felt their poverty,
> their struggles and disappointments. These filled my life, magni-
> fied like horrors in a dream. My father and mother were coura-
> geous, even gaily so. They did everything possible to make me
> happy, and I gaily responded with an effort to persuade them that
> they were succeeding. But all unsuspected, I lived through a child-
> hood that was a nightmare.[8]

For although the Wilders had fetched up finally in a place where they
could stick to the land, the margin that supported Rose's days in school
and the comforting book adventures each night was perilously small.
They put in a small crop of corn on the clear portion of their land the first
spring, and that summer Rose picked berries to sell in town or to trade at
the store for staples. In time, money from timber purchased a cow, which
yielded butter to sell or trade as well, and a small frame house replaced
the windowless cabin, which became a barn. But they were far from
living well, and at times even the daily meals were problematical. Years
later Rose bitterly ascribed her bad teeth to early and continued malnutrition. Once she started a rabbit in their woods and chased it into a hollow
log, where she barricaded it in with stones. It provided rabbit stew that
night and cold rabbit in her school lunch the next day. She went barefoot
on principle, pretending not to want shoes when they were offered: she
knew what shoes cost.[9]

From time to time in her later years Rose would look back over that childhood with profound dejection, wondering what had gone wrong. In such moments, she suffered a sense of present misery rooted in a false start in life, some early damage from which she had never recovered. Lying in a sickbed in Tirana, Albania, in 1927, she noted in her journal "Influences: 1 to 16: no affection, poverty, inferiority." We have seen enough of the early poverty of the Wilders—a poverty at times almost absolute, a matter of food and shelter—to acknowledge the justice of the one claim. And even as the family had risen by daily small steps toward some measure of security, the child had come into a painful double consciousness of economic and social inferiority. As she grew into her manifest talents and intelligence, her very gifts and quick perception magnified the distance that a few dollars a year set between her and the daughters of the first families of Mansfield. In the schoolroom, she regularly defeated them in the spell-downs. "This did not add to my popularity, but it was my one chance to feel superior to the town girls. They might laugh at my clothes, but they couldn't laugh at my spelling."[10] The father of one of these town girls owned a sundries store, where Rose regularly admired the spools of penny-a-yard ribbon in the window, hoping to buy when the apple trees began bearing. The proprietor once invited her in, and she never stopped again, filled with the shame of being unable to put down her penny.

But however severe these disabilities, Rose had listed "no affection" first. This can only be a charge against her parents, but her father seems to have been largely unproblematical in her emotional life. Helen Boylston testified that Mama Bess ruled the family with an iron hand, and to understand Rose's charge is to look again at those powerful evocations of the mother's presence in the daughter's reminiscences. Certainly they are in themselves loving images of an admired matriarch; behind them stands the archetype of the embracing mother of Rose's childhood dream. But except for this dream-vision, the affection flows from daughter to mother, not the other way; and in more than one instance the scene is deflated by the mother's accusation or reprimand. One revealing sketch by Rose looks back to those earlier years in De Smet. It places a little girl in her grandmother's care while her mother works; on returning, the mother asks, "Has she been a good girl, Ma?" Sometimes Grandma would have to say that she has not been very diligent. "A little sigh, no more than a sad breath, would come from Mama's chest." Such evidence stands against the broader backdrop of the generalized guilt Rose seems to have carried from her earliest years; and it needs also to be assimilated to the occasional attempts she made in middle age to see her relationship with her mother clearly. At one extreme are the idealized visions, written for a public audience or for a correspondent before whom Rose must posture herself and her family. At the other are her journal entries in which she tries to speak honestly to herself. These latter will have their appropriate place further on, but their essence is captured in one brief entry from 1933: "She made me so miserable as a child," Rose wrote bitterly, "that I never got over it."[11]

There is no specific charge. Indeed, there is almost nothing apart from Rose's occasional jottings to testify to the private character of Laura Ingalls Wilder in any respect—except the mother's confession to a recurring dream of traveling a frightening road in a dark wood.[12] At most we can hypothesize from a life so trammelled with hardship and insecurity as hers an emotional life so narrow and disciplined as to leave little margin for spontaneous affection. And the Puritan ethos of our culture had always placed discipline ahead of love in shaping the lives of children. The impulses and standards Rose's mother brought to bear on her daughter were probably not much different from those of most frontier mothers in her day, although the success Mama Bess finally made of her life suggests an energy and tenacity above the common; doubtless she was characteristically diligent in the attempt to shape her daughter. Thus, we might say, Rose had to struggle both with a child's irrational guilt (why did *she* not get diff-theer-eeah? what could she recall of her brother's death? why were her parents' hopes dashed again and again? and who burned down the house?) and with a parent who held her to severe standards by damaging strategies that increased her burden of guilt with every willful impulse.[13]

In the light of one psychoanalytical theory, the case is almost clinical. Psychoanalyst Alice Miller has written of her insights into the cases of children damaged by demanding parents who relentlessly controlled them by adult standards of behavior. The result, Miller argues, is that such children see themselves as instruments of the parents' vision, and thus are never permitted to accept the legitimacy of their own desires. Robbed of their childhood, they grow up with a certain vacancy or hollowness at the core of their being. As adults, such victims tend to suffer alternately from feelings of grandiosity, when the internalized tyrant is temporarily appeased, and of depression, when it seems that no accomplishment will satisfy. Gifted children, quick to intuit the nuances of feeling in the family drama, are especially vulnerable, Miller believes, and thus the title of her book, *The Drama of the Gifted Child*. Glimpses from later years suggest that Mama Bess had perfected a style of domestic martyrdom that her daughter was helpless against. At age thirty-eight, Rose would complain that "she still thinks of me as a child. She even hesitates to let me have the responsibility of bringing up the butter from the spring, for fear I won't do it quite right!" As a middle-aged woman Rose would come to recognize these strategies even as she succumbed to them, but as a child she could only suffer uncomprehendingly.[14]

IV

A few years of marginal existence in their new home made it clear to the Wilders that Rocky Ridge Farm was years from becoming a paying proposition. The place was really barely habitable, and a cash income was needed. By 1898 they had moved into a rented house in town. The precipitating opportunity was probably the death of Mr. Cooley, who had traveled to Mansfield with them. Cooley had taken over management of a hotel and also worked as a drayman for the railroad. Almanzo, always good with horses, took over the dray operation, while Mama Bess took the occasion to board the men building the road to nearby Ava. Even in town, the Wilders developed a reputation for keeping to themselves, but it was clear to neighbors that they were just barely eking out an existence.[15] Rose now found herself to be a town girl again—nominally, at least, for without doubt the family spent their spare moments at Rocky Ridge, working toward the day when it could really be a place to live. The house that her mother envisioned would be completed only after Rose had left home, and we can imagine the intervening years as a gradual transition between two homes.

For her parents, life in town was a necessary evil, but it had its attractions for a growing girl. There was a little more money; in time, her dresses were as good as anyone's; and there was the endless absorption in the petty details of small-town life that began with the distinction between town girls and country girls and ended with the distinction between girls who succeeded in marrying and those who did not. Rose saw with the accurate eye of the outsider. As she grew into adolescence, she found herself still behind the barrier of those differences that had marked her as "Professor" Kay's youngest and brightest student. In high school, she seemed to be embarrassed by her relative poverty, recalled one of her contemporaries, Blanche Coday Anderson; Rose, it was clear, wanted to belong just as Blanche did. If Rose had a close friend in these days, it was probably Blanche Coday; but if Blanche seemed to have made the inner circle, Rose felt herself walled out. "I was too shy, too sensitive to break it down. I was not invited to parties. I was 'left out.' I was hurt and lonely." And she was sure she would never marry.[16]

She was not quite friendless, of course. In addition to Blanche, her friendship with the Cooley boys continued, and there was the stationmaster's daughter, Ethel Burney, who eventually married Paul Cooley.[17] But an incident from those days suggests that Rose could be a difficult friend even for those who knew her best. Playing a game called "Truth," she and the Cooley boys agreed to enumerate each other's faults but not to get angry:

> I began, with Paul. I had not candidly stated more than half his faults when his face began alarmingly to swell and darken, his fists clenched, his eyes stared; he began to jump up and down, his face became purple. I continued—always being one to finish whatever I began; . . . but the thumps of Paul's feet . . . brought parents invading, demanding explanations, asking Paul what on earth was the matter with *him?* He was able to speak only in gasps; he gasped, "I promised—not to get—mad—and I'm not—mad but (in a rush) Oh iflhadn'tpromisedI'dbe so MAD."[18]

Probably Rose was simply marginal rather than central to the social life of the school and felt it with the keenness of a growing critical intelligence. Hers was the isolation of the precocious child in a commonplace world, and doubtless the boys as well as the girls found her intimidating. As, no doubt, did her teachers. For as the sullen and frightened little country girl verged into adolescence she began to find that the difference between the world she discovered in her books and the one she had to accommodate herself to in school was intolerable. The result was rebellion and a number of school years begun but never finished because she could not get on with her teacher. The earliest instance was probably the one she described as an example of her problems: on the first day of the school year a new teacher gave her class an exercise in "transposition" (paraphrase). The lines were Tennyson's "Break, break, break! On thy cold gray stones, O sea, / And I would that I could utter the thoughts that arise in me."

> When his attention returned to us, he asked for my transposition. I said the lines could not be transposed, they were poetry, and what they meant was not what they said. . . . He turned to a boy, Charlie Day, and asked him for his transposition. Charlie Day stood up, proud in successful achievement, and read:
>   Smash on your rocks, O Ocean, and I wish that I could say what I think about it.
>   This I could have borne, suffering but enduring, if the teacher had not turned the incident to my moral profit. Let this be a lesson to you, Miss Wilder, he said; you fail because you do not try; you see that Charlie succeeds in doing what you did not attempt. Perseverance is the chief virtue; without it you will accomplish nothing in life. If at first you don't succeed, you must not weakly give up; you must....I stood up, slammed my books on the desk, said in fury, "I will not stay here to listen to such stupid, stupid....!!" and went home.[19]

She kept up with her studies in her free time at home, lying on her stomach eating apples in the haymow of their barn in town. She skipped most arithmetic and forever after coped with figures by her own methods, but she taught herself algebra from a textbook from sheer joy of the material. What uneasy arrangement must have obtained between her,

her parents, and the school we can only imagine. She seems to have been among the Sixth Readers who subscribed their nickels for the invaluable Prescott, for she recalled that class's serious look to their futures as childhood's end drew near:

> Should you stay at home (and work, of course) or work your way through an academy? What was the right balance between duty to parents and obligation to one's self? (Nobody questioned his duty to parents who had given him life, nor the debt he owed them for supporting him from infancy through the Sixth Reader.) Was more education practical? . . . Should one work for money, or work for learning? The argument was perennial.[20]

Dreamy and odd, a writer of fanciful stories and poems, recalled a classmate years later. A schoolbook survives from her years in the Mansfield High School, which seems to have run only to the tenth grade. In scribbled notes on blank pages and in margins, we can glimpse an adolescent bored and frustrated, periodically in trouble, and already given to a novelist's analysis of behavior and motive. " 'A friend who ceases to be a friend never was a friend,' " she wrote on one blank page. "I am afraid that was, and is, only too true about Blanche, and I cared for her a great deal more than anyone knows, and care for her yet, for that matter." Another entry captures a small classroom drama:

> Oct. 9, 1900. I am standing in a corner, diligently studying my general history lesson for tomorrow morning. . . . I was drawing a cat, and Mr. Bland said to Scott Coday, "What was Thoreau's philosophy?" and Scott answered, "I don't know." Whereupon Mr. Bland said, "Is that right, Rose?" Naturally somewhat astonished, I gasped, "Why, Scott didn't answer the question at all, did he?" And Mr. Bland coldly remarked, "Rose, you may take that corner, I am tired of your doing something else when you should be reciting." Poor Mr. Bland.

Some of the entries seem to be scribbled notes to her seat-mate in the silent classroom. The subject, not surprisingly, is often boys and romance, but the details suggest a Rose Wilder who is already an odd assortment of interests for her classmates to cope with.

> Yes, I was standing by the window, & J. J. was beside me, & we were talking. You know I'd taken my collar off in school because it hurt my sore throat. Well, he was looking down at me and talking, & I leaned back against the wall & looked up at him, & just then she said, "Oh Rose, you remind me of Hattie Mears at a dance." And I didn't think it was a compliment at all. Say, did I look so silly as H. M.? Really, now, honest.
>
> Glad you think so. I do too. We were talking about "Boin" Harvey's views on bimetallism & *that* isn't a sentimental subject & I didn't feel one bit like H. M. looks, so I don't see why I should look that way.

Another entry carries an air of prophecy:

> I wonder why he said that. Did he mean I'd be an old maid because
> he was so conceited as to suppose that if he didn't want me no one
> else would? Or did he suppose (still conceited) that just because
> I wasn't so struck with his charm as to want to go with him I
> wouldn't want to go with anyone else! Or did he suppose that I
> am naturally adapted for an old maid's life? Cats, you know, &
> knitting, & a fondness for solitude & a dislike of sweethearts! Or
> did he—but what's the use of wondering? Only, do you think he
> thought I was sentimental or what, that he said an old maid *novel-
> ist?* Oh, say, I wish you'd ask him.

And a list, prophetic of her later prodigious letter-writing, notes her
seven "most important correspondents," including her Aunt Grace in De
Smet. An eighth, fallen into disfavor, has been crossed out. And what,
finally, are we to make of the judgments lurking in a thirteen-year-old's
mind as she annotates her ancient history text? "Sept. 27, 1900. If only such
men as the Spartans lived in these days, life would be worth living."[21]

So her education continued, in contention with a school that formally offered her nothing beyond the curriculum for the tenth grade. To
her good fortune, however, a family arrived in town who owned a whole
wall of books, and Rose one by one borrowed them all. Most impressive
were the works of Marie Corelli, popular romancer of wicked London
society, whose use of adjectives, Rose found herself reflecting spontaneously, was *masterly.* She read all of Bulwer-Lytton and whole sets of other
English novelists and, finally, Eugene Sue's *The Wandering Jew* in two
volumes, sitting in the swing at the farm. Early in this blood-and-thunder
novel she would discover two young girls, Rose and Blanche, involved in
the adventures. The original folk-story had intrigued her as a child, and
now as her imagination expanded beyond Mansfield it fastened on that
mythical wanderer, unlimited in his experience of the world, as an ideal.[22]

V

She could not have known it at the time, but she was already caught up in
a dilemma that would define her life. On the one hand lay the growing
perfection of the home on the land that her parents were working toward:
powerful bonds of love and obligation grounded in a deep-seated pastoral myth were already in place. On the other lay the world revealed to
her by her reading but concealed by the horizon as seen from the Mansfield town square: her fulfillment lay somewhere out there. In between
was Mansfield itself, a ragged cluster of homes sheltering fewer than five
hundred souls, none of whom could share her growing aspirations. Already she was equipped for her parents' country life: she could milk a
cow and drive a team and split firewood; she could rise to the excitement

of an Ozark fox hunt—twenty or thirty mounted men, sixty dogs, and the sound of hunting horns; and she was a talented cook and worker with her needle.[23] Or she could commit herself to Mansfield, and become what town girls became when they grew up: wife and mother—or old maid—in a petty hierarchy defined by rigid canons of respectability. Or she could leave.

Rose's most thoughtful measure of this time of growing up in Mansfield would come thirty years later, when she turned her attention to those years for a series of short stories for the *Saturday Evening Post* and *Ladies' Home Journal*. In 1935 she collected these stories into a single volume and prefaced it with the title essay, in which the burden of *Old Home Town* became clear. It marked her remembered rebellion at the narrow and crippling ethos of nineteenth-century small-town America. The stories are all narrated by an observant adolescent girl, bookish and awkward with boys, whose mother is already defensive about her chances of marrying. All turn on the struggles of various victims of a small-town culture in which the second greatest crime is to be an old maid and the greatest to yield to a spontaneous impulse from the heart. The victims are mainly women: spinsters, widows, adolescent girls, discontented wives; and their oppressors are in the main parents and husbands, but the spirit of Mrs. Grundy reigns over all. Speaking in her own voice in the preface, Rose recalls a veneer of petty gentility over the general penury, a mindless respectability that a child questions at her peril, and beneath it all an implicit set of values that she could only formulate once she had broken away:

> It was a hard, narrow, relentless life. It was not comfortable. Nothing was made easy for us. We did not like work and we were not supposed to like it; were supposed to work, and we did. We did not like discipline, so we suffered until we disciplined ourselves. We saw many things and many opportunities that we ardently wanted and could not pay for, so we did not get them, or got them only after stupendous, heartbreaking effort and self-denial, for debt was much harder to bear than deprivations. We were honest, not because sinful human nature wanted to be, but because the consequences of dishonesty were excessively painful. It was clear that if your word were not as good as your bond, your bond was no good and you were worthless. Not only by precept but by cruel experience we learned that it is impossible to get something for nothing; that he who does not work can not long continue to eat, that the sins of the fathers are visited upon the children even unto the fourth generation; that chickens come home to roost and the way of the transgressor is hard.[24]

The last story in the series sees the narrator, who has left town at age seventeen for business college, established as a sophisticated world traveler, having transcended the narrow horizons of her origins.

It is a tale often told in our literature in the years between the wars: the flight from the village, the escape from the dead hand of the Puritan tradition. The earlier models were Sherwood Anderson's *Winesburg, Ohio* and Sinclair Lewis's *Main Street*. The point, however, is not that Rose's book was derivative, but rather that she had participated in her generation's rebellion against the inherited past. *Old Home Town* makes the judgment of her adolescent years explicit; but even in the 1930s, and particularly in the pages of the mass-circulation magazines she wrote for, the genteel tradition still proscribed writing directly about the authentic experience of those years. Only in 1967, and then only in a private letter, could she tell the stories that she could not write for the magazines:

> When I was a "youth"—I mean when I was ceasing to be a girl and becoming a young lady . . . there was an unmarried young lady in our town . . . who gave birth to The Son of God, Jesus Incarnate again, as foretold in the Bible and as she herself testified. Strangely— as I thought, even then—nobody in town believed her, though all unquestioningly believed that every word of the Bible was the literal word of God dictated by Himself to his scribes.—There was another girl whose father whipped her unmercifully with a black- snake whip and sent her to her aunt in Kansas City for an abor- tion; the aunt sent for the child's father who went to Kansas City and married the girl. They returned to Mansfield. Five months later her mother and sisters—who in the interim had not spoken to her; nobody in town did—went away somewhere—St. Louis, Memphis, I don't remember where—and the husband frantically begged neighbor women to come help the girl, the baby being prematurely born. . . . Twenty-five years later this girl, then mother of five, was scornfully refusing to speak to a young girl reputed to be rather "fast," saying virtuously to me that she felt it our duty to maintain morality.—Another girl in town was taken ill in the night, seized with fierce pains; her mother sent for the doctor and was appalled to see a baby born. The girl had laced herself tightly enough to conceal her condition completely. She was not spoken to, by her family or anyone else, so long as I knew.[25]

It is clear what the young Rose found oppressive about her daily life in Mansfield. Less clear is what visions filled her imagination as she dreamed of the future. The geographical frontier that had defined the future for her parents and grandparents had been officially closed in 1890; by and large, the occupation of the continent was completed. What lay ahead, as America edged into the twentieth century, was the virtual annihilation of geographical space by the automobile, the airplane, the telephone and telegraph, the radio and the motion picture. The railway had made Mansfield possible, and the telegraph kept it in touch with the remote world, but little had really disturbed the town as yet from its nineteenth-century sleep. The new frontier was yet to be defined in the minds of Rose's generation in the technological expansion of human experience that would make possible a world no one in Mansfield could dream of. By age sixteen, Rose had already traveled widely in her reading: no doubt her sense of a wider world was compelling. As she dreamed of the Wandering Jew, rocking to and fro in the swing by the Ozark cabin, the sentence of that mythical wanderer did not seem too hard to bear for the chance of seeing the world. Louisiana would be the first adventure.

VI

There were two crucial visits to the Wilder home in Mansfield in these years, both by members of Almanzo Wilder's family. His redoubtable sister Eliza Jane was central to both, though present only at the second visit. Eliza Jane Wilder, unmarried as a young woman, had been a Dakota homesteader too; but after struggles on the land that would have broken many a man, she had given up on Dakota, this in the year before Rose was born. She traveled and worked widely in several states and spent some time in Washington, D.C., as a clerk in the Department of Interior. But by 1893 she had returned to her father's farm in Spring Valley, and while there she had married a prosperous rice farmer visiting from Crowley, Louisiana. She was then forty-three. She moved with her husband to Crowley, where a child was born in 1894. E. J., as she signed her letters, persuaded her younger brother Perley to join them in Louisiana, and in 1898 her elderly parents, James and Angeline Wilder, sold out their Spring Valley property and invested their considerable estate in Louisiana rice plantations. On their way to Louisiana they stopped in Mansfield for a long summer visit. Traveling with them was their oldest daughter, Laura, a widow of fifty-four.[26]

This visit had two significant results. First, Rose's mother and her older sister-in-law shared the same first name: Almanzo had already felt the difficulty when they were courting, and reaching past his wife's middle name, Elizabeth (also the name of his sister Eliza), he had come to call his wife Bess or Bessie. During this visit the distinction became confirmed as a family convenience, and for Rose her mother became Mama Bess. The salutation would head her letters home all her life. The second result was perhaps more significant, as it established Crowley as another base the family could turn to in time of need. In the next year James Wilder would lose all of his new investment and die a broken man, leaving one branch of his family now located in Louisiana with Eliza Jane as its most significant member. From the remains of his father's estate, Almanzo Wilder received five hundred dollars, with which he apparently bought the rented Mansfield house they were living in. It was, perhaps, just the infusion of capital they needed: in the years that followed, they found it possible to build the dream home at Rocky Ridge and return to live there permanently. No doubt the sale of the town property was instrumental to this return.[27]

VII

The second visit was by E. J. herself, some years later and apparently just about the time that Rose had gotten all she would ever get from the Mansfield school. E. J. by this time was a woman well disciplined by adversity into a general competence in the world. Perhaps she saw in Rose something of herself, a woman of high abilities not destined for the common fate of early marriage and a housewife's lot. Perhaps too the visit resulted from a plea by the Wilders: there is a story in other branches of the Wilder family suggesting that Rose was slipping out of parental control, and mention is made of a worrisome dalliance with a Latin tutor who had been hired by her parents.[28] The facts are blurred in family gossip generations old. In any case, the result was an arrangement for Rose to spend a year in Crowley, where the school boasted a curriculum beyond Mansfield's best offerings. Nominally it was a high school; Rose would describe it later as an ambitious ninth grade. In 1903, at age sixteen, she left home for the first time to live under her aunt's care and to test her abilities in higher education.

There was first a principal to be persuaded of her qualifications: she had no records from Mansfield to show. To enter the graduating class she would have to pass examinations in American history, English history, two years of Latin grammar, algebra, plane geometry, civics, and American literature. Drawing on her random study for the past ten years, she took and passed examinations in all but Latin and plane geometry. She offered to take make-up classes in these while studying Caesar and Cicero and solid geometry with the regular class, and despite his doubts the principal admitted her. She completed all of the Latin and all of the geometry, in addition to the normal curriculum, in one year. She stood at the head of her class of seven in Latin, wrote a Latin poem, and read it at the graduation exercises. She was seventeen years old and had completed her formal education.

In this hectic life she also found time for a beau, but little time for sleep. The whole Crowley experience would be the kind of exercise in sustained energy and efficiency that would mark her career intermittently:

> Well, before Thanksgiving I had two or three of what used to be called suitors, and by Thanksgiving my heart belonged to—is it funny or sad that I can't remember his name? He was Prince Charming, the only one I have ever known. He was from Chicago, he was visiting his sister, he was an Older Man, a graduate of the University of Chicago, he must have been all of 24 years old; his

manners were polished until they glittered, he drove a phaeton and pair. . . . He drove me to school every morning, in the phaeton. Every evening after school he was waiting for me, in the phaeton. It had red wheels, rubber-tired. I hurriedly left my books at my aunt's (she was out of her mind about me, fearing the worst for my virtue) and we were off deliriously for the evening. We ate in *restaurants*. We drove for hours and miles along those dusty white roads in the moonlight, between the cypress trees dripping Spanish moss, by the gleaming dark bayous where the alligators slept in piles, past the rice fields and through the sleeping tiny towns. . . . My virtue was not at all endangered. I MUST be in by 10. And almost always I was at my aunt's by midnight.

Now to work. There was a long screened porch, buried in vines, along the side of the house by my room—porch called in Louisiana a gallery. There I had a table under the light, with my books on it. I did the exercises in Latin grammar, I did the lesson in Caesar and the lesson in Cicero, and I could not keep my eyes open. I must be brightly up before sunrise, to curl my hair, etc., etc. and be ready before HE came to drive me to school. And I don't remember how I discovered a way to do the next day's geometry problems. But I did, and it worked for the rest of the school year. This way.

LOOK at the problem: to bisect the cone...* Set the alarm clock two minutes ahead. Sleep (I had only to stop trying to keep my eyes open, let my head down to the table.) Bong! the alarm! You're awake, to bisect the cone. . . . Q.E.D. Get the solution down on paper. LOOK at the next problem and repeat from *. In 12 minutes—oh, say 15—the six problems were solved, I was sleeping on my bed until the alarm clock woke me to tomorrow and the beau in the phaeton.[29]

What else could fill her time in this year? Apparently political enthusiasms as well. The resentful populism that had failed nationally with William Jennings Bryan in 1896 had thrown up a new hero for those who still hoped for justice under a new political and economic order. Eugene Debs became the first socialist candidate for the presidency and mounted a heroic speaking schedule across the nation. It was natural for those who found the white and golden asters along the Mansfield sidewalks to be political symbols to find in Debs a figure to embody their resentment of the established order. E. J. herself was a tireless worker for Debs, and her enthusiasm rubbed off on her visiting niece. "When I was sixteen I was an ardent Socialist," Rose recalled. "That was in the days when we read Edward Bellamy's 'Looking Backward,' meanwhile ourselves looking forward to a perfect world which would painlessly arrive when everyone voted for Debs."

Rose was one of his young enthusiasts, passing out copies of the *Appeal to Reason*, the western newspaper that supported his cause, to the residents of Crowley. She even, she later claimed, made campaign speeches of a sort on his behalf.[30]

The school and the town had become another arena in which she could test her abilities—and to discover again, as she had in Mansfield, that the way of the talented newcomer is a lonely one. Her own accounts of this year in Crowley were written in letters long after that time, versions determined by a selective memory and the pose she assumed for her correspondents. One of her classmates in Crowley remembered her, no doubt correctly, as a gifted but hopeless outsider: "Rose Wilder was with us only one year. . . . She was different, cared only about her art and writing. She was messy, not like any of us. Stayed to herself most of the time—didn't come to our parties. . . . She would have been very attractive, but she was *messy*. Didn't know how...."[31] Memory, in this case reaching back eighty years, perhaps conflates Rose's later literary career with her school days, but the mark of artist and writer was probably already apparent. The aged voice trails off in exasperation at the former classmate who "didn't know how." In Crowley no less than in Mansfield, Rose's manifest talents had served to isolate her, and the remaining details have the ring of truth. Sixteen-year-old girls are merciless and sure in these judgments of ineptitude: the charge of personal untidiness is corroborated by others who knew her later.[32] In time Rose would master the forms of social intercourse, but for years she considered herself awkward in their niceties. Her graduation picture reveals a sober, almost sullen, childish face, faintly uncomfortable in adult finery and hairdress. But for the moment she was not untidy.

VIII

When she returned to Mansfield in the summer of 1904, Rose had ended her formal education but had begun a life of romance and politics. No doubt the whole experience was marked with a new access of confidence in certain of her abilities but also with a newly sharpened apprehension about her future. Better educated than most in the town and with a romance with a college man to measure Mansfield swains by, she had also taken the measure of her capacities for work and had begun to glimpse the chances of a life in the wider world. Marriage was the obvious alternative; but although there were some faint suitors, apparently both Mansfield and Rose had decided that whatever future she might have would not be the conventional one of Mansfield wife and mother or languishing spinster daughter.

In retrospect, she saw the problem clearly as a personal one that was also representative of change overtaking the country:

> When I was seventeen, not one young man had asked me to marry
> him, though two had almost done so, and I did not discourage a
> possible public belief that they had. Another change which was

affecting America became for me a personal problem. As soon as the young men of my town reached marriageable age, those who had courage and ambition went to the cities. In my mother's girlhood the young men who were left would still have been eligible, but now there were two reasons why I would not have married any of them, in addition to the fact that I was not asked. One reason was that I was courageous and ambitious myself, and these men were not.

The other reason was the high cost of living:

> It was an age of riotous expenditure. . . . Telephones were everywhere; the shirt-waist and the straight-front corset had ushered in an era when women's fashions were changing every year; the milliner's best hats bore the outrageous price of four dollars; everyone who was anybody had a bicycle. . . . these young men were in no position to marry and maintain a household on any such scale as that.[33]

The tone is flippant but the problem was real. The era of mass consumer-delights was at hand and Rose's seventeen-year-old's notion of happiness did not include the "narrow, relentless life" of her old home town. "We rebelled against it. We wanted a land overflowing with milk and honey, where everybody would be free and good and happy."

> That way of life against which my generation rebelled had given us grim courage, fortitude, self-discipline, a sense of individual responsibility, and a capacity for relentless hard work. The qualities had been ingrained in the American character from the first. These were the qualities with which the millions of Americans . . . set out to get what they wanted, and got it, and lavished it on their children: freedom, ease, comforts, luxuries. . . .[34]

And so, with most of her parents' virtues and few of their values, Rose could do nothing but leave. Her friend Ethel Burney had learned telegraphy from her father, the Mansfield station-master; and Paul Cooley had picked it up, too. For Rose, mastery of the Morse Code and the telegraph key was probably a matter of days. It would provide her with an exit from her old home town.[35]

BACHELOR GIRL, MARRIED WOMAN

If I'd ever made the best of things . . . I'd be stuck in Mansfield yet.

Shortly after her return to Mansfield from Crowley in 1904, probably in the summer of that year, Rose Wilder boarded the train that would take her west to Kansas City. Here she began her career as telegraph operator. Her first job, she said, paid her $2.50 a week and provided the first margin of independence. "I used to long and dream," she wrote years later,

> of a sometime coming (and I damn well meant to MAKE it come) when I would be so rich that I would not know precisely, every minute steadily, how much money I had; usually one dollar, one quarter, a dime, two nickels, and a postage stamp (then 2 cents). All in my purse, of course. And when I mailed a letter, there would be two nickels, a dime, a quarter, a dollar. The nickel's worth of salted peanuts for supper today and tomorrow left only one nickel, one dime, the quarter and the dollar. $1.40.[1]

The extra dollar was probably for a rented room. She was seventeen and self-supporting—a "bachelor girl" was the phrase in vogue. She knew no more than most seventeen-year-olds what she would make of her life, except that it would be something different, something more, than sleepy Mansfield could offer. The Wandering Jew was ready to wander, driven by a sense of need as strong as it was undefined. "I don't 'make the best of things,'" she would write twenty years later:

> I never have and I never shall. Making the best of things is . . . a damn poor way of dealing with them. If I'd ever made the best of things . . . My God, I'd be stuck in Mansfield yet. . . . My whole life has been a series of escapes from that quicksand. It may be all right as a philosophy for the lucky ones that haven't had to fight like the devil for every scrap they've ever got. A person who starts out as a mal-nutrition child in an Ozark log cabin and gets even as far as I've got, does it by raising hell about things, not by making the best of them.[2]

The next decade would see her cross the continent east and west, change careers three times, find a husband and leave him, bear a child and lose him, and attempt suicide. It is also a decade that for the biographer affords little information, few points of reference, and great latitude for conjecture.

Probably that first job at $2.50 a week was as a clerk in the telegraph office, but soon she was a full-fledged telegrapher in the main office of Western Union in Kansas City. Her first assignment had been as a night operator at the branch office in the Midland Hotel, but with characteristic energy she found both day and night jobs, and double income, within her scope. Once she had mastered the mystery of the revolving glass door, she delighted in the white-marble, red-plush, gilt-and-crystal elegance of the Midland; no doubt it reassured her that life offered such rewards for industry. And it was easy: "Just sat there and mechanically sent messages, thirty an hour, sixteen hours. I didn't even think, just existed. Never knew what words I was sending, they were seen by my eyes and sent by my fingers without touching the brain at all." Daytime work at the main office was simply work, but the night shift at the Midland was sheer indulgence. In the long evenings she would signal to her friend Gladys at the Postal Telegraph desk across the lobby. The two companies were competitors, and neither woman would leave her desk while the other stayed; but with equal loyalty they could desert together for the public dressing room on the mezzanine, where with a spirit lamp and hot curling irons they would style their hair and talk.[3]

To her claim to have worked sixteen-hour days seven days a week at this time she added another three hours a night in reading. She had read Darwin and Herbert Spencer in her teens, she said, and Schopenhauer, perhaps somewhat later, which would have occupied a few evenings, and there would have been time also in the slack hours at her telegraph desk between messages. It was probably in this time that she learned to use a typewriter, which quickly became a natural extension of her hands. The story is that a notice came down from Western Union that all operators who could not type were to be fired: she took a typewriter home that night and taught herself to use it. Only years later, when she had worn the letters off the keys, did she realize that she was a touch-typist.[4]

She was earning sixty dollars a month, working a double shift, and apparently finding time to spend it on smart clothing, as suggested by a photograph of a very stylish Rose Wilder from about this time. In one of her visits to Sedalia she saw her first motorcar and rode in it at the unbelievable speed of almost twenty miles an hour. And there was time for men as well. A young woman telegrapher working the evening shift in a hotel lobby would inevitably attract the attention of traveling-men. One of them just might have been her future husband. And a young local man named Julian Bucher, whose father owned a saloon, appears in her correspondence; while Paul Cooley remembered a man named Johnson who visited her during a return to Mansfield. But this was not a subject

she recalled with pleasure some twenty years later in a cryptic but suggestive note in her journal: "When I was seventeen I went further to smash in
struggling with sex. Not that it was really a struggle; I was a rag-doll in its
hands." The possibilities of whatever happened at age seventeen reach
backward to her days in Crowley with the suitor from the University of
Chicago, run through the Mansfield swains who would not ask her to
marry them, and extend to her first days on her own in Kansas City. Der-
eliction seems more likely in those first days on her own than under
the watchful eyes of her aunt and mother. What the experience amounted
to is impossible to say; but in her own mind, it seems, by 1905 her age of
innocence had passed. She had had to find her own way; her mother had
given her no guidance, but had left her as an adolescent to worry with
her friends whether a man could give her a baby by kissing her.[5]

And so all we can say about Rose Wilder for some three years is that
she seems to have been working in Kansas City as a telegrapher and
experimenting with life. Her first twenty years had passed, and when
twenty years later she assessed them she was grimly judgmental:

> The first twenty [years] were wasted. . . . I didn't fit my environ-
> ment, and I didn't know any other. But I have never fitted any
> environment. . . . It may be my life has been determined by the
> futility, the inferiority, the vanity, the stupidity of me in those first
> twenty years. There was nothing but vanity in my wanting "edu-
> cation." My real desire was for money, clothes, social position (!),
> good times, admiration. I hadn't an inkling of the real world of
> books and thought.[6]

On October 20, 1906, the *Mansfield Mail* noted the return of Mrs. A. J.
Wilder from a visit of several weeks to Kansas City. Probably Rose's work
allowed her few opportunities to come home to Mansfield. The bond
with Mama Bess would be one she was never to break; but she would
wrestle much of her adult life with the sense that those twenty wasted
years were her mother's fault, and that more years were wasted in the
same expense.

||

It seems unlikely that the young Rose Wilder worked two shifts at the
telegraph key, seven days a week, subsisting each evening on salted
peanuts, without respite throughout these years. More likely is that this
memory reflects brief or occasional stints of double duty and intermittent
shortness of funds. And given her restless nature, it would have been
surprising had she remained in Kansas City much longer than she did.
But the event that moved her on seems to have been the great national
telegraphers' strike of 1907. Rose Wilder was very likely among those who
posted picket lines at the offices of Western Union and Postal Telegraph.

She later said once that the strike ended her telegrapher's career, which was not quite true; it did, however, enforce a hiatus and a series of relocations that led shortly to another career. The strikers began in high spirits: they held rallies and staged a picnic in Swope Park, and a substitute operator who showed up at the Midland Hotel found that someone—perhaps Gladys or Rose—had made off with the telegraph key. But within a few days it was clear that the companies were determined to wait the union out; Rose Wilder, without job or income, soon came back home to Mansfield to await developments. On November 9, the union capitulated; the companies in many cases refused to reinstate strikers, but it took back women in greater numbers than men, apparently because they were thought to be more docile employees. Rose did not return to Kansas City that November, but she was shortly posted to Mount Vernon, Indiana, as manager of the Western Union office there.[7]

She was also the telegraph operator, clerk-cashier, and janitor; her staff consisted of one messenger boy, age thirteen. Now she worked only ten hours a day, only six days a week, and her salary was fifty dollars a month, of which she was able to save half, she said. Moving up and on in the world, she was putting Mansfield behind her, despite Paul Cooley's plaintive postcard confessing his loneliness and hoping for a reply. There she stayed, it seems, until April of 1908, when she boarded a train for a new position in San Francisco.[8]

The next year is as obscure as it was momentous. The motives for her move were never mentioned, save for a brief reminiscence about having crossed the country in that month on her way to "Gillette in San Francisco." Gillette Lane might have been one of the traveling-men passing through the Midland Hotel; a postcard from Julian Bucher mentions his having written to "Mr. Lane" and specifies "It is your move now, Rose," which leaves room for the possibility of an early connection of Rose with Gillette Lane. If so, her relocation to San Francisco would seem to bespeak some arrangement between them. Her address in San Francisco for some time was the Avon Hotel, where presumably she continued work as a hotel telegrapher; although it seems likely that at some point she took over the important stock market wire from New York, which required her to transform the telegraphic dots and dashes into a continuous flow of market figures. In this time she met Bessie Beatty, who would become her friend, mentor, model, and, eventually, a chief object of scorn and resentment over a period of thirty years. In this time also she married the man whose name she would carry the rest of her life.[9]

Bessie Beatty, called Betty by her friends, was a woman not quite a year older than Rose, a native Californian who, as a young reporter on the *San Francisco Bulletin*, made something of a name for herself in 1908 with her reporting of the visit of the U.S. fleet when it anchored for several weeks in San Francisco Bay en route around the world— Theodore Roosevelt's grand symbolic display of America's international power. Beatty and Rose shared an apartment at 1418 Leavenworth in 1908–1909; in the same apartment building lived a reporter for the rival *San Francisco Call* named Claire Gillette Lane. His usual name was Gillette, although Rose sometimes called him Claire; and if Rose had not met him in Kansas City she must have met him here. But if she had known him earlier, he might well have been her introduction to Bessie Beatty. There is no conclusive evidence either way. Gillette Lane and Rose Wilder were married on March 24, 1909. Rose was twenty-two, her husband just the same age; they were married, in fact, on his birthday. The witnesses were Louis J. Stellman, another newspaperman and photographer, and his wife Edith, an artist, who would become part of her circle of San Francisco friends. In some augury of the future, Rose broke a mirror on her wedding day. And shortly she quit her job as telegrapher to become, very briefly, a housewife (or "parasite," the fashionable term among advanced thinkers). The newly married couple left San Francisco soon afterward to visit Missouri and the bride's parents.[10]

At this point in her life, two new worlds seem to have opened up for Rose to explore with the passion and energy she had brought to each enterprise before; they were very different but not mutually exclusive, and the tension between them would plague her throughout her life. The first was the opportunistic pursuit of money and success in the commercial world; on this model she would conceive of herself as a disciplined businesswoman. The other was the life of the mind—of books, ideas, literature and art; on this model she would strive to understand her world and write about it. Gillette Lane and Bessie Beatty as journalists stood on the fringe of that second world, and through Beatty Rose would eventually come to work in it. Gillette Lane, however, was drawn to the other; and with him Rose set off on another career, leaving telegraphy behind for good.

When later she could candidly examine her reasons for marrying, it all became quite clear to her: "When Gillette came along, I wanted him because (1) I wanted sex, (2) I took him at his own stated value, as representing success and money and the high cultural level of newspaper work. When I married him another reason was added; I was tired of being a working girl and wanted the freedom and fun of a home." In time, all these reasons would fail her, but the last failed almost immediately: "The most decisive moment in my marriage was probably that moment when I was coming back to the apartment at 1418 Leavenworth Street, with the 15 cents worth of lamb chops ("French chops") for dinner, and suddenly asked myself, 'Is this all there is to it? Is there nothing more, never will there be anything more than this in all my life?' "[11] Domestic life had paled rapidly; and for the next several years the something more her heart desired was to be sought on her husband's terms. For despite his claims to the high cultural level of newspaper work, Gillette Lane was attracted more to the possibilities of success and money in advertising and promotional work than to the intellectual demands of newspaper writing; he responded more to the lure of the big commission than to the certainty of the small but regular salary; and he had a taste for the appearances of prosperity although prosperity itself had so far eluded him. Or so Rose would draw him in her letters and in her novel *Diverging Roads*. He was an American type, the Salesman, who would be limned definitively by Arthur Miller. Something in Rose, grounded in those years of hardscrabble poverty on the farm, responded vigorously to this new vision; and together they set out for five years of a footloose, wandering life in search of big commissions. The Wandering Jew might well have been, in one of his lives, a traveling salesman.

Apparently Gillette Lane had at one time made his living traveling the small towns of the Midwest conducting promotional schemes on commission. He would develop subscription campaigns for local newspapers; or he would for a fee write booster articles for a town's business development, place them with a newspaper, and take a commission on the increased subscriptions the articles brought in. Some such life seems to have been his and Rose's in the months following their marriage, and it seems likely that they operated through the small towns in southern Missouri, perhaps using Mansfield as a base before settling in Kansas City. Probably they were frequently separated in that first year, as Rose waited in rented quarters, or at home in Mansfield, for his return from his forays. During much of 1909 she would have been unable to accompany him, for she was pregnant.[12]

The episode of the birth of Rose's child is among the obscurest in this obscure period; she mentions it only twice in all of the surviving letters from this time on, although it was on her mind as late as 1944, when she wrote to console a friend on the loss of child. "My own son died thirty-five years ago. It isn't true, what people say, that you will ever forget, but in time you do learn that unhappiness and loss are part of living. . . ." It was, apparently, an early death, a late miscarriage, or a stillbirth; and there were medical complications for Rose requiring an operation in Kansas City. The event probably left her unable to bear children; and it remained one of the fixed reference points in her emotional landscape as the years went on.[13]

Whatever the complex causes, the years of her marriage were among the most difficult of her life. She was depressed, ill, underweight, and fortifying herself with patent medicines, probably opiates, long after the operation. During the spring of 1910 she was working as a newspaper reporter for the *Kansas City Post* and the rival *Journal;* her sprightly accounts of scandals, crimes, accidents, food shows, and baby pageants are the first appearance of her public voice and contrast sadly with her actual misery at the moment. "A girl working in Kansas City for $60 a month can live well, dress nicely, and save $125 a year," she reported. "At least, so the ninety members of the domestic art class at Westport High School say, and they have figured it out in every detail." The article frames in gentle irony the theories of a high-school project that Rose had already tested and was testing again in the daily scramble of a working life.[14]

In the meantime, Gillette Lane apparently pursued his promotional schemes; and probably Rose was beginning to have doubts about the future of her marriage even as she embraced the vision of success that her husband brought her. Some vacancy in her inner life remained unfilled, psychic bruises remained unhealed, and the bonds of matrimony soon began to chafe. In later years she would look back on the period as "a kind of delirium. Partly because I was a fool, and partly because of the mental effects of my operation in Kansas City. I wasn't physically normal between 1909 and 1911, nor mentally normal till 1914." Sometime late in 1910 Rose and Gillette left Kansas City and began to work their way eastward across the country. Letters back to Rocky Ridge came from Louisville, Cincinnati, New York, Boston, and Maine.[15]

IV

December of 1910 found them lodged in the Waldorf-Astoria Hotel in New York City, from where Rose sent her mother a series of postcards describing the lavish decor they enjoyed for seven dollars a night. This would be their base of operations, she declared, without stating what those operations would be. And at this point the trail all but vanishes except for two fragmentary letters that place them in Maine, where Gillette seems to have had a salaried position in advertising while Rose sold advertising space; at one time in later years she claimed also to have promoted patent medicines, perhaps the very ones she dosed her body with, and Del Monte canned fruits, eating "every dodgasted one of their fruits, in every imaginable recipe."[16] The letters seem to suggest that she and Gillette were temporarily living apart, working at separate jobs perhaps connected with the same promotional campaign. Prophetic of the future, however, is Rose's advice concerning some small books her mother hoped to produce. Probably these were to have been home-published collections of fairy-tale verses for children, some of which would later appear in the *San Francisco Bulletin*. No other evidence remains of this enterprise, but it is the earliest appearance of Laura Ingalls Wilder's aspirations as an author and her daughter's guidance through the details of a project.[17]

Another letter from the same period suggests to Mama Bess a series of articles on poultry raising and other aspects of farm management for a farm journal, and further indicates that some such manuscript has already been attempted—with the inept help of Gillette Lane. Another letter advises that she should set up a small enterprise marketing her own farm products and her neighbors' on commission; it envisions finally a self-sustaining operation that would pay a steady income with little effort. The whole conception bears the mark of her husband's thinking on Rose's own. But the most striking passage in this letter is one that captures in a single episode the essence of the good life that the young Lanes were pursuing. Gillette apparently had incurred some minor injury in a railroad mishap, and the couple had capitalized on it shamelessly:

> We got $1,000, and all expenses, out of the rail-road, and since our hotel bill for less than three weeks was $160 we thought we did very well. I never did live quite so expensively, as you may gather from the figures, and it once in a while scared me, but we thought it best to do it for the impression on the railroad, and I guess it was a good idea, for they paid us nearly twice as much as they would have otherwise. Up here in Maine $1,000 looks awfully big, and since Claire wasn't permanently hurt in any way and his salary didn't stop a day there's not a chance in a hundred that we could have got even half that much out of a jury. But we made such a bluff of rolling in wealth and being able to fight the thing till kingdom come, and also of Claire's being a high-salaried man of wealth, that they were impressed and came through with a great deal more than they meant to. Which isn't much, and if it had happened in California we could have got five times as much. But this is Maine, where they barter. We went down to see the president of the road in our big overcoats, Claire wearing a new hat and I in my fur one. . . .

The ethics of the situation are disturbing; it is tempting to lay off the responsibility onto Gillette Lane. But a further explanation perhaps lies in Rose's inherited antipathy toward the railroad companies that had taken advantage of the prairie settlers: in one of her mother's letters is preserved the assertion (an old saying, she calls it) that "a man who won't steal from the R.R. Co. ain't honest."[18]

Sometime in 1911 the couple returned to San Francisco, even to the same apartment house, and probably to the apartment Bessie Beatty had vacated for a new address.

V

Back again in San Francisco, Rose renewed her acquaintance with the world of professional writers. At about this time she worked at a salary for the Pacific Hardware and Steel Company, but her circle of friends continued to be the newspaper people she had come to know through her husband. Bessie Beatty was a fixture on the *Bulletin* now, and through her and Gillette's other acquaintances Rose came to know working newspapermen such as Lem Parton and Roi Partridge; Louis Stellman and his wife Edith she had known earlier, probably as friends of Gillette's. At this time Rose began to turn her hand to kinds of writing beyond the limited reporting she had done for the *Kansas City Post*. She, Bessie Beatty, and Lem Parton collaborated on a mystery-thriller called *The Emerald* that would never be published but that would tease her thought with possibilities years later. But serious writing would be some years off, for with Gillette she turned to a new career in selling farmland.[19]

Many of the large California estates and old cattle ranches, some of them with titles going back to Spanish days, had succumbed to the pressures of growing population and rising land prices and were being broken up and sold as small farms. Rose and Gillette went to work for a land company that was subdividing a number of these properties; the Stine and Kendrick Company ran advertisements in the San Francisco newspapers describing fertile parcels and including a coupon for interested parties to clip and mail in. From such leads the Lanes would contact potential clients and escort them out to the properties where small-time buyers might stake a few hundred dollars against the future and where persuasive agents might carve out their own future from the earnest money of other people's dreams. Other potential buyers were to be found by canvassing among the oilfield workers around Coalinga and Bakersfield, who could then be taken by train to the estates near San Jose and Sacramento. Heretofore Rose and her husband had worked as a team in the main, but in this new enterprise it was clear that more was to be gained by dividing their efforts in hopes of doubling their commissions. By such a logic did Rose come more and more to work on her own and to find that she could rely more on herself than on Gillette Lane.

Such, at least, is the inference to be drawn from the autobiographical novel Rose later wrote about her life in this period. *Diverging Roads,* which ran in *Sunset* magazine in 1917–1918 and was published as a book in 1918, tells the story of a small-town girl who begins life as a telegrapher and finds her way to a career as a free-lance journalist. It cannot be read literally as a transcription of Rose's life, but its themes perhaps suggest the emotional dilemmas she picked her way through in these years. Its heroine, Helen Grey, is a naive young woman with fairly conventional yearnings for marriage and a life in a vine-covered cottage; but as she enters the wider world she finds herself caught between small-town standards of respectability and a growing sense of her own potential. In her innocence she can recognize neither predatory males nor women of easy virtue, but neither can she accept the prudery of Mrs. Grundy. When a handsome, sophisticated young salesman sweeps her off her feet and into marriage, she thinks that the dream of the vine-covered cottage will be realized; but a few years of living hand-to-mouth, one jump ahead of the bill collector, with a man whose own dream is of the big score that will net him millions, leaves her feeling emotionally abandoned and hardened to a protective self-reliance that permits her to divorce him. As the crisis resolves itself, she has the opportunity to remarry to a childhood sweetheart who would realize her earlier dreams; but she chooses instead the uncertain but freer life of a traveling journalist, buoyed up by her recent successes and the examples of several independent women professionals who have become her friends.[20]

The marriage offer from the childhood sweetheart is probably pure fiction, although that figure might have been modeled generally on her oldest male friend, Paul Cooley. And the character of the irresponsible husband is probably an exaggeration of Gillette Lane's actual flaws. But a series of episodes rings with a particular emotional intensity that makes them significant quite apart from their status as fiction. In one scene a lonely, married Helen has been reading William James's *Pragmatism* and finds herself taken by its redefinition of truth: "It says there isn't *absolute* truth—truth, you know, like a separate thing. Truth's only a sort of quality, like—well, like beauty, and it belongs to a thing if the thing works out right." Later she reads in a library a book on the social history of marriage and the place of women as property within that institution. Here, certainly, we can see Rose memorializing in her fiction her own farewells to the moral absolutes of her upbringing. In another memorable episode, the abandoned Helen Grey finds in the depth of her despair the strength to take her life into her own hands—to take up her husband's failed efforts as land salesman and to make a success where he could not. And finally there is an effusion of satisfaction as the heroine finds her place as competent professional writer among women friends similarly independent. *Diverging Roads* is not great fiction, and it is not simple autobiography; but it is an imaginative post-mortem of the death of innocence and the resurrection of a disciplined and confident mature woman.[21]

A more significant symbolic death and resurrection had come by way of an incident darker than she could assimilate to the popular fiction of *Diverging Roads*. She would later describe the years between her marriage and her break with Gillette Lane as a time not only of physical but of mental ill health; and at some point in this period both combined to move her to the edge of her endurance. "It is really much better to be

killed quickly than little by little," she would later write of her failed
marriage; and in time she made a confessional article of her attempt at
suicide: "The value of my own experience with marriage was that it made
me as unhappy as anyone can possibly be. If only the usual events of the
usual marriage had happened to me, I should probably have accepted
them and managed to live without being either happy or unhappy. Most
people do, and I am not an unusual person." On a more intimate note,
she reflected to a friend that Gillette was, in some way, slightly mad, and
that the strain of continuing among friends to appear to love him was
more than she could bear. According to her published account, she succeeded in drugging herself into unconsciousness with chloroform on a
handkerchief, only to awaken later with a bad headache and a keen sense
of her own absurdity. In time, she would date from this incident the gradual emergence of a mature determination to accept life's manifold blessings while trying to live without illusions.[22]

One of the illusions she was learning to live without, though, had to
do with romantic love. She would always remain alive to the sudden flare
of passion, and even to the reality of enduring affection; but what she
could not reconcile herself to was the suffocating claim of another on her
essential self, the emotional dependency that left neither partner free or
whole. No lover could block her view of a wider horizon nor of deeper
mysteries that made passion seem trivial. Such, certainly, was the burden of her later complaints about marriage, and of a poem that seems to
come from these years:

> On the trees and the rooftops the gray skies come down
> In sudden silver rain, and the air stirs with fear
> More strange than the memories of the old human town.
> For the feet of the rain were on earth before man was here
> And the rain will be when earth has forgotten him
> As the moon has forgotten life. The breath of the rain
> Is a silent whisper of spaces where even the stars are dim
> And there is no knowledge of hope or love or pain.
> I am afraid. "Oh, love! Something to cling to—
> Hide in.—Safety—Just for a moment beneath the eternal skies.
>
> Love me! Love me—give me your lips, your eyes—*you*—It is you,
> *You* that I want...." You, safe from surprise
> Of change, older than mountains, younger than dawn,
> Part of me, soul of me—Ah! God! I could kill,
> Tear, break, destroy you!
> The moment is gone,
> And we are two. Two again, and alone, and still.
> We are mysterious as rain and space and change.
> Who are you? What am I? Tomorrow will not see
> Our shadow-shapes...Your eyes are strange,
> And strange things move behind them. Can you be

A refuge from the dark between the suns,
Being yourself a darkness to your own eyes?
Yes, dear, I love you. The thin chill that runs through me
Comes with the closing-down of the gray skies,
That's all.
I am fleeing again on the hunted trail that runs
From nothingness to nothingness through empty skies.

But at the moment such a vision had not fully clarified; rather, she was merely setting some things behind her, finding a way to live with Gillette Lane while opening herself up to a second round of possibilities in California. Somewhere, something ought to satisfy.[23]

VI

Diverging Roads might well be an obscure epitome of Rose's life from 1904 to 1918. The actual track, of course, is not so clear-cut; and there is evidence that the writing career Rose would come to was starting well before she left Gillette Lane, and that the break with him was gradual and, finally, good-natured, whatever the failings and intermittent pain on either side. Apparently the first few years of selling land went well indeed, yielding at times commissions of a thousand dollars a month. They had a motorcar, a fire-red 1912 Thomas Flyer sedan, "a purely wonderful car, the pride of the town, the admiration of the highways." But their work took them far from the highways, and Rose learned to change punctured tires and to carry a reserve supply of gasoline in a five-gallon can on the running board beside the tool box.[24] With the fire-red Thomas Flyer they followed a life of dusty desert roads, small-town hotels, finely honed strategies to bring clients to the point of purchase, and frequent separations. They returned to San Francisco often; but their bases of operations were probably San Jose and Sacramento, from where they would foray out into the farms, the towns, and the oil fields, beating up business. The outbreak of war in Europe in 1914, however, sent a shudder of uncertainty throughout the country; prospective buyers preferred money in the bank to a mortgaged parcel of unimproved real estate. Commissions dried up and the Gillette Lanes had to look for another career.[25]

The letters from this period are only in half a recounting of her experiences in San Francisco; the other half of their divided concern was to coach Mama Bess in the early stages of her own writing career. Rose had begun to draw on her contacts among her newspaper friends to do some commissioned feature articles, while for some time Mama Bess had nurtured hopes of making some earnings by her pen and had even written her own mother about plans for writing a "life story" in some way.

The obvious markets for her immediate experience, however, were the small journals aimed at local farmers and their families; she was beginning to place some small pieces in the farm supplement to the *Kansas City Star,* and soon she would begin publishing regularly in the *Missouri Ruralist* under the name of Mrs. A. J. Wilder. For the moment, the writing careers of mother and daughter were proceeding in step, and Rose was full of advice on how her mother might develop material for her audience— or how she might adapt material Rose had already written. "I have just finished writing a very fair story of how a certified-milk dairy is run," she wrote; " . . . it is very interesting stuff. I thought if you could get some local names to hang it upon you might resell my stuff bodily for say, the first story for the Ruralist, or perhaps to the Kansas City Star."[26]

Occasional newspaper assignments and publicity work were part of Rose's scrambling effort to keep the bills paid. The Gillette Lanes no longer had the motorcar; and they were living in a small apartment—a kitchenette and a sitting room with a wall bed—so that she could not even contemplate the luxury of inviting her mother for a visit.[27] The letters to home reveal an aching concern for money and a curious detachment from the affairs of her husband. Gillette *seems* to have been working . . . but it is not quite clear: "It is my belief," she wrote her mother, "that Claire has gone to work for the Carodoc people. They are a big advertising agency here and they have been negotiating to get him for quite awhile. . . . they sent for him and offered him forty a week and 20% of the net earnings of the whole company. He said he was going to take it, and he has been going down town regularly ever since, so I believe he has gone to work for them." The letter goes on (apparently after some break) to reveal that he *is* now working, and it gives a picture of their hand-to-mouth existence.

> Claire got eighteen dollars today, and we nearly threw a fit—the first real money we have seen for ages and ages, except what you sent. So the rent is no more hanging over us like a piece of black crape. . . . here we have been running carefreely around with people who have to hire secretaries to count their money, and Claire has been casually talking millions with men who are as powerful in London as here, and dining at Tait's with champagne at twelve dollars a bottle, and I went to a lecture in the white and gold room of the St Francis today at which the cards were five dollars, and was an invitation affair besides—and afterward ran into Techau's for a bite and saw the check for the four of us—$11— and all the time inside the gnawing mad wish for twenty dollars for the rent man, and the wonder if the gas would be cut off tonight![28]

Gillette was working only at temporary promotional jobs, despite vague plans in regard to New Zealand and Guatemala; Stine and Kendrick owed them deferred commissions that would never be paid; and Rose could only cultivate prospects. It was not uncommon for the San

Francisco newspapers to sponsor charity events to raise money for worthy causes—orphaned children, for example; presumably the publicity would expand circulation. Through Bessie Beatty, Rose was involved in this kind of work, as well; she mentions "working a benefit for the poor children of the Juvenile Court—which will clear at least five thousand dollars for them—how I wish I were one of the beneficiaries! Of course I am not doing it for sweet charity's sake, any more than any of the others—I am doing it as a policy stunt—want to get acquainted, and want to know people. There is a lot to be got that way."[29] And, in another letter: "As far as spending my time in making the right sort of acquaintances, I DO mean it in a 'climbing way.' It's easy enough to know the right sort of people, and there's every advantage in the world in knowing 'em—if anyone means to climb at all she might as well climb all the time, and if she meets people at all, meet the right sort."[30] It was probably in this year (1914) that Gillette arrived home on December 5, Rose's birthday, with no money but bearing dozens of red roses for his wife. Pockets, purse, and larder were all empty, and we can read an obscure index to the state of her marriage in Rose's prompt action. She peddled the flowers door to door "for a charity" to recover the money for their evening meal.[31]

How many irons could she keep in the fire? She had by this time also written a play, which she had high hopes for. And she was apparently still connected intermittently with Stine and Kendrick's land company, which was subdividing the Chowchilla Rancho in the San Joaquin Valley: "Dairyland Farms" were offered for one hundred dollars an acre on ten-year contracts. It was in Stine and Kendrick's San Jose office that Rose received the telephone call from Bessie Beatty offering her a position on the *San Francisco Bulletin*. She left for San Francisco on the next train. It was January, 1915.[32]

VII

Her recollection of another watershed in that month was quite specific as she considered the years of her marriage: "I got rid of Gillette in January, 1915. Then the Bulletin days. . . ."[33]

The roses in December had not been enough. She was twenty-eight years old and beginning a new life.

ULLETIN DAYS

The worst thing about life is the necessity of trying to do something with it.

The decade had been a progress from innocence through experience to a self-conscious, somewhat brittle maturity. Girlhood notions of a simple domestic life had vanished under the pressure of her own powerful, if vague, ambitions and the complex disappointments of her marriage to Gillette Lane. In effect, she could not reconcile her developing notions of personal fulfillment with the inevitable bonds of marriage. Love itself was another matter, as she would later write to Dorothy Thompson, citing a scrap of verse (perhaps her own) she had carried in her head:

> Now that you are gone, loving lips, loving hands,
> Now I can go back to love—
> I can run and stand in the wind on the hill,
> Now that I am lone and free,
> Whistle through the dark and the cleansing chill,
> All my red-winged dreams to me.

In time, she would come to describe marriage as "the sugar in the tea, that one doesn't take, preferring a simpler, more direct relationship with tea."

But for the moment, in whatever sense she had gotten rid of Gillette Lane, the formal divorce was yet some three years away, during which time they apparently lived more or less apart in San Francisco in more or less amicable relations. Perhaps remembering this time, she would describe love's ending: "not quite being able to disentangle one's self, never quite having the ruthlessness to strike the hands on the gunwale with the oar till they let go." But Gillette Lane from this point on fades from her life. He himself would go on to a modest career in real estate and insurance, and would marry twice more, leaving his third wife with the conviction that his marriage to Rose had been the one great love in his life. He and Rose corresponded for a few years, but he would be remembered only in occasional reflections on her past and would leave little more than his baffled exclamation, at some point in the dissolution, to echo in her thoughts: "Why can't you, just once, be *human!*"[1]

By her own developing standards, she was simply all too human in striking out for a perceived good while caught in a web of stifling circumstance. As her heroine in *Diverging Roads* would discover, there was no *truth* in her marriage anymore. By "human" Gillette probably meant simply conventional, with all the implications of absolutism that convention carries, while in her own clearing vision the easy absolutes of her upbringing were rapidly eroding. A decade later she would discover a description of eighteenth-century heroines that was also, she declared, a description of herself as a girl: "They are faithful by instinct, and do not dream of the possibility of being anything else. They possess no morality, but all the virtues; for human beings are moral consciously, but good by nature."[2] For instinct and nature we can read convention, which would always hold Rose strongly in little ways while in larger ways she rejected it; the struggle to be moral consciously would in time loom as the one significant issue. For the moment, however, it was enough to be free.

II

During the years of her marriage she had kept in touch with Bessie Beatty. And when in late 1914 Beatty was given charge of a new feature in the *San Francisco Bulletin*, a women's page, she quickly found herself in need of material and assistance, and her thoughts turned to Rose. She adapted some of Rose's letters to appear as a continuing column, and she called Rose to offer her a position as her assistant at $12.50 a week. By February of 1915 Rose was installed at Bessie Beatty's shoulder in the crowded, windowless room at the rear of the *Bulletin*'s quarters, working sometimes twelve hours a day to fill the page and bring it to press.[3]

On the Margin of Life was the banner at the head of Bessie Beatty's page; below it ran the interpretive subtitle: "Truth is seldom on the written page. We must search the margins and read between the lines." Actually, the page offered its women readers a steady supply of truths, large and small, to answer the dilemmas of their lives; the metaphor of its title aimed rather at the marginalized lives of women and the strategies by which they found the space to flourish or just to survive in the larger culture. Rose's first column reflects a thoughtful if lighthearted assessment of the relations between the sexes; it is easy to guess at its origins in some earlier letter to Bessie Beatty. "How on earth can men act as they do and still call themselves the logical sex?" the voice queries. "Why, if they had the smallest bit of logic in their entire make-up, three minutes of reflection would show them how absolutely illogical they are." There follow ten paragraphs of representative masculine foibles:

> It's a man who looks at the sandy ford of the river and decides it is too much trouble to put the chains on the wheels, and drives blithely in. And, if you've ever noticed, when the automobile stalls

in two feet of water, and he has to get out and jack up the car and
put the chains on anyhow, he is very bitter with his wife about it,
especially so if it was she who suggested the chains while they
were still on dry land.[4]

The narrator is identified as "the woman with interrogative eyebrows,"
an appellation for Rose probably invented by Bessie Beatty, and the column extends over several days. Later columns shift to more general topics, although the personal note is still apparent: "After all, we never again
feel so old in all knowledge and wisdom as we are at seventeen, when we
know nothing of either; we never again feel so old in world-weariness
and loss of all illusions as we are at twenty-four, when illusion is just
beginning."[5] By February she was appearing with a small column almost
daily, and although the topics are diverse, a recurrent theme is the gentle
deflation of illusion and self-deception in personal relationships.

Probably Rose was writing these little pieces in her evenings after
her day in the editorial offices with Bessie Beatty. Paid space-rates in
addition to her salary as editorial assistant, she could now look forward
to a small but steady income. At about this time she moved into quarters
in the great house at 1019 Vallejo on Russian Hill, and from here began to
flow a series of lighthearted pieces about the inhabitants of her room-
ing house. Downstairs lived a diminutive artist, Berta Hoerner, who also
worked for the *Bulletin* and who had already illustrated some children's
verses by Rose's mother in Bessie Beatty's pages; shortly Berta would also
illustrate some of Rose's pieces as well.[6] As her columns accumulated, a
certain kind of career was beginning to open up to Rose: given the right
circumstances, she might have parlayed her style and perspective into a
position as a regular columnist. But the confines of the women's page
were too restrictive, and she soon began to turn her energies to broader
fields.

Her new career would be as a writer of lives, both biographical and
fictional, and at times a blend of the two. In the grand scheme of things at
the *Bulletin*, she was to concoct serials to hold the continuing interest of
readers as editor Fremont Older built the *Bulletin* from a marginal, loss-
ridden publication to a position as one of San Francisco's leading newspapers. Older had earlier achieved enormous gains in circulation, largely
by initiating graft investigations into city government. His talent as an
editor was for hiring talented people and giving them the freedom to
work at their best. Serial stories were for him not merely a means of
maintaining circulation: he wanted them to be the best of their kind,
however hazy his notion of literary standards might have been. Sophie

Treadwell, later to write *Machinal*, had been Rose's predecessor; and Older would hold Rose to a standard that he could sense but not define. Rose's first serial fiction was "A Jitney Romance," a lighthearted piece of fluff that she herself thought little of; Older called her into his office and suggested that she could do better.

"I said, well, but what had that to do with it? This was a newspaper serial, wasn't it?" When Older pounded his desk and roared that he wanted the very best writing for his newspaper, Rose could not believe him. "I felt precisely as if J. P. Morgan should say he desired a life of poverty." She challenged him: would he print, say *Les Miserables*? And with another blow of fist on desk Older rose to the challenge: "If Victor Hugo'd walk in here with the manuscript of *Les Miserables*, I'd print every word of it! I'd be damn glad to!" "He wanted good stuff," Rose recalled. "He believed in the good taste and even in the average mentality, high mentality, of the mass of newspaper readers. But fundamentally, all the time, what he wanted was readers."[7] Older's literary theory was, in short, populist rather than elitist; and Rose herself would later struggle in the dilemma of such a commitment.

Older was then at the peak of his powers, a bald, cigar-smoking and demanding taskmaster with a soft heart for anyone's troubles. He was one of the few men Rose would ever admire without reservation, while he apparently found much to admire also in this vital neophyte journalist with the gifts both for prodigious work and lively conversation. In later years her letters would cheer his troubled old age, a recompense she would pay him for his own gifts to her. Her years among the spirited writers who labored under him at the *Bulletin* would be a charmed period in her life; and at the parties at his ranch she encountered the San Francisco liberal establishment and a raffish circle of artists, intellectuals, and freed criminals Older took an interest in. As a writer of serials, she accepted Older's standard and worked hard at it, without illusion. Sinclair Lewis had preceded her at the *Bulletin* and Maxwell Anderson would follow her; and although these writers clearly felt the call to greater things, Rose made no such claims for herself. She did not aspire to another *Les Miserables*, but with such encouragement from Older she felt free to turn her best energies toward narratives that would daily tantalize the *Bulletin*'s readers into the next issue of the paper. She soon found herself able to spin these stories out at a rate of fifteen hundred words a day for weeks at a time. She achieved local recognition if not fame in San Francisco journalism; until 1922, as she leaped from opportunity to opportunity, her byline and picture would appear daily in the *Bulletin* for months on end.

One of her first efforts was a serial "autobiography" of the young daredevil flyer Art Smith, "as told to" the enterprising newspaper writer. The whole affair was a function of the San Francisco International Exposition of 1915, which nominally celebrated the opening of the Panama Canal but was designed to celebrate the city's vigorous recovery from the 1906 earthquake and to call attention to San Francisco's heightened status as the natural terminus of the greatly shortened east-west sea route. Among the early attractions were the aerial acrobatics of Lincoln Beachey, who was already renowned for such stunts as flying a plane within the confines of a large exhibition hall. Late in her life Rose claimed to have flown with Beachey in San Francisco; certainly by this time she had flown in a plane, this in a day when most planes were single-seated, custom-built contrivances with no provision for passengers save for a jury-rigged perch on wing or fuselage. Beachey crashed to his death in the early days of the Exhibition, and Art Smith, boy aviator from Fort Wayne, Indiana, quickly replaced him. To extensive newspaper coverage Smith flew stunt maneuvers enhanced by smoke trails and fireworks over San Francisco Bay. Shortly after his arrival, Rose interviewed him and transcribed a version of his life-story, which ran in the *Bulletin* over a period of four weeks and was later published separately as a small book.[8]

The story of Art Smith was followed shortly by an even larger coup. Henry Ford had come to the Exposition to promote the cause of his Peace Ship, which to considerable publicity had sailed to warring Europe in the name of world peace. Ford's fame as an industrialist lent credibility to his peace efforts, and in the early years of World War I the two strands of public interest combined to make him a powerful focus of journalistic scrutiny. Rose tracked him down aboard the battleship *Oregon*, which was visiting San Francisco Bay as part of the celebration, and from a series of interviews, augmented probably by some secondary research, pieced together a story of the young farm boy from Michigan and the struggles that led to his triumphant fame and fortune.[9] "Henry Ford's Own Story" ran in the *Bulletin* in November and December of 1915 and was published as a book in 1917 by the Century Publishing Company. Rose's connection with Century was aided by an Associated Press reporter named Guy Moyston, at the time merely a professional acquaintance but later to become much more to her.[10]

IV

The 1915 Exhibition was also the occasion of a long-awaited visit of Mama Bess. The idea had been raised in letters before Rose caught on at the *Bulletin*, but there had been no money for railway fare and no room for her in the small apartment Rose shared with Gillette. Rose's editorial salary, however, augmented by rates for her serial work, enabled her to send the necessary funds. And she and Gillette were now living apart. Mother and daughter had been separated since 1911, and the coincidence of Rose's new prosperity with the lure of the Exposition justified Mama Bess's long train ride west from home for an important reunion with her wandering daughter.

Mrs. A. J. Wilder was at this time simply that, an occasional columnist for a farm magazine, known to her readers under her husband's name plus the honorific Mrs. The writer Laura Ingalls Wilder had not yet come into existence, but her later fame would justify publication of the letters she wrote home to Almanzo during her trip to California. Prosaic, laconic, yet stretching dutifully into description of what she finds interesting, these letters reveal a commonplace mind and a commonplace style, but also a temperament vigorously alert to the surface of the world and the economic realities beneath it. She was forty-eight, her daughter twenty-eight; they were meeting for the first time as adults on Rose's home ground.

The mother's letters find Rose at home in the apartment on Russian Hill; downstairs lives the "little artist girl," Berta Hoerner, while Bessie Beatty lives across the street. Gillette Lane appears occasionally in attendance upon his mother-in-law, suggesting that the split was perhaps papered over to spare Mama Bess's feelings. Whatever transitional relations Rose retained with her husband during the period in which she "got rid" of him appears to have been within the range of her mother's expectations. There is little mother-to-father comment on the relations between daughter and her husband: Gillette is not working regularly but has a few short-term reporting jobs; Rose is carrying them both as they wait without much hope for deferred commissions from the failing real estate company. And as a subtheme, we find that Mama Bess has come to San Francisco for some money: she hopes, if the commissions arrive, to recoup a $250 loan to the hard-pressed young couple. Meanwhile, in a way deeply revealing of the way money would define the relations of mother and daughter, Rose is paying her mother for her visit—an occasional twenty-dollar gold piece to make up for her lost efforts on the farm at home. Mama Bess reports the accumulation with some satisfaction and returns home with more wealth than she brought.[11]

The most significant strand in these letters concerns the relations between mother and daughter as writers. Rose's mother had broken into print in a modest way as early as 1911, writing for a rural audience about farm topics; and early correspondence shows Rose eager to give her mother the benefit of her experience in writing advertising to develop marketable ideas. The writing enterprise, in fact, occupied the entire family: the *Missouri Ruralist* in 1912 carried an article by Almanzo Wilder that was certainly not written by him, but probably by his wife with help from Gillette Lane.[12] The San Francisco letters reveal a continuing role for Rose as mentor, although nothing could be more different from Rose's easy and vigorous style than her mother's pedestrian prose. One passage, however, suggests that the benefits did not flow one way only, but rather that Rose had drawn freely on her mother's family stories of life on the Dakota frontier. Rose had written "Behind the Headlight," a serial "autobiography" of a railroad engineer of which she was ostensibly the editor. Actually it was a composite of several interviews with old railroad men; and its recreated dialogue and setting, its careful pacing of dramatic incident, and its strong romantic plot make it a fictionalized narrative however true its main outline and incidents might have been. Part of the fiction was literally an import from Wilder family history, as Rose engrafted onto the engineer's days on the Dakota railways tales her mother had told her. A similar easy ethical slide lay at the heart of her story of a San Francisco police detective, "Ed Monroe, Manhunter." According to Mama Bess, the anecdotes of criminal life actually came from an ex-convict working in the circulation department of the *Bulletin*. The ex-convict was probably Jack Black, who would a decade later publish his own memoirs. In this period, however, he also narrated some of his prison adventures to Rose, who wrote them up as "The Big Break at Folsom."[13]

Entangled literary and ethical questions emerge at this point, questions concerning the truth of the narrative and the identity of the narrator. The pull of invention upon fact is as old as narrative itself, and the special discipline of historical veracity arises late and survives with difficulty. Realistic fiction and modern history seem to have grown up as complements to one another; and what Rose was practicing was a blend of the two that finds its earliest antecedent in Defoe and that has continued to flourish as a sub-literary genre in the face of all criticism. More significant, no doubt, are the values served by this genre that account for its popularity. From the story of Art Smith—and the ensuing lives of Henry Ford, Charlie Chaplin, Jack London, and Herbert Hoover—until her final writings, the story remained one simply of heroic romance, the reassuring interpretation of life as successful struggle against circumstance to a point of peaceful reward. Doubtless this was Older's sound assessment of broad public taste; but it was one that Rose could work within comfortably. From the writer's point of view, particularly facing the practical problem of increasing a paper's circulation, the issue scarcely rises above the level of producing a marketable commodity. All of her life Rose would cheerfully describe herself as a competent hack writer. By the time of Mama Bess's visit, Rose's beginning salary of $12.50 a week had risen to $30.

Technically, in adopting the first-person pronoun in writing of the engineer or of Art Smith or, later, the burglar Jack Black, Rose became not an editor but a ghostwriter; while in writing the life of Henry Ford she posed as objective recorder. But the effective distance and difference is not great, as the personal details of the specific story are assimilated to

the underlying Ur-story. So far as is known, such minor figures as Art
Smith did not object to the fictioneering liberties with their lives. Ford,
however, would later record his distaste for the results of his casual interviews with this San Francisco reporter;[14] and the ethical issue of the
authenticity of Rose's versions of the lives of the famous emerged dramatically as she engaged the lives of Charlie Chaplin and Jack London.

V

Chaplin was at the height of his fame in the spring of 1915 when he
granted Rose a series of interviews at the Essenay Studios in Los Angeles.
The ensuing story, ostensibly in Chaplin's own voice, ran in the *Bulletin*
in July and August of 1915 and consisted of a narrative of Chaplin's childhood adventures in poverty and his eventual triumph in American films.
Much of the drama derived from Dickensian portraits of Chaplin's mother
and father, complete with recreated dialogue in a novelistic mode. It
makes a good read even today, and again Guy Moyston was able to negotiate a contract for book publication, this time with Bobbs-Merrill. The
title page implies Chaplin's imprimatur and thanks Rose Wilder Lane for
"invaluable editorial assistance." Perhaps Chaplin never saw the series
as it ran in the *Bulletin*, but when he saw an advance copy of the book
version, he was angry enough to threaten legal action to stop publication. Copies were actually in the warehouse when Bobbs-Merrill acceded
to Chaplin's demands and withdrew the book. A few copies made their
way into the world, but by and large the suppression was complete. Rose
wrote a remarkable letter to Chaplin in the course of the affair:

> Your present attitude of course puts me in a perfectly frightful
> position with the Bobbs Merrill people. I suppose I deserve it for
> not making sure that the arrangement would be all right with
> you. . . .
>   I suppose that your feeling is simply that you should have some
> money from the book if it should appear. It is natural enough to
> want money, but I wonder if you are not exaggerating the possible
> profits to be made from book publication? My own profits from it,
> even if it sold up to the very limit of our expectations, would be
> only a few hundred dollars—perhaps worth half a day of your
> time. As matters now stand, it appears that your action will result
> merely in my losing the amount—which I need not say would
> make much more of an impression on my bank account than on
> yours—and also in your losing the publicity value of the book, a
> publicity which even Theodore Roosevelt in his palmiest days was
> glad to utilize. . . .
>   You've lived a life which makes a corking book. I have written
> the book—and really, it is no more than true to say that it is a book

whose popular appeal is greater than that of a book any other hack writer is apt to write. . . .

It is in the interest of both of us to have the book published. I admit it's more to my interest than yours. . . . But it is to the interest of neither of us to stop the publication of the book. And if the situation is allowed to develop into a real scrap, we'll both be in the position of the two men who fought over a nut and brought the matter to a judge who ate the nut and divided the shell. I don't see a bit of use in the world in letting the lawyers have the nut, do you?[15]

Something must be said about such a letter, but it can be deferred for a glance at Rose's later biographical enterprise, a fictionalized "life"—or, perhaps better, "impression"—of Jack London in 1917.

VI

The famous novelist had died unexpectedly in 1916 at age forty, and public interest in the details of his life was high. Portraits and reminiscences were frequent in the press and in magazines, and it is not surprising to find Rose pursuing an opportunity to expand the genre she had worked so naturally in before. She had now developed a connection with *Sunset* magazine, which on the basis of her work on Ford and Chaplin had commissioned her to do a series on London. Her engagement with that work is preserved in part in her correspondence with Charmian London.[16]

Charmian had her own plans for a biography of her husband and had actively discouraged a number of biographical enterprises. Rose arranged an interview with her ostensibly to gather material for the series of articles on "the personality and adventures of Mr. London" that had been commissioned by *Sunset*; she suggests that Charmian should share with her "a common interest in the worth of the articles"—a charmingly ambiguous statement that can be read as an avowal to work responsibly or as a tacit threat to publish irresponsibly. By the time of her next letter, after the requested interview, she asserts as news that *Sunset* now wants "a semi-biography . . . a sort of free-hand sketch of his life," and she apologizes for seeming to have come for the interview under false pretenses. Subsequent letters from Charmian reveal her uneasiness but also that Rose has made a striking impression on her as "an interesting and brainy woman," one whose career as a writer Charmian was reluctant to impede.[17]

Charmian found her fears justified not by Rose's first installment, which she found unobjectionable ("fiction, for the most part—charming fiction, too"), but by *Sunset*'s advertisements for it, published in the *Bulletin*. She found these to be "yellow, offensive, lying"; but she reassured

Rose that "you are not in the least 'yellow'."[18] The rest of their correspondence charts a growing disappointment on Charmian's part, although her animus is directed more at *Sunset* for its irresponsibility and at herself for not having demanded that Rose check copy with her. Rose acknowledges the inadequate, hybrid nature of her work: "Of course the whole thing is fictionized—but I hope merely in the matter of color and handling." But she defends herself on several matters of interpretation, particularly her portrait of London's father, as based on sound evidence from other sources: she claims to have scoured the Oakland waterfront and to have talked with many who had known London—everyone from Johnny Heinhold to the mayor of Oakland. As her series on London continued, Rose had to contend both with Charmian and with Jack London's sister, Eliza, who put the matter succinctly: "What Jack London himself wrote about his own life is mixed with fiction. But *you* are supposed to be writing his biography."[19] Charmian understood more clearly what Rose was about, and did not object in principle to a portrait mixing material from *Martin Eden* and *John Barleycorn* with facts gleaned from research; but she resented the occasional inaccuracy she might have corrected and the interpretations she deemed in error. Even though her threat of legal action had won her the right to offer corrections in proof, by the time the series was concluded she was bitter in the extreme at *Sunset* for exploitative tactics and disappointed at Rose's failure to achieve a sketch worthy of the man.[20]

It is easy to take Charmian's side in this: few relatives of biographical subjects are satisfied with the lives that are written, and their natural claim to special knowledge must be respected. On the other hand, the biographer is never to be required to accept the interpretations of interested parties. What is most fascinating is how Rose was able to do such damage to Charmian, if not to Jack London himself, and still retain Charmian's respect, even admiration. Rose's letters present herself as a struggling young writer eager to break into a major magazine, yet one caught between the magazine's exploitative demands and her continuing work for the *Bulletin*. Her visit to Charmian and the skill of her writing were, apparently, enough to prepossess the widow in favor of her endeavor and to persuade her to assign most blame to *Sunset* for requiring such things of a writer. All of it is just close enough to the circumstances to be true; and Rose's letters to Charmian are powerful instruments of persuasion and justification as the proposed work evolves from a sketch to an eight-part biography and from a serial to a full-fledged book.

Yet it is possible to read into the whole enterprise a subtle and continuing calculation on Rose's part, particularly in her disarmingly casual claim of having little interest in publishing a book that might vie with Charmian's intended biography: "I have not seriously contemplated its publication in book form. I am a lazy creature when it comes to cashing in my opportunities—it is the story which interests me, not the profits." To which Charmian finds herself seduced into replying, "Publish your book if you can, later on. I shall not stand in your way—even if I could." If this was a calculated strategy on Rose's part, it was one in which she finally overplayed her hand—not in her letters to Charmian but rather in the work she accomplished, which Charmian ultimately judged to be "very largely an erroneous interpretation of Jack London."[21] Even though it was by then quite clear that Charmian had found the whole enterprise offensive, Rose could not resist bringing to her the offer of a book publication: so far had she come from her initial interview and disarming lack of interest. She professes that she will not publish without Charmian's permission—then asks if any changes might make the work acceptable.

> Is it possible, by alterations which will not involve changing the entire structure of the story, to make it acceptable to you for book publication?
>
> Century publishing company offers me fifteen percent royalty. The royalty is not as high as I have been offered, but I like the connection with Century. I like the connection, indeed, more than the money. It might be possible to arrive at some financial arrangement with you.[22]

Charmian's objections, however, despite her goodwill of a year earlier, were by now insuperable: "It was pretty fiction . . . but it was not biography and IT WAS NOT NECESSARY TO GOOD WORK." Century, she suggests, "would not care to buy a lawsuit with a manuscript."[23] And so the matter ended—however, with a real regard for Rose evinced on Charmian's part and a real regret at standing in her way. The nature of Rose's regrets are less clear. Her correspondence throughout acknowledges Charmian's moral right to refuse permission; and her final letter claims that her own decision is a moral one as well: "Can you not see," she wrote, "that were I the sort of yellow person to be terrorized by threats of the law I would also be the sort who would make the story absolutely law-proof and disregard all the motives which do in fact actuate me, and have from the first?" Her letter rings with sincerity:

> You have been hurt, and I regret that. Whether you believe it or not, I really do. I wrote the story with the tenderest regard for all the persons concerned in it. I still believe that you have read in it many things which the stranger, reading it, does not see. I believe that if you saw me more clearly your attitude toward me would be very different, and you would neither accuse me of lying to you nor of desiring to use you as a stepping stone. These things do not hurt me as deeply as they would if they were true, and I can quite appreciate the viewpoint which makes them seem true to you. But I do sincerely regret the whole situation, and the Century company incident does not add a featherweight to that regret. As you

say, they will take something else of mine. One book does not
make a career. I do wish that you could believe that my first
thought on receiving the offer was for your feeling in the matter,
and that I had not the slightest intention of attempting to over-rule
it in any way. Indeed, I wrote them immediately that I could not
accept it, and only on second thought did it occur to me that I
might have exaggerated your objections, and that at least I might
write you and be finally informed of them.[24]

Yet the sincerity would be less suspect were the Chaplin affair not in
the background, and thus the suspicion that the moral high ground is
assumed in the face of another lawsuit. There is certainly the possibility
of a deep-laid deception here—indeed, considering the persuasive sincerity of Rose's whole series of letters, of self-deception underlying it all.

VII

During her visit with Rose, Mama Bess had admired the view from Telegraph Hill and had mentioned that Rose hoped to move there—despite
the disreputable neighborhood of Italian fishermen surrounding. Early
in 1916 Rose did make the move to "The Little House on Telegraph Hill,"
as she would then head her letters, sharing a shabby, leaky little domicile
with Berta Hoerner.[25] Although the formal divorce action would not be
completed for almost two years, the move effectively marked the end of
her life with Gillette Lane and the beginning of an exhilarating period of
growth and independence. Her year at the *Bulletin* had given her a sense
of her abilities and had opened up indefinite vistas for her future; the
year following would consolidate her career as a professional writer and
as a woman in control of her own destiny.

Now free of Gillette, she could concentrate her attention on a new
circle of friends. These ranged from working journalists and writers into
the bohemian fringe of artists and intellectuals. We can imagine her
throwing herself into this new life with the storm of energy that she
brought to every new enterprise. These were, or ought to be, finally, her
kind of people. But friendships are seldom equal investments on all
sides; and Rose, who had never had companions who could share her
interests and aspirations, committed herself to these people with a generosity she would later regret. To her tea parties came Bessie Beatty,
publicly beloved for her work with abandoned children and exploited
women, something of a professional virgin, subtly manipulative and
powerfully ambitious; Elmer Hader, a painter and illustrator engaged to
Berta Hoerner; Associated Press correspondent Guy Moyston; Lem Parton of the *Bulletin* and his wife Mary; an otherwise nameless Dmitri, per-
former of a notorious Russian dance; boozy Frederick O'Brien, Manila

newspaperman, with a manuscript no one would read; Jacques Marquis, a journalist and musician born to a prosperous Swiss family; his American wife Annette ("Peggy"), a photographer; Austin Lewis and Anna and Rose Strunsky, socialist friends of Jack London; novelist C. C. Dobie, author of many San Francisco stories. Charmian London was invited, and promised to come, but did not. "A real gaiety" prevailed, Rose recalled fondly; "all of us could be crazily happy till dawn on rice pudding and oranges and cigarettes." Surely the women among this group were the friends for whom, when they sallied out for drinks or dinner, smoking cigarettes became a gesture of liberation. Rose told the story of purposefully and fearfully lighting up in restaurants, only to be reproached again and again by waiters and managers who insisted that in respectable places women did not smoke. But it was necessary to make the gesture, and thus the habit that stayed with her for life.[26]

This was a time of great intellectual and emotional stimulation. Always an avid reader and talker, keenly aware both of her own good abilities and of the voids in her formal education, she had until this period worked in realms far removed from the world of ideas. Her ingrained assumptions were essentially Protestant and individualistic, the inheritance from pioneer parents, however tempered by her infatuation with Eugene Debs. But her naive faith in Debs had waned during her real estate days, she recalled, as she "fought for commissions and sales, too busy getting them to worry about the Golden Rule in business, especially as I never happened to encounter it there." And the religious certitude of that inheritance would be set aside: "there wasn't any Eden ever, you know," she wrote to Mama Bess. "Drunk on Darwin, Huxley, Spencer, my generation nonchalantly abolished God," she later observed, and Marx and Freud were part of the heady drink as well. Moral absolutes, under the eye of science, became simply conventions as she and her cohorts sought to ground themselves in a newly discovered natural order that underlay the shattered culture of the nineteenth century.[27]

What fell into place was a melange of ideas that essentially substituted a romantic naturalism for the departed theism and a social meliorism for the discredited gospels. As she had come to maturity in an urban business world, she had encountered the easy adaptation of the earlier tradition of individual struggle to the Darwinian hypothesis: social Darwinism had become a cliché by her adult years, and she had read Herbert Spencer while still a telegrapher. But for her new circle of friends, ideas were a stock-in-trade. The *Bulletin* regularly carried editorials on the leading issues of the day written by her friends, and the intellectual life of San Francisco was energized then as now by the proximity of Stanford University and the University of California across the bay in Berkeley. Rose would still have heard echoes of William James's presence, as well as current lectures by David Starr Jordan; Bergson's ideas were in the air; and the instinctive, self-serving energies that had carried her in her business career found a new challenge in the vaguely socialist liberalism of many of her friends. Certainly the limitations of social Darwinism were on her mind as she wrote, not merely in her willingness to consider government solutions to social problems in "Soldiers of the Soil" and "The Building of Hetch-Hetchy," but also in her fiction and her local color pieces. In "Myself" her heroine is lectured on "survival of the fittest" by her business-school teacher, whereupon she immediately gets her first job by keeping from a more needy classmate news of an opening that she might fill it herself. And in one episode of "The City at Night," Rose ironically invokes the Darwinian phrase as a hard-working immigrant boy, sole support of his family, learns of the death by disease of his infant sister.[28] Years later Rose would proclaim that at one time she had been a Communist, which was probably an overstatement; but from this period until her visit to Europe she accepted as more or less inevitable the eventual arrival of a benign socialist order. She was attracted to Jack London's theoretical socialism, and when she recalled in a letter to Dorothy Thompson their generation's enthusiasm for the Russian Revolution ("The sun is rising in Russia," they said to each other), she was remembering an attitude, if not a creed, that she shared with many of her contemporaries.[29] That she was willing to debate the Bolshevik war resisters who organized under Jack London's name shows the pragmatic streak underlying her fling with socialism, but it is likewise no surprise to find in her FBI file that in 1919 her name was on the mailing list of the Finnish Singing Society, identified by the FBI as a propaganda group associated with the IWW. The mailing address was 1413 Montgomery, The Little House on Telegraph Hill.[30]

It was a time of growth in many directions. What she had wanted as a girl in Mansfield, her dreams fed by fiction and unratified by experience—dreams of fame, romance, wealth, glamor generally—began to come into focus as specific possibilities. The most authentically realized passages in her *Bulletin* romances were those describing the poverty-child who discovers new worlds of affluence, manners, and learning that leave her uncertain of herself, resentful and ashamed of her origins, and greedy for fulfillment. Typical is the heroine of "Myself," whose experience with a wealthy lover leaves her gasping for riches and whose romance with a distinguished novelist finds her making mental notes of books to read. In some innocence, Rose had taken Gillette Lane's babbitry as sophistication, only to find in her new life new standards. The energy she had thrown into telegraphy, then into advertising sales, flowed into these broader channels but still with little direction save toward some kind of personal fulfillment. Her divorce had freed her and given her a certain facile sophistication ("Marry at eighteen and get it all over with by twenty-five," she remembered saying); but what should follow was not clear. "I still had no practical sense whatever, but lived in dreams and fantasies. My thirtieth birthday shocked me into a sort of sanity for a moment, and then I forgot it."[31]

VIII

Ranging out from her core of professional friends were the artists and intellectuals of the Bohemian order. Rose's solid middle-class grounding afforded her a healthy suspicion of the pretensions of the artistic life; she gives them a satiric portrayal in several of her serials. But she found these people interesting just the same, and in a letter in her middle years she reminisced about one of the more exotic incidents from her early days in San Francisco. "Did I ever tell you the tale of how I tried to fatten Gertrude Kanno?" she wrote to her agent, Carl Brandt, mentioning a notorious if not notable sculptress who had been the mistress of Joaquin Miller, the flamboyant "poet of the Sierras" at his ranch (the Hights, he spelled it) above Oakland. There Gertrude had met Kanno, a Japanese poet working as Miller's handyman, who succeeded Miller in her affections:

> Kanno was a Japanese poet of the greasiest description, whose poems were uttered aloud as he emerged from the subconscious in the early mornings, and I've always suspected that Joaquin Miller's nobility—when Gertrude and Kanno appeared before him hand-in-hand and confessed their love...Well, anyway, they had all been living together on The Heights, and Joaquin was noble; he sent the two of them away to Washington, where they were legally married on the seashore and the story was good for two columns with pictures everywhere. Then they came back to The Heights. At this point I enter the picture, young and generous and kind. Gertrude and the Japanese lived beautifully together in a six-by-ten shack made of redwood boughs and filled completely with Gertrude's model-stand and clay. They slept on the ground beneath the stars, most romantic, and they lived on rice. Whenever the rice ran out, Kanno would build another few feet of stone wall for Joaquin Miller, who would give him a dollar, which bought more rice.
>
> But something happened; Joaquin paid for no more stone wall. These two then began to call on their friends just at meal-time. Most of their acquaintances could endure Gertrude, but the Japanese was *really*—not because he was a Japanese, but just because he was Kanno. It was too much to bear. In a few months food supplies absolutely ceased; people sat stolidly a whole day through, starving themselves, rather than feed those two. They were starving, quite literally. My heart was wrung. I returned to town just at the worst; Gertrude had crossed the Bay with the last dime. Kanno couldn't come, having no ferry fare. Gertrude was a skeleton, really.
>
> "Gertrude," I said, "Come and stay with me." She was dying,

but all she needed was rest and food. Tenderly I cared and cooked for her; five meals a day, most delicate and nourishing food. People asked, what was I doing nowadays, and others replied, she is fattening Gertrude. It was true; I did nothing else. And she did recover, she could stand and walk without trembling, she began to have a normal color; days and weeks passed, and she began to have rounded flesh upon her bones. Till one night I was awakened from weary sleep by Gertrude, violently shaking me. It was an attack. "False friend, lying traitor!" she said. "I see it now, I see it all, don't think I don't know—you are killing my Art!"

She was fairly strong by that time, and always much taller and bigger than I. We had quite a scrap in the dark, all complicated by my bed clothes, but partly by physical exertions and partly by telling her not to be a fool I got some reason into her. About one o'clock I got her back to bed in her own room, and collapsed into mine. I slept instantly from exhaustion, and was awakened by one wild ceaseless peal from the doorbell. Kanno, with broad-brimmed hat and huge black cape, came charging through the door. "Where is my wife? Foul fiend, what have you done with my Gertrude?" One shriek of great joy on the stairs, and Gertrude in my borrowed nightie was folded into the black cape. I went to bed, and so did they.

I was awakened by Gertrude. "Where are the bath-sheets? My darling likes them better than towels. He's taking a bath now, I don't know how to light the water-heater and it sounds as though it'll explode. You'd better look at it." She gathered up all the bath-sheets and my bath-salts and vanished into the bathroom. I went down to the kitchen to rescue the house from the gas water-heater. My room was next the bathroom, so I stayed downstairs, fitfully dozing in a chair, till dawn. The two then descended, happy.

I have always had a weakness for happiness; there is so little of it, it seems a pity to spoil any. So I prepared a truly mammoth breakfast, which they ate, and when they wanted more I prepared that, too. Replete, they sat together on the window seat in my living room. On the rug at a little distance I sat cross-legged— always the best posture for meditation—and meditated how, without injury to their sensibilities and pride, I could get rid of them. For Kanno was really unspeakable. And after all, Gertrude was now well-fed. . . .

Kanno's long rank hair was parted in the middle, like that of a Japanese doll, and his eyes gazed out of it at me with the expression he thought was hypnotic. "Eyes like the sea," he said. I didn't get it, partly because I was tired, and partly because it sounded like a string of oily zzzzz's.

"What?" I said.

He repeated, "Eyes lige zee zee . . ."

The bread-knife was lying on the window-seat; there was where Gertrude had put it when I asked her to slice the bread for toast! And as its point went into my shoulder I regretted that I hadn't found it, but had cut the bread myself with another knife, instead.

I was at a disadvantage, being cross-legged on the floor, and I really thought Gertrude would kill me before I got the knife away from her. She did cut me rather badly, but only surface wounds. Kanno didn't do anything; merely sat.

My rug was ruined; it was never the same again after coming home from the cleaner's, and the cleaning company said they wouldn't be responsible. I spoke harshly to both of them, and Gertrude never forgave me. The next time I met her was on the street, and, wearing the dress of mine which didn't fit her, and in which she'd walked out of the house that morning, she cut me dead. She was thin again, too.[32]

#

By the time Rose had broken off negotiations with Charmian London, early in 1918, she had left the house on Telegraph Hill to live briefly at 1120 Arch Street, the Berkeley home of one of her married friends, Alice Danforth. The Jack London project was over for now, but not out of her thoughts forever. At the moment, however, she had another novel in progress, the demands of which, she had written Charmian London, kept her from staying fully abreast of Charmian's contention with *Sunset*. *Diverging Roads* would be the last in a series of romantic serials that had begun with Rose's earlier work for the *Bulletin* in 1915.

These serials had been shamelessly clichéd romances. *Diverging Roads*, however, brings into focus an unromantic problem common to all these romances—a problem that Rose doubtless saw to be of concern to many of her women readers but also one that she felt keenly herself. This was the conflict between marriage and career as destiny for the modern woman. All of Rose's heroines are working girls—a nurse, a stenographer, a telegrapher, a copywriter—propelled into the work force out of necessity or, at least, out of a revulsion against entrapment in poverty by an early and unpromising marriage. They succeed at work while hesitating between suitors—one attractive and wealthy but finally irresponsible, the other an exemplar of pedestrian virtue despite his lack of charm and sophistication.

In the early stories, conventional marriage to the upright young man finally solves all problems, including the career; but by her next-to-last effort of this kind, Rose was self-consciously bringing the career problem to the fore. The heroine of two linked serials, "Myself" and "——— and Peter," is not only successful but happy in her work and foresees a satisfying future in her advertising career. But she also sees a lonely future and marries a struggling attorney who agrees that they will have a "modern" marriage with two careers. The second serial analyzes the strains of such a marriage, as neither partner has proper time to devote to the simple cares of a life together. Earlier she had resisted the illegitimate route to success by marrying the boss's irresponsible son; now she must fight off the temptation of an internationally renowned novelist who would carry her away to a glamorous life. A philosophical dimension is afforded by a woman radical who denounces marriage as a medieval property arrangement and who preaches free love and state-raised children. Under such pressures the heroine strives vainly to "have it all" (her own phrase); in time, she solves all problems by keeping her husband, quitting her job, having babies—and beginning a career as a novelist.[33]

This was Rose's engagement with the "women's problem" as it presented itself in her day. Buried in it, doubtless, lay her own personal version of the dilemma, although, presumably in the interest of her readers, she enforces on her heroine a self-abnegation and compromise that she could not achieve in her own life. Rather, her sympathies lay with the striving careerism of her heroine. In *Diverging Roads* and her association with the Century Publishing Company she would find an opportunity to explore imaginatively the natural limits of her own career.

We have already glanced at this novel as a kind of epitome of Rose's life since leaving home. More broadly, it also limns in an intellectual background by which she sought to understand the pressures driving her toward another life. She poses the marriage dilemma acutely by making her heroine a young naif who works as a telegrapher only so that she and her childhood sweetheart can accumulate the money to marry. But the skills and satisfactions she discovers in earning a living also reveal the pleasures of a free and independent life. In the version serialized in *Sunset*, the faithful, plodding childhood sweetheart reappears as her ill-fated marriage dissolves and the mature lovers are reunited—another concession to popular taste. But in the expanded book-version published by Century, Rose could no longer betray her heroine. Rather, she allows her to reject the temptation of a saving marriage to find her way—as her author had—to a second career as a journalist and a new life among broad-minded, independent women, such as those who gathered with her on Telegraph Hill. Near the end of the book, these women gather for a free-ranging discussion of marriage, the upshot of which is that they accept the need for love and children but not necessarily the need for marriage: "We don't need husbands," one of them cries. "We need wives. Someone to stay at home and do the dishes and fluff up the pillows and hold our hands when we come home tired. And you wouldn't marry a man who'd do it, so there you are." Rose would describe *Diverging Roads* as "the only book I've ever seriously written—a novel whose subject was the destructive effect of woman's freedom (financial and personal) upon the old institution of marriage."[34]

There remains in this connection a mysterious lover of Rose's during this period. She mentioned to Charmian London that she anticipated being married in the spring of 1918, but that the man in question had enlisted in the Canadian Flying Corps. The idea is hard to square with her suspicion of the bonds of matrimony all the rest of her life, and it is entirely possible that the tale was a strategy simply to gain Charmian's sympathy. A later journal entry mentions a certain "Austin" as successor to Gillette Lane in her affections, and the name recurs again in her correspondence with Dorothy Thompson. A possible candidate is Jack London's friend and socialist mentor, Austin Lewis, who appears from time to time in her letters and diaries in wholly noncommittal terms. He was, perhaps, the distraught lover she mentions in one letter illustrating the curative power of comedy against the chafing of serious affections:

> I remember once sitting on a park bench with a man and having a dreadfully emotional scene—at least, he was emotional—and his tearing off vowing to go to the devil, or kill himself, or something, and I put on my Tam, which I'd taken off to enjoy the breezes, and picking up my gloves, and so on, and was leisurely departing, reflecting on the woefulness of life, when he returned violently and demanded his eyeglasses. He had taken 'em off in stress of excitement, and he had a lecture that afternoon and couldn't read his notes without 'em. Well, we looked everywhere, and they were completely vanished. Would you believe it, it was not till late that night, when I was taking down my hair, that I discovered 'em. They'd been in the Tam.[35]

X

Rose's romantic serials were, in large measure, trivial, or, when they touched serious themes, these were trivialized by her concern to achieve conventional romantic endings. And her "biographies" were never serious biographies, but rather biographical outlines supporting fictional embroidery. Her most authentic work for the *Bulletin*, however, was simply as a wandering feature writer in such series as "Soldiers of the Soil" (1916), "The Building of Hetch-Hetchy" (1916), and "The City at Night" (1917).

"Soldiers of the Soil" is a story of the small farmers of the valleys around San Francisco, implicitly projected against the background of the European war and the attendant concern for food production. As pictured in the *Bulletin*, Rose sets off in a jaunty campaign hat and walking skirt to hike and hitchhike the agricultural environs of San Francisco. The circumstances play to her strength, as each day offers a new adventure to be captured in a vivid vignette. A thematic question runs complexly through all her interviews: is it possible for a man with no capital to get a start as a farmer—in short, to be a pioneer? The answer in most cases

seems to be no, although there are heroic exceptions; and among deraci-
nated day laborers tramping the roads seeking work in the orchards and
fields there is a disturbing nativist resentment of "foreigners" (mainly
Oriental and Italian) who work inhumanly hard for a success that these
native laborers cannot bring themselves to achieve.[36]

The Hetch-Hetchy Dam, which would create a reservoir to meet
San Francisco's need for a water supply, was under construction in 1916
and was an obvious subject of interest for the *Bulletin*'s readers. Rose's
experience selling farmland to oil-riggers in the California valleys made
her a natural candidate for an exploration of the dam site and the progress of construction. She was in her natural element as she recounted her
travels by wagon, horse, and foot into the construction camps in the
Sierra wilderness. The grand design of the Hetch-Hetchy project recedes
and each daily column is laden with vivid, closely focused anecdote and
character portrayal. We meet the lonely snow-gauger on the Sierra watershed, connected to civilization all winter by a single telephone line; the
gentle giant, acknowledged in all camps as the strongest man in the
Sierras; and the stoical steam-boiler operator who works all day in a rain
of sparks, his clothes regularly ablaze. Rose takes a turn at operating a
steam-dredge, and catches on fire herself.[37]

If these earlier series had put Rose on her natural ground, "The City
at Night" let her explore a setting she had adapted to readily. As a transplanted farm girl, she found the city exciting always; and her developing
talents for vivid reportage served her well as she turned to explore the
hidden corners of San Francisco at night. Later she would turn these
same skills to travel writing in Europe and the Middle East; but in exploring the lives of those city denizens who lived unseen by most *Bulletin*
readers, she was cultivating a sense of the everyday exotic. She put out to
sea before dawn with Italian crab-fishermen; she visited Bohemian cafes
and commiserated with the poor children who scavenged in the produce
market; she observed the rituals of a charismatic Russian religious sect
and the pathetically respectable parlor-dances of ethnic Sicilians. With
an underworld guide, she interviewed a sad young cabaret singer in an
after-hours nightclub and actually made an illegal purchase of opium
from a dealer who assumed that her guide was breaking her in to a life of
prostitution. And she mingled with the prostitutes in notorious Bartlett's
Alley, observing their cynical cooperation with a police round-up staged
to satisfy the anti-vice movement in the city.[38]

This last episode was probably in conjunction with one of Fremont
Older's campaigns in behalf of the outcasts of society. The *Bulletin* had
run a serial of a prostitute's life and, on Bessie Beatty's page, the pathetic
story of "Babe of Bartlett's Alley," a young prostitute rescued from the
streets by a woman benefactor in whose home she slowly died of tuber-
culosis. At about the same time, a young San Francisco minister took up

a campaign against the open prostitution tolerated by the city within an area known as "the Line." Older was sympathetic to the persecuted women and angered by the hypocrisy of both the church and the city; with his blessing, Beatty and Rose helped one of the madams to present her own protest—by showing up, accompanied by her sisters several hundred strong, at the minister's own church with a petition saying, in effect, if we are turned out in the streets, will you take us in? He, of course, would not, nor would his congregation; but the point was made.[39]

XI

Although Rose seldom confronted it directly, the war in Europe runs like a dark thread through these years of her own rapid growth. The war had brought the end to land sales, which had propelled her willy-nilly into the world of journalism; and the uneasy period of recession had kept Gillette Lane only marginally employed while his wife outgrew him. As the nation drifted closer to war, *Bulletin* editorial writer Robert Duffus recalled, San Francisco never engaged the problem as closely as did the eastern cities; and only gradually through personal impingements did it become real to the little circle of people around him. Duffus had voted for Wilson in 1916 on his promise to keep the nation out of war, as had Rose; and Duffus's editorials for world peace carried Fremont Older's support as well as Rose's; yet the surge of events was finally unavoidable. Now, as American men were called into uniform, Berta Hoerner's fiancé, Elmer Hader, began his military training at the Presidio, leaving Rose a memorial painting of the view from her old home on Telegraph Hill. Then, with the advent of the Russian Revolution, Fremont Older in the autumn of 1917 sent Bessie Beatty off by way of the Orient to cover events in Russia in a continuing column for the *Bulletin*. It was an assignment Rose would certainly have coveted, even resented, given the way she came to see Beatty not simply as model and mentor but as one whose accomplishments were as much by guile as by skill. Rose, by contrast, was sent to Hollywood to interview movie stars, and her columns—on Douglas Fairbanks, Mary Pickford, William S. Hart, Dorothy and Lillian Gish, as well as an equal number of names now long forgotten—ran sometimes on the same pages of the *Bulletin* in an implicit comparison that was inescapable.[40]

XII

The precipitating event in a redirection of Rose's career was the resignation of Fremont Older as editor of the *Bulletin*. Owner R. A. Crothers, who had bought the paper as an investment, had long chafed under some of Older's liberal campaigns, but had been forced to give Older a free hand because of steadily growing circulation. Crothers's nephew, a young Stanford graduate, stood to inherit ownership and had developed notions of making the *Bulletin* generally more genteel and respectable. Matters came to a head over the Mooney case. Tom Mooney, a labor radical, had been convicted of throwing a bomb at a 1916 Preparedness Day rally in support of American entry into the war; the evidence turned out clearly to be perjured, and Older's paper argued forcibly for Mooney's release from prison. Powerful conservative forces in San Francisco would have been glad to see Mooney hanged on general principles, and in time the pressure was more than Crothers could bear. He ordered Older to drop the Mooney case, and Older resigned—only to be offered the editor's position, and a free hand, at Hearst's competing *Call*. Crothers was disappointed, but consoled himself that he would save $10,000 a year on Older's salary; he could not foresee that the *Bulletin* would soon be wallowing in red ink in Older's absence.[41] For without his presence, the little band of talented, independent journalists he had gathered around him broke up. At this point Rose began a series of journals that would run intermittently through her middle years: "A chemical breaks up its molecular formation in process of becoming something else, and so does a world. The Bulletin is dead. Funeral early in 1919. No flowers. Only members of the family will be present at the interment."[42]

It was the war, ultimately, of course, that was breaking up Rose's world—losing Fremont Older his position and destroying the *Bulletin* as the nexus of the lives of Rose and her colleagues. In her journal she ticked the losses off one by one, charting the scattered locations of her friends. Most important, perhaps, was the return of Bessie Beatty by way of Europe, only to depart at once for New York to be interviewed for the editor's position at *McCall's*; she traveled with Older and his wife, for Older had been called east to discuss his new position on the *Call*. Rose resigned from the *Bulletin* on July 12, four days before Older cleaned out his desk. Crothers offered her more money to stay on, but her loyalties were with Older at the same time that she was beginning to feel the tug of a free-lance career. She had been living for some time in Bessie Beatty's vacant apartment at 1644 Taylor; but now she moved for a month to Sausalito, 17 Alexander Avenue, where she recorded in her journal the play of light and shadow in the view across to Alcatraz during the moments between her final efforts at the revised version of *Diverging Roads* and her attempts to teach herself French. Nearby was the house of Frederick O'Brien, whose manuscript about his South Seas adventures she had agreed to revise. She noted in her journal an elaborate incident between the two houses involving some missing raspberries-and-cream, complete with spontaneous poems commemorating the event. "This is foolishness," she concluded, "but that's the only way to spend life. It buys more that way than any other."[43]

She was unemployed but unworried. Her connection with *Sunset* had given her enough confidence in a free-lance career to refuse Crothers's offer of a raise to return to the *Bulletin*. By August 6 she had turned in the last chapters of *Diverging Roads* and then occupied herself with housework. "And a most curious feeling of being anchorless at sea." She was discussing the possibility of going to the Orient for *Sunset*, as the heroine of her novel had done; and presently the project went forward far enough that she requested a passport to Siberia. But she remained uncommitted: "The worst thing about life," she wrote, "is the necessity of trying to do something with it." She had the South Sea manuscript in hand but could not bring herself to work on it. "I am incorrigibly lazy. But the real trouble is that the war overshadows everything." Her revulsion at the war reached some kind of climax as she sat one evening in the Greek Minerva Cafe listening to the strains of "Over There." "I went home then," she recalled, "sick of seeing drunken men and prostitutes dancing to 'Johnny, get your gun, get your gun, get your gun. . . .' "[44]

Clearly, something had to happen to move her off dead center. From out of the blue—at least, from out of Washington, D.C.—came a telegram to move her: "Will you consider work for Red Cross publicity bureau in London to go as soon as possible if agreeable. Kindly wire night letter collect salary expected and when you could go if at all. Work would be magazine writing." The date was September 27, 1918.[45]

An INTERLUDE AND HERBERT HOOVER

5

. . . there is still three-fifths of the world for me to discover.

Probably Bessie Beatty had passed along Rose's name to the Red Cross, for one of her stops on her return from Russia had been in Washington to report to the Red Cross on what she had found in her travels. The Red Cross was involved, of course, in far-flung relief efforts; and to the extent that their work depended on the voluntary contributions of Americans, they needed an elaborate public relations machine. The Publicity Bureau needed writers, and with most men in uniform these writers were often women. Rose wired her acceptance and left San Francisco on October 11 for Washington, D.C. But before she left, she struck a deal with Fremont Older in his new position at the *Call* to write a series from England on the food problem there and the role of English women in addressing it.[1]

The trip across the country permitted a brief visit to Mansfield, her first in seven years, where her parents had been active in their own way in Red Cross work: to a benefit auction, the local paper reported, Almanzo donated a Leghorn rooster, two hens, and a bushel of Irish potatoes, while Mama Bess contributed her own rooster and fifteen thoroughbred Leghorn eggs. By the middle of October 1918, Rose had arrived back home and was accompanying her mother on trips to St. Louis and Kansas City.[2]

Home and parents had been much on her mind in these transitional days. Her repeated publications in *Sunset* had earned her a page for a self-profile, complete with portrait photo, that would appear with the second installment of *Diverging Roads* and just the month after she left San Francisco. She took the opportunity to congratulate herself on her parentage:

> My mother loves courage and beauty and books; my father loves nature, birds and trees and curious stones, and both of them love the land, the stubborn, grudging, beautiful earth that wears out human lives year by year. They gave me something of all these loves, and whenever I do something that I really can't help sitting down and admiring, I always come plump up against the fact that I never would have done it if I hadn't been wise enough to pick out these particular parents.

She also took the occasion to frame a brief and perky credo:

> I love life because it is always, always interesting. Pessimists say
> that life is bitter and cruel and hard to bear; optimists say that it is
> bright and joyful and full of hope. I think they are both right. Pain
> and joy, happiness and suffering, as they enter an individual life,
> are alike in the one quality of being always a new experience, and
> therefore interesting. The value of life, to me, is that it is so big,
> and we are so small, that we can never get hold of all of it; there is
> forever something more, still unknown.[3]

It is a statement at once facile and sincere. In the background, no doubt,
are William James and Henri Bergson, both popular forces in the intellectual stream she had been sipping from, and who served to support a kind
of naturalistic, if not natural, piety, by which she might with some faith
embrace the flux of life and eagerly anticipate its changes. "I have never
been out of the United States," she had written as she prepared this
profile, "though I have seen most of them, so there is still three-fifths of
the world for me to discover." Behind these words, of course, lay her old
fascination with the life of the Wandering Jew; and perhaps she recalled
them as prophetic when, shortly afterward, the opportunity to work in
England had presented itself. After a brief visit with her parents, she left
for Washington, D.C., to report for work with the Red Cross Publicity
Bureau. Her official date of employment was October 18; she would re-
sign less than a month later, on November 15.[4]

||

What intervened, of course, was the Armistice, which has hung over
these last few pages with all the irony of history. Peace threw all things
into uncertainty, among them the need for publicity writers in England
or newspaper serials about wartime food problems. Rose stayed in Washington just long enough to write a feature article for the *Call* on the problems that the end of the war would pose for the country.[5] At complete
loose ends again, unemployed and without prospects, what better to do
than to go to New York City?

Bessie Beatty was now in New York, installed as the editor of
McCall's; and Berta Hoerner had come to say goodbye to her fiancé,
Elmer Hader, who had, unfortunately, shipped out to France just before
her arrival. The sensible thing, Rose knew, was to return to San Francisco, where an assured job and salary awaited her with Fremont Older.
But at Beatty's urging, and perhaps spurred by the example of Beatty's
success in her move to the great city, Rose wired her changed intentions
to Older and settled down for a new and improvised career. She and
Berta rented a three-story house at 31 Jones Street in Greenwich Village.

So naive were they that the location and the name itself meant nothing to them.

The immediate problem simply was money. Berta had none; Rose had one hundred dollars, which the landlord immediately demanded for the first two month's rent.

> We borrowed $25 from Bessie Beatty, and lived that winter on 50 cents a day; split pea soup, nothing else. . . . We slept, heaven knows why, on a bedsprings (which someone gave us) on the floor, under newspapers and all our clothes; and woke in the mornings deeply impressed, like waffles, by the bedsprings. No heat. The place seemed infested by rats at night, but we soon discovered that it was a ghost. . . . By day Berta worked at her drawing board and I at my typewriter, wearing all the clothes that could be super-imposed and frequently warming our hands in our armpits.

Under such stringencies they mailed a joking notice to their friends postponing Christmas until the third Wednesday in July. The third floor became Berta's studio, while at her typewriter Rose mined several short excerpts for *Asia* and *Century* from the Frederick O'Brien manuscript and cobbled together a couple of magazine articles probably based on her background reading for her Red Cross appointment. But the great coup was her version of the story of Cher Ami, the carrier pigeon that had saved the Lost Battalion in France. She carried the manuscript blithely to Philadelphia to editor Edward Bok of *Ladies' Home Journal*, who read it and bought it on the spot:

> Berta and I discussed for a couple of weeks, and even dreamed on the bedspring, how much LHJ would pay for that piece; we decided $50 and privately I thought of $75, but suppressed that thought to avoid being disappointed. . . . The envelope came; with flopping hands, while Berta held her breath, I opened it. Check for $750. My god. We were so rich that I didn't write another word all spring.[6]

III

The concluding recollection is not quite accurate, for she was at work that spring to exploit the connection with Bessie Beatty at *McCall's* for her own benefit and her mother's. She wrote a romantic story about farm life for Beatty; but at the same time she was busy at her mother's material as well. Beatty had decided to run a series of articles entitled "Whom Will You Marry?" in which older women would pass on to young readers the wisdom of their experience with marriages to men in various occupa-tions. Beatty knew Rose's mother from her visit to San Francisco and commissioned her to write the lead article on life as a farmer's wife. The article is a succinct and optimistic analysis of the advantages of such a life, dramatically framed in a visit to the older woman by a young neighborhood girl contemplating such a marriage. In style, tone, and dramatic force it is a quantum leap beyond Mrs. A. J. Wilder's articles for the *Missouri Ruralist;* and from a letter Rose wrote her mother shortly before its publication we can understand why. Rose, it is clear, had substantially edited and rewritten the manuscript before it could be accepted—much to her mother's chagrin, apparently:

> Don't be absurd about my doing the work on your article. I didn't re-write it a bit more than I rewrite Mary Heaton Vorse's articles or Inez Haynes Irwin's stories. And not so much, for at least your copy was all the meat of the article. About the trusts—the editors thought, and so do I, that if one went into the economic factors of the farm situation at all they should be gone into more thoroughly. . . . I did not feel competent to cover these aspects, nor even to touch upon them, without an amount of research that I had not time for. . . . So I'm afraid I agree with cutting out that part, and I'm awfully sorry if you don't like it.

The letter then continues with several pages of close criticism of another manuscript her mother has written, urging her particularly to observe how Rose has handled the transitions in her revisions of the successful article about to be published. It is clear that Rose has established herself as a skilled doctor of other writers' problematical materials, and she offers her mother the same services she has given her professional peers. "Whom Will You Marry?" marks the first appearance of Laura Ingalls Wilder as a writer beyond the parochial scene; its vetting under her daughter's hand marks also the conditions under which she would in time come to fame. But one of Rose's offhand remarks in this letter carries an unintended irony: "I have not had time to go over the children's stories. I glanced through them, and think them good. But they are not so important as the articles, for there is no opportunity to make a name with children's stories."[7]

IV

Everyone's world was shifting rapidly in new directions in 1919. The house on Jones Street was leased for the year, but before that year was out Berta would be married to Elmer Hader upon his discharge from the army. He set up his studio with Berta in the Jones Street house, but they would shortly depart, taking most of the furniture Rose and Berta had collected, for Nyack, where they would live out the rest of their lives. Rose stayed on in the Village but did not consider herself part of it, although she circulated freely among working writers and artists around her; and later she would identify her closest brush with American Communism with this period, when the success of the Bolshevik Revolution in Russia had transformed many socialist intellectuals into philosophical revolutionaries.[8]

She was fascinated, she later claimed, with the historical novelty of the Bolshevik experiment in skipping the capitalist phase in the Marxist sequence, and angry at foreign efforts to interfere with its progress. As for the likelihood—danger or hope—of an American revolution, her common sense left her skeptical. "Unfortunately," she recalled a few years later, "I knew a lot of people of all shades of opinion,"

> and by still more unfortunate nature, when an argument starts I automatically take the unpopular side. When I raged at the Lusk committee and the excluding of legally elected men from legislatures because they were legally elected socialists, half my friends said I was a Bolshevik—and ceased to be my friends. When I refused to give time and money to the revolution, and said that Herbert Hoover was a great man, the other half of my friends said I was a soulless bourgeois, and borrowed $5 from me.

"My New York friends," she recalled much later, "were all engaged in the problems of splitting the socialist movement and forming a section of the Third International here: Jack Reed, Bob Minor, Kenneth Durant, Albert Williams, Max and Crystal Eastman, Floyd Dell, Ernestine Evans. . . ." Some of these, Reed and Minor and the Eastmans, she probably knew casually; but the others were members of the Haders' circle and she would see much of them when she was in town. They, at least, had the distinction of cleanliness, conventional morals, and good manners: the various excesses of the Bohemian life held little attraction for Rose, and her hesitation about committing to the radical cause was probably as much a visceral revulsion against some radicals' dress and manners as a suspicion of their doctrine—although she could not help admiring the dedication by which some went cold and hungry while working selflessly for the cause. "I was rather despised by almost everyone I knew," she wrote, "because I was bourgeois; I worked; I paid my bills; I wore fairly good clothes—clean, at least, and I paid the cleaner instead of giving money to the Mooney defense." In the Village, she said, her bases were Washington Square, a pastry shop, and Floyd Dell's orange-painted kitchen at 11 Christopher Street. Probably she gave up the house on Jones Street to the Haders in the spring of 1919, and for much of the remainder of that year she was elsewhere. She had yet to finish her work for Frederick O'Brien; and she had already begun considering another biography, this time of Herbert Hoover.[9]

In the Village she had met a writer who went by the name of Jane Burr, who kept a summer hotel in the small community of Croton-on-Hudson, an hour by train from New York City. Croton had become something of a colony for left-wing radicals: John Reed lived there, as well as

Max Eastman and Albert Rhys Williams, and Floyd Dell was married there early in 1919 under Jane Burr's maternal sponsorship. Dell, who was just Rose's age, had by 1919 become something of a left-wing hero, as associate editor of *The Masses* and one of several of the editorial staff prosecuted unsuccessfully by the Wilson administration for opposition to the war. In a gesture of proletarian solidarity in the class struggle, he listed his occupation as "worker" in the New York City directory. On John Reed's insistence, Dell and his new wife bought a tiny house on Mount Airy Road above the village of Croton, and that spring he and Rose cemented the most durable of her friendships when she settled in at Jane Burr's Drowsy Saint Inn for six weeks to complete her work on Frederick O'Brien's manuscript.[10]

She had had the manuscript in hand since the preceding fall, and her success in placing excerpts from it gave her some sense of its possibilities for publication. But the work would prove, finally, to be freighted with more frustration almost than she could bear over the next ten years. According to her letters, she took the work as an act of mercy: she depicted O'Brien as a pathetic drunkard hanging about the San Francisco Press Club and literary soirees, boring people endlessly about his manuscript of his adventures in the Marquesas Islands. By her agreement with him, she would get an initial fee of five hundred dollars for making the manuscript publishable and one-third of any royalties once it was published. Somehow O'Brien got hold of her copy of the agreement: perhaps it was left behind when she lived temporarily in his house in Sausalito; one story has Berta carelessly leaving it in a hatbox. But Rose had her five hundred dollars guaranteed and few expectations for a large sale for the book, so in the spring of 1919 she turned her best efforts on it to clear her desk for a projected life of Herbert Hoover.[11]

From her own repeated claims and from available manuscript evidence, her work on O'Brien's manuscript was a wholesale revision, even to the extent of inserting an episode of her own composition. This six weeks in Croton became one of those idyllic interludes by which she would measure her frustration in later days: work and living and life's pleasures seemed to unroll together in one fabric, gathered, she recalled, in the image of the burgeoning spring leaves in the rain outside her open window. "I wrote White Shadows," she reminisced, "sitting by an open window in Croton and feeling those little leaves in the rain." In the evenings after work was done, she would walk up the Mount Airy Road to visit with Floyd Dell and his bride. Albert Rhys Williams, who had covered the Russian Revolution in a full-dress suit, his other clothes having been stolen, was also living at the Drowsy Saint; and suffrage activist Doris Stevens lived nearby. The women particularly struck Dell with their skill as raconteurs: "My goodness," he wrote to his old friend Joseph Freeman, "the times I have sat up all night listening to those gals tell stories!" Such evenings led to a life-long friendship with Rose and a continuing correspondence that left Dell, near the end of his long life, still so admiring as to annotate one of his letters from her: "I have known many good story-tellers . . . and of them all I think Rose was the most delightful."[12]

Her own recollection of these days and of Dell was equally fond, despite their later drift apart in politics. And she could tell an equally delightful tale of which Dell was the butt, and which caught the essence of her ambiguous response to these high-minded people whose theories could not quite shake her own sense of reality. When the great socialist writer H. G. Wells had come to the United States, Dell and Max Eastman and another writer from the staff of *The Masses* had called on him as representatives of the American movement, taking him to dinner at some considerable expense to themselves. Rose and Marie Dell waited with anticipation for a report on the evening, but Floyd returned crest-fallen.

> They had taken Mr. Wells to the Brevoort, given him a dinner regardless of cost, expressed their admiration, adoration, reverence, waited to hear his wisdom; he had said nothing but commonplace politenesses until they ventured humbly to tell him something of their own efforts in the class-struggle here. THEN he had spoken these terrible words: "There are no classes in the United States," and had risen and said goodnight. None of them had been able to speak.
>
> "I myself could not imagine what he could have meant," Rose concluded, "until I was in Europe and discovered what classes are."[13]

V

A biography of Herbert Hoover was probably a project that began to coalesce as soon as Rose saw that she would not be going overseas for the Red Cross. Probably it had been suggested to her even earlier, during her association with Charles K. Field of *Sunset*, who would appear as her coauthor; she later claimed it was commissioned by Field specifically to boom Hoover's presidential stock.[14] Hoover was already a famous man, first for his successes as a mining engineer and later as food administrator during the war; his connection with Stanford University made him a famous Californian as well. His articles on wartime food production and distribution had run in the *Bulletin* concurrently with a series Rose had done entitled "The Embattled Farmers"; thus her interest in the food problem extended naturally to Hoover in his national and international role, for now he was to save Europe as director of the American Relief Administration.

Once O'Brien's manuscript was off to the publisher, Rose returned to Rocky Ridge Farm late in the summer of 1919; with her fee from O'Brien in hand, she could afford an extended vacation. On her arrival she wrote at once to the Haders. It is the earliest surviving instance of the epistolary virtuosity that would mark her correspondence with her friends, suggestive of what Bessie Beatty had found as copy for her pages and exemplary of the verbal energy that would for years make a letter from Rose the equivalent, often, of a variety magazine. Four single-spaced pages detailed her train ride home, complete with her opinions on Sherwood Anderson's *Winesburg, Ohio*, sketches of other travelers, dramatic recreations of her taxi and hotel experiences—all levitated with a grace and wit that reveal the entertaining presence she had been among friends she clearly missed. And, intermittently, phrases gently mocking the leftist rhetoric of the circle she had just left:

> Dear Comrades—
> Having come so far on my journey back to the people, I am at this moment sitting on the second floor of a plain but comfortable peasant's hut in the Ozark wilderness. . . . In such humble surroundings, with what longing my heart turns to those dear comrades whom I have left in that beloved New York. . . . But I have given it up willingly, even gladly, in order to go to the people. No doubt the people will give a tea-party for me soon, and then heaven knows I shall suffer for my convictions![15]

In September, Jacques and Peggy Marquis arrived from San Francisco by automobile, a truly adventurous trip in 1919; they were on their way to new careers in New York via Chicago, and when they left on the twenty-fifth, Rose went with them.[16] At about this time, the Haders removed to Nyack; Rose, her old connection with Berta and Elmer now on a different footing, did not remain long in the city. It was also about this time that she met, probably through Doris Stevens, liberal lawyer Dudley Field Malone, who would later become entangled in her problems with Frederick O'Brien; they were friendly enough at this time for Rose to write a play performed at his Christmas party. She then returned to Rocky Ridge for the Christmas holidays on her way back to San Francisco; she stopped over in Topeka, Kansas, to interview a cousin of Herbert Hoover's, and by February 1920 she had interviewed Hoover's brother Theodore, now on the faculty at Stanford. A letter from Hoover's uncle in Oregon reached her on Russian Hill again, now at 1017 Vallejo.[17]

By this time she had written the early installments of the Hoover biography, which would begin appearing in the April issue of *Sunset*, and she was negotiating with Century for book publication. During March and early April 1920, she struggled to complete the final chapters, but her mind was not on her work; her diary devotes more space to summaries of European affairs than to her immediate problems. The charmed circle from her old days on the *Bulletin* had vanished. Aside from Louis and Edith Stellman and Fremont Older, there were few of her old friends around to keep her company; she was adrift again in the city she loved, while all America, it seemed, had gone to Europe. At some point in 1919, *Collier's* had offered her a chance to go to Mexico and report on the pursuit of Pancho Villa, but she had turned it down because she still had hopes of going to Europe.[18] Guy Moyston had been posted by the Associated Press to Europe in 1918; he had written her from aboard ship on his way to Danzig, from where he was under orders to try to get into Russia. He succeeded, crossing from Finland in the same train with Emma Goldman and a group of anarchist deportees. Now he was in Holland, awaiting a chance to go to Berlin.[19]

Meanwhile, Rose made her way to Los Angeles to interview a man who had known Hoover in Australia and China; while there, she visited Upton Sinclair in Pasadena and spent a day with Gillette Lane's mother, finding, apparently from wedding photos, that Gillette had remarried and gotten much stouter. Returning to San Francisco, she renewed her friendship with her domestic friend Alice Danforth, bearing gifts for her children and admiring the improvements to their house in Berkeley. She read Upton Sinclair's recently published *The Brass Check,* which attacked the press for sacrificing truth to the profit motive and which could well have caused her some uneasy reflections on her own motives for writing. She complained to her diary of her misfortune to stand between radicals and conservatives on every issue and to be damned by both; but her metaphor reveals her native empiricism. "Why is it supposed to be wrong to fall between two stools? It is the fault of the stools; we should all sit on the good solid earth."[20]

On March 20 she again received a telegram calling her to Europe for the Red Cross.

VI

The telegram came not directly from the Red Cross this time, but from Elizabeth (Bessie) Breuer, a writer Rose had met in New York. Breuer was now working for the American Red Cross publicity arm, and her task was to recruit seasoned magazine writers to keep the work of the Red Cross alive in the public consciousness. It was, in fact, ideal work for a certain kind of free-lance writer: there would be the basic work of writing press releases and items for the Red Cross's own organs, but there was also a ready market in American newspapers and magazines for stories about postwar Europe; and while living on the Red Cross stipend a writer could carve out stories for other publications as well. Apparently, so long as the Red Cross work was mentioned from time to time, a writer was free to exploit any market while drawing the Red Cross salary. Rose reached an agreement with Fremont Older for a serial travelogue to be called "Come with Me to Europe" and left California for Washington, D.C., on April 10, 1920. The trip, she recognized, would be another watershed in her life; at the back of her mind was a determination to stretch her itinerary as far as Baghdad, a dream that had been with her since reading *The Arabian Nights*. The next day, as the Overland Limited wound slowly across the deserts of Nevada and past the Great Salt Lake, she was moved to reflect on the innocent Rose Wilder who had made the same passage, but heading west, twelve years before, "in April 1908—going out to Gillette in San Francisco."[21]

There was yet a little personal persuasion to be done before the job was hers. Bessie Breuer was willing to hire her, but apparently Rose had not sufficiently impressed someone in her earlier one-month stint for the Red Cross in 1918; her personnel record showed a grade of B for both ability and interest. Several interviews were necessary to clear her for re-employment, and there were additional difficulties with the Bureau of Passport Control: probably her association with socialists, Communists, and other radicals had been duly noted. In any event, she had to gather testimonials from Bessie Beatty, Fremont Older, Charles K. Field, and several others, as well as call on California's congressional delegation, before her passport application was finally approved at the end of April.

As she waited, she continued work on the Hoover manuscript. She went to New York to talk to Hoover himself, and then to Atlantic City to attend a Republican Weekend banquet, where she duly noted Hoover's rising political fortunes. In New York, she touched base with old friends and collected new acquaintances: Bessie Beatty's apartment was one center of importance, and another was developing around the Haders, whose gift for friendship would soon make their Nyack home a gathering place for a unique circle of journalists, writers, and artists. She said hello and goodbye to the Haders, Floyd and Marie Dell, Frederick O'Brien, and to Lucille ("Dee") Wollenberg, an old *Bulletin* friend now in Boston; she saw Jacques and Peggy Marquis, now en route to visit Jacque's home in Switzerland; she met Ruth Comfort Mitchell, Ernestine Evans, and Mary Austin and spent a pleasant evening with Kenneth Durant, who would in time become the American correspondent for *Tass*. It was probably in this period that she attended a meeting of the American Communist Party, in the company of Harold Rugg, an event that she would later identify as her furthest swing to the left.[22] In Beatty's apartment she met the editor of *Good Housekeeping*, who commissioned several articles from her, as did Gertrude Emerson and Elsie Weil of *Asia*. Other new acquaintances included the invalid Clarence Day, not yet famous for *Life with Father*; Stella Karn, an aggressive young publicist with a background in circus life; and Stella's friend Mary Margaret McBride, a young newspaper woman from Missouri whose fame awaited the popularity of radio in the next decade..

In such company, Rose felt her energies and her confidence rising: "Whatever happens," she confided to her diary, "I am really going to write this summer—write hard and a-plenty, as Bill Hart would put it. I feel simply brimming over with stories."[23] With her career assuming international dimensions, she obviously needed an agent to handle her affairs while she was in Europe. She signed on with Carl and Zelma Brandt, a major agency, and with them concluded a contract with Century for publication of her Hoover book. During her visit with Hoover, he had asked her for a statement of the issues involved in the Sheppard-Towner Maternity Bill pending in Congress: she finished it at 3:00 A.M. on May 4 and, as soon as the stores opened, bought new shoes, a hat, and veil at Wanamaker's.[24] Her ship to Europe, the *St. Paul* of the American Line, sailed at noon. She found her cabin and slept until six that evening.

"COME WITH ME TO EUROPE"

6

*I so much like real things—the realities that come naturally from the
depths of us like—what shall I say?—the way trees grow.*

By the time she awoke, no doubt, the ship had cleared New York harbor; so her description for her San Francisco readers of the Statue of Liberty was probably based on an earlier harbor excursion. The great lady, she said, reminded her of nothing so much as a "large, somewhat too fat woman in a nightgown, clutching its folds with one hand and holding a candle in the other. Irresistibly you think of mice and of alarms and excursions by night on cellar stairs."[1] The tone is not so much facetious as premonitory, as she promises her readers common experience seen with a fresh eye and reported without cant.

The crossing was uneventful, save for the good luck of winning the ship's pool two days running. But already on ship she was discovering in the young people she talked to the restlessness and rootlessness and eagerness for new experience that would mark the generation after the war; it would become a theme in her daily column. And another theme begins to emerge as she talks with a young French girl returning to France after a visit to the United States: beneath the exotic, the picturesque, the hallowed and the traditional glories of Europe lay an ingrained backwardness that the American would find appalling. As they travel on the boat-train from Cherbourg to Paris, they regard the countryside with different eyes. "Remember," warns the mademoiselle, "there is not a single bathroom under one of those damp thatched roofs."[2]

The battle with and for plumbing becomes a rich comic vein in Rose's accounts of her adventures, culminating in her encounter with a concierge who orders Rose out of the house when she inquires about installing a bathroom at her own expense. The problem was a metaphor, of course, for the larger issue of evaluating a different culture, which in turn would require an evaluation of her own American-ness. She would go through several stages with this problem, and would not solve it with this trip to Europe. The problem of the plumbing would not be solved until October, when, after several moves, she chanced upon adequate quarters. Meanwhile, the larger problems to contend with were matters of her professional and emotional life.

The two emerged together within days of her arrival in Paris, as she dined in Montmartre with Bessie Beatty, Carl and Zelma Brandt, and a new acquaintance, Arthur Griggs. Griggs was a Francophile American, several years younger than Rose, who had made Paris his home; he was in the employ of the Agence Littéraire Française, handling the American market. He was looking for someone to translate for American magazine publication a series of stories written by the aging Sarah Bernhardt. At the table he found an interested editor in *McCall's* Bessie Beatty and an ideal translator in Rose, whose spoken French was still unreliable but whose reading knowledge was adequate to the job; she had, moreover, a reputation for salvaging troublesome manuscripts. The occasion had other consequences, however, as the association quickly blossomed into a romance. She found Griggs interesting in part because he knew Paris intimately, in part because, she wrote Berta Hader, "he is the first man I've known fairly well who has not volunteered the story of his life, so he stands alone against an unknown background." Griggs became her guide to Paris, and for the next year they would be regular companions whenever Rose was in town. One of the first places he took Rose and Beatty was to the Bal Tabarin, where the naked women dancers, Rose observed, all needed baths. The maître d' informed them that the next week's attraction would be something called the Week of the Demi-Vierges. Beatty, more shaky in her French than Rose and unaware that the term described a young woman who would grant any sexual favor save the last, said nonchalantly, "And I bet I'm the only *demi-vierge* in the place."[3]

||

Rose's first trips out of Paris were obligatory for any journalist—trips, that is, to the battlefields of the Argonne Forest and Belleau Wood, which gave her several vivid and touching columns for her San Francisco readers. She posed before a shattered building at Château Thierry for a Red Cross publicity photo; a copy went to the Haders with her notation, "R. W. Lane & other Ruins." Her first extended trip beyond Paris, however, was to Switzerland. Jacques and Peggy Marquis were visiting Jacques's family at the family estate, the Château du Chatelard in Montreaux. A companion to the nearby Château Chillon memorialized by Byron, the Marquis family home sat among its vineyards on a hillside overlooking Lake Geneva. This was Peggy's first visit to her European in-laws, and as a middle-class American girl from Los Angeles she was both astounded and intimidated by the traditional ways of her new family. Rose was called for a visit to share her consternation and amusement, which again Rose turned into chatty columns on Swiss laundry methods and social customs and a visit to the Marquis family's ancient wine cellars, where she discovered, she claimed, that the wine had no effect on drinkers within the cellars—but addled the brain immediately upon the return to daylight.[4]

Although she did attend an international women's conference, this trip was largely a personal indulgence, and after a few days she returned to Paris to prepare for a serious fact-finding trip to Vienna. The intervening week was filled with daytime work on the Bernhardt manuscripts and evenings in the Latin Quarter with Arthur Griggs. The night before her trip to Vienna was apparently a fateful one, as a long walk along the Seine ended with "a two-year compact," some kind of understanding between herself and Griggs. It left her both exhilarated and uneasy the next day, as she filled her hours on the train with a journal that mixed her impressions of the landscape with more intimate reflections addressed to Griggs.

It is very likely that Griggs never saw the missive that ensued: in later years, Rose would from time to time not send letters that had been really mind-clearing exercises for her own benefit. Her intermittent journal writing had begun a few years earlier in San Francisco, and seems to mark the beginning of a conscious concern for finding a significant center to her life. It would have to come, she realized, from some inner certainty, some still point within the flux and reflux of an increasingly complex subjective life—"the ceaseless chatter in my own head," she would call it. Most who knew her would have been surprised to find, beneath the witty and self-confident charm she had developed as her public character, the fears and doubts that occasionally sent her spinning into circle after circle of self-analysis. She was determined to make something of herself in this trip to Europe, and the strain of measuring each day's accomplishment against a standard she could not quite grasp would at times yield effusions such as the one she now directed nominally to Griggs:

> There are so many things I would like to say to you—and I suppose I shall say none of them. Human beings are so helpless when it comes to giving others any light in this groping darkness between us all. But I think you will see more clearly than most of us. I hope I gave you something—just a little something—that makes you happier and more content. . . . I so much like real things—the realities that come naturally from the depths of us like—what shall I say?—the way trees grow, from some inner essential principle of them, just expressing itself. . . . I would like to think that when you have fancies about me now they are just quite simple memories of realities we had together. I would feel somehow that you were giving me something more genuine in your thinking about me that way. . . .

Nowhere in this skittish love-letter does she say that she loves him. The texture of the whole epistle is symptomatic of what she fears worst: into a journal of her experience, on which her writing is to be based, intrudes the personal yearnings of her hungry heart. Within two days she is looking for a letter from Griggs at her hotel, and her diary records the wail directly: "Ow! No mail from Paris! No telegram—nothin'—." The next day she telegraphed him.[5]

Despite her anxious heart, she turned her attention vigorously to the business at hand. If in Paris she had found life difficult, sharing with the Parisians the shortages of a country just past a war, the difficulties of the victors had in no way prepared her for the misery of the vanquished. The Austrian people had made great sacrifices during the war, and the terms of the peace had so dismembered the Hapsburg Empire and so disrupted normal trade and food production that Austria consisted of little more than a starving Vienna surrounded by a reduced countryside that could not support it. The whole city was showing the signs of years of malnutrition. Rose noted it at once in the listless, shuffling people; and she encountered it at first hand when the Red Cross assigned her an interpreter, a cultured, educated woman, fluent in many languages, who had not the strength to work consecutive whole days and whose typical gesture was a hand to the forehead, symptomatic of the headache that accompanied persistent hunger. At dinner in her hotel, Rose found that she could charge her meal to her account—except for the bread and butter, for which she must pay cash to the waiter who bought it personally on the black-market. And when she returned to her room unexpected and found the maid rummaging on her dresser-top, she feared for her money and a valuable pin, lent by Peggy Marquis, carelessly left in sight: but the terrified maid unclenched her hand only to reveal a stale roll that Rose had left behind. It was for her children, she pleaded.

The children of Vienna were to be Rose's special concern during this visit. The Red Cross was providing support to the children's hospitals and Rose was to gather material for an article about these hospitals. It was a depressing business: she found a whole generation of children stunted and retarded by years of malnutrition; an apparently precocious infant of two turned out to be six years old. There was enough food to keep a limited number alive but not, the doctors feared, to bring them to normalcy; while outside the hospital mothers awaited the death of present inmates that would make room for their own starving children. The whole rooftop of one hospital was an open-air ward for tubercular children, sun-brown and naked, who, to show appreciation for American food, proudly gathered around to sing "Way Down upon the Swanee River." The pathos struck her to the heart, but in front of the children she must smile, which she did until the smile froze to her face.[6]

And yet, over against the seemingly hopeless condition Europe had brought itself to were the manifest glories of its culture and tradition, and over against them both the innocence and vigor of Rose's native land. She had been in Europe less than six weeks and in Vienna less than one when she wrote her mother a long letter from the Hotel Bristol.

> At that, the Americans come close to being the most humanly decent, and certainly physically the most perfect, of all the peoples I have so far seen. . . . You have no idea how different is the aspect of crowds on the streets and in all public places—they seem the rags and riff-raff compared to American crowds. A traveler from Mars could see that Europe has been a battle-ground for centuries—the people are short, ugly, mis-shapen. I have yet to see one handsome man or one beautiful woman. . . .
>
> On the other hand, they have a love for beauty, both in material things and in ideas, that America does not even understand. They have no running water or telephones worth the name, bath-tubs are luxuries and such a miracle of comfort as the American upper-berth is undreamed of—but every city street is lined with trees and every public building is built for beauty and not for profit. . . . My little French secretary . . . looks at me with bewildered eyes above a *Saturday Evening Post.* "But these—these are magazines for boys and girls, aren't they? They're so *young.*" And I can only reply with the old phrase, "America is a young nation." One has to see a little of Europe to realize it. We *are* so young, with all the crudities and illusions and bombastic self-assertions over hidden self-distrusts that go with youth. Europe is old and cultured and wise and cynical—and golly, how she envies America![7]

She fled Vienna in extreme depression, but in Prague she found much to smile about spontaneously. Here were a people prosperous and well fed, confident in their colorful ethnic identity, and deliriously happy with their new freedom from Hapsburg rule. Their political ideal, indeed, their political model, was clearly the United States, she found, even to the point of celebrating their own independence on the Fourth of July and flying the American flag beside their own. But she had no sooner reached Prague than she collapsed in a faint and was taken to a Red Cross infirmary to recover. She laid the blame on her experience in Vienna, and struggled up to meet with Alice Masaryk, daughter of an American mother and wife of the new nation's leader. Somewhat renewed from her Vienna experience, she was able to return to Paris in better spirits, to be met at the station by her French secretary and Arthur Griggs.[8]

The following weeks were spent in regaining her health, writing up her Austrian and Czechoslovakian experiences, searching for an apartment, and seeing Paris in the company of Arthur Griggs and Marjorie Thirer, a footloose and very young American girl with great talents for dancing, drinking, and taking up with strangers, yet withal, possessed of a saving good sense and a spontaneous charm—Daisy Miller all over again. Recalling her own youth at age twenty, Rose wished she could have been such a one. As it was, Marjorie drew out Rose's maternal and protective impulses, but also her wry reflections that the war had altered all the values by which she might offer Marjorie any guidance; the best she could do was to take her in to live with her for a time. Her French secretary had searched Paris for weeks and had found Rose only a small room at the Hotel Metropole, rue Cambon. Marjorie, however, shortly found them vacant rooms at 9 rue de la Grande Chaumière, near the Red Cross Publicity Bureau and the Café Rotonde. In her new quarters, Rose worked through several nights at her typewriter; all of Paris danced in the streets celebrating Bastille Day while she worked, and they celebrated all night while she tried to ignore the din. She took the occasion of the Bernhardt translations to interview the aging actress, who was still performing at age seventy-nine, and found her a magnificent wreck still avid for theater gossip from San Francisco. But once her desk was cleared, Rose had to take time to attend to her health, which by now included a badly infected throat and problems with her teeth. A Red Cross doctor recommended against a tonsillectomy, but despite daily swabbings the infection would not clear. She slipped into a pattern of morning work, afternoon naps, and nighttime ramblings about the city. In two months in Europe she had completed the Hoover book, several articles for the women's magazines, and part of the Bernhardt translations, as well as the early portions of the daily columns that would go back to Fremont Older. Yet her indulgences left her feeling guilty. "Life goes by as meaninglessly as a river," she lamented to her diary. "My thirty-third year is already half-gone, and I have the energy of a butterfly at sunset. Nothing accomplished, nothing done, have earned this day's repose." A week later she, Griggs, Marjorie, and Marjorie's companion for the evening ended their night on the town by sitting in the rain in front of a Champs-Elysées cafe and singing Gilbert and Sullivan until midnight. Such times were, she could tell herself in her better moments, "the utterly wasted days that make the others worthwhile."[9]

By September her health was no better, but she had put behind her enough work, including now some children's stories for the *Junior Red Cross Magazine*, that she could consider another trip for more material. Her life had settled a bit: a chance meeting with Dorothy Dulin, an artist who had worked with her in her *Kansas City Post* days, solved the problem of a permanent residence; for Dorothy and her husband were moving to smaller (and warmer) quarters, and Rose could have their apartment at 5 rue Schoelcher—a large studio with unreliable central heat but with a bathroom and hot running water, a kitchen, a bedroom, and huge arched windows overlooking the cemetery of Montparnasse. Her income from her writing was picking up, and at this time she wrote to her mother committing herself to an annual five-hundred-dollar payment toward her parents' support on the farm. Her sense of responsibility seemed to expand with her income, for also at this time she wrote to Berta Hader that she was considering adopting a French war-orphan, a child for whom she could make a home, complete with nursemaid, in her new apartment. Other people would always have a ready claim on Rose's money; and although Jacques and Peggy Marquis were now together in Paris, on their way back to New York City, they were close to a separation, and Peggy came to Rose for a six-hundred-dollar loan. With such burdens did Rose set off on another trip of exploration. On September 21, after farewell drinks at the Rotonde with Griggs, Marjorie, and the Marquises, Rose left on the Orient Express for Warsaw.[10]

IV

Here occurred another chance meeting, one that would have long-term significance. In a confusion over sleeping-berth assignments she encountered two young Red Cross nurses, Helen Boylston and Kitty Van-Buskirk, on their way to Poland after an assignment in Albania. Their stories of wartime experience Rose found enthralling, and she inserted them bodily into her column for her San Francisco readers; by the time the train reached Poland, the three had fallen into a free and easy camaraderie that Rose found to be the type of the new life young women were forging for themselves. Rose soon was using Helen Boylston's childhood nickname (Troub, for Troubles); it was the beginning of a long and important friendship.[11]

Again Rose kept a journal in the form of a letter to Arthur Griggs. A new kind of interference began to insert itself between Rose and the experience she must transcribe and interpret for her readers. Much about Poland she found fascinating: its similarity to the American Midwest, the resurgent nationalism in its war to expand its border against Bolshevik Russia, its admiration for America—expressed when two boys carrying buckets of milk and chocolate said merely "Amerikansky Hoover" and knelt to kiss her feet. But in addition to occasional lapses into her personal feelings for Griggs, she slips into a long and nostalgic digression about her childhood at Rocky Ridge Farm. Homesickness and her love for Griggs flow into one stream of sentiment by the end of one journal as she tries to comprehend the flux and reflux of her feelings while traveling in a strange and fascinating new land; as always, she is struck passionately by the plenitude of life and the poverty imposed by the necessity to choose: "My dear," she laments, "I wish I could live all the lives on earth—*All* of them."

I'm lonesome as the dickens for you.

Only—I'm afraid if I saw you I'd kiss you—or you'd kiss me, or somehow we'd be kissing. And I don't want to be kissed, I want to talk. I'm wild to be talking to someone who understands, and thinks, and is awake and alive to all this exciting, fascinating, hideous, mad world—someone who is wise, and amused, and clever, and sweet without being sickish, and cynical without being bitter, and kind without being kindly, and decent without being intolerant, and—But why so many words? I'm mad to be talking to *you*—[12]

As in Vienna, she was struck with the natural integrity of the national culture, from high to low, just as she had to remark the changes recent history had wrought. The Red Cross was headquartered in the summer home of a Polish countess, whose elegant chambers bespoke a life of leisured refinement; yet under the stress of war-begotten poverty, the countess had taken to sleeping with her shoes on because she had no maid to help her dress and undress. Warsaw Rose found almost as short of food as Vienna had been; yet the Opera and Ballet were full nightly and the productions surpassed those Rose had seen in New York, and the people were as hungry for books as for bread. And in Poland she found a radical feminism that made the American version seem pale: women soldiers paraded the streets; women politicians spoke in the Diet; and women, she was told, had been the primary protectors of the national language and culture under foreign dominion.

Her trips beyond Warsaw led her into the most striking of her adventures so far in Europe. A visit to the salt mines at Wiliczka discovered a virtual underground city with elaborate salt-crystal carvings, a chapel and choir, and musical entertainment that culminated in spontaneous dancing and singing, mingling miners and visitors alike. But much as she admired the Poles, she felt that there was something central to Slavic character in her hosts that she could not penetrate. It was connected somehow with their indifference to a frightful beggar whom she encountered in Wiliczka, a grotesque figure with no arms and only one leg, wearing a red cape and hopping hideously after her automobile, winking and leering familiarly as he came; someone threw him some money, only to hear him howl frighteningly when he could not pick it up. And it was connected somehow with their casual acceptance of a shot fired at them by a guard at the Czech border. The bullet passed through Rose's hat: their concern was not for her life but for her hat; and the guard, after all, was only a frightened boy.[13]

V

She returned to Paris on the eighth of October, momentarily sated with travel and longing for home—wherever that might be. For she was beginning to face the paradox that the only destination that held its thrill was home, yet, "as you travel, you make little homes everywhere you go and all of them . . . tug at your heartstrings." She had, in fact, retained her San Francisco and New York apartments as long as she could through subleases; and now the landscape slipping by her train window held little interest as she read from an old paper-covered Shakespeare, heading back to her Paris home.[14]

At the moment, that home consisted of unsatisfactory quarters at 9 rue de la Grande Chaumière, where the running water ran continuously, the sheets were changed every month, and her maid's little boy made a constant din. But within the week she was able to take possession of the Dulin's apartment at 5 rue Schoelcher and begin nest-building. Her only furnishings were a few cushions, which she threw from the balcony to the ground three floors below, where Marjorie Thirer and a young American boy named Pendleton awaited with a pushcart to haul her possessions to her new home. For weeks the furnishings and appointments would occupy Rose and Marjorie, and the accounts of their triumphs filled her letters to Berta Hader. By this time she had given up her New York apartment and had her possessions there shipped to France, and soon she was installing the *lares* and *penates* of her life in her new home.

In truth, the domestic exercises were a kind of therapy for depression. She felt her health slipping again: she fainted once more on November 7 during dinner at the Laperouse, and she was in bed too ill to move, off and on, for the next two months. Her diary records many blue days and sleepless nights that seemed to verge on nervous collapse. She was now writing a newsletter for the Red Cross and fifteen hundred words daily for her newspaper column; she was revising the Jack London manuscript toward an eventual novel; she was also working on a series of children's stories for the *Junior Red Cross Magazine* and completing the Bernhardt translations, which apparently involved substantial editing and revising as well; she had accepted a similar assignment with the memoirs of the Armenian dancer Armen Ohanian; and she had been asked to ghost a travel book from someone's notes—a task she reluctantly turned down. In addition, she was keeping up a voluminous personal and professional correspondence and a complex social life. By any measure, her output was prodigious, and it reflects a natural vitality that she was pushing to its limits. After completing the Bernhardt material, she went on a weekend birthday spree with Arthur Griggs—and by the following Monday was guilt-stricken again: "Rotten mood because nothing done," she recorded.

But her relationship with Griggs was beginning to falter too. They spent much time together, but when she was too busy or too ill to accompany him, he went off on his own adventures and returned to sleep away the odd afternoon on her couch, a beast they had dubbed the White

Elephant. She watched him sleep one afternoon and mused in her diary: "A. G. came in at noon, much the worse for wear—is now sleeping on the White Elephant. A profound emotional disturbance going on underneath. I hear echoes of it vaguely. But feel more like work than for the past week. Work for me is a symptom of dis-ease these days." Later that evening was a talk before the fire and the end of their two-year compact.[15]

This apparently amounted to a loosening but not an abandoning of their ties, for they continued in regular company. As a salutary domestic ritual they determined to put on a traditional American Thanksgiving dinner with their friends. Marjorie, Pendleton, and the Dulins were enlisted, and for weeks in advance they all scoured Paris for such rarities as cranberries, canned corn, and baking powder. Rose was by now in the reign of the third of a succession of household maids, each the cousin of her predecessor, and two of these were called in to help with the dinner. The two young Frenchwomen were aghast at the idea of oyster soup: cooked oysters were fatal, they knew; and they peeked with alarm through the kitchen door as the crazy Americans tried to poison themselves. The dinner lifted the spirits of these American expatriates; at the end of the evening they found that the French maids had spurned turkey, dressing, and mince pie and had, instead, made themselves an omelette.[16]

Another form of therapy carried Rose quite out of herself. Her friendship with the Dulins, both artists, awoke in her an interest in drawing; and as an experiment she sat in at a class, sketching from live models. Suddenly she found in herself an unexpected facility as lines flowed effortlessly from her charcoal to the paper. "And I am perfectly happy while it's doing it," she wrote ecstatically to Berta Hader; "I have never been so happy in all my life." The master teacher praised her talent, and for a few days she saw the possibility of a new source of joy in her life. But her supervisor at the Red Cross office objected to this diversion of her efforts, and she herself came to see that she could not spare the time from her writing. Reluctantly she gave it up, promising herself an indulgence in her old age that she could not pursue just now.[17]

Depressing too was the developing problem with Frederick O'Brien. Rose had nothing but pity and contempt for O'Brien, except for his sense for a good tale; but she had wrought better than she knew in her work on *White Shadows on the South Seas,* for it had become a best-seller and had gone into multiple printings. The book would be reprinted in several editions in the decade of its popularity and would also become a movie. Already in 1920 O'Brien was suddenly prosperous and famous; in San Francisco people "went to Frederick O'Brien" as they would go to a monument, Fremont Older wrote Rose. Her chagrin was immense, for O'Brien had repudiated the royalty agreement with her, and he had her only copy of the contract. A final insult was to find advertising copy she had written herself now announcing another printing of the book. "He'll live all the rest of his life in the glory of White Shadows, but I'll have the mean horrid despicable satisfaction of knowing that he knows he can't write, anyhow," she lamented to Berta Hader. In time, however, this would not be satisfaction enough.[18]

December fifth marked her thirty-fourth birthday, another holiday to be gotten through in a foreign land distant from her family or friends. She reported a successful dinner to Berta Hader; her diary noted that Griggs's birthday would be on the fifteenth, and they feted each other with dinner and gifts. Back at Rocky Ridge Farm, Mama Bess held a party for Rose as well; in a house decorated with her photographs, the guests were treated to a reading of her letters, and all sat down to write Rose their Christmas greetings. Mama Bess had reason to be grateful, for Rose had just sent her $125 as the first quarterly installment of the $500 promised for 1921. It amounted approximately to a tithe of Rose's income; in the back pages of her diary she kept track of her earnings month by month, and by December it amounted to $5,506.35.[19]

Christmas came and went as a quiet and private day with Arthur Griggs; it had been preceded and was followed by more sleepless nights and nervous prostration; she noted a complete collapse on December 21. "There is always the question of my health standing the strain," she wrote, "but it seems equal to it so far." By New Year's Eve she was up and about again, and Griggs took her to the first opening since the war of the famous Bal Bullier. The press of the crowd awaiting entrance was all but impenetrable; Griggs got them in by telling a doorman that they were a couple on honeymoon. From a balcony above the ballroom, they watched as all classes of Paris life danced happily below them. After midnight the orchestra began a sensuous Apache dance, and Rose was witness to a spectacle of a special French madness. It was sexual energy made musical. The dancing public would not let the orchestra stop; the conductor was assaulted and the orchestra literally played for its life as the crowd danced itself into exhaustion. Afterward, Rose and Griggs walked the night streets to Notre Dame, then taxied home at 4:00 A.M.[20]

VI

The new year of 1921 began auspiciously with an important new friendship. A few weeks before, a tall, blonde, strikingly beautiful young woman had begun work at the Red Cross Publicity Bureau; her name was Dorothy Thompson, and in time she would become the most influential woman journalist of her day. At the moment, however, she was a neophyte. She had dined at Rose's apartment several times in December; and with another journalist, Kate Horton, they spent the first two days of January in a walking trip along the valley of the Loire. In Dorothy

Thompson, Rose found a companion who could equal her enthusiasm for hours and hours of good talk. The experience cemented a friendship that would be vital for years; and even after they had drifted apart, their nostalgic letters would commemorate these days. On her return to Paris, Rose found Arthur Griggs in no condition for good talk as he suffered in the last stages of a forty-eight-hour party. By now, she had found herself deeply uncomfortable with the effects of alcohol on her own mind and body; although she would continue on principle to tolerate its importance to the men in her life, she seldom drank herself. But the issue was, it seems, a tender spot in her relations with Griggs. "Hideous evening and night," she noted in her diary.[21] Late in January Rose fled to London, on the pretext of business but as much in the hope of seeing Guy Moyston, who remained a valued friend from her San Francisco days.

Moyston had sought out her address from the Haders during his assignment in Dublin; he and Rose had exchanged letters and had narrowly missed seeing each other in their travels across Europe. London seemed a possibility at the moment, but he was called to Dublin before she arrived. In her disappointment she made a few desultory attempts to discover material and conferred with a London agent to handle manuscripts for her in the British market, among them a revision of her Jack London story that she was revising as a novel. She had arrived full of energy and determination:

> I have felt ambitious today. I say to myself that I will conquer England. It is simply a matter of conquering myself—self discipline. I always tangle up my life so foolishly. I must finish the Older serial, the Bernhardt series, produce A.R.C. copy. The Poland story may sell & relieve immediate finances. . . . Jack London is a gamble at the English market. I am not ashamed of the book.

"I give myself three years," she continued the next day, trying to plan a program for her career. "After Constantinople trip will have definite understanding regarding [the Red Cross] newsletter and stand in readiness to fill orders. Otherwise no more hack work, except possibly Ohanian book. . . . One good book a year, with all I can put into it." One day later, however, she looked back over these hedged and conflicting impulses and found herself mired in self-doubt:

> The difficulty is, fundamentally, my own harum-scarum mind. I do not want things in an orderly manner, but helter-skelter, all at once & when that chaos is added to the chaos of living the result is messiness and frustration.
>
> I want a home, love, money, and the envy of others, i.e. "success." And there are thirty years of blundering to make up for. The home will accumulate if I will use intelligence in buying and keeping.[22]

In another entry from about the same time she recorded her impressions of her readings in Arnold Bennet: "Nice little cardboard walls all around him . . . a pleasant interior, so refined and neat, and sanitary, too." Which provoked her to compare Bennet's complacent certainty with her own gaping self-doubts:

> Walls. Damn it, we have to have them! Corsets for our mind, to keep 'em from wobbling all over the place. Bennet can point to his "achievement." Why should I ask what it's worth? I who haven't accomplished even a conviction that the reason I don't produce books is because it isn't worthwhile. I've got to produce some, just to prove to myself that my opinion of the grapes is unbiased.

She contemplated going on to Ireland, but a cable from the Red Cross in Paris called her back to plan a trip to Montenegro.[23]

Baghdad had been more or less jokingly her destination since she left the States. Her discussions with her Red Cross supervisor raised the possibility of going for material as far as Constantinople, and she and Dorothy Thompson had talked of taking a freighter through the Suez Canal and returning to the States by way of Siam and China—and possibly, for Rose, a triumphant return to San Francisco on the order of that accorded Bessie Beatty on her return from Russia. More immediately there was reason to go to Montenegro at the behest of another new friend, Elsie Benedict, a young woman from California who had become deputy director of the Junior American Red Cross in Europe. The work in Montenegro needed publicizing, and Rose might go beyond the Balkans to Constantinople in time.

The interval in Paris was filled with the arrival of Troub Boylston and Kitty VanBuskirk from Poland. They had been worn down, finally, by the work there and were returning home. They moved in with Rose and filled her odd moments with play and talk. From them Rose first heard of Russian roulette among the Polish army officers; one of Kitty's friends had finally blown his brains out after four years of gambling on the spin of the cylinder. And the officers had devised a new version of blindman's buff, played in a dark room full of men. One stood in the middle with a pistol, while the one who was "it" called out, "Here I am." Then he tried to dodge the bullet, as did his friends around the room. It was, for Rose, an image of the madness in Europe. And time, no doubt, for a drink at the Rotonde, where Rose sipped tea as she watched the dissipation about her.[24]

And if not the Rotonde, there was the special relief and gaiety of Mardi Gras. Rose reserved a box at the Bal Bullier, and she and her new friends all went in costume. Rose resurrected a famous gypsy costume from her San Francisco days, "with some glittering additions." Arthur Griggs went as a Turk, Kate Horton as a countess, Troub as a boy. . . .

> Kit was absolutely stunning in an Albanian harem costume . . . enormous wide trousers of rose silk, with six-inch cuffs of solid

gold embroidery, and a jacket of the same solid stiff golden, and a sash of bright blue and a golden chiffon-cloth veil.

Dorothy went as the stunningest of Paris students, in corduroy trousers, a silk shirt open at the neck, a Roman-striped sash, a blue tam, a mustache and a pipe. We collected a dozen eager admirers, a tall and absolutely charming Indian Prince in white and silver with a tall turban, and an Apache or two, and several unimaginative evening-dressers, but they could dance, and a Roumanian peasant, and champagne popped on every hand, and the two orchestras relieved each other without a pause, and the floor was something I can't describe—a million costumes, all more colorful and witty than the ones you'd seen a minute ago. We came home at five o'clock in the morning, with blistered feet, and sang all down the boulevards, while the dawn was just coming up the sky.

But damn it! I'm getting no work done. . . . [25]

Despite her guilty conscience, her diary shows thirteen installments of her San Francisco column completed in this week. She saw Dorothy Thompson off to Vienna, where her dispatches for the *Philadelphia Ledger* would soon begin her meteoric career. Meanwhile, Arthur Griggs failed to keep a dinner engagement, sending a friend with an explanation instead; Rose was enraged all night, and Griggs's arrival at 5:00 A.M. prompted a diary entry so bitter that she blotted it out. After another spate of work she treated herself to a walking trip from Melun to Barbizon, where a moonlight stroll in the forest in which Robert Louis Stevenson had composed his "Forest Notes" so entranced her that the next day she leased a cottage, Les Iris, for the coming summer: it was to be a retreat for herself and Arthur Griggs. On her return to Paris, Kit and Troub left for New York, bearing a pile of her manuscript material to be delivered. The same afternoon Rose entrained for Rome, her destination Montenegro and points east.[26]

VII

In Rome she met Elsie Benedict, who was to be her guide to Montenegro. The way to Montenegro lay through Bari—a den of thieves, they found—and across the Adriatic to Ragusa (now Dubrovnik), where Rose encountered what she could only understand as a psychic experience: the childhood dream of the walled city, which had recurred many times in her adult years, stood before her in every detail down to the large cat asleep in the chair. The mural on the wall was of Mother Ragusa embracing the children of all nations. The experience remained a genuine mystery all of her life, unassimilated by the determined rationalism of her later years.[27]

Montenegro occupied her for the month of March. The way there lay down the Dalmatian coast, as lovely as California's, then all but straight up five thousand feet to Montenegro along a switchback road so steep it was called the Ladder. At the top she found a limestone country practically without soil, where the inhabitants lived in stone houses indistinguishable from the landscape and still swore by the pagan spirit Bog, whom Rose identified as the bogeyman of her childhood. Here again she found American women, far from home but marvelously competent, dealing with the civil devastation left by the Austrian army. Surrounded by starving and homeless children, an incompetent government, and disbanded soldiers turned brigands, these women met daily crises and still managed to turn an old harem into an American home in which every night they dressed for dinner.[28] It was but a boat ride across Lake Scutari to reach Albania, which she had heard tales of from Helen Boylston; she planned to pass through on her way back to the Adriatic coast and thence toward Constantinople. But it would be two years before she would reach Constantinople. The Albanian adventure would be the high point of her years in Europe and would mark her life forever.

VIII

In the town of Scutari (now Shkodre) she encountered a familiar situation—two competent young American women running a children's school and clinic. But Betsy Cleveland and Margaret (Alex) Alexander were just about to embark on a trip of exploration into the mountains of northern Albania to consider locations for new schools for which they had raised private funds. Rose could not pass up the invitation to join them; and on April 12 they set off on horseback with an escort of teamsters with a packtrain, two gendarmes, an Albanian civil servant as interpreter and, at the last moment, a young Moslem boy, Rexh (Redge) Meta, whose garb consisted of the traditional red fez and American pajamas. After the first day's journey the horses and teamsters turned back; the rest of the journey, save the last day, would be on foot through a country wilder even than Rose had found in California's High Sierra.

To their knowledge, only one foreign woman had ever been into these regions ahead of them. It was not merely the remote fastnesses of the mountains that gripped Rose: within them she found a people who, save for their rifles, were still embedded in a culture of the early Middle Ages. Beneath a veneer of primitive Christianity lay a more primitive sun-worship and a theogony in which she detected analogues of early Greek religion: Zeus and Athena were living presences to these people. Beneath their nominal acknowledgment of civil law lay an ancient traditional law that kept them in constant blood-feuds; and their history still consisted of an oral tradition that connected them with Alexander the Great, Philip of Macedonia, and Aristotle. In their simple and difficult lives she found much that she thought no longer possible in the modern world: an inflexible code of honor, a natural grace and nobility, and a casual heroism. Here, indeed, were a people whose lives grew naturally as trees. As a woman, her presence guaranteed the safety of the men traveling with her through the land of their enemies, which prevented several deaths; one tribal leader offered to take her in marriage—not for her charms, but because as a literate, modern woman she could help bring his people into the twentieth century. She was struck by his self-lessness even as she recognized that the modern world would obliterate just the simple harmony of life that tugged at her heart.[29]

Albania was also the first country in which she encountered a vital Moslem tradition. Centuries under Turkish rule had not brought Islam to the mountains, but the civilized lowlands had become largely Moslem. It was the faith of young Rexh Meta, whose family had been slaughtered by retreating Serbs in 1915, when he was but a child. As Rose came to tell it, Rexh had survived the massacre beneath a pile of bodies, and carrying an old silver-mounted rifle longer than himself, had made his way across the mountains to Scutari, killing occasional Serbs along the way. Once in Scutari he had become the head of an informal family of refugee street-children, caring for them until the American relief team took them in. He had quickly learned English, and now he attached himself to Rose, acting as guide, adviser, and interpreter in situations where she was clearly beyond her abilities. His age at this time was, by different accounts, either twelve or fifteen; it could not have escaped Rose that the baby boy she lost in Kansas City would have been almost of an age with this Moslem orphan. She was convinced by the journey's end that Rexh had saved her life. In gratitude, she would later do all she could to ease his.[30]

For the journey had been for the most part in a drenching rain; Rose had been wet to the skin for days, had slept in unheated quarters, and had eaten little and seldom by the time the party reached the village of Shala. There she fell ill with fever and pains in her chest; fearing pneumonia, she determined to return to Scutari at once, ahead of the main party, which had a further mission. A Shala man was found to guide her, and Rexh volunteered to return as her protector. After a day's march along mountain trails in the rain, Rexh discovered that her Shala guide had deliberately detoured through the land of his enemies because, in a woman's company, he could pass with taunting impunity under the noses of those sworn to kill him. Thereafter Rexh took charge. He found a donkey for her to ride and a second guide to assist her, and after another day's long traverse of a mountain range he brought her safely down into Scutari by moonlight. Within a week Rose had recovered sufficiently to write with some humor of her adventure to her mother:

[An Albanian mountaineer] slings a Mauser across his shoulders, takes the chain of a donkey in his hand, and walks straight up what you would call an utterly unclimbable mountain side, literally dragging the weight of the donkey behind him, and singing as he goes in a voice that rings from all the mountain peaks around. They don't seem to know what it is to be breathless; even when I and my packs were on the donkey, it never fazed 'em a minute. Only then another man walked behind holding the donkey's tail, so that when he fell off the edge of a four-inch trail they simply lugged him on without mishap. I don't know why the donkey's tail never came off. You read about these precarious twelve-inch trails—I give you my word I looked forward to a four-inch one as to a haven of safety, and a trail ten inches wide would have looked to me like Fifth Avenue. You go across a thousand-foot slide of decomposed shale . . . and it slides as you go, and if you slide with it, you'll go gaily avalanching eight hundred feet or so and then drop off into two thousand feet of space and fall through the thatched roof of the peaceful family in a house below. But when the donkey slides the man behind holds him by the tail, and the man ahead tightens up on the chain—without losing a note of his careless song.[31]

But the Albanian experience had temporarily sated her desire for adventure. Constantinople and Baghdad would be deferred as she returned to Paris to rest and to assimilate what she had discovered.

IX

The Albanian adventure would, in fact, become the basis for another serial for her San Francisco readers, which would later be gathered as *Peaks of Shala*, certainly the best of her books. But before she could incorporate this episode into her writing, her personal affairs entered another crisis. She arrived in Paris on the morning of May 5 and had lunch and dinner with Arthur Griggs. The next day she packed for a trip to Barbizon and the cottage she had leased there, but on the day following she entered in her diary a note at once cryptic and clear: "Not going to Barbizon. Final end of one episode. . . . Unpacking and going through papers. Damn miserable but tremendously relieved."[32] The affair with Arthur Griggs was over.

It was a time for old friends and new beginnings. The new apartment had lost its charm—and had developed a leaky roof—and Rose began to cast about for a different one. Her domestic tribulations there occupied a chatty correspondence full of girl-talk with Berta Hader, revealing that in her year in Europe her hair had become quite grey. Rose Strunsky, who with her sister Anna had been among her radical friends in San Francisco, arrived in Paris and moved in with her for a time.

Dorothy Thompson passed through on her way to England. Doris Stevens, an old friend from her days in Croton-on-Hudson, had come to Paris with lawyer Dudley Field Malone; both had been active in the suffrage movement and were now on the verge of marriage. And Guy Moyston had arrived from Ireland, where he had been the primary correspondent covering the Sinn Fein rebellion: he had, in fact, interviewed Eamon DeValera after being led blindfolded through Dublin streets to the revolutionary leader's hideout. By now Moyston had served overseas long enough in his Associated Press job to qualify for home leave before being reassigned to London, but he began his vacation with a trip to Paris to visit Rose. Together they retraced the walking trip along the valley of the Loire that she had made with Dorothy Thompson. Moyston found Rose with an ache in her heart and a willingness to be consoled beyond simple friendship.[33]

Rose was clearly distraught and attempting to control herself through her work. It was at about this time that she sat one day at her typewriter in the Red Cross office, turning out one of her regular columns to bring home Europe's misery to American readers; in a room next door, Moyston was talking with her friends, Arthur Griggs perhaps among them. Under Rose's fingers, the copy in her typewriter runs suddenly into four pages of therapeutic self-analysis:

> A Letter From Europe.
> The pink and chubby Kewpie with cocky smile and the bow of tulle about its middle has become a figure of tragedy in Vienna, according to George W. Bakemen of the Red Cross, who is in charge of that organization's relief work in Austria. The Kewpie, Mr. Bakemen says, has come to mean two things to Viennese women: America's charity and their own broken pride.
>   Last year several thousand American layettes were distributed, each of them containing a baby-blanket with printed Ye Gods, how nervous I am, and of course it shows in the way my typewriter sounds; I wonder how much of such hypocrisy is justifiable?

There follows line after line of stream-of-consciousness, devoted generally to her shame at her pretenses and at the deeper insecurity that makes the pretenses necessary; she longs for an "inner unshakable calmness," "the poise [that] must come from within," that will make pretense unnecessary. As in her letter to Griggs, she is again longing for the realities that come naturally from depths, as a tree grows. And as she writes, she recognizes that she is at the same time engaged in self-therapy: "a self-expression, a conscious flowing-out through my accustomed medium, the typewriter, helps; as a strong river current straightens out the weeds in its path." Into the stream flow voices from the room next door:

> . . . they are laughing next door; what is he thinking? I have him down in my notebooks, yet I do not understand him, no one

understands another, what does he think of me, how dizzily vast and innumerable the factors in any human relationship; yet this is all of the past and I must hold to the new thing; no one can by will power make a genuine attachment and how much of my feeling for the other man is self-enforced, not spontaneous at all, yet it seemed true, the truest thing I have ever known; they all do.

Finally the spasm runs its course; a block of white-space rolls through her typewriter as she regains control: "Now I must get to work; it's over; has been quite ended for some minutes."[34]

Shortly after Moyston's arrival, he and Rose went together to a party in Sherwood Anderson's quarters. Among the guests were Ernestine Evans, Anderson's friend since his Chicago days and Rose's since her time in New York; Edna St. Vincent Millay and her current lover, Griffin Barry; and Esther Root, who would in time become Mrs. Franklin P. Adams. Anderson was on his first visit to Europe; as one of the revolutionary voices in modern fiction he was something of a lion in avant-garde circles. Rose, however, had thought him a bad writer and now found him to be a poseur as well. The meeting would have been of no particular significance except for the affair of the Quatz' Arts Ball, which led to Rose and Guy being embedded for posterity in Anderson's novel *Dark Laughter.*

The ball was the annual bacchanalian revel of the Ecole des Beaux Arts, in which the students and their friends first banqueted, then paraded through the streets in outrageous costume as preliminary to a wild ball and general orgy in the Luna Park auditorium. Tickets to outsiders were at a premium, but Rose gained access through her friend Jamie Dulin, who had connections with the Académie Julien. Her diary entry for June 10 is brief but sufficient to the imagination:

> Quatz' Arts ball—Jamie & I to Jeanne's apartment, she & sister
> and we to Julien's Academy—dinner—rioting thro' the streets—
> Maxim's—taxi to café—into Luna Park auditorium—Ye Gods!
> Taxi at 6 A.M. through the Bois and home to breakfast.

Two days later she was still recovering, and at some time in the next few days she and Moyston were again in Anderson's company, for in *Dark Laughter* Anderson would create a woman writer named Rose Frank and her friend a newspaper man recently in Ireland; the woman Anderson portrays as shaken and distraught over her experience at the Quatz' Arts Ball. The scene becomes a part of Anderson's strategy for exploring his theme of sexual repression, Rose Frank being one of its victims. The book would become Anderson's first big commercial success, and he was shrewd enough to recognize that many of his readers were captured by prurient interests, particularly in the scene with Rose Frank. Rose Lane, when she discovered it, would be outraged at Anderson's distortion, which revealed, she thought, merely his own vile mind.[35]

X

Meanwhile, she had rented her unused cottage at Barbizon to Ernestine Evans and Rose Strunsky and had for herself leased a new apartment at 8 square Des Nouettes; and after Guy Moyston sailed for the United States much of her time and energy again went into redecorating. In a riotous letter to Fremont Older, she described the joys and tribulations of hiring French workmen, who had no idea of American standards of efficiency but who delighted her by bringing an accordion to work and by inscribing her freshly plastered walls with witty political cartoons while awaiting the paperhanger who would not come.[36] By this time she had completed writing up her Albanian adventure, and she was again considering how she might get to Constantinople and Baghdad. She was finding, too, some covert connection between her romantic involvements and her childhood: the long account of her childhood at Rocky Ridge that she had written for Arthur Griggs had ended "and that little girl grew up—somewhat—and became me—and I became yours." Now, as another romance with Guy Moyston was commencing, she found herself drawn further back into her childhood in a short story she called "Innocence"; here she plumbed even earlier memories, of her days in Florida, in a story that presented a startling image of evil through a child's eyes. It would be her best work in short fiction, and would be recognized by an O. Henry Award in 1922.[37]

Late in August she heard from Moyston that he was sailing for England, and on September 3 she arrived in London for a two-week visit that would establish their relationship on a new footing. Since her divorce from Gillette Lane it had become obvious to her that she needed both love and freedom, but not obvious that the two could be reconciled. What caused the failure of her relationship with Arthur Griggs is not clear, but it seems equally likely he could not rise to her standards of loyalty or of detachment. Helen Boylston, however, simply thought him an amiable idiot.[38] In Guy Moyston Rose seems to have found a man she could, for the time being, love and keep at arm's length; the evidence of his character suggests a hard-drinking, essentially decent, but skeptical and detached observer of life who valued his friends but kept his feelings in check. His visit to Paris had renewed a friendship but had started something else as well; and as Rose moved into this new affair she kept her eyes open and all but foundered on her apprehension. Her diary entry for her first full day in London runs through a page of quotidian details and debouches in a cry from the heart: "O, these days of sheer misery."

Her diary notes reveal a vacation full of fun—sight-seeing and theater—beneath which an emotional struggle left her enervated. One diary page details the facts of the day and ends cryptically, "I am no longer romantic." A longer journal entry for the same day is more revealing, as she tries to assess the impulse that drew her on this trip and the caution that casts a pall over it:

> All the miracles are inside us. My emotion seemed genuine, the most real thing yet. Nothing happened, and it simply is not. Taking it seriously—that's what's wrong. I had no sense of humor about it. I was so damn serious. . . .
> And yet I must have someplace in which to keep my heart. I can't work so long as it keeps on wailing alone in the cold.

Apparently Moyston was having something of the same struggle. "Dinner with Guy," she noted, "who says he has no sentiment." By the time she prepared to return to Paris, she was ready again to discipline her heart. "One has to keep on just the same and let it wail." While in London, she had also received a letter from Dorothy Thompson in Vienna, who was contemplating marriage: "Letter from Dorothy, asking advice. Wrote her eight pages of it!" It is a letter that unfortunately has been lost.[39]

XI

Back in Paris Rose plunged into the routine of Red Cross publicity work and an attempt to finish her translation of Armen Ohanian's memoirs. Here she faced much the same problem she had in writing of Hoover's experiences in Australia and China—how to write credibly of ground she had not covered. She wrote to Moyston requesting detailed maps of the Middle East and mentioned vaguely her intentions soon to make that long deferred trip. In the meantime, Elsie Benedict was back in Paris; she suggested a walking trip in Brittany, and in early October the two took a train to Concarneau, which became their base for a week's exploration of the Breton countryside. As always in these trips into the corners of the world where ancient traditions remained untouched by contemporary life, Rose found herself entranced with the local color and the beauty of an integrated and unself-conscious culture. In the streets of Concarneau, they met a wedding procession coming from the church, "children in front, bride & groom arm in arm, and two by two the guests, women in full length lovely shawls of black lace, men in velvet jackets & flat hats with ribbons hanging behind." Such were the kinds of notes she often made for use in travel-columns; but here she slipped into a pensive recollection of the provincial culture she had left behind.

> There is a lot of difference between this environment and that of my childhood, and much to consider in the difference. There is

probably very little incentive to change here; although one does see the Breton girls in Paris, and it seems to me that some successful painters and actresses have come from the Breton peasantry. There is nothing which prevents. And after all, what did the "incentive to change" mean in Mansfield? Discontent and a cheap pretentious imitation of city life. I am the only girl who really left Mansfield. The others took Mansfield with them to Kansas City. And I am not an exhibit for the defense. These peasants have beauty and mystery—emotional values—in their church. They have charm and contentment in their lives: they *do*, it is in their faces. They have creative joy in their handwork. Query, does the Mansfield Embroidery Club?

A few nights later, in bed in her hotel room, she looked more deeply into the discontent that separated her from the simple peasant life. "I have the blues," she acknowledged.

> Why is that hell in all of us? A fundamental discord, it is: an agony of mal-adjustment to life, or to our conditions of life? Or is it because we can not accept the mystery, the unknowableness, the mists? We want solidities. Religions gave people that. The walls enclosed space in which one could move confidently. Shut off the view, but gave that in exchange. Now we've broken down the walls, and we're sick with dizziness.

The next day, they encountered an American tourist, a vulgar woman who forced her acquaintance on them and who clearly had brought her Mansfield to France with her. And in the village of Baye, they met a charming peasant woman of fifty who queried them about Pont Aven, a place she had never seen. The question marked the difference between the integral peasant culture Rose had admired and her own restless energies, for she and Elsie had just walked the distance in less than two hours.[40]

Rose was exchanging long letters with Guy Moyston now—more friendly and chatty than romantic, although there is clearly a standing joke between them about marriage. She was clearly in a position to avoid entanglements, for the Red Cross job was about to end. Budgets had been cut and the publicity department would be closed at the year's end. It was time to take seriously her intention to see the Middle East.[41]

Peggy Marquis had returned to Paris, without husband now and eager for a round of nightclub dancing and, beyond that, foreign adventure. She and Rose decided to leave for points east on the new year; Siam was their distant goal. Rose's agent had placed *Peaks of Shala* with Harper, which was interested in pictures from Albania; and by a happy coincidence, Peggy Marquis was an experienced photographer. The two women decided to travel first to Berlin to buy cameras, then to work their way through eastern Europe to the Mediterranean and Albania. The Red Cross owed Rose transportation back to San Francisco; and although it was irregular she persuaded her superiors to give her the cash in lieu of a ticket. A small advance from Harper swelled her purse; she sublet her apartment, newly leased and decorated just six months before, and bought a new wardrobe. As the year drew to a close, her thirty-fifth birthday passed without notice; and a miserable Christmas, without presents and with a bad dinner in a restaurant, left both her and Peggy depressed. On December 30 she met with Doris Stevens and Dudley Field Malone, and Malone agreed to represent her in a lawsuit against Frederick O'Brien over her rights to royalties from *White Shadows on the South Seas*. There was no New Year's Eve celebration in the flurry of last-minute arrangements. On January 1, 1922, Rose and Peggy left Paris for Berlin.[42]

$\mathscr{T}$HE ROAD TO BAGHDAD

*The happiest moment of my life was the moment I lighted
a match in the sunshine, in the Tartar market of Tiflis.*

Rose arrived in Berlin ill again, this time with ptomaine, but after a long sleep in her room at the Adlon Hotel she emerged to explore a new city. The other Americans in Berlin, however, by which she meant mainly newspapermen, were a sad lot, "like blind men in a treasure trove where they can help themselves, and where they can get only a few pebbles"—these pebbles gathered mainly in the Adlon bar and a few cafes. Her guide to the treasures and to the nightlife of Berlin was a new friend, the emigré Russian Isaac Don Levine, now an American newspaperman and later to become an important friend and sometime adversary. Under Levine's guidance she found magnificent theater and a German middle class and intelligentsia both cultured and thoughtful— although, she later came to believe, fatally detached from politics, which would permit Hitler to emerge in a neglected polity. These were the early days of the doomed Weimar Republic; Rose was witness to the over-whelming inflation that would swamp that government and that would leave her incurably suspicious of governmental monetary policies. The police were enforcing a rule of expelling currency-rich foreigners after a short stay lest they buy up too much of scarce goods. Rose took ad-vantage of the exchange rate to splurge on more new clothes. And she and Peggy gained new respect for the German dye industry when they experimented with German rouge: it was meant for application in a weak dilution, but they inadvertently touched it to their cheeks in full strength, which painted them at once bright as circus clowns.[1]

While she explored Berlin a new job emerged as well. The Near East Relief Agency (NER), which had come into existence to aid the suffering Armenians during the war, embodied a mission parallel to that of the Red Cross. While still in Paris, Rose and two other members of the Publicity Bureau, Major C. D. Morris and Frank America, had applied for posi-tions with the NER, and surprisingly all three were taken on: Rose was to receive support for three months in the eastern Mediterranean. A con-firming telegram came on January 10; the agency was willing to advance her travel money; so she delayed in Berlin even longer to collect this bonus for her Middle East trip. Her work for the NER was not to begin until September, which would allow for a leisurely approach to Constantinople and points east. After three weeks in Berlin, Rose and Peggy boarded the train for Vienna.[2]

The visit to Vienna was a brief one to see Dorothy Thompson and to stage their visit to Albania for pictures for Rose's book. The stricken city was even uglier than it had been the year before: hardships had provoked riots, most buildings were without heat in midwinter, and nighttime taxi-drivers, full of hostility toward foreigners, held them hostage on the dark streets for triple-fares. Morality was a luxury most could not afford in Europe, Rose decided, pondering how far she would sink under similar hardship. Dorothy had been in London for a brief vacation but was promised home within a week; Rose and Peggy had use of her apartment. This was to be their mailing address until further notice, so Rose was busy sending letters and telegrams to a host of friends, editors, and publishers: her movements from here on would be unpredictable, she knew. The first unpredictable element emerged when her telegrams to Albania brought replies that the mountain passes were buried in snow; it would be March, at least, before the area she needed to photograph would be open. A month or more was to be filled. They spent a week with Dorothy Thompson on her return; then they decided to try what might be found between Vienna and Albania in their period of grace.[3]

The month of wandering by railroad and hired cars began a series of travel articles for which Rose did the writing and Peggy the photography. For more than a year their theme would be the conquest of exotic places by two intrepid American women living out of a purse called the Mutual Fund. Their first stop was Budapest, where Dorothy Thompson had many connections; she followed to join them in a few days and to present to them the man she would soon marry, a Hungarian Jew named Joseph Bard. Rose had already warned this beloved younger woman about marriage generally, and her apprehensions were not eased by her assessment of Bard himself, whose morals she suspected at once. For the moment she held her tongue, though, and she and Peggy bent their way toward her dream city of Ragusa.[4]

Rose had traveled briefly in Yugoslavia and Albania, but as guest of the Red Cross and with access to their quarters. Now she and Peggy, whose foreign travel had been confined to France, found themselves on their own and subject to a different order of civilization than in the great cities of western Europe. The problem presented itself most critically as they sought quarters each night. Rose would write later about their stays in "the usual Balkan hotel."

> . . . two story, rough boards, stone-paved ground floor cafe, stairway to bare rooms with iron bedsteads (no rugs or curtains) and

candles or kerosene lamps. Blow out the light and the onrush of
roaches and bedbugs was *heard*. Before you could scratch a match,
the whitewashed ceiling was black—and I mean literally black—
with the bugs. . . . While the lamp burns, you order four dishes,
set one leg of the bed in each, and fill the dish with kerosene. Over
the lower sheet on the bed you spread a layer of Keating's powder:
when ready to sleep, you roll yourself deftly in the upper sheet,
tucking in its ends to make a neat package of yourself and bringing the last end over the tucks so that no folds lead inward (not
easy to describe, but it can be done). The final last fold, held open,
lets you blow out the light and quickly, quickly, you roll that and lie
on it. All snugly wrapped up, lying in Keating's powder and in
wrappings more or less smeared with it, on which the bugs patter
down like rain from the ceiling.[5]

An intervening visit to Sarajevo, to see the place where the Great
War had begun, yielded an article, as did the return to the ancient walled
city she had been destined to visit, she thought, since childhood. Ragusa
had reassumed its Slavic name of Dubrovnik, she found, but the charm
remained as she stood on the ancient wall looking out toward the island
chapel built by Richard the Lion-Hearted returning home from his Cru-
sade. Around her circled the local pigeons, descendants of mail-carrying
birds so valued that they had been made citizens of the city.[6]

II

Rose decided to approach Albania by the sea; a coasting steamer carried
them two days down the Adriatic to Albania's port city of Durazzo (now
Durrës). Progress had come to Albania, in the form of a Ford automobile,
one of four in the country, which took them up over the coastal mountains and forty miles inland to the capital city of Tirana, beyond which lay
the cloud-topped peaks of the Dinaric Alps. Rose found herself falling in
love with the country all over again; she felt herself in living contact with
a civilization more ancient than Greece and Rome—here young Cicero
had dissipated, and in the country's money old Greek and Roman coins
circulated with American five-dollar gold pieces. But Peggy could not
help wishing that progress had reached the bone-jolting road along
which Albanian peasants drove their laden donkeys and water-buffalo
carts, and upon which their taxi had halted with a flat tire. They were
received, however, with great courtesy by the Albanian government:
"Such a lot of care I've had," Rose wrote to herself, "—telegrams, guards,
soldiers. I've never been so cherished."[7] Six weeks in Albania would
provide not only the pictures Rose needed but also two more proposals of
marriage and a genuine Balkan revolution.

The first proposal came from a young Moslem nobleman, one of several men who regularly accompanied Rose and Peggy on evening walks into the countryside. These were cultivated, sophisticated Albanians, Moslem southerners most of them, and educated in Constantinople, London, Paris, Vienna—even at Harvard—who had assembled to see their country through its birth pangs. Rose and Peggy were staying at Red Cross guest quarters while they arranged for the mountain trip, and Rose interviewed government ministers in an attempt to understand the nation's political situation; the ministers and their friends became after-hours escorts and protectors of the women out of a required gallantry as well as a real curiosity about these exotic, unveiled American women who blithely assumed all the freedoms of men. Rose respected most of them, and enjoyed their company, although Mr. Martini came to be known to Peggy and Rose simply as the Cocktail. Rose's suitor, she knew, already had one wife; when he asked for her handkerchief as a token, she gave him a yellow one, which happened to be Peggy's. Peggy vowed from time to time to claim either the handkerchief or the suitor who went with it.

The second proposal came with the revolution, which began on the very evening of the gift of the yellow handkerchief. Elez Yusuf, a mountain chieftain, had ridden down into Tirana—to talk with the government, he later claimed; he was accompanied by a hundred or so of his horsemen. As they approached the city, they met a body of government troops; shots were exchanged, the government troops withdrew, and Elez Yusuf occupied a section of the city and barricaded his forces. The minister of interior in the Tirana government, Ahmet Bey Mati, had only a few raw recruits at hand, but Elez Yusuf did not know that. The situation that night was tense; the ministers would tell Rose and Peggy nothing, but insisted that they stay in their rooms. Rose ventured out and was shot at by a nervous guard. At four in the morning the minister of public works and the secretary to the minister of foreign affairs tapped at the window and asked permission to visit the women. The secretary, Djimil Bey Dino, was a handsome and educated man who had been particularly attentive to Rose. Until dawn they amiably discussed Albanian history and culture; the unspoken question was who was protecting whom.

There followed a day, and then another day, of negotiation, mediated by the British minister, a personal friend of Elez Yusuf, who came in from Durazzo; Dino had sent for him to gain time while Ahmet brought in troops from the countryside. On the afternoon of the second day, Rose sat in the window of the Red Cross office, awaiting developments; with her sat Dino, who spoke of the beauty of her white hair in the sunlight.

> Was I, if he might ask, in love? I replied, O no, not at all. Then my heart was quite free? Quite, I said, and very fond of freedom. At this moment the lid of Tirana blew off, a rifle grenade hit the Red Cross dining room and scattered tiles in every direction, the

machine guns started, and about two thousand rifles went busily
to work. The government had got its soldiers, and was attacking.
He said, Please get out of that window. . . . And then he asked me
to marry him. No, not exactly that, either; he said that he would
tell me why he was unhappy; it was because I had broken his
heart. And he said a great many other things. While he was saying
them a bullet came in and took a lot of plaster off the wall behind
us, but we did not notice it much. And then Peggy came in and
had something almost like hysterics. . . .[8]

It was a romantic moment. Rose would for some time contemplate with
something like regret the possibility of the serene and ordered days of an
upper-class Moslem woman and the satisfaction of a life in Albania.

Hot fighting continued all night. Rose and Peggy sat on the floor of
the Red Cross school, where refugees from six nations shared dinner
while bullets whizzed overhead and occasionally through their windows.
The next day, having surrounded the rebels with fresh troops, Ahmet
Bey ordered the town crier to proclaim that the quarter held by Elez
Yusuf would be torched and the defenders shot. While negotiations continued, the residents of the doomed quarter were permitted to move out
with their possessions as the deadline was extended hour by hour. At
four in the afternoon, Elez Yusuf walked out of the barricades and
stepped into the first automobile he had ever seen; with the British minister he rode to Parliament House and swore an oath of loyalty to the
government, for which he was given safe conduct home with his men.
The next day Ahmet Bey marched to Durazzo to put down a second
rebellion, and later Rose could see hanged men on the roadside and fires
in the hills, where government troops were burning the villages of the
rebels who had supported the Durazzo uprising. Rose suspected Italian
conspiracy at the bottom of it all, for under the League of Nations mandate,
Italy could occupy Albania if a stable government were not formed.[9]

At this juncture, Peggy left for the interior mountains to retrace
Rose's earlier journey and take pictures; it was by now mid-March and
the mountain passes should be open. Rose would remain in Tirana and
write up the travel articles for which they had already gathered material.
It was in this interval that she came to know a man she would admire as
much as she did Fremont Older: Ahmet Bey Mati, the most strikingly
capable minister in the fledgling Albanian parliamentary government.
Mati was simply a regional name, taken from the river that watered his
ancestral lands, where his family had long ruled; his family name was
Zogu, and he in time became the ill-fated King Zog of Albania. When
Rose came to know him in several all-night interviews, he was a young
man still in his twenties, educated in Constantinople but still a mountain
warrior in a Western business suit. He had distinguished himself as a
fighting man in the skirmishes that ended the war in Europe; what Rose

admired now were his keen political instincts and his ability to hold Albania's fragile government together by sheer force of his personality. With Serbs threatening in the north and Italy in the west, and with ancestral memories of danger from Greece and centuries of domination by the Ottoman Turks, Ahmet had also to face down internal dissension and to attempt to bring his country into a relationship with the great European powers. Rose found him simply fascinating. While his soldiers outside the ministry building composed impromptu songs honoring his valor, Rose noted the one thing in his life she envied: "the best part of life is purposefulness."[10]

At the same time, she was beginning to love the idyllic life of Tirana itself. It was still in many ways a medieval town surrounded by feudal estates, peopled by an ancient race who had not yet succumbed to the ills of Western civilization. With a California climate and hemmed in by beautiful mountains, Tirana offered a refuge for a driven woman, an escape to another time and another culture that could be appreciated properly only by a jaded modern appetite. After a week of empty pages in her diary, she summarized her days in Lotos-land:

> All these beautiful days in Albania, which I shall never forget. When it rains, a fire in the fireplace in my room, and I work on the Older serial and eat oranges. . . . And Zotni Martini takes me for walks, singing all the way down the Durrazzo road—and we lunch at the Cafe Internationale. And the band from Korça has come. . . .
> . . . later we went to the room of the cafe piano player, & there was music and we danced and sang Albanian songs and dances. And we walked home under a sky of stars, saying nothing but singing all the way.

It was at about this time that she wrote a note to herself on an Albanian picture postcard: "I have not realized the absolute necessity of an anchor, as it were, before. I am certain, now."[11]

Meanwhile, Peggy Marquis was living a different kind of adventure. She had managed to retrace Rose's earlier route back into the mountains and get some pictures, but her hardships were the equal of Rose's earlier ones. Rose wrote the account from Peggy's report:

> Mrs. Marquis went into the mountains alone, with only Albanian guides, nearly lost her life more than once, and suffered such hardships that when I met her on the plains six weeks later I hardly recognized her. The pack-mule carrying the cameras and plates fell down a waterfall, and the camera with which the pictures were made was rescued by an Albanian who swam the rapids to get it. The mule was a total loss. The camera was, naturally, full of water. Mrs. Marquis took it to pieces on the floor of a mountain cabin by the light of the fire, dried it in fragments and put it together again with the aid of a pin and a hairpin, which are

still in it. . . . Nevertheless, it made the photographs, on plates which she dried one by one with a handkerchief, while the Albanians and their goats slept on the floor around her.

After this, such terrible storms came down on the mountains that the Albanian government became seriously alarmed for her safety, and sent gendarmes to rescue her, and then more gendarmes to find the first gendarmes. None of them reached her. Food had given out in the mountain villages, and she nearly starved.[12]

In fact, food was so short in the village where she and her four Albanian escorts were trapped that it was clear that the visitors had to leave. It was possible, they thought, to climb on the crusted snow through one mountain pass and descend onto the Scutari plain below. The village sent four chiefs to escort them, as was required by mountain courtesy. Peggy climbed until she was exhausted, then demanded to rest. Grim-faced, her guides would not let her, for as the sun rose higher the spring snow would begin to avalanche. And the avalanches began: first the sound, a loud rushing in the air; then the mad dash to safe ground, two men dragging Peggy when she fell. She remembered nine avalanches before she lost count. In time they were met by another mountaineer, whose home was beyond the ridge: he had heard of their coming by the mountain "telephone," a high-pitched vocal call by which mountain messengers communicated from peak to peak, and he had come to guide them. Finally Peggy could no longer even stand; she demanded that they leave her, and her interpreter pulled out his revolver. "I'm sorry," he said, "but we must kill you. We can't carry you, and the avalanche might not kill you quickly. If you can't run, we must shoot you and ourselves." For under tribal law, Peggy was their charge, and their honor demanded their own deaths if they failed her. She got up and staggered on; but in time it occurred to her to say, "After this, don't mind me. If you're going to do any shooting, please begin with yourselves."

In time, after a thirteen-hour trek, she was safe in the guide's mountain cabin, and while she rested her guides went back over the dangerous terrain to recover her cameras and much of their other gear, which had been abandoned in their mad dash for safety. And in time she made it down the mountainside to the plains, where in the interval Serb troops had occupied the route to Scutari. Peggy's American identity got her through Serb lines, and her status as a woman protected the Albanian men who were her escort. Sun-blackened and tattered, she rendezvoused with Rose aboard a coasting vessel that would return them to Trieste, and by April 24 they had reached Vienna again. Three days later, and a week from medieval Albania, Rose and Peggy saw *Ariadne auf Nauxos* at the opera, Richard Strauss conducting.[13]

In truth, Peggy was not the only one who needed rest and rehabilitation. Rose's throat was bothering her again, a tooth was abscessed, and although she did not know it she had contracted malaria: she had been delirious on the boat to Trieste. After consultation with friends in the Red Cross she went on to Budapest for treatment, where on May 4 she entered a private sanitarium. That evening she wrote a letter about the Albanian situation to Herbert Hoover, and the next morning her tonsils were removed. As she recovered, Peggy developed the Albanian pictures, and after looking them over they decided to return to Albania for more photographs. After a week of recuperation, however, Rose could not pass up the opportunity to accompany the Budapest police on an all-night raid in which plain-clothes security police checked identity papers in bar after bar, casually brutalizing young prostitutes and arresting people on vague suspicions. It was her first actual experience with the realities of a police state. She and Peggy also discovered the fabulous Gellert Turkish baths, a tiled fantasy in an undersea-motif that would produce a *World Traveler* article and an experience Rose would remember fondly even to her last year.[14]

A week later, after rail passage to Trieste and a coastal steamer down the Adriatic, she and Peggy were back in Tirana at the Hotel International. She felt better, now that the tonsils were gone, but she was not well. The next evening she fainted on the stairs after dinner, and after two days of illness she had her abscessed tooth lanced, with considerable relief. As her health improved, the charm of Albania reasserted itself, although Peggy did not feel it always:

> Went walking in the field of flowers—sang in the evening . . . May nights of Ramazan—stars, locust trees masses of shadow-tones, tops black against the sky. Square lantern hanging in the catalpa tree, large leaves clear bright green, shadows of other leaves black velvet appliqué upon them—Little table under the stars, soldiers singing and the hadji's call—White arches of shops illuminated— and Peggy is bored.[15]

Peggy left for Scutari again, and again Rose remained in Tirana with her writing. She completed the serial for Older and caught up on her voluminous correspondence. She renewed her acquaintance with young Rexh Meta, who was now studying at the Tirana Vocational School under Betsy Cleveland's sponsorship, and committed herself, in her own mind, at least, to supporting him through his further education as though he were her son. The Albanian year was well into summer now; mountain travel would never be more easy or safe, and once Peggy had returned from her work in Scutari they determined on one last exploratory trip before leaving the country. Near the end of June they traveled by foot and horse up over the western mountains into the Mati, home territory of Ahmet Zogu. The Mati they found to be a land of primitive castles and feudal customs, inhabited by a Moslem tribe as striking in its way as the Catholic tribes of the Shala region they had visited in the north. It was a beautiful country and her heart ached to make it her own; on an impulse she dug into her funds to send a gifted Mati boy from the town of Klosi down to the vocational school in Tirana to share Rexh Meta's good fortune. But at the same time that she felt an incipient surrender to Albania, she also felt, paradoxically, the pull of her own country and home. One morning she awoke weeping for home; some unremembered dream haunted her, and only later did she notice that the day was the Fourth of July.

A week later, still in the mountains at Pateni, she sat down with her notebook for one of her periodic stock-takings. She was, she reminded herself, on her way to San Francisco; she had one hundred dollars in hand but prospects of more; but she was not satisfied with her self-discipline:

> I must make a habit of thinking out carefully on paper the details of any project before I embark on it. The Mati trip is a failure because I did not do that.
> I must not be misled by my romanticism.
> I must take care of my dress and my personal appearance.
> I must get myself, somewhere, a house. To decide where, I must see America first. Probably near New York, somewhere on the Hudson. The climate is bad, hot in summer and cold in winter. Building is expensive and servants impossible. I do not like New York. Also it is far from anywhere else that I like to be. It is the center of my market. There I am in touch with all the editors, and with the Library and the Museum. Also as a fiction writer I must write American fiction, & in America is my material. New York is the place to make a success. . . .
> It will be a purely selfish life. No little boys from the Mati being sent to the Tirana Vocational School.[16]

IV

Rose and Peggy arrived by ship in Constantinople on August 11, 1922. They were met by Major C. D. Morris, who had been Rose's supervisor with the Red Cross and who would continue in that role with the Near East Relief. Both women were ill; Rose had her bad tooth pulled immediately and went to bed for a day and night, got up for one day and went back to bed for two, and after spending a night in fever and delirium it was clear that the tooth had not been the problem. At the American hospital, Rose's condition was quickly diagnosed as malaria. Peggy joined her there the next day for a week of hospitalization for the same malady, and from that point on Rose noted her quinine days in her diary. "We were utterly wrecked by the mountain trip," she wrote to Guy Moyston:

> . . . and we came on as wrecks to Constantinople, where we spent a week or so in the American hospital. Albanian malaria, than which there is no malaria than whicher. Even the malaria of Albania is superlative. Yes, I still love the country, and so does Peggy, though she slanders it unmercifully; we are going back someday to stay. We take sixty grains of quinine twice a week, and spend between times recovering.

Despite the gay tone she could affect when feeling well, the illness struck her spirit as well as her body. She would recall, later, having been so ill that she had lost the fear of death.

They had just a few days left at the end of August for rest before embarking for Batum on their way to Armenia. As their ship beat its way slowly up the coast of the Black Sea, Rose found little to note in her diary save a fried cockroach that was served with her chicken.[17]

The Transcaucasus Peninsula was an area of international tension to rival the Balkans. Occupied by the ethnically and religiously distinct Georgians, Armenians, Azerbaijanis, and other minorities, the region lay between the emerging Soviet Union and the collapsing Ottoman Empire. Russian and Turkish troops had marched back and forth across the lands of these unhappy peoples, and in 1915 the Turks had begun a systematic extermination of the Armenian population as an unreliable and dissident element in the empire. By 1917 the plight of the remainder, many of them children, had led to the formation of the Near East Relief effort from the United States; and Rose's job, as it had been for the Red Cross, was to observe the relief efforts and to write of them for the American audience to promote donations to the cause.[18]

By 1922, Armenia's long-term fate had been sealed. There had been a brief period of independence bolstered by a federation with the two neighboring states, but Soviet troops had occupied the land and local Communists were taking over civil government; by the end of the year all three states would be assimilated into the Soviet Union. Rose and Peggy arrived in this transitional period. Disembarking at Batum, they traveled inland by a train made up of converted boxcars and named the *Maxim Gorky,* to Tiflis (now Tblisi), the major city in Georgia—retracing by rail, Rose noted, the route of the ancient Argonauts.[19]

It was Rose's first encounter with Bolshevism in practice. Her experiences in Europe had by now made her skeptical of schemes for the improvement of mankind; and Tiflis she found the paradoxes of the new order striking. As she and Peggy haggled in a shop for an enameled belt one afternoon, the room was suddenly darkened as shutters dropped and the entrance closed—but business went on by lamplight. By Party decree, she found, all shops must close at three so that the workers might have a leisurely stroll in the parks before dinner—as had been the custom of the privileged classes before the revolution. Meanwhile, business went on as usual behind closed doors; and Rose was moved to recall her own days of voluntary double-shifts at the telegraph key as she had simply sought more income. Later she visited the Workers' House, a social center established in the elegant Hotel Metropole, now commandeered by the revolution. The center offered cheap food and a library of books confiscated from wealthy homes, but it was almost empty of patrons. The workers, she found, preferred the traditional local pleasure-gardens, where they could choose their entertainment and their food and pay for it. In the countryside, however, she found a new series of paradoxes—in one village a hideously debased peasantry who, by and large, preferred the new regime, which took only a portion of their produce, to the old, which had taken both food and money. "The tsar of the world is dead," they told her over and over. But in another village was a prosperous sect of Christian pacifists, traditionally communal in their land holdings, who had suffered little under the Turks. Even these, however, had little interest in the terms of their new freedom, complaining of the constant meetings to elect new local Communist officials. "Why doesn't the government go ahead and govern, and let us alone?" one farmer complained bitterly.[20]

From Tiflis they could range southward on inspection trips into Armenia. They found a country in which the dramatic signs of suffering had passed: the refugee populations were mainly dead, leaving behind empty towns and villages, their buildings devastated not by war but by the refugees who had torn them down to burn the beams and timbers for fuel. The surviving population lived in conditions so degrading as to make her experience in Vienna seem mild; years later she could still recall her visit only with a shudder, and the Near East Relief workers only with admiration as "the finest men and women who ever lived . . . the best that God and human aspiration have made." These workers had made efforts to get agricultural production started again, and they had established orphanages to care for as many of the homeless children as funds would permit: "In Armenia . . . where not one mud hut remained standing, they found little terrified wild creatures hiding in holes, bones and naked skin scabby with dirt and sores, clawing the earth for grassroots to eat and peering for grubs with eyes oozing the pus of trachoma. The Americans caught them, cleaned and salved and bandaged and fed them."[21]

In addition, Rose found local Communist commissars attempting to cope with civil administration. She visited NER orphanages and interviewed Communist officials diligently, taking copious notes as she attempted to understand the problems of the ruined land. She found one commissar planning to appropriate the total harvest from the farmers, then to redistribute it in payment for work on irrigation canals. But when she interviewed a local peasant, she found him simply resigned to starvation when the government took his grain. She and Peggy agreed that Peggy would write the lighthearted travel adventure required by *World Traveler*, while Rose would concentrate on the serious and unpleasant details of the Near East Relief work.[22]

It was winter and they were often cold and ill; there was seldom fuel enough to heat the NER buildings, let alone the peasant homes they had occasion to visit. The two women had left a trunk containing their winter clothes to be forwarded from Tiflis, but it arrived empty, the contents stolen, and they could not be angry at what privation forced upon these people; they simply improvised skirts and jackets from old blankets. They traveled by rented open motorcar or in train compartments converted from old boxcars. It was physically and emotionally wearing work. Rose had her three-month commitment; but by early November she confided to her diary, as she battled a flare-up of malaria, a "definite break in my endurance." There was nothing of the relative comfort and settled civilization of Europe to sustain her spirits, nor was there the exotic charm of an untouched primitive culture to justify the physical privation, as had been the case in Albania. There was little more than an unremitting spectacle of an obliterated civilization whose survivors perished daily of hunger, disease, and cold.[23]

"It was in Armenia that I learned fear," she later wrote to Fremont Older, "and the lesson went fairly deep." Not that she found herself in personal danger, as she had in Albania. Rather, "Armenia first revealed to me the inherent cruelty of mankind." She was well aware of the history of cruelty of Turk against Armenian; but when she was shown the site of an actual massacre she discovered another dimension to the region's history:

> Hundreds of human skeletons lay in a heap at the base of a high cliff. Skulls grinned among the bones and from the ground around it. Leg bones and rib cages were scattered farther away where hyenas or dogs had dragged them. There were little skulls and tiny backbones.
> What had been done was plain. The living had been herded to the rim of the cliff, hemmed in, to jump or to be slaughtered.

But when she inquired further into this atrocity, she found evidence to convince her of an Armenian hand here, and the victims to have been Tartar villagers. And even as peace settled over the land in a new political order, she found the systematic torture of Armenian by Armenian in Erivan, as the Communists consolidated power, a revelation: the sounds from the torture chambers kept her awake at night. Such atrocities were simply normal in this benighted land, she concluded, and could not be judged by Western standards. But even on her the inevitable indifference to human suffering began to rub off. In Etchmiadzin, she viewed the *Catholicos,* head of the Armenian church, garbed in a blaze of jewels at the ordination of a bishop; afterward she sat down to a sumptuous feast at the archbishop's table in the company of fat and happy monks. "And would you believe that I ate with appetite, that I enjoyed it all . . . ?" she lamented, while outside starving children grubbed for pine nuts beneath the trees. "They're always dying out there," the Archbishop remarked, thinking of her publicity work for NER. "Did you bring a camera?" And then the newly ordained bishop set off alone through the winter snows toward a posting so remote and so certain of hardship that Rose could think of him only as a martyr to his faith.[24]

Against such a background, her own best efforts depressed her. In an NER outpost at Djalal-Oghly, she paused to reflect in her journal: "Life goes by and nothing comes of it—nothing. No meaning. Everything you've collected turns meaningless—like the things left in the dresser-drawer that you don't know what to do with when you pack. Little bits of uselessness. And yet that's all that's left in your hands from the days that have gone. And all the other days will be just the same."[25]

To read Peggy's published account of their experiences is to discover little more than the engagement of an American sensibility with the quaint and exotic features of a foreign land, as two curious women travel in an unreliable Ford with a feckless guide and chauffeur. They encounter a Tartar camel caravan carrying packing crates labeled "bacon"— which the Tartars' Moslem faith would prohibit them from carrying, could they but read the label: the women collapse in tears of laughter. They spend the night in the home of a Georgian peasant family, sharing the only bed while the family sleeps upon the great masonry stove. And they discover a little Germany, complete with language, colonized in the eighteenth century by German peasants offered land by Catherine the Great. Rose's articles dip below these surface oddities to underlying realities: she discusses politics, taxes, and farming with her peasant host, and she plays his point of view off against that of the church and the local commissars in assessing Armenia's future. And she gives her readers a capsule history of the region even as she tugs at their heart- and purse-strings to support the Near East Relief orphanages. It was thoughtful and compelling writing, and probably the NER got its full money's worth from the weeks of newspaper columns and the several magazine articles Rose placed as a result of her appointment.[26]

What Rose got from it all is less easy to say. What struck her most were the aeons of human suffering the region had endured, populated by warring nationalities who could think of peace only in terms of exterminating their neighbors. It had marked the people with an acceptance of misery and brutality incomprehensible to an enlightened Western mind; really, the clue to understanding it all, she thought, lay in a reading of the tribal wars in the Old Testament. In the midst of the most recent chaos she found two alien forces for order at work: the American NER workers, briskly efficient and ingenious at organizing orphanages and agriculture; and the Communist functionaries, idealistic and ideology-driven, with a sense neither for business nor agriculture and liable to make terrifying mistakes. Neither seemed capable of making a lasting impression; but the Americans were clearly temporary visitors, while the Communists were there for a long stay. What was emerging for Rose, however, was a sense of the uniqueness in the world of American culture—more vital than the European and transcending by light-years the struggles of this primitive and forsaken land. Democracy for these people, she thought, could never advance past the village level; beyond that, she concluded, the autocracy of the Communists was better than that of the tsar: "At least it has brought peace." But, as she told her San Francisco readers, such experiences were making her more than ever proud of her fellow Americans, who had brought with them the only decency she could find in this backwater of civilization.[27]

V

The two women were in Erivan, capital city of Armenia and in the shadow of Mt. Ararat, through much of November. Technically, Rose's appointment was nearly over, and although Major Morris wired her suggesting she return to Constantinople, the continuing hostilities between Greece and Turkey made travel by sea impossible for the time being; Britain had closed the sea routes to Constantinople. Faced with the chance of an entire winter in the Caucasus, Rose and Peggy made their way back to the more comfortable city of Tiflis, and arrived strained close to the breaking point. In such a taut emotional state, Rose was susceptible to transient surreal states of mind: the flare of a match in sunlight, the flame vibrant but almost invisible in the brighter glow, somehow gave her such a spasm of joy that she recalled it in her journal years later, and repeated the incident several times to Guy Moyston. It was, perhaps, like the growing tree, the flowing river, another figure of the life lived simply by the energy of abiding passion; but her own energies were running perilously low.[28]

Another incident was more specifically premonitory of the future. As she drove out from Tiflis to inspect some outlying villages, she and her chauffeur stopped on a wind-swept plateau for lunch, and she walked off toward the horizon while he tinkered with the engine. Once out of sight of the car, she seemed to be not under the sky but in it. "It was like being quite alone on the roof of the world," she wrote Clarence Day.

I felt that if I were to go to the edge and look over—holding carefully, not to fall—I would see below all that I had ever known; all
the crowded cities and seas covered with ships, and the clamor of
harbors and traffic of rivers, and farmlands being worked, and
herds of cattle driven in dust across interminable plains. All the
clamor and clatter, confusion of voices, tumults and conflicts,
must still be going on, down there—over the edge, and below—
But here there was only the sky, and a stillness made audible by the
brittle grass. Emptiness was so perfect all around me that I felt a
part of it, empty myself; there was a moment in which I was nothing
at all—*almost* nothing at all. The only thing left in me was Albania.
I said, I want to go back to Albania.[29]

As their strength returned, Peggy and Rose decided to try one last
trip of exploration in the Caucasus. They had seen much of Georgia and
Armenia, but they had not been to the Moslem state of Azerbaijan, although they had encountered many of the distinctively robed Tartars
on their travels. Having by now learned that getting on a train required
either the brute strength to fight a mob or some official connection, the
women went straight to the director of the railway and secured a private
compartment on a train to Baku, the great oil-producing city on the Cas-
pian Sea. The boxcar compartment smelled of disinfectant, but it was
clean; and by dawn of December 11 Rose found herself passing through a
landscape like that of the California oil fields. At the stations, children
were selling strings of tiny boiled lobsters, which she and Peggy ate
using hairpins in place of lobster forks.

Ostensibly, Rose was covering the meeting of the state delegate
assembly, and she took copious notes on plans for industrial and agricultural production. But the incident that struck home to her was her
experience with currency exchange rates. As seasoned travelers, she and
Peggy had discovered that rates were always better on the street than on
the government exchange, and in Baku they set out to change a ten-
pound note. Their inquiries in the streets, however, produced only baffled stares or withdrawal; the women suspected fear of the police, or
cheka. Finally one man led them to an imposing building where he indi-
cated they should buy some tickets to enter. Which they did—and found
themselves admitted to a huge room filled with hundreds of haggling
men of many nationalities. Rose and Peggy had, in fact, bought themselves seats on the state currency exchange! They showed their ten-pound
note and immediately received bids of up to 144 (million roubles to the
pound). Peggy instinctively said 146, and throughout a morning of haggling the women held their "bull" position out of sheer amusement.
Finally a Persian broker met their price and delivered them mounds of
roubles by way of a porter with a wheelbarrow. Whereupon the *cheka* did
arrive, and Rose and Peggy found themselves before a commissar who
lectured them on the dangers they posed to the state economy, driving

the rouble down with their ten pounds sterling. They were permitted to leave with their bales of money; but they found that prices had already risen as a result of their speculation. Rose had seen galloping inflation in Weimar Germany, and here again she found reason to ponder the relationship of government to a nation's currency.[30]

Rose's thirty-sixth birthday had passed almost unnoticed, except for a surprise cake from one of her NER friends. As the year drew to a close, the sea-lanes to Constantinople were again opened. December 31 was Armenia's last day of independence before its formal assimilation into the Soviet Union, and on that morning Rose and Peggy left Batum by ship. "At last out of the Caucasus!" Rose noted. New Year's Eve was spent at anchor in the harbor of Trebizond, in the shadow of a Turkish cruiser and an American destroyer. At Rose's suggestion, their ship flashed a New Year's greeting to the destroyer, but they received no reply.[31]

VI

The Bosporus was such a clutter of ships that they waited in vain for official permission to disembark. By now they had learned to deal with some degrees of Eastern inefficiency: they bribed a passing boatman to take them ashore, and then bribed the customs official to pass them through after hours. And when that night the horse-drawn taxi stopped in a darkened street as they proceeded toward the Hotel Tokatlion, and the surly driver demanded a tripled fare, Rose simply stood up and beat him on the head and shoulders with her umbrella.

Once resettled in Constantinople, she turned to some additions to the forthcoming *Peaks of Shala* while Peggy explored the social life of the European and American colony in Constantinople, often to the small hours of the morning. In their hotel they encountered the Countess Alexandra Tolstoi, the great novelist's daughter, adrift since the revolution: she assumed that as Rose was always at her typewriter she must be Peggy's secretary, and treated her accordingly. But she also sold the women two winter coats from her baggage. Ship passage could not be had to Egypt, and most of the NER personnel Rose knew were relocating to Athens, so the two women decided to relocate with them and trust to finding passage to Egypt from there. On January 20 they arrived in Athens and took up lodgings in the Hotel Grande Bretagne, where they would spend the next five months.[32]

Once beyond the strain of life in Armenia, Rose found the far horizons of the East beginning to beckon again. She wrote to Guy Moyston that she was considering going on to Persia by way of Suez; and while in Athens she met B. D. MacDonald, a Scottish traveler familiar with the Middle East, with whom she planned a trip to Baghdad in September.

And the *World Traveler* was anxious for more travel stories from the Middle East. So while Cairo was necessarily the next stage on their journey, they would have to mark time until September. Meanwhile, as Rose wrote to recoup depleted finances and recuperated from a malarial flare-up, Peggy dashed off to Crete and Corfu, and then to Budapest to retrieve some clothing they had stored there. Rose visited often with the international community in Athens, who watched with avid speculation the international power-plays around the Bosporus. Turkey had driven the Greeks out of their colony at Smyrna and Athens was awash with refugees. From accounts in the Greek press, Rose expected the Greeks to be at the gates of Constantinople; if a war flared beyond these sporadic skirmishes, there would be writing to be done about it, and she wanted to be at hand. Peggy had already picked out the shops she hoped to loot in Constantinople. The domestic situation in Greece seemed ripe for revolution, though; the government had seized all gold accounts, and Rose and Peggy, with much of their money in dollars, were caught in a rising currency market that quadrupled their local debts and raised their hotel room from four to sixteen dollars a day.[33]

Guy Moyston was back in California now, resigned from his Associated Press post and having some success as a free-lance playwright. As Rose thought of his life in the States, she was conscious of how her European experience had changed her.

> Really . . . we forget that there can be anywhere on earth that isn't overrun with refugees and hysterical about the next war. . . . Men come to Europe and do one of two things; either go all to pieces, or plug along at a job for a bit and then go back to America and fit in without a single jolt. Women come to Europe and don't 'go to pieces' morally or physically or legally, but somehow . . . they just don't fit in any more. Either in Europe or in America.

As she turned outward to Moyston to describe her malaise, she turned inward to her journal to describe it to herself as a metaphysical crisis in faith. Even as she sat in her hotel room, attempting to hack out articles for complacent American readers, everything suggested that life was provisional, all certainty mere assumption:

> Dizziness at the edge. Life is thin narrowness of taken-for-granted, a plank over a canyon in a fog. There *is* something under our feet, the taken-for-granted. A table is a table, food is food, we are we— because we don't question these things. And science is the enemy because it is the questioner. Faith saves our souls alive by giving us a universe of the taken-for granted. When a table is molecules, atoms, electrons, mysteries still unanswered, and food is not bread & meat but calories of unknown that will have only guessed-at effects in the mysterious commonwealth of our bodies—who are we? Nothing but a dizziness about to fall—where?[34]

And as local backdrop to her metaphysical angst, a glimpse into primitive certainties that she and the West had long left behind, as she paid an
Easter visit to Delphi and the rituals there. With some perspective, she
would describe it years later:

> That Easter I walked alone in the rain (no tourists then; no buses)
> up the Sacred Way, past the ruined temples, the lovely columns
> . . . at night in the rain, all the way down that long, long, narrow
> valley to the sea. The Pascal lambs were roasting over the bonfires
> in the darkness, and after the feasting there was singing and dark
> figures leaping over the flames. Rites at least two thousand years
> older than Christianity, of course. All indescribably WILD and
> strange.[35]

As the Greek spring merged into summer, a desperate heat wave
set in. Rose continued to work in her hotel room, clad only in wet chemise
that dried on her as she worked, while a second chemise soaked in a
basin nearby. Peggy returned from Budapest; Rose confined her visits to
Corinth and Megara, and a few cruises aboard an American destroyer,
courtesy of some officers she had met. The Armenian book came to nothing and her finances continued to ebb. She borrowed $750 from Major
Morris and decided to return for the remainder of the summer to Constantinople to live in a house near Robert College, subleased from the
wife of a Standard Oil executive; there, at least, currency was stable and
expenses could be projected with some confidence. And there she and
Peggy would mark time while waiting to meet B. D. MacDonald in Cairo
in September.[36]

VII

Now it was Peggy's turn to relapse into malarial chills, and as she languished in her bed it became clear that she was tiring of the Middle East
adventure: she became petulant about her discomfort and longed for
Europe. Rose continued at her typewriter. "There must come a time
when luck must turn," she reminded herself. She adopted a blue-eyed
cat for companionship and met Louise Bryant, who continued in an afterglow of notoriety since the death of John Reed. Finances did not improve,
and Rose turned next to her other good friend in the NER, Frank America, borrowing a thousand dollars on a note cosigned by Peggy. With that
much to carry them to Cairo and beyond, Rose and Peggy left at the end
of August. Frank America came out to their ship to see them off. He
stood waving to them as the pilot boat took him ashore, and Rose felt a
sudden pang at the parting: "dear F.A., and seemed the last bit of security
in the world." He had taken over Rose's rented house and, no doubt, her
blue-eyed cat as well.[37]

As they slipped down the Turkish coast that night, a shore battery fired at them in a sort of nervous rebuke. The next morning they anchored in the Gulf of Smyrna but were not permitted to land. Rose had already written about that devastated city from other's accounts, and she spent the day gazing at its ruins, quite without thought or feeling, she found. She was reading Trollope's autobiography, and after copying a passage from that supremely confident and productive author into her journal, some stray association moved her to add, "Economy is undignified with white hair: it is an admission of failure in life. But can't one be dignified in admitting failure?"[38]

In fact, a cluster of problems involving economy, failure, and a loss of self-confidence was gathering for Rose. Late on September 1 she and Peggy registered at Shepheard's Hotel in Cairo after an exhausting day passing through customs and a humiliating medical screening. A sign in the hotel room offered an intriguing set of options:

Ring once for the waiter,
Twice for the maid,
Three times for the Arab.

The Arab appeared like a genie, and Rose could only think to ask for ice water, which she had not had since leaving New York City. It appeared, and on this augury of good fortune she set out next morning for two days of sight-seeing, which ranged from the lovely mosque of Mehmet Ali, an Albanian emigré, to the obligatory pyramids and Sphinx. The pyramids did not impress her as would the ruins of Baalbeck, but the gaze of the Sphinx, she sensed, was inscrutable only to Western eyes: the older races of the East, she was sure, recognized in it the wisdom that has seen the rise and fall of civilizations of which her own was merely the most recent. Meanwhile, confrontation with Egypt had made Peggy's yearning for a familiar culture undeniable.[39]

She had decided to return to Switzerland and go on to Paris and New York. There was a stormy confrontation regarding her original debt to Rose and money still owed to the Mutual Fund. Rose had been carrying her, it seems, for most of two years; and now Peggy also needed money for her decampment. The details of the final arrangement are not clear, but apparently Peggy left Rose to recoup the debt from her husband, while Rose turned over to Peggy three hundred of the thousand dollars they had borrowed from Frank America. Peggy kept the cameras and, as it turned out, some of Rose's baggage and clothing as well. Rose blamed her own weakness of character in allowing herself to be taken advantage of, but she also wrote bitterly of Peggy in her journal: "A woman with the mind and character of a spoiled child. A liar, a coward, selfish, unscrupulous, mean and vain and malicious. No loyalty, no tact, no sense of obligation. Shallow emotions. . . . She knows what she wants and goes after it. She had her plan ready before we separated in Cairo. What was it?"[40]

B. D. MacDonald was in Cairo as he had promised, and Rose left with him immediately after her settlement with Peggy for Jerusalem and Damascus. She was traveling now in country she had known imaginatively through her Bible and tales of the Crusades since childhood; her father's name, Almanzo, harked back through his family's English ancestry to the Crusades, altered from the Moorish *Almancar.* She made the obligatory stops at the Christian shrines and sent picture postcards to her pious Grandmother Ingalls in South Dakota. But Baalbek stunned her imagination in a way the Christian settings, or even the Greek temples, had not. Like the Sphinx, the great stone temple raised to the pagan god Baal, Lord of the Flies, bespoke of reaches of time and depths of the human spirit that her tradition could not grasp. On the other hand, the beautiful city of Damascus, with its fountains and palm trees, set a standard of serene Eastern civilization that she found as refreshing as it was exotic. She and MacDonald tarried two weeks in the Victoria Hotel, exploring the charm of the city.

In the midst of such challenges she was finally overwhelmed with a desire for home. She had received a letter from Mama Bess, and on the way to view an Arab religious festival outside of Damascus she made the decision. If she could make it to Baghdad, she would abandon Siam, the Orient, and a triumphal return to San Francisco. The next day she telegraphed Cook's Travel in Beirut for rates. "I can't realize that I shall actually be going home," she noted in her diary. "I wonder if I shall someday really be changing cars at Springfield?" Her resolve had carried her just three weeks longer than had Peggy's.[41]

In fact, that change of cars was yet some months away, and there was yet one test of her resolve to be met. In 1920, as she had begun her foreign travels, she had lightheartedly announced Baghdad as her destination, and in Damascus she was closer now than she had ever been. At the moment, however, travel to Baghdad seemed unlikely. There was, of course, an ancient route still traveled by camel caravans, but these left by no predictable schedule and the prospect of days of travel by camel no doubt daunted even Rose. Just the year before had been the first automobile crossing of the five hundred miles of desert, and there was a weekly mail service driven by desert veterans, but there were no real roads and no reliable guides for ordinary travelers. As Rose made her plans to turn back, she went to bed one afternoon with a bad cold. At four o'clock, MacDonald came in with a new guest at the hotel, a Major A. L. "Desert" Holt, who said that he could get them to Baghdad. After hearing him out, Rose got up from her bed, had a tooth filled by an Arab dentist, packed for Baghdad, and was back in bed at eleven.

Desert Holt had been attached for several years to various British missions in the Middle East and had served with valor during the 1920 Mesopotamian insurrections against the British. He had explored extensively by Ford automobile in Transjordan and Mesopotamia, surviving bandit attacks and seventeen days as a prisoner of one raiding party. He was the very type of the British colonial officer: hardy, brave, overwhelmingly self-confident, and a little mad. He was just returning from England with his new bride and posting to a new assignment in Baghdad. He had never traveled the Damascus-to-Baghdad route, but the fact did not particularly concern him. All they needed to do, he said, was to find the air-furrow to Baghdad.

In 1921, Holt had been commissioned to make the first ground survey for an air route for a Cairo-to-Baghdad mail service. Fliers had discovered that automobile tracks on the desert were visible from high in the air; R.A.F. pilots searching for Holt during his desert captivity had followed these traces. The obvious next step was to lay such a trail deliberately, so in May 1921, Holt and another officer, starting from opposite ends of the route, laid a track from Amman, Jordan, to Ramadi, on the Euphrates River, across a desert heretofore traversed only by camels. Within six months, however, most of the marked trail had eroded away and needed renewal, which was accomplished with a Fordson tractor and a double-ganged plow. Holt and his partner chugged the whole distance from Amman to Ramadi in fourteen days, laying behind them two wide and deep trenches, easily visible from the air. All Rose and MacDonald had to do, Holt said, was to follow established tire tracks east from Damascus until they hit the air-furrow, which would guide them to Baghdad; what was more, he and his bride would go with them.

On September 27, the party set out in two Ford Model Ts. Holt had his own machine, equipped for desert travel with special tires and springs; Rose and MacDonald rode in a rented car with a hired Arab driver and his mechanic. Both cars were crammed with extra gasoline and built-in water tanks from which the travelers drank with individual rubber tubes. Holt drove like a madman, far outdistancing the rented car in his special machine. Rose and MacDonald had to track him by dust on the horizon, then catch up when he chose to wait for them. From time to time, the Fords would become stuck in some hole, and Rose's experience driving in the California deserts came into play as she helped jack the wheels out of the sand. They discovered one long-abandoned hulk of a car, its crankshaft broken. By the end of the second day they were quite lost in the Syrian desert, although no one would admit it.

The "trackless desert" had, in fact, sometimes too many tracks and sometimes too few. Obvious trails would lose themselves in gullies and flint-beds or end in wind-blown sand. At a critical point, the party chose the most likely path, a double set of wheel tracks that led them confidently on for miles. And ended. A wide loop in the desert revealed that the previous traveler, as confused as themselves, had lost heart and doubled back on his trail, scoring a double highway to nowhere. They had followed his trail for a hundred miles. The two Arabs began to weep.

Their situation was dangerous. The Fords required not only gasoline but water regularly, and they were down to four quarts for cars and people. They were at least two hundred miles from Baghdad. Holt opined that their best bet was to run due east and hope to hit the Euphrates before their water ran out. They might have to abandon one car and use its water in the other's radiator. Then Mrs. Holt lost her wedding ring, and they swept and sifted a vast patch of sand before pressing on. Holt was fearful of bandits and sought to keep off the skyline. The hired driver and his mechanic scuffled over their water bottle and were separated only by force. As they made camp that night in a sheltering ravine, MacDonald thought he heard voices. The women alternated with the men keeping guard with rifles at the ready. Rose turned to a back page of her diary to write a few lines:

> . . . on a moonlit night, while standing guard against Bedouins, on the Syrian desert between Damascus and Baghdad—when the moon is under a cloud the desert is very dark, when it comes out, the desert just escapes being white. No sound but the blood in your ears & the voices of your fancy. Also strange shapes, & the rocks move. Fountains of darkness on the horizon, also the skyline swings as on a ship.

The next day Holt admitted what Rose had known since the day before—that he hadn't the slightest idea of where they were. But as he scanned the horizon, a distant mountain reminded him of Tel-el-Eshauer, a peak he had seen while laying the air-furrow. But now he was seeing it from a different angle. If he was right, it was within ten miles of the wells of Rutba, which were on their route. He set off at top speed, and his companions could only follow. When they caught up with him two hours later, he was gazing down into a small ravine at foraging camels and two men. Rose and MacDonald covered him with rifles as he approached the herdsmen and found them friendly.

The herdsmen led the travelers to their encampment at the wells; and Holt explained to Rose that these people were the Saluba, a tribe wretchedly poor even by the severe standards of desert life. They traced their ancestry not to Semitic origins but to the European Crusaders; and as Rose picked her way through yards of mud and camel dung around the wells, and drank deeply of water the color of tea, she must have pondered the ancient connection between her father's name and her hosts. A sheep was killed in their honor and consigned—head, tail, wool, and all—to a stew-kettle. Under a tattered tent three feet high, the lost travelers ate mutton with their fingers and asked their hosts the road to Baghdad. Set on the right path, they came across the air-furrow the next afternoon.

They were still ninety miles from the Euphrates, but it gave them a comforting sense of contact with the British Empire.

The journey from this point on could only be anticlimactic. Its imaginative background had been the old tradition of the Garden of Eden and the later tales of a valley rich in harvest ruled by Haroun el Rashid, visited by Ghengis Khan. But as the Fords reached the Euphrates, the old tales were as nothing to the sullen river flowing by barren banks through a desert prospect as far as the eye could see. On the evening of the sixth day they crossed the Tigris on the Maude Bridge and entered Baghdad.

Here, sadly, was nothing from the Arabian nights, a city not even to be compared with Damascus, Rose thought. The soft colors of the buildings were merely stucco over mud brick. The tiled minarets of the mosques against the sky drew her eye; but although she had been permitted to enter the lovely mosque of Mehmet Ali in Cairo, here Christians were not welcome visitors, the British officers told her. She stayed a week in a small hotel next to a water-bottling plant. The high point of each day was tea with her British friends. The civilization of Baghdad was not to be compared to her other experiences in the Moslem world; her deepest impression was of a more ancient presence beneath the scruffy local culture and the banality of the European foreign-service life. She felt it most as she rowed out on the Tigris and looked back on the city rising out of foundations laid by Nebuchadnazzar. The boat, manned by naked bronze-skinned boys, was as primitive as if from prehistoric times. Through half-shut eyes, she said, she gazed through the present into the past and dreamed strange dreams.[42]

It was time to go home. There would be no triumphal return to San Francisco from a trip around the globe. Her experience from Armenia to Baghdad had marked her in a way that she finally put clearly in 1949. "And in Baghdad, where India comes up the Tigris to smudge clean Arabia, I turned back. The fabulous East was the easier way home but I had seen enough of its human misery, its killing toil and ignorance and humility, its so-called 'spirituality' born of hopelessness and starvation, and the revolting snobbery of Westerners too stupid to recognize their own brutality."[43] Holt was in Baghdad to stay, and MacDonald was off down the Tigris on his way to Bombay. Rose could not return to Damascus the way she had come; rather, she and her driver and the rented car took the northern route along the Euphrates to Dier-el-Zor and then westward to Palmyra and Damascus.

It was a jolting, nine-day trip, including three days in quarantine at Abu Kemal, at the Syrian border, where the French army controlled passage. This was an established route; there was no desert camping. Rather, each night was spent at a *caravanserai*, the desert equivalent of a motel:

In reality, it is a barnyard filled with goats, sheep, camels and camel drivers, surrounded by a twenty-foot mud wall. Against three sides of the wall, shoulder high, is a platform; on the platform are windowless rooms. You may spend the night rolled in your blankets on the bare platform, or on the bare floor of a room. All the other occupants of the caravanserai spend the night bleating, grunting and squealing, or tootling Arab music, talking, singing, dancing, fighting, honking your automobile horn, eating and drinking, or biting, buzzing and crawling, according to their various forms and unrestrained wills. It is a picturesque and colorful sight to see them doing it—those that are large enough to be seen.

The humor came after the fact, and was written for the *World Traveler* audience. She loathed the persistent sand flies, hated the French border guards; her taste for the picturesque was sated. "To think that I'm sitting in this picturesque damn town on the Euphrates, when I want to be at home," she noted at Halithe, where the police had halted her car for the night for some unspecified danger, probably bandits, on the road to Annah. She tarried with pleasure only at Palmyra, King Solomon's Tadmor of the Old Testament and still bearing that name for her Arab driver, to visit the tomb of Xenobia, the Bedouin queen who had defied the Roman Empire for a five-year reign. In the background, Rose heard a Bedouin child singing the Missouri Waltz. Pausing in Damascus only long enough to gather her possessions, she left at once for Beirut and sailed for France on the night of October 20.[44]

VIII

The *Belgrano* carried Senegalese troops below decks and three first-class passengers above: Rose and the two French officers in charge. For ten days she had little to do save look forward to home and backward on her recent experience, and talk with the young French lieutenant anxious to practice his English. She turned to her journal to take stock of her foreign adventures:

> I gave myself three years: the three years have gone, and here I am, circumstances unchanged. If three years of my life mean anything they must mean it to and in me. . . .
> Finances certainly much worse than three years ago. Friendships, if any, gone. Career in worse shape. Gain is apparently little but worthless and fading memories. Unless at last I have grown to adult intelligence.[45]

She landed at Marseilles, took a train to Paris, and quickly found temporary quarters in the empty apartment of a friend of the Dulins. She had not been in town five days when Peggy Marquis arrived, ready to resume the friendship on the old terms and looking for a place to live. Rose did not invite her to share her quarters. She spent her time with the Dulins and in buying a new wardrobe for her trip home. Ernestine Evans arrived in town on her way to the States, and the two women sailed together on the *Leviathan* on November 20, 1923. "Last of France quite unemotional," Rose noted tersely in her diary.

She was exhausted by the time she boarded ship, unable to take a turn about the deck without trembling. The crossing was uneventful, save for a meeting with a man who would in time assume considerable importance in Rose's life. Garet Garrett, later to be a major political writer for the *Saturday Evening Post,* struck Rose as a "little involved self-conscious and conventional man." Nonetheless, they talked for hours about "maternity and matriarchy"; "utter piffle and staleness of old times," Rose wrote to herself: it all seemed part of a life she had left behind long ago. But from out of that past came a host of friends to meet her at the boat: Mary Margaret McBride and her companion Stella Karn, Berta and Elmer Hader, Bessie Beatty, Kenneth Durant. Within days she made connections again with Helen Boylston and Clarence Day; there was Thanksgiving dinner with the Haders, and her diary records a whirl of meetings with editors, publishers, and her agents. "Wasted time and futility," she scrawled, conscience-stricken, across the bottom of one page. The next day she did nothing but read Katherine Mansfield. "Would such stories of America sell?" she asked herself. "Let us have no nonsense about it. I do not write for the Lord, but for cash." Gone, it seems, was her London resolution to do no more hackwork; she was broke and in debt, and taking shape was a scheme that would require considerable money.[46]

Three weeks slipped by before she could catch the *St. Louisan* for Missouri. She changed at St. Louis, then again in Springfield after an all-night ride. "Like a dream," she wote on December 20. "Mama Bess met me at Mansfield station." Mama Bess found Rose physically altered by her experience; a picture from this time shows a pinched and haggard face, almost unrecognizable from earlier photos. After a day of rest, Rose went to town with her father in the lumber wagon to claim her bag and to meet the people on the streets of her old home town. She had been gone for four years, and she was home for Christmas.[47]

$\mathscr{A}$ MISSOURI INTERLUDE

> *I somehow always have this idea that as soon as I can get through
> this work that's piled up ahead of me, I'll really write a beautiful
> thing. But I never do. I always have the idea that someday,
> somehow, I'll be living a beautiful life. And that, too. . . .*

She had gone abroad to seek adventure, fame, and fortune. She returned to Mansfield world-weary, homesick, in debt, and physically
debilitated. Within days she felt the old alienation; within weeks she
felt hopelessly trapped; and within months she was getting fat. Two
days after Christmas she began a story she called "Autumn," in which
a globe-trotting successful woman writer returns in triumph to her old
home town; she is gently patronized by her domestic sister for being
unmarried; she in turn pities the thickening bodies and minds of her old
friends she meets at a party in her honor; and she is finally exhilarated
by relief at meeting an old beau, who still held a grip on her heart, and
discovering him to be a cautious, platitudinizing bore unworthy of her
affection. Her return to old bonds has been a discovery of freedom, she
reflects as she drifts off to sleep: "To each human being one thing is
stable. That is the thing not yet examined. . . . So all the ecstasies and the
heartbreaks come to one end, and the end is freedom from them all.
Freedom. And the good years yet to be lived!"[1]

There was no old beau in Mansfield for Rose; and the pitying sister
probably represents the tacit judgments of Rose's old friends and Mama
Bess: the whole imagined situation merely objectifies the distance Rose
discovered between herself and her origins. She was something of a local
sensation, with her foreign clothes and exotic tales. "I am a lion for miles
around," she wrote Guy Moyston; she spoke at a meeting of her mother's
club in a black lace dress just after the new year; and from then on people
would ask, having no other way to grasp her experiences, "What is the
weather now, where you have been?" But the isolation, the reversion to
country life, her mother's constant presence were more than she could
accept with equanimity. "This life is almost intolerable," she recorded in
her diary on January 10, 1924. "I do not know how we shall endure it until
I can get away. This is the sort of hell that taught me endurance, but now I
am old and have so little time left to live peacefully."[2]

But if at thirty-eight Rose was feeling her age, her parents were older and showing theirs, and her sense of obligation was overpowering: she could not grasp the freedom her heroine discovers. Her father was sixty-seven and had suffered the cold of winter severely ever since his stroke in Dakota Territory; Rose longed to send him to a warmer climate for the winters. But her mother, ten years younger than her father, seemed to be the real problem. "I don't know whether I shall ever be able to get away from Mansfield again or not," she wrote Moyston. "My mother is old and not very well, and wants me to stay here." Actually, there is little evidence of Mama Bess's actual ill health; she would live on vigorously till age ninety, and her husband till ninety-two. Rose's bondage was more emotional than circumstantial.[3]

The practical consequences, however, were that Rose became the family slavey. Guy Moyston made the mistake once of implying a sentimental, Whittier-like view of winter on the farm, and Rose could not take it:

> No it am *not* jolly on the farm when the snow flies. You just try it once, with the well frozen, I mean the bucket frozen in it, and the floors dirty with muddy feet and dogs and wood-dirt and ashes-dust, and the whole front of the house shut like a tomb because no one has the strength to keep it warmed, and three human beings living in one room with the dogs, and the swill having to be cooked for the hogs, and a sick lamb in the corner, and—well, you just try it once.

And the worst of it was that her parents could see no reason why she could not live her own life in these circumstances.

> My people can't see why I shouldn't settle down here for the rest of my life. They're too old to do the work, and a servant can't be got; money won't hire one to do the work that has to be done in a farmhouse. . . . Sometimes it seems to me I'll go mad and fall to biting the trees—me scrubbing the floors and washing windows and bringing in wood and washing dishes three times a day and peeling potatoes and waiting on the pigs. . . . It's either do it or see my mother—who's simply broken down under it and should be in a hospital. What the hell can one do? . . . Their point of view is perfectly good; let me stay here and do my writing and we will all be rich. Only it doesn't work out that way. After a full day of slavey's drudgery in the dirt I can't write. My mother says to go ahead and write and she'll do the work. But I can't do that either. And on the other hand I simply can't cut and run and live happily on the Coast, leaving them in this rotten mess. Besides, I've been away five years, and I'm their only child, and all that.

By the time she had been home six weeks, however, Rose was trying to lay practical plans for some means of escape, and relaying these schemes to Moyston. She hopes to get her father to sell off the stock, and most of the land if buyers can be found; the upkeep of the house and an income for her parents she thinks she can afford once she is out of debt. She could send her father to California for the winters, and take her mother to Paris, and maybe she could get to San Francisco again to see Fremont Older and her friends. . . . And then there was Albania. "Guy, if I can't get back to Albania next spring," she wrote Moyston, "it will be the hardest thing to bear that has ever happened to me." Her hopes spiral out and out, but always come back to the need to write something that will bring in some money.[4]

But it was not simply the work and the worry that oppressed her; it was, she said, "a sense of solitary imprisonment." The isolation from good company and good talk dulled her spirit, and when free time opened up for her to work she could not take advantage of it all. She could write about twenty-five hundred words a day, she said, then she could merely wander around distracted, wanting something to happen. "I want street-cars and trucks and telephones ringing—things to interrupt me so I can go on working." Instead, the interruptions were the galling ones of her inevitable situation. "Papa & mama quarreling as usual about the farm." "Drove with Papa to the Fry's sale: in the afternoon to town with Mama Bess to get washing." In defense, her mind at times slipped into a daze: "There is an insulation over everything. The unreality of solitary days. I read Schopenhauer and L. H. J. [*Ladies' Home Journal*]. Life goes by, gets away from me, and soon I shall be dead, and everything insulated forever." To her delight, Moyston sent her newspaper clippings, book reviews, and magazines unavailable in Mansfield. There was no radio, and only the local newspaper, and library books came by post from Springfield, fifty miles away. "Dear Guy," she wrote, "nothing that breaks into print sends a ripple to our shores. A week ago I wrote to a friend in bewilderment, 'What's a teapot dome?' Since then I am informed that it is an oil scandal."[5]

||

There were days of relief. In Paris she had met a writer named Catherine Brody, who had preceded her back to the States to a newspaper job in New York. Rose had urged her to visit Rocky Ridge Farm, and shortly after the new year she stopped for a few days on her way to California. And in February B. D. MacDonald came in from the west, in the last stages of his trip around the world, a reminder of the plan Rose had abandoned. He tantalized her with an invitation to travel with him retracing Marco Polo's route to the Orient. The visit that gave her life, however, was Guy Moyston's. He had had some little luck with a play in California, and had spent some time unsuccessfully trying to write movie scripts. Now he was heading east again, and accepted Rose's invitation to visit. He arrived at the end of March and stayed for three months.[6]

Almost no record remains of these days. Rose and Moyston had been exchanging letters several times a week; now, happy with her lover at hand, Rose had fewer letters to write and less need to reflect to herself in her diary and journals. Springtime in the Ozarks is a lovely season, and she started a nature journal in which she minutely described the daily and hourly changes as spring advanced. She and Moyston began a collaboration on a magazine serial and on a play, projects that would occupy them for the rest of the year; and Rose was finally transforming her biography of Jack London into a novel, reading to Moyston from the manuscript as she progressed. There was a five-day fishing trip with Mama Bess's friends to nearby Table Rock Lake. Moyston got on famously with Rose's parents, particularly as he discussed Prohibition and politics with Mama Bess, and by the time he left he was carrying several friendly bets on the year's presidential nominations and the outcome of the election. In the evenings he and Rose had a private time together as they went out to the pasture to bring home the cows; his pratfall into the stream became an instant family legend. As darkness gathered, they would sit on the porch, smoking cigarettes and companionably talking. When Moyston left, even Nero the Airedale pup missed him, mournfully wagging in his vacated room. The loss was exemplary for Mama Bess, Rose wrote: "There was a large empty space in the house after you left, and my mother said, 'Now can you imagine what it is like when you go, and there is *nobody*?' "[7]

It was an arms'-distance romance that these two lonely and cautious old friends were developing. "I have a very special kind of caring for you, you know; you and the Major and Frank America, three of all the people I've known that I really trust and love. And you most of all. . . ." "It's good to have you say you like me . . . I'd be very stupid and blind if I didn't care a lot for you," she wrote as she anticipated his arrival; and once he had gone, the letters take a more intimate note, yet savingly tart: "Very much love, my dear. And while I don't agree that it's intellectual, I do quite agree that it isn't a question of 'purely physical personality,' not even in [the] most sublimated physical personality. If you could be you as a hunchback in a leper colony, those circumstances wouldn't make any difference." They continued their collaborative writing by mail, and Rose jokingly suggested a kind of authorial marriage of names, by which they would create a fictitious author, Lane Moyston. And as she learns of Guy's ill health and physical exhaustion, her letters become clucking, detailed exhortations to rest and seek treatment. She, she reports, is in blooming health, at 141 pounds and, on a diet, counting down: "I estimate that at this rate I shall weigh 28 pounds in six months." He sent her father some lovely long woolen underwear, English imports, against the coming winter. And they laid plans for a rendezvous in New York in the fall.[8]

It was to be either in Croton-on-Hudson or in Nyack. Rose weighed the relative advantages at length. She had fond memories of Croton from the spring of 1919, and Jane Burr and the Dells were old friends; Nyack offered the company of the Haders' circle and the older friends from San Francisco. Berta Hader's notions of propriety, however, amounted to a "Volstead act [prohibition] against kissing," which "would have the lamentable effect of the real Volstead act, as far as our inclinations went." Life together in Croton would be simpler, because although "in that transplanted Greenwich Village, the Villagers would put the same construction on it that the Mansfield villagers put upon your being here," the group at Croton would "just take it as a matter of course." "We could spend our days in reading plays and our evenings in walks and our nights in innocent childlike slumber," she continued, "without any strain upon our nerves or consciences. BUT . . . it would put you in the tacitly assumed position of having an interest in me which you don't want to be assumed by anybody. And with some of my new acquaintances in New York . . . a Croton address might not be an asset."[9]

The dilemma seems quaint today, but it points up that feature of Rose's temperament that had set her apart from Greenwich Village and its ambience even as she had lived there: a formal conservatism that was a matter of style rather than of conviction. "The trouble with me . . . is that I have the tastes and the instincts of a perfect lady, and yet somehow I've missed having quite the mind of one. I like things delicately in order; I like the clearness and the dignity of lives lived conventionally." Radical freedom was instinct with her, but flagrant promiscuity, unwashed bodies, and dirty tablecloths were something else. Unlike many of her friends, she did not condemn Puritanism: ". . . it was a thoroughly sound reaction against a corrupt state of society. . . . It produced some of the best thinkers and fighters and pioneers in history." "Better, say I, far better, depravity clothed than depravity naked."[10]

She was beginning to face consciously the dilemma of desire and duty. The girl who had thrilled to the story of the Wandering Jew, reading in the swing at Rocky Ridge Farm, had also absorbed conventions as laws from her heritage; and as her rebellious conscience kept her at Rocky Ridge now, hacking out stories to support her family, she felt achingly that there was another life she ought to be in tune with: "I somehow always have the idea that as soon as I can get through this work that's piled up ahead of me, I'll really write a beautiful thing," she lamented to Moyston. "But I never do. I always have the idea that someday, somehow, I'll be leading a beautiful life. And that, too. . . ." And it was but a step from personal longings to the metaphysical. In one letter she wrote touchingly of a baby owl her father had found, its mother missing, as it faced the family dog. She lifted it to the low limb of a tree. "There it stood, and looked blindly in the sunlight down at Nero, and flapped its wings with all the courage of a lion. . . . There is something very beautiful and terrible in the world—at the core of the world, of life—something neither beautiful nor terrible, but both, inseparably—if only we could *get* to it—could only know it somehow. But one gets only a glimpse, now and then, indescribable, ungraspable, only a *feeling*. . . ."

What she longed for was some natural and authentic assertion of her place in the world, just as she would submit willingly to destiny "blowing like a dark wind among the planets." She had sensed some such balance in the Moslem world, especially among the desert Arabs: " 'Inshallah,' they say, and smile . . . 'If God wills'. . . and you like to think that somehow they have struck the balance, and know—without thinking—how important and unimportant they are. Instead of eternally wavering, like us, with pain and struggle from our little feelings of importance to our tremendous sense of unimportance and impotency." Her life, sadly, was just such a wavering, as she pined for a life according to heart's desire—in Albania—and submitted to her mother's claims on her, and as she longed to write something worthy of her best talents while she frittered away her days in work she did not respect. Meanwhile, time was her enemy, and more and more temporary consolation could be found in the simple handwork—sewing, knitting, baking—she had been born to:

> I am dizzy with the speed of time. Weeks and months and years speeding by, and somehow no progress—getting nowhere—like a treadmill. That, I think, is why I take such pleasure in making something with my hands; one has that feeling of having accomplished *something*.
> One never has the feeling about a stack of good paper covered over with little black typewriter-marks.

She read George Bernard Shaw's *Saint Joan* and was not impressed, but she was even more strongly appalled by the decline of Shaw's talents with age. "Guy, my dear, if this is the gulf yawning at the feet of—how old is he? Seventy?—we birds of time have but a little way to fly, and by all the gods we should be getting in the hay while the sun shines. . . . If I fall as far as Shaw—What a fall!"[11]

In the end, they engaged two of Jane Burr's thirteen rooms at the Drowsy Saint Inn in Croton. From the Dells, Rose learned that she could have Max Eastman's house there for the year, but she reluctantly declined: "I suppose I'll have to come back to the farm. Mama Bess will be broken hearted if I don't." But she stopped at Nyack first for a visit with the

Haders, where Moyston and Elmer Hader met her train on the seventeenth of September. She then tracked down the ebullient Troub Boylston, who was working as a private nurse. Troub was introduced into the Hader circle and became an occasional companion to Rose and Guy as they circulated from Croton to Nyack to New York City during the next three months.[12]

It was, from all evidence, one of the happiest times in Rose's life. She and Guy worked together on the serial and on a play of Moyston's that he called *Smoke*. Between times there were long walking adventures in the countryside around Croton, rambles in Moyston's Ford, and runs down to the city for theater and shopping. By mid-November, Jane Burr's unheated rooms, however, had diminished their enthusiasm for Croton, and they moved to separate rooms in the Judson Hotel in New York City. Here Rose organized an informal Friends of Albania society, with an eye to providing funds for relief and education. She was also trying to develop for Mama Bess a bridge between her parochial writings for the *Missouri Ruralist* and a national market.[13]

Since 1911, Rose's mother had written regularly for this regional farmers' journal. Her forte had been practical hints for managing the farm home, although in time she became something of a columnist, offering a few prosy thoughts each month on moral and ethical issues. Sometimes she incorporated parts of Rose's letters into her material. In the course of 1924, however, Rose had begun to develop a connection with *Country Gentleman*, which the Curtis Publishing Company offered to a rural audience as an alternative to the more urbane *Saturday Evening Post*; despite her wistful assertion to Moyston that her natural talent was for the *Harper's* kind of story, under the pressure to earn money Rose had begun a series of contrived Ozark hillbilly stories for *Country Gentleman*. Now, with her agent, she was attempting to bring her mother into this market as well.[14]

The instrument was a short article Mama Bess had written describing the development of her kitchen into a model center for the farm wife. While in Croton, Rose took the amateurish effort in hand and simply reconceived and rewrote it from beginning to end, as she had done with the earlier *McCall's* article. She revised the lead, cut out detail, reorganized the development, and invented a dramatic interlocutor to emphasize a country-city contrast. Mama Bess complained rightly that it was now Rose's article, but Rose argued that she was offering instruction, by which her mother might break into the national market. Mama Bess's resentment shows through Rose's letter, and Rose lectures as though to a recalcitrant student. For all of this, Mama Bess got $150, less the agent's commission, and Rose's reassurance that later articles should fetch two hundred dollars.[15]

For Thanksgiving, Rose and Guy went up to Croton to visit Floyd and Marie Dell; Christmas they spent in the city with Rose's friends from *Asia* and with Clarence Day. Free time was drawing to an end for both of them; by late December, Moyston was away to rented quarters in Palisades, but he sent violets back to Rose. Her letters to him were now frankly loving, full of pleasant recollections of their time together, yet expressive of what she understands to be a special detachment they share:

> I feel so strongly the coming toward us of a new year. . . . There's this, at least, to say. Let's live it gaily. Life has been good to us. And even when it's not kind, it is always, somehow, good in itself. I want the new year to be kind to you, my dear. So very much, I want it to give you everything you want. No one knows. But anyway, nothing that comes can destroy that eternal change that is the core and the goodness of living.
>
> When I think of you and me in our relation to each other, the thing I want most is that we will continue to want the same thing. . . . Please, O unknown fate, let us both keep wanting something for ourselves, something outside ourselves—freedom, or integrity, or whatever word that comes to mind, since none of them fit. Don't let us lose what we have, and come down to the scrambling and hurting of clutching at each other.[16]

IV

On the tenth of January, 1925, Rose arrived in Mansfield again, full of new hope and new plans, but still subject to the old fears. She had been summoned abruptly by Mama Bess, who had fallen ill. Helen Boylston mentioned the event as illustrative of the way Mama Bess could yank the chain that held Rose to her. "Rose was very much her mama's slave," she recalled, "and Mama said, 'Come home.'" Rose persuaded Troub to join her on the return to Missouri for an indefinite stay: in her mind, no doubt, was Troub's skill as a nurse, but she was also an amicable companion and was interested in trying her own hand at free-lance writing under Rose's tutelage. Back east, in care of Troub's father in Portsmouth, New Hampshire, waited Rose's latest investment for life at Rocky Ridge, a nearly new 1923 Buick sedan, sporting nearly new tires, a new blue paint-job, and only ten thousand miles of service. It would follow them to Mansfield by rail. Rose's father met them with the lumber wagon to carry their baggage; Mama Bess met them with a taxi to carry them home.[17]

Within a week appeared the issue of *Country Gentleman* that carried both Rose's first Ozark story and Mama Bess's kitchen article. Another of Rose's stories had been accepted and she had plans for more; on the strength of such success, she hoped shortly to lay up ten thousand dollars in bonds for her parents, the income from which would free her to leave home again. She was almost out of debt now; an advance from her publisher on the Jack London novel had allowed her to repay the loan from Frank America. For her own part, Rose was beginning to participate in the great American fantasy of getting rich on the stock market. Troub had a small inheritance that she had put into the investment company of her former employer, George Q. Palmer; it was showing a nice return, and Rose began to plan opening an account of her own.[18]

In effect, she was making use of adversity, although this involved various kinds of self-betrayal and hypocrisy. Her short story "Autumn" had brought her $450 from *Harper's*, as would "The Blue Bead," which won an honorable mention in the *Harper's* prize competition for 1925. This kind of story, she told Moyston, was her best work. But her contrived Ozark tales for *Country Gentleman* earned her six hundred dollars each, with the prospect of higher fees later, and they were easier to produce. What was emerging was a series of connected stories about Abimelech Noah Baird, a backwoods boy whose native shrewdness enables him to rise to prosperity and station as a small-town lawyer. The character was based loosely on her parents' friend, a Mansfield banker named N. J. Craig, but Rose had also known the Ozark culture since childhood. The contrivance of their plots aside, however, she was interested in capturing the authentic Ozark folkways and idiom, and as the stories progressed she consulted Craig about them. But she could not bring herself actually to read the rural journal that was paying her for this material.[19]

Another kind of bad faith was involved in an article she wrote for *Country Gentleman* in this January of 1925. "A Place in the Country" paints a loving picture of her parents' life on Rocky Ridge Farm, giving due credit to the satisfaction inherent in the work of rural life. As narrator, she recounts her own early conviction of the inferiority of country life as opposed to that in the city, and she recalls an attempt to persuade her mother to give up the farm to live in St Louis. But now, older and wiser, she must admit that the landscapes framed by her mother's windows are the equal of those she has seen in the Louvre; and that her mother's life, on balance, has been as good as her own. Such a message was, of course, just what the readers of *Country Gentleman* would like to hear, but it sorts ill with Rose's complaints in her diary and in her letters to Moyston. In time, her own history would authenticate the sentiment on her own terms, as she would find a way to have a country life without the country labor and a home to herself without the drag of her parents. But in its moment it sounds like nothing so much as an attempt to put the best face on a dreaded future, a capitulation not merely to her audience but to her mother.[20]

A similar capitulation occurs in an article published in *Cosmopolitan* in the same month and written during her stay with Moyston in Croton. "If I Could Live My Life Over Again" offers an eloquent description of the pressures and opportunities that led her to leave the small town, marry and divorce, choose a career and a single life over a marriage and family—all in pursuit of personal happiness. But she ends by acknowledging that the woman who has led the conventional life of self-sacrifice has chosen the higher and the better path, and she avows that could she choose again with her mature knowledge she would have remained married. Nothing in her life suggests that this sentiment is personally true. At worst, she conveniently concedes to the moral norms of the magazine audience; at best, she has probably been meditating, in her current unhappiness, on alternative fates, just as she had contemplated the advantages of becoming a Moslem wife: had she never known freedom, a serene and honored bondage might have had its own joy. Both articles come out of a scrutiny of her past as it has delivered her into her present dilemma. She acknowledges, for the sake of her readers, bonds that she cannot accept for herself. Mama Bess, no doubt, was warmed by the portrait of her life in the first article; the second, which set Mansfield to clucking over Rose's shame, she did not deign to notice.[21]

Guy Moyston found his own dilemma in his relationship with Rose. Their affair in London had been, for him, a casual one; Rose, seeking consolation after the loss of Arthur Griggs, had been hurt further by Guy's indifference. Now there was a complex reversal of positions. He was in love and wanted to marry; she was in love, too, but wanted to remain free. "I always wanted love," she wrote to him:

> I wanted the kind of love that would be, profoundly, my whole existence. Deep down, nourishing me, like a tap-root. I have always been willing to pay anything else I have, or could have, for that. But . . . being constantly with any other person, even you, is incompatible with other things I want. I like loneliness. I'm used to it; it is such a habit with me that I miss it when I don't have it . . . I don't want to be tied to anyone by the mass-pressure of everyone who knows us; I don't want all my movements to be dependent upon the movements of someone else, as though we were handcuffed and leg-chained together; I DON'T WANT TO BE CLUTCHED.
>
> Why did you say it is impossible? If we try as hard, if we aren't any more discouraged by little failures along the way, why can't we come as near to making a success of it as people make of marriage? Do you really think it is as difficult, for you and me, as marriage would be?[22]

Apparently Moyston did think it more difficult. "Don't try to build a dream, dear, on the cornerstone of something I can't give you, or anyone," she warned. "I don't want to be married. I'm not a wife. I can't help it, I just am not." What she viewed as their unique achievement he considered a preliminary to a more conventional relationship; but her imagination had long since foreclosed that possibility. A sketch for a story from about this time focuses the problem she faced:

> A story of Telegraph Hill and the two who loved each other there.
> The little brown house and the eucalyptus grove, and the ferries
> on the bay. All through it there must be a sense of *going*. Nothing
> static. And he says, Don't you see, marriage and the babies, that's
> the real current; that's the real going on. You will be only standing
> still. And she loves the things that are housewifely, the linens and
> the polished woods and the little curtains at her windows. But
> don't you see that I love them because they're always unattainable
> for me? The things I never can keep. Nor truly have. For the work
> of a housewife is a resistance to the going of things. And I, who am
> going too, can not set myself against that stream. Already my
> curtains are fading, and I must be going on. No, for you can not
> keep me, and I can not keep this; that is the tragedy.

Moyston seems to have had traditional masculine notions of protecting
and supporting the woman he loved, and he interpreted her reluctance
to accept his expectations as a kind of rejection. A growing petulance in
his letters can be detected in her replies to them, as they corresponded
several times each week. In point of fact, the protection and support was
more nearly Rose's contribution than his; and it is easy to find in their
relationship a mother-son configuration as their letters become less frankly
romantic and more humdrum. He had given up a career in journalism to
become a playwright, a leap similar to the one Rose had already made
successfully; in their collaboration on his work, her support becomes as
much emotional as technical as she rallies him from depression; and it
is possible to detect his latent hypochondria and her displaced mater-
nalism in her long paragraphs devoted to his physical and emotional
complaints.[23]

But the dependency was mutual: Rose needed a sounding board for
the bafflement and frustration of her daily life; and her visit to old friends
at the Haders' parties had resulted in a rift over the O'Brien case. Legal
preliminaries had drawn on for years; and in the interval O'Brien had
been lionized as a best-selling author, even by Rose's friends who presumably knew of the original agreement between them. Rose interpreted this
as hypocrisy and disloyalty, and she had come to feel that Moyston was
the only one of her old San Francisco friends she could trust. She recalled
herself in those halcyon days on Telegraph Hill as "warm-hearted, generous, credulous, kind, really profound in my affections and loyalties." "I
once loved them and trusted them absolutely," she wrote with some
bitterness, "and now I'm afraid of them." She had always been out-
spoken, and willing to carry her opinions and affections to the furthest
degree; but as she had ventilated her feelings regarding O'Brien she had
encountered a condescending tolerance, suggesting to her that these valued old friends had developed a habit of discounting her claims generally. It was a matter of a style, no doubt, that at its extremes disrupted the
smooth surface of amicable discourse; and as she fumed over the matter

she wavered between paranoia and self-knowledge: "they can always murmur, 'Dear Rose—but of course, we all know what *Rose* is. . . .'" The old connections would continue, but on Rose's part never with the same confidence.[24]

Meanwhile, the Buick had arrived and the Jack London book had been published as *He Was a Man*. Rose hated the title, taken from *Hamlet*; it had been chosen by her publisher. And she was not particularly happy with the book itself, which fell between her attempt to achieve a critical analysis of character and her need to serve up throbs and thrills for a popular audience. "It's so awful—and yet not awful enough," she wrote to Moyston. She had intended "a study of an egotist," "the most stupid sort of human frailty," while her reviewers found only a "mawkish adulation" for Jack London. London had continued to engage her imagination equally for his flawed affirmation of his individuality and for the vast wealth and popularity he had won as a writer; but she also projected into his story her own sense of a life unaccountably off-center since birth, which left him unable to value any accomplishment even as he strived for some new good. To the hero's baffled wife, she gives Gillette Lane's baffled complaint against her: "Oh, why can't you be *human!*" To the hero and the lover who replaces his wife, she gives that perfect consonance of desire and mutual freedom that she was unable to explain to Moyston. And to the hero, she gives the moment of pure happiness she had mysteriously experienced in Tiflis, as he strikes a match and watches the flame flicker almost invisibly in the sunlight. It was a symbol she would use again to describe her admiration for Dorothy Thompson, who came to embody for her an ideal union of passion and purpose, a life whose outer form was generated naturally by an inner principle of being. All of these intentions were apparently lost on her readers, as they were on Mama Bess. "She'll have her copy of HE WAS A MAN on her shelf forever," she wrote Moyston, "and never read the first chapter or any other. She'd hate it. She hates anything at all that has to do in any way with sex. You may remember that she read part of the manuscript. She did it because she thought she ought to, to please me, and I just didn't give her the first part. She read until she came to Frisco Jack's woman, then said she'd as soon read about a movement of the bowels."[25]

Rose felt better about the Buick, "absolutely new to the eye, all kinds of dinguses, an engine that purrs down to a whisper . . . or up to an 80-mile roar." Mama Bess and Almanzo were alive with anticipation, as was Rose: "Nothing that has recently occurred in Mansfield is going to make the sensation that that car will, when unloaded." When it did arrive, it was promptly named Isabelle, and Mama Bess took to driving readily; but Rose's father, although an expert with horses, was a more difficult learner. "The first time he tried to drive," Rose wrote

> . . . he narrowly escaped smashing a couple of other cars on the
> highway, jumped an eight-foot ditch, and tried to climb a good-
> sized oak tree. You see, he had been used to driving a team, and
> when the two cars telescoped down on us, he simply braced both
> feet *hard*—one of 'em on the accelerator—and pulled back on the
> steering wheel with all his force, saying in a firm voice, "Whoa!"
> I . . . went head first into the windshield, just as the oak tree up-
> rooted under the car and lifted the rear wheels off the ground. . . .
> I thought it showed great intelligence in us, when the road got so
> dangerous with cars, to quickly leave it and climb a tree.

While Rose rested with swollen eyes and a purple-and-yellow nose, Troub
picked glass fragments from her face. But as spring merged into summer,
the new automobile, with a restored radiator and front axle, gave them a
new mobility as they ranged through the hills and small towns of Rose's
Ozark home.[26]

V

As her income picked up, so did Rose's spirits. Sales of *He Was a Man* were
enough that she could project a small income from it into the next year;
her Ozark stories were finding a ready acceptance at *Country Gentleman*;
and Harper had optioned her next novel, which would be based on a
collation of the Ozark stories. With this much certainty in her life, she
could make plans for another escape from Rocky Ridge. She heard time's
chariot rattling behind her. "I don't see any immortality, any eternity, for
my life, and I care like the devil that my life's so short; I value intensely
every moment of it; I am greedy for every little scrap of the little time
I have." And her old daydream of the Wandering Jew rose up again.
"Indeed," she wrote Moyston, "I'd as soon die quite dead,"

> as go to Heaven, with all the exciting places left unseen, all the
> languages unlearned, all the *living* unlived. It's greediness, is
> the matter with me. It's not being able to get a firm enough grip on the
> moment, to squeeze out of it all that might be squeezed. The only
> thing that would take that trouble from me, would be to be—as so
> often I've wished—the Wandering Jew. All I want is just to live as
> long as this old earth does, to survive through the glacial periods
> somehow, and see what happens next.

Moyston apparently made the mistake of suggesting that one might be
resigned to being merely "happy enough," which provoked Rose to one
of her tirades of self-definition: "Damn it, I don't intend to be happy
enough. I don't 'make the best of things.' I never have, and never shall.
Making the best of things is (to me) a damn poor way of dealing with
them. . . . A person who starts out as a mal-nutrition child in an Ozark

log cabin and gets as far as I've got, does it by raising hell about things, not by making the best of them."[27]

She could not raise hell with her mother, however; rather, she had to plan carefully. By the middle of the summer she had worked out for herself the terms of her obligation: she would give her mother another year of her time and would commit herself to building investments that would guarantee her parents an annual income of one thousand dollars. Until that nest egg was accumulated, she would continue her yearly support of five hundred dollars. But even as she was working out the formal terms for her release, she was beginning to understand the psychology of the bondage she labored under:

> My mother can not learn to have any reliance upon my financial judgment or promises. It's partly, I suppose, because she still thinks of me as a child. She even hesitates to let me have the responsibility of bringing up butter from the spring, for fear I won't do it quite right! And it is partly because my income has to her the doubtful quality of magic. I don't work regular hours, I don't get any salary, I haven't any property, not one hen that will lay eggs, not one cow that will give milk. My money appears, somehow. . . . Where is perseverance, thrift, caution, industry—where are any of the necessary virtues? Simply not in me. It is really, a sad thing for my parents. . . . They would have had comfort and joy and pride from me, if I had married fairly well, had a good home, been steadily lifted a little in the world by my husband's efforts, become, let us say, a socially successful woman in Springfield. . . . This unaccountable daughter who roams around the world, borrowing money here and being shot at there, learning strange languages and reading incomprehensible books even in her own language, is a pride, in a way, but a ceaseless apprehension, too.

Mama Bess had not believed in the Buick when it was promised and was hard-pressed to believe in it when it was out of sight, even though she had learned to drive it. Rose had bought it with the five hundred dollars promised for 1925, and to make it up to Mama Bess, who was "so sensitive and strange about money," she had substituted a promissory note from Moyston, secured by some of his rubber stocks, on which he paid regular interest to Mama Bess. By such creative financing Rose could satisfy both her mother and her own conscience and still have the luxury of the automobile. But her mother was suspicious of it all.[28]

Letter by letter to Moyston, Rose's plans grew, shifted, and grew again. At one point, a buyer for the farm seemed imminent, and Rose queried Guy in detail on the possibilities of moving her parents to a retirement in rural England; she also hoped to find a way of settling her blind Aunt Mary somewhere other than South Dakota, where Grandmother Ingalls had just died. By March of 1926, Rose calculated, she would have accumulated enough money to stake herself to another trip to Albania, even allowing several months in Paris to study languages; and, she hoped, Moyston could join her for an April vacation in Brittany; perhaps he could spend some time in Paris as well. She began to draw elaborate plans for a Moorish home, complete with inner courtyard and pool, to be built in Albania. Her letters at times throb with anticipation and excitement; gone are the heavy blues of the winter before and the girlish passion of the letters following her New York visit with Moyston, as gradually the prospect of a life abroad competes with her longing to be with her lover. "There are those two things that I care about more than anything else," she wrote Moyston; "you and Albania. . . . I've got to work out my obligation here, at any rate, until *I* feel right about it, before I can do anything for myself. I feel, somehow, that it's a sentence to work out, and that then I can go, to you and Albania."[29]

VI

However affectionate he may have been in person, Moyston's letters were apparently cool, detached, and ironic; and although she complained at times that his love did not show in his writing, her own letters by the end of the year had developed a certain distance as she balanced the needs to sustain her one intimate relationship and to plan a life in which he would be but an occasional participant. But Moyston himself was developing interests beyond those he shared with her. He was having no success placing his play; and he found himself with the opportunity to become a director of a company that would distribute contraceptive diaphragms in covert connection with the American Birth Control League, headed by Margaret Sanger. Rose's business sense took fire at this opportunity; her letters were full of encouragement and advice, but rife with warnings as well: she did not trust reformers, whose dedication to their cause permitted them too often to take advantage when they could. But she had a clear sense of the demand that should make such a business a success; and in a touching note she reveals a personal naivete (probably feigned) and a vigorous interest in the case of her friend: "Would it be possible for you," she wrote Moyston, "without embarrassment to yourself, to get—I don't know. Whatever's required. And could it be sent without danger of criminal prosecution, by express? I'm asking because of Mrs. Craig. She's half mad with this continual terror, and nine children. . . ."[30]

When she was not writing, Rose and Troub were often on the road, gathering material for her Ozark stories. She took an active role, although under some duress, in her mother's club work and entertained a circle of Mansfield women of her own generation; indeed, the routine felicities of domestic life, from cooking to embroidery and redecorating, were a regular delight and distraction in her life. And as steps beyond the routine, she shaved her head to promote a new growth of hair; she began a study of Greek and of the ukulele; she started compiling an Albanian-English dictionary; and with Troub she took up photography, converting Mama Bess's kitchen to an occasional darkroom full of chemicals. There was much the Wandering Jew might experience even within her limited circle. Troub occupied her attention professionally, as well; she was desultory in her attempts at writing, but she let Rose read her diary of her time at the front in France, and Rose urged her to submit it for publication. *The Atlantic Monthly* accepted an excerpt and asked for more; and Rose had the satisfaction of seeing another career launched with her help.[31]

But if all this while Moyston, Albania, and her hopes for her future beckoned her eastward, her past and a powerful nostalgia drew her back to the west. Her days on Telegraph Hill had been an enchanted time for her, and she had kept up a correspondence with many friends in San Francisco, particularly with Fremont Older. She could go back to work for him at any time, she knew; she did not want to return to newspaper work, but she did want to see Older, who stood as a rock of integrity in her thoughts. And she wanted to give Mama Bess the experience of a cross-country automobile trip. In mid-September Rose, Troub, and Mama Bess left in the Buick, en route to California by way of Kansas, Colorado, Utah, and Nevada. Rose and Troub shared the hours at the wheel until Rose found that the driving-nerves that had sustained her during her days selling land were no longer equal to the task. As they crossed the Tioga Pass outside of Yosemite, vision obscured by a hay wagon ahead, a dog attacked the wheels of their car, and Rose quit driving abruptly.

To revisit San Francisco was a bittersweet experience for Rose. Some old friends could not find the time for her, and others were unexpectedly kind. They spent a long weekend at Fremont Older's ranch; in Rose's honor he offered a Sunday picnic, where most of her friends from her *Bulletin* days came to greet her. She paid a sentimental visit to her old haunts on Telegraph Hill, a little dismayed to find the area now gentrified with fences, landscaping, ornamental walks, and, where Italian children used to play, a parking lot from which automobiles now looked out over the ocean. The new occupant of her little house was suitably impressed by her return; she and her old friends still persisted as legends, and it was rumored that Dmitri still did his Russian lion dance on her old couch at parties there. Coppa's Restaurant had moved and was catering to a more prosperous clientele, but Papa and Mama Coppa remembered her and would not let her pay for her meal. She spoke on Albania at the Foothill Club in Santa Clara and spent a day with the Danforths in Berkeley, where she had written *Diverging Roads*. But inevitably she discovered that the five years' absence from her old haunts had changed her beyond measure. "There was not a moment that I couldn't have wept," she wrote Moyston, "because I was not me any more, but only a ghost that remem-

bered old and lovely things. It was really in San Francisco that I realized
that I am middle aged." She found, of course, that she had hoped to do
more than she could; and again time pressed heavily on her, now embodied in Mama Bess, who had worried from the time they had left about
getting home again and whose peace of mind was the driving force in
their schedule. They hurried down the coast to Los Angeles, where an
old friend from her days on Russian Hill arranged a tour of Universal
Studios for them. Then they made their way back across Arizona, New
Mexico, and Texas toward Missouri. The trip had taken six weeks; "6
weeks *spent* on California trip," Rose noted emphatically. Once home,
Mama Bess decided that she had enjoyed it. Rose found waiting for her a
letter from Moyston, complaining faintly that she had chosen to make
this trip when he had wanted her to come to New York to visit him.[32]

Moyston spent Thanksgiving at the Haders, and sent Rose a report
of the festivities and of the new house they were constructing on their
land overlooking the Hudson River. He was finding himself in an increasingly difficult position, between his real regard for the Haders and Rose's
resentment of what she considered their disloyalty. His description caught
her at a curious time, as she recalled the old parties on Telegraph Hill and
looked forward to new ones in Paris:

> It hurts me a lot, remembering the real gaiety that used to prevail
> on Telegraph, where all of us could be crazily happy till dawn, on
> rice pudding and oranges and cigarettes, to think of the Nyack
> parties, which are so different. They don't seem half so happy, to
> me. There used to be such spontaneous joyousness. Youth, per-
> haps. Maybe I just don't grow up. Just wait till you see me in Paris!
> Well, and probably you'll be seeing three of me at the time, but
> every one of 'em will be HAPPY. Oh, Guy! It just doesn't seem
> possible it can come true. But it will, won't it? Please tell me you're
> sure it will?

For Christmas Guy sent her one gift that was a harbinger of the future
and one that was a memento of the past. The first was a sewing kit for
travel; the second was a copy of Sherwood Anderson's *Dark Laughter,* in
which they both appeared in the erotically charged atmosphere of a discussion of the Quatz' Arts Ball.[33]

VII

She had now served her second year's sentence at Rocky Ridge and she
had the wherewithal for her escape—almost six thousand dollars, she
noted among her New Year's Resolutions, mostly from the growth of her
investment with Palmer and Company. Nineteen twenty-six was to be "a
year mostly of investment rather than income. Principal hope for New

Year's 1927 finances is in P. & Co." Moreover, *Hill-Billy*, a gathering of her Ozark stories in novel form, was in proof and was being read by Moyston and Floyd Dell; it would provide some royalties in 1926. She professed little regard for it, as a confection aimed at a very average reader's taste; but she had made an effort to preserve the idiom and culture of the vanishing mountaineer, and the implicit theme was the supplanting of a corrupt political regime by a legitimate one. These were precisely the concerns that had gripped her in Albania and that she would confront on her return.[34]

She was ready to articulate some of the motives that drove her. In response to a review of *He Was a Man*, she had written to say that:

> . . . the restlessness which was Gordon Blake's is mine—the common unease and discontent of Americans which makes us the greatest builders, the greatest destroyers, most incessant movers, the always seeking and never satisfied people. . . . somewhere there is something we want and no obstacle can halt our determination to get it. This is the American, the twentieth century spirit. Therefore the soul of America is a baffled, tormented thing and at the root of all our life there is a bitterness.
>
> I know a land where life is simple and the struggle of our century is very far away. This is Albania. It is not civilization. I shall live in Albania because, for me, that little Balkan country is richer in happiness than all the twentieth century, because it has kept what all the scientific minded civilizations have lost: a sense of the beauty and the mystery of life. A land where every morning the sun brings Allah's inscrutable gift of a new day and from tall white minarets the muezzin gives thanks for it.

A similar sketch for Moyston admits to some premonitions:

> . . . the West is civilizing the East. Soon there'll be no refuge under heaven. I shall die, a very old, very brown, very dirty woman trudging behind the camels somewhere in the midst of the Arabian desert, and the desert will bleach my bones. Except that probably even before that time the Bedouin will be traveling in Fords and listening to the muezzin through radio.[35]

The brighter vision, however, had sustained her through her two years of duty at Rocky Ridge. As the new year of 1926 began, she arranged to reoccupy her Paris apartment on April 1 and booked reservations on the Cunard *Ausonia* for March 20. By now it had been decided that Troub Boylston would accompany her on the Albanian adventure. Early in January she and Troub went to Springfield to make application for their passports, and this symbolic act moved her to make her first diary entry in two years: "life begins again with new passports." Thoughts of New York and Paris made work difficult; as a desperate remedy, she and Troub began reading Samuel Richardson's slow-moving *Pamela* "to keep from

going mad with anticipation." Some comfort and some cash for an old
wound came in February with the settlement of her case against Frederick
O'Brien; after attorneys' fees, she netted less than a thousand dollars.[36]

She allowed herself three weeks in New York to meet with her agent
and editors, to visit old friends, and to see Guy. He had written earlier to
say that their plans for April in Brittany conflicted with the demands of
his new job; but September seemed a possibility. Her last letter before
leaving Mansfield shows a slight apprehension:

> Dear Guy, it is such a long time, really. Fourteen months. Seriously,
> I expect I'll really be awfully shy at seeing you again. And you'll
> probably not feel anything at all, specially. You'll just come down
> to the station to meet me, quite sober and matter-of-fact. And I
> won't look quite as you have been remembering me, partly because
> memories imperceptibly drift away from the reality, and partly
> because my hair is short and my clothes will be unfamiliar to you. I
> don't really expect you to be so awfully overjoyed. . . . Things
> never really pick up exactly where they were dropped; they start
> again from a new beginning.[37]

Things did not pick up well at all. Within two weeks there was a
misunderstanding and hurt feelings on Rose's part, apparently over Guy's
commitments to friends that made her doubt her standing with him. Her
note draws back from love to the safety of friendship; his reply asserts
regret, unchanged feelings, but admits that he does not have the capacity
for the romantic love she seems to need. There was one more rendezvous
at a party given by Genevieve Parkhurst of *Pictorial Review*, and he saw
her off at the boat with a book and a box of candy. The relationship was
patched up and projected into plans for his visit to Europe; but she had
sounded a premonitory note even, perhaps, as the affair had begun—
when she had recorded in her notebook a series of personal definitions,
one of which reads: "Love—a name given by men and women to their
mutual exasperation with the discrepancy between what each wants the
other to be and what each finds that the other is."[38]

$\mathcal{T}$HE ALBANIAN EXPERIMENT

9

. . . an implacable circle of reality moves with us wherever we go.

On the evening of March 30, 1926, Rose resumed possession of her Paris apartment at 8 Square Denouettes, where her former maid Yvonne waited with a good dinner ready. Rose could not have her April in Brittany with Moyston, but she was quick to claim another indulgence. She and Troub enrolled immediately in the Berlitz School for language study. They embraced a daunting schedule, but Rose was in her glory. "Guy, it's simply *heaven*," she wrote on April 10. "We study from 10 to 12, and 2 to 4, every day. French, Italian, German and Russian. After next week I'm taking on Greek, & Troub Serbian, and maybe I'll take Serbian, too, and maybe some more Albanian if we can find the teachers." After dinner, they would study their grammars and practice conversation until midnight. They were something of a sensation in the Berlitz School. But even though the capable Yvonne was at hand to cook, clean, and do their shopping, their enthusiasm was overreaching their time and energy; plans for Greek, Serbian, and Albanian had to be dropped, but their study in four other languages continued until mid-July.[1]

There was time for little else in Rose's life except her correspondence, for which she saved her Sundays. The long letters to Moyston began again. She yearned to show him Paris in April; he reported to her his evening parties in company with Rebecca West and Fannie Hurst, as well as some unspecified lurid Greenwich Village doings. They made plans for a September reunion in Brittany, for the moment on a renewed footing:

> All our, "I love you," "I don't love you" trouble . . . was because we were using different meanings for that misdemeanoring verb, which should have been in jail centuries ago for disturbing the peace. If you and I would trade our definitions of it, we'd exchange positions, too. That was the sudden bit of light I got on the situation that last afternoon while we were talking . . . don't let's bother to say anything about it. Our relationship remains the same—the happiest and most richly satisfying I can imagine.[2]

She was conscious that this was a watershed year for her. Shortly before leaving for Europe she had written a rather melodramatic autobiographical article for *Cosmopolitan*, in which she claimed to have found the secret of happiness. What rings most true in this account is the description of the unhappiness of her childhood and marriage, the latter put in only the most general terms. Happiness emerged only slowly, she asserted, after the rebellion of her body at that suicide attempt by chloroform, after which she began to see that nothing would fully satisfy, but that life itself, in its wonderful and interesting variety, was a great gift. "And if one neither seeks nor expects happiness anywhere else, it is there. Just to be alive, *if nothing else matters to you*, is to be happy."[3]

It was a point of stability she could oscillate through but not maintain, as certain powerful objects of desire pulled strongly at her imagination. She was verging on forty now, and the unfocused ambition that had driven her as a young woman had clarified into a limited constellation of hopes. The day after beginning language study she looked with cautious optimism to the future: "Five years from now I hope to be at home in at least six languages, to have the house in Albania, and to have begun writing—perhaps." At the heart of this constellation was the old longing for a kind of integrity in her life, one that would let her meet the world confidently on its own terms and then to write about it as a free agent rather than a market-bound hack. The middle term, the home of her own, was a powerful symbol of the integrity of the self; it would be at once a sanctuary and an outer sign of what dwelt within. The Albanian home had been on her mind since it had flashed upon her as she wandered on the steppes of Soviet Georgia: ". . . my house would be built on the shore near Durazzo, a house of clay-brick, plastered and whitewashed, its rooms built around courts, and some of its archways leading into walled gardens."[4]

She had reason enough to be cautiously optimistic. She had sufficient money to carry her for a year, her writing looked likely to produce a regular income, and her investment account was growing nicely. Moreover, the friendship with Troub seemed to project itself tranquilly into the future, which promised congenial companionship and shared expenses. Their Russian teacher was a multilingual Pole who remembered Troub from her days in Warsaw; he was also a professional architect, and as he began to visit in the evenings for additional lessons and wide-ranging conversation, he also offered his services in planning a home to be built in Albania. In six languages they struggled over architectural terms as the plans developed. It would overlook the Adriatic; with a colonnaded courtyard and a swimming pool, it was also designed with loopholes for rifles, for easy defense by servants during rebellions. Rose was serious enough about this dream to pay her architect friend preliminary fees for his services. She sent a sketch to Guy Moyston.[5]

Spring and early summer were cold and wet in Paris, and not even the joys of languages and architecture could save Rose from occasional depression, especially when it became clear that Moyston would be prevented by family problems from joining her in Brittany in September. A bright spot was the arrival of Dorothy Thompson from Berlin, where she was rapidly making a name for herself as a journalist in international affairs. She and Rose fell into each other's arms with shrieks of joy and there were two long evenings of good talk. But with the course of language study drawing to a close and September now free, the actual move to Albania was at hand. Rose gave up her apartment and through a contact at the American legation in Albania rented a house that was to serve as interim quarters upon their arrival. They decided to buy a car and drive to Albania.[6]

||

The car would be named Zenobia, in honor of the Bedouin queen who had ruled ancient Palmyra in defiance of the Romans and whose story Rose admired. This latter-day Zenobia was in fact a 1926 Model T Ford sedan, maroon in color. Brief diary entries suggest trouble in getting permits to drive the car and documents to take it out of the country: a full account, years later, was perhaps somewhat embellished, but it remains a richly comic story that focused Rose's exasperation with state bureaucracies:

> One requirement was twelve passport pictures of that car, taken full-face, without a hat. I exaggerate; regulations said nothing about a hat. But this was a Ford naked from the factory; not a detail nor a mark distinguished it from the millions of its kind; yet I had to engage a photographer to take a full-radiator-front picture of it, where it still stood in the sales-room, and to make twelve prints, each certified to be a portrait of that identical car. The proper official pasted these, one by one, in my presence, to twelve identical documents, each of which was filled out in ink, signed and counter-signed, stamped and tax-stamped; and, of course, I paid for them. One was given to me.
>
> After six hard-working weeks, we had all the car's papers. Nearly an inch thick they were, laid flat. Each was correctly signed and stamped, each had in addition the little stamp stuck on, showing that the tax was paid that must be paid on every legal document; this is the Stamp Tax that Americans refused to pay. I believe we had license plates besides; I know we had drivers' licenses.
>
> Gaily at last we set out in our car, and in the first block two policemen stopped us. European police-men always go in pairs, so that one polices the other. I do not know whether this makes it impossible to bribe either, or necessary to bribe both. I never tried to buy a policeman.
>
> Being stopped by the police was not unusual, of course. The car's papers were in its pocket, and confidently I handed them over, with our personal papers, as requested.

The policemen examined each one, found it in order, and noted it in their little black books. Then courteously they arrested us.

No one had told us about the brass plate. We had never heard of it. The car must have a brass plate, measuring precisely this by that (about 4 × 6 1/4 inches), hand engraved with the owner's full name and address, and attached to the instrument board by four brass screws of certain dimensions, through four holes of certain dimensions, one hole in each corner of the brass plate.

My friend wilted on the wheel. "It's too much," she said. "Let's chuck it all and go by train."

"Gentlemen, we are completely desolated," I said. "Figure to yourselves, how we are Americans, strangers to beautiful France. Imagine, how we have planned, how we have saved, we have dreamed and hoped that the day will arrive when we shall see Paris. At the end, here we are. We see with our eyes the beautiful Paris, the glory of French culture and French art. Altogether natural, is it not? We seek to conduct ourselves with a propriety the most precise. In effect, gentlemen, what is it that we have done? Of what fault it is that one accuses us? You see our passports, our cards of identity, our permission to enter France and to remain in France and to enter Paris and to live in Paris, and, unhappily, to leave France and to depart from Paris, for all joys must end, is it not? That is life. In fact, you have well examined all these, and you see that all are altogether completely in order, is it not? And the receipts for our rent, and for our window tax, and for our foreigner's tax, and for our income tax, and the quittance of our lease, all well made, is it not? all well viewed by the authorities. Good, that is that. But, it must be, the good logic always, is it not? It sees itself that we, we have committed no fault. It is not we who lack the brass plate; it is the car. Gentlemen, one must admit in good logic that which it is that is your plain duty; arrest the car. Good. Do your duty, gentlemen. As for us, we repudiate the car, we abandon it, we go ———— "

We were detained. The policemen accepted my logic, but courteously they said that the car could not stand where it was; parking there even for one instant was forbidden. My friend suggested that the salesman would take it back. Courteously the policemen said that, without the brass plate, the car could not move an inch from where it stood; that was forbidden.

"In all confidence, gentlemen," we said, "we leave this problem in your hands." We hailed a taxi and went home.

Mysteriously next day the car was in the sales-room. In two weeks the brass plate was beautifully hand-engraved. Exactly two months after we had paid for the car, we were able to drive it.[7]

Indeed, Rose's diary for August 2 notes in large letters, "WE HAVE THE FORD. And I had hysterics when they told me."

The incident was, perhaps, symptomatic of broader changes in France since they had left—Rose two and a half years ago, Troub four. On their first visit they had come as part of the great American rescue of war-damaged Europe and had often been treated with the deference due benefactors. Now Europe was lapsing into normalcy, and in France particularly they found an anti-American sentiment over the war debt to the United States. Minimally this resentment showed itself in occasional gratuitous insults, but on Bastille Day Troub found herself trapped in a taxi among crowds of celebrating Parisians. She was recognized as an American and attacked in anger: one man climbed to the top of her cab and assaulted her with his umbrella.[8]

And, sadly, Europe was moving into the twentieth century. Much of the attraction of Europe lay in the deep historical integrity of its culture. The comparative thinness of their own culture struck Rose and Troub as it had many Americans for generations, and the transformation of that rudimentary culture by industrial technology and commercial exploitation had left them feeling deeply ambiguous about the American ideal of Progress. Thus, as Troub wrote, their immediate love for the remnants of that older civilization they found abroad:

> It was a great relief to live in lands where there is stability; where the unity of the family life is a sacred and binding thing, very lovely to see; where education is real and very thorough, and where the atmosphere of culture is such that even the illiterate peasant absorbs it, for he sings arias from the operas as he walks behind his plow, and he will show you with pride and real appreciation the beautiful old things that have been handed down through the generations of his family.[9]

But, as Rose wrote Moyston, "Europe will very soon be no refuge for us."

> The machines are getting it. Albania may briefly save me. . . . Perhaps there will be nooks and crannies here and there in modern civilization, in which you can hide yourself for the remainder of a lifetime. You say, England and Germany are industrial countries. True; but they have been partly saved by the remnants of another civilization, remnants which until recently have had enough life in them to resist, and to prove a handicap to, modern industrial civilization. The Great War killed the last of them.

When Rose had first visited Albania in 1921 there had been no automobiles. On her return a year later, there were several, one a taxi that had transported her and Peggy Marquis from Durazzo to Tirana. Now she was about to enter with her own machine, the latest improved model of Henry Ford's genius for industrial production.[10]

The early weeks of August were filled with preparations to leave. Their days no longer filled with language study, Rose and Troub had time to renew a social life in Paris. Rose's agents, Carl and Zelma Brandt, were in town; and in a party in their company Rose encountered Arthur Griggs, now with a wife. The evening was, coincidentally, the wedding date of Bessie Beatty, who was being married to an actor in an elaborate ceremony at Fremont Older's ranch in California; at the end of the evening, the party sent off a congratulatory telegram. Rose had persistently questioned Moyston about the wedding plans of her former mentor, and she had made a trip to Barbizon, where she contemplated Les Iris, the country cottage she had once rented for her trysts with Arthur Griggs. *Diverging Roads* had been the thematic title of her first novel, and as she set off for Albania she was looking back over roads not taken. Her hopes for the future lay with the money she had invested with George Palmer, who was in Paris for a visit. She and Troub took him for a spin around town in their new Ford, and then on August 20 they were on the road to Albania. Troub by now was doing most of their driving.[11]

They had already started to draw on their profits from their Palmer accounts to finance their trip; and in gratitude for the treasures he was heaping up for them they kept a journal of their adventures, in alternate hands, in the form of a continuing letter to him. Later this would be revised as a letter to Mama Bess, which she read to a gathering of the Justamere Club back in Mansfield. The story quickly became a mock-romance in which the intrepid Zenobia bore the three intrepid heroines—Yvonne traveled with them—through comic adventures in exotic lands. A visit to the gaming tables at Monte Carlo netted Rose three hundred dollars and an appreciation of the addictive properties of gambling; their passage through Italy cost them stolen baggage and any lingering good opinion of Italians generally, although Rose did note a conspicuous invigoration under Mussolini. On the sixth of September they shipped from Bari across the Adriatic to Durazzo with Zenobia as a deck passenger; the next morning their last adventure was transferring the Ford from ship to shore:

> How she was got off the high deck of the steamer none of us know. Somehow she was lifted off it and lowered down into a tiny sail-boat hardly big enough to hold her. And the bottom of the little boat was full of barrels, empty, lying on their sides, so that she couldn't possibly get a wheel-hold on them. In this fashion she was brought wobbling to the wharf, which rose a good five feet above her headlights—a sheer wall.
>
> When I saw her she stood there swaying. Two planks, eight inches wide, had been inserted under her front wheels, and led upward at an acute angle to the edge of the wharf. Under them the lapping water licked its lips. Troub was at the wheel, enclosed in the glass box of that sedan. On the wharf a wild-eyed Yvonne clutched all our purses and stared, frantic. Some twenty or thirty Albanians swarmed over Zenobia and the sail-boat, tipping the boat, the car, and the planks first to one side and then far to the other. I expected the whole thing to collapse momentarily.

Zenobia made one desperate struggle. Under her hind wheels the slender boards cracked and twisted. She lurched and sobbed, and gave it up. But with one determined shout all the Albanians urged her to try it again. "All*ah!*" they yelled. Her poor wheels slipped among the barrels, and both plank-bridges tipped side-wise at an angle of 30 degrees.

I turned away, unable to bear the sight. A stern Yvonne took me by the shoulder and turned me around. "I don't want to watch it," I said.

"You will save *mademoiselle* when she goes to the bottom," said Yvonne, in a voice of ice and steel.

Of course, I can't swim....

The Albanians rigged ropes around Zenobia's body, and tied others to her front bumpers. In long lines upon the wharf they manned these ropes. Other Albanians half-stripped, and went overboard into the water to help hold the boat steady, while Ze-nobia's hind wheels were lifted and boards placed beneath them. These boards broke. Troub called, "Rose, I can't see. Are the front wheels all right?" The front wheels were on the very edge of those bending, tipping boards. What did she mean by all right? The whole thing looked all wrong to me. She yelled, "Never mind, I can't hear you!" All the Albanians were yelling, "All*ah!* All*ah!* All*ah!*" Troub gripped the wheel. With an awful lurch Zenobia thrust her front wheels over the edge of the boat. The two planks shrieked aloud and sagged toward the water. "All*ah!* All*ah!*" yelled the men at the ropes, rhythmically straining backward. Zenobia lurched again, shook all over and swayed horribly. "All*ah!* All*ah!*" yelled the Albanians.

There was a frightful confusion of rending and cracking and yells.

"Save *mademoiselle!* Only save *mademoiselle,*" babbled Yvonne. "As for the car, we can proceed on foot."

Just as Zenobia's hind wheels struggled over the edge of the wharf one of the planks collapsed completely. Its fragments fell into the Adriatic. But the ropes held.

Zenobia stood on the wharf. Yvonne said, "Grace a le bon Dieu!" Troub said, "Rose, gimme a cigarette."

We had arrived in Albania.[12]

Their rented house was in the Rruga Tiekos off the Durazzo Road in Tirana. Recently built, it had been occupied by members of the American legation; it boasted a toilet but no bathtub. What it lacked in amenities it made up in charm and setting. Behind a gate and front courtyard its fifty-foot facade of blue stucco spanned the lot; through the ground-floor en-trance a straight hallway gave a glimpse of the rear courtyard, while on either side of this entrance curving steps rose to the second-floor living quarters. Below were four rooms for servants, above two bedrooms and bath, a dining room, and an enormous (thirty-five by fifty feet) living room with fireplace. The landlord had agreed to build an outside kitchen at the rear. The three women arrived with no furniture and only the clothes they were wearing.[13]

But shortly the baggage shipped from Paris arrived, and within weeks they were more or less comfortably installed, with some furniture bought and a carpenter engaged to make more. Rose supervised the installation and painting of interior woodwork; the mammoth living-room floor was painted dark green and finished with a compound of beeswax and turpentine; and workers commenced laying up mud-brick walls for the kitchen, which Rose described in great detail for her father's interest. Through the local foreign-service colony they found an array of servants: an aged gardener, a cook, and a *kvass*—a combined porter, foot-man, and butler who, by tradition, also represented the honor of the household to the community. The capable Yvonne supervised them all, as undaunted by their Albanian as they by her French. Zenobia went into rented quarters in a local garage. An American neighbor gave them a small gazelle for their garden, and they settled in for the good life they had planned for in Albania.[14]

Much of the good that they remembered was still there. They were in a city still largely untouched by urban bustle. The only sounds intrud-ing on them were the daily calls to prayer by the Moslem faithful, the spontaneous singing of wedding parties and workmen, and the tinkling of bells on pack animals passing in the streets. Quiet autumn nights gave them a moonlit view of the distant mountains as winter came on with a California grace. They could have as much or as little social life as they wished in the foreign-service community; they joined the tennis club—a little rabbit hutch of a place, Rose said, with uneven courts—not for ten-nis but as a social base; and they renewed their acquaintance among the ministers in the Albanian government. Late in October arrived a Victrola they had ordered, and the new records and sensational sound brought an eruption of dancing into the community. Their huge living room, with its waxed floor, became a perfect dance hall, where for a time much of the Albanian government might be found in ample periods of leisure. Djimil Bey Dino, who had offered his love to Rose during the uprising of 1923, came to call; now fat and married to a woman he had never seen before his wedding, he was minister to Rome, and as they danced he talked to Rose of moonlight walks she had forgotten and hinted romantically at what might have been.[15]

Even as she reached to grasp the life she dreamed of, Rose recog-nized its instability, at odds both with her personal circumstances and the march of history. Part of the dream was to write from an authentic impulse, but she needed her income from commercial fiction—unless the

Palmer account should grow large enough to free her from that writing. In the meantime, she must write for an American market from a foreign land. She needed also to secure her parents' future while living independently from them, in effect earning a double income; yet while away from Rocky Ridge she worried about their welfare. And Albania itself was slipping into the modern world, giving up its ethnic culture even as its fragile independence was threatened by Italian ambitions.

Within a month of her arrival she was attempting to settle things at home. Mama Bess was enough taken with the success of Rose's stock-market winnings to want to invest some of her own savings; "Stocks [are] leaping around like corn in a popper," Rose wrote. "Fortunately, we can't lose."

> I will have Mr. Palmer add $500. from my account to the $500. you send him, and invest the $1,000. for you in some good security that will pay you 8 percent. . . . But do not [let] this lead you into the sinful extravagance of trying to save it. The only proper use for money, for you two now, is spending. And I say again, you need not worry any more about money. If I were to drop dead this minute, I have enough to double your present income if you never touched a cent of the principle. . . . if you take a notion to do something . . . that costs more than your income warrants, you need only let me know. You can have it.

As she pacified her conscience in regard to her parents' future, she continued to be uneasy about the future of Albania. Ahmet Zogu, who had struck her as an authentic national hero during her last visit, was now president and soon would become king; Rose was fascinated and fearful as she watched his efforts to maintain order at home and balance on the international stage. Ancient blood-feuds made Ahmet subject to assassination for purely domestic reasons; and Mussolini hoped, by fomenting internal rebellion and applying economic pressure, to capitalize on Italy's right under the League of Nations to occupy Albania if its government failed. Ahmet hoped to maintain support from England in return for oil concessions, but England and Italy had a natural community of interest in Abyssinia. "I have not seen Ahmet," Rose wrote to Guy Moyston,

> who is indeed now the closest of prisoners, ringed round by gendarmes ten deep—outside a closer circle of imported Russian Guard—and then by about half the army, every time it is necessary for him to leave his house. . . . The political situation here is very critical. Mussolini is about ready to take the country. It comes down to a life-and-death struggle between Mussolini and Ahmet, and since . . . England has abandoned Albania to Mussolini, I really have little hope of the country's being saved.

Among her Albanian friends was a man she discovered to be one of Mussolini's agents; incensed, she told him that, despite their friendship, if she learned of a plot to assassinate him, she would not warn him of it. He gauged her anger and found it formidable: "I've always known you tell me the truth," he said, "when you tell me anything. I was warned you'd poison me, but I didn't believe it. I think you would use a gun."[16]

Wrapped up in the political situation, the local social life, and a new house and garden, she was unable to get down to her writing; and only the timely arrival of royalties from *Hill-Billy* prevented her from drawing down her Palmer account. She was now able to live just exactly as she had wanted to live, freed by servants from mundane tasks so that she might . . . well, that was the problem: with nothing for the moment that *had* to be done, too often she did nothing:

> It is so much more simple . . . to have plenty of servants. I like to get up in the morning, and come out of the bathroom to find breakfast hot on a well served table; and come out of the dining room to find my room spick and span, looking as though no one had ever even thought of undressing in it last night, or sleeping in it. And when I want a fire, I like to say, "Fire, please," and have it blazing. And when the bell rings, I like to know who is there before whoever it is knows I'm here, and be able to be at home or not as I like. All this, to me, is not complication, but simplification. . . . And besides, I really do like a fairly large household—of people who are satisfied and happy and busy and NOT entitled to demand my time. I like to see Lazar and the cook and the gardener cozy in the kitchen after lunch and dinner, smoking and telling stories. I like to hear whistling from the nether regions where Lazar is doing the lamps. I like to see Yvonne settled in the garden with her lap full of sewing, and the gazelle browsing near and the cat walking wild-beast-bristly circles around it, and Yvonne enjoying them both like anything,—but getting the curtains hemmed just the same.[17]

In fact, this brief period of almost absolute freedom brought her not to productive work but to a month of private reflection and self-analysis as November moved on to December and her fortieth birthday. On a blank page in one of her notebooks appears a single startling notation: "The leprosy of death, which attacks everyone at about 40." For two weeks she kept a journal entitled "My Albanian Garden," a record of the idyllic passing days interspersed with passages of disturbed introspection. Portions of this remarkable document have already been cited as keys to understanding her earlier life, but here extended excerpts are needed to capture the dramatic confrontation with self she found as she settled in to live the Albanian dream.

As she and Troub drove out along the Durazzo Road one evening, she was depressed by the decline of the picturesque ethnic Albanian costumes into rag-bag European clothing:

There seems to be a lack of self-respect in this precipitate abandoning of characteristic costume. . . . The army has a lot to do with it; all the young men of Albania have been put into uniforms; they get the idea of the stereotyped coat and trousers from that. Also the idea that European clothes are more "civilized" than Albanian. But somewhere along the road I got a new angle on the question, by thinking that Albanians, after all, are only following the road that all peoples have traveled; from leisure and beauty to speed and utilitarianism; why should we cherish the irrational wish that one tiny corner of the earth could stand out against the current? Let me gather what may still be saved of the real Albania, which very soon will hardly be a memory. . . .

Thus, even as she settled in for the life of serene delight she had imagined, she could see the coming changes that would make it impossible. Already she was hedging her bets, calculating a series of books she might make of the Albanian experience before it all vanished before her. "Then let me go back to Rocky Ridge Farm, and be an individual, myself. Nothing can be done about it." The evening landscape itself offered a metaphor for her thoughts:

The sunset was very brief. . . . The mountains were sliced off along their tops, neatly, in a straight line, by dark blue mist that covered the eastern sky. Beneath this line, between the nearer mountain peaks, the far valleys and farther mountain peaks were revealed in sunshine. They were vaguely beautiful—something as lovely as our waking dreams of lands we shall never see. We continue to cling to the belief that when we see them they will be beautiful, but an implacable circle of reality moves with us wherever we go. . . .

These were evening thoughts: mornings seemed better, as she rolled a fresh sheet into her typewriter and began her daily stint. The mood would last, however, only until she was forced to measure her accomplishment against her vague aspirations. "There is something in the briskness of the morning that makes me feel strong and jubilant, as though I could manage my life at last. These moments are few, and quickly vanish in the grubbiness of facts; time will escape me while I toil upon Ozark stories, and few of the things I wish to do will ever be done."

Two days later she would record the same rhythm of work and idleness, then descend to the very center of her being:

I worked only a little while yesterday morning; the second Ozark story drags, and I can't get *into* it. I stopped before noon, and filled in sketches of the front gate and of the house. . . . Fun messing around with them. But unprofitable, and I don't know why I always yearn to make my activities profitable—in some vague, unconcrete sense of profit—when nothing really is, or can be. Why do I still want to "accomplish something?" The weakness of it is in the vagueness of the "something." Anything definite that I wanted to do, I suppose I could. Few human beings are freer than I, and of the mediocre ones, among whom I belong, not one in thousands has more talent than I. And I come back to the old unsatisfactory explanation, that my trouble lies in wanting too many things, but none of them passionately.

In one month I shall be forty years old. The first twenty of them were wasted—what do I mean by that? I didn't fit my environment, and I didn't know any other. But I have never fitted any environment. . . . It may be my life has been determined by the futility, the inferiority, the vanity, the stupidity of me in those first twenty years. There was nothing but vanity in my wanting "education." My real desire was for money; clothes, social position (!), good times, admiration. I hadn't an inkling of the real world of books and thought. When I was seventeen I went further to smash in struggling with sex. Not that it was a struggle; I was a rag-doll in its hands. When Gillette came along, I wanted him because (1) I wanted sex, (2) I took him at his own stated value, as representing success and money and the high cultural level of newspaper work. When I married him another reason was added; I was tired of being a working girl and wanted the freedom and fun of a home. The most decisive moment in my marriage was probably that moment when I was coming back to the apartment at 1418 Leavenworth Street, with the 15 cents worth of lamb chops ("French chops") for dinner, and suddenly asking myself, "Is this all there is to it? Is there nothing more, never will be anything more than this in all my life?" I was twenty-one then, and very old, and my life was practically over.

The rest of that was a kind of delirium. Partly because I was a fool and partly because of the mental effects of my operation in Kansas City. I wasn't physically normal between 1909 and 1911, nor mentally normal till 1914.

I got rid of Gillette in January, 1915. Then the Bulletin days, and my life on Telegraph Hill. I still had no practical sense whatever, but lived in dreams and fantasies. My thirtieth birthday shocked me into a sort of sanity for a moment, and then I forgot it.

In 1920, Europe. I was really through with sex by that time; Arthur Griggs was an accident of circumstances, of my own fantasy (which by this time I did really, though dimly, recognize as fantasy), and of the excitement I felt because I was in Paris. It was an accident, but I let it use up my time, my energy, and my money, for a year. I let it keep me from any advantages of being in Europe, and from any profit through my connection with the Red Cross.

That ended at the same time that Red Cross support failed. After that I let myself be exploited by Peggy, for two years. They were pleasant. At least I learned to wear evening clothes, and to see some social distinctions. The financial collapse caused by Peggy's exploiting—which was caused by my own negligence in not listening to my own common sense—took me back to The States. Where I should have gone two years earlier. And I did not dig myself out of debt until 1925.

One year at Rocky Ridge, piling up money to follow another dream; Albania. And now I am here, and forty years old, and by this time too much experienced in "fresh starts" to believe that I shall really make one. . . .

What IS Albania, to me, really?

Living is pleasant here, and cheap. We can be very comfortable and lazy. The country is no more beautiful than any other beautiful country. The climate is Californian. The people are like people anywhere.

It is far from financial source of supplies. Living is cheap, but we are spending a great deal of money, and will undoubtedly continue to do so. I work, and let the money go, as always, in satisfying momentary desires for material things. I can lose my life here, bit by bit, as I have always lost it.

As to my work. If, during the next two years, I can write for money, and at the same time, more or less, get ready to write something. . . . I should divide my work into two fields, and make one of them worth while. That is, one of them should express me. And there's nothing to express. . . .

The world is too big for me to grasp and handle. I don't know anything about the world; about history or geography or philosophy. I don't know anything about any part of life, because I've never lived any of it; I've only muddled about in dreams. Does everyone muddle about in dreams?

Damn it, I've got to get back to that Ozark story.

At her best moments, she projected a serious trilogy of novels about Albania, recognizing that if "it is to have any value at all . . . it must come from an inner meaning, a beauty put into it . . . from some sort of rearrangement, some establishment of order, in me, in my attitudes and philosophy." At this point she gave herself two years to make something of her Albanian experiment; later she would commit herself to three; while at other times she seemed to regard her return to Rocky Ridge as imminent.[18]

The disturbance rippling through her private thoughts erupted in her correspondence as well. A letter from Fremont Older, apparently dwelling on his loss of vitality as he reached seventy, prompted an agitated response from Rose, who had admired his crusader's energy at an age well past her own. "I think the only thing you really need is a good scrap," she wrote on Thanksgiving Day:

There's not one human being in a hundred thousand who is gifted with the energy you've got. It's a gift I would give almost anything to possess. It is the one magic thing; and it doesn't, really, wear out. When I saw you last summer, there you were, as full of it as you were when I first met you eleven years ago. It's that energy that's marvelous; it makes you more alive every minute than most people are in their whole lives. If you don't go unconsciously try-

ing to smother it under a notion that you are old because you are
seventy. . . .

   You see, this is a vital point with me. Not only because it's *you*
who are speaking so agedly, when I feel that it's only an idea you
have. . . . But also because I am so near forty myself that I feel
forty. And forty is really a frightful birthday. . . .

And in this month she was also corresponding with Guy Moyston regarding Bessie Beatty's surprise marriage at "forty-odd." Beatty had always struck Rose as a sexual tease and a professional virgin, one who
used her charms as an adjunct to power while never maturing sexually
beyond adolescence. Now Beatty had the nerve in speaking of marriage
to quote, disapprovingly, Rose's own conversation of years before: "Marry
at eighteen, and 'get it all over with' by twenty-five." "My idea," Rose
explained, "was that it was a mistake to carry the 18-year-old person,
unsatisfied and unfulfilled, all along with one through one's whole life;
and at forty still be looking for the 'ideal mate' and 'the great love' and all
the rest of it." And even as she wrestled with her own problem of "growing
up at growing up time," she could be so direct and honest as to confess to
Guy—in a three-page descriptive letter—that she had dreamed that he
was to marry Bessie Beatty. "You aren't engaged to anybody, are you,
Guy? Honest, Dimples darling, it was an awful dream. I feel *miserable.*"[19]

   There were signs that Moyston was moving more and more into a
life that she could not share. His plans to buy a new car sent her into a
spiral of resentment that he could find money for that but not for a trip to
Europe. His new business concerns occupied much of his time; and he
had been successful, without Rose's help, in launching a dramatic sketch
into production off-Broadway, and then later for a short Broadway run.
He contemplated buying an old farmhouse, or perhaps building a home,
near Croton, and she leaped in to advise at great length on buying, designing, and remodeling: she would love, she explains in great detail
even as she plans her Albanian home, to buy and renovate an old farmhouse. Meanwhile, she was looking at possible building sites near Tirana:
one problem, she found, was that under Albanian law she could own
land only within the city. She and Troub climbed to the top of a minaret in
Tirana and surveyed the town below with a telescope.[20]

   Thanksgiving week brought a new rebellion in the hinterlands. The
government commandeered all automobiles to transport troops to the
troubled area; but Rose's friends at the American legation officially requi-
sitioned Zenobia, thus protecting the automobile, which was then required to fly the American flag as it traveled Tirana's streets and the long
exposed road to Durazzo. Rose's dreaded fortieth birthday passed without note, and December passed in celebrations both of the Christmas
season and of Albanian political holidays among the foreign service colony. Rose and Troub hurried to knit sweaters as Christmas gifts for their

servants, and astonished and delighted them with gift baskets on Christmas Eve. A boys' choir from the technical school arrived in their courtyard, offering them traditional carols in Albanian accents beneath a moonlit sky.[21]

IV

The new year began with a series of earthquakes and alarms about a war between Italy and Yugoslavia over Albania's strategic position on the Adriatic. Rose and Troub slept with coats and shoes at hand, to be able to rush into the streets if necessary; the temblors separated their fireplace from the wall and left daylight cracks in their house. The international tensions strained their confidence in the future of Albania and made their plans to buy or build a house subject to constant revision. Yet they continued to pursue the good life; Rose described in great detail the luxury of living each day attended by servants and presiding at the end of each afternoon at a tea in three languages for friends from the polyglot community. When not working at their writing, she and Troub spent long hours planning an elaborate flower-garden. Their broker, George Palmer, sent them advice and seeds; and they ordered more plantings from an American seed company, which sent them in plain envelopes inscribed only with Latin botanical names. With little knowledge of what would come up, they turned their plans over to their Albanian gardener, who spoke no English and read no language. Among his accomplishments was a chrysanthemum bed edged with lettuce.[22]

Rose continued her intermittent journal of garden thoughts, mixing her observations on the weather and the garden with contemplations on the course of her life. On a fine morning in January she and Troub skipped work and went walking, finding a house for sale that pleased them immensely:

> There is no reason, I suppose—if I can get the money—why I should not own half a house in Albania. . . . At any rate, advertising literature is arriving daily now, and without money I can sit furnishing that imaginarily-owned house with ten thousand dollars' worth of electric plants, plumbing, electric fixtures, furniture, rugs and silver. Which I do. . . .
>
> And at other times I build a house on Rocky Ridge Farm, and furnish it as lavishly. . . .

Which leads to calculations of how much she will have to earn and how many stories it would take to earn it.[23]

She had written nothing for the market for a year. She began with a short story aimed at *Country Gentleman*, which was rejected because "it had too many snakes in it." How many were enough was not specified, so she had to content herself with half the price she had expected—this from *Harper's*—and with seeing it selected by Edward J. O'Brien for his *Best Short Stories of 1927*. In February she started an Ozark serial for *Country Gentleman* that she called *Cindy*. It was a romance of feuding Ozark clans in nineteenth-century Missouri, and it was one of the few works she admitted real shame over. With great reluctance she forced her way through the spring months to its conclusion, fighting off daily the distractions of random reading, domestic busy-work, and international politics, all of which interested her more than the pot-boiler in her typewriter. She loathed her lack of discipline, connecting it with her failure ever to complete the round-the-world itinerary in 1923:

> One should have the strength to rise above all such things. There is, really, at the heart of me, a wilting. A spirit that isn't strong should at least have the charms of frailty—delicacy, sensitiveness. But I remain the grubby midwesterner without his robustness. . . . Lawrence held on and kept going, kept fighting, kept even a vividness, for some twenty months on the Arabian and Syrian deserts. And I wilted after one comfortable trip across to Baghdad.

In the interval, she borrowed freely to support her new life—from her friend N. J. Craig's bank, in Mansfield, on security provided by Mama Bess, from Frank America again, from Clarence Day, and from Moyston. Much of the borrowed money went into improvements to the rented house; by March, as she wrote Moyston, she and Troub had decided to wait a few years for prices to fall, meanwhile remodeling to match heart's desire. Workmen added a screened balcony overlooking the garden and new fireplaces in every room.[24]

Rose's correspondence with Moyston continued at a reduced rate: the passion and discontent that had produced almost daily letters from Rocky Ridge had abated, and the rate fell to biweekly missives, in their contents hard to distinguish at times from her letters to Fremont Older or Clarence Day. Presumably Moyston's letters were falling off as well; he returned to California by tramp steamer for the winter, and then, on his return to the East, he enrolled in a play-writing class at Yale, which with his new business pulled him in directions as compelling to him as was Rose's Albanian home to her. Rose sent a six-page letter to greet him in California, and ended it with a query as to the state of their relationship: ". . . won't you draw up to the typewriter and tap out for me your attitude toward our relationship, and some notion as to what you imagine will become of it in the future? This isn't a request for any demonstrations of affection, it's just simply a desire to know what you think. And don't think, Guy, that whatever-there-is-between-us isn't going to change."[25]

Whatever his reply, the correspondence continued good-naturedly at its reduced rate as she pushed forward with the serial and fought off the distractions of her domestic life. She had to intervene to save the life of her Greek cook, who had inadvertently insulted the family of Suleiman, *kvass* to the American legation. Suleiman arrived with pistol in hand; all of Rose's persuasion was needed to postpone the confrontation until the cook could be spirited away and out of the country—leaving Rose with the problem of finding a new cook, which she solved by importing one from Austria. She and Troub helped a Moslem neighbor nurse a new baby through three critical nights of illness, only to see an Albanian doctor arrive and kill it with a powerful purgative. And then her old friend from Berkeley, Alice Danforth, arrived on a poorly financed trip around the world accompanied by her two children, who literally tore the house apart. After two weeks of misery, Rose advanced Alice passage to Vienna and wrote Dorothy Thompson a frantic letter to find them cheap accommodations.[26]

Despite such distractions, *Cindy* was finished by the end of June, and Rose and Troub celebrated with a motor trip through northern Albania. They traveled in a circle through small Albanian towns, making a point to visit the homes of their Albanian servants and spending a night in the home of the redoubtable Suleiman. When Zenobia broke down with a flat tire, they made the mistake of getting out for an exploratory walk along the mountain road, and were promptly arrested by gendarmes who appeared as by magic. The border tensions with Yugoslavia accounted for the standing orders to arrest wayfarers, and they were let go with stern warnings to remain in the car. Rose noted that she had now been arrested in four countries—this and other anecdotes in one of her mammoth seven-page letters to Moyston on her return. It was part of an effort to explain to him the charm the country had for her. But she also acknowledged that his own interests could have the same pull. On returning to the East from California, he was full of news of his play-writing class at Yale. "I didn't know that I should lose you so entirely by coming to Europe," she closed her letter. "You remember that you used to mean to live over here, too. That you were coming over last year. But The States have somehow got you. I doubt if you'll ever leave."[27]

As she awaited word on the fate of her serial, world traveler B. D. MacDonald arrived, chaperoning a group of American college students through Europe. Rose and Troub took him adventuring with Zenobia on a hilarious trip that ended with near fatal injuries to the faithful Ford, whose useful life was now ended. On July 22, Rose learned from her agent that *Cindy* had sold to *Country Gentleman* for $10,000. In effect, she was freed from work for another year.[28]

V

Her response to her sudden wealth was to go shopping for a dog—in Budapest and Vienna. She and Troub had seen a magazine advertisement depicting a pedigreed Great Dane, which they had ordered by mail. But the dog had been sold, and they deferred the idea. Now the notion reappeared with new charm, and with their *kvass* Teko they set out for Budapest by boat, rail, and finally by rented automobile. Part of the pleasure of the trip was to give Teko his first glimpses of modern civilization. The tradition of his job made him both servant and protector, and they marveled at his courage in confronting the routine dangers of modern travel. In Budapest they sent him to the zoo while they shopped, and had the delight of his descriptions of animals he had never known to exist: with elbow to his forehead he described the great beast whose arm grew between its eyes and terminated in two fingers with which it accepted money. They bought, of course, clothes and household goods, including a German ice-maker that no one ever learned how to operate. In Vienna they set out to buy a Great Dane, and ended with a ball of fluff, a Maltese terrier named Mr. Bunting—the first of a line of such dogs that would be Rose's companions for life. Their orgy of spending completed, they returned by way of Venice and arrived back in Tirana on August 25.[29]

Every act bespoke the permanence of Rose's intentions to remain in Albania. Yet the previous May she had confessed to Moyston that she would probably have to come home in the next year to "stay there a while with the family"; and within a week of her return from buying furnishings and curtains for their house, she could write to him that "I am trying to dodge the only solution, which is, to go back to Rocky Ridge and get servants and boss them. I would then be doing my duty of taking care of my parents." Taking root in the back of her mind was a picture of an English cottage she had seen in an old turn-of-the-century magazine she had received from her mother, part of a batch she had requested as she considered a new group of stories to be set in her childhood. She confessed to Clarence Day her suspicion that the Albanian venture was a mistake—that its very delights scattered her energies. But nonetheless, the next month she and Troub were seriously considering a twelve-room house that would soon be available.[30]

VI

As usual, her letter writing was her favorite dissipation—a distraction from the fiction-writing she felt she ought to be doing and a substitute for the good talk she craved but found too seldom in the company she kept. About this time she began to save carbon copies of her letters, perhaps because, as she had said to Guy, she recognized that the best of her was in her letters; in any event, she was not above copying a felicitous page of description to Moyston into a letter to Clarence Day or Dorothy Thompson or Fremont Older. To these correspondents she poured out her thoughts both personal and cosmic in five- and six-page single-spaced letters: ". . . you know how I take any idea in my teeth and run off with it, like Mr. Bunting with a stolen slipper—ears flapping and eyes shining and teeth clenched," she reminded Moyston. It was as though, having cracked the serial market, which put her on the verge of a lucrative income, and having established a growing stock-market account, which promised her financial independence, she sought escape from the tight focus of her energies in a centrifugal whirl of thought. Her problem was that she despised the center these thoughts fled from, but she had no idea of where her center should be.[31]

The flaring match in the sunlight in Tiflis—and the sudden access of happiness it brought her—remained a central metaphor in her imagination. She repeated it in a letter to Moyston as a figure for the fusion of energy and purpose that she longed for but could not achieve. What, really, could she do that was worth doing? And worth the loss of all of the other myriad blandishments of the lovely world? Again and again she lamented to Moyston that she was too greedy to sacrifice anything willingly. Yet again she was finding that the good that she reached for never satisfied her need. The real curse of the Wandering Jew was not to wander eternally but to carry the implacable circle of reality with him.

"What I most want is money," she confided to her journal, "but also I do want to write something that says what I want to say." But from that point her analysis carried her past a defensive deprecation of her own gifts inward to doubt the reality of her own identity. Moyston had urged her to take her role as a writer more seriously. "The reason I can't take myself seriously as a 'creative artist,' Guy dear, is because I'm not one."

> . . . it's somehow not in me to bear very patiently with my own mediocrity. If I can't—and I can't—be Shakespere or Goethe, I'd rather raise good cabbages. And that is why I would not write at all, except that there is more money in writing than in cabbages, not only more money, but more freedom. . . . That is why I'm not "filled with my art." I ain't got no art. I've got only a kind of craftsman's skill, and make stories as I make biscuits or embroider underwear or wrap up packages.

In the same vein, Clarence Day wrote to chide her for her habit of despising all but her best. "It seems to me," she replied, "more that I don't, really, have any respect for anything I do."

> I hate the falseness in it so. I really do hate it. And yet I can't get away from it. It's something in *me* that's wrong. It's that I'm not stable enough, that I'm not *anything* enough. It's that I'm so damnably easily suggestible; I can fall into any hypnosis, and do. And I don't really know what *is* me, my attitude, my opinion, my vision of the real, the thing I *want* to do or say. . . . it seems to me that there's nothing there, that it's all derived—no, not even derived;

that it's all assumed, put on, seized upon to cover a nothingness.
You say you respect my quality, my gifts. My God, what *is* my
quality? Do you see anything in me that's *mine*? I don't.

She realized that she was heir to the skepticism of her age, and she
envied the refuge that faith, or simply commitment, provided. Beneath
her eyes was the remnant of medieval integrity that persisted among her
Albanian neighbors. She paid a call on the Moslem household of her
landlord, which was preparing for the wedding of his sixteen-year-old
daughter—a marriage arranged by the two families. The simple good
cheer of three generations of women living under one roof, passing their
days amicably in spinning, weaving, and gossip while resting comfortably in the web of tradition and ancient law at this crucial moment touched
her with a disarming envy. Could there be an integrity of life—or of
writing—without belief? When Moyston had enrolled in his play-writing
class at Yale, his course of study provoked her into a series of long letters
that argued that the theater, the arts generally, were insignificant in modern culture—merely a recreation for the intelligentsia at best, a soothing
opiate for the mass audience at worst. Great art came from lyrical passion, she argued: the elevation of technique over content was symptomatic of decadence, whether in the smoothly crafted *Saturday Evening
Post* story or in the experimental gibberish of James Joyce or Gertrude
Stein. The great work came from a deep faith that made its own rules and
compelled the rapt attention of a wide audience, as had Greek and Eliz-
abethan drama: the true artists of the twentieth century were jazz musi-
cians and baseball players, she suggested, while the last great novel was
Uncle Tom's Cabin. "All of which doesn't prevent you and me from living
quite pleasantly and comfortably, and perhaps some day making a fortune out of the useless amusements we provide."[32]
Through this whirl of thought and feeling she was trying to work
her way toward some compensatory faith in a purely existential integrity,
one that acknowledged the meaninglessness of the natural order while
finding interest in its ceaseless variety and satisfaction in some personal
order. She had been reading George Borrow's *Lavengro* and had been so
struck with passages that celebrated the simple glory of the world as
solace for human losses that she copied out a page in a letter to Dorothy
Thompson, who was despondent over the failure of her marriage; and
some such argument was the burden of her exchange with Fremont Older
in this year, as she tried to lighten the gloom that had settled around him
in his age. Rose was distressed at his depression and melancholy. In their
exchange of letters she argued vigorously that altruism was not natural to
humankind and that justice was not part of the world's natural order—
and, in fact, that it would be dangerous if reformers could impose these
ideals on human behavior, for such tampering might disturb the natural
balance achieved over centuries of evolution.

> If men were kind, what you would have would be a crowd that
> could not go forward because every man in it would be stepping
> back to let someone else go first; and they would keep stepping
> back to the unicellular amoeba and so on off the field of creation.
> There is no remedy for the miseries of creation, because misery is
> the heart of creation. That is, conflict is. . . . But suffering, like
> happiness, is only an incidental by-product. Inevitable, but not
> important.

While she conceded that people like Older and herself might very
well feel pity, it was, by and large, a defect in their equipment for survival; and at best they should recognize it as a personal taste rather than a
moral law. The tender sensibilities of American liberals was a sentimental
cultivation, a luxury of wealth; she found more admirable and more natural the equanimity with which her Albanian neighbors could accept a
public hanging or the death of a child. A tough-minded realism might at
the same time accept a life lived by personal values while acknowledging
that these had no universal significance; the important thing was the constant excitement of life itself:

> It's enough for me, just to be alive, just not to be dead yet. Just to
> see, and hear, and think about, this fascinating, interesting vari-
> able world. I don't care whether it's beautiful or not, I don't care a
> damn whether a single thing in it is arranged to suit *me*, I don't
> care whether there's intelligence in it, or justice. . . . That's what I
> really mean when I say that I don't care about ideals; I don't care
> anything whatever for them, in comparison with the way I care
> about being alive. . . .

And to Older's concern for the ethics of daily life, she offered a purely
empirical theory: out of the conflicts of life emerged a practical morality, a
rudimentary code of behavior that worked because experience revealed
that it promoted life. American business, she argued, was based on honesty in commercial affairs, without which it could not flourish.[33]

VII

And then, suddenly, it was time to go home again. After investing fifteen
months and two thousand dollars in the Tirana house, she had resolved
the conflict between the Albanian dream and her sense of responsibility
to her parents. Typically, the new scheme presented itself to her in a
vision of a new house. "Houses are abiding joys," she had written to
Dorothy Thompson while in the throes of remodeling her rented house;
"they are the most emotion-stirring of all things." That had been in March.
In December came a brief notation in her diary: "So ends the Albanian
house."[34]

Troub, ever adaptable and agreeable, was ready to leave as well.
With some intention of returning, they sublet the house on Rose's forty-
first birthday to an American member of the diplomatic corps and sold
off their furnishings. Zenobia had already been sold some months earlier. On December 10 they sold their beds and retreated to the large home
of Colonel and Mrs. Stirling of the British legation, where they had arranged to take room and board until they could decide on their passage
back to the States. Dorothy Thompson had predicted that Albania would
become Main Street; Rose wrote her that it had instead become the Via
Mussolini. The country had become more and more entangled econom-
ically with Italy, but the precipitating event for Rose may well have been
when she was walking with Mr. Bunting and met "an Italian creature
who kicked him." To Fremont Older, however, she explained that she had
found herself ill from abscessed teeth, unable to write, and cut off from
her American markets. The combined weight of these mixed motives
were more than she could stand against, although she continued to maintain that she had always intended to return to the States every two years
or so and might yet return to Albania. However, even as she decided to
give up her Albanian house, her imagination had clarified her future in a
vision of another: "In the Tirana house, planning an English one on Rocky
Ridge," she confided to her journal.[35]

If her approach to age forty in the previous year had prompted an
uneasy self-analysis, the fortieth year itself had been marked by a deliberate attempt to locate herself philosophically in some minimal, last-
ditch stand in the conflict between desire and death, marked primarily in
her letters to Fremont Older. Interestingly, she had some trouble keeping
her true age in mind this year, declaring the approach of age forty to
Older as her forty-first anniversary drew near. The year was marked as
well by the challenge of marriage posed by her friends Bessie Beatty and
Dorothy Thompson, which reflected on her arms'-length romance with
Guy Moyston. She could never understand why Beatty, given her temperament and career, had chosen marriage so late in her life; and as the
year drew to a close she heard also from Dorothy Thompson that she and
Sinclair Lewis were to be married. Rose had advised Dorothy against her
first and disastrous marriage to Josef Bard and had more recently consoled Dorothy's heartbreak when Bard left her early in 1927. Her words
then had echoed some of the tough-minded resignation to loss that she
was trying to learn for herself:

> Sometime you will look back on all this, and be glad it happened.
> Someday you will know that you never loved him, that you only
> loved your image of him—something made out of yourself, maybe
> out of the best that was in you. . . . Whatever it is, it dies. And in a
> strange way, you will be glad of that, too. Because after all, always,
> every day of our living is a little bit of dying, and that's all right. It

really is. There's something in you that's deeper than even this thing that's happened, and that will go on, my dear.

Rose loved Dorothy like a younger sister and prized her above all her friends, and she had been deeply hurt when their correspondence had dropped off after Dorothy's marriage to Bard. "Every woman has love affairs," she had written Dorothy. "It's the rarely fortunate one who has a sincere friend—I mean a *friend.*" The correspondence and the friendship had been renewed with Dorothy's period of grief, but Rose was uneasy now about the projected marriage to Lewis. "I feel a thousand years older," she wrote, "since trying to recall a person I once used to be, who also cried whole-heartedly, 'I am in love, thank God, again!' And you know so well what I think—and feel—about marriage."

> There may be a man who can love on a hill in the wind, one who won't clutch and cling and muddle—you see, I'm *really* not pessimistic!—and if there is, I hope you've got him. As to keeping him forever—I can imagine nothing more wonderful than always *wanting* to keep a man. . . . It's this not wanting to keep them, and yet not quite being able to disentangle one's self, never quite having the ruthlessness to strike the hands on the gunwale with an oar until they let go—that's the horrible thing. That's always my ending.

She put off Dorothy's invitation to meet her and Lewis in Sicily, preferring, she said, to see her old friend when the first blush of romance had faded enough not to distract their conversation.[36]

In this context Rose was reassessing her relationship with Guy Moyston and with men generally. In 1921, as she had turned from Arthur Griggs to Moyston, she had acknowledged to herself a need for a place to keep her heart from "wailing alone in the cold." Reviewing that journal entry in 1927, she discovered a change: "when it stops wailing," she noted, "it really *stops*. I don't seem even to *have* any, any more." Moyston's failure to join her in Europe had disappointed her deeply, and her side of the ensuing correspondence suggests an emotional disengagement that would protect her from expecting more than he could give. At the same time, she recognized that she could not give what most men seemed to want. She had been reading W. L. George's *Gifts of Sheba,* and she paused to contemplate George's suggestion that "the only man a modern woman can live with is one who doesn't care a damn for her." In her journal she mused:

> I have been contemptuous of all the men who have said they loved me. Except Austin [Lewis?], & I was beginning to doubt his pretenses. He was right in never teaching me anything, & so was A. G. but neither could keep it up. My attitude toward men has always been essentially exploiting. This is a point always missed. I wanted what they had, not what they were. And got it and went on. No enduring relationship is possible. But why should it be

> thought desirable. An ideology from much more primitive soci-
> eties. No: permanence is the one thing we all want—because it's
> impossible. We're so *tired* of becoming, want to *be*.

A few days later she began on the facing page one of her periodic stock-
takings: what to show for the eight years since she began this journal?
First on her list is "End of love affairs," followed by "Some common
sense, but not so much as the usual girl of twenty." "Am I, at forty," she
concludes, "beginning not to have any hopes any more?"[37]

At the year's end she subjected herself to another of her annual
assessments. "I fear to plan ahead, because nothing that I have intended
has ever been realized. Nevertheless, an ambition much reduced in seven
years—I now want $100,000 and a house when I am 45. I now have roughly
$16,000." Her New Year's resolutions were simply to write a thousand
words a day and to go back and settle at Rocky Ridge. The growth of her
stock-market account made the financial goal seem reachable, and with
enough money she could hire help and live as well as she had in Albania.
This sense of prosperity tempted her into one of those gestures from the
heart that, as she had said to Older, disabled the idealists of the world.
She had kept a watchful eye on young Rexh Meta, the Albanian boy
who had guided her out of danger during her first venture into the mountains. He was now about eighteen and had finished his secondary curriculum at the Tirana Vocational School; he was bright, idealistic, and fluent
in English. Albania was in need of educated young men, and the government was willing to finance some part of his study abroad. From somewhere, perhaps from one of the British officers, came the idea that Rexh
should go to Cambridge, and in the week before she left, Rose offered
him five hundred dollars to make the enterprise possible. Implicit was
the promise that more would be forthcoming if it were needed, and at the
moment Rose's finances were in better shape than were the Albanian
treasury's.[38]

The housing arrangements with the Stirlings seem to have been
more or less indefinite; as the year turned over into 1928, Rose simply
noted that in that year she would return to Rocky Ridge. But on January
23 came a cablegram from Mama Bess containing some disturbing news
that Rose did not record, but it apparently precipitated an immediate
departure. The last few days were filled with long walks and regrets for
the beauty of the country she was leaving. On January 27 they left Durazzo
harbor on a coastal steamer for Greece, where they boarded the *Saturnia*
for the voyage home. Off Palermo, the beauty of the mountains and the
bay at sunset struck Rose again with the sense of the romance of life when
it is untouched by the implacable circle of reality. "I hate to be middle
aged," she wrote, "but no man can give me the romance I want." A brief
landing in Lisbon and a glimpse of the Azores shrouded in fog gave her
dreams of these new destinations for later travel. They landed in New

York on February 16, to be met by George Palmer. Rose had to pay $450 duty to enter Mr. Bunting into the United States.[39]

Rose and Troub checked into the Berkshire Hotel and embarked on another splendid round of shopping, and Rose arranged for much-needed dental work for her abscessed teeth. Guy Moyston did not arrive until the twenty-fifth, when he came down from New Haven. There was a ritual trip to Nyack to see the Haders and their friends, and it was more pleasant than she had expected. Rose and Guy returned to the city that evening by bus and talked in a cafeteria until 1:00 A.M. Clearly, they had gone as far as they could go together. "The end of the beginning in London in 1921," Rose entered in her diary. "Paris was first, but not really the beginning." The next day, she sent him a note calling off a planned weekend in Croton, pleading her dental surgery: "On the whole, it's been a happier seven years than unhappy, hasn't it?"

> You might just mention to me sometime that, on the whole, you don't regret our going to the valley of the Loire, nor even that evening on the hill at Rocky Ridge when all the cows stood 'round and stared at us so wonderingly—I would be glad to hear you say, if you can sincerely, that the happiness has been *almost* worth the pain. Because I'm sorry that I've hurt you so much—I didn't, you know, ever mean to.

She refused to see him during her recuperation, and when he sent flowers she sent him a gentle note of thanks and farewell, quoting from memory the whole of Frost's "Diverging Roads."

> Two roads diverged in a yellow wood, and I—
> I took the one least traveled by.
> And that has made all the difference.

"Too bad I didn't write that myself," she concluded. "Anyway, I live it." She couldn't sleep for toothache and dreaming of Albania. Troub conferred with publishers regarding a book-length version of her war memoirs, then departed to visit her family in Boston, taking Mr. Bunting with her. Five days later Rose was back home at Rocky Ridge Farm.[40]

EXPERIMENT AT ROCKY RIDGE

10

There's a series of geological adjustments . . . going on in my mind.

On her way home from Albania, off the coast of Spain, Rose had turned to her journal again to take stock and plan her future:

> It is encouraging that I acted with decision, taking my losses, about the Albanian house. And again with decision, to avoid financial losses, in leaving the Stirlings.
>
> I will spend no more time, effort or money in realizing dreams, until I have a safe and solid $50,000.00 properly invested. I shall try to do this by the end of 1930. Six thousand a year contributed to the Palmer account should do this. Ten thousand a year earned. One serial and a few short stories. This seems to mean three years in The States, mostly in Rocky Ridge farmhouse, and it involves delicate personal adjustments with the family and Troub.
>
> If I can only make it a fresh, sunny, open-air life—without all this smothered smoldering.
>
> A busy life, active and energetic. At the same time, a *learning* life, studious. So that when I'm free to go again I shall be ready.

Again, a new start with new resolutions. Somewhere ahead lay the good life in which character and purpose and beauty would fuse in daily enterprise. All would depend on the growth of the Palmer account, which in time would free her of the twin worries of writing for the market and providing for her parents. It seemed just within her grasp. Even as she laid these plans on board the *Saturnia*, Mama Bess was hosting another of her Justamere Club parties, noting Rose as joint hostess on the invitation even though her return was yet a month away—so eager was the mother for the prodigal daughter's return. Within days of her arrival in Mansfield Rose found herself absorbed in the old life of club meetings, dinner parties, and social visits. A despairing scrawl stretches across a week of empty diary pages: "Days on the farm do not fill diaries."[1]

Not that she hated the parochial life with a constant passion. The Ozark spring was beautiful, and on a good day she could confess to her diary, "Nothing nicer than Rocky Ridge." In a mindless blur, she could all too easily fill her days with baking, cooking, embroidery, and planning parties—all the trivial pleasures that kept her from the writing that would pay her bills and free her to leave again. Often she dreamed of reconciling her equally strong domestic and itinerant impulses by having a string of homes across the globe, and only when moments of reflection revealed to her the impossible conflict did she turn to her private journals to record her frustration. "I shall never have anything I want," she noted one day, acknowledging again, for the moment, that the implacable circle of reality would encompass any of the current schemes that crowded in upon her.[2]

II

Among other things, she wanted a remodeled old farmhouse and a modern English cottage and an Albanian home. The growth of the Palmer account made two of the three possible in the present circumstances. A month after her return she had plans for a foundation-to-rooftop remodeling of Rocky Ridge farmhouse, which would bring electricity and plumbing into the home that had already become something of a local showplace. This would become a home for herself and Troub. Her parents would get the English stone cottage, built over the hill on the east forty. The Albanian home would come later. As she considered her plans for this compulsive building, she attempted to forestall regrets with clear-eyed prediction of her own folly: "It is another life-wasting mistake that I shall make."[3]

She would have to draw down her Palmer account considerably to build the new house, but the stock-market was booming and Carl Brandt was getting her better prices for her latest stories. If she could get her parents settled and establish her own income from dividends, she would be free to travel as she pleased and write what she wanted—whatever that might be. The emptiness she suspected at the core of her being had as its reflex a paralysis of freedom as she considered what she might write when not under duress. "Convictions—completely blank!" she entered in her journal on April 23. Somewhere in her random reading she encountered an admonitory passage that so struck her that she transcribed it into her journal. "Create a circle for your life and eliminate from it all that is unsuited to your constitution . . . eliminate from it everything clashing with the highest ideals which you wish to realize—then you have some possibility of a harmony." To this passage Rose appended her question: "And what of the 'constitution' to which nothing is alien, everything (and nothing: that's the answer) 'suited'?" She was even beginning to question the validity of her own impulse to write letters, as she read in the recently published letters of Joseph Conrad. "Conrad's sincerity is striking," she noted, "under the various phases of himself shown in his letters to different persons. The same quality of adjustment not only in mood but almost in fact, that makes some persons accuse me of posing and lying, is in him. But underneath there is a firmness and a sincerity that I haven't. Perhaps I shall achieve it when I am fifty." When Clarence

Day suggested that he and Rose make a book of some of their letters, she could not agree: ". . . mine are cheap little showings off," she said; "I cut capers and am a little Jack Horner. I am sincere, but only with the surface of my mind, and the sincerity is all mixed up with smartness." At one point, she connected her "showing off" with her use of simile, and from time to time she experimented in her letters to Day at writing descriptively without them.[4]

A connected issue was the integrity of her professional writing. Carl Brandt persuaded her that she should permit *Cindy* to be published as a book with the argument that it would raise her prices for her next serial. She agreed reluctantly, and was humiliated by the thoughtless and tasteless advertising copy that came from Harper's marketing staff. As its publication date approached, she agonized over the dilemma it posed. "I hate the publication of *Cindy*—which will be out next week. Because it is cheap, it isn't true, it says nothing worth saying. I wrote it as a serial, for the money. I didn't want to write it for itself. Now I need money for these two houses, and see nowhere to get it but from another serial, for which I have no idea." Carl Brandt continued to cajole her for more manuscripts, and she produced a couple of stories that he placed with *Ladies' Home Journal*, another Ozark story for *Country Gentleman*, and another slip into excellence that she hoped the *Ladies' Home Journal* would take at her new rates of $1,200 but that ended again with the high prestige and low price ($400) of an appearance in *Harper's*. The two *Ladies' Home Journal* stories, she thought, had at their centers serious studies of relations between wife and mother-in-law, between mother and daughter, but no one, she complained, seemed to see past the contrivance of their plots. And what did her books have in common, she lamented to Brandt, except that all of them were prodded out of her by editors, none came spontaneously from herself? "All that's not what I'm talking about, when I say that I can *almost* write a real book. It is true, Carl. There's something in me that all this copy I turn out doesn't touch. That it doesn't have anything to do with. I almost really have something to *say*." But the closest she could come to identifying this hidden center was to speculate on a book that had the quality of fireflies in the Ozark twilight. In response to her pleas, Clarence Day continued to argue that a substantial core could be inferred from the best qualities even of *Cindy*; and Floyd Dell, also levied upon for support in this crisis, suggested vaguely that the strength of her writing lay in her awareness of natural beauty.[5]

She could submit to this painful self-scrutiny because she hoped shortly to be able to afford it—afford, that is, to go her own way with her writing. She did not aspire to Conrad's massive authority, nor to the evanescent charm of Virginia Woolf ("I haven't an intelligence competent to meet her"), nor to the social vision of H. G. Wells, whose productivity she admired but whose optimism she found to be a covert religion.

She found a kind of fidelity to experience she admired in the novels of Frances Newman, whose style caught both the permanence of the self and the transience of the moment. If she could find such a modest ground for herself to work on, she could be content; out of such work could flow a sense of integrity that could not be compromised by the market she now hawked her wares in. She connected her outrage at the tawdry promotion of *Cindy* with the sense of violation she had felt when Sherwood Anderson made a sexual display of her in *Dark Laughter* and the more recent discovery that "that unspeakable slimy little Hungarian Jew, Josef Bard"—Dorothy Thompson's first husband—had made her a character of easy virtue in his novel, *Shipwreck in Europe*. The sexual metaphor connects both her sense of having prostituted her own talents and having been violated by her publishers. Carl Brandt alluded to a writer who claimed that one achieved real virginity from age twenty-nine on, which approximately described Rose's hopes in retrieving a reputation she had too lightly let go.[6]

Her chagrin at her own record and prospects became especially keen in May of 1928 at the unlikely conjunction of Sherwood Anderson and Herbert Hoover in her emotional life. She had felt little regard for Anderson's accomplishments as a writer, and less for his character as a result of his treatment of her in *Dark Laughter,* but in May she chanced upon his earlier *A Story Teller's Story*, a loosely autobiographical account of his development as a writer. The book momentarily stunned her with its rejection of the formulaic magazine story, its moral commitment to "truth of essence" in fiction, and its concluding exemplary tale of the magazine writer of slick fiction who, when he longed to write the truth, found himself so crippled that he could not. In a daze of emotion she sat down to write Anderson a long, rambling letter of admiration in which she acknowledged the heroism of his stance and presented herself as a worst-case instance of the alternative. "You hate plot-stories. (Hurrah! A man who succeeds in really hating, *hating* plot stories, without writing 'em!). . . . (I don't say *I* do it; no, I write the plot-story-cut-to-measure. I'm not talking about me.)" Upon cool reflection, she decided not to send the letter, but kept it in her files. The Hoover incident cut her from another angle, when she found in a *Saturday Evening Post* article by Garet Garrett a claim that Hoover had bought up and suppressed her book on him because it had so glamorized his life. Apparently Hoover had mistakenly asserted a wish as an accomplished fact, and it was not even clear that he had Rose's book in mind, but the report put her in the embarrassing position of seeming to have written an unauthorized libel and to have accepted money for its suppression. Hasty telegrams to the *Post*, to her agent, and to Charles K. Field and Fremont Older in California sought some way to set the record straight, but she had finally to accept the humiliation in silence. Not that she disagreed with Hoover's judgment of her book: "I'm not particularly proud of it," she wrote Fremont Older. "I think it is, really, a cheap bit of work." But the whole affair, she lamented, made her seem not merely a hack but an unscrupulous one as well, particularly among Frederick O'Brien's friends.[7]

But beneath the discontent with her work lay the deeper problem of her stance toward life itself: if that were authentic, the work would take care of itself. Her ideal, in many respects, continued to be Dorothy Thompson—"a song, a poem, a flame in the sunlight"—and Dorothy's second marriage after the failure of her first brought to a head Rose's suspicion of marriage-for-love as a compromise of that integrity. She had continued to puzzle with Fremont Older over Bessie Beatty's marriage (". . . if I so far lost my present identity as to fall into matrimony, I wouldn't *marry* a Bill. Darling as he is."); and Clarence Day's unexpected announcement of his marriage cast a pall over their correspondence and provoked Rose into another of her unsent letters, in which she attempted to describe how the conventions regarding married men and unmarried women must inevitably distance them from each other. ("What complete idiots men are," she entered in her diary.) And when Dorothy Thompson wrote of her old life with Josef Bard and her new life with Sinclair Lewis, Rose detected a self-deprecation in Dorothy's relations with both men that amounted to self-betrayal. Deeply upset, she wrote a letter analyzing the damage Bard had done Dorothy that was also an implicit warning against Sinclair Lewis. Bard, she argued, had been so clearly Dorothy's inferior that he had used the charm of his European culture to denigrate her talents and undermine her self-confidence, leaving her with artificial values and a diminished integrity. Now there was the danger that her life would be submerged in that of her new husband: "Now you write, and *you* are gone. . . . It's a break between you and the world that was yours, the world you created—I say it so badly. Where does the light of the candle go, when it is blown out? . . . I so desperately feel that you *should* be reached, set burning again....Your light means too much, is too rare, precious, to be lost." Upon reflection, this letter too she did not send, replacing it with a vaguer warning and a hope that they could talk about a letter not sent when they met again. But as their correspondence continued, with Dorothy reporting on her domestic happiness with Lewis, Rose could not refrain from some serious jesting about the dangers of marriage to a woman's integrity:

> You know I can't like your husband ever—except by forgetting that he is. You would have gone to Albania with me, long ago, if you had thought of marriage as I think of it. You know—as one thinks of the sugar in the tea, that one doesn't take, preferring a simpler, more direct relation with tea. And when I met Fodor in Vienna and heard that you were happy, slim, and gay again, I thought that you'd come to the same, "No, thank you; Lemon please," point of view.[8]

Fremont Older was the other model of integrity in her life, and with him she could discuss her personal concerns against a background of history and metaphysics. She freely acknowledged using him as a sounding board for ideas as she "boxed the compass" of her opinions, searching for some stability. "There's a series of geological adjustments, so to speak, going on in my mind—and perhaps character—just now," she confessed to him. "Earthquakes and volcanoes and tidal waves accompanying. And what's really in this pouring out of letters to you is a confusion, a struggling with ideas and points of view." Older was a longtime liberal crusader, and her letters to him were a working out of her own repudiation of much that she had accepted during her San Francisco days as received liberal opinion.[9]

The modern loss of God, she conceded, left a wholly natural world in which "all animals but men know how to live and die." But for his self-consciousness, man could live in the world as easily as fishes in the sea; that self-consciousness, however, condemns him to a search for meaning. The facile conclusion, that the search reveals nothing but determinism, yields the liberal absolution of the individual of responsibility for his conduct, which accounts for the general decline in order in society, while an afterglow of Christian meliorism assumes a spark of natural goodness that can be retrieved. Another, more strenuous conclusion might be reached, however, which accepts the world that science reveals while finding certain virtues empirically "true," that is, promoting life and order. The individual then assumes the obligation of testing values and taking responsibility for the outcome. Her experience among the Armenians had disabused her of any notion of natural human goodness; natural cruelty seems more the case, struggle and conflict the necessary norm, and evil a kind of moral laziness—but even hate was far better than a flabby determinism.

This welter of dynamic choice inevitably changes the world, Rose acknowledged, however much she deplored most of the changes. What began to emerge from this boxing of the compass was an attempt at acceptance of a complex, evolving universe which, when seen personally (as Older saw it), was full of pain and disappointment, but when seen with a detached imagination—that of the Wandering Jew—presented a glorious spectacle of ceaseless variety and interest. "What on earth is happening to me, dear Mr. Older? I can recall the time, not long ago, when such sentiments would have given me a permanent wave." Older scrawled at the bottom of one letter, "This is *not* a gorgeous world," to which she replied:

> Tell me it isn't, when you've lived twice ten thousand times as long as the Wandering Jew, when there's nothing around any corner that you don't know to weariness, when all the Encyclopedias are primers to you, and when nothing but the long-time-expected and

often-experienced ever happens to you any more. And I will reply;
it isn't that the world isn't as gorgeous as it's always been, it's only
that you're tired and need a rest.[10]

It was a view compounded of Darwin, Herbert Spencer, William
James, and Bergson (at least), which assumed as a goal a detachment that
she could seldom achieve. One of Older's columnists mistook a hint from
a letter of Rose's to write of a transcendental leap, "letting my spirit become a part of all other spirits." Rose protested vigorously: "personally I
shall hang on to whatever small bit of my spirit is painfully evolved by
me, and keep it out of the cosmic consciousness to the very last gasp."
Later, she wrote of herself as much as of Older: "If you wouldn't *care*
about the world, you'd see it unprejudiced, and enjoy the incredible and
astounding spectacle of it. If you must care, then let go and really *be*
emotional, as most people are; love it, and hate it, and fight it and accept
it and scorn it and worship it and then begin all over again." This pas-
sionate alternative seems close to the unself-conscious fusion of character
and action, thought and feeling, that she saw embodied in Older and in
Dorothy Thompson—and that she could no more maintain for herself
than she could her idealized detachment. To Dorothy she wrote of the
problem as well, invoking again her favorite figure: "The myth of the
Wandering Jew is really the expression of the human heart's desire. Immortality is a poor compromise between that desire and the observed
fact." And she copied out for Older a passage from Conrad's letters that
she found seductive: "the fidelity to passing emotions which is perhaps a
nearer approach to truth than any other philosophy of life." "My real
concealed notion about that," she added, "is that it's a slick excuse for
sloppy thinking. But Oh boy, what a beautiful slickness!" This letter
came just weeks after she had confided to her journal her final assessment
of Guy Moyston: "Guy refuses. A refusing attitude is a narrowing, dry-
ing one. Too self-protective. A seed protecting itself from all contact with
soil because it fears cut-worms. And now he can't write. . . . Naturally."[11]

Out of this dialectic effort, however, began to emerge a view of her
country and its place in history that would carry her a long way. Early she
had outgrown the thoughtless nineteenth-century patriotism that was
her natural inheritance, and she had embraced as a young intellectual a
fashionable disdain for the cultural thinness of her country, for its relentless commercialism and industrial ugliness. Her travels in Europe had
begun as a pilgrimage and had ended in retreat, as she came to see
European culture, for all its grace and beauty and classical resonance, as
a spent force poised for one last gasp of a war.

The future, however inhospitable, belonged to the United States,
where the restless energies of a free people would propel civilization into
an unimaginable future. She and people like her were, unfortunately, "a
remnant of Greek civilization left over in the midst of forces making a

new, and quite other, civilization." Her problem was that of an amphib-
ian, able to live in the new world only if she could retreat at times to her
original element—some enclave of peace and harmony; and she cited as a
cautionary example the sentimental and impractical Hellenism of George
Cram Cook, whose pastoral ideals led him to a life in flea-ridden Greek
villages and death by glanders. The issue coalesced neatly for her around
Dorothy Thompson's marriage to Josef Bard, in which she saw Bard's resentful parasitism, his envious air of superiority in the face of Dorothy's
natural force, as a symbol of European decadence. "As human beings,"
she had written Dorothy in that unsent letter, "there was no comparison
between you."

> In tradition, the only difference between you was that he was a few
> centuries behind you. As a European, he was nearer the sources
> of a common culture and therefore knew them better; as a Euro-
> pean, he knew languages and histories and variations of culture.
> It was an accident of environment that equipped him with these
> things that, to us as Americans, seem valuable. To him as the
> European, they appeared to be exactly what, today, they are; a
> heritage from a great past to a weakling present, of no value except
> as last weapons against an inevitably conquering civilization-of-
> tomorrow that has nothing whatever to do with them.

"Be happy," she concluded, "and come home to a country which may not
be God's own (since we have abolished God) but is most certainly the
greatest country on his footstool."[12]

If Josef Bard was the representative European, the representative
American was Herbert Hoover. Rose continued to admire him despite his
dismissal of her book, and she argued his case with Fremont Older, who
had voted for Al Smith. In Europe she had found the American Relief
Administration a model of honesty and efficiency in comparison with the
Red Cross and the Near East Relief; and Hoover knew "the whole round
globe" as well as Smith knew New York City. Thus he could put American international relations on a business-like footing and cut through the
mingled disdain and sycophancy of the European view of the United
States. "If Christ had run on the Democratic ticket, I should still have
been for Mr. Hoover. We don't want this country crucified. . . . I prefer
the idealism of the Ford factory to that of the revolutionary; it has more
effect on the world."

> This is the largest, most powerful . . . most prosperous Empire in
> history. It also happens to have an economic system that distrib-
> utes its wealth more equally than any other. It has no spiritual
> qualities (no country has ever had); but it does have moral ones
> (which no other country has). For the first time in history, we have
> a vast people which has somehow perceived the practical use for
> moral qualities, and therefore has 'em. Idealism that doesn't have

practical uses has never got anywhere. . . . I *like* to see a hard-headed and hard-boiled business man, with an international point of view and a large stock of practical humanitarian ideas, running it.[13]

III

Whether as cause or effect of such geological shifts going on in her thoughts, she entered the summer of 1928 in a state of nervous exhaustion. She laid it to twenty-five years of accumulated overwork, "almost as bad as though I'd married twenty-five years ago and been keeping middle-western house ever since." She hated the affectations of "nervous" women, but she had to admit that her nerves were bad: "It *is* nerves, but not the psychological ones; the little actual gray-white ones that run around in the bones and branch out into the skin and so on. . . . I'm practically flayed, and can't do anything about it." In such a state did she embark on a systematic redeployment not only of her thoughts but of the practical conditions of her life.[14]

In June Troub arrived from the East with Mr. Bunting and a new roadster named Janet to find Rose full of plans for their new life together. A tenant house was to be built for a hired man, a full-time cook/housekeeper was to be installed, the new house was to be built for her father and Mama Bess, and Rocky Ridge farmhouse was to be modernized for Rose and Troub to live their own lives in. Already Rose had a new desk she had ordered in New York, which was so wide that the door to her room had to be altered. In the meantime, they could glory in their new radio, a super-heterodyne eight-tube Radiola model that Rose had admired in the home of George Q. Palmer. Troub had serious intentions of settling down to a career as a free-lance writer now that her war diary had just come out in book form. But she was not under the economic pressure that Rose faced; she had a small inherited income in addition to her Palmer account, and she had no dependents, so her engagement with the new life was at once freer and less serious than Rose's. Pending completion of the new living arrangements, she pitched a green tent on the hillside above the farmhouse; there she worked intermittently at her writing, and there she and Rose held Albanian teas in memory of their former life. And Troub bought a horse named Governor, on which she ranged the hills about Mansfield.[15]

By midsummer Mama Bess had agreed to the new house, but she would have nothing to do with the planning or supervision of the construction. Rose estimated that it would cost her four thousand dollars, but "it would solve all problems." And problems there were: Rose was under constant levy by her mother for trips, visits, and conversation; and then as she worked in her room, distracting conversations rose from the rooms below. Mr. Bunting and Nero, her mother's dog, could not be trusted together. And the house was simply crowded. Construction began in August, and as summer moved into autumn Rose found she could leave no detail unsupervised. She and Troub made trip after trip to Spring-field to consult with the architect and builder and to choose fittings and appointments, while at home they spent hours daily observing the build-ers' progress, at times halting work while they called for changes. Rose found studding in place for a nine-feet-two-inch ceiling, and had it taken down and replaced at eight feet, three inches. She changed bathroom plans on the job and sent back to Springfield a load of flooring that displeased her. She found plaster painted instead of tinted, finished floors to be refinished, damaged tile to be replaced. She accepted the chimney, although it did not seem straight. Electricians came to wire the new house and at the same time installed wiring in the old farmhouse, and although it took intervention of a lawyer to prod the Public Service Commission to install service lines, in time electricity flowed to both houses and the old kerosene lamps were put away at Rocky Ridge Farm. [16]

All this time the social life of the community flowed on around and through Rose's life—a series of distractions that she could resent but not deny. With two automobiles in the family, long day-trips and weekend excursions were possible, sometimes in company with the Craigs and others of Mama Bess's friends. Genevieve Parkhurst stopped on her way to California and was feted by the local ladies. Major Leslie Barbrook, a British army officer Rose had known in Albania, showed up as an Ameri-can immigrant on his way to mining work in Arizona, and had to be given a tour of the region. Just as he left, a Dr. Zentary she had known in Budapest arrived. The *Mansfield Mirror* noted almost monthly appearances of Rose as guest speaker at club meetings around the region. And the Justamere Club continued, and Rose could not stay out of its machina-tions: "Justamere meeting: Mrs. C. N. Clark & Corinne Murray black-balled; reconsidered & elected members: we think Mrs. Davis did it, but all agree it was a mistake." Through it all, Rose fell into periods of nervous exhaustion. "Am almost at ebb tide," she noted on October 19. "Have decided to go to the Mayo brothers as soon as time and money allow." The November 10 entry concluded, "Crise de nerfs in night & didn't sleep." Four days later: "Read article saying that play—i.e. purposeless activity—is necessary to health. But I don't know how—have never played." [17]

As the new house neared completion, Rose went on a spree of buy-ing in the Springfield furniture store and spent the night awake at the banality of the whole enterprise. The new house was beginning to present itself as a Christmas gift for her parents, and the spending contagion spread to Troub: Rose's ordered birthday gift had not arrived on December 5, but Troub went to nearby Seymour and came home with a new 1929 Buick sedan, "all curves," that they had admired since summer. When the globe Troub had ordered arrived a little later, Rose was just as delighted; and for Mr. Bunting there was a new Scots terrier puppy as companion. Three days before Christmas the new house was ready for the parents to move into: once Rose had cleaned it and installed the furniture, Mama Bess made her visit and pronounced herself delighted. Rose would rent Rocky Ridge farmhouse from her for sixty dollars a month. Christmas itself, despite a barometer from Troub that no one could read, could only be anticlimactic.

As the month ran down into the new year of 1929, Rose and Troub furiously cleaned and cleaned out the old farmhouse and had painters in to refurbish the whole interior. They had a house to themselves again, Mama Bess and Almanzo a short walk over the hill or a short drive down the road away. On the last day of the year they cleaned the attic while painters worked in the dining room. They did not realize that it was New Year's Eve until the radio informed them of it after supper. Doubtless also forgotten was the long discussion they had had earlier whether to have an apartment in New York or to live at the Berkshire Hotel, and that sometime in this year of ferocious nest-building Rose had copied into her journal a poem on wanderlust by an unknown author:

> Yonder the far horizons lie,
> And there by night and day
> The old ships sail to port again,
> The young ships sail away.
> And come I may, but go I must,
> And if men ask you why,
> You must lay the blame on the sun and the stars,
> The white road and the sky.[18]

When Rose did her year's end accounts, she found that the new house for her mother had cost not four thousand dollars but eleven thousand. At such a price had she replaced the house she had burned down when she was three years old. But George Q. Palmer had more than doubled her stock-market account in the year, and to avoid drawing it down further she borrowed from Troub and from her friend Craig's bank. Prosperity still seemed just within her grasp. She made due note of money she still owed to Mama Bess and to the reliable Frank America. Her New Year's resolution for 1929: "I will be happy, be healthy."[19]

IV

She had moved Mama Bess far enough away not to be an hourly distraction, and she had again her own establishment: a large and comfortable home, a congenial companion, and freedom to order her days to her liking. A hired man in the tenant house did the maintenance and heavy work of the place and the live-in cook/housekeeper was installed in her parents' old bedroom. Her growing investments and quarterly dividends served as a cushion against future need. Now if ever should come the work that would define her better self, tap that sense that she had something to say that was hers alone. But it did not come. Rather, she found herself oppressed by the responsibilities of the two homes and unavoidably subject to the old panic and depression when her daily stint at the typewriter did not produce regular checks in the mail. On January 10 she noted, "First time I ever kept a New Year's resolution for ten days." But by February she complained that she felt as though her mainspring were broken, and a short automobile trip one day touched again her longing for the wider horizon: "No tongue can tell how *I want to get away from here!*"[20]

In truth, the earthquake changes she had sensed the year before were consolidating, but not into configurations she could tap for income. Her happiest times at her typewriter came in her correspondence with Fremont Older. She delighted in playing devil's advocate, challenging his liberal, humanitarian beliefs with outrageous arguments—for the systematic chloroforming of habitual criminals, for instance. And although she wrote with tongue in cheek, she was in fact mapping a larger hardening of the sympathies that she had shared with Older and her San Francisco friends of the decade before. Her experiences in Europe and the Middle East had disillusioned her of any faith in natural human goodness, classical Western civilization was fast eroding into anarchy in Europe and had barely made an impression in America, everywhere standards were dissolving. Walter Lippmann could write a preface to morals but not of morality itself. At one time—in tribal Albania, or nineteenth-century America—harsh experience had produced harsh moral codes that enforced order. Contemporary humanity needed strong leaders to whip it into shape, such as Hoover in the States or Ahmet Zogu in Albania. Genevieve Parkhurst, visiting again, found her growing cynical. Rose hoped she was merely seeing things clearly.[21]

In part this repudiation of her former views probably reflected her disappointment at her old friends, who, she thought, had betrayed her faith by continuing to adhere to Frederick O'Brien. She had tended always to overinvest in friendships, and her resentment was proportional. By the same token, she had underinvested in her relationships with men, so protecting herself against romantic claims as to drive Moyston, for one, away in frustration. Now, as she hardened herself against her general disappointment in humanity and distanced herself emotionally from people once dear to her, she began to invest heavily in surrogate relationships that would be at once more reliable and less demanding. One was with her dogs, to an extent not uncommon in dog-lovers, no doubt, but with a fervency and dedication that would mark the rest of her days. Another was with her informally adopted son, Rexh Meta, now installed at Cambridge and in need of money and counsel.

Mr. Bunting and his new brother got the regular baths, grooming, and play of infants in the household. And on Rexh was lavished the clucking, mother-hen attention that had been a strong feature of Rose's relationships with Arthur Griggs and Guy Moyston. At Cambridge, Rexh was doubly and triply isolated: the only Albanian, one of the few Moslems, and inadequately and irregularly supported by the financially pressed, disorganized, and corrupt Albanian bureaucracy. His letters were affectionate ("Dear Mother"), thoughtful, optimistic, idealistic; hers were solicitous and occasionally hectoring, as she offered him unsought advice on his studies, his tutors, his health, his future, his relations with the Albanian government—the list could go on.

> I am worried about your living conditions, for they are really important. If you come out of Cambridge knowing everything in every book there, and with dyspepsia, you will be in worse condition than if you'd never gone to England. Health is much more important than you can begin to realize, at your age. When you're as old as I am, you'll realize that good sound teeth are more important than a title, and that the best head upon earth is no use whatever without a strong, healthy, energetic body.

Although Rexh had a good natural intelligence, he had been indifferently educated in Tirana and had considerable preliminary study to make up before he could pass his entrance examinations. His first try was a failure, but his second was successful: on October 7, Rose received a single-word telegram, "PASSED." She wrote him a letter of congratulation and enclosed a check for five hundred dollars.[22]

Thus Rexh's needs were added to the burden she felt for her parents' support, and she began to work doggedly at the old vein, turning out several more stories for Country Gentleman and Ladies' Home Journal. She had high hopes for a serial named "Romance," based on her Albanian experiences, and its rejection threw her into another depression. She turned immediately to other stories; "nothing stopped Conrad," she reminded herself. Away from the typewriter, she threw herself into refurnishing the farmhouse and landscaping the grounds, conducting French lessons for some local young people, and, always, club meetings and day-trips with her local friends and her mother's. "I am very happy when I am not working," she admitted to her diary. A new name begins to appear in her diary, that of Corinne Murray, who with her husband ran the local laundry. She seems to have been a cut above the general intelligence of Mansfield; as a Catholic, she introduced Rose to a priest from nearby Cabool, who was "the only person I've met in a year and a half who understands my usual English—it's horribly disconcerting to try to talk to these one-syllable people—and who not only isn't quite taken aback by an idea, but indeed is actually interested in it." Father Gillison offered her an engagement with religion quite the opposite from the local "Holy Rollers," whose meetings were an occasional entertainment. Rose and Gillison played chess together at times, a game she had taken up with Corinne; it occupied many of their evenings, though Rose seldom won.[23]

The year slipped by in a rhythm of such little joys and similar alarms. Troub was called one night to deliver a baby at the tenant house, and again to shoot a rat beneath the refrigerator. Mr. Bunting ran away, and for days Rose searched and advertised in the county, until he was found sixty miles from home. Her fainting spells began again; she fell and bit through her lower lip in a brutal cut. She began to develop a sense of the immense momentum of everyday reality. "I believe that most lives are exciting," she wrote one day in her journal, "intensely emotional daily, about little things, that most Americans are vaguely decent persons, vulgar, self-centered, insensitive, stupid, but well-meaning." It was at about this time that she read Vina Delmar's *Bad Girl* and argued to Catherine Brody that "it illustrates the so-shallow, almost externalized, whole life of ordinary, perhaps the only simply healthy people. And that *therefore*, and for no other reason, Vina Delmar may be a great realist." And then she woke one summer morning with a title and theme in mind: "*Victory.* . . . Given a quite commonplace life, to achieve within it a sense of completeness & victory. Bunting wants to run away, I let him go—and thought, victory only through defeat. Yield and relax, give up (not the fight) the struggle. Death is perhaps like that." Was this the book she was meant to write?[24]

Catherine Brody had come for a long stay, and Genevieve Parkhurst for several shorter ones, so for a time four typewriters were at work in Rocky Ridge farmhouse. Rose offered them a quiet place to work and congenial company and conversation in the evenings, an informal writers' colony. From them she got the intellectual stimulation and moral support most of Mansfield could not give her; for although Rose had a social circle of local women she saw regularly, she could not but chafe under their narrow vision and occasional mistrust of her manners if not of her morals. It was worth her reputation to smoke in public, and as for the occasional male visitor, well. . . .

> The Embroidery Club met last week—it meets every month—and at the conclusion of the afternoon, delicious refreshments were served to the members and guests, who then left thanking their hostess for a very enjoyable afternoon. I always spend the afternoon hemstitching a sheet. Verne Freeman and Jessie Fuson talk mostly about flowers. Maude Reynolds Hensley picks at me, hav-

ing a concealed (not too well concealed, even to my face, and O ye Gods behind my back—!) opinion that it's queer how I got my money, and anyway I haven't got as much as I'd like to make out, and more than that, she can remember me when. Troub's back ruffles up and she dashes to the fray. For example, Maude says, giggling lightsomely and staring, "Do you know, I never saw a *lady* smoke—ah—before." And Troub answers with the friendliest astonishment, "Really? Why, how queer. Where have you been all your life?" Or Maude says, "Of course, *our* dog is registered." And Troub pounces; "Registered? Not with the American Kennel Club?—No, I wouldn't have thought so. Who was his grandfather? —Oh, don't you? We always get *at least* that much of a pedigree, with our dogs." It makes Troub mad to have Maude pick on me. It makes Maude mad to see me hemming *linen* sheets. Maude agrees with the washerwoman, Mrs. Young, that there's something awfully funny about the number of sheets this house sends to the wash. Who ever heard of changing beds every other day? Anyone can guess what that means—(whisper)—*men*. Mr. Craig's car has been *seen*, standing in our yard, at *midnight!* Well, no wonder the sheets have to be changed so often. The Bridge Club is meeting at my mother's, tomorrow night. I am doing the refreshments. . . .

The recipient of this delicious letter was Mary Margaret McBride, who had by now made a successful transition from newspaper reporting to writing free-lance articles for the major magazines. She was trying to write some short stories and had sent a couple of manuscripts to Rose for criticism. Rose "ran them through the typewriter," and offered voluminous advice, as she had done for Troub, for Louis Stellman, and, of course, for Frederick O'Brien. That tender subject had surfaced again in a column by Heywood Hale Broun, and Rose was at some pains in a letter to him to protest that her "ghosting" did not extend to the facts of the narrative: "if it be protested that 'ghosting' is outside literary ethics, I think that point of view very far fetched in this case. My effort was to put on paper Mr. O'Brien's personality and his stories *as he told them* in conversation." Was this in fact the kind of book she was meant to write? The sense of having been used, and badly paid for it, presented itself inevitably in a sexual metaphor; it connected with her sense of having been abused by Sherwood Anderson, Josef Bard, and the copy-writers for *Cindy;* and in a further extension of the metaphor she could sympathize and rage with Dorothy Thompson at the corrupt world that writers labored in. For Dorothy, at about this time, had found her book on Russia plagiarized by Theodore Dreiser—who, she claimed, had spread the rumor that they had been lovers, and that she had used the opportunity to steal from *his* notes.[25]

A challenge to self-knowledge appeared as Rose encountered a questionnaire in the final number of the *Little Review.* She could not refrain from writing out the questions and her responses in her journal:

1. What should you most like to do, to know, to be?
   I should most like to travel in strange remote parts of the earth and to enjoy it while I'm doing it—not getting too tired and dirty.
2. Why wouldn't you change places with any other human being?
   I would change places with any young woman—about 20—with intelligent, simple, harmonious parents, good health, good breeding, and a cultured background.
3. What do you look forward to?
   I look forward to a mediocre old age.
4. What do you fear most from the future?
   I fear most being crippled or (inevitably) losing my teeth.
5. What has been the happiest moment of your life? The unhappiest?
   The happiest moment of my life was the moment I lighted a match in the sunshine, in the Tartar market of Tiflis. The unhappiest moment is that recurrent one in which I realize Time and Death.
6. What do you consider your weakest characteristics? Your strongest? What do you like most about yourself? Dislike most?
   The characteristics weakest in me: self-confidence, prudence, forethought, industry, will, unity of purpose, discrimination, presence of mind. Strongest characteristics: restlessness, tenacity, imagination (fancy), impulsiveness, generosity with money or things, desire to *acquire* (things, experience, information), nervous irritability, morbid sympathy, vanity, recklessness. I most like my intelligence. I most dislike my appearance.
7. What things do you really like? Dislike?
   I like: dancing, good talk—ideas in talk, luxurious living, beautiful houses and gardens, the Winged Victory, Italian Primitives in the Louvre, the sea, the desert, salted peanuts, the "rich" feeling in getting checks, linen sheets, lyric poetry, good department stores, Fifth Avenue, moving pictures or the theatre, smoking, dawn, sensation of physical cleanliness. Dislike: other people's untidiness, personalities, vulgarity, lack of symmetry, stupidity, dieting (all care of the body), dogs, work (especially writing cheap stuff), automobiles, poverty, desserts.
8. What is your attitude toward art today?
   I have no view of art.
9. What is your world view? (Are you a reasonable being in a reasonable scheme?)
   I am a partly reasonable being in chaos.
10. Why do you go on living?
    I enjoy living.[26]

And so she did, moment by moment and day by day in the simple pleasures that required little labor or thought. It was a sunlight life, but nothing ignited her to flame; and in those recurring moments when she realized Time and Death she sought some scheme that might kindle her into action again. On August 15, 1929, she turned to her notebook with a plan: "I resolve that next year I shall travel." She would give Rocky Ridge farmhouse over to the tenant farmer with a caretaker's salary of four hundred dollars a year; if she continued her rental payments to her mother at sixty dollars a month, "for about $100.00 a month I can buy freedom. I must first pay off debts." No doubt this scheme continued at the back of her mind through September and October as she and Troub readied Rocky Ridge farmhouse for the winter with a new automatic steam-heating system and traveled back and forth to Springfield and St. Louis for shopping and dental work. They were in St. Louis on October 29 when the stock market crashed—and they could not believe the news, or, at least, could regard it merely as a temporary low in a market that would always rise. Of more concern was that Troub had lost two valuable rings. Only a week later could they take it seriously, and only after a lapse of years could Rose come back to her diary and note the event that would reshape her life: "This was the day of the Great Crash—the evening that I said to Troub, knowing it but not believing it, 'This is the end.'"[27]

Rose at three,
Spring Valley,
Minnesota.

Rose and Spookendyke, ca. 1896.

Rose at seventeen,
Crowley, Louisiana.

Rose, ca. 1906,
perhaps in her
Kansas City days.

Rose in San Francisco,
ca. 1918. Published in
Sunset, it marked her
emergence as a writer
for national magazines.

Laura Ingalls
Wilder in
middle age.

Gillette Lane,
ca. 1912.

Rose at the
Hetch-Hetchy
Dam site,
ca. 1916.

Rose on one of her
walking tours in
France, ca. 1921.

Rose in exotic
costume, Europe,
ca. 1923.

Ragusa (Dubrovnik),
the city of Rose's
dream-vision, 1920s.

Rose and
Isabelle, 1925.

Dorothy
Thompson,
ca. 1922.

Helen
Boylston at
Rocky Ridge
Farm,
ca. 1925.

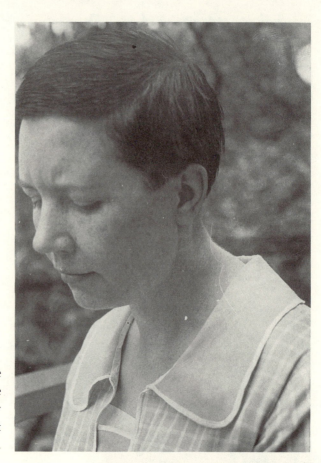

Rose at Rocky Ridge
Farm, 1925. Picture
probably taken by
Helen Boylston and sent
to Guy Moyston.

Rose and dogs
at Rocky Ridge
Farm, 1929.

Fremont
Older,
ca. 1930.

Rexh Meta in his Cambridge
robes, ca. 1932.

John Turner in
Europe, 1939.

English stone cottage Rose built for her
parents at Rocky Ridge, ca. 1930.

Farmhouse at
Rocky Ridge,
ca. 1957.

Rose interviewing Harold Stassen's mother, 1939.

Laura and Almanzo Wilder, ca. 1942.

Rose in her
Danbury
kitchen, 1960.

$\mathcal{T}$HE GHOST RETURNS

This kind of writing is called "ghosting," and no writer
of my reputation ever does it.

What gradually became abundantly clear was that any hope of financial independence had ended with the market crash. The end was not dramatic, as it was for those speculators who had bought heavily on margin and found their paper fortunes gone overnight. Rather, Rose and Troub (and Mama Bess) had mostly invested money already in hand, and for some time they could look upon occasional rallies in the long decline of the market as signs of a return to normalcy. The first great drop did alarm them ("Troub nearly insane with depression," Rose noted in November); but then they settled in to continue their usual round of life while waiting for things to improve. Palmer and Company was late with its annual report of their accounts, but continued with optimistic weekly newsletters, which Mama Bess, noting their blank reverse sides, prudently used as scrap paper. Rose and Troub had fallen into the habit of drawing dividends plus part of their capital gains each quarter, a practice Rose sometimes noted by putting the word "dividend" in quotes. The company managed to pay fourth-quarter dividends, but shortly George Q. Palmer began to close out individual accounts, carrying their remaining assets in the larger company account and ceasing individual reports. By April of 1930, the newsletter was no longer optimistic, and by June Rose's portfolio had lost half its value. The "dividends" that she and Troub continued to draw from their accounts were clearly neither earnings nor gains, but Troub continued in a thoughtless optimism and Rose could not quite bring herself to believe that she would have to rely solely on what she could earn from her typewriter to support the establishment she had built up around her. Once it was finally clear to her what had happened, she summarized her personal crash in her journal:

> This period of "depression" is as interesting as a war and I am
> sorry I have not kept a record of it from the first. My experience
> has been apparently . . . typical of America-in-general, i.e., the
> Middle West which *is* America. I believed everything, was completely on the surface, up on the crest of the wave. . . . The little
> breaks in the market did not disturb us because the market always

recovered; they were explained as "technical adjustments." The break on Friday—Nov., or Oct., 1929—worried me a little. I spoke of it to Troub who said in effect, "Don't be a fool."—On the next Tuesday when we got Monday's paper & she read the market news aloud, I said—"Our accounts are gone—this is the end." One of these feeling-whitefaced-&-staring moments. But that wore off in time. A kind of momentum carried us on. Underneath, however, worry began.[1]

Before the shock of the new order settled completely upon her, at the end of 1929 Rose treated herself to a trip to New York City. She could afford it only because Genevieve Parkhurst offered her accommodations in her apartment; but even so she spent money she soon regretted. Her spirits were revived, however, by renewing old friendships; and it was worth the trip just to see Dorothy Thompson again, the first time since Paris in 1926. And finally she met Sinclair Lewis, whose marriage to Dorothy had provoked Rose's defensive growls and deep-seated fears. Lewis's notorious initial charm, however, won Rose over at once, and an evening of wide-ranging talk dispelled her misgivings. "I like him," she confided to her diary. "So few men . . . have minds that run under their own power," she wrote Dorothy later. Mary Margaret McBride and Stella Karn took her to the theater; she met with Major Morris and Frank America to talk over old times in the Near East Relief; she saw the Haders and went to Croton to visit Floyd Dell; Guy Moyston and Jacques Marquis took her automobile riding; and ex-convict Jack Black from her San Francisco days, whose newspaper autobiography she had "ghosted," himself now an author and lecturer of some notoriety, sent her roses on her birthday. She arrived back in Mansfield on December 24 bearing special pastries bought in New York to be served at a Christmas Eve party for the Justamere and Embroidery Clubs. The new year brought her usual sober assessment of the past and future: 1929 had been a "wasted year"; for 1930 she resolved to "pay debts; save money; try to read systematically."[2]

||

Her problem was to write enough to pay current bills, let alone outstanding debts, and it would be a long time before she would again have money to save. The year would be a painful one of failing self-confidence, random distractions, and periodic depression. Actually, her production would not fall off significantly from earlier or later years; it simply could not meet the commitments she had assumed to her parents, to Rexh Meta, and to her own sense of how she ought to live; and as she flogged her brain for ideas for stories and puttered through days when she could not work, her guilt and frustration erupted through the daily trivial entries in her diary. January 30: "This life is really nauseating." February 16: "Two years in the States. Comfortable & hateful place built here. Parents comfortably established." She awoke on March 2 remembering her earlier realization that "I shall never have what I want." Now, she feared, " 'I shall never have more than I have now.' But I do not want to believe that this is the end, though contentment would be a relief, restful." March 30: "So horribly blue that dying seems a relief."

As the Depression deepened and advertising revenue dropped, the magazines became cautious in buying fiction, preferring to draw for a time on backlogs of already purchased manuscripts. Rose began to encounter successive rejections of her work; and when in May Carl Brandt reported a sale to *Country Gentleman*, it was the first money she had earned since the preceding October, before the Crash. In the interval, Troub carried them from her private income, which left Rose further in debt. They began to consider other sources of income, for a time cattle-farming, which Troub, who spent long hours on horseback with the dogs, began to think an ideal occupation. In April, Dorothy Thompson arrived for a brief visit en route from California to New York to join her husband. Rose had paved Dorothy's way to a meeting with Fremont Older, delighting in bringing together her two most admired friends: Dorothy she described to Older as "one of the most beautiful of living creatures"; Older she prefigured as "an old oak, embittered by many storms, that nevertheless dwarfs all of these younger growths." The two women continued their correspondence during Dorothy's California sojourn, as Dorothy reported on Rose's old haunts and on a striking visit to Robinson Jeffers. On her return trip, Dorothy arrived in Mansfield seven months pregnant, which drew out Rose's maternal solicitude; but she also brought Rose the rumor of a traveling correspondent's job for the *New York Evening Post*. Rose eagerly made application and solicited Fremont Older's good word for her; but that job too was frozen by a budget-conscious management.[3]

As usual, her correspondence with Older provided an outlet for her thoughts about broader social issues. Ostensibly, she was continuing her debate with him over prison reform, but what regularly emerged was her insistence on individual responsibility and initiative. As one who had begun in poverty and had energetically supported herself and others for twenty-five years, she was appalled at the coddling of prisoners Older advocated and she resented them as a drain on the working poor. Older waxed rhapsodic over an upright old well-digger he had discovered living contentedly on a pittance of earnings and a small pension and wanting little more than a warm place in the sun: Rose pointed out that it was a good thing for the old man that someone else worked hard enough to produce a surplus to support his pension, and she praised the taste for luxury that kept people working. It was clear to her that Older's vision of a whole society was obscured by his sentimental concern for individual pain, while she was willing to accept suffering in the world as the natural consequence of normal human striving. "There's probably no such thing as Life; that's probably just an imaginary abstraction we've created in our head. There's probably nothing but living things. Living seems to depend on killing, too; nothing lives without doing it. . . . Agriculture begins in a discrimination against often very beautiful plants, which must desire to live as much as any others do."[4]

By midsummer she was behind in her payments to her mother and to the furniture store in Springfield. Rexh would need $250 by October 1 and she did not know where she would get it. Her head was empty of ideas for her own work, but she read ceaselessly. Sigrid Undset's *Kristin Lavrensdater* left her emotionally bent for days and provoked her to "resolve to fight my lifelong habit of constant and indiscriminate reading, which in my case has been little more than a drug habit." But by August she noted, "Have continued to read steadily." She rediscovered the native Ozark fox-hunting culture, and spent a number of lovely evenings on the hillside, listening to the hounds in the distance pursuing the fox that by tradition would be run but never killed.[5]

Into the midst of these distractions her mother brought her a manuscript to work on. Although Rose did not know it, she was about to begin the most important work of her life. For at least twenty years, Mama Bess had thought of writing the story of her life as a child on the American frontier. Now she had completed a factual, first-person narrative of her life from her childhood in the forests of Wisconsin to the prairies of Kansas and Dakota—in effect, her autobiography. Rose took this in hand much as she had Frederick O'Brien's *White Shadows*. During a ten-day stint in May she lopped off the early section set in Wisconsin and ran at least two drafts of the remainder through her typewriter, producing a manuscript of about a hundred pages entitled "Pioneer Girl." She thought it might run as a serial in one of the women's magazines and she sent it off for Carl Brandt to consider. She then worked up the earlier portion into a third-person narrative of twenty-some pages entitled "When Grandma Was a Little Girl" that she and her mother envisioned as text for a picture-book for small children, something similar to the books that Berta and Elmer Hader had been doing. This she apparently sent off to Berta Hader, perhaps over Mama Bess's signature, as her mother's "juvenile" with a request for Berta's help in placing it with a publisher.[6]

During this period Mama Bess made it known that for her wedding anniversary, August 25, she would like to make a trip to her old home in South Dakota and, as Rose noted, "will need, must have money then." Rose promised that she would get the money for her by that date. But two weeks later no money had come in, and the day after Rose had written Rexh promising him his $250 for Cambridge Mama Bess brought up the subject again. "My mother came over for the afternoon and says they can not afford to make the trip to Dakota. I am a fool and a failure. Why was I such a fool as ever to get into this mess?" Two days later she was back at work revising her mother's manuscript ("She says she wants prestige rather than money," Rose recorded, failing to note that this was a luxury she herself could not afford.) She was still working on it a week later when Carl Brandt wired that he had sold another of Rose's stories. She at once telephoned Mama Bess offering the Dakota trip as an anniversary present; Mama Bess pondered the offer a week before deciding not to go. "They will not go to Dakota," Rose wrote, "but want the money to spend on ponds & meadows here—and may go south in the winter. God! I need money." Three days after this she completed her mother's "juvenile"; ten days later she paid Mama Bess $250 of the annual five hundred she had promised and turned again to another rewrite of the "pioneer story."[7]

The events of the summer epitomize the bondage Rose labored under; and it is not hard to see Mama Bess jerking the silver cord. The little girl who had been made to feel her parents' misfortunes so keenly still suffered when her mother denied herself pleasures, and Mama Bess had perfected the power of the martyr's covert control. Despite all that Rose had lavished on her in recent years, no tribute would be enough; and now as Rose began to stumble while the nation collapsed around her, her mother made sure that Rose would feel her burden of guilt again. By September Rose had finished for the time being with her mother's manuscript and turned to another formulaic domestic-adventure story for the women's magazine market—something, she hoped, that would bring in another check. "Did 4 pp. new story. Walked over and spent afternoon with my mother, who walked home with me, I heartsick at all this wrangling & eternal pulling & tugging at me from all sides. Why can't I be left alone?" Her spirits were not helped when she finished the story and the visiting Genevieve Parkhurst opined that "it will sell but isn't the work I should be doing. It *is* bad policy. Went walking on the hilltop with my mother who wants a new will." A week later she had begun another story, which hit a snag. "Tea on hilltop with my mother who again talks about property and wills. Said I wished I'd never made a cent, then she and papa could be supporting me." In her distraction, it seemed also that her oldest stays were failing her. She had written Fremont Older, seeking in his wisdom some light on the country's situation but had been disappointed in his reply: "All friends fail in dry times," she wrote at the head of one of his letters. Carl Brandt's reticence about her manuscripts she interpreted as rejection of her need for support. "Letter from Carl who has sent Dangerous Curve to L.H.J. & will wire any good news. Urges me to come to New York. But he is really indifferent. Why not when Older is?"[8]

III

She did want to go to New York, not only to get away from the farm but to push her work with editors. But she did not have the money to make the trip as she wished, as she explained to Rexh Meta:

> . . . if an editor sees me wearing an old hat or a coat that doesn't look as though it had come from one of the best and most frightfully expensive shops, then he thinks that my work can't be very good or I'd be more successful than that, and even if I do succeed in selling him something, he offers me his very lowest price for it. While on the other hand if I appear lavishly prosperous and give him the impression that I don't need money at all and don't care whether I sell anything or not, then he pays me his highest prices for fear if he doesn't I'll simply say he can't have my work. It's all very idiotic, but that's the way it is. So if I have to go to New York, I'll have to live at what is called "a good address," and I'll have to have new clothes. And how to do that with no money is a problem.

Indeed, as she confessed to Rexh, she had less than ninety dollars in hand. A partial answer came with an invitation to visit Mary Margaret McBride, whose Park Avenue address would provide an appropriate base of operations. And on her arrival on October 15 she was greeted with a telephone call from Carl Brandt's office that another of her stories had sold to *Country Gentleman*. It was only her third sale of the year; it brought her income for the period to little more than three thousand dollars, but it solved the immediate problem of financing her stay.[9]

In New York in the autumn of 1930, she found concentrated the fear and misery of the Depression that had touched her in Mansfield, but her report of it to Mama Bess was tough-minded and breezy. Hoover was doomed, she saw, and she was amazed at the terror that the tiny group of American Communists ("hardly a chemist's trace in our population") had produced in the business and financial community, who were afraid of revolution among the unemployed. "And right away hundreds of thousands of dollars are thrown as it were to the pursuing wolves. Whereas in reality there's no more communism among these masses of unemployed than there is in your living room." The apple-sellers on the street corners she saw from the point of view of the farmers, claiming to have discovered that the phenomenon originated in a promotional scheme by the agent of the Oregon Apple Growers, "and the whole population of greater New York is walking about helplessly with hands full of apples."

> The unemployed thereby makes from $2.50 to $5.00 a day. This unemployed thing is rather absurd, anyhow; there are only about 3,000,000 out of work in the country, and even in the best of boom times, we normally have about 1,500,000 unemployed. But the idea

is certainly selling the Oregon farmers' apples. And what with lavish aid from Wall Street, being unemployed is quite a good occupation in this town.

There was the usual round of parties with old friends, but this was a business trip in which Carl Brandt set up meetings for her with editors she wished to see. Brandt had not been enthusiastic about her mother's manuscript, but Rose pushed it, unsuccessfully, as a nonfiction serial with editors at *Good Housekeeping, Ladies' Home Journal,* and *Saturday Evening Post*. Graeme Lorimer of the *Post* termed it "most intelligent writing," she reported to her mother. Lorimer had suggested that it might be fictionalized, but "I know you don't want to work it over into fiction," Rose concluded. There is no indication of what success she had in promoting her own work, although apparently she told Thomas B. Costain of the *Post* some details of her father's life that he thought would make a good story. Her business with editors concluded, she went up to Croton to visit the Dells again, where Floyd, perhaps echoing Genevieve Parkhurst's concern over Rose's wasted talents, loyally predicted that within three years she would write a good book, "real yet romantic . . . true without being dull & beautiful without being a lie." She also picked up some news that gave her a bit a jolt. "Did I tell you Guy Moyston is getting married?" she wrote her mother. Moyston's bride was a young editor at *Harper's Bazaar,* twenty-seven years of age.[10]

At this point there was little to keep her in the East any longer, but her stay was prolonged by the announcement of the award of the Nobel Prize for literature to Sinclair Lewis. Rose had, of course, seen Dorothy Thompson again; and when, in the next week, the Nobel award was announced, Dorothy turned immediately to Rose to provide care for her baby, now six months old, while she accompanied Lewis to Stockholm for the award. Quite apart from the obligations of friendship, the idea appealed to Rose. She would have charge of a Westport home within commuting distance of the city, and she would have at hand a French maid and chauffeur and a German nurse on whom she could practice her languages. She took time to companion Dorothy through some painful dental surgery in New York and then went up to Westport on November 30.[11]

She took with her a piece of desperately needed hackwork. For she had met Lowell Thomas, who was then still largely a print journalist. His forte was narratives of exotic adventure, his own and other people's; as a world traveler and associate editor, he had published frequently in *Asia,* and he knew her friends Elsie Weil and Gertrude Emerson of that magazine. No doubt he had heard of Rose's work on *White Shadows;* he approached her to commission at a thousand dollars each the revision of some first-person narratives he had collected from obscure adventurers. As she settled in for what would be a three-month stay in Westport, she turned her attention to the first of several manuscripts she would ghost for Thomas. She needed the money badly, and the work so occupied her that she did not have time even to answer Rexh Meta's several letters inquiring about her. "The Sinclair Lewises returned from Europe on March 3rd [1931]," she was finally able to write him from Rocky Ridge. "Up till midnight on the first I was working like mad to finish a book."

> The fact is that I was doing all this secretly, for another person who has more money than literary talent hired me to do two books at $1000. a piece. This kind of work is called "ghosting," and no writer of my reputation ever does it. . . . I wrote one whole book in November and December, and another in part of January and February. Something like 180,000 words in all. That was why I was working from sixteen to eighteen hours a day and toward the last twenty hours; and of course I had no time to write a letter even to you. I got the check for the second book on March fifth and sent you half of it. . . .[12]

She never faced squarely that her reputation as a ghost for Frederick O'Brien had gotten her the job, nor that what she was doing for Lowell Thomas was exactly what she was doing for Mama Bess. For during her stay in Westport, she had also been forwarding her mother's interests. Berta Hader had been successful in interesting children's editor Marian Fiery of Knopf in "When Grandma Was a Little Girl"; and when Rose went from Westport to Nyack for a visit on February 15 she found that Fiery had already written her mother, expressing strong interest in the manuscript if it were expanded to twenty-five thousand words and filled with authentic detail of pioneer life. The book would become not a picture book for little children but a story for young readers. Rose discussed the matter with Fiery and wrote her own letter of instruction to Mama Bess. Most revealing, perhaps, is that Mama Bess seems at this point to have had little idea of what Rose had made of her original manuscript, as Rose has to tell her not only where to find it in her files but also just what it is: "It is your father's stories, taken out of the long PIONEER GIRL manuscript, and strung together, as you will see." Rose has seen immediately what has to be done in the new format: the action will expand from one winter to a cycle of a year, and on this axis will be strung as much remembered detail as can be retrieved from the original manuscript and from some other tablets that Mama Bess has filled with her recollections. Rose urges her mother to start writing down the material at once. "If you find it easier to write in the first person, write that way. I will change it into the third person, later." And on the matter of the ghostly hand behind the manuscript, she reassures her mother that "I have said nothing about having run the manuscript through my own typewriter, because the changes I made, as you will see, are so slight that they could not even properly be called editing."[13]

IV

"Heartsunk, arrived Mansfield," she entered in her diary for March 20, 1930. Indeed, she had no work of her own going forward; on her horizon loomed two more manuscripts for Lowell Thomas and the promised revisions of her mother's juvenile. Among her baggage as she returned was a large bundle of letters, the hundreds she had written to Guy Moyston, now returned to her upon Moyston's marriage; she read them over and put them away, and in time she would even think quarrying something from them for publication. She had severed another relationship in this watershed period as well: after more than a decade with Carl Brandt, she had begun to question his judgment regarding her manuscripts and she had heard rumors of his failing powers. Just before leaving New York she had a meeting with George Bye, who was agent to Catherine Brody and Lowell Thomas; he agreed to add her to his list of writers and, later, to handle her mother's work as well. Rose's thanks for this second service were deprecating: "It's really awfully decent of you to bother with this small fry. . . . And I don't expect you really to bother."[14]

Within a month she had completed a third manuscript for Lowell Thomas, and shortly after she had mailed it off Mama Bess brought her more manuscript pages to be worked into the juvenile for Knopf; Marian Fiery had wanted a better title and it now was called "Little House in the Woods." Rose was working on a short story of her own at the moment and set her mother's pages aside until she had finished. She was also anxiously awaiting an installment payment due for her ghost-work: "Very blue & miserable all day. Wrote Lowell Thomas I want that $500.00." "L.T. should be reading my air-mail letter today." The check arrived and with it an infusion of energy; in four days of steady work she enlarged her mother's book to the required length. On the third day of this outburst, her mother arrived to check on progress. "Almost finished juvenile. My mother came over in afternoon & read it. I gave her $500.00 check & am paid up with her till 1932. She & my father stayed to dinner." Three more days of work produced a clean copy, and as the last pages came out of the typewriter Mama Bess arrived to read the final chapters. The next day, May 27, it was in the mail to Marian Fiery; "I don't know just where or how I come into this, do you?" Rose queried Fiery, pushing herself into the background as a mere adviser to her mother. The same post brought Rose a rare relief. "Letter from Rexh says he will not need money from me next year."[15]

The following week brought Rose relief of a different sort, as her parents left on the long-deferred trip to South Dakota: ". . . astounded to see them start on the trip," she noted. "Dreamed parents returned tonight, I raged that I must leave here." She had in fact been working since February on a plan that would send her to Venezuela for Lowell Thomas;

in the end it came to nothing, in part because Thomas was in difficult financial straits as well. Rose was working on another manuscript for him and he was having trouble finding money to pay her: "L. T. wants me to wait: says times are desperate." He ended by giving her checks postdated by several months. After three weeks her parents returned, their platitudinous "East west, home is best" driving her into a silent fury. As the summer heat deepened, the locusts sang deafeningly in the trees at night and Rose could not sleep. Her stories did not sell, and as she waited for Thomas's checks she had to put off the wages due her cook and hired man. She endured a series of trips for dental work in St. Louis and Springfield, while Mr. Bunting's illnesses drove her to distraction. From New York came word that Stella Karn had lost her publicist's job; she and Mary Margaret McBride would have to give up their Park Avenue apartment. On September 19 came the word from Knopf: "My mother's juvenile is accepted . . . . Am feeling grand."[16]

The euphoria would be short-lived, for still more calamities were gathering on the horizon. Even as Rose negotiated through her new agent for just the right contract for Mama Bess, decisions were being made at higher levels at Knopf to cut costs by discontinuing their juvenile department. Word reached Rose in early November, and as she and Mama Bess tried to confront this disappointment life trickled maddeningly by. Now between projects for Lowell Thomas, Rose was trying to get her own work on track again; a new story tentatively called "Courage" was taking shape in her mind but she could not get it to move on paper. From San Francisco, Older tried to put her on the track of another ghost job: the Countess Alexandra Tolstoi was on a lecture tour describing her experiences following the Russian Revolution and was interested in putting a manuscript into publishable form. George Bye suggested that such books were a drug on the market; but Rose pleaded for encouragement: "This kind of thing doesn't cut down my own output. I can keep working on my own stuff right through a job like this"; but "my connection with a ms. like this must not be known at all." The Countess's typing was bad and her English was worse, and Rose decided finally not to attempt this job for the woman who had sold her a winter coat in Constantinople, who had dismissed her as Peggy Marquis's secretary, and who now had no recollection of having ever met her.[17]

Stymied in her writing, Rose worked with the hired man clearing rocks in the gorge behind the house, hoping to find a cave and spring, planning to build a rock garden; in the evenings she hemmed curtains while Troub read aloud from Rose's old newspaper serial, "Soldiers of the Soil." Mr. Bunting had run away and been returned for reward so often that now he was kidnapped and held for the usual five dollars in ransom. Into this stalled life on November 19 came a bombshell from the East that Rose recorded in headline letters in her diary: *PALMER INCOME STOPPED.*

I was playing chess with Corinne, & Troub handed me the letter to read. What an awful fool that girl was! Naturally I didn't turn a hair, & she sat on the divan staring at me wild-eyed all the rest of the afternoon and starting & saying "wha-a-t!" when spoken to. Corinne naturally all agog—When Corinne left, Troub announced her decision: at last, after five years of idleness, she was going to start out as a short story writer. I told her definitely I could not support her while she was doing it and that she had better go to New York & get a nursing job while I still had the money to pay her fare. This was decided.

The next day Troub wrote to a former employer asking for a job, then went to town for a permanent wave. She would go back East to her father temporarily; he too had lost his savings in the market, but his income as a dentist held up. Troub would take the Buick and attempt to sell it, applying Rose's share of the proceeds to the large debt Rose still owed her. On December 3 she departed, taking Mr. Bunting's companion, the Scots terrier Sparkle, with her, as well as Rose's check for $125 and leaving Rose a bill for her new traveling clothes. Four days later Troub was in New Hampshire, and Rose was in Rocky Ridge farmhouse alone. A partnership of six years was over.[18]

In the interval, some good news had come. Marian Fiery had lost her job at Knopf, but she retained a faith in the manuscript of "Little House in the Woods"; apparently she passed it along to Virginia Kirkus of Harper Brothers, who accepted it on a single reading. Mama Bess was given this cheering news while Rose and Troub were still trying to come to terms with the Palmer bankruptcy, which they kept from Rose's mother because she, too, had money invested there. Apparently there was some hope that one of Palmer's funds would survive with Mama Bess's money, but a December 9 telegram from Troub brought news that dashed that hope. Rose had advised the investment, so the blame for the loss was hers. "Too horribly upset about my mother's money to work," she noted. "Wrote letters all day. Have $963.84 in bank." She carried the tidings to her mother the next day: "She took it very well, considering."[19]

Troub gone, Rose's birthday had passed on December 5, 1931, with only a quiet dinner with her parents. "Forty-five today—and the world calls me *old!*" she observed. Despite his reassurances of the summer, Rexh again needed money, $110. She cabled "Money coming," and although she had less than fifty dollars not immediately committed, she was able to raise one hundred dollars to send him:

> The Springfield bank that went busted is going to pay about 5% of its deposits soon, and I had a telegram from my literary agent saying he's almost certain he's going to sell a story—the last one I sent him—for me. So I borrowed $75, which will be covered by the bank payments, and there you are. The point is that I can't be any worse off than I am; and if that story does sell I will have enough

to go on for two months more, and if it doesn't, I might as well
have nothing at all as to have this $100. which won't meet my bills
or do anything else for me. So you might as well have it.

As the letter left, a cable came from Rexh: "Better news. Cancel money."
She wrote him to keep the money for his future fees. The story she mentioned did not sell, and she went back to work on "Courage," hoping
to be able to go to England in June for Rexh's graduation. Just before
Christmas Mama Bess received news that her story, now entitled *Little
House in the Big Woods,* had been named a Junior Literary Guild Selection.
She now had prestige, and the money would soon follow. Summarizing
her own year, Rose wrote: "I am forty-five. Owe $8,000. Have in bank
$502.70. Paying $60 a month rent to my mother for this house." She
glanced to the top of the page, on which she had calculated since 1927 the
growth of her Palmer account, now defunct. Then she had written, "ambition much reduced—I now want $100,000 and a house when I am forty-
five." She now repeated in conscious irony her observation of four years
ago: "Nothing that I have intended has ever been realized!"[20]

V

Nineteen thirty-two would be a year of crisis and clarification. The early
months were spent in what she called an "agony of despondency," which
at best was a dull worry about bills and at worst an occasional attack of
panic. She had earned no money since October; by February she had no
idea how she would meet her March bills; and it would be April before
she earned anything again. Corinne Murray, now her closest friend, presented the laundry bills that Rose paid with outer calm and inner terror.
Genevieve Parkhurst wrote to borrow a hundred dollars, and Rose sent a
check. From South Dakota came a pathetic request for aid from her Aunt
Grace; Mama Bess perhaps helped out here. Late in January, Mama Bess
arrived with the proofs of her forthcoming book, and as Rose took a
break from correcting them she chanced upon a *McCall's* article entitled
"Are You Living Your Own Life?" In her diary she scrawled an emphatic
NO! She continued her work on manuscripts from Lowell Thomas, which
promised some more income from someone else's work; and when Thomas
suggested the chance of a trip to Malaysia for him, she spent a joyful day
reading up in the encyclopedia, then crashed into despondency again as
she assessed the likelihood of such a trip. In March, Mama Bess brought
her another manuscript, a compilation of Almanzo's early recollections
entitled "Farmer Boy." As Rose began this new task, she wrote to Genevieve Parkhurst and George Bye requesting any kind of work. Genevieve responded with a commission for an article; George Bye wrote,
"This is an awfully dark hour." Late in March arrived author's copies of

Little House in the Big Woods, "very well done." Mama Bess was now an author with a national audience.[21]

In April, checks from Lowell Thomas and Genevieve Parkhurst lightened the gloom somewhat, as did a breakthrough of a sort by her agent: George Bye placed a story of hers with the *Saturday Evening Post*, but at a humiliatingly low price. Rose would for years rail at the *Post* for paying in prestige rather than in cash; but this sale was the beginning of a connection that would be of major importance for her writing. And now, with money on hand to pay bills for a few months, she could pause to take stock of her situation:

> May 14, 1932. The boom, the famous "1929 bull market," did this for me: it took me out of the irresponsible "artist" class into the responsible householder class. The crash left me with nothing to support this position, yet because it is an obligation to my parents, to my servants, to—idiotically—the dog Bunting and the horse Molly—I can not bring myself to abandon it. Otherwise I would be rejoicing in going back to the days when I earned my daily bread usually the day after I had eaten it & lived wherever I happened to be.

It was time now to wrestle with her feelings, even as she wrestled with the circumstances of her life. In time, the long fret subsided into the peace of exhaustion, a delusive resignation:

> May 28, 1932. Looking for a notebook to write vagrant thoughts in, came across my diary of 1918. It brings back so vividly those young days in Sausalito. Fourteen years ago. I ask, what is my gain in fourteen years, and do not know.
>
> This morning, picking faded roses from the white-rose bush, in a chilly before-breakfast time, it came to me that my recent discovery of peace is really a surrender. "Come unto Me, all ye who are weary and heavy-laden, and I will give you peace." I too would believe in God if my subjective experience had coincided in time with a religious ceremony. I only sat on my bed, looking at and listening to the blessedness of rain after drought, and the cool refreshment of earth and grass seemed to spread through me. That was day before yesterday. Nothing has changed in my circumstances, I am still deep in debt, held here where I hate to be, grown old, losing my teeth, all that—and never anyone knowing I am here, so that I feel forgotten in a living grave. But for two days I have *felt* peace. The fever is gone.
>
> May 29. Then after all this, last night the agony came back as soon as the light snapped off. I am old, I am alone, a failure, forgotten, here in this alien place, I am losing my teeth. . . . I could not fight it. Turned on the light and read Sedgewick's LaFayette till my eyes burned out. This morning I accounted for the seizure by Mr. Palmer's letter of yesterday, saying that Troub has new clothes very becoming, & that when he was at the St. Regis

the other night she came in with her own party—Teresa, Major
Barbrook, and another man. I am so furiously envious of Troub, of
course. But now it occurs to me that all that nightmare misery
probably came from my idiocy in eating a whole plate of crackers
with a glass of milk after I went to bed. All my trouble is still my
old trouble of almost twenty years ago. I am not leading my own
life because any life must coalesce around a central purpose, and I
have none.

June 8, 1932. For days I have been blue, despondent, maintaining such cheerfulness as I could, only by great inner effort. I have
not been able to work. All this I have ascribed to my own personal
situation—growing old, needing dental work that I can't pay for,
having only enough money for one more month's expenses, seeing it slip between my fingers like sand, receiving no letters, being
quite forgotten by everyone, being a failure.

None of these facts had anything to do with my despair. My
whole trouble was that I am not master of my material in writing
my mother's second juvenile. It was a little job that seemed incon-
sequential—and is—and therefore it was able to do all this to me
without my knowing it—The truth is that for better or worse, no
matter how hopelessly a failure, I am a writer.

I am a writer. Nothing else in the world is so important to me—
to my own inner self—as writing is.

Recorded and for the first time realized, this eighth day of June,
1932, in my forty-sixth year.[22]

She had in fact been working on the manuscript of "Farmer Boy"
intermittently since March; from time to time Mama Bess would stop by
to read what she had written. Rose devoted most of May to it and did not
finish until August, shortly after completing the three-part story called
"Courage" that she had had in hand for almost a year. This conflict between her own and her mother's work was real in terms of the time it took
away from writing that would earn her living; she did believe that writing
for children trivialized her talents; and a latent resentment of her mother's
hold on her was beginning to surface. But this regular immersion in
family history had led her to a body of material that she could make use
of on her own. For even as she had wrestled with her private fear and
depression in her notebooks, she had been trying in her social and business contacts to whistle up the courage to go on. "But what's all this
gloom about, anyhow?" she questioned George Bye. "Me, I'm still blithe
in the best of all fascinating worlds." To Marian Fiery she wrote, "I don't
believe this terror of the future is justified by the facts."

The more I see of the public temper in this depression, the more
I'm reluctantly concluding that this country's simply yellow. Our
people are behaving like arrant cowards. And it's absurd. Nothing's fundamentally wrong; we're going to pull out of this quite all
right. Only we'd do it much sooner if everyone wasn't cringing

and crying and yelping like a scared pup. In spite of this hysteria of fright, I believe this winter is going to be better than the last, basically, and that by next year times [will] definitely be better.

She was beginning to think of the current depression in terms of the hard times following the Panic of 1893, which had dislodged her parents from South Dakota and fetched them up in Missouri—and they had come out all right. Just the previous year, during her visit to New York, she had spoken to Graeme Lorimer of the *Saturday Evening Post* so strikingly of her parents' and grandparents' cheer and courage during the legendary "hard winter" in Dakota that he was still thinking of it more than a year later. "Rose Wilder Lane told me the last time I saw her that she thought Easterners were yellow because they were so blue—even those who still had plenty to eat and a place to sleep," he wrote to Bye. "She told me of the struggles of her parents against pioneer conditions in the middle West and how they were still able to find something to laugh about no matter what their losses and hardships." He suggested that "an article which vividly portrayed these pioneer conditions could be made to speak for itself and it would be very wholesome medicine right now."[23]

"Graeme Lorimer's note confuses me rather," Rose wrote Bye, "because I can not do a first-person pioneer story myself. My gray hair makes me seem more ancient to him than I am. . . . Would they take a third-person fact-story of the HARD WINTER of '73, about my father and mother?" Bye suggested that Lorimer had confused Rose and her mother's book; but there is a certain confusion on Rose's part as well, as she seems to struggle to separate her writing identity from her mother's and her mother's material from her own. She followed up on the idea, however, with a synopsis of "The Hard Winter," which she suggested could be the basis of a series of short stories. Lorimer was not interested in this project, but he did encourage a single work to be distilled from it. To read that synopsis is to read a synopsis of what Laura Ingalls Wilder would eventually publish as *The Long Winter.*[24]

All of this stirring up of family history went on while Rose was struggling simultaneously with a Lowell Thomas manuscript, her mother's "Farmer Boy," and her own growing manuscript of "Courage." This story took as its material some of Mama Bess's accounts of the grasshopper plague, Charles Ingalls' trek east to earn money for his family, and the great winter blizzards on the plains; but it was an awkward size for magazine publication, really a novella, and she did not have much hope for it. Small checks from Lowell Thomas carried her through the summer, and as an act of faith she sent $150 to George Q. Palmer to buy her some good stocks—and persuaded Mama Bess to reinvest as well. But there was no money to travel to England for Rexh Meta's graduation from Cambridge, nor was there money to meet her domestic obligations if she went to the Far East for Lowell Thomas, and by the end of the summer she was in severe straits again: "Total assets in the world—$498. Can't work: no ideas." She decided to discharge Mrs. Carter, her cook and housekeeper. They wept together at the parting.[25]

But by now Rose had finished "Courage," which, as it had taken its material from family tales of the frontier life, now took a new title from a hymn sung for years in her mother's family and invoked by Mama Bess against the troubles of the Depression. As *Let the Hurricane Roar,* it was sold to the *Post* early in September of 1932. In the same month, Harper refused "Farmer Boy." Rose took her money and, with Corinne Murray driving, left on a motor trip across the country, arriving ultimately in New York City.[26]

OURAGE

All we have to do is remain invincible. . . .

The year and more Rose had been occupied with *Let the Hurricane Roar*, rolling revision after revision through her typewriter under the title of "Courage," had been a period of clearing vision as she tried to summon up the courage to face her problems; the working title had been deeply thematic and reflective of her own concerns in a way unlike anything she had ever written. Ultimately the process would become metaphysical and historical, but for the moment it involved simply herself and her family lore. In reimagining what she had always known about the struggles of her grandparents, Charles and Caroline Ingalls, to found a home on the prairie frontier, she discovered a model of the strength she needed to face the problems of immediate historical circumstance and her own chronic shortcomings. Earlier, when the burden of obligation had rested more lightly and the future had seemed brighter, she had doubted the reality of her essential self and the possibility of a personal subject matter; and she had plucked at Carl Brandt and Floyd Dell and Clarence Day for answers. To Clarence Day she had written, "Pioneer America, maybe. That is all right; but I don't care about it. Don't dislike it and I readily admit all the admirable qualities; I'm simply not interested. I was brought up on pioneer stories, and never a spark from me." Now the spark had been struck and she had produced the one work of hers that would remain continuously in print, a minor classic of frontier literature. In the process, she had discovered something she had managed to evade through years of hackwork: "I am a writer."[1]

But it did not really represent a discontinuity in her thought. Somewhere at bedrock was the Darwinian naturalism she had assimilated early in her intellectual life and that had given her first, an intense imaginative apprehension of life as individual struggle all along the biological chain, and second, a vision of history as the spectacular natural resultant among myriad contending lives: the Wandering Jew would be privileged to see it all, and she resented missing any of it. Within such a vision she was alive to the heroism both of the great man who could seize circumstance and alter history, such as Ahmet Zogu or Herbert Hoover, and of the little man, whose determined pursuit of his own interest, many times com-

pounded, equally made history: such was the burden of her letters of
social analysis to Fremont Older, Dorothy Thompson, and Rexh Meta.
But now Hoover was floundering, as was Ahmet in Albania; and if certitude were to be found anywhere it would have to be in more ordinary
people.

She had long had a suspicion of those who would cut themselves off
from the natural flow of human desire, such as the various blue-nose
Puritans, over-refined intellectuals, effete artists, hypocritical radicals,
and poseurs generally she had known. A few years earlier, she had responded with a "roar about [E. M.] Forster" to Dorothy Thompson's
report that he had asserted curiosity to be an attribute of a fourth-rate
mind. "Curiosity's our only salvation . . . ," Rose had fumed. "My protest is really against this habit of the intellectuals, of discarding the essentially *human* attributes as beneath their own high level intelligence. It
isn't a high level when it does that. He might as well say that hunger's an
attribute of a fourth-rate body. Curiosity's the hunger of the human mind."[2]

She would rapidly come to a similar mistrust of those who would
impose unnatural order through tradition or law, or accept an order alien
to basic human experience, the essentially Old World expedients. Her
experience in Europe had left her with a conviction that its civilization
was a spent force and, conversely, that American civilization was a fresh
start and the wave of the future. "I think I must stay in America and write
American stuff," she had advised herself the year before. "Sometimes I
can almost *feel* this." Now, as her country struggled in a dark hour, her
mother's attempt to recapitulate her own history brought Rose to seek in
it a way of understanding the nation's dilemma. *Let the Hurricane Roar*
was an exemplary tale of courage and self-reliance for Americans down
on their luck. Its heroine, a young woman alone in a sod dugout during
a Dakota winter, summons a traditional optimism as she writes to her
absent husband:

> We are having hard times now, but we should not dwell upon
> them but think of the future. It has never been easy to build up a
> country, but how much easier it is for us . . . than it was for our
> forefathers. I trust that, like our own parents, we may live to see
> times more prosperous than they have ever been in the past, and
> we will then reflect with satisfaction that these hard times were not
> in vain.

And shortly after, her native optimism tested by a blizzard that cuts her
off from all aid, she looks out over the frighteningly indifferent landscape
and discovers in herself an exhilarating insight:

> In that instant she knew the infinite smallness, weakness, of life in
> the lifeless universe. She felt the vast, insensate forces against
> which life itself is a rebellion. Infinitely weak and small was the

spark of warmth in a living heart. Yet valiantly the tiny heart continued to beat. Tired, weak, burdened by its own fears and sor-
rows, still it persisted, indomitably it continued to exist, and in
bare existence itself, without assurance of victory, even without
hope, in its indomitable existence among vast, incalculable, life-
less forces, it was invincible.

The story was, Rose wrote later, "a reply to pessimists. It was written
from my feeling that living is never easy, that all human history is a
record of achievement in disaster (so that disaster is no cause for despair),
and that our great asset is the valor of the American spirit—the unde-
feated spirit of millions of obscure men and women who are as valiant
today as the pioneers were in the past." So Rose had discovered what she
believed, and discovered as well the book she was meant to write. But to
live out that belief in her own life required a daily grapple with despair.[3]

||

Her trip to New York following the serial publication of *Let the Hurricane
Roar* was her usual one to friends in Nyack and Croton, and to her agent
and friends and publishers in the city. Earlier she had heard the view of
the future from the liberal East, where Genevieve Parkhurst offered a
fashionable theory of restructuring the country from the top down:

> Our whole system is cracking under our eyes and a newer & big-
> ger future [is] looming before us—one in which we will outgrow
> our swaddling clothes & come of age at last. Even the great finan-
> ciers know that the day of vast fortunes is over, that a five day
> week & 7-hour day is here, that industry will have to take smaller
> dividends so there will be work for all, and leisure, too. Some do
> not want to acknowledge it and they are staving it off—or trying
> to, rather—but judgment day is here.

But Rose was suspicious of the view from the top, and on this trip she was
interested in seeing how the country outside of New York was faring.
One of her first stops was a visit to earliest memories, as in Spring Valley,
Minnesota, she discovered people who still remembered the Wilders'
year of recuperation following their flight from the plains. "Mrs. Lamson
says, tell my mother to bring back the pie tin full of ginger bread she took
to Florida 41 years ago," she wrote back home. Her itinerary was a meandering line across the upper Midwest and Canada, through New England, and a return through Maryland, Virginia, and West Virginia. She
was heartened by the resilience of middle America, she said: everyone
reported that locally they were doing all right, but that they had heard it
was "tough everywhere else"; and for the destitute there were many

local relief agencies. Whatever the future might bring, it would be what the people wanted:

> . . . created by a hundred million human beings who are not so helpless as to create a manner of living that they don't like. The mass effect is the sum of innumerable little choices made hourly by these millions of individuals. . . . This country is created by, for, and of the lower classes, the hoodlums, roughnecks & hard boiled guys. The civilization they produce will be, obviously, not an aristocratic civilization. Nevertheless, this is not to say that it will not be a civilization.[4]

Rose returned from New York early in December of 1932, buoyed by a good reception of *Let the Hurricane Roar* among readers and editors. She had changed publishers, moving from Harper to Longmans, Green, who had agreed to bring out a hardcover edition of her novella in March. She promptly went to bed for three weeks of influenza; as she recovered, she copied into her journal passages from a letter from one of her readers, a well-educated businessman from Chicago. His family had been pioneers like hers, and he understood what she had been at in *Let the Hurricane Roar*:

> It is the kind of story which the American reading public needs to get back in thought to the American philosophy of life, in a time of great stress and personal complexity for us all. The realism did not distort the picture, as Hamlin Garland and so many who have written of the pioneers did, in losing the fine theme of achievement and artistic sense of mastery of a job and creation of something "out of the raw." It concludes on a high note of achievement, which I feel has been lost in our fiction dealing with the Rise of American Civilization. . . . If the American philosophy of life is to be understood and correctly interpreted, the pioneer experiences must be given realistically, but with the optimistic faith of the pioneers.

The writer summarized the history of his own parents, whose lives on the Nebraska plains paralleled that of the Ingalls in Dakota:

> The facts are not unique. It is the story of millions of the inarticulate pioneers who have made America and American civilization. Their composite experiences have gone to make what I believe to be an American philosophy of life, more fundamentally distinctive in civilization than anything which has come into world thought since the time of the Crusaders.
> The story of the American pioneer has not yet been truthfully told. It is a story of gigantic achievement, physically, spiritually, morally, which in the telling should reveal the primal forces which have gone into the making of America. A story which, rightly told, should lead the world back from the defeatist thinking of the

socialistic, militaristic, caste formula in which European thought
is so hopelessly involved. . . .

This story would, then, develop the broad theme that would sustain
Americans in the dark hours of contemporary history: ". . . triumphant
vindication of the freedom of the soul and of the power of men and
women under stress and trial to endure and to develop personal strength
and power from struggle, and to achieve satisfying places in life for themselves, and for those who come after them in the endless chain of life in
which we are all links."[5]

Rose could not have put it better herself. *Let the Hurricane Roar* had
opened the theme in her imagination; but it would be several years before
she could turn directly to it again. Meanwhile she had to earn a living
and deal with her mother's claim on this pioneer material.

Implicit in her own family history was the question of what becomes of
the pioneer once the pioneering is done. Her own parents had struggled
on the plains and had failed; and thirty years of hard-scrabble farming in
Missouri had given them a marginal prosperity that, without Rose's subsidy, threatened to disintegrate as they aged. Unimpressed with pioneer
virtues, she had herself shaken the Missouri clay from her shoes as soon
as she could, to become radically cosmopolitanized by the time she returned to her roots. And even as she longed for exotic adventure and
acknowledged a bohemian freedom from conventional morality, her natural style was a middle-class gentility in everyday life. Which was just
what her mother's had become, just as rapidly as she could afford it.
Mama Bess's endless club work, teas, and social hours, all duly reported in
the local paper, was mainline small-town American respectability through
and through, and Rose chafed under it even as she went compulsively
through its rituals. In more ways than she liked to admit, she was her
mother's daughter; and as they drew closer than ever before in the production of her mother's books, Rose began to experience a complex revulsion, something of a delayed adolescent rebellion. "Not feeling so good,"
she noted one day. "Walked over to my mother's and contemplated what
I'm coming to in twice ten years."[6]

She went one day with her parents to visit some neighbors—from
all the signs, Rose noted, grimly hard-working, immaculately respectable, dirt-poor farmers. Rose was taken with the simple sincerity of their
life:

On the way home I remarked thoughtlessly that I had had a nice
time. My mother brightened pathetically. "Did you really? You

weren't bored?" Before I could collect my idling mind she added, still brightly, "Seeing how the other half lives." Suddenly I was profoundly, coldly angry. I could have killed. But my anger had no focus, no direction. It was not against her or anyone else. "What do you mean?" I said, icy. She looked at me. I could feel the murder in my eyes. Hers seemed expressionless. "Just common ordinary farmers," she said, turning again to the road ahead. "What am I but a common ordinary farmer," I said, or something inside me said. It did not seem to be my voice, grating through my throat. She did not say any more. . . . I would as soon spend a day with them as with the Craigs, but my mother's sense of social distinctions keeps her from comprehending that.[7]

In fact, Rose was well versed in the social distinctions that marked her mother's rise to social eminence in local circles. While growing up in Mansfield she had felt painfully the difference between town girls and country girls, between the moneyed merchant class and the hard-pressed dirt-farmers; and in fleeing Mansfield she had at once been climbing out of her origins and fleeing Mrs. Grundy. While still in Albania she had begun thinking of drawing on her life in Mansfield at the turn of the century for some stories; old magazines sent by her mother revived old memories; and as her store of rural hillbilly material grew thin, she shifted her focus to the small-town society she recalled from her youth.

Over the next few years she would produce a series of such stories for the *Saturday Evening Post* and *Ladies' Home Journal;* ultimately she would collect them as a book called *Old Home Town.* The first of these, entitled "Old Maid," had been the instrument by which George Bye had moved her out of *Country Gentleman* and into the more prestigious *Post;* and with the success of *Let the Hurricane Roar* the editors there were more receptive to her other stories and raised her rates. All of the stories in this series were the "plotted" stories demanded by the magazines; but the unifying subject was the grip of small-town respectability on the spontaneous impulses of the human heart; and once collected into *Old Home Town* they would become a deeply ambiguous assessment of the impress of her mother's generation upon her own.

For the moment, however, as the money for *Let the Hurricane Roar* trickled away in monthly expenses, she returned to Mama Bess's *Farmer Boy. Little House in the Big Woods* had begun with Mama Bess's desire to preserve her father's tales; but under editorial pressure and Rose's revision it had become a winter's tale of hearth and home heavily invested with instructive detail of daily pioneer life. It is possible to see at the core of *Farmer Boy* a similar collection of Almanzo's reminiscences from his childhood, but it too became a compendium of farm-life skills; and its deepest theme was the connection between work and food. Whatever the reason for its initial rejection, Mama Bess brought it back to Rose in January of 1933. Rose had visited her father's old home in Malone, New

York, on her most recent trip east; and with a keener sense of place she made the *Farmer Boy* manuscript into what it should have been before it was sent out initially, a proper companion piece to *Little House in the Big Woods*. After a month of intermittent work, mainly cutting her mother's clogging detail and softening the focus of individual chapters into idyllic scenes, it was restructured into another nostalgia-laden cycle of the seasons. Sent out again, this time it was accepted.[8]

Rose knew that for the sake of her own career she should be striking further into the ground opened up by the success of *Let the Hurricane Roar*, but a profound depression, compounded of ill health, resentment at her confinement, and fear for the state of the nation was settling around her. Her journal for 1933 is the bitterest she ever penned; "not," she declared, "a record of the years of my life, but of the years of my death." It is filled with self-loathing and with scathing portraits of her mother, Troub, and Catherine Brody, who had returned to spend the year with her:

> I want to finish work on my mother's juvenile by the end of this month if possible. There's a curious half-angry reluctance in my writing for other people. I say to myself that whatever earnings there may be are all in the family. Also I seize upon this task as an excuse to postpone my own work. But there can be no genuine pleasure in generosity to my mother, who resents it and does not trouble to conceal resentment. Generosity stripped of all selfish pleasure *should* be left pure generosity. In fact, it also becomes resentment. Suggesting that there actually is no such thing as pure generosity. Maxwell Aley sent a clipping of the trade-advertisement of Hurricane; splendidly done and I was very happy over it. So was Catherine, who insisted upon showing it. With an instinct of self-preservation I concealed it, knowing my mother was coming, but innocently C. brought it out. My mother said she didn't have her glasses & refused to look at it. Later, when Jack & Corinne had seen it and it was put aside, my mother went quietly, got her glasses, read the advertisement with an air of distaste, & interrupted our talk about other things:
> "Why do they place it in the Dakotas?"
> I = "I don't know."
> She = "The names aren't right."
> I, alarmed = "What names?"
> She = "Caroline and Charles. They don't belong in that place at that time. I don't know—it's all wrong. They've got it wrong, somehow." Effectually destroying the simple perfection of my pleasure.

It is a striking scene in a tense family drama. Clearly, Mama Bess has read nothing of Rose's story; clearly she resents Rose's intrusion into her material and the liberties fiction has taken with the facts of her parents' lives. And apparently Mama Bess took her chagrin abroad into the community, for there persisted in Mansfield the gossip of her anger and resentment at Rose's use of privileged materials.[9]

In the interval before the acceptance of *Farmer Boy,* the book version of *Let the Hurricane Roar* was published, to be greeted by a supportive editorial in the *Saturday Evening Post,* uniformly good reviews, and good early sales. Rose began sketching a plan for a massive, ten-volume work of fiction for which *Let the Hurricane Roar* would be the prelude. This would be nothing less than a fictional refutation of Spengler's *Decline of the West,* an interlocking series of contemporary tales ranging across the continent and all classes, carrying American history implicitly in its action as it traced the emergence of new cultural configurations out of the breakup of European traditions. "American life is the chaos of unresolved conflicts. Of opposing forces in action. Follow the line of one of these forces, and a pattern—perhaps original in aspect—must emerge. Just as a battle becomes a diagram in textbooks of military strategy. This pattern should create the form of a work of fiction. . . . " This would be the novel written by the Wandering Jew, of course, and even as she planned it she doubted her abilities:

> If ever I write my beautiful great novel and no one cares, I will be
> so *hurt*—and as always, coward that I am, I shrink from risking. . . .
> Courage is what I most lack. Intelligence next—the intelligence to
> see where, and how, I disagree with Spengler. Because I *feel* a
> vitality in America, and though it has followed Spengler's pattern
> to the megalopolis, I do not believe we are nearing civilization yet.

And the next day she had lost confidence altogether and had confronted herself in self-knowledge: ". . . suddenly I was overwhelmed with despair. I knew I haven't the powers to do such a thing, and saw myself as the absurd and piteous ambition that attempts and fails to do more than it can. I saw the cheap, thin, wobbling work that will come of all this effort— the smiles of critics and the blank incomprehension of readers. All the rest of the day I was sunk."[10]

IV

In February Mr. Bunting was hit by a car on the highway; carried home, he languished quietly for a few hours and died as Rose and Corinne played chess. Next day he was buried on the hill above the farm. Although Bunting's place would be taken soon by a puppy offered by the hired man, Rose was grief-stricken and guilt-ridden for months, given to periods of uncontrollable weeping. It would be too simple to say that the loss caused the depression that crippled her for most of the year; rather, the excess of grief, which she recognized herself, was a symptom of the deeper malaise that was grounded in her balked and frustrated life and compounded by unrecognized illness. Her own analysis connected her grief with the loss of that spontaneously happy and unthinking engagement with life she had shared in her moments with Bunting; her guilt was a matter of failed responsibility to him. No doubt this was in large measure a natural grief; but we need not sentimentalize to understand what a heavily laden surrogate Bunting had become for other failed relationships. "I know very few people," Rose wrote just before this loss. "My acquaintance is not wide, and I have no friends. There is no person upon whose loyalty I could rely." "Just once more being in love—having someone to try to please, to shine before—would make me really a good writer, I think. But for so long I have not even seen a man who could interest me at all."[11]

She was getting close to some home truths about herself at this point. "I myself," she went on, "would be loyal (to the last ditch) to a number of persons,"

> but this would be because of an inexplicable inner necessity to act in accordance with a certain picture of myself. It would actually be an inability to destroy certain dramatic, histrionic values. . . . Self-interest does not play its proper part in my life. That is the core of the reason why, if dramatic values demanded, I could be a heroine or saint, capable of any self-sacrifice. That is also why I'm so easily exploited by anyone who takes the trouble. I have never really felt that I am I; I feel no identification with myself. My life is not *my* life, but a succession of short stories and one-act plays, all begun by chance and left unfinished.

It was the old sense again of the disintegration of her own personality, certainly a threat in the emotional stretch she made between the despair of this journal and the chirrupy letters she continued to write to her correspondents, between the nighttime weeping and the daily cheer she maintained with her mother, Catherine Brody, and the social life of Mansfield. For in Mansfield, Rose had no confidants: to all appearances, she would always bear her burdens with gaiety and fortitude, and even among her correspondents there was no longer anyone she could open herself up to. Guy Moyston, Clarence Day, Floyd Dell, and even Dorothy Thompson had all withdrawn into the deeper loyalties of marriage. Only to her journal could she confess the anxieties that lay beneath the daily acts of courage.[12]

The reflex of her compulsive generosity, however, was the exploitation and paranoia she felt when it did not buy unconditional gratitude. Catherine Brody was with her by invitation, living on a small advance from her publisher while she worked on her next novel. Rose had felt so strongly Catherine's need to get on with her work that she had asked George Bye to advance Catherine an allowance out of her own fee for the serial publication of *Let the Hurricane Roar,* rather than waiting for Catherine's publisher's advance. She had also written on Catherine's behalf to Upton

Sinclair, hoping he could forward her interests as a fellow radical writer, and to Sinclair Lewis by way of Dorothy Thompson. And she had even helped Catherine with the planning of her novel. When Catherine finished the first draft, her editor wanted to see it; uncertain, Catherine asked Rose to read it first, and Rose took the manuscript to bed with her that night:

> While I was reading, C. B. came in, in her nightgown, her brown face smeared with white pore-cream. Enthusiastic, I said, "Catherine, it's grand! it's—"
> She snarled. I never heard just that sound before. Petrified me. And this snarl ran into words before I could blink.
> "Argh! Rose, this time you've just *got* to be *honest!* Do you think it's worth going on with?"
> "Yes. I don't know what you mean by saying that this time I've got to be honest. I won't say another word, not one."
> I . . . asked if she had a duplicate rough draft. So that if this one were lost in the mails—
> "I'm not going to send it to Maxwell Aley." Face twisted into a mask of sullen ugliness—hatred. "He can't see that. I'll tell him he can have it for mid-winter publication. What do I care if he has a novel on his fall list?"
> Here is a writer in her thirties, with no money to live on, scornful of doing writing (or anything else) for money. . . . Yet viperishly refusing any kind of help, hating anyone who in careless hospitality so much as asks her to tea. . . . In Maxwell Aley she has a sympathetic publisher. . . . In me she could have, has had, a sincere friend who tremendously admires her work, would gladly do anything to help her in any possible way. And this is her attitude toward us.[13]

The portraits continued, sketches from life in many ways better written than anything in her fiction. Loving ones of her local friends Corinne Murray and Ruth Freeman, whose lives were uncomplicated by any higher aspirations than the duties of friendship and motherhood. A devastating, resentfully jealous one of Troub Boylston, who for years had paid her way with good fellowship, and who would continue to live her grasshopper life to the end:

> A letter from Troub says she has Ida Wylie's Connecticut house rent free for the summer, with use of a Buick convertible coupe and Eva LeGalliene's riding horses. . . . A crowing triumphant letter. There is a woman well into the thirties, with no more sense of responsibility than a spoiled child—lazy, untidy, careless, self-centered, short-sighted, and completely insensitive, with the New Englander's curious pride of intellectuality based on nothing—no achievement, no effort toward achievement. And she always gets what she wants. . . . It is true that she doesn't want much and has no pride to interfere with any easy means of getting it. She doesn't

want more life, but less: she cares only to get through each day with as little effort or discomfort as possible, and like a child she will be happy with a feather or a colored pebble. She will have a happy, carefree summer in Connecticut, spoil Ida Wylie's house a little, probably ruin the car, and somehow land nicely on her feet for next winter in New York. While I, who must pay for everything I get, will never get anything I truly want.[14]

Even more devastating are the cameo portraits of Mama Bess, whose starched respectability and sense of social station cast her in the role of moral arbiter for Rose and Catherine. Mama Bess had sought to dissuade Catherine from traveling to Springfield with N. J. Craig, who was offering Catherine advice on her novel about banking: "Could she not arrange for Corinne to take her in Bruce's car, and meet Mr. Craig in Springfield? etc. With a curious deep satisfaction she said, 'The talk about him is getting *thick*, thick.' " A few months later Mama Bess arrived to play out another little moral drama of her own confection:

> My mother came for a purpose. She always does. Sitting on the divan, in her flowered ruffly pink-flowered-and-blue transparent dress, she said Mrs. Lynn is going to give a pot-luck next week, C. B. and I are invited. C. B. said at once, joyfully, "Oh, let's go! It'll be fun." I agreed, we talked about it, my mother interrupted— half-laughing annoyed, irritated, yet pleasantly aware of important excitement she was about to let loose—"Why won't you let me finish what I'm saying!"

The excitement turns out to be that among those bidden to the party are a couple recently involved in a gossipy divorce case.

> So she said we girls could do as we pleased, of course, but she wasn't going. I asked her why. . . . She said, "Well, I can tell you my point of view. If we go, it will be printed in the paper, it will go to Hartville. Everybody will read it, all those people that heard all that divorce trial—" She said, "It's bad enough now because I drink beer, but still, in a way, it does something for beer because Mrs. Wilder drinks it, but if we are at a party with Reuben Williams they'll just say, 'The Wilders have gone tough.' " She repeated that a couple of times, "gone tough," with explosive force as though the word "tough" were obscene.[15]

The episodes are richly comic, and they reveal Rose's quick sense of her mother's limitations. But at the deepest level the relations between mother and daughter pivoted on matters not of decorum but of power and money. In the financial stress that gripped the country, Mama Bess was having her own problems with money, but she, like Troub, had a way of always getting just what she wanted. Her response to the Depression was to take her remaining savings and pay off the mortgage on Rocky Ridge Farm; beyond that, her finances were mingled with Rose's in an excruciating tangle. Rose was committed to an annual subsidy and monthly rent for Rocky Ridge farmhouse, on which she was falling behind; in addition, Mama Bess had put some of her own savings into the new house, for which Rose had given her an interest-bearing note. Mama Bess began offering schemes of self-sacrifice: she suggested one day selling the new house with forty acres; the price mentioned was less than half of what Rose had put into the building, but the interest on the sum if invested would yield a small income. Rose, of course, would have to turn Rocky Ridge farmhouse over to her parents again—but her heart leaped at the idea of being free to travel again, despite the loss in such a sale. The plan came to nothing; but within a few days Mama Bess returned with a new scheme. In a harrowing domestic drama, we can glimpse the strategies of martyrdom Rose had been struggling against as long as she could remember:

> It's amazing how my mother can make me suffer. Yesterday, Sunday, she was here, and asked to see the electric contract. I must have known, without knowing, what was coming, for I *ran* upstairs, saying I'd bring it down, telling her—behind me—that she needn't come. Of course she came. She sat at my desk, I in my typewriter-chair. And while she put on her glasses and slowly, very apprehensive, read the contract, I closed my typewriter into the desk as if clearing decks. Then she began. Cheerful, almost playful, and brave. She has it all planned. Cut off the electric bill and she can manage indefinitely. She's going to "let me go." Well, after all, she didn't have electricity before; I've given her six "wonderfully easy years." How she hates it that I'm her "sole source of support." Implicit in every syllable and tone, the fact that I've failed, fallen down on the job, been the broken reed. But never mind, (brightly) she's able to manage nicely, thank you! And it's true enough that to live like a Digger Indian's no aesthetic hardship to her. But the additional labor would be.
>
> So I sat all the time smiling, and softly murmuring vaguely, that "I wouldn't cut off electricity." Why need she? Something must happen—"I wouldn't do that if I were you—" Perhaps an hour of simply hellish misery. Toward the end I cut very careful patterns in paper with the tiny scissors. Helped a little as a distraction, helped a little more to keep some self-respect—saying to myself, "I *can* cut beautifully proportioned patterns." (Even though I'm no other earthly good.) At last I said, almost unconsciously, without *any* premeditation, that I'd give her a check of $60.00, February rent. She demurred, without real force. I got up, came to this other desk, wrote the check and gave it to her. She took it only on condition—that I'd tell her if I needed it back!
>
> We both knew the interview was over, the instant the check changed hands. By tacit consent went downstairs and my mother at once, without speaking about going, put on her hat and started home.

The curious thing is, that she's sincerely reaching for some kind of companionship with me. She's trying to be friends. She wants to "talk things over." She wants genuine warmth, sympathy. She has not the faintest notion what she's doing to me. But underneath, there's not a trace of generosity in her. . . .

She doesn't intend to let me get away with owing her a penny, not any more than she'd give a tramp a crust of bread, or a neighbor a taste of first strawberries. She's going to get every cent she can, as soon as she can. I don't believe she *thinks* this, but something in her knows exactly how to put the screws on me. She made me so miserable when I was a child that I've never got over it. I'm morbid. I'm all raw nerves. I know I should be more robust. I shouldn't let her torture me this way, and always gain her own ends, through implications that she hardly knows she's using. But I can't help it.

That $60 check leaves me without money for this month's bills. It gives her a $150 bank balance, which she'll save most of, to pay next fall's taxes. She was pleased, self-satisfied, on the street in Mansfield, Saturday, when Mrs. Wilson looked at her palm & told her she could get anything she wanted. "I always have," she said complacently, & repeated this when she told Mrs. Craig what Mrs. Wilson had said.

Mama Bess's electrical service had been saved. But two months later Rose had her own service disconnected, and Rocky Ridge farmhouse was lighted by oil lamps again. [16]

V

In one of his best-known stories, D. H. Lawrence wrote of a house that whispered of the need for more money. Certainly Rose heard the whisper throughout Rocky Ridge farmhouse this year, and it resonates agonizingly through her notebooks and letters. In time, probably at the next temporary infusion of cash, electricity was restored, but there seemed little hope for sustained relief. Harper's contract for *Farmer Boy* cut initial royalties in half. George Bye sold a few more of Rose's magazine stories, but at reduced prices; these funds would get her through the year, and she could look forward to royalties from *Let the Hurricane Roar*. Her publisher assured her that in any normal year it would have been a bestseller, but that the depressed economy had hurt sales badly. Rose recognized a connection between her own depression and the nation's, and she had become a close follower of economic statistics—boxcar loadings, steel output, auto production, bank clearings. The two Mansfield banks were wobbly but still open, and when Roosevelt announced the bank holidays they calmly ignored his edict and went on with local business. Nonetheless, Rose held some of her checks on New York banks rather than depositing them locally, fearing she would not get her money out. Her income tax for 1932 was forty dollars, which she chose to pay in quarterly installments in 1933. In her more buoyant moments, she recognized the danger in the whisperings of the house and her purely economic motives:

> I knew that the house-plans, housekeeping, this morning's thoughts of rebuilding this place—all futile, worthless trash. I must resist these, as a temptation, an opiate. My business is with this marvelous, fantastic, cruel, mysterious world, and with human beings in it, and knowing them and putting them into patterns of words. How silly and how cheap, these extensions of *me* into wood and stone and wool. It is nothing but the most trashy vanity.[17]

Her earlier admiration for Hoover was considerably chastened; she saw him now as one of the ironic victims of history, a man disabled by his very abilities from offering effective political leadership. In the preceding summer she had put her worries to paper:

> For the first time I am worried about general conditions. Momentum becomes exhausted. Besides, Hoover's appeal to the Senate is bad. It is alarming without being arousing. His effort to avoid admitting any danger, while at the same time stating it, is psychologically bad. This country desperately needs one of the good old slogan-makers—a Roosevelt or a Bryan. Hoover's intelligence is his weakness: it keeps him seeing problems all around, instead of dramatically.

In the next year, she found that she had wished for too much. "March, 1933: We have a dictator, Franklin Delano Roosevelt, a smart politician."[18]

Her misgivings about Roosevelt would not diminish, but would grow apace as she saw greater and greater power gathered to his administration and his skills as a slogan-maker used to further programs that struck her viscerally as wrong. Her own response to adversity was simply to work harder, improvise solutions, ride out the storm, and look hopefully to the future; whereas to suppose that remote politicians and bureaucrats could beneficially intercede between individual lives and the great natural forces that swept through the world was simply political hubris. The world would right itself through the myriad individual choices made, not through government intervention for some hypothetical general welfare—as she had recently written to Dorothy Thompson: "no one can serve the Greatest Good to the Greatest Number; he doesn't know what the greatest good for them is, and he can never be in touch with the greatest number. The greatest good to the greatest number will obviously be reached when each individual of the greatest number is doing the greatest good to himself."[19]

Her first chance to engage this premise in public argument came in the summer of 1933, when the *Saturday Evening Post* commissioned her to write an article on American wheat production. *Let the Hurricane Roar* had established her credentials as a writer on sod-busting pioneers, and her earlier work on farm life and food production during her California years made this a familiar assignment. She made a two-week trip into Oklahoma and Kansas, wrote the article, and collapsed into her bed for a month of illness under the care of Catherine and Corinne. The article appeared in the September 23 issue of the *Post*—without Rose's name. It purported to be "by a grain trader," and carried that fiction throughout the narrative, presumably because Rose, as a fiction writer and as a woman, would carry no particular authority on this subject for the *Post*'s readers. Essentially, the article was an argument against government intervention in the grain market and in the economy generally. In the background were the drought and dust-storms of 1933; the recent moratoriums on the banks, the stock market, and the Chicago Board of Trade; plans for subsidized acreage reduction; and the general climate of economic uncertainty generated by the activist programs of the Roosevelt administration. The drama of the account involved the forces that would set the price of wheat: on the one hand were the natural forces of weather, supply and demand, the millions of self-interested decisions of farmers and consumers, and the old-time responsible trader who made an orderly market by adjusting these forces one to another; on the other were the clumsy intervention of government agencies, the resulting disruption of normal calculations of self-interest, and the inevitable distortion of the market by speculators gambling on such unnatural forces. Thus did the descendant of Charles and Caroline Ingalls confront the New Deal, finding in it natural faith replaced by cynicism and moral courage by manipulation.[20]

VI

There was some lightening of her depression by midsummer, but relapses came, and as she catalogued the ills of her failing, middle-aged body she began to note a recurrent pounding in her head. She felt constantly exhausted, and she wondered if she could still be suffering the drain of her operation twenty-three years before. But much of her problem, she believed, was not physical; and if it was not, she should be able to surmount it by will. "I am mentally sick," she confessed to her diary. "Don't know if will can break this." She was fond of quoting Mary Margaret McBride: "All we have to do is remain invincible." Her will carried her through two grueling weeks in the wheatfields, but the strain of the trip, and the promise of a check from the *Post*, sent her to Springfield for medical examinations that revealed a major thyroid deficiency. Daily medication and a month of rest brought her body somewhat closer to normal, although the pounding in her head persisted and her spirits continued low, even lower once she realized that her new medicine was not a cure-all. Corinne Murray moved in to care for her, and shortly she became in effect Rose's live-in companion and housekeeper. In her sick-bed one day in September Rose turned again to her journal:

> I really felt bed a refuge, an escape. Forty years I've thought I had courage and I have none at all. My whole life seems to be always to have been at cross-purposes, all its effort lost. Nothing at the end, all cruelty & mistakes, probably that's why I can't stop crying about Bunting, & no medicine the doctor can give me will stop this pounding inside my skull. The cure's something I've got to do, somehow, myself—and I feel too weak and don't really care. All one's life one says at intervals, "I wish I were dead," and at last one really does. . . . [21]

But on that day another cure arrived.

On a cold and wet September afternoon, he stood there on the kitchen porch, an undersized boy of fourteen, ragged and rain-soaked and dirty and asking to work for food. As she answered his knock, the household dogs at her heels, Rose without thinking latched the screen door against the dogs, and the look on the boy's face broke her heart. She first put him to work weeding the flower bed, then gave him dinner and a cot for the night in the garage. The next day he was obviously sick, so he stayed on. Corinne scavenged some secondhand clothes for him, and with a bath he was transformed into an attractive young man. Against her better judgment, Rose was hopelessly smitten, and John Turner moved into Rocky Ridge farmhouse and into the emotional void left by Guy Moyston, Mr. Bunting, and the distant Rexh Meta. [22]

As Rose recovered her health, Catherine Brody had returned to New York, so there was a vacancy for John Turner in the old farmhouse and in Rose's life. Within days she had him enrolled in the high school and engaged in French lessons under her guidance; new clothes from the Sears Roebuck catalog fit him for Mansfield society. He proved bright and tractable and humorous, but reserved about his past; he had been orphaned a year before in Oklahoma and had drifted about in Texas, he said. Gradually it emerged that his late parents were really from Springfield, that he had had some minor scrapes with the law, and had lived most recently with an uncle at nearby Ava, where his brother still remained. Their uncle treated them decently, but John had suffered under his aunt's hostility: in a typical gesture, she had sewed up the pockets of his trousers so he could not lounge with his hands in them. Finally, he had run off, and had been on the road for six weeks when he wandered up to Rose's door. Under her care and feeding he throve rapidly, gaining pounds in days and inches in a few months. She put him on an allowance and assigned him household chores, which he performed intermittently;

in time, as he chafed under Rose's daily close supervision of his life, disturbing instances of deceit would occasionally present themselves, but little beyond the latitude traditionally allowed adolescent boys. Within a month he had engaged Rose's affections; he was not a lover, but he was someone she could strive to please and shine before; and she began to feel some ease in the emotional stress that had drained her all year. "Idiotic, but John seems to be pulling me into integrity again. I feel now, sometimes, how precarious the existence of 'I.' A feeling of there being only a thin thread toward safety, but that I hold it and shall get out in time." "John is a deep joy to me," she wrote in her journal as the year turned toward winter. "There is endless interest, amusement, fascination, charm, in such a relationship with a child. I feel responsibility, but it is no weight on me, no burden at all. The boy has his own strength, his own character, and his interest and affections are not directed toward me. Whatever I get from him is pure gain and there is nothing to lose."

It is a curious entry for a woman who has just adopted an adolescent child about whom she knows almost nothing. She might have written the same thing about Mr. Bunting. It is almost the only optimistic note in her journal for this year, and the optimism blurs her self-knowledge and common sense. She would always give more than she got in personal relationships, and expect more than could be returned. Her connection with John Turner would be no exception.[23]

As the year ended she fell ill again, suspecting her infected teeth, and the despair that had covered the year drew in upon her again. "1933 the worst year yet. Only cheer is that John came," she noted, holding fast to the thin thread she had caught hold of. She began to fear that her bad health was permanent, and that her mother's worst worry at her divorce from Gillette Lane would be realized:

> This year is ending dismally. I am too sick to work and haven't money to last 2 months and pay income tax. . . . I want to keep on going but do not quite see how, and there is no alternative—rather than justify my mother's 25-year dread of my "coming back on her, sick," I must kill myself. If she has to pay funeral costs, at least she will cut them to the bone and I will not be here to endure her martyrdom and prolong it by living.

In December her forty-seventh birthday passed without comment. New Year's Eve was spent with friends at a roast-goose dinner, where Mrs. Wilson, the local seer who had read Mama Bess's palm, now read Rose's. Her prophecy suggests that Mrs. Wilson, or the town gossips, had been studying Rose closely. Rose wrote it into her journal as a kind of buoy to cling to:

> This is a period controlled by Fate, in which it makes no difference what I do. It is coincident with a nervous breakdown. Nothing

organic is wrong, my health will improve, this period of helplessness will pass, and I [shall] embark upon a clear, straight line
of triumphant success. I shall live to be 90, in good health and with
sufficient money. I am too much dependent upon other people. I
am suicidal. I shall make a number of long journeys, all safe and
comfortable. I can quite well dispense with "the other sex."[24]

"CREDO"

I am now a fundamentalist American. . . .

R ose had now to learn to be a mother, but she was starting late in life and the child had had fourteen years to grow into a character already significantly shaped. She had always over-involved herself in the lives of those she loved, and she now addressed herself to the details of John Turner's life with a vigor that was often more than he could stand. Ingratitude may well be her final judgment on John Turner, but even a child given a better start in life might have struggled under Rose's constant attentions. To the normal pressures of adolescence, no doubt, were added rebellion at her careful scrutiny and a growing knowledge that he would always owe her more than he could repay.

Once he was clean and clothed and enrolled in school, she put him on an allowance, part of which he was obliged to save, and assigned him chores, mainly washing the evening dishes while she dried. It was an opportunity for regular conversations, and if he sometimes skipped out it was perhaps because the grilling became too intense; there were occasional rows, and there were times when he reduced her to tears, but there were also times when Rose noted that he was simply sweet. She began going to high school basketball games, where John played on the freshman team; she planned and hosted elaborate parties for Halloween and birthday; and Rocky Ridge farmhouse became the locus for comings and goings of young people Rose had never known before. She kept track of John's savings, his spending, his school chums and his girlfriends, his school grades and his teachers; she wrote him poems; she put him on a curfew, which he regularly broke and for which she regularly forgave him, even when he lied about the reasons. In time, he was given charge of a cow, probably one from her father's herd, and the money from the cream check became his. When his savings reached five dollars and went into a bank account, Rose doubled them from her purse. We can understand his anger, if she could not, when he sullenly vowed to save enough to repay her contribution. And daily she agonized over his language, uncouth and ungrammatical; to which he quite naturally replied that he hated English and would never learn to speak it. In all of this, we can perhaps glimpse obscurely a version of the daily oppression Rose had felt as a child under her mother's eye. Her diary charted the ups and downs of this new relationship with all the anxiety of a new love affair, which, in a sense, it was. "I do not like my life but I adore John." But again, "John a hopeless hillbilly and hoodlum." He, a self-absorbed teenager, and hardened by recent misfortune, could barely acknowledge her concern. "I said I worry about him because he is precious to me. He said he can't understand it. I said, 'Maybe you will when you are older and have children of your own.' It didn't occur to me, until he thought it, that he isn't my child."[1]

She understood that he was filling a need in her. Physically she continued to waver in and out of good health, but her emotional life began to stabilize somewhat as this new charge gave her a different future to plan. On a springlike February day, they drove to Ava to a basketball game; the farmers along the way were burning off their fence rows and woodlots, and the gold flames against the gray smoke and the black trees struck her with a sudden beauty. "I felt well and energetic, ready to work again, full of hope & confidence, and wondered why I plan for John, why do I not take wing and *live* once more." Why indeed? Her need for affection and approval had always worked against her own best interests. This new entanglement was perhaps a balance against her mother's hold on her, but it served equally to hold her in place. And it was increasingly clear that she no longer had the vitality to seek another Albania; the implacable circle of reality all but defined her horizon now. "Literature has so little to do with the realities of normal living," she wrote, listing the affairs of her kitchen and house, "which are all these small cozy matters, and such tragedies as the burning of the garage and the scorching of a roast, the failure of a cake, the loss of a basketball game." Most of 1934 would be spent in an emotional convalescence, in which her exertions for John Turner were a kind of necessary therapy. "This mother-&-son love affair with John does not have the effect that other love affairs have had. I wish to have money, even to be greatly a Success, in order to give him things and to impress him, but the wishes are conscious and weak. Of course no literary success would seem important to him as such."[2]

But for most of the year she was unable to work, and unable to concern herself about money until it was all but gone. "The mainspring of the mechanism seems broken," she recorded in her journal. She wrote to borrow five hundred dollars from Fremont Older, almost as a test of his affection and expecting to be refused, and was pleasantly surprised when he wired that a check was on the way. He was in bad health and depressed by age; but from her invigorating letter of thanks and support any reader would have thought her to be in blooming good spirits herself. Later she borrowed again from the bank, even though her friend N. J. Craig tried hard to steer their conversations away from finances, apparently fearing such a request. In this interval Mama Bess brought her a third juvenile story to work on: she had quarried out of "Pioneer Girl" an expanded account of her life in Indian Territory in Kansas, a story again based on her father's tales of a time before her memory. For this story, she and Rose attempted some historical research and even made a fruitless automobile trip attempting to locate the old homesite. Mama Bess called it her Indian story, Rose entitled it "High Prairie" as she worked on the manuscript during five weeks in May and June, and in time it would be published as *Little House on the Prairie*.[3]

By midyear of 1934 Rose had fumbled her way through two magazine stories that failed to find buyers. Once she had Mama Bess's manuscript off her hands for a time, and desperate for funds, she borrowed from George Bye against royalties due from *Let the Hurricane Roar*. This loan could carry her through most of the remaining year: she paused long enough to knock off one story that suddenly rolled easily from her typewriter, perhaps because she had found its germ in one of her mother's anecdotes. She mailed it off to Bye, then took John on a trip to visit a new friend in Florida. This was the historical romancer Talbot Mundy, whose series of connected stories about a Roman adventurer called Tros had the makings of a novel, so his publisher thought. Somehow the manuscript came to Rose for an opinion; she was enthusiastic, made some suggestions, and fell into a lively correspondence with Mundy, who was living in a small beach-house near Osprey. His invitation and Bye's loan gave Rose a chance to get away for a month of sea-bathing and sunburn, including a trip to Havana. Rose returned invigorated to find that *Saturday Evening Post* publisher George Horace Lorimer so liked her latest story, "Object Matrimony," that he had raised her rates by a third, to twelve hundred dollars. Something of a blockage had been broken; she quickly wrote and sold another story to the *Post* and then another to *Country Gentleman*. She had solved her finances for the year—repaying her debt to Older, full interest to her mother, and rent in advance for a year. Talbot Mundy's *Tros of Samothrace* was published and gratefully dedicated to Rose Wilder Lane.[4]

In October, Catherine Brody returned for a long visit, just in time to get involved in the elaborate Halloween costume party Rose planned for John. Soon she and Rose were also contemplating extensive rebuilding plans at Rocky Ridge to accommodate an enlarging household. For on the horizon of Rose's consciousness was John's older brother Al, still living in backwoods poverty at his uncle's farm near Hunter Creek. John had concealed the connection until he was recognized on the basketball trip to Ava; but once the connection was revealed, Al had come to visit several times at Rose's invitation. John had seemed reluctant to admit him at first, saying enigmatically, "You don't know Al. *And, to be frank, you don't know me.*" John's caution was perhaps to protect his own interests, perhaps a child's attempt to warn Rose against himself; but in any event Al Turner would prove to be a lesser problem than John. Rose met with the uncle, offering to support Al through high school. The argument was persuasive, and in November Al Turner arrived to join Rose's household.[5]

It had been a year of recuperation. Although there were relapses, her health improved as singly and in pairs her teeth were left at the dentist's. She seemed to be on track with her writing again and she could with equal enthusiasm plan a rebuilding at Rocky Ridge and an escape from its trammels. By the end of the year she was writing away to Stanford for enrollment information and planning a savings program both to get her away from Rocky Ridge and to send John to college. The Montgomery Ward Company sponsored a scholarship program, whereby mail orders sent in on forms bearing a child's name earned a commission payable toward college fees—so Rose explained to Fremont Older, sending him a letter extolling Ward's services and enclosing some forms with John's name on them. No doubt other correspondents received similar letters.[6]

||

Catherine Brody was called away to Hollywood to a movie-writing job. Her relationship with Rose had always been mutually uneasy admiration, and Rose noted in her diary that this was the end of it. Occasional letters continued, but by and large Catherine dropped out of Rose's life. Mama Bess was probably glad to see her go, if she had been "talked about." Years later, after Rose had left, Catherine would step off a train in Mansfield on a transcontinental trip, resplendent in a fur coat that made the townspeople take notice, to make a call on Mama Bess, only to be turned away as she telephoned from the station. For the moment, however, Catherine's departure left Rose with two teenaged boys as her household companions, although she was aided by the ever-present Corinne Murray. Two new occupants no doubt complicated living arrangements within the farmhouse; shortly Rose had a small cabin erected near the farmhouse on the foundations of a garage that had burned the year before. It was a combined bunkhouse and workroom for the boys, who were both interested in model radios, and it would become a popular site for young people's parties.[7]

Meanwhile, Rose was engaged in a deliberate effort to integrate her popular magazine fiction with her emerging social consciousness. For several years she had been reexamining the Mansfield of her childhood in a series of stories seen through the eyes of an adolescent narrator named Ernestine. Each story satisfied the implicit requirements of slick-paper fiction: a domestic crisis was resolved in a neat twist of plot; the dramatic situation was rendered realistically, but circumspectly in regard to sex; and heart's desire was satisfied after threat and struggle. The general air was of quaint, archaic moral dilemmas before the modern enlightenment. These stories had found their places in the *Saturday Evening Post* and *Ladies' Home Journal* between 1932 and 1935, but their scattered appearance had obscured the unity of their locale and themes. The various victims of communal and parental authority, punished for seeking unsanctioned fulfillment of heart's desire, were all enacting the revolt against Mansfield values that had driven Rose in her original flight. No individual story is thesis-ridden: some victims triumph through a trick of plot rather than through moral enlightenment; others simply escape to a freer world, as does the young heroine by the end; but nowhere is the moral atmosphere of the community explicitly challenged.

It is easy to see here Rose attempting to reconcile her own enlightened views with the conventional values of the magazine readers who paid her way: she might genteelly titillate but not offend. But as she began to play mother to John Turner she came unavoidably to contemplate her own adolescence and the tutelary role connecting generations—her mother's to hers and hers to John's. "When I first saw myself in John's eyes as a survivor of a way of life which nothing in his experience equipped him to understand, it struck me at once that here was material for a story."[8] She did not write this story, but the impulse to interpret her own adolescence gathered around the Ernestine stories; and as she attempted to draw these together in a single volume called *Old Home Town*, she began to uncover ambiguities that had not been manifest in the stories individually. To contain these, she labored during the first three months of 1935 to frame a prefatory essay that would draw the stories together thematically, redeeming their original triviality and achieving a moral resonance by means of the title essay through which the series would be screened. The apparent strategy would be to portray a small town through the growing ethical consciousness of the adolescent narrator, the whole framed in the more comprehensive ethical vision of the preface.

However, once her moral imagination seized this material whole, Rose seems to have betrayed both her heroine and the various victims of her stories. The escape into cosmopolitan freedom that Ernestine and some of the stories' heroines achieve would seem, certainly, to be grounded in Rose's own experience and to reflect her immediate longings; and indeed, by the end of the preface, she acknowledges that the old home town has become so cosmopolitanized by the radio, the movies, and the automobile that escape is unnecessary: anyone can be as free as he chooses. Nonetheless, in the emotional center of the preface, she comes down not on the side of the freedom denied in each of the stories, but rather on the side of the original powerful Puritan ethos of the nineteenth-century pioneers that had decayed into mere respectability in the town she remembered.

With a force and seriousness that had never appeared in the stories themselves, she characterizes the community in broad strokes of reminiscence: she paints a moral geography of the town, framed between the schoolhouse and the cemetery, the right side of the tracks and the wrong; she details the daily, weekly, and yearly cycle of routine and the complex conventions that carry the force of law. We have noted this passage before, as embodying all that the young Rose had sought to escape. It is worth repeating here, as a marker of what she had returned to accept:

> It was a hard, narrow, relentless life. It was not comfortable. Nothing was made easy for us. We did not like work and we were not supposed to like it; we were supposed to work, and we did. We did not like discipline, so we suffered until we disciplined ourselves. We saw many things and many opportunities that we ardently wanted and could not pay for, so we did not get them, or got them only after stupendous, heartbreaking effort and self-denial, for debt was much harder to bear than deprivations. We were honest, not because sinful human nature wanted to be, but because the consequences of dishonesty were excessively painful. It was clear that if your word were not as good as your bond, your bond was no good and you were worthless. Not only by precept but by cruel experience we learned that it is impossible to get something for nothing; that he who does not work can not long continue to eat; that the sins of the fathers are visited upon the children even unto the fourth generation; that chickens come home to roost and the way of the transgressor is hard.

These were the empirically discovered moral truths she had mentioned to Fremont Older. And even as she was willing to acknowledge the modern cosmopolitanizing of the village, she found a wavering in her conception of the freedom once found in flight, now available to all in the modern liberal dispensation:

> Now some of us seem to see, in our country's most recent experiences, an unexpected proof that our parents knew what they were talking about. We suspect that, after all, man's life in this hostile universe is not easy and cannot be made so; that facts are seldom pleasant and must be faced; that the only freedom is to be found within the slavery of self-discipline; that everything must be paid for and that putting off the day of reckoning only increases the inexorable bill.
>
> This may be an old-fashioned, middle-class, small-town point of view. All that can be said for it is that it created America.

The language rings with the conviction of submission. In this reach of her imagination, at least, Rose had come to heel behind the values of her mother's generation, while in other reaches she still dreamed of a free life in the great world as it unrolled into the unknown future. The prefatory essay to *Old Home Town* teeters on that dilemma, which would in essence become her continuing problem as a social thinker: to cosmopolitanize the strengths of the small-town ethos that she had, like her heroine Ernestine, earlier rejected.[9]

Old Home Town was published in August of 1935, while Rose was living in the Tiger Hotel in the university town of Columbia, Missouri. Earlier, she had finished the manuscript during a month's retreat at the Old English Inn, a resort at Lake Taneycomo south of Mansfield. By such flights and perches she was breaking away from Rocky Ridge Farm.[10]

Once Catherine Brody had left, Rose had seen *Little House on the Prairie* through proofs and had written a small piece under her mother's name to be sent out to *Child Life.* She had started a piece of fiction in the pioneer mold entitled *Free Land,* but put it aside to finish *Old Home Town,* and it was pushed further aside when George Bye got her a contract, with a substantial cash advance, to write a book on the state of Missouri. The need to get away became a more frequent motif in her diary as her health improved; in May she had finally given up most of her remaining molars and accepted the need for extensive bridgework. "The rest of my life toothless," she wailed to her diary, but the sacrifice seemed to restore her vigor. And she had to accept the death of Fremont Older, the news discovered in *Time,* severing the last link with her glory days in San Francisco. Her final letter to him was a cheering one on adjusting to ill health; what scared her, she said, was the Roosevelt dictatorship, particularly his struggles with the Supreme Court, and the proliferation of government "make-work" jobs—even in Mansfield.[11]

One sign of her renewed vigor was the return of the old detached metaphysical angst that had for a time been displaced by more pressing concerns of mere physical health. In the interval between the completion of *Old Home Town* and her immersion in the Missouri book, she paused again for one of her characteristic soundings for the bottom of her convictions. She mused on the contrast between the Islamic submission to flux and fate and her Western determination to bend time and circumstance to will:

> You westerners are right! the Young Turk said to me; we were sitting in the open door of a box-car, jogging down to Aleppo. He said, We must stop submitting to God; we must stand up and fight God, as you do. We must have railroads, motor cars, airplanes, modern armaments; Islam will die if we don't. Islam will die if you do, I said. Yes, he said; but we must survive, we must fight; we must stop submitting to God and defy Him, fight him in the western way, or The West will destroy us completely. What will

it profit you to win the whole world and lose your soul? I asked
him. God knows, he said. But why do I have to tell you, a Westerner, that you Westerners are right? You can't tell me we are, I
told him; because I don't believe it.

In a revealing movement of thought, the Western will-to-knowledge
becomes identified with pain itself, submission with an opiate. She had
discovered in her dental surgery that novocaine did not affect her:

> Has anyone ever written anything true about pain? The early Chris-
> tians must have known. Many people must know. The goodness
> in the worst of it, goodness that's a thing-in-itself perceived: not
> moral at all. . . . when the chisel goes through bone into nerve
> and consciousness goes out, it goes out clean and fighting and
> *knowing,* aware of a reality. I tell you that pride and dignity are
> quite as much of an obstacle between *you* and that *knowing* as the
> "jelly of fear" can be. What I tried to say, is that possibly fear *knows*
> danger more clearly than courage does.

Then after a page detailing the glories and tragedies of her garden, she
touches bottom again:

> I do not care what becomes of me. All I want is to *know.* Not intel-
> lectually. Yes, the intellect is human, the distinguishing human
> trait, function, even principle. But not (I say), *vital* principle. The
> vital thing is *one* thing, deeper than all forms of mind; we share it
> with everything living. Trees have minds and so have we. . . .
> What I want to know is what the beaver knows and the wasp
> knows and what—sometimes, a little—artists, poets know—*not*
> intellectually, but by a kind of direct unreasoning contact. . . . We
> all, I tell you, *know* what can't be thought or said.

And at bottom she discovers simply the two figures that define her
imagination:

> I am not doomed to enough life. What I get tired of is the struggle
> *to* live. Years & years of clothes, food, trains, short stories, prices,
> thoughts and thoughts and thoughts, the ceaseless chatter in my
> own head, and books and people and land and oceans—for one
> little swift flash of life. Once, in a Tartar market, while the inter-
> preter went into a shop, I leaned against a wall and struck a match
> to light a cigarette. The flame burned in the sunshine, invisible,
> while I looked at it. And there's nothing whatever to tell, or to
> think. I'd live as long as the Wandering Jew, on the chance of one
> more instant of such *life.* [12]

Between this vital principle and the occasional personal contact with
it lay the realm of history, which always engaged her imagination when
the exigencies of daily life could be put aside. It was this vein that was
tapped when George Bye put to her the offer to write a book about Missouri for a series by the McBride Publishing Company. The fifteen-
hundred-dollar advance was a temptation as well, as was the necessity to

travel, if only in her home state. "I must learn Missouri," she had counseled herself in 1931. "This is untouched literary material. Which I should be able to understand. Any material can be made a vehicle for whatever one can say about life." Now the opportunity had fallen into her lap. She was able to do a little work at home, but by July of 1935 it was clear that to do what she wanted she would have to work in the archives of the State Historical Society in Columbia. She located in the Tiger Hotel, named after the athletic teams' totem animal, a few blocks from the University, leaving John and Al Turner and Rocky Ridge farmhouse to weekend visits, frequent letters, and the interim care of the watchful Corinne Murray.[13]

Her enthusiasm for the project was unfeigned. "I see the book as the *story* of this state," she wrote Bye. "States have character; at frontiers they mix as even France and Germany do, but each one has its own individuality."

> I'd like to show Missouri's nature, not by description but in action, as one shows the character of a person in a story. Beginning with DeSoto's entrance; sketching in the Indians, the wilderness, the topography; going on to the struggle between Chouteau and St. Louis; the life of the rivers; the Spanish and the French, and the invasion of the mountaineers. . . . All this makes a distinctive character, the quality of Missouri, something felt in Missourians— so that you couldn't, for instance, imagine that Mary Margaret McBride came from anywhere else.

She bought a secondhand Ford just for the project, and with Corinne Murray spent several weeks touring the state. After finding her way to the appropriate material in the archives, she settled in for several months of sustained writing. A measure of her diligence is that her diary entries ceased for half a year, and her correspondence became almost perfunctory.[14]

Never did she work so hard for so little gain. As the manuscript neared completion at the year's-end deadline, it became clear that she and the editor at McBride's had very different conceptions of what the book was to be. She had produced a dramatic and anecdotal history of the state; he wanted a topographic book with a decided contemporary flavor. After several abortive attempts at revision, she gave it up, vowing that she felt honor-bound in her failure to return the fifteen-hundred-dollar advance if the publisher would release the manuscript to her. She had already spent the advance in expenses, of course; and she could not afford to devote more time to the project; but she made the pledge in self-righteous anger at having been badly used. "They will get the money as soon as I can spare it," she wrote Bye; "they can not get it sooner, and any attempt to do so will merely exasperate me and decrease my earning power. . . . I think I am behaving damn well under the circumstances." But she did not regret the episode: "It got me away from that damned farm."[15]

Some measure of her distraction during this time away from Rocky Ridge is that she could not bring herself to resume her diary. She had filled the old one, but she put off buying a new one and writing in it until almost April of 1936, when she forced herself into one of the periodic summaries that seemed to mark the lowest ebb of her spirits. "This year began in such anxiety and fear that I could not bear to make a record of the days," she began,

> and so abandoned the old habit, and did not buy a new five-year diary, my last one being fragmentarily (for last year) filled. I am still too much afraid to sleep, and this is the time in which I have become definitely no longer middle-aged but an *old* woman in appearance. And perhaps really—How do I know what it might be like if I were to live to be sixty or seventy, as I might so easily have done, and always thought I would do?[16]

The entry marks the failure of her Missouri book and this attempt to engage history. In the same interval, however, she had produced almost without effort a piece that would stand her in greater stead. It had doubtless been ripening at least since *Let the Hurricane Roar*, and it probably began to come into focus a year earlier during a "long discussion about life & America's destiny" with her mother. But its fruition probably had something to do with the visit of Garet Garrett, a featured writer of economic articles for the *Saturday Evening Post*. Rose had known him since their shipboard meeting in 1923; he had written the article on Herbert Hoover that had given her such humiliation about her book on Hoover; and in the summer of 1935 he was touring the Midwest for a series of articles on the New Deal farm policy. She knew the country and the subject; matters of decorum and propriety aside, she was an ideal traveling companion for his research; and for two weeks in his car they toured Illinois, Kansas, Nebraska, and Iowa, not omitting a trip to Rocky Ridge Farm. There is just a hint that what began in business led to a brief romance; but it is not at all unlikely that he was also just the person she needed to whet her political ideas against. He was one of the few people of real intellectual substance she had talked to since her last visit to New York City at the end of 1932.[17]

The trip was a real eye-opener, her first direct contact with the agricultural policies of the New Deal. She and Garrett were equally appalled at the freedoms the farmers were asked to sacrifice for the presumed benefits of the various farm programs, mainly strict production and marketing agreements; but what particularly struck Rose was the operation of the Resettlement Administration, an agency of the Agricultural Adjustment Administration, which they saw at work in Polk County, Illinois. Here, on marginal land, were poor farmers—some who had lived on the land for years, some who had recently taken up cheap land when city jobs had failed—under siege by government agents whose mission was to move them off the land. The grand scheme was to reduce marginal production and redevelop eroded farms as grasslands, but the reluctant farmers stood in the way. The carrot was the offer of government employment in the redevelopment, government loans to take up better land, government-planned community centers; the stick was the threat of condemnation. Rose could think of nothing so much as the agricultural reforms she had seen in Soviet Georgia and the more ominous news of Stalin's collectivization of Soviet farms. "Communist Terror in Illinois," she would later call it. By the time she and Garrett reached Kansas, she had undergone another formative experience, reacting both viscerally and consciously against the national defeatism by which so many farmers were acceding to such drastic measures. She was ready to resist, if she could but find some small way to exert leverage.[18]

The piece she wrote just after Garrett's departure was entitled simply "Credo." Adelaide Neall of the *Saturday Evening Post* had solicited a personal article from her, probably as a result of political opinions intimated in a "Who's Who" profile the *Post* had done of her earlier in 1935: "I am now a fundamentalist American," Rose had written then; "give me time and I will tell you why individualism, laissez-faire, and the slightly restrained anarchy of capitalism offer the best possibilities for the development of the human spirit." Invited to expand this premise, Rose sent Neall her "Credo"; but for some reason it was returned. Six months later, Rose sent it to George Bye (who was a Roosevelt supporter, and later agent for Eleanor Roosevelt) as part of a continuing correspondence about politics. "I'd like you to understand why I'm a Jeffersonian Democrat," Rose wrote, "and will vote for anybody—Hoover, Harding, Al Capone— who will stop the New Deal." Despite his liberal politics, Bye was so struck with the force of the piece that he resubmitted it to the *Post*, where it was read by different eyes and published immediately.[19]

"Sixteen years ago I was a Communist," Rose began, distorting her own personal history a bit and making an impossible claim to have been present at Jack Reed's organization of the Communist Party in America. She had, no doubt, been at some meeting in Reed's presence in New York, but it was not the historic one she claimed. This stretch of the truth, however, is not central to her argument; but rather is a reach for rhetorical authority. She then recapitulates her early commitment, as a morally conscious intellectual, to the extension of human freedom by seizing economic control from the capitalist and ceding it to the state—a notion that she had held unexamined, she claimed, until her visit with a Russian peasant family in 1922. Her host was probably the same peasant who had asked, "Why doesn't the government go ahead and govern, and let us alone?" In this new context, Rose re-creates a new dramatic scene, as he complains of the Communist government:

"It is too big," he said. "Too big. And at the top, too small. It will not work. In Moscow there are only men, and man is not God. A man has only a man's head, and one hundred heads together do not make one great head. Only God can know Russia."

A westerner among Russians often suddenly feels that they are all slightly mad. At other times, their mysticism seems plain common sense. It is quite true that many heads do not make one great head; in fact, they make a session of Congress. What, then, I asked myself dizzily, is the State? The Communist State—does it exist? Can it exist? . . .

The picture of the economic revolution as the final step to freedom was false as soon as I asked myself that question. For, in practical fact, the State, the Government, cannot exist. . . . What does, in fact, exist, is a man, or a few men, in power over many men.

A philosopher might say that Rose had simply discovered the theory of nominalism, that only particulars are real. But this is not to diminish the force of her discovery that she had really, so to speak, been a nominalist all her life, and that the discovery had profound implications for a theory of government. From such a premise she could logically defend her deepest social instincts: that individual experience is primary; that freedom is mankind's natural condition; that society is a derived concept, at best an occasional epiphenomenon; that anarchy is an ideal condition; that government is a necessary evil, to be held in check against its natural tendency to tyranny. Out of such bedrock assumptions she could erect a theory of history that discovered America's greatness in its experiment with minimally limited anarchy, an anarchy that had permitted unprecedented experiment, innovation, and, finally, prosperity. By contrast, Europe had barely emerged from the dead hands of feudalism and monarchy and was already sinking back into another form of tyranny, that of state socialism. Implicitly, the present danger was that under the stress of the Depression, Americans would yield up their freedom for the promised security of the New Deal. She thinks not, at least not in her old home town and the other communities she has visited across the countryside:

The spirit of individualism is still here. Not half of the reported unemployed have ever appeared on the relief rolls; somewhere those millions who have not been helped are still fighting through this depression on their own. Millions of farmers are still lords on their own land; they are not receiving checks from the public funds to which they contribute their taxes. Millions of men and women have quietly been paying debts from which they have asked no release, and somehow being cheerful in the daytime and finding God knows what strength in themselves during the black nights. Americans are still paying the price of individual liberty, which is individual responsibility and insecurity.[20]

Roosevelt, the New Deal, and the forthcoming elections of 1936 received no mention; but the *Post*, which opposed the New Deal editorially at every turn, was glad to find such an eloquent spokesman for its cause and featured "Credo" as a lead article. As a statement of principle it had been gestating in Rose's thought since 1929, but its basis in her experience went back to her earliest childhood. "Sweet are the uses of adversity," she had written over and over in her school copybook. For twenty-five years she had ridden the crest of opportunity, discovering new resources within herself at each slip and recovery; since the Crash, she had discovered the principle of her deepest reflex, the frightening but exhilarating pathos of individual freedom. The exemplar was that terrifying rebel and skeptic, the Wandering Jew; and the dream of achieving the dearly bought amplitude of his experience might be replaced by the reality of a life absolutely free to pursue it—"within the slavery of self-discipline," as she had written in *Old Home Town*. "The question," as she now put it to her readers in "Credo," "is whether personal freedom is worth the terrible effort, the never-lifted burden and risks of individual self-reliance." Any answer other than a yes could only be a betrayal of American history.

"Credo" was a strikingly popular piece, and its reception gave a real lift to her spirits. One businessman brought it to the attention of the National Association of Manufacturers, recommending wide distribution; and Herbert Hoover himself wrote to praise it, saying he would try to get millions of copies into circulation. Longmans, Green brought it out almost immediately as a pamphlet entitled *Give Me Liberty*. Rose was particularly interested that this reprint be priced cheaply enough to reach a wide audience by way of newsstand sales; she offered to sacrifice part of her royalties to keep the price at fifty cents. She found local evidence that its message needed widespread iteration: some twenty University of Missouri students called on her, and "all wanted to know what one asked in these words, 'Of course, we understand you wrote that for the money, but what do you *really* think? You don't mean you think there's any good in capitalism?'" These same students told her that there were six members of the Communist party on the faculty; and in looking over literature anthologies, she found that they included "Stuart Chase, Veblen, and redder moderns." She had scoffed at the notion of a Red menace in New York in 1930, but she was much readier to see the evidence now.[21]

IV

Meanwhile, Mama Bess had been forging ahead with her fourth juvenile manuscript, quarrying out and expanding portions of "Pioneer Girl." The first three books had enjoyed good sales and were producing a small but significant income; she reported to Rose an eight-hundred-dollar

check for the first half of 1936. By midsummer she delivered the manuscript of *On the Banks of Plum Creek* to Rose: "I have written you the whys
of the story as I wrote it," Mama Bess noted. "But you know your judge-
ment is better than mine, so what you decide is the one that stands." Rose
turned from her other work to deal with it: "have to finish my mother's
goddam juvenile, which has me stopped flat," she entered in her diary.
Two months later she had a finished manuscript ready to return to her
mother, along with a letter instructing Mama Bess how to mail it to George
Bye. She included a draft of a letter for Mama Bess to write to Bye, requesting him to negotiate better terms for this book. Mama Bess complied, copying Rose's letter verbatim in her own hand.[22]

But the arrival of Mama Bess's manuscript on Rose's desk was coin-
cident with an obscure contretemps that can only be guessed at from its
results. In the same diary entry that notes "my mother's goddam juvenile," Rose summarizes a bad week: "This week is all shot to hell by my
mother's yowls. I have written Corinne to take everything on the farm
and I will close the place. End 9 years of an utterly idiotic attempt." The
decision was sudden but apparently easy to make. Rose's earlier plan had
been to stay in Columbia only long enough to finish research for the
Missouri book; the project was dead for the moment, but she had hopes
of revising it for publication by Longmans. At the same time, she had to
work steadily for the magazines to keep her income flowing, and such
divided attention seemed to require that she stay in place. Doubtless,
too, she felt a real relief to be away from the farm and her mother's daily
ministrations; certainly her writing was going better since she had left.
Meanwhile, she had tried to keep that establishment running by means
of weekend visits and frequent letters, while Corinne, the boys, and
Mama Bess came up to Columbia for occasional visits, which Rose had to
host. It was a fragmented life that cried out for simplification. What Mama
Bess's yowls were about we can only guess, but she cast a jaundiced eye
at the unusual arrangements at Rocky Ridge farmhouse. In truth, there
was probably some justice in her complaints, as she saw the Rocky Ridge
farmhouse, scene of years of her own labors, taken over by strangers and
her daughter an absentee landlord. She did not approve of the presence
of John and Al Turner, who were in trouble over appropriating the tires of
an abandoned car, nor of Corinne Murray's upkeep of the place. Upon
some provocation, finally, she ordered Rose "to come back at once to stay
(and throw Corinne out) or get out myself." And she ordered the hired
man to kill Rose's dog, which he did.[23]

In any event, Rose could not bring herself to return to Rocky Ridge
Farm. Corinne took the furnishings to her home in Mansfield. Rose had
already brought the boys to Columbia for the summer for special tutor-
ing in math, and as events unfolded they would not return either. She
and John had talked about sending him away from Mansfield to finish

high school; their choice settled on New Mexico Military Institute, and once she had made enough sales to the magazines to see a year ahead, she enrolled him for the fall term. Al she enrolled at the University High School in Columbia to complete his senior year, with promises to help him if he enrolled at the university. Mama Bess's books were beginning to provide an income that promised fair to free Rose from worry about her mother's future. Perhaps an occasional visit would be all that she would need.[24]

The summer passed in a swelter of heat and maternal solicitude. In her ninth-floor apartment, the city heat of a Missouri summer rising around her, Rose found herself writing as she had in Athens, between showers and without clothes. John and Al, lodged nearby, diligently picked their way through algebra with the aid of a tutor, a graduate student at the university. With no chores to do, John blossomed into a charming and occasionally thoughtful young man, for whom Rose began to entertain high hopes; Al, always less trouble, she also found considerably more naive. She sent John away to the Colorado mountains for two weeks before seeing him off to New Mexico by way of Texas, where he was to spend a couple of weeks at the Texas Centennial. George Bye suggested that she write of her personal experiences with her informally adopted sons, but she refused: "I can not think of a worse atrocity than exploiting them in print, for them and their friends to read, their misfortune and our relationship. . . . Youngsters need mothers, much less for the incidentals of food and shelter than for an assurance of emotional safety, one refuge where they are absolutely certain of not being betrayed."[25]

The role of mother to this unorthodox family was one she took seriously, and it did in time find its way into her writing in passing references to her "sons" and their struggles in the world. She had kept a watchful eye on the Turner boys' problems in school, and she was appalled at the lax standards she found in the high schools: the boys learned little because little was demanded of them, she decided. The contrast with her own meager schooling and her hungry self-education struck her strongly, of course, and she saw little in the university student body to make her believe that higher education was any better. Her growing contempt for formal education tracked nicely with the radical individualism of her other views, and she would argue vigorously for the superiority of experience in the "real world." One day a student from the university, Norma Lee Browning, came to interview her for the school newspaper and, incidentally, to show her some of her own writing. Rose liked what she saw, in person and on paper, and encouraged her—to quit school, study writing under Rose's tutelage, and find her education in the world around her. Browning was stunned, but she demurred: she had, after all, only another year to finish her degree. But she had been marked forcibly by the impress of Rose's personality: in this graying, matronly woman she had found an intellectual energy and a commitment to the living power of ideas that made her own university education seem pale. She would soon be drawn back into an orbit around Rose as model, mentor, and finally, life-long friend—becoming for Rose much that John Turner never would be.[26]

John Turner was planning for college, of course, as was Al, and Rose encouraged them as she had Rexh Meta—allowing that, as the world stood, a degree was a key to advancement however much it might delay a real education. As summer turned into fall, Norma Lee Browning went back to her classes, John was gone to New Mexico, and Al was in high school all day; and Rose was suddenly reminded of the remainder of her family across the sea. Rexh Meta wrote to say that he was getting married soon, to a childhood sweetheart he had courted, often without hope, through the traditional Moslem approaches to her father. Rose had followed the courtship for several years, offering advice and consolation through its many convolutions. Now all difficulties were resolved, save one that Rose could see without being told. She was broke at the moment, but she borrowed two hundred dollars from George Bye to send Rexh and his bride Pertef to Budapest on their honeymoon. And shortly she found that she could write about this son, a charming short story about an Albanian boy's tragic youth and the courtship of his childhood sweetheart, "The Song without Words."[27]

BETWEEN TWO WORLDS

14

> *One thing I hate about the New Deal is that it is killing*
> *. . . the American pioneering spirit.*

It was an irony to be transcended that her powers began to return even as she felt herself slipping into a profound isolation from her times. Although she never put it this way herself, in a sense the nineteenth century was ending for her. Her personal markers in this transition would be the deaths of the two great editors she most respected, Fremont Older and George Horace Lorimer. To Older's biographer she wrote, the year after his death, "something is gone; the world is not the same; a light clicked out, and I do not care for anything, not anything, as much as I did. So I shall not mind dying as much as I would have." Lorimer died in 1937, and the news prompted Rose to write his son a touching letter of condolence that linked Older and Lorimer in the same way. "To me it is a comfort in my own sense of loss, to know that the greatest American of my time had a life which near its end gave him completeness and satisfaction."[1]

The election of 1936 was a severe blow to Rose. Heretofore, she and Garet Garrett could console themselves that no one had ever voted on the New Deal, and that the nation might yet be retrieved from the course Roosevelt had mapped for it. But in November the nation did vote on the New Deal, and there was no mistaking that she and Garrett would represent a minority position for a time to come. Both of them were finding it difficult to write under the prevailing climate of opinion: the great modern writers, Rose suggested, succeeded on the strength of their hatred for the modern world, while those who affirmed traditional values did it in the weak and trivial forms of magazine fiction. In the middle, however, was the writer like herself, "who has felt sometimes a possibility of writing strongly and truly, [but] has felt at the same time an inexplicable lack of strength to do so . . . was it a perception of one's helplessness against the times?" "It seems to me," she wrote Garrett, "that what has happened is a closing of that gap between Faulkner and Kathleen Norris."

> America has at last become one people, united in an affirmative.
> You and I, what we are and what we remember and represent, this
> has been finally, definitely rejected. The time for the negations,
> the rejections and contempts, of the Huxleys and Faulkners, is past,

and the thinness of the Faith Baldwins will not be enough now. There
will be writers who will speak, as Mark Twain spoke, out of this af-
firmative audience and to it, and they will be great writers again.

And I think it will be a hundred years, or five hundred, before
what America was will begin to stir again in history and to find its
voices. . . . I am still au fond so American that I am an optimist
believing in Life. Anyone who believes in Life must love and have
faith in his murderer.[2]

Whatever her intellectual relationship with Garrett, it was in some
attenuated sense a romantic one as well. She was nearing fifty now, he
seven years older—short, fat, and balding, with a voice husky from an
old bullet wound and missing some fingers as well. They had kept up a
correspondence after their 1935 trip through the Midwest, and in her
isolation he was one of the few minds she could reach out to for understanding. His letters just before and after the 1936 election are marked
with a deepening pessimism, hers with indignation. People asked him
what was wrong with Roosevelt's economic plans. "It wasn't that they
didn't understand what I said," he complained. "It was that what I said
didn't interest them. . . . They wanted manna and water out of the rock.
I wanted people to stay hard and fit and self responsible, for the sake of
going on." She lamented that even the Republicans accepted the New
Deal as new, rather than a reactionary return to state authority, a counter-
revolution. "If there be any immediate hope at all (of this country's avoid-
ing Europe's debacle) it is that somehow, from somewhere in this multi-
tude, young men will come, knowing what America, the American revolution, is in principle . . . wanting to fight for it."

In this bed of sympathetic principle, something like love bloomed,
crusty and irritable on his side, quietly supplicating on hers. He likened
himself to a barnacle on a rock. "Only two things can pry me off. One is
death and the other is a female. That is why I hate females. . . . You are
not that kind of shell fish. And if you were, what would be the use of
sticking side by side to a sea cliff?" In April she wrote to him: "I have
done no work since the first of March. If you will write to me, no matter
what, just a word, a few lines, only that there may just once be your blue
envelope in the postbox, I swear that this time I shall not answer. This
time the resolution will hold; not a word in reply from me." Her diary for
the next two weeks notes again and again no mail, no blue envelopes.
"What stands this twice-a-day blow over the heart?" But the heart in time
reconciled itself to this loss as well.[3]

||

She would be surprised to learn from George Bye at the end of the year
that she had earned nine thousand dollars in 1936. It was her best year

since 1926, when she had received ten thousand dollars for her serial *Cindy*. She was receiving from two thousand to twenty-five hundred dollars for her short pieces now and she felt increasingly confident as her income rose. In her budget calculations she mentally set aside a thousand dollars to send John and Al Turner to Europe to broaden their education.[4]

She had a large work in hand now. For several years she had worked intermittently on a novel called "Free Land," and on a factual narrative called "Hard Winter." Probably one coalesced into the other at some point, as both drew on her parents' stories of frontier life in Dakota. She seems to have first conceived of it as a three-part serial on the order of *Let the Hurricane Roar*, but as the year progressed it began to double in size. After *Let the Hurricane Roar* she would draw more and more on her parents' Dakota experiences for her short stories as well, and her work and her mother's were approaching a convergence. For Mama Bess was now at work on a manuscript she called "Silver Lake," and as Rose wrote home with a detailed questionnaire about life on the frontier, her mother warned her off of at least one incident that she planned to use herself.[5]

A harder problem was to achieve some convergence between her fiction and her emerging ideology. A decade earlier she had lamented to Moyston, as she now did to Garrett, that good if not great writing depended upon a consonance between the writer and the values of the age. But whereas in the twenties she had felt alienated by the materialism of the machine age and longed for the premodern integrity of European culture, she now found herself extolling the prosperity achieved by American culture and fearing its loss in some collapse into a version of European statism. Her very premise threatened to undercut her work, and she knew it. "I know that Mr. Lorimer and others on the staff are disappointed in me, because I did not follow HURRICANE with more fiction in that genre," she had written to Garrett: "I tried, but I could not do it. What I believe is not true unless it is true in its time; and I can not write today of what America was, except in tones of loss and sorrow and pessimism . . . and that is not true in me." She repeated the dilemma to George Bye, asking his advice. "You see the thing from the outside, as I can't. Here is a certain facility with words, and a name for whatever it is worth. I suppose I will go on writing for another twenty years. What would you do, in my place?" Bye's answer has not survived, but we can assume that he replied with only the most genial kind of encouragement. She wrote on, as she always did, under the lash of necessity, hoping to make *Free Land* something more than an exercise in nostalgia.[6]

Faith is easy when confirmed by events and supported by other believers shoulder to shoulder. When it is discredited by events and abandoned by friends, the mettle of the true believer is tested. Every arena becomes more restricted, the narrow fellowship of the remaining faithful becomes more highly valued, and tolerance is sacrificed to ideology. Rose found herself caught between an honored past and a frightening future, the one a ground for unswerving optimism and the other promising only despair. "Cognitive dissonance" is a term thrown up by the psychobabble of our day, and it certainly describes the stress of holding old beliefs against all evidence from the present. From this time on she would be subject to an increasing brittleness of temperament, a dissociation between the natural charm and vitality of her engagement with the world and the watchful suspicion toward a hostile world that verges on paranoia. Once she had been able to dismiss Communism as a European aberration that could not take root in the States, but the growing membership of the Party and its larger voice in the intellectual medley of the nation increased her fears; and from her perspective the measurable distance between the threats to personal freedom by the Party and by the Roosevelt administration continued to diminish.

The two threats seemed to coalesce as she contemplated the election, the leftist inclination of some of the university faculty (who presumably had cast the few votes for Earl Browder) and Roosevelt's attempt, following his victory, to pack the Supreme Court. She had herself cast a despairing vote for Landon (the only one in town, she claimed), and she had since the beginning of the New Deal viewed with alarm the recurring criticism of the Supreme Court as an obstacle to Roosevelt's programs. As she later told the story, a young faculty wife diffidently asked her what she thought of Roosevelt's plan. Rose told her that she thought it would wreck the Constitution, and also that she planned to send a telegram of protest to the state's congressional delegation. The young woman wanted to sign, but was afraid to because her husband's position would be jeopardized. She returned home, but later that day a stream of visitors came to Rose's room to sign the telegram, 632 in all. These were, Rose said, the common people speaking out against Roosevelt's plan.[7]

The leftist writer Anna Louise Strong came to Columbia, and as a member of the city's intellectual community Rose was invited to a dinner in her honor, and pointedly absented herself. She good-naturedly tolerated the irony that George Bye was Eleanor Roosevelt's agent, and was thus invited to the Inauguration, and even the compounded irony that Eleanor Roosevelt had read *Let the Hurricane Roar.* "I've never doubted that the Roosevelts are personally charming people," she wrote.

> Who does Mrs. Roosevelt think are the new pioneers? One thing I hate about the New Deal is that it is killing what, to me, is the American pioneering spirit. I simply do not know what to tell my own boys, leaving school and confronting this new world whose ideal is Security and whose practice is dependence upon government instead of upon one's self. . . . All the old character-values seem simply insane from a practical point of view; the self-reliant, the independent, the courageous man is penalized from every

direction, and must increasingly be, until he is liquidated. How can I wish my boys to be kulaks? that road ends in Siberia.

And in one of the increasingly radical movements of thought that would make her seem to some people slightly loony, she raises the possibility of political assassination:

> I hoped that Roosevelt would be killed in 1933. If there were any genuine adherence to American political principles in this country, any man in public life with the simple decency to forget his own personal picayune interests and stand for them, I would make a try at killing FDR now. . . . When a man embodies political principles, what he is personally makes no difference whatever, either to history or to me.

Today such a letter could get her jailed, or at least visited by the Secret Service. It is more than mere bravado, and it gains resonance from her earlier acceptance of assassination as a political instrument in Albania. But it was probably not so much a threat as it was a rhetorical symptom of her anxiety. From the sunnier side of her nature came a more typical anecdote that reflected, she thought, Roosevelt's true status with the American people. She told of sitting in a packed movie theater where the end of the newsreel was devoted to Roosevelt. "The President was an anti-climax to football," she wrote Bye.

> . . . first there was a lapse of attention, then restlessness, then a growing sense that the smile and the waved hat expected well-merited applause . . . and a spattering response, sincere but perfunctory. Suddenly on the screen flashed the words, Mickey Mouse . . . and from the heart of every one of the thousand burst a roar of deafening applause. Oh why? I cried in my embittered soul, O why didn't the Republicans nominate Mickey Mouse?[8]

III

It was time to relocate again. She had cut her ties to Rocky Ridge Farm and had uprooted the boys from rural Missouri as well. John Turner had not had a happy year at New Mexico Military Institute. His grades were at times very good, and he did complete his high school degree, but his adviser reported that he was not working to capacity and that socially he was not adjusting well; the burden of several letters was that John was in many ways immature and probably not ready for matriculation at a major university. Typically, Rose concluded that travel and experience in the world would be good for both of the Turner boys. Al had completed his high school work as well, and she offered to reward them both: either she would buy them motorcycles to travel to Mexico, or she would send them to Europe, but she recommended the second as Europe seemed on the verge of destroying itself for good. With such advice, both decided to visit Europe. John would spend a year studying in Paris to finish his preparation for college. Al Turner had less definite plans, but he would go abroad for the summer. A friend of his would accompany him, while for John's companion Rose recruited his math tutor, Charles Clark, a recent PhD in chemistry from the university who was going to an appointment at a research institute in Paris. The boys' passage was booked from Montreal in June of 1937, and in the middle of that month Rose and John left the Tiger Hotel by bus for New York City. As he went on to Montreal, she stayed behind to find lodgings for the time it would take to complete *Free Land*.[9]

Although it was not clear to her at the time, she had left Missouri for good. Her heart had quailed at the prospect of the move, largely because at New York prices she would have to live in diminished circumstances. She had really lived in considerable comfort for nominal rent in Columbia's Tiger Hotel; and as her friend Mary Paxton Keeley planned the building of an elegant little house, Rose fought off the temptation to buy and refurbish a home in Columbia. As the old lust for a home of her own reasserted itself after two years in a hotel suite, she appealed to George Bye for help in finding suitable quarters in New York. In a hilarious letter, she catalogued all the possibilities of New York quarters, mentioning particularly the Grosvenor Hotel "for around $100. a month, with nothing extra charged for smell of plumbing." In her Columbia suite she had a thirty-mile view and morning sun; "at the Grosvenor I can gaze at an airless airshaft and wish those hellish traps would be as decent as mousetraps and strangle us to death *quickly*." On her arrival in New York, she settled briefly at 5 Prospect Place; her funds were down to seven dollars until she wrote and placed another story with the *Post*. The twenty-five hundred dollars it brought, along with an advance from George Bye, would support her boys in Europe and her own needs while she finished *Free Land*. Presently she relocated to the Grosvenor Hotel, 35 Fifth Avenue. It would be her home for the following year.[10]

Gazing into the airless air shaft of the Grosvenor, Rose forged ahead with *Free Land*, working, she recalled, fourteen to twenty hours a day. She was now squarely within her parents' pioneer experience as she attempted to draw together her writing and her ideology. *Let the Hurricane Roar* had been her mother's parents' story, which Mama Bess was now retelling from her own point of view; *Free Land* would become in large measure Almanzo Wilder's story, the one Graeme Lorimer had urged Rose to write. Almanzo, now eighty years old, emerges dimly in this family of two outspoken, hard-driving women as a taciturn, industrious lover of horses and farming whose occasional indulgences were a cigar and a game of pool. In the interests of authenticity in her narrative, Rose plied him with letters and a questionnaire about his early life; Mama

Bess went to work on him too, and pried out of "the oyster," as she called him, details that were new to her after fifty years of marriage. His responses to Rose's queries, free-form in spelling and innocent of punctuation, provided both the axis and significant detail for her retelling of the family story in *Free Land*.[11]

The title was consciously ironic, an echo of the complaint Rose and Mama Bess bridled against throughout the Depression: "But everything is changed now; there's no more free land." Their response was that there never was any free land: only hard work conferred ownership. "We often talk of the thing you mention," Mama Bess wrote to Rose, "there being no opportunities now."

> If we had had such opportunities when we were young we would have been rich. If we were only a little younger than we are we would do something about them. Anyone who will half try can make money surprisingly now. How they can keep from it I can't see, nor what they do with the money they can't prevent themselves from making.
>
> . . . Of course, nobodys else [*sic*] business is any of mine. But I find my heart is getting harder. I can have no least sympathy for people any more who can do and will only holler that there is no chance any more.
>
> I wish they *all* might have the opportunities we had when I was young *and no more*. Wouldn't it be fun to watch 'em?

Free Land would pose dramatically just what those opportunities had been.[12]

IV

Even as Rose struggled with *Free Land*, Mama Bess's literary career was taking a national turn. Each of her three books had been well received, the third, *Little House on the Prairie*, particularly. The fourth, *On the Banks of Plum Creek*, was in press in the autumn of 1937 and she was working on the fifth, which would be entitled *By the Shores of Silver Lake*. She now found herself invited to address an audience at a Book Week celebration at the great Hudson's Department Store in Detroit, Michigan. Publishers, booksellers, librarians, and authors would be gathered, a professional whirl that Rose would have handled easily but that would be a new challenge for her mother. The Wilders now had a late-model Chrysler automobile, but the long trip to a large city was daunting until they found a younger friend in Mansfield who agreed to accompany them and take over the driving. Mama Bess's talk was scheduled for October 16, and on her arrival at the Statler Hotel she found a letter from Rose awaiting her, complete with verbatim instructions on how to manage the hotel service and to make contact with her editor from Harper's.[13]

The talk itself is almost the only text by Laura Ingalls Wilder in her career as novelist in which Rose had no direct hand, although the ideas were probably the result of years of discussion, and the daughter is easy to hear behind her mother's voice. For her Detroit audience, Mama Bess located her impulse to write in a desire to preserve her father's stories, which she put off until she was past sixty, "when I wrote my first book, *Little House in the Big Woods.*" After its success, she continued,

> I began to think what a wonderful childhood I had had. How I had seen the whole frontier, the woods, the Indian country of the great plains, the frontier towns, the building of the railroads on wild, unsettled country, homesteading and farmers coming in to take possession.
> I realized that I had seen and lived it all—all the successive phases of the frontier, first the frontiersman, then the pioneer, then the farmers and the towns.
> Then I understood that in my own life I represented a whole period of American history. That the frontier was gone and agricultural settlements had taken its place when I married a farmer.
> It seemed to me that my childhood had been much richer and more interesting than that of children today, even with all the modern inventions and improvements.
> I wanted the children now to understand more about the beginning of things, to know what is behind the things they see—what it is that made America as they know it.

We can detect here, certainly, a consonance with her daughter's interest in drawing on the pioneer past to revitalize the flagging present. The identification of herself as a representative American type sounds like Rose's kind of historical analysis. And certainly, as Mama Bess continues her talk, we can hear echoes of the great, multivolumed series of American novels Rose had once projected:

> Then I thought of writing the story of my childhood in several volumes—a seven volume historical novel for children, covering every aspect of the American frontier.
> After the work was well started, I was told that such a thing had never been done before, that a novel of several volumes was only for grown-ups.
> When I told my daughter . . . about it, she said it would be unique, that a seven volume novel for children had never been written.

It is an interesting document: in essential ways true enough, no doubt, yet shot through with a disingenuous pose of autonomy that would have infuriated Rose if the speaker had been, say, Frederick O'Brien. In Mama Bess's own words, "All I have told is true, but it is not the whole truth." When Rose saw the text of the talk, she simply wrote, "Detroit talk came and it is *fine*. No wonder you made a great hit."[14]

By this time, the house on Rocky Ridge Farm was occupied again. Once Rose had decided she was not coming back, Corinne Murray and her husband continued in residence for a time. But with Rose no longer sharing expenses, there was no advantage to their remaining, and they moved back to their quarters in town, probably at Rose's urging. Rose's parents took possession and gradually moved back in—Mama Bess so flamingly resentful of Corinne Murray's books left behind that she savagely threatened to burn them. The little English cottage, all that remained of Rose's stock-market fortune, would be rented and, in time, sold. It had always been more Rose's idea than theirs, and the old farmhouse represented the toil of all the years since 1894. There Mama Bess resumed her work on the next volume of her life story.[15]

Rose could no longer offer immediate counsel and supervision, or even come home on weekends any more. She would continue to receive Mama Bess's manuscripts by mail, and the counsel would go out by return post. She was still trying to bring Mama Bess's narrative skills, which were essentially those of an oral storyteller, up to the standard of a modern novelist. Nothing puts more clearly Rose's contribution to her mother's work than a letter that tries to explain to Mama Bess her shortcomings: "As to similarity in our writing, of course. You often write lines and whole paragraphs that I feel are what I would have written or anyway wish I had. What you haven't developed is structure, a kind of under-rhythm in the whole body of the writing, and a 'pointing up' here and there. And you often fail to put in detail." Rose then suggests the value of copying long passages of another writer's work in developing a critical sense of style. She recommends, in a profound irony, that Mama Bess copy over one of her already published books, presumably to help internalize all the changes Rose had made in the original:

> Copying gives you the attitude of the writer, not the reader. You will find many things that you want to change, and when you do, just change them, write them your way. But you will see that in each paragraph there is a rhythm, a sort of broken-tune, underneath, and that the chapters and the whole book have their rhythms, too. And when you want to break these rhythms you will figure out why, and see and feel the rhythm you substitute. You will also note the details as they come in. . . .

There follows a densely packed page-and-a-half of prosody, phonology, and prose poetics generally. It is hard to believe that Rose really expected this all to stick; there is an undercurrent of showmanship and display, as in many of her letters; and the effect is not so much to instruct Mama Bess as to demonstrate an arcane craft that she will never learn. But Rose has it to throw away: "A good bit of the detail I add to your copy is for pure sensory effect. Take a chapter like GRASSHOPPER WEATHER in PLUM CREEK. You have your copy and I do not remember it in detail." It is a revealing letter, in which the tenor is to encourage Mama Bess, but the burden is to remind her, in her new fame, of her dependence on the ghost behind her books.[16]

V

As the fall of 1937 declined into winter, and Rose sat gazing into the air shaft of the Grosvenor Hotel, she had not only her aging parents in Mansfield to distract her from her work, but also her surrogate family of three sons in three different places. Al Turner was back from a summer in Europe and enrolled in the University of Missouri at Columbia; he was twenty now, and apparently his arrangement with Rose was that he would attempt to live independently at that age. She let him go, but she kept him under proxy observation by her friend, Mary Paxton Keeley:

> Mary, he can not possibly do it. He has about twenty dollars
> . . . This is going to be the toughest time he ever had. I'm letting him walk right into it. . . .
> At the same time, I don't want it to break him. I don't want him to see nothing to do but give up. . . . Let me know if he is not getting enough to eat, or if there is something he really should do and can not do for lack of money.[17]

Her concern was misplaced, for Al Turner proved able to care for himself, and in time he would go on to a good career as an engineer with the McDonnell Douglas Company.

John Turner and Charles Clark were bicycling in Germany as Rose wrote of her concern about Al. In jest, John sent her a picture postcard of a man some Americans still found comical, Adolf Hitler. John and Clark had spent the summer in England and Paris and would return to Paris for the winter, where Clark would take up his research appointment and John would live at the Fondation des Etats Unis and enroll for classes at the Sorbonne. His letters show a quick and lively mind and an appropriate gratitude for the opportunity Rose has offered him, as well as a boundless confidence in his own opinions. Rose's intentions were clearly to make of this eighteen-year-old rural Missouri boy a cosmopolitan sophisticate, such as she wished she had been at that age. She suggested he stay a second year in Germany, and she had hopes of sending him on to Albania—to meet Rexh—and to the Middle East before bringing him home for schooling. John's intentions hovered between enrolling at Cal Tech or Princeton and joining Al at Missouri. Rose's hopes for him were always higher than his own, and the intensity of her expectations would always be more than he could live up to.[18]

Rexh Meta offered her at once fewer worries and more consolation. He had been a man since he was a child, and she could count on him to chart his own direction and manage his own life. He was languishing in civil service jobs beneath his abilities and watching his country deterio- rate under Italian pressure and domestic intrigue; he was a true patriot, zealous for Albania's development, and saw his fate to be clearly tied to his country's. With no sense of comedy, he wrote of an abortive insur- rection led by an Albanian who had been influenced by *Mein Kampf.* In October Rexh's wife delivered a girl, who was named Borë-Rose, or Snow Rose, in honor of her father's benefactor. Rose sent an elaborate assem- blage of gifts, from books on care and feeding down to and including disposable diapers and an offer to send more regularly. To her offer to supply whatever else could not be bought in Albania, Rexh struggled with masculine ignorance and Moslem modesty to request for his wife a nursing brassiere. But by far the heaviest burden of his correspondence with Rose concerned itself with the purchase of land and a house. Rose still had dreams of an Albanian home, and what began to emerge at this time was a plan to provide Rexh with funds to buy land and build on it, with the understanding that the home would have a place for her when she was able to come. His letters report the search, the plans, and the negotiations in detail. Rose had hoped to remain a silent partner, but as Rexh began to bargain for property clearly beyond his means, he was suspected by some of having corrupted his government post by taking bribes or embezzling. To protect himself, he had to name his benefactor, which nonetheless cast him in a problematical light in Tirana society.[19]

This odd family she had assumed responsibility for was a constant distraction as she tried to go forward with some work that would win for her the money they needed. *Free Land* was growing into a big novel; Adelaide Neall, Rose's closest contact at *Saturday Evening Post,* was wait- ing for its delivery, and in September she wrote to George Bye, quoting a letter from Rose:

> Oh, I am heartsick about this story. The only hope is that I was hopeless about the bit you saw. You did say that the blizzard was cold. . . . This thing wears me out and I don't dare get outside of it and look at it because then I know it's no good and am scared everyone will agree with me this time. I'm somewhere near the 40,000th word. With I think about 20,000 more but faster ones to go before I can prove up on this cursed land. I'm plowing it with an ox-team now.

"I imagine," Neall observed to Bye, "this is Rose's usual state of mind when she is part way through a serial. What would you think about suggesting that she show us the 40,000 words she has written?" Rose was persuaded to turn over the partial manuscript, which was enough to warrant advances from the *Post* and from Bye to support the completion. By November she was turning in the final revision to the *Post* in sections, and once it was done it amounted to an eight-installment serial that would run in the *Post* over a two-month period. She received twenty-five thousand dollars, by far the most she had earned for anything. It was almost as much as she had lost in the stock market crash of 1929. She went to Philadelphia to spend Christmas with Adelaide Neall, then to New Jersey to visit Garet Garrett.[20]

VI

Her serial done and money in hand, Rose could turn again to her mother's work. Mama Bess's sense of her career as a writer had been given a lift by her reception in Detroit, and she now had several irons in the fire. She thought again of her old project of publishing children's verses, some of which had appeared variously over her name and Rose's in the *San Francisco Bulletin* more than twenty years earlier; and she approached Berta Hader with the proposal that they do a book together, Berta to furnish illustrations. The letter is remarkable for its thinly veiled calculation and a self-conscious puff of pride. "I have a large field of readers," she said truthfully, "because, as of course you know, my books have a large and increasing sale."

> I feel sure that my name will guarantee a good sale for the book of which some would undoubtedly be to readers unacquainted with your work. Your name would do as much for me. So I think a children's book carrying both our names will be sure of a satisfactory sale at least and be valuable to us both in increasing sales of your other books and my other books.[21]

Another project she floated concerned a manuscript that still remains problematical in the Wilder canon. The posthumous *First Four Years* was conceived and apparently outlined if not actually drafted sometime before 1937. Mama Bess's title for it was "The First Three Years and a Year of Grace," a story of her early married life. Late in 1937, she apparently wrote to Ida Louise Raymond, her editor at Harper's, that she had a "grown-up book" in mind. Raymond replied enthusiastically, and Mama Bess consulted Rose on the project. Her letter repeats one that Rose has lost:

> I thought it might wangle a little more advertising for the L. H. books if I said I might write the grown up one. It was not a promise and if I didn't it wouldn't matter. So I wrote that I had material for one in my head etc. Then I asked you if you ever expected to use the framework of The First Three Years and wondered if it would be worth while to write the one grown-up story of Laura and Almanzo to sort of be the cap-sheaf of the 7 volume children's novel.
>
> I could write the rough work. You could polish it and put your name to it if that would be better than mine.

Rose was not enthusiastic. "As to your doing a novel, there is no reason why you shouldn't if you want to, but unless by some wild chance you did a best-seller, there is much more money in juveniles." Whenever it might have been written, this manuscript would have to wait until after the death of both writers to find publication.[22]

The major problem at hand was the manuscript of *By the Shores of Silver Lake,* which Mama Bess had sent to Rose to work on. The surviving correspondence concerning this manuscript is the most extensive of any concerning Mama Bess's writing, and it shows her emerging *amour-propre* as a writer bumping against Rose's professional expertise. She had doubtless taken seriously Rose's encouragement that the writing of fiction was a craft that could be learned, and when late in 1937 she sent to Rose the manuscript of *Silver Lake,* it was clear that she had invested considerable thought and self-respect in an effort that she hoped could stand on its own merits.

Rose's detailed critique upset her. Rose thought the opening scene did not properly lead in from the previous book, she found much material too old for a children's book, and she found problems with a wavering point of view. In a series of letters, Mama Bess argued strongly for her material. "I truly think the way I have handled it is best," she wrote, while conceding that "you know best" and "without your fine touch, it would be a flop." And where she was not defending her technique, she assumed the legitimate priority of literal fact, what had really happened in her life. Rose had to read her a lesson in the truth of fiction as opposed to the truth of history, striking hard at her mother's naive assumption that the details of her life could stand without artistic justification: "You will just have to take my word for it."

"To make the changes you want to make in Silver Lake, it will have to be practically rewritten," Mama Bess complained by return mail; and a few days later, "Don't work on Silver Lake until you hear from me again. I am going over it carefully once more. . . . I was in hopes that I had profited enough by your teachings that my copy could go to the publishers, with perhaps a little pointing up of the high lights. If it could, then perhaps I could do the following two without being such a bother to you." Within a week or so, however, she had capitulated under the strain of trying to solve the problems Rose had pointed out to her. "Change the beginning of the story if you want. Do anything you please with the damn stuff if you will fix it up."

By and large, it seems, Rose had her way with the manuscript, working it over in the course of the following year. But not before writing her mother a conciliatory letter in an attempt to restore her confidence. "You don't know how much good your letter did me," Mama Bess replied, "and I can't tell you. You see I know the music but I can't think of the words. . . . Anyway your letter picked me up and gave me courage. It is sweet of you to say the nice things you did about my writing and I will try to deserve them more. . . . I am beginning Hard Winter as you suggested, with the strangeness of the geese not stopping at the lake."[23]

𝒻REE LAND, NEW HOMES, LOST SONS 15

Now we will have a place we can call home . . .

ree Land was serialized in eight parts in the *Saturday Evening Post* in March and April of 1938. Its early installments found a wide readership among those who prized the pioneer past, and she was invited, along with Dakota artist Harvey Dunn, to address the South Dakota Society of New York. In expanded form, *Free Land* was published as a book in May. It was Rose's most serious and sustained effort as a novelist, and it received uniformly good reviews and rose at once to the best-seller lists, where it remained until August. It had appeared just as the Pulitzer Prizes for the year were in the news, and the *New York Times* took the occasion to offer an editorial review of *Free Land* and recommend it to the Pulitzer committee for next year's award. Finally Rose had written a book that brought her both money and recognition.[1]

Her research for the Missouri book had given her certain insights regarding American character and history, and these had coalesced with family history to make possible a story that she and her admiring readers regarded as representatively American. In five years, from age nineteen on, her hero David Beaton pits his courage, skill, and endurance against the Dakota plains in the effort to make a farm for his wife and children. His trial by blizzard, drought, storm, bad luck, Indians, horse-thieves, and assorted minor calamities is met with laconic humor and unshakable optimism—a sustained trial that seems incredible in simple recitation but that is grounded in natural circumstance, firmly conceived character, and the actual history of Rose's own family. Plotting is minimal, confined to the comic relief of David's sister Eliza and her reform of a charming rascal; the real action is episodic, tied to the cycle of the seasons and the human rituals of marriage, birth, and death. By the end of five years, David is still on the land: his substantial capital gone, his substantial debt hanging heavy, but his optimism undampened. "I couldn't sell out today," he tells his father at the end, "every tot and tittle I own, and pay over half what I owe. But it's a good country. I'll be right here, father, when this farm's worth something."[2]

"This is a false ending," one reviewer complained, ". . . the only false note. . . . It leads one to believe that David conquered. Some did and do conquer. But the odds!" Rose's reply appealed to history: many made good in Dakota, she pointed out, and between the droughts some were actually prosperous. But the real issue was a conception of optimism; she quoted a poem from somewhere in her reading, an epitaph presumably from a Greek island tombstone:

> A ship-wrecked sailor, buried on this coast,
> Bids you set sail.
> Full many a gallant ship, when we were lost,
> Weathered the gale.[3]

In fact, Rose had gone to some lengths to avoid a facile optimism. Young David's early marriage, a cliche of romance, turns out to be a mistake of the heart, but one he resigns himself to live with. His later career is framed in that of his father, who watches his son struggle to repeat his own successes as farmer. The older man, first and last, is given to quiet moments watching the stars, when it is clear to him that life, finally, is tragic—when he recalls his own grandfather's summation: "My life has been mostly disappointments." The words were Almanzo Wilder's in a letter to Rose, and they reach back to his failure as a plains pioneer. In *Free Land*, the rhythm of struggle and setback suggests that, even at the end, nothing is guaranteed for young David Beaton, though Rose does permit herself an ironic *deus ex machina* as David's father resolves to advance his son some much-needed cash—charged to his future inheritance. "I don't know as you noticed it when you was to home," he tells his son, "but ever since you young ones was born to mother and me, I wanted you to have an easier time than we did."[4]

The point, of course, is that David most certainly has not. But he has the character of the ancient Greek sailor, or the Albanian mountaineer, or the teenaged heroine of *Let the Hurricane Roar*: a life-affirming optimism that sustains him against all odds. This understated heroic pathos Rose would ultimately find a basis for in a simple metaphysics, but she had long since found it manifest in human nature: it derived, for her, from that very ground of life she had truly grasped on only rare occasions, the knowledge that human life shared with all creation. One remembers her touching discovery of the defiant young owlet in the tree at Rocky Ridge, her throbbing identification with the flame in sunlight, her invocation of a deeper strength for Dorothy Thompson's grief in her divorce, the lift of the heart that came with her gaze toward the Albanian mountains. But it was the essence of this vision that it could be grasped but not held, pursued but not maintained. Thus, eventually, her acceptance of adversity, even her perverse love of failure—for the sake of the vital moment when it is transcended and human nature knows itself.

From such a ground, through a series of implicit major and minor premises, flows a social and political theory that surfaces in Rose's narrative in the thoughts and actions of her characters. David Beaton is a homesteader, but his father has never liked the governmental homestead program:

> He did not believe in giving, or getting, something for nothing. He believed in every man's paying his own way. . . . The Beatons, men like them, had paid for that public land, had worked and paid taxes to buy it from France and Spain and to settle the war with Mexico. It belonged to the people who had worked to pay for it; it should honestly be sold to lighten their taxes. . . .
> "Who supports the Government," he had asked. . . . "We do, don't we? the people? Well then, don't it stand to reason the Government can't support the people?"

But from a corrupt premise corrupt practices flow, as throughout the book the requirements of the Homestead Act are routinely flouted. Even David Beaton lies about his age to file a claim, asserting a natural right prior to the legal fiction. "He pushed back his hat and felt fine. Beating a legality was a satisfaction, like paying something on an old grudge. A man knew instinctively that Government was his natural enemy." Rose is but a step from pamphleteering.[5]

Only one reviewer, however, was wholly adequate to Rose's intentions in *Free Land,* and that because he had read her pamphlet *Give Me Liberty.* Burton Rascoe, writing in his *Newsweek* book column, said little directly about *Free Land* except to endorse it as "one of the most tonic and engrossing novels that has come along in years." His preamble, however, invoked a kind of populist wisdom embodied in "We, the People" as opposed to the articulate theories of philosophers and intellectuals. Satisfied with the self-evident truths of the American tradition, such a citizen "is largely unaffected by all the vociferous winds of doctrine and does what he feels is his patriotic and social duty without bothering his head about the howling of these winds."

> This sort of American, in cities, villages, and on farms, is the American Rose Wilder Lane understands and sympathizes with so well that her little book "Give Me Liberty" might be considered the most eloquent and most revolutionary utterance of the decade in America, if only because it is so completely American in tone and feeling, and so at odds with the theories of the intellectuals who are in such a dither about the hobgoblins of Fascism and Communism that they are challenging us to choose one or the other.
> We common people, clothed in our barrels, will just say: "What's the rush? Fascism may be O.K., Communism may be O.K., but we have been experimenting with Americanism for a long time in theory and have given it only a brief trial. Let's see if it will work. If it doesn't, the experiment can't be any tougher on the plain man than the experiments in Fascism and Communism."

"Mrs. Lane," Rascoe concluded, "in a dramatic novel, has revealed to us a national soul of which we all partake and which some of us may forget we have."[6]

Rose was deeply gratified to find her ideas restated so clearly. Someone in the Midwest had alerted her to Rascoe's review, and when Isaac Don Levine brought her a copy and read it aloud, she was moved to tears. "I do so much want our country to be aware of what it is," she wrote Rascoe at once.

> I try to help that understanding, and it seems to me that I always fail completely because my abilities are so inadequate. But when you see what I try to do, then I haven't wholly failed and perhaps next time I'll do better.
>
> You live somewhere not far away, don't you? I have bought a little farmhouse here—23 x 24—with old apple trees and lilacs. Everything is terribly upset now, all my books still in boxes, the whole place in that state where everything is somewhere else. . . . Perhaps when my little house is painted and papered, you would come to a house-warming?[7]

||

Rose was indeed in a new house now. She had been living in hotels for over three years, and the money she had received for the serial version of *Free Land* made it possible for her to pay off her debts, mainly a large one to Helen Boylston, and to think of reestablishing herself in a home where her domestic impulses could flourish again. She had thought briefly of buying and renovating a row house in Philadelphia when Adelaide Neall raised the prospect, especially when it seemed that Garet Garrett might join them:

> I love major operations on houses. They are my sin, my vice. If a house has good foundations, is basically well-built, that is all I ask. My greatest joy is piles of plaster, blue-prints, carpenters and masons underfoot, yells of "Look out!" with crashes, and me in the midst casting an eye along levels and surfaces and saying, "That's a quarter of an inch out, there." I would rather have a house to make or re-make than a house made. Much rather.
>
> For myself, basic condition is all that needs to be good. Foundations, timbers, joists, plates and rafters. All surfaces of a house, even shingles and partitions, are temporary to my eye, anyway—like dresses and hats. Nothing but character is solid. Windows, doors, interior walls, balconies, baths, wiring, plumbing, ceilings and floor surfaces come and go, fluctuating, changing, unstable as (actually) stone. (Water is much more stable, of course.) Just so one has the fundamental honesty, soundly there, one has a good house.[8]

This paean to the joys of remodeling was both expressive and pro-phetic. Early in 1938 she began looking for a place in Connecticut after sounding out John Turner on the idea; he had responded enthusiastically from Paris, writing "now we will have a place we can call home." Rose had meanwhile renewed her old acquaintance with Isaac Don Levine, who with his wife Ruth had established a summer and weekend home in Norwalk. Levine had watched Rose running rapidly through her money from *Free Land*, and fearful that she would spend it all, he encouraged her to invest in a property and joined her in her search. In March, with twenty-six hundred dollars and a nine-hundred-dollar mortgage, she bought a small farmhouse on a few acres just outside of Danbury. A two-story clapboard with a big porch and a big attached woodshed, it had been owned by a Czechoslovak immigrant family whose breadwinner had been out of work for three years. With some guilt Rose took over the immaculate little house, including two cats who refused to move. For the next twenty years it would undergo dramatic changes and transforma-tions as she worked her will and imagination upon it. The Albanian house had been a romantic dream, Rocky Ridge a failed experiment, but the house on King Street would at last become a home. On April 1 she moved in, aided by the Haders, who drove down to New York from Nyack and carried her to Danbury in their car. Cold weather and snow set in, and for two weeks she did nothing but stoke the ancient coal range in the kitchen, read, eat, and wash dishes. But she was content for the moment, and plans for renovation blossomed ahead of the spring flowers. "Rooted here already more than ever at Rocky Ridge," she noted in her diary; and shortly she was writing enthusiastically to Mary Paxton Keeley in Missouri, with whom she exchanged housewarming gifts, about her daffodils, forsythia, and huge lilacs.[9]

Inevitably there was a reaction and a let-down. As summer came on, the yard and garden got out of control, her gasoline lawnmower would not work, constant rains warped her doors and mildewed her books, and into the midst of this expanding mess walked John Turner, back from Europe. Genevieve Parkhurst came to help pull weeds, and Frank America reappeared to drink coffee and talk. And Norma Lee Browning and her husband arrived to reestablish the acquaintance begun at the University of Missouri. The little house was crowded and awk-ward; there were not enough beds or bookcases; sleeping and cooking were improvised; and John would need money to enter Lehigh in the fall. She was having trouble regaining her writing impetus after the suc-cess of *Free Land*, and the old blues returned. "Don't know why I live, or live here." "Should work and can't. What to do with a meaningless life? Am dumb, dull, empty. Blue as hell. Cried all night."[10]

She was, in fact, passing over another major watershed in her life. The popularity of *Free Land* made her briefly a minor celebrity; media attention came from a radio interview by her old friend Mary Margaret McBride, who had transcended the Depression by creating a hugely popular radio persona as hostess of a talk show. And her renewed friendship with Dorothy Thompson, whose newspaper column and radio program made her, *Time* said, an equal with Eleanor Roosevelt as an influential woman in the land, let Rose feel herself briefly among those whose opinions mattered. But *Free Land* had also effectively ended her career as a fiction writer, although the realization would strike her only slowly. Increasingly her life would be absorbed with her home and garden on the one hand and with political and social theory on the other—the first, in a complex way, an enactment of the second. At the heart of both was a fierce commitment to the primacy of the self-sufficient individual; but it was as though her energies, divided between the practical and the theoretical, could no longer find the free space where imagination could explore the unity of the two in a story. She would continue to work the shadowy ground of revising her mother's fiction: she completed substantial work on *By the Shores of Silver Lake,* which would be published in 1939, and there would be three books beyond that. But by and large the writing for the rest of her life would be theoretical and polemical; and against the tide of history her views would seem increasingly isolated and idiosyncratic.[11]

No doubt part of the reason for her falling spirits as the year wore on was the collapse of a project to which she had devoted considerable emotional energy. In an attempt to retrieve her investment in the aborted Missouri book, she had conceived of a series of forty-eight such state-books, each by a native writer, that would form a composite history of the United States. She would be the editor of the series, helping these writers to make the connections between the stories of the individual states. She wanted not an academic history, but such a history as a novelist might write, in terms of the personal motives and actions of the significant characters of each state's history. At the root of her conception was a regional and populist (and, finally, republican) vision of the country as a secondary complex of primary individual and local interests, both at any moment and over the course of time: "American history is actually an orchestration; it was a history of tribes, which became a history of colonies, which became a history of States, united but diverse. The United States is actually a history of States, more than it is a history of Union." As her preamble made clear, such a history would be a salutary counter to the temper of the times:

> It seems to me that the time is ripe for a re-assertion of American values. There is a genuine American spirit in this country, which

for the past two generations has not had a voice. Indeed it has
never been made fully self-conscious, because since the Revolutionary period of the late 18th and very early 19th century, the
attitude of articulate Americans in general has been one of criticism based on European standards. This people is, on the surface, volatile, hysterical, given to swift extremes and reactions,
but beneath this restless surging it is a profoundly patient and
profoundly skeptical people. As Dorothy Thompson has said, the
characteristic American expression is, "Oh, yeah?" I think that the
New Deal has carried Europeanization as far as the American people will willingly permit it to go, and that at present this people
blindly feels a reaction toward the principle of individual liberty,
which is the essential American principle. I think that there is
what 'the intelligentsia' would call a cultural lag, among the intelligentsia who are still speaking in criticism of America—a criticism
based on European ideas of the proper function of The State. I
think that any literary effort toward making the American spirit
more self-conscious by explaining it to itself in rationally intelligi-
ble terms, will be welcomed with enthusiasm.

For this project, she hoped to enlist such writers as William Allen White,
Walter Edmonds, Kenneth Roberts, Ellen Glasgow, Zona Gale, and
Stephen Vincent Benet. Not surprisingly, she found few writers willing
to sacrifice the year she had spent in state archives preparing her Missouri book. William Allen White agreed to do a book on Kansas; but the
rest "replied with cordial lectures at me for not sticking to fiction," and
the project died.[12]

And like many Americans, she was increasingly oppressed by events
in Europe. Her own perspective had established American history as a
unique experiment in personal freedom, defined by its revolutionary
difference from Europe, and she feared that America would be dragged
into the growing conflict. The American people, she was convinced,
would not voluntarily enter another European war, and much of her
energy flowed into a series of efforts to awaken a popular opposition to
the drift of events. In January of 1939 she published another essay in
political theory in the Saturday Evening Post, "The American Revolution,
1939." It grew naturally out of her earlier "Credo," and was notable
chiefly for her rhetorical strategy of adopting popular Communist terminology (some of which came from Thomas Paine) and turning it back on
the enemy. In a survey of world political history, she identified the earliest primitive tribal organization as essentially communal (for her, a kind
of minimal communism) and traced successive governmental forms,
including Athenian democracy, as efforts to seize and hold power over
the community. An essential leaven was introduced with the Judeo-
Christian belief "that all men are equal in the sight of God and that a
human being is a human soul, with not only certain duties but certain
rights." The political expression of this insight was the American Revolu-

tion, establishing the ideal of personal liberty and individual rights and beginning an experiment in government based on the premise "that a man is free to the extent in which he is not governed—simply not governed." "Rather than permit government to invade society, the free society must invade government. This invasion is a revolutionary necessity, which liberals will someday perceive and act upon."

The person who believed this, she asserted, was the true liberal, and the political dynamic was a struggle between those who would advance the experiment in freedom—the continuing revolution against government—and such counterrevolutionary forces as American communists and their sympathizers who promoted a European-style class struggle, fascists who found authority in the leader, businessmen who sought to buy political power, misguided altruists who would attack corruption by subjecting individual rights to the tyranny of majority rule, and social theorists who measured America by European standards. All of these suppressed the natural vitality of a free people, destroying creative energy in a retreat to controlled security. "At this moment," she asserted, "the counter-revolution is so strong that government hardly permits society to function." Herbert Hoover wrote to congratulate her on her eloquent statement of what he still believed in.[13]

Public opinion, she hoped, might be so mobilized as to keep America out of the growing European conflict. She had felt betrayed by Wilson's failed promise to keep the country out of the First World War, and the discovery in 1932 of Wilson's secret House-Grey agreement with England confirmed her suspicion of presidential powers in foreign policy. The native isolationist sentiment in the country itself had found expression in the movement for the so-called Ludlow or Peace Amendment to the Neutrality Act, which would require a national referendum to declare war, except in case of attack by foreign powers. She had no great expectation that the amendment could be passed; but she hoped that the debate might sharpen the national consciousness of the threat from Europe and make it more difficult for Roosevelt to lead the nation to war. Most of her few publications for 1939 were in support of the amendment, and she urged Mary Paxton Keeley, as she did everyone she knew, to write in its behalf—"the ONLY thing that will keep your boy and mine in school through college." Her private belief was that Roosevelt had already signed secret protocols with England, and in her correspondence with Mama Bess, who was venomous in her contempt for the Democrats, we can hear the crackle of political animosity turned personal. "Your article on the Ludlow amendment in Liberty is great, so plain and fair and true," Mama Bess wrote:

> But I simply gnashed my teeth when I read Mrs. Roosevelt's. It evaded the truth—you proved that presidents could not be trusted.

She said trust them. Also she tried to scare people by completely ignoring the fact that a vote would not be taken in case of attack.

My opinion is that Roosevelt has already made his secret agreement and Elinor [*sic*] knows it. Your article touched them in a tender spot by speaking of such a thing.

In May of 1939, Rose traveled to Washington to appear before the Senate Judiciary Committee, which was holding hearings on the amendment. In the brief paragraph that ends the *New York Times* account of the proceedings, we can detect the flurry of consternation as the last witness, a private citizen—plump, graying, middle-aged—inserts her purely logical and idiosyncratic view into the public record:

> Rose Wilder Lane, the only other witness today, told the subcommittee she appeared not as a pacifist but as a revolutionist. Despite her quick explanation that she referred to the American revolution, and that she advocated the proposed amendment as a means of preserving American democracy, Senator Borah took alarm. He tried to get the witness to say that she meant "Americanism," but she stuck to her own terminology.[14]

IV

As summer passed and the fall merged into winter in Danbury, Rose was again alone in her new home. John Turner had spent the end of the summer in Columbia, boning up on French with a friend of Rose's for his entrance exams at Lehigh; and his exultant telegram ("Les examinations etaient tres faciles. Be home tonight.") marked the start of his college career. Optimistically, he joined a fraternity; but by December Rose received the kind of letter mothers seldom expect but too often get: "Please do not be alarmed. I am flunking French and philosophy." He was also chronically ill from infected tonsils, and an operation scheduled during the Christmas holidays found Rose short of cash; her mother offered a loan, but she borrowed instead from George Bye. To Bye she pleaded the necessity of new clothes for a series of lectures in Boston; her modest fame for *Free Land* and *Give Me Liberty* had translated into a number of speaking engagements for women's clubs and book clubs, as well as for a manufacturers' association. Thoughtful businessmen had found her an eloquent spokesman for laissez-faire economics; and this connection would develop later into a position with the National Economic Council that would offer almost the only outlet for her political views. But her own economic crisis of the moment was real. The money from *Free Land* was gone; she was slipping out of the lucrative *Saturday Evening Post* market; and until much later in her life she returned to the short-range strategies and improvisations that had always been her normal economic style.[15]

The regular travel back and forth from Danbury to the city, however, was more of a strain than she had anticipated, even though Danbury's main charm had been that it was somewhat outside of normal commuting distance from the city. In the summer of 1938, however, she had reencountered the young woman she had met as a student at the University of Missouri in Columbia. Norma Lee Browning and her husband were living in a two-room East Side apartment as they tried to make a start in the world, and when they called on Rose she welcomed them with open arms despite their education. And she was intrigued with the convenience and economy of their quarters. At about the same time she came upon a *Woman's Day* article about a New York City decorator, Dorothy Lambertson, who had transformed a ten-dollar-a-month cold-water walkup flat into a charming *pied-a-terre* apartment. Rose rented a place in the same building with Browning (up five flights at 550 East Sixteenth Street) and enlisted Lambertson to decorate it and furnish it for her with second-hand items refurbished. The whole enterprise was as much a symbolic gesture as it was a matter of convenience. The block of tenements was, from a middle-class view, a slum; some nearby were actually condemned; but Rose was struck with the idea of transforming a hole-in-the-wall nightmare into comfort and convenience with ingenuity and elbow grease; and her populist sentiments made the thought of living among people who were respectably poor attractive. With a coal-stove and cast-off furniture she and Lambertson contrived another showplace to grace the pages of *Woman's Day*. Actually, it was little different from her life in Paris, Rose recognized. She hired Tony, general handyman and porter, to carry coal up the five flights of stairs, and her neighbor Mrs. Stankowicz to clean; but they were less servants than helpful friends, she claimed. And as for that great marker of American civilization, the bath, Rose bathed as her neighbors did: "We bathe as the last Empress of Austria bathed in her palaces. We bathe as Washington did, and Jefferson, and young Henry Ford, as all Americans bathed forty years ago and all Europeans except the richest bathe today. We bathe, and daily, in small movable tubs."

She was quick to define a place for herself in her new society. From time to time she would phone Schrafft's or Longchamps and order cookies for a tea party for the whole building. The gesture carried with it some resonance from her benevolence to her Albanian servants and from her determined participation in the Mansfield Justamere Club; Bessie Beatty had years before accused her of loving to play Lady Bountiful; but by now Rose could justify the impulse as rooted in her natural political commitments.

Norma Lee Browning recalled the time vividly. An unnamed and pompous magazine editor once braved the neighborhood and five flights of stairs to visit Rose, panting and disgruntled; they stepped down the hall to visit Browning and on their return found themselves locked out.

The only way in was through a neighboring apartment and across a ledge to Rose's window—a mission on which Rose dispatched her editor friend with considerable glee. But when a building inspector arrived to order a concrete partition between lavatory and stool in her bathroom, she was not amused: crying "Storm Trooper!" she chased him down the stairs, neighbors watching in excitement. She then called the president of Chase National Bank, owner of the building, and declared that she would accept a bathroom partition only when Mayor LaGuardia had one too.

She would divide her time, summer and winter, between Danbury and her city flat for several years; and she thought of herself so self-consciously as one of the building's community that she took the opportunity to reply at length to a passing reference in the *New York Times* to the "little people" of the tenements. Their poverty, she pointed out, was relative only to the great material prosperity made possible by American enterprise. "The material conditions of living in this neighborhood are those of all prosperous Americans about thirty years ago," she wrote; "they are superior to the conditions from which Europeans generally have retrogressed since the World War."

> Yet today THE TIMES applauds the discovery that people living in such conditions are people. So thoroughly has Marxian "ideology" permeated American thought that economic classifications rule it, and a rental of only $8 a month automatically means that we are not human beings but mere units of "the masses," "the under-privileged," "the slum-dwellers," a population-group existing as the inert butt of benevolence, uplift, and governmental action.
>
> It should not be necessary to say—it should be taken for granted—that my neighbors are the equals in intelligence, morality, love of family and home, pride, gayety, courage, and hope and charity, the equals of human beings anywhere.

The letter is much longer, but it does not flag in its eloquent defense of the natural equality of humanity and its alarm that this equality was threatened by the forces of "counter-revolution" in "this present overwhelmingly reactionary world."[16]

V

By the summer of 1939, Rose had company in the Danbury house again. Norma Lee Browning was an aspiring writer, working hard to start a career, as was her husband, photographer Russell Ogg. Rose invited them to spend the summer with her; while her husband worked at an addition to Rose's house, Browning worked on her writing under Rose's demanding tutelage. It was, for Browning, a time of broader education as well, as her own developing political impulses found a shape in Rose's settled beliefs. And more broadly still, Rose became and remained simply an exemplary figure—"always a wonderfully vibrant, zestful, and exuberantly *alive* person," Browning would recall, having seen little evidence of the occasional depression that Rose would take to her journal. This young couple Rose left in charge of her house while she undertook a trip across the country, ending with two months in Bellingham, Washington. The opportunity was provided by John Patric, a vagabond freelance writer who had sought her out because he shared her political views; Rose seized upon the trip, in Patric's automobile, as another chance to check the temper of the people in hard times.

She stopped over in Minnesota with a commission from *Woman's Day* to interview the parents of Harold Stassen, the boy wonder recently elected governor of the state. Along the way, she was impressed with the number of itinerant families, more or less self-sufficient, living out of automobiles and trucks while they worked where they could. Further west, however, she discovered another of the heroic "little people" who so fired her imagination. In Jackson Hole, Wyoming, she encountered a displaced Missourian named Charles McCrary, who had moved west when a fire destroyed his machine shop. He had for a time taken over a small coal mine near Laramie, where he was able to make a meager living until the fees required by the National Bituminous Coal Act put him out of business. For a while after, he and his family had been self-sufficient vagabonds, traveling and working out of two trucks and a trailer: when Rose met him, he had just managed to build a county bridge almost single-handed, using salvaged materials and equipment and heroic ingenuity, for a mere fifteen hundred dollars.

Rose saw McCrary as a type of the real American; she began a serial fictionalizing his career and sent the first installment, concerning his coal-mining operations, to the *Saturday Evening Post*. "The Forgotten Man" was refused, however, because the editors thought it was simply anti–New Deal propaganda: what they had hoped for was another *Free Land*. Rose argued that she could not write it otherwise; and Adelaide Neall wrote a concerned letter to George Bye that marks the shift in Rose's sensibility and mode of conception: "Rose is certainly a sufficiently skilled craftsman to tell a story and let her message or propaganda or what have you develop from that story." The skill remained, of course, but the patience and the faith in her imagination did not; and the failure of "The Forgotten Man" floats in the wake of her career as a buoy marking a permanent change of direction.[17]

She returned to Danbury to find that Russell Ogg had made great strides in remodeling her house and to greet John Turner, adrift again. He had given up on Lehigh after one semester, and Rose had staked him to an apartment in her building while he tried to get his life in order. A week after moving in he moved out, leaving for Missouri with intentions to

marry a girl there. After some time in Missouri and a period in Fort
Wayne, Indiana, he reappeared in Danbury, unmarried and declaring his
intention to become a journalist. Rose arranged a number of interviews
for him with newspaper and magazine editors, including one with Dewitt
Wallace of *Reader's Digest,* who cordially turned down John's first article.
In time, he found a post as a rewrite man on the Danbury newspaper, but
it paid no salary, only space-rates, and in little more than a week Rose
noted in her diary a letter from New York: "John says he has skipped out
again." By the end of the year he was in Ottumwa, Iowa, looking for work
but telegraphing for money.[18]

Returning to such problems had pitched her again into one of her
periodic depressions; in her diary she recorded the old effort of will:

> October 3, 1939. This whole week has been spent in depths of
> gloom & idleness. This morning I feel well again. I have cleaned
> the house and I turn over a new leaf. It is true that I have a talent
> for writing, and I am not going any more to deny it. I am going to
> try every day to live as I know a person should live, and I am going
> to write or try to write something every day.

She forced her way through an unpublishable short story; but in 1939 all
she would achieve would be some occasional pieces for *Woman's Day* and
some promoting the Ludlow Amendment. And the early revisions of her
mother's next book, called in manuscript "The Hard Winter."

It had taken Rose more than a year of intermittent work to bring *By
the Shores of Silver Lake* to publishable form; and in the meantime Mama
Bess had completed the next manuscript in her series. She was concerned
that the long interval since her last book would lose her readers, and even
as the final draft of *Silver Lake* was being typed for the publisher, she was
pressing Rose to accept the next manuscript. She sent it off just as she
and Almanzo left on a trip to South Dakota. "I expect you will find lots of
fault in it, but we can argue it out later. If the ms. is with you, it will be
where you can work on it when you please and get it over with when you
like." Mama Bess was seventy-two now, and quite naturally concerned
that accident or death might forestall completion of her series: she in-
structed Rose where to find the notes for her next book. "You could write
the last book from them and finish the series if you had to."[19]

The trip was an indulgence for the Wilders; the year before, in fact,
they had taken a longer one west to Oregon. But they were living in
relative prosperity now, with rent from the stone cottage and interest
from bonds and savings—most of which came from Rose's annual donation, which she continued even yet, probably to maintain, for tax purposes, the fiction that she stood as head of the household. But a large
measure of the Wilders' well-being came from the continuing royalties on
Mama Bess's books, which by now amounted to over two thousand dollars

a year. Mama Bess had pinched pennies and stretched narrow resources for so long that thrift and hard bargaining were second nature; she was still battling the electric company by having the service shut off if her bills were too high. But in moments it came to her that she was now safe; and she wrote to recommend her old-fashioned style of thrift to a daughter who had always seemed extravagant and improvident. "If you are comfortable, a little money ahead or at least your bills paid so you don't have to worry over them will add greatly to your happiness," she wrote Rose: "Don't I know! I haven't gone alone down that long, dark road, I use to dream of, for a long time. The last time I saw it stretching ahead of me, I said in my dream 'But I don't have to go through those dark woods, I don't have to go that way.' And I turned away from it. We are living inside our income and I don't have to worry about the bills." And at least once her gratitude swelled up into a letter of tribute to her daughter's lifetime of ministration.

> . . . I thought again who we had to thank for all our good luck. But for you we would not have the rent money. You are responsible for my having dividend checks. Without your help I would not have the royalties from my books in the bank to draw on.
>
> I looked up to admire the new window curtain in the dining room and there was the dining table you gave us, with the chairs around it.
>
> Over the new, blue, glass curtains in the bedroom are the blue and rose drapes you gave me and beside the window is the dresser with the lovely mirrors and drawers full of the beautiful jewelry you have given me.
>
> I thought about you all day and when night came I lay on the Simmons bed you gave me and pulled over me the down quilt, a gift from you. I looked across the room at Manly in his Simmons bed covered with his down quilt both gifts from you as well as his chest of drawers I could see on his side of the window.
>
> It is always that way. When I go to count up our comfortableness and the luck of the world we have it all leads back to you.
>
> And so, snuggled under my down quilt, I went to sleep thinking what a wise woman I am to have a daughter like you.
>
> Very much love,
> Mama Bess
>
> Oh Rose my dear, we do thank you so much for being so good to us.

Rose had earned the tribute, of course. But had she received the affection as a child, she would not have had to transform her mother into a dependent to win it now, in her own middle age.[20]

Mama Bess returned safely from South Dakota and went to work on her next manuscript. She was, by now, carrying on a correspondence of her own with George Bye, although it is likely that each letter went by Rose's instructions as both maintained, for their joint agent, the fiction of

Mama Bess's autonomy. Rose had had the "Hard Winter" manuscript since June; but in September Mama Bess wrote about it to Bye: "The book to follow 'By the Shores of Silver Lake' is now taking shape on my desk. . . . Do you think there would be any chance to serialize the story?"[21]

VI

These were, of course, the darkening years in which the world descended into the second great war, years in which many thoughtful Americans saw the world divided into a contention between Fascism and Communism. For many, Communism seemed the lesser evil; for some, it promised salvation. Hitler had taken Austria and Czechoslovakia and threatened the rest of Europe. England and France lacked the means and the will to oppose him. The great unknown quantity was Russia, which, by the logic of power politics and geography, was naturally a counterpoise to Nazi Germany. The atmosphere in the United States was also clouded by the long-established liberal view of the Soviet Union as the harbinger of a new and just social order; Rose herself had formed her early views at a time when it seemed that "the sun [was] rising in Russia." Recently, the Spanish Civil War had enlisted the sympathies of most liberals as a struggle against Fascism; and to the extent that the Spanish Loyalists included Communists within the alliance of groups against Franco, that sympathy afforded Russia a natural reservoir of good will among many American intellectuals.

Rose, of course, saw the terms of this analysis as irrelevant to the American experience, except to the extent that involvement in the European war would increase the power of American government over its citizens. In practical terms, both were dangers to be confronted and argued down as the occasion arose. Thus an eloquent letter on anti-Semitism to the *American Mercury*. As for many small-town midwesterners, even today, Rose's experience with American Jews was late and infrequent; unlike urban easterners, for whom the ethnic identity was a primary category, the Jewish identity was one of the last things that struck her as she met people. Thus an easy theoretical tolerance, even innocence, of an issue deep-laid in other segments of society. Dee Wollenberg, Catherine Brody, and Isaac Don Levine—some of her best friends were Jews (as was that "slimy little Hungarian," Josef Bard); and it was with a certain self-righteous passion that Rose seized the opportunity to defend these friends on the principle of natural human freedom. Each great enemy in American experience has sought to restrict basic human freedom, she wrote to the editor of *American Mercury*: "Our enemy today is no longer the Established Church, nor British soldiers, nor slavery: it is this importation from Fascist Germany called anti-semitism."[22]

The threat from the left, however, seemed to her much more immediate; for American Communism still wore a quasi-respectable face,
although it carried an anti-Semitic virus as well. Rose found herself
embroiled in a complex skirmish here, as her militant anticommunist
stance damaged and almost lost her the old friendship with Dorothy
Thompson. Isaac Don Levine, a Russian emigré Rose's equal in militancy,
had gained access to a Russian intelligence officer named Krivitsky who
had defected to the United States. Krivitsky had stories to tell not at
all flattering to Stalin, alleging, among other crimes, that Stalin secretly
admired Hitler and hoped for a rapprochement with Nazi Germany. Levine
interviewed Krivitsky thoroughly and ghosted a series of articles over
Krivitsky's name; Rose paved the way through her association with the
Saturday Evening Post for publication of this material. Rose considered the
testimony confirmation of her deepest antipathies; but among readers on
the left, Krivitsky's allegations challenged the special virtue that had
attached to the Russian Communist program since the revolution, and
they disquieted those who hoped to preserve Europe from Hitler by
adding Russia to the balance of forces against Germany. Krivitsky's first
four articles appeared in the months just before the Hitler-Stalin pact was
signed in August, 1939.

Dorothy Thompson was by now a national figure, not simply as
Sinclair Lewis's wife but in her own right as a journalist and commen-
tator on contemporary events. Rose continued to be on her guest list, but
Dorothy moved among the nation's leaders, and some estrangement was
to be expected. She agreed with much in Rose's position, but she was
always more pragmatic than ideological and her values had a strong
European cast. Thus, what Rose found as likely truth in Krivitsky's articles, vetted by Isaac Don Levine, Dorothy found more problematical.
Her natural mistrust of ideologues and axe-grinders made Krivitsky and
Levine himself less than disinterested witnesses in her eyes. Her skepticism met Rose's ideological fervor in a test of an old friendship.

The heart of the matter was really a misunderstanding. Dorothy had
addressed the International P.E.N. Congress at the New York World's Fair
on May 10, 1939, shortly after the first two of Krivitsky's articles had been
published. The air was heavily charged with anti-Nazi sentiments; most
talks turned on the perilous situation in Europe. In such a setting, Dorothy's remarks on Krivitsky, which she intended as illustrative of a journalist's difficulty in finding truth in a politically charged atmosphere, could
easily be interpreted as an attack on Krivitsky's credibility—especially as
they seemed to echo a vicious anti-Semitic attack on him by the *New
Masses* a few days earlier. A report of her remarks in fact then suffered
just such a distortion in the *Daily Worker.* At the worst, it seemed as
though one of America's leading journalists had been captured by the
Stalinists. Rose apparently heard of the matter from Levine, and there

seems to have been a telephone conversation in which Rose challenged Dorothy with this distortion and in which Dorothy spoke of Levine with some hyperbole as a man with an axe to grind. An exchange of letters followed, in which Rose wrote:

> My friendship for you has been genuine since 1920. It ends now, not because yours is a pretense, but because you are not the Dorothy I thought I knew and have been defending.
>
> Once you were a fine person, sensitive, intelligent, witty, poetic, ardent for truth and justice, sure in judgements based on moral and humane values. Now you are coarse and stupid. You surround yourself with sycophants and exploiters who would betray you. . . .
>
> For half your lifetime I have signed notes to you "with love" and meant it. I could not believe what my reason told me. So I appealed to your honesty, your love of justice, and your patriotism; I told you that your charge against Don Levine is a mistake or a lie, I asked for a chance to prove that it is not true. You prefer to discard a genuine friendship.

Eventually, after several exchanges of letters, something like the truth emerged and Dorothy's apology for her affront to Levine smoothed the waters. She and Levine were two of Rose's oldest and dearest friends: caught between them, Rose turned for ideological reasons to Levine and all but lost Dorothy as the tensions that shortly would bring about World War II here brought close friends to the limits of their love for each other. Rose's friendship with Dorothy would continue amicably, but it would never be close again. An increasing ideological brittleness was making Rose's personal relationships more and more problematical. Her friendship with Isaac Don Levine would in time founder on a similar but nastier contretemps.[23]

VII

Rose had a personal stake in events in Europe in the person of Rexh Meta. In the flush of prosperity following the publication of *Free Land*, she had sent him several thousand dollars to purchase land for a home. He kept her apprised of the negotiations, and once the purchase had been made he sent her an elaborate map siting its location in the hills above Tirana. Then followed a complex scheme whereby a paper sale would be recorded to her—this to make a confiscation or forced sale to the government more difficult, a possibility he truly feared. She in turn sent him a drawing and a floor plan of a futuristic house with a walled garden that she had found in an issue of *Ladies' Home Journal*. With modifications to accommodate her, it was to be her Albanian home where she would live at times as a visiting grandmother. All such idyllic plans, of course, pivoted on continued peace in Europe—or, as Rexh hoped, a short war that Albania might, in its insignificance, survive.

The events of 1939 cast all in doubt. In April Italy moved to annex Albania. Rose sent a cable offering what help she could; Rexh received it even as Italian warplanes were swooping down on Tirana. His letter a month later revealed his family to be safe and the country calm, but all plans for the future put in abeyance. Rose offered a haven if he chose to emigrate; but Rexh was naturally hesitant to land in a new country with no means of support save her charity. He suggested that she might have some influence with the Albanian foreign minister in obtaining him a diplomatic appointment in the United States: the minister was Djemil Dino, the ardent bureaucrat who had offered Rose his hand years before, but Rexh seemed not to know of that relationship, and Rose apparently did not attempt to intercede by that route. As an alternative, Rexh planned to send his wife and daughter to Rose for a time, perhaps to visit the World's Fair, and he might be able to visit briefly as well. But as the European war came to open hostilities in September and as Germany began its march across Europe, even Rexh's optimism failed. It had become impossible for him to send money out of the country, so Rose assumed payments on his life insurance to a company in England. His last jittery letter was written just before Italy declared war on England and France; in it he commends his family to Rose's care should he not survive, and specifies the distribution of his insurance money.[24]

They would never meet again. And she was about to lose John Turner as well. He had turned up once more, broke and aimless. Rose wept as she confided her pain to Norma Lee Browning. Since John's time at Lehigh, Rose had maintained a joint checking account for him in New York with the understanding that he would draw on it with her permission. She now authorized him to draw fifteen dollars a week until he found a job. He overdrew and did not find a job; instead he applied for the Coast Guard Academy, but failed the examinations. His frustrations were leading to outbursts of anger, and one day in June of 1940 came the last, as he rose raging from the table at some trivial remark by Rose. He smashed his chair against the floor and walked out of the house and out of Rose's life, but not before dipping into her checking account, leaving it overdrawn. "I have heard nothing from him directly," she wrote in her journal, "do not expect to and do not want to. If he had kept his head three days longer I would have deeded him this house, as I had told him I would do on his 21st birthday." Shortly after, she did have a phone call from him; she broke into tears and begged him to write her at times. There were a few letters for a while, and one more brief visit; in time she rooted him like a weed from her heart.[25]

John Turner would discover his own ideas about what his life should

be after his twenty-first birthday. He found his way by enlisting in the
Coast Guard, where he served throughout the war, rising through the
ranks to a spot commission as Lieutenant Commander. Later, he would
complete three engineering degrees and go on to a successful career.
Such achievements, of course, would redeem his early false starts, but he
could never share them with Rose. Her hopes for him as he grew up had
always outstripped his unformed resolution and abilities, and his sense
of guilt could only compound with each failure. "I was sponging off her
and losing my self-respect," he would say later, recalling those days. In
that time, and in his own way, he had seen matters more clearly than she
did. Upon his Coast Guard enlistment, he sent her a letter of apology,
and its reasoning touched the heart of the problem between them:

> I feel that I should be grateful to you and that I owe you something.
> This feeling has produced the usual results—I almost hate you. Yet
> I have continued to accept your generosity until I almost hate
> myself. I am going to try again to do what I almost succeeded in
> doing last winter. To break completely and to stand entirely on
> my own feet is the only way that I will ever be able to really be
> myself. . . . Please don't think too badly of me, and please don't
> take this too hard. You have been everything to me that my mother
> never had a chance to be. I do admire and respect you. This is the
> first time that I have been really honest with you.[26]

WAR AND THE DISCOVERY OF FREEDOM

16

Every human being, by his nature, *is free.*

ose had been wildly wrong about the oncoming war. She had regarded the Munich Pact as marking an understanding between England and Germany, isolating France and neutralizing Russia, and ensuring European peace under German domination while England expanded its influence into the Middle East. Even as Germany assimilated Austria and Czechoslovakia, signed the nonaggression pact with Russia, and moved into Poland, she could write hopefully in her diary, "I do not expect war." Her analysis was grounded merely in wishful thinking; her native midwestern isolationist instincts would not let her believe that affairs in Europe could pose a crisis for her country. She took comfort from the sentiments of the ordinary people she knew: a fire extinguisher salesman assured her "that an attempt to put this country into this war will mean armed revolution here," a thought she deemed important enough to transcribe into her journal.[1]

The date was May 10, 1940, the day that Germany invaded the Low Countries. She and Don Levine had an engagement to go to Stamford to see Isabel Paterson's blossoming shag-tree; but all plans were cancelled as he called that morning to give her the news from Europe. She joined the Levines in their home and held a tense vigil with them as the radio brought successive broadcasts, and it was clear that a difference would strain their friendship. "Don and Ruth want this country in the war *now*," she recorded that night. "They both . . . turned against me."

> Three times I said, There are valuable things, the most valuable to me, our friendship. Don replied merely that he is sick, physically sick: he will take a rifle and fight; he will die before he will submit to Hitler. Ruth answered once by explaining that Don and she are pro-Ally. The second time by saying this is hard on "those of our faith." I said passionately, "Ruth, you are no more Jew than I am English: we are *Americans*." She was polite. I taxied to Stamford, saw the shag-tree.

The hurt rankled overnight, and she turned to her journal again to clarify her thoughts. What emerged was a paradigm of midwestern American innocence:

I begin to think, or feel, that I have been wrong again in refusing to follow the general pattern. I am a damn fool about so many things. Because the Jew as alien to me, apart from my kind, from all other humanity, has never existed in my own consciousness, I have not been able to see his existence in the world. I do not know what "the Jew" is. Facts are that he is not a race, a nationality, nor, as an individual, often, the adherent of a religious faith. I do not know what the reality is. I have been unable to see that any reality, The Jew, actually exists. I have never felt in myself any reaction whatever to The Jew as such. For thirty years I never even was aware that, for instance, Dee Wollenberg called herself a Jew. I never thought of Don Levine otherwise than as an individual human being, himself. Asked, I would have said that he was a naturalized American of Russian birth. When I met Ruth, no thought entered my mind regarding her race, religion, or whatever it is that's called, Jew. I saw a beautiful and charming young woman whom I liked at once. Yet yesterday she coldly repulsed my efforts to save what has been a genuine and deep emotional attachment and did this by saying that Hitler's actions probably do not mean to anyone else what they mean to "those of our faith." What does she mean by "our faith"? I don't believe she is any more devoted to the Jewish religion than I am. I don't believe she even knows what it is, how it differs from any other belief in God. Why do these persons who call themselves Jews, set themselves apart from me, repulse humanity in me, strike me this blow of asserted differentness, apartness, whenever an incident or a divergence of opinions threatens to hurt our friendship?

Why indeed? Reading this account years later, Ruth Levine was appalled that what she had seen as an honest difference of opinion could have wounded Rose so deeply. The Levines were not religious Jews, and their grief was really for the culture of Europe generally. Except that they, and many others, could not imagine the extremes to which Rose's radical individualism and particularizing mode of thought could carry her. Ancient categories and deep-laid traditions crumbled beneath her instinctive analysis, but few could see with her eyes. She was braced for the uneasy difference by the time, a month later, that she listened with the Levines to the news of the fall of Paris. The Levines wept openly; Rose, with a preternatural calm, merely allowed that within a century the event would be of little significance.[2]

Europe was a doomed culture in its death throes, and her country was well out of it, she thought. The best thing that could come of it would be "the explosion of the Communist lie that has poisoned the whole world for an entire generation." Nonetheless, she followed the news closely, keeping daily, sometimes hourly notes from the broadcasts in her journal. Heroism, especially in a doomed cause, always touched her: the spirited defense by the Finns was 1776 over again, she said; and she jotted phrases from Churchill's first speech as Prime Minister into her notebook: "a mar-

velous speech—a historic document." And when she found a moving poem identifying the fallen European capitals with Thermopylae, that went into her notes as well. But in time, the carnage tested even her faith: "I ask myself, may it be that the whole effort of human freedom was a mistake? that the effort is too great for the results, which perhaps after all are too largely material?" Isabel Paterson, who shared many of her views, suggested that the Allies, rotten with collectivism and the Marxist lie, could not fight well; but that the Germans had thrown these aside for an older lie, that of despotism. Rose noted, "But to me, despotism has a kind of authenticity, a (on the wrong basis) coherence, a truth of a sort. At least, there *is* a despot, whereas the collective has no existence whatever."[3]

In the spring of 1940 she had fallen again into one of her depressions, and again she tried to write herself out of it by resuming her journal. Diary and journal entries had been spotty since she had left Rocky Ridge, and in her mind the lapse was a symptom of her inability to work.

> It is necessary to begin again the habit of keeping a notebook. Something must be done to enable me to write fiction. I have no ideas whatever, no spark, I see no stories, I do not desire to write. I am living on borrowed money now, after writing no fiction since Free Land in '37, two years ago this past winter. What has become of my ability to write a story when I had to? Have just looked through old notebooks of twenty years ago; that "I" no longer exists. What interests me now? I kept those notes because I was interested. Perhaps, in gear, the wheels may turn the engine. But truly I would prefer to die.
>
> No argument against suicide has any reality now. Only I don't like to leave a mess, debts, a nuisance of funeral and probate, etc., that would only annoy people. I ought to pay Rexh's insurance and not leave John with no one to live on—and "off of." Nobody cares enough about me not to be irritated by the little nuisances my suicide would bring on the few who know me—George, John, Ruth & Don. Probably I will die fairly soon, anyway. The problem is, How to write enough to keep the bills paid till then.

She directed her observations strenuously outward, noting down the weather and her conversations with the taxi-driver before the old worry broke through again: "O god I must get some money somehow."[4]

||

The borrowed money was from Mama Bess, who had sent her five hundred dollars to see her through this dry spell. Rose had just put the finishing touches on the manuscript called "The Hard Winter," which she had received from Mama Bess almost a year before. More obviously, perhaps, than in Mama Bess's earlier manuscripts, we can trace in "The

Hard Winter" mammoth and defining evidence of Rose's hand in converting her mother's primitive narrative into a lively and publishable manuscript; simply put, she rewrote the manuscript—expanding, condensing, and shifting material, sharpening drama and dialogue, and composing new episodes out of whole cloth—just as she had done, presumably, for Jack Black, Frederick O'Brien, and the manuscripts from Lowell Thomas. Similar conversions had been required on Mama Bess's earlier books, ever since *Little House in the Big Woods*; but by now Rose seems to have abandoned any pretense at instructing her mother. Final copy of "The Hard Winter" was in Bye's hands in May, and in June Mama Bess was in correspondence with him regarding a contract. In the year since completing "The Hard Winter" she had projected the continuation of her story into two more volumes rather than one; and she was still hinting of an adult novel to come after that.[5]

The Harper editors did not like the title, which they found depressing despite its historical authenticity; the assumption was that any book intended for children should not be "hard" or arduous. The quibble sent Rose into a tirade about the coddling of modern children, which, in her view, consisted in sheltering them needlessly and harmfully from the truths of life. It was a note she had touched in several published and unpublished essays; and it was connected with her determined faith in the common-sense wisdom of common people when not misled by politicians, educators, and intellectuals. This reservoir of truth was an article of faith with her by now; and from it she inferred the inevitable continuation of the American Revolution as the abuses of freedom continued. She was willing to do her part, if she could just find a place to exert leverage. She was incensed by an editorial by Dorothy Thompson in *Ladies' Home Journal* in which Dorothy advocated compulsory labor camps for American youths; and she wrote to Mary Paxton Keeley suggesting "a sort of modern version of the Committees of Correspondence that began our revolution for personal freedom in the 1760's." "Each one of them would send ten postcards, to others who would send ten postcards"; and the result would be a hundred thousand informed citizens protesting "such communist-nazi ideas as . . . compulsory labor camps." Rose offered to serve as a nucleus, supplying each patriot with the names and addresses of the others. Such forlorn hopes would characterize her life; but she seldom despaired of this kind of effort, although the passage of the Selective Service Act in September of 1940 dimmed her vision considerably. "Liberty is extinguished on the whole earth," she lamented in her journal. And Harper editors would not accept "The Hard Winter" as a title; they suggested "Little Town on the Prairie," a title Mama Bess noted and reserved for her next book. "The Long Winter" emerged as a compromise title by the time the manuscript was published late in the year.[6]

By the end of the summer of 1940, Rose was down to the last one hundred dollars of the money from Mama Bess, and she was not sure she could earn more. Her journal had lapsed again for several months, and she tried to goad herself into action by summarizing her life since leaving Rocky Ridge: "I try now, once more, to reassemble whatever I am and to continue to exist, I do not know why." She was earning small sums from time to time for needlework and short feature articles, some anonymous, for *Woman's Day*, really a minor magazine. She hoped for some regular arrangement with the magazine to count upon, but for all her good relations with editor Eileen Tighe she felt that she was treated with a casual disregard, even by the office help: the respect that had come with *Free Land* had vanished. "This is really the end—like that."

"*Free Land* exhausted me," she realized one morning. "I have no ideas for fiction." She dreamed from time to time of stories to write, but they vanished on waking or crumbled as she turned to her typewriter, and she ended by writing letters. Fortunately, she now had no dependents: Rexh Meta was unreachable and John Turner had walked out of her life; and aside from taxes, she had only to feed herself, which was often too much trouble, and to find funds for small improvements to her house. She felt herself slipping into obscurity, and it was galling to contemplate the successes of those she had once rubbed elbows with as equals. The Haders were successful authors and illustrators of children's books; Mary Margaret McBride, Dorothy Thompson, and Lowell Thomas were successful in another medium in these halcyon days of radio; and even Helen Boylston had established a writing career with her nursing stories for girls. Apparently Rose had entertained some hope—on some implied promise—of succeeding to Mary Margaret McBride's position on her radio talk show on McBride's transfer to another network. Certainly Rose's gift for conversation might have made her a success; but her penchant for ideological dispute probably worked against her. In any case, the succession went to Bessie Beatty, of all people the one Rose could resent the most. "Depend upon the Irish," Rose fumed, recalling the help she had given Mary Margaret with her writing. "It is incredible what a fool I have always been. To think that Stella [Karn] had only to ask me to put Mary Margaret in SEP sixteen years ago and I did. I make her 'important,' and she disdains me because I'm not—. Dee [Wollenberg] is genuine. Anyone else?"[7]

No one close to her knew of these bouts of depression, nor of the perilous state of her finances. Ruth Levine would spend nights with Rose while her husband was away on assignment; she remembered Rose's constant good cheer and came to love her dearly even as she learned to discount some of the extravagances of her style of conversation. And when put to the test, Rose could still hold her own with those accustomed to a wider stage: Ruth Levine once hosted a luncheon for Rose, Ayn Rand, Isabel Paterson, and Clare Booth Luce; and in such formidable company the honors for talk went to Luce, but Rose was at her ease and in her element in the conversation. In a more domestic setting, Norma Lee Browning was a regular visitor; to her, Rose was like a doting grand-mother, characteristically to her elbows in flour as she baked almost daily and prepared meals for guests but seldom ate much of what she cooked; she ate irregularly, as solitary people often do—bread and coffee and oranges, usually. She would dress for her appointments in the city, but at home her habitual carelessness of dress became a sloppiness, her stock-ings awry and her hair caught up in a net or turban. Company was ther-apy for her, but her nerves were frequently at a stretch and even the handyman hanging wallpaper was sometimes more than she could take. "I feel better when I am not solitary in the house," she noted, "yet as 4:30 approaches I am so eager to be alone that I can hardly bear the tension of waiting. The whole secret of living is in adjustment to other people. But I don't know how it's done." She began noting the astrologer's advice in her newspaper, finding the odd coincidence that gave the day its logic. She joined the Dorcas Society, the local equivalent of Mansfield's Justamere Club, which met at the King Street Church just across the road from her house and served to keep the conventional surface of her life engaged; but all the while some realignment of her inner life was taking place. An obscure crisis seemed to pass late in September of 1940 as she suddenly shed old worries: "Some finality ended yesterday a period in my life. A new era begins." She was going to interview Herbert Hoover for an article; the expenses would eat into her tiny reserve. "That does not mat-ter. I will make money." A note from Norma Lee Browning passed along the rumor that John Turner was in Texas, which Rose noted without com-ment. "It is all past, gone, finished," she recorded. "Forgotten. I am free of the past."[8]

To be free of the past really meant to shed the career she had been making for twenty-five years. She would be free of old friends who could not follow her into ideology. She would be free of the effort to write fiction, which meant freedom from the bondage of high fees for her work. Except for some hopes for Rexh Meta, she was free of responsibility for her adopted family, and free finally of the drag of Mama Bess's financial worries. Small fees for occasional articles could meet her simple needs; a smaller circle of friends, who shared her political views, would suffice for her social contacts; and her energies could be focused on a voluminous correspondence with other lonely and embattled watchers of a country gone sadly awry. Somewhere in all of this she had passed the midpoint of middle age, and she was now free to grow old and, as she felt compelled by circumstances, militant and defensive—and crotchety. In effect, she had retired. And the long passages of painful self-analysis in her journals, the "ceaseless chatter" in her head, had ended as well, as though she had lost contact with her inner self even as she had engaged the larger problems of history and politics.

At about this time she wrote a long, polemical letter to Adelaide Neall protesting, among other things, what she saw as the *Saturday Evening Post*'s policy of paying writers in prestige rather than in high fees: it was, she argued, an abuse of power restricting a writer's freedom. Her argument involved a radical revision of her own personal history with the *Post*, which was perhaps what Neall had in mind as she penciled a note across the page: "Our wild Rose at her wildest."

The nominal occasion of this letter was a forthcoming radio broadcast of a dramatization of *Let the Hurricane Roar*, starring Helen Hayes. The *Post* held radio rights, and the fee to Rose was a good one, but she protested the adaptation as a moral if not illegal infringement on her rights to her literary property. She was often alone now, except occasionally for a young woman named Virginia Manor, an acquaintance of Norma Lee Browning's whom Rose had taken in out of some vague sense of responsibility, and she was reaching out more to local neighbors for company. On the evening of the broadcast she invited one of these, a woman who owned a dairy farm, to come in with her children and listen with her. Afterward, in conversation, the woman offered the opinion that everyone ought to go to church: Rose, catching a whiff of a coercive philosophy, ordered her out of the house. Yet it was a measure of Rose's considerable charm that the family seemed not to resent it overmuch; the children recalled her years later with a certain admiration and respect, the daughter particularly for Rose's concern for her education apart from formal schooling. Something of the same hair-trigger militancy had earlier led Rose to dismiss, violently, an immigrant peddler from her New York apartment when he dared to complain about life in the United States; but he missed the chance to know her well enough to appreciate her crotchets. In the community, she was becoming something of a character; to a small circle of sympathetic friends and correspondents she was a respected mentor; while to some of her older friends she seemed sunk in a monomania. "Floating between sanity and a bedlam of hates," Ernestine Evans wrote of her to Berta Hader. "Strange, erratic girl," Jane Burr wrote to Floyd Dell.[9]

IV

The winter of 1940–1941 saw Rose again in the city. She had fallen into the practice of subleasing her city apartment until the weather turned cold;

this year, as she awaited the end of the lease, she was exiled to the Algon-quin Hotel, luncheon home to the famed Algonquin circle (which she hated for their brittle intellectualism) until January, when she could return to her beloved flat. There she turned to the manuscript of her mother's next book, which would be published later in the year as *Little Town on the Prairie.*

The manuscript was ready for Bye in July. Rose warned him of its imminent arrival with a curious reference to Mama Bess: "She writes me that the new manuscript is almost ready and she will send it to you without my seeing a good part of it." It had been more than two years since Mama Bess had finished her version of *The Long Winter,* and this new book had been disentangled from a matrix of material that contained another as yet unwritten. Rose wrote very little of her own in this period, and it seems likely that much of her time was spent on revisions of her mother's material. Mama Bess did not work from a typewriter, and any manuscript she sent directly to Bye almost certainly had passed through Rose's hands and typewriter first; yet on July 3 Mama Bess also wrote to Bye promising three copies of her new manuscript by post from her. Both letters, by mother and daughter, seem to be part of a strategy to preserve the illusion of Mama Bess's independent status as an author.[10]

In *Little Town on the Prairie,* the fictional Laura enters adolescence and romance, and to read the book with an ear alive to the rhythms of Rose's own fiction is to find echoes of her style throughout—as is the case, in fact, with all of the Little House books. And at least since *Little House on the Prairie,* Rose had been heightening the ideological potency of her mother's stories by emphasizing the primacy of the individual and med-dling role of the government. Now, to read the manuscript of *Little Town on the Prairie* in Mama Bess's hand page-by-page with the published ver-sion is to find that Rose again made radical revisions, moving whole chapters and writing additional material as well as pointing up the drama and dialogue of almost every scene. Nowhere does the story leap more clearly to the eye with Rose's ideological imprimatur than in what she accomplished with Mama Bess's rudimentary chapter entitled "Fourth of July," in which Laura goes to town for the patriotic celebration. There she listens to a speaker give a short history of the nation's wars and recite the Declaration of Independence—most of which appears in the text. In a clearly sacred moment, Laura, with "a solemn, glorious feeling," listens to the words she knows already by heart. At the end, "No one cheered. It was more like a moment to say, 'Amen.' But no one quite knew what to do."

> Then Pa began to sing. All at once everyone was singing. My country, 'tis of thee, Sweet land of liberty, Of thee I sing. . . . Long may our land be bright With Freedom's holy light. Protect us by Thy might, Great God, our King!

The crowd was scattering away then, but Laura stood stock still. Suddenly she had a completely new thought. The Declaration and the song came together in her mind, and she thought: God is America's king.

She thought: Americans won't obey any king on earth. Americans are free. That means they have to obey their own consciences. No king bosses Pa; he has to boss himself. Why (she thought), when I am a little older, Pa and Ma will stop telling me what to do, and there isn't anyone else who has a right to give me orders. I will have to make myself be good.

Her whole mind seemed to be lighted up by that thought. This is what it means to be free. It means, you have to be good. "Our father's God, author of liberty—" The laws of Nature and of Nature's God endow you with a right to life and liberty. Then you have to keep the laws of God, for God's law is the only thing that gives you a right to be free.

The passage is wholly Rose's creation, and in it she has made her mother not merely a romantic but also an ideological heroine. Equally significant, perhaps, in the story's dramatization of Laura's determined work to earn money to send Mary to the school for the blind, is Rose's suppression of the fact, embedded in Mama Bess's determinedly authentic account, that Dakota Territory provided funds for Mary's tuition, room and board. This information did not reach print: no government handouts would be permitted for this family.[11]

The conceptual underpinnings of the Declaration of Independence reach deep into Enlightenment philosophy, of course; Laura's naive discovery short-circuits centuries of political evolution with all the force of revelation. All a child, and most people, would need, of course; but Rose was herself searching for the bottom of her convictions again and she would shortly produce a small book in which she tried to find the deep structure of her political consciousness in a simple reading of history. On one of her visits to Herbert Hoover, he had complained to her that he could find no book for Stanford students that expressed the fundamentals of American political philosophy. The problem took root in her mind; she needed only an opportunity to attack it. The popular appeal of her *Saturday Evening Post* articles seems to have caught the attention of an editor at the small John Day Publishing Company, and he requested from her a book on American political philosophy that would develop her ideas in some historical depth. Out of this commission would come *The Discovery of Freedom*, a small volume that still stands as a handbook for the ideological right. She would work intermittently at revising this book into a definitive treatise until the end of her life.[12]

Much of the preliminary work on the book took place in a trailer park in McAllen, Texas. Even as war began with Japan and Germany, Rose was on the road with Norma Lee Browning and Russell Ogg and their travel trailer, heading on a tour of the Southwest. They hoped to follow the harvest north and find some articles in the experience; she hoped to find inspiration for some short stories as well. But in Texas Russell Ogg fell severely ill; although they did not know it, he was feeling the early symptoms of diabetes. Alarmed, he and his wife returned to his home in Missouri for medical advice and treatment; he went into a Kansas City hospital while she went to work in a defense factory. Rose, meanwhile, remained in charge of their parked trailer in McAllen for three months. She was infatuated with the climate and the vegetation. The Rio Grande Valley in winter, she wrote George Bye, was all that Florida and California claimed to be.[13]

In mid-April she was back in Danbury after three days and nights on a bus from Texas. Her father had written her in Texas, offering to pay her fare to Mansfield, but although she had not been home in five years, she had refused. She had finally cut the tie of obligation to Rocky Ridge Farm, largely by establishing an independent income for her parents from her mother's books. She now settled in at her Danbury home for the summer to complete the manuscript of *The Discovery of Freedom*, which would go through at least two versions before she would let it go to press. For long weeks she did not even go to town, letting her neighbors do her shopping, and the grass grew tall around her house when she found that in wartime she could hire no help to cut it. A family of groundhogs emerged from the wilderness to mow small patches at her doorstep as she worked. Only the alarm of infected teeth sent her to town, and with the loss of her last molars she found herself nibbling her food like a rabbit, or a groundhog, with her remaining incisors.[14]

To read her letters from this period to George Bye, Dorothy Thompson, and Mary Paxton Keeley is to realize how the entry of her country into the war had sharpened her concern about its long-range future. She was confident of the outcome of the war, but she was alarmed at the growth of governmental powers and the ready acceptance of government planning by business and the general population, particularly as the wartime alliance with Russia served to legitimize what she saw as collectivist tendencies in her own country. Many from her generation had been sentimental socialists and parlor Communists since the Russian Revolution, and too few, she thought, had had their eyes properly opened to the Russian menace, even by the twistings and turnings of policy required by the Hitler-Stalin alliance and its later dissolution. Power once usurped by government would not be readily returned, she feared, and collectivist habits of thought once engrained would vitiate the national energies. "Can't you see," she would write to Dorothy Thompson, "that the 'ending up' of the communist effort, and the fascist, and the nazi, are inevitable in the nature of things? Can't you see that the New Deal is essentially the same effort as all these, and that its end is inevitably the same end?" A mere request from Bye for some pink Texas grapefruit from McAllen had sent her into a bitter jest about the wartime respectability of Communism: they were not pink, she wrote him, they were red:

> These are no times for half-measures, George. Can you look at Stalin's battle for democracy, and find around you any intellectuals who still feel that being merely pink is enough? Texas grapefruit, too, are doing their part. . . . the pinks are as out-of-date as in Columbia's halls of learning. How can I send you pink grapefruit? You would be called a Trotskyist.

Other letters, prompted by a legal phrase on one of her checks from *Woman's Day*, lamented the erosion of belief in property rights as essential to personal freedom; and the news that the *Saturday Evening Post* would, under a new editorial policy, become more "liberal" and supportive of the war effort prompted her to insist on the difference between supporting the war and supporting the Roosevelt administration:

> But does it have to be pro-New Deal to be American? I thought all Americans were in this war. My own idea is that Americans have got to fight and win this war in spite of New Deal handicaps on production; and that to save America we've got to lick the Japanese and the Germans and then get rid of the New Deal. And I'll bet we're going to do it. Being anti-New Deal to the marrow of their bones isn't keeping millions of Americans from caring just as much for America and doing just as much to win this war as any of the millions on the New Deal payrolls. . . .

A call from a *Collier's* editor, saying that he was forced by vote of the editorial board to reject a story of hers that he personally liked, provoked her to a tirade against the flight from individual responsibility into collective mediocrity—Fremont Older, or George Horace Lorimer, would have made the decision themselves. The world seemed infected, she thought, and the war was not the largest problem. Few seemed to share her concern, and to those who did she turned for a sounding: "Mary, what do you truly think about affairs in general?" she wrote to Mary Paxton Keeley back in Missouri:

> I mean of course the war's got to be fought and Americans will win it, and of course Hitler & everything the name stands for is too abominable for words. But we are certainly agreed on that & I needn't ask what you think of it. What I want to know is the rest— what do you think is ahead of us, beyond and apart from the war? What do you think is *happening*, actually, and what will be the outcome?

Such were her concerns as she worked her way through the drafts of *The Discovery of Freedom* in the summer and autumn of 1942. She at last had

found a gardener, a man more toothless than herself but still willing to
work at age seventy-eight.[15]

V

The book was published in January of 1943 with a further descriptive
subtitle: *Man's Struggle Against Authority*. Since the publication of *Give
Me Liberty* as a pamphlet, she had hoped to reach a wide audience with
her political convictions; and now again, in simple and direct language,
short paragraphs, and a vigorous and hortative style, she attempted to
put her deepest beliefs into a form any reader could understand. "Every
human being, *by his nature,* is free." What could be simpler? The book's
spiritual father was Thomas Paine, but the vision was broadened to include the world revealed by modern science and energized by industrial
technology. The opening lines reach back two decades to her terror of
the interstellar winds drifting through the voids of space, but a shift in
emphasis permits her to ground a new vision in a simple metaphysics
intended to make her argument both scientific and logically consistent:

> Here is a planet, whirling in sunlit space.
>   This planet is energy. Every apparent substance composing it
> is energy. The envelop of gases surrounding it is energy. Energy
> pours from the sun upon this air and earth.
>   On this earth are living creatures. Life is energy.

From such a premise she could infer all she needed. Human energy was
self-directed, hence free; but the slightness of individual strength against
the forces of nature made cooperation—hence the brotherhood of man—
a necessity, thus a fact of life. Yet the structure of this cooperation—
the social order—was a secondary phenomenon, an abstraction from the
myriad free choices and manifest only in shifting and vanishing situations. Her narrative and analysis from this point turned on this paradox,
as she attempted to account for the emergence of the closest approximation of ideal human freedom in the social order that had given her birth.
Formally, she considered herself to be writing history, but the beginning
paragraphs suggest a creation myth, a story of the founding of a people
and a nation that legitimizes their place and aspirations. And this was in
fact the intent of the history she wrote, shaping her years of wide, self-
directed reading into an account of the emergence of the American people as the embodiment of the faith that would save the world, a faith in
the absolute primacy of the isolated individual.

It was a history at once political and religious, to the extent that she
defined religious faith as "whatever a majority of individuals believe to
be the nature of the universe and of human beings," thus grounding any
responsible act in this faith. Such a stance permitted her then to divide

her analysis into the Old World and the New, the Pagan Faith and the Revolution, false dogmas and the liberating truth. The old, the pagan, and the false are simply the belief that "all individuals are, and by their nature should and must be, controlled by some Authority outside themselves." The names for this Authority are legion: the gods of primitive tribes (primitive communism), the Party (modern Communism), the Leader (Fascism), the Divine King (monarchies), the State (socialism) the Majority (democracy); but these all manifest themselves in the authority of a despot. Set over against this darkness of history are a series of moments at which a revolutionary insight occurs: that man controls his own energy and is responsible for his own actions. She identifies the first of these moments with Christianity from Abraham to Christ, the second with Mohammed, and the third with the American Revolution. And only since the third of these revolutions, and its consequences in western Europe, has mankind been free enough to turn his energies upon the world and make his life safe, prosperous, and happy beyond any civilization before. Thus against the darkness of history and the contemporary nightmares of reaction—Communism and Fascism—the United States and the western rim of Europe have stood alone as embodiments of the discovery of freedom.

There was much else by the way in this succinct book, which was an odd mixture of prophetic zeal and curious lore gleaned from her foreign travels and random reading. There was much to demonstrate the dead hand of the state on creative human energy. Abandoning her youthful complaints about the machine age and the uniformity of American culture, she now accepted implicitly the opposition of man and nature and the blessings of the Industrial Revolution. She regretted the American failure to achieve the purity of the Constitution's intentions, lamenting the lapse of the presidency into political partisanship, the confusion of democracy and republicanism, and the atrophy of the Electoral College: she truly believed that most people would, like her exemplary Russian peasant, prefer to ignore government, turning that hard task over to representatives to wrangle out a few minimal rules for them. And she saw the American Revolution as a continuing one, incomplete in the United States (or regressing temporarily under successive exigencies of the Depression and the war) and a model for the future for the rest of the world. "Americans know that all men are free," she concluded:

All over the world there are men who know it now. The pygmy Republic has become a colossus. And too late and too little, the Old World tyrants attack this Revolution with its own tools.

Win this war? Of course Americans will win this war. This is only a war; there is more than that. Five generations of Americans have led the Revolution, and the time is coming when Americans will set this whole world free.[16]

On its appearance, the publisher made little attempt to promote the book; it was, perhaps, as complex a disappointment to him as had been her Missouri book to another publisher. Most newspaper reviewers ignored it, and the occasional journal reviewers divided over it according to their temperaments; few could accept equally its fervent tone, its radical argument, and its idiosyncratic learning. Joseph Mau, writing for *Book Week,* complained about "the extraordinary range of subjects about which Mrs. Lane knows so many things that are not so. . . . it needs to be exposed, but it does not deserve it." Bernard De Voto observed that it was "certainly on the side of the angels and it is certainly exciting reading, but it calls for a constant exercise of critical and historical control." The kindest review came from Albert Jay Nock, himself the author of *Our Enemy the State,* who acknowledged some questionable points in her argument but conceded that they were all "*obiter dicta.* None of them has any bearing on the actual substance of her work. When it comes to anything fundamental, Mrs. Lane never makes a mistake. She is always right. In this respect the book is really remarkable." Herbert Hoover, who had read the book in manuscript, had privately judged it "a most difficult book to appraise." But he had found its "basic ideas superb" and "some chapters brilliant," and on its publication she prevailed upon him for a short letter of praise to her publishers to use in promoting it.[17]

With such praise she had to be content. Her heart's blood was in this book, which she conceived of as a primer of what every American should know. But it fell almost unnoticed into a nation preoccupied with the practical matters of daily life in a time of war.

ATRIOTIC SUBVERSION

I'm subversive as all hell!

ineteen forty-two had ended with influenza and a fire. One morning in December she staggered down from her sickbed to find the wood-shed in back of her kitchen ablaze; and although she managed to put out the flames with an extinguisher, she inhaled enough smoke to put her in the hospital, seriously ill. So as the long Connecticut winter dragged on, she watched sick in body and depressed in spirit, under the occasional care of Virginia Manor, as the nation's brief and narrow interest in *The Discovery of Freedom* flickered and went out. She was convinced that there was a conspiracy of silence against it among the liberal New York reviewers, and the initial sale was so poor, little more than a thousand copies, that in time she returned the advance to her publishers. She began feeding huge flocks of birds outside her kitchen window and pondering her stance against a world in which she was becoming increasingly irrelevant.[1]

Among work of which she made no mention was her completion of her mother's final manuscript, *These Happy Golden Years*, which was by now at the publisher and which would appear in the spring to good reviews. With this last effort for Mama Bess, Rose had completed what would be the most significant work of her life. What had begun as a project to make her mother a little extra money had become an enterprise of a decade and more in which her mother had become a world-renowned author of children's classics. By and large, it had become also an enterprise that would in time support them both for the rest of their lives. For Rose herself it had become, indeed, a resented demand upon her energies; but as she and her mother had wrestled together to discover the coherence of fiction in the facts from Mama Bess's memories, Rose had also drawn on this family lore for her own best fiction. Not only could she count on small but continuing royalties from the sales of *Free Land* and *Let the Hurricane Roar*, but Mama Bess's income would increase annually as the readership of her books increased worldwide. And eventually, of course, Mama Bess's income would come to Rose.

Mama Bess apparently still had hopes that she and Rose could make the transition that would bring the fictional Laura into the adult world. "I have thought that 'Golden Years' was my last," she wrote George Bye; "that I would spend what is left of my life living, not writing about it, but a story keeps stirring around in my mind and if it pesters me enough I may write it down and send it to you." The reference was probably to "The First Three Years and a Year of Grace," which perhaps she had not yet completed, and which, if it was completed, Rose probably had not yet seen. In time, neither Rose nor her mother could bring herself to the work that would make this story into an adult companion to the children's books. Both had, in a sense, exhausted the Wilders' life as material for fiction; such a book could only become another *Free Land*.[2]

||

There were yet some battles to be fought, and some ways yet of claiming an audience for her views. Her letters to Herbert Hoover continued to express a basic optimism about the country, grounded in her faith in the common sense of ordinary people:

> Sunday I attended services in this little neighborhood church. The congregation numbered seven. The minister is a teacher, he teaches economics in Danbury High School. A year ago he preached an ordinary sermon, and the congregation dispersed after a few remarks about weather and crops. He is now preaching from Ezekiel, on responsibility. Sunday he said that for thirty years he has taught that economics are the basis of social values, and it is not true; the real basis is individual responsibility, and he now doubts that it is even social responsibility; isn't it perhaps the individual's responsibility to his own moral standards? The seven stood discussing this on the church lawn until everyone was late for dinner. They were unanimous that "this social idea" has gone too far. A woman whose mind has never been out of her kitchen said, "You can't do anything by law. Everything comes from inside a person, out. It can't be put onto anybody from the outside."

Rose had, on her arrival in Connecticut, been struck with the way some Connecticut workmen, still strongly ethnic, retained vestiges of a European class consciousness; and she had upbraided Dorothy Thompson for speaking of the "villagers" near her Vermont farm ("don't you hear the European accent in your word?"). The men Rose hired to carry out her rebuilding brought their own cold lunches to eat in the yard; she invited them into her kitchen for a sit-down hot meal with her, as was the Ozark custom. Her account of her experience with her workmen had been twisted by columnist Heywood Broun to make her sound like an economic royalist and a Lady Bountiful; her sputtering reply had drawn on her working-girl, union days as a telegrapher, while stressing that artificially high union wages destroyed jobs. Dorothy Thompson was not moved from her middle-of-the-road positions, and did not become the "voice for America" that Rose wanted to hear. She would have to do it herself.[3]

Dorothy Thompson's voice now reached millions weekly from her radio program and her columns in the *New York Herald Tribune*. Late in 1942, Rose had found her own access to an audience in the pages of a small weekly Negro newspaper, the *Pittsburgh Courier*. She had first noticed the paper for its conscious concern for individual freedom, obviously a racial issue. Rose's radical individualism left no more room for a concept of privilege by race than by class; and the story of the *Courier's* owner, a rise from orphan poverty to prosperous entrepreneur, was one that she warmed to easily. A correspondence led to an offer of a weekly column, "Rose Lane Says," which she began by rehearsing some of the passages from the manuscript of *The Discovery of Freedom*. The *Courier* had a provincial base, but its outlook was decidedly national and international—cosmopolitan enough to feature Indian and Chinese columnists as well as a middle-aged, middle-class white woman in its pages. By 1943, she had another subject to explore with her readers, as wartime rationing began in earnest and Americans began to struggle with the artificial regulation of scarce commodities. She was convinced that government controls of prices, production, and distribution would suppress the natural productivity of the American people and needlessly distort the economy. Against the background of a short history of the inefficiencies of planned economies, she granted the good intentions of the government but raised the question of the government's role in personal economic affairs once the war was ended; clearly she was attempting to educate a voting public for a future repudiation of the New Deal.[4]

In her private letters, her tone was less moderate, and the occasion of rationing became one in which her principles demanded a personal symbolic act. She would not, as she later said, ask some official "for permission to LIVE":

> I have no ration card and shan't have one; every time the radio says, "You MUST get your ration card," I turn purple with rage and snap it off; no radio lives to say MUST to me. I do not believe in rationing, in principle; I am certain it causes more shortages than it relieves; for instance the meat shortage now was caused by "control" of feeds, and price-fixing, which made farmers kill off their calves and young stock because of uncertainty about what orders would be issued next. Also, I can live without buying any food, so let those who can't, have whatever is in the groceries. All I need is flour and salt; even sugar I rarely use, I still have most of a 25-lb sack Norma Lee bought while I was west. . . .

As spring came, she planned a large garden and negotiated with neighbors to go shares on a cow, a few pigs, and some chickens. It would be the Ozarks at the turn of the century again: homemade butter and cheese, fresh meat and vegetables in season, and hams and home-canned foods in the winter. And remembering the scarcities of Europe after the last war, she had already in 1939 hoarded six cases of Ivory soap against an uncertain future. For a long time she had informally traded baked goods to her neighbors for occasional rides to town. Only the rationing of cigarettes would stump her, if it should occur, and she looked forward to the chance to quit a habit of twenty-five years.

Alarmed, Mary Paxton Keeley offered to send her rationed goods from Missouri, as Rose herself had sent scarce items to her old friend Elsie Jackson in embattled England. "Thank you a lot," Rose replied, "but you mustn't send me rationed things. I intend to get along without them. And if you think a minute you will see that I can't refuse to get a ration card and at the same time take coffee and sugar and so on from people who do; that would be just taking a stand and then getting out from under the consequences." She went on to elaborate the principle. "Of course it does not matter what we get along without. It isn't that I mind not having anything."

> But it seems to me that what our boys are fighting for, America's real meaning, is going to get lost behind their backs if we who stay at home don't defend it. If we let our country be national-socialized, if we let ourselves submit to politicians' "control" of everything we do and get so used to it that we don't get rid of every one of these restrictions upon personal freedom just the minute that the war is won, then this whole war will be just waste motion and lost lives. For what is the use of getting rid of Hitler if we let our own country adopt his political philosophy? As Roosevelt says, it is the Nazi philosophy that must be got rid of. And it can not be got rid of by believing it. It can only be got rid of by "little people" like you and me, who won't submit to bureaucratic regimentation.

And so she prepared for her own hard winter. In time, she had twelve hundred jars of home-canned food of all kinds safely stored down cellar.[5]

The spring of 1943 brought her yet another battle, really more of a picket-line skirmish, but one that vaulted her briefly into the national news and gave her another hearing. She was accustomed to listening to radio commentator Samuel Grafton, who one day asked his listeners' opinions on an extension of Social Security. Rose had seen the end of Bismarck's version of Social Security in the chaos of the Weimar republic; she could see the economic implications of an unfunded national obligation that operated like a Ponzi scheme; and she was appalled that her government should presume to choose for its citizens how they should prepare for their old age. She had recently spoken on the radio against Social Security, and the facts of her argument were fresh in her mind. On a postcard she scribbled a brief message: "If school teachers say to German children, 'We believe in Social Security,' the children will ask, 'Then why did you fight Germany?' All these 'Social Security' laws are German, instituted by Bismarck and expanded by Hitler. Americans believe in freedom, in not being taxed for their own good and bossed by bureaucrats." Fearing that her professional name would draw undue attention—perhaps hoping that her message would carry the force of a voice from "the little people"—she signed her married name, Mrs. C. G. Lane, and gave her address.[6]

In the Danbury mails, her postcard passed under the eyes of the Danbury postmaster, who, in the tense wartime atmosphere, thought it subversive, and copied the message and sent it to the state FBI headquarters. What followed was an exercise in error, bureaucratic bumbling, and general bad judgment that left the Bureau with egg on its face and spread Rose's name and picture across the nation's newspapers. It also produced an FBI file of over one hundred pages. The first error was that her name was miscopied as C. G. Lang, and when an FBI record search yielded no one by that name at her address, the matter was turned over to the state police, who sent out a young trooper perhaps overly impressed with the importance of his mission. The remainder of the story is best told in Rose's own words, for that is what made it to the papers. In a piece entitled *What Is This—the Gestapo?* she cast herself as a character in a small drama:

> Two weeks later she was digging dandelions from her lawn, when a State Police car stopped at her gate. A State Trooper, uniformed and armed, walked up to her. He said that he was investigating subversive activities for the F.B.I., and asked her whether anyone in her house had sent a postcard to Samuel Grafton.
>
> She said that she had sent one. The State Trooper leafed through a sheaf of papers clipped to a board, found a typed copy of the words she had written, held this before her eyes and asked sternly if she had written those words.
>
> She said, "Yes, I wrote that. What have the State Police to do with any opinion that an American citizen wants to express?"
>
> The trooper said, more sternly, "I do not like your attitude."
>
> A furious American rose to her full height. "*You* do not like *my* attitude! I am an American citizen. I hire you, I pay you. And you have the insolence to question *my* attitude? The point is that *I* don't like *your* attitude. What is this—the Gestapo?"
>
> The young State Trooper said hastily, "Oh no, nothing like that. I was not trying to frighten you."
>
> "You know perfectly well that your uniform and your tone would frighten a great many Americans in this neighborhood who remember the police methods in Europe. You know, or you should

know, that any investigation of opinions by the American police is outrageous!"

"Oh, come now," the trooper protested. "At least give me credit for coming to you, instead of going around among your neighbors and gathering gossip about you. I only want to know whether you wrote that postcard."

"Is that a subversive activity?" she demanded.

Somewhat confused, the trooper answered, "Yes."

"Then I'm subversive as all hell!" she told him. "I'm against all this so-called Social Security, and I'll tell you why." And for five minutes she told him why. "I say this, and I write this, and I broadcast it on the radio, and I'm going to keep right on doing it till you put me in jail. Write that down and report it to your superiors."

By the time it reached print the story had been polished by several tellings in letters to her friends, no doubt ("it's really too bad that only the dandelions heard me," she wrote Dorothy Thompson in one version). But someone drew it to the attention of the National Economic Council, a small New York–based group of conservative businessmen and laissez-faire theorists who published occasional pamphlets and a monthly review of books. *What Is This—the Gestapo?* was published anonymously under this imprint and mailed widely throughout the country. When the story was picked up by the national newspapers, the FBI was forced into embarrassed denials of impropriety, and Rose had suddenly a wider national exposure than her books had ever gained her.

Locally, her new fame won her an audience before the Danbury Lions' Club, to whom she gave a talk warning against creeping socialism, the New Deal secret police, and Communist-inspired books in the schools; this talk was also reported to the FBI by a Danbury informant as "seditious." As a curious cap to this story, and an indication of the complex consistency of her thought, Rose wrote directly to J. Edgar Hoover himself, acknowledging the necessity of a national secret police to protect the country in time of war, in fact praising his work—but insisting on the necessity of keeping it within the limits of "American principles": "To this end, whenever a policeman or an investigator puts so much as a toe of his boot across the line protecting any American citizen's right to free thought and free speech, I regard it as that citizen's duty to refuse to permit this, and to raise a loud yell." Which, of course, she had. She might have been less charitable to the FBI had she known the extent of their records on her, which included the fact that she ended by inviting the trooper into her kitchen for cookies. Also included were her association with the *Pittsburgh Courier* (itself under surveillance for subversion) and her 1919 connection with the Finnish Singing Society in San Francisco, identified as a propaganda wing of the IWW.[7]

IV

The FBI files also contain a record of her next exercise in subversion, which was an attempt to reduce her income below taxable levels. Even as she found herself no longer able to produce the fiction that had commanded high fees in the national magazines, she had also found the demands on her income dropping; and in this change of circumstance and attitude she found a new and sweet use of adversity. She would boast from time to time of living on less than a thousand dollars a year; and to avoid income tax was, of course, the next logical step in her exercise in self-sufficiency. The immediate occasion was probably a fee of $1,750 for a *Reader's Digest* reprinting of *Let the Hurricane Roar*. This had always been her most popular book: its message of struggle against overwhelming adversity was appropriate for a wartime audience, and no less a person than Sinclair Lewis had recently thought to offer it in an anthology for a book club. But the *Reader's Digest* fee effectively doubled her income for the year, and the tax-bite was correspondingly large. Through George Bye she found an attorney who was willing to try to set up a trust to receive her income and pay out all but her necessary expenses to charity. By now, no one depended on her income but herself; her mortgage was paid and she really needed only enough to buy a few staples and pay her taxes. She was receiving sixty dollars a month for her *Pittsburgh Courier* column, which sufficed for her needs, and she would have the satisfaction of seeing little or none of her earnings going to a government she vociferously condemned. It is not clear that she actually carried this scheme to its end; the exploration of the possibility stands merely as a symptom of what was on her mind. Probably the same impulse lay behind her refusal of a job with the Office of War Information (OWI), tendered from her old friend Bessie Breuer, who had gotten her the job with the Red Cross that had taken her to Europe years before—although it is hard to imagine Rose working for the government on any terms. She described her stance and her strategies in another talk to the Danbury Lions' Club, making a story which was duly picked up by the news wire-services and widely reprinted. A reporter from a New York newspaper had called for an interview and quoted freely from her remarks. "NOVELIST HAS GIVEN UP WRITING AND INCOME TO FIGHT NEW DEAL" was the heading next to her picture:

> Rose Wilder Lane, novelist, has taken to the storm cellar until the Roosevelt administration blows over. She calls it "resisting regimentation."
> "I stopped writing fiction because I don't want to contribute to the New Deal. . . . The income tax was the last straw. I don't see why I should work to support the Writers War Board, the OWI and

all such New Deal piffle while men are dying and there is work to be done at home."

"I raised a pig, butchered it last fall, 600 pounds of beautiful pork. I get around the butter and sugar rationing by making my own butter and using honey as a substitute for sugar."

She smiled. "Would you like to see my wealth?" Leading the way down to the cellar she pointed to rows of canned vegetables and fruits on the shelves. "Eight hundred jars. Corn, peas, beans, tomatoes, pickles, green peppers, beets, berries, all raised in my own garden. That's genuine social security."

She spoke earnestly. "The thing to do, if you think such practices are wrong, is to resist them. The American people did it with prohibition. The colonists did it when King George III tried to overtax them. The New Deal is going back to King George's economy and scarcity. I feel very hard times are coming. . . ."

The column was clipped and sent to the FBI by someone who had attended the earlier Lions' Club meeting; it was, the informant claimed, "extremely seditious."[8]

So too thought the *New Republic*, although its editorial comment did not use the word. Rather it chastised her for carelessness with the facts. Rose had, by this time, her private mental catalog of bureaucratic horrors inflicted on the nation by the New Deal, excesses of regulation that had distorted the economy. She cited some of these for the visiting reporter, and no doubt her ideology ran her into exaggeration. Holding her to the letter of truth, the editors investigated—to the extent, at least, of querying the very bureaucrats Rose had criticized—and found little substance to her charges. The point, of course, was that for Rose even that little was significant symbolically of the larger evil that had installed the bureaucracy in the first place. "Mrs. Lane's Sitdown Strike" was the editorial lead, and the conclusion accused her of "her own little private revolt against the war effort." Such were the polar conceptions of patriotism in the grim year of 1944.[9]

V

There were other battles large and small to be fought in these years. One was so important as compulsory military service in peacetime. Another was so simple as local zoning, which she opposed vigorously and eloquently in 1945–1946 with a small band of like-minded confederates. A sparsely attended town meeting had set up the zoning commission; when she heard of its arbitrary authority, she joined with six others (the Independent Citizens Committee) to mobilize public opinion against it. It was a classic case in citizen action, as they aroused the community by telephone, postcard, and letters to the editor. When the commission met to consider regulations, an overflow crowd of one thousand descended on city hall; the meeting was moved to the high school auditorium, then adjourned for a week as the beleaguered commissioners sought to deal with a hostile audience. The local paper described Rose's appearance and her claim that "the plan to enforce the regulations is similar to tactics employed in Germany."

> Mrs. Lane, who owns a home and three acres of land in King Street district, says she has no intentions of letting any group of public officials tell her how she is to operate and develop her home and land.
> She has written an open letter to the citizens of Danbury in which she describes the regulations as a trend toward a socialistic form of government. "Socialism is the police-enforced obedience of individuals to regulations imposed on them for the 'common good'," Mrs. Lane wrote.

Rose clipped the item from the paper and added her own annotation: "Report omits mob-meeting after adjournment, which demanded I speak. I said, 'We must abolish the zoning commission.' " Which the voters did, after Rose and her committee researched the law, persuaded them that they could, and petitioned for a town meeting to address the matter.[10]

It was minuteman, guerilla warfare, and she found it exhilarating to lead citizens against an overweening government. The Independent Citizens Committee had for a time a status beyond its size; really it consisted of Rose and one other woman who did the spadework, a realtor whose brother provided legal advice, and a few workers from the local hat factory. When a grateful citizen forced on Rose a ten-dollar donation, it was their first and last cash income. Pressed for details of their organization, Rose's friend, Madelaine LaCava, said that the committee simply gathered to deal with occasions as they arose. A few years later they gathered again on the occasion of a school-board budget that they thought was secretive and exorbitant. In days they again mobilized the town; a packed assembly hall, divided between the local educational establishment and tax-paying townspeople, alternately hissed and applauded speakers as the committee moved an alternative and much lower budget. As the meeting became entangled in parliamentary maneuvering and sank into chaos, Rose moved adjournment and a ballot referendum. The desperate presiding officer grasped the straw, the motion passed, and shortly so did the committee's alternative budget.[11]

The national debate over compulsory military training offered her another chance to sharpen her principles in practice. At the heart of her notion of a nation's military strength lay the old idea of the volunteer state militia, locally raised, trained as a unit, and inspired by attachment to the local soil. A country worth defending would be defended voluntarily, her heart and her reading of her country's history told her. She had been appalled by peacetime conscription in the months before the war; now, as the country began to look to the end of the war and the possibility of having to maintain a large standing army, the specter of permanent and compulsory conscription began to walk the land. *Woman's Day* commissioned opposing articles from her and from Bernard De Voto. Rose used her opportunity to argue from the history of Europe that compulsory conscription actually weakened a nation's military strength as it weakened the spirit of its citizens. At the heart of her argument she quoted Ortega y Gasset: "It must be emphasized that the warrior spirit is one thing, and the soldier spirit quite another. The soldier spirit [is] the degeneration of the warrior." "Permanent conscription [she went on] made soldiers of our enemies. Englishmen and Americans are warriors, free men who—when they must—fight for a cause they support and the truth they know."[12]

VI

Thus the war years passed as she fought her own battles on her three-acre patch of independent soil, dividing her time between her garden, her kitchen, and countless hours at her typewriter, where she wrote countless letters to the small band of fellow thinkers she had found across the land. As the war ended and, shortly after, wartime rationing and price controls as well, someone from the *Chicago Tribune* recalled her notoriety of 1943 and sent a reporter to Danbury to see how she was faring. "He found her more of an individualist than ever and with a cellar full of meats, fruits and vegetables to prove that anyone with similar convictions and ambitions could have sat out the war without a ration card." Virginia Manor was with her again, working in New York but by now something of an acolyte, and in the interval Rose had acquired two Maltese terriers, avatars of the beloved Mr. Bunting:

> Although she hadn't done any canning from the time she was 12 until she began her self-subsistence a few years ago, Mrs. Lane refuses to consider herself a pioneer in undertaking to feed herself, her young companion, Virginia Manor, who also writes, and her two dogs named Jonathan Edwards and Henry David Thoreau.
> She has taught Virginia how to churn butter and this product along with all the others, is made at a fraction of retail store cost. Virginia keeps the household books and maintains their inventory, but no attempt is made to figure production costs.
> The only items on the cellar shelves prepared with the use of sugar are the jellies and preserves made by Virginia who explained: "I had a sugar card when I came here but I know better now."[13]

This interview, as well as the earlier ones, mentions that Rose has sons in the military service; an earlier one also mentioned a son in a concentration camp. John and Al Turner had dropped out of her life, but she continued to invoke them as a proof of her patriotism and a shield against criticism. The case of Rexh Meta remained to the end a different matter. She had had no direct word from him since his last letter on the eve of the Italian occupation of Albania, although he did manage to get through to her a request to keep his life insurance paid in case he was killed by the Fascists. From friends abroad and from Elmer Davis in the Office of War Information, Rose managed to learn that Rexh and his family had at first been interned in an Italian concentration camp. His father-in-law was given a post in the puppet government established by the Italians and was able to get the family returned to Albania, where Rexh's long association with the British was enough, apparently, to ensure his arrest by the Communist partisans who took control of Albania at the end of the war. He was sentenced to thirty years in jail without food, although his wife was permitted to bring food in to him. In time, Rose found a means to forward money to Pertef through friends in the American Red Cross.

Rose's fear was that this son would be executed, or taken to a Russian labor camp and worked to death. Her hope was that some unofficial word indicating U.S. interest and influence might spare him that fate. It was to this end that she wrote Mary Paxton Keeley back in Missouri, who was a childhood friend of Bess Truman: "Just that, would save Rexh. A word from Mr. Truman to the State Department, or to OWI, or to his own secretary, would do it, entirely unofficially and not involving anyone officially in any way. Just a hint, from the right person, that there ARE Americans who are watching Rexh's case and will know what happens to him." Whether this appeal bore any fruit cannot be known. But even as she launched this appeal in the direction of Truman, she turned to Herbert Hoover as well. To him she explained that any aid to Rexh Meta and his family must be indirect, for her anticommunism was well known and might provoke retaliation against Rexh. Years later she claimed that some unspecified agreement was reached whereby Rexh's life would be spared if she would never speak out against the new regime in Albania; the claim is probably one of her late self-dramatizations, and it is more likely that she decided to hold her tongue out of simple prudence. She loathed Communists more than death itself, but she never spoke against those in Albania. To the end of her life she continued to send money for support of Rexh's family, and the aid would be carried on by her next "adopted" child.[14]

For even as the Turner boys receded from her horizon and Rexh Meta was all but lost to her, she had discovered another young man to bind to her with her attentions. *Reader's Digest* had reprinted *Let the Hurricane Roar* because the wife of one of the editors had recommended it. During one of his conferences with Rose, at the White Turkey Inn in Danbury in 1943, editor Burt MacBride had brought his son Roger along with him. Roger MacBride was fourteen years old, bright and interested, and through him Rose began to explore the role, not of mother now, but of grandmother.[15]

$\mathscr{C}$OLD WAR WARRIOR

I feel fine. . . .

There had been no journal ruminations for many years, but on January 14, 1949, Rose turned again to the notebook she had last opened in 1941. It was time for one of her periodic stock-takings:

> Well, this probably proves something Pollyanna-ish, though I don't know about a new era's beginning 8 years ago. Here I sit alone and contented in my new-made house with the two Maltese, David & Junior. Workers have been in the house since last May. Fireplaces are built in the living room and study, bay window in my bedroom, new closets, new furnace room, new porch upstairs between bedroom and study (former lumber-room) and below it the little porch with three arches which shall be a breakfast room when I have my planned new kitchen. . . . I began all this with no money. It is all paid for, I can't think how. I feel fine, though now I can't see without glasses, wear an upper plate, have only 6 lower front teeth left, and pains, maybe arthritic, in my knees. Troub, fat and crippled with arthritis, is living in her own house in Weston near Cobb's mill. Betty [Bessie Beatty] died suddenly at Berta's house on Easter Sunday last year. John sent Christmas card from Columbia, Missouri, last month. I ignored it. Nothing much happened in the unwritten interim, except the war, increasing socialization, Roosevelt's death. . . . My mother has sold Rocky Ridge on installment plan, $50 a month. Communists are taking China and Truman (elected to everyone's stupefaction) has just appointed Dean Acheson Sec. of State.

Thus she catalogued her interests, personal and political, at the beginning of her sixty-third year.

The entry is striking for the narrowing of its emotional range. Old friends have been sloughed off, the bleeding wound from John Turner stanched, the childhood home she had lavished her fortune on is consigned without comment to strangers, and the war just ended is leveled with the death of Roosevelt and the triumph of his hated policies. She has drawn a circle within which her energies would be focused: her house, which would become a monument to home improvement, and her political evangelizing, which would become more zealous and hard-bitten as it became more marginal to the national political scene. And gone forever, it seems, is the painful scrutiny of her inner life that had characterized earlier journals. The ceaseless chatter in her head had fallen silent. "I feel fine."

The end of the war had ended rationing and the need for the dramatic posture of self-reliance. The deliberate suppression of her income continued, however; and as labor and materials for the expansion of her house became available again most of her small income from royalties went into her house. She wrote almost nothing that would command a fee, though, and kept her expenses pared to the bone. Hours freed from gardening and canning could be diverted to her domestic expansion and to the mounds of daily correspondence with her small network of fellow thinkers.

For several years she had written her weekly column for the *Pittsburgh Courier,* instructing her readers in elementary government, political history, and laissez-faire economics. In 1945 her column in that paper ceased; later she would claim that the editor, a "New Dealer," could no longer tolerate her views. But she was also about to transfer her energies to a new forum. She had become editor of the National Economic Council's monthly *Review of Books,* a position offered to her on the death of Albert Jay Nock, a political theorist she admired except for his espousal of the Single Tax principles of Henry George. She had always been a compulsive, omnivorous reader but by now she had given up on the nihilism (as she termed it) of modern fiction and had turned more and more to history, economic and political theory, and international relations. As in everything that took her interest, she was self-taught to the point of lay authority in these subjects. Now she could promote, to a self-selected readership, books she considered important, and warn against those she found pernicious. With correspondence and book reviews, she was bound to her typewriter as much as ever she had been when her support of others had depended on it, but her audience now was scattered, accessible only through the daily mails, and in search not of entertainment but of education and moral support for a minority view that history seemed to have passed by. Young Roger MacBride, first at Philips Exeter and then at Princeton, now called her Gramma; he came to spend weekends, to pull weeds in her garden or perform other chores; and after work she would fix a chicken dinner and talk with her new acolyte long into the morning. Like Norma Lee Browning, MacBride found himself receiving another education, an alternative to his classroom learning that was compelling by the range, focus, and energy this other grandmother brought to the political and economic arguments she had spent two decades in refining.[1]

These were the early years of the cold war. Since the Russian Revolution, the prospect of Soviet Communism had been largely a theoretical concern for Americans, dividing intellectuals over the broad issues of

social justice and drawing many well-meaning people into leftist pos-
tures against the horrors of Fascism. Now, however, to Rose and to many
like her, the problem was immediate and all-consuming: the Russians
had the atomic bomb; and although her country had won the shooting
war against Fascism, it seemed to be losing a larger struggle against communism, as from Berlin to Shanghai great areas of the globe fell to the
Red menace. And at home the country seemed riddled with subversion,
treachery, and false doctrine. Her beloved Balkans had been betrayed at
Yalta, the Nationalist Chinese deserted shortly after, Alger Hiss stood as
a symbol of internal perfidy, Keynesian economics bid fair to reduce her
country to bankruptcy, and every month seemed to produce some new
encroachment by her government on the natural—necessary—freedom
of its citizens. Rose had always been impressed by the militancy and
dedication of the early Communists, and in these dark days for the republic she began to shape herself in their image. From her independent
little plot of ground, seated daily at her typewriter, she sought to kindle
what flame she could. A few people were interested in what she had to
say, fewer still would engage her thoughts in an exchange of letters. The
essence of her life in these years runs through her hortatory book reviews
and her private correspondence. The first of these represents hours of
daily reading; the second, hours of daily writing. Her letters to Jasper
Crane, for instance, would eventually run to hundreds of pages.[2]

||

The scholar must acquire a taste for old book reviews, but in this case the
reviews matter less for what they tell us about the books, many now
forgotten, than for what they reveal about the reviewer. By and large
Rose used the occasion to reiterate and expand the ideas she had drawn
together in *The Discovery of Freedom*. Her readers needed to know modern
history, both European and American; the history of socialism and communism and the lives of the men who shaped these alien doctrines; economic and political theory generally; as well as the specific history of the
Roosevelt administration in its manifold treacheries. Many of these works
had deficiencies of conception or vocabulary that she was quick to point
out; but once the reader saw them clearly he would also see clearly the
essential points of doctrine that she had now refined.

Over and over she came back to them, first principles and necessary
inferences: that the essence of human life is in the free-standing individual rather than in the social collective, that individual action is freely
chosen, that choice implies individual responsibility, that the essence of
government is coercion to impede individual action. At some point in the
sequence, first principles flowed into corollaries: that a hostile universe

required human cooperation (hence the brotherhood of man), that the ideal state was simple anarchy but minimal government was needed to keep the peace and deter foreign aggression, that the ideal society was a complex, self-regulating structure of competing and cooperating individuals whose energies working freely would transform the world.

By now her view of history was complete as well. It was not a world fallen from grace but one still struggling toward it. Until the American Revolution, the world had been characterized by societies whose individuals had viewed themselves as controlled from outside themselves, whether in primitive communal clans whose primary category was "the people," or in theocracies whose powers came from gods, or in later despotisms and monarchies whose rulers held all power and granted occasional privileges. Out of Judeo-Christian and Moslem conceptions of individual responsibility had come an ideal that had flowered into a political system only recently in the New World—and that had been under attack, and recently in retreat, from reactionary collectivist regimes ever since. In the future lay the real world revolution, in which the American ideal would be completed at home and would subvert the outworn ideologies of the Old World. Rose's writing was at its most poignant as she invoked the vision of an embattled nation on the edge of history, threatened by forces of darkness from without and by traitors from within.

In effect, she had found a way around the safe and debilitating, all-inclusive logic of determinism. Forces such as the id or history or economics were simply old gods with new names, who vanished once the individual decided to choose his actions. At the same time she could claim to be scientific, or at least empirical, in her deepest beliefs: individual freedom was a hypothesis tested and proved in American history, and further back lay the older truths of the Judeo-Christian tradition. Despite her attendance at the local King Street Christian church, she was no more naturally religious in her old age than in her youth: "I am not a Christian, but I am a theist," she wrote to one of her correspondents; and her mind skipped easily from the knowable Creation to an unknowable Creator, and back from there to the traditional moral laws, which she believed to be empirically tested laws of human nature.

All of this aside, there was the practical matter of protecting these gains in the present moment of history. National defense was a legitimate function of government, and she was glad to have a strong military presence in the world; although she was unconvinced that Russia would attack the United States when internal subversion had served so well against other countries. Internal subversion was a threat she could appreciate, having seen Mussolini's agents at work in Albania; the fate of Czechoslovakia was not lost on her; and she was glad to have the FBI on guard against subversives, even if it had looked in on her in a momentary lapse of judgment. She did not think it impossible that a coup might strike at the national government; but she took heart at the original federal nature of the union, which would leave forty-eight state governments with their militias as bulwarks against complete subversion. She had never considered herself an intellectual, most of whom were Marxists or, at least, socialists or Keynesians, she feared; but she did discover and admire the theories of Friedreich Hayek and Ludwig von Mises.[3]

The social scientist, reviewing the list of symptoms, would find a clear case of American right-wing pathology: an implicit monism that denied the chance of legitimate compromise with its opponents; a privileging of a past era; a sense of embattled danger from conspiratorial forces; an anti-statist political theory; a conservative economic theory. Having made his analysis, he would look for the causes in a sense of displacement from a previously honored status, and a corresponding resentment. The biographer, less clinical and schematic, cannot risk losing his subject in such a scheme: to dismiss Rose as a right-wing ideologue is to dismiss the pathos of her journey to that position and to reduce her pilgrimage to a reflex. Certainly that track lies somewhere in her baffled attempt to re-create in her own life something of her mother's triumphant assertion of will over circumstance; that effort had ended with the failure of her enterprise at Rocky Ridge and the loss of her fortune in the Depression. And just as she had summoned up her energies and optimism to face her own hard winter, she had found her pioneer assumptions betrayed by a national government that seemed determined to destroy initiative and create a dependent populace. The intervening years had truly been a period of reaction, as she attempted to recapture an honored past in her mother's books and to rationalize the values of that past in her own books and essays and in her personal daily confrontation with the world. The social scientist has a name for it all, this "condition of those who have more of a stake in the past than in the present." It is the Quondam Complex, he declares. Luckily, Rose never lived to hear the term; and finally it does not quite square with the forward reaches of her views.[4]

For despite whatever complex might underlie her commitment to the values of an earlier time, she was passionately engaged with the problems those values revealed in the present and optimistic about their resurgence in the future. The question was, what could an aging woman of limited means *do*—to forward the continuing revolution and to confound its enemies? Little actions, symbolic gestures, small-scale attacks and skirmishes could exercise her own integrity and embolden others to do their duty.

A book reviewer can warn against a bad book, but it is another stage of the battle to try to suppress its sales. In August of 1947, Rose came across a college textbook, *The Elements of Economics,* by Professor Lorie Tarshis of Stanford University. She devoted the whole of one issue of her *Review* to exposing the fallacies of this book's Keynesian assumptions and the insidious appeal of its rhetoric. "I cannot do justice to this textbook's charm for the immature," she wrote. "I cannot convey the impact of its grave passages upon their deepest and best emotions." While she conceded that the Keynesians were "emphatically . . . not communists," she warned that their economic assumptions undermined the very basis of human prosperity. "In the broad troop-movement of the Marxians, they advance in the center. They come to save capitalism as Hitler rescued the Sudeten Germans."

> *The Elements of Economics* plays upon fear, shame, pity, greed, idealism, hope, to urge young Americans to act upon this theory, *as citizens.* This is not an economics text at all; it is a pagan-religious and political tract. It inspires an irrational faith and spurs it to political action. From cover to cover there is not a single suggestion of any action that is not political—and Federal.

She ended with a list of fifteen colleges that had adopted it; in the next month's *Review,* she made room to recur to this book and furnished an expanded list of colleges where it would be used to educate the "young Americans [who] . . . will be voters in 1950 and 1952."

> Do you want the new voters of 1950 to learn now that the American economy produces poverty, depression, unemployment and world war? that the Russian economy is superior because it is planned? that nothing but Federal spending can maintain capitalism, and that Federal spending "being under social control" can be any amount of money that printing presses can print, with no fear of disaster?
>
> If you are an alumnus of any of these universities, if you know anyone who is, if you know the parent of a student in any of them, if you pay taxes to support any of them, or if you can write a letter or use a telephone, do you imagine that there is nothing you can do?

There was a kind of war here, she understood. She had lately read of publishers yielding to left-wing pressures not to publish Hayek's *The Road to Serfdom,* and in this case she had a chance to right the balance, however little. Her review and its appeal had its effect, however minimal. Several schools found their choice of the Tarshis text called into question; and from at least one school in Texas came a letter from a dean to the FBI, asking if the chairman of his department of economics was a Communist. And in a correspondence with his university's president, Herbert Hoover lent the weight of his influence to an attempt to have the book removed at Stanford.[5]

Ideology selects its own society. Rose was no longer a fiction writer nor even a journalist anymore; and the years of her ideological campaign mark also the substitution of new friends for the old network of writers and journalists. Even the Haders became identified with the naive American left and the follies of her own youth. Into the void left by such renunciations came two kinds of friends. The first were a number of the ordinary good people of the community with whom she shopped, visited, and attended movies, and whose essential decency she always believed was both an American strength and weakness: typical were the women of the Dorcas Society ("the nicest good women imaginable, the 'American innocents'"). The second was a small band of ideological warriors, reliable in opinion and tested in their own battles. To follow out Rose's connections with such figures as Joseph P. Kamp, Merwin K. Hart, and Jasper Crane is to take a fair sample of the American radical-right in these postwar days of national paranoia at both ends of the ideological spectrum. And it will illustrate how difficult it was for an essentially decent woman to keep her ideological skirts clean in the nasty battles some of these figures chose to fight.

Conspiracy theories have always lain at the heart of extremist politics in America; and there is a long and unhappy history of targeting minority groups as conspirators against the public weal. In the postwar period, Communists had largely replaced Catholics and Jews as the target group, and with some justification, given their ideology. Rose's antipathy was real and virulent; Communists were enemy enough for her; but she never associated herself with the impulse toward witch-hunting and persecution that would typify the excesses of the McCarthy era. Rather, she was more concerned with promoting the individualist values that would stand as a counter to collectivists generally. But among those who shared her values were some who carried with them the scent of the old anti-Semitism, as conspirator groups coalesced in their imaginations. For Rose, the enemies of her enemies were apt to be her friends, which put her in some very problematic company.[6]

Joseph Kamp was, according to his stationery, vice-chairman of the Constitutional Educational League. He was its spokesman and writer, its representative to the world, perhaps even its only member. Like Rose, he was a self-taught historian and theorist, deeply patriotic and reflexively anticommunist. To give him his due, he was equally antifascist although less preoccupied with the Fascist danger. He kept close track of the careers of American Communists, "fellow travelers," and the members of alleged "front" organizations. A slashing and vitriolic writer, he authored and distributed a number of pamphlets (*Fifth Column Conspiracy in America, Vote CIO—and Get a Soviet America*) and one book, an "expose" of the World Government movement in the years just after the war. He was particularly attentive to left-wingers who had changed their names presumably to hide Jewish origins. He came to Rose's attention when he was called before the Special House Committee to Investigate Lobbying, which was concerned with the financing and distribution of his material. The committee demanded his contributors' list; he asserted that the committee lacked jurisdiction and refused to produce the list. Cited for contempt, he was given a jail sentence—and a four-page spread in Rose's review. She knew him only by name at the moment, but their community of interests made them natural allies and in time close friends. In the years that followed, Kamp and his wife were frequent guests at her Danbury home and its caretakers during her absences.[7]

The scent of conspiracy is strong in Kamp's writing; he begins his *We Must Abolish the United States* with an account of a visit to his offices of a "spy" from the United World Federalists. The odor runs strong through the world of Merwin K. Hart, as well, though the enemy this time was an older and more traditional one. Hart had been the founder of the National Economic Council and its first president, but in the complex of enemies these warriors feared he fixed upon those that threatened his militant Christianity. First among these were, of course, the godless Communists; and to the extent that Franco had opposed the Communists in Spain, Hart had been a supporter of Franco. Such an attachment made him, of course, a crypto-Fascist in the rhetoric of the Left. The same reasons that led him to support Franco made him want a strong Germany reestablished to oppose the Russians; he had been against the requirement for unconditional surrender, and he had opposed the Nuremberg Trials on principle. Complexly entangled in his vision also was a militant anti-Zionism: in December 1959, in an evangelical essay in the *Economic Council Newsletter* he took the occasion of a book entitled *World Faith* (which endorsed a hypothetical world religion as adjunct to a world community and world government) to discover a Zionist conspiracy "to suppress American consciousness of Christianity." His United States was manifestly a Christian country, and Christianity was rolled together with patriotism and free enterprise in a stance against Communism, socialism, Zionism, and the New Deal. By any standard he was an extremist: he had proposed legislation specifying resignation or death for Communist public officials, and the rhetoric of his essay was a Christian warrior's call to arms against Zionism.

Rose had read widely in Jewish history and culture, she had always had valued Jewish friends, and she was on principle scrupulously fair in her assessment of the place of Jews and other minorities in American society. But Hart was friend and fellow warrior; her Christian sentiments were of a less fervid strain than his, but her native sense of the Jews as exotics, and the wall she had encountered between herself and the Levines, made her suspicious as well of the divided loyalties of American Zionists and their influence in the United States. And when Hart, as a result of his article, found himself under attack from Rose's old friend

Isaac Don Levine, Rose again found herself caught between two valued comrades. In essence, Levine charged Hart with being a Fascist and anti-Semite; Hart in turn charged Levine with being a Communist dupe and anti-Gentile. From a distance of forty years, in their dispute they seem to share equally the honors for ideological overkill. Earlier, Rose had found herself forced to choose between Levine and Dorothy Thompson over an issue that was, at its root, a matter of anticommunism, and principle had triumphed over sentiment. This time, Levine was lost, as his attack on Hart obscured for her his own long and principled struggle against Communism. "After thirty years of absolute mutual loyalty, he made me the victim of the most total treachery," she wrote Dorothy Thompson. Her friendship with the Levines would continue on the surface, but a growing discomfort over this rupture on the part of the Levines was among their reasons for a move to Maryland.[8]

Rose's friendship with Jasper Crane was of a different order, however, just as Crane was of a different order from Kamp and Hart. Crane was a retired executive from the DuPont Corporation, a devout man and a charitable Christian. After some correspondence, he invited her to visit; and a friendship emerged that prompted Rose to long and chatty letters. His perspective was that of a businessman who saw his work as labor in the Lord's vineyard and the fruits to be a better world for all. His letters to her were in the main stiff and unimaginative; but his personal presence was apparently winning, for her letters to him came to be a running commentary on her life and thoughts.

Alluded to in this correspondence is one of the more obscure episodes in her battle against the Communist enemy, the rescue of the Romanian immigrant Jon Ovezea from deportation to his native land. Ovezea was a young Romanian airplane pilot, by conscience an anticommunist, who in 1946 had despaired of emigrating to the United States on his country's limited quota and had stowed away on an American ship. Held on Ellis Island for return to Romania, he came to the notice of Rose and some of her friends who hoped to save him from what they feared was certain death if he was returned. He and similar politically motivated illegal immigrants from Communist countries could hope to avoid forcible repatriation only through a special act of Congress, and such a bill had been introduced on his behalf by Representative Howard Buffett of Nebraska. While the bill was pending, the Immigration and Naturalization Service, apparently with little or no notice, loaded a ship with several hundred such refugees for immediate deportation. Rose found in the haste and secrecy of the operation implications of Communist influence within the government. As she told the story, Ovezea persuaded a sympathetic guard to telephone the pastor of the Romanian Orthodox Church in New York City, who alerted Buffett to the clandestine sailing, who in turn succeeded in getting Ovezea taken off the ship and returned to Ellis Island.

As his fate was being decided, Rose became part of a support group, including Crane and Merwin K. Hart, who came to Ovezea's aid with testimonials and affidavits. In time, he was allowed to leave for Honduras; and, by a chain of events that can only be imagined, he was by then married to Rose's young protégée Virginia Manor. Within a year the couple was settled in Los Angeles. The whole point of Rose's interest, of course, was that Ovezea was a refugee of conscience from Communism; she claimed, on unspecified evidence, that others in his situation were granted entry if they simply joined the Party—which, presumably, would link them with highly placed and influential members of the State Department.[9]

The correspondence with Crane was probably based on mutual support. He was dazzled by the play of her intelligence in letters that expressed many of his values more forcefully than he could himself. She, in turn, found in him an access to the thinking of active American capitalists—the big business that should, she thought, be fighting the encroachment of government power at every turn. No doubt it helped her own sense of destiny to be in touch with such sympathetic figures as Crane and Hoover and to use them as sounding boards for her recurring sense of outrage. No note is so consistent in her letters to Crane as the sense that if they all continued to work together for what they believed in, they could in time wrench the American people and the republic back onto the abandoned track.

There were so few of them, though; and she wrestled with the dilemma of keeping her efforts within an ideologically pure group or embracing the occasional ally who was right in some ways but not all. "I have come most reluctantly to the conclusion that Lenin was correct in his view that the almost-but-not-quite-right ally is more dangerous than the open opponent," she wrote to Crane. "It's the not-completely friend who can betray you; the outright enemy doesn't have that opportunity." The subject was the followers of Henry George, such as Albert Jay Nock. But at other times she was willing to encourage curious alliances, such as with the religious right, as represented by Carl McIntire: "It seems to me that the tactical value of Dr. McIntire's movement would be that it enlists the unintelligent emotional people against, instead of for, collectivism; and they are so easily caught by the socialists' lovely fantasies." She had reviewed one of McIntire's books and had corresponded with him, but she could not take him seriously. Nor could she find much fellow feeling with Ayn Rand, whose skills as a writer she admired but whose antireligious fervor she found, during one long and harrowing argument in her Danbury home, to be irrational and whose larger views she found elitist. Considerably purer was the group that gathered at Princeton in July 1946 to discuss "the principles of Freedom." The capitalization was Crane's in his invitation to her; she did attend, and spent a session in conversation with a group that included the presidents of Princeton and of Carleton College, Norman Vincent Peale, and Felix Morley. The group continued for some time; with typical optimism, Rose saw it as "the beginning of the development of a whole school of thinkers and writers reviving American thinking." She saw the necessity of attracting young Americans, as she had already enlisted young Roger MacBride. Meanwhile, she continued to read and take notes toward a revision of *The Discovery of Freedom*, which as a popular simplification of a complex matter had never satisfied her. With Felix Morley she began a correspondence regarding the distinction between "freedom" and "liberty," the first a natural condition to be manifested politically in the second. This and similar problems would occupy her free time until her death; the definitive treatise she projected would never be written, but would lie forever latent in notes and drafts sufficient to fill a large suitcase.[10]

IV

As Rose began her sixty-third year in 1949, Mama Bess was about to turn eighty-two. She had sold Rocky Ridge Farm on a life-lease and had ceased writing, her life story now told, and the increasing popularity of the books had long since erased any worry about money in her remaining years. In Mansfield she was the local celebrity, as impressive for the royalty checks she deposited regularly at the bank as for her literary reputation. As the beloved Laura of her books, she was basking in a growing international adulation that filled her mailbox and kept her busy with replies. A library in Detroit was named for her, and in gratitude she donated to the Detroit Public Library her handwritten, fair-copy manuscripts of *The Long Winter* and *These Happy Golden Years*; a similar donation of the *Little Town on the Prairie* manuscript was made to the Pomona, California, Public Library.[11]

    These gifts would, in fact, ultimately betray her secret. At least one of Rose's friends, Ernestine Evans, had long suspected Rose's hand in the books; and certainly the Haders, who had seen the earliest manuscripts, knew something of the matter. But it would be many years before curious scholars would begin to compare the pedestrian efforts of Laura Ingalls Wilder's manuscripts to the published versions that had passed through her daughter's typewriter. That anyone would ever be interested to make the comparison probably never crossed Mama Bess's mind. But she did have some qualms of conscience in her prosperity. In July of 1949 she wrote to George Bye, assigning 10 percent of her royalties to Rose. The most she would acknowledge to Bye, however, was that "I owe Rose, for helping me, at first, in selling my books and for the publicity she gave them. . . . This arrangement should have been made long ago."[12]

    The arrangement approximately doubled Rose's income and would in fact bring her more money than anything she had written since *Free Land*. There is no sign that she ever mentioned the matter to anyone; but for the first time ever between mother and daughter, money was regularly flowing the other way. Certainly it was a demonstration that Rose had finally succeeded in ending her mother's fears of poverty. Rose had not been back to Rocky Ridge since she had left Missouri in 1937, but within a few months of this gift from her mother she would be called back by the death of her father. Almanzo James Wilder, farmer and horseman, hero of several of his wife's books and model for David Beaton of his daughter's *Free Land*, died on October 23, 1949, full of years at ninety-two. He had never been a problem for Rose; her letters reveal a tender and indulgent love, as for an overgrown child; and except as a literary model, there is no evidence that he touched his precocious daughter in any significant way. She and his wife had had flourishing careers, but his life, as he had said, had been mostly disappointments.

V

Mama Bess was alone at Rocky Ridge now, and as long as her health permitted she remained busy with correspondence with readers—many of them children, teachers, and librarians. The burden had become so heavy that Harpers composed a form letter that could be used for many occasions. Other letters she attended to personally, and she admitted an occasional interviewer—but not Catherine Brody, that loose woman in a fur coat. A small group of younger neighbors gathered about the town's most famous resident, and she came to depend on them in many ways. Still, Rose recognized that the old claim on her time could not be denied from Danbury. The years until her mother's death were marked by a number of long visits to Rocky Ridge Farm, usually in the winter.

She was an aging woman herself by now. At the end of 1951 she turned sixty-five and became eligible for Social Security benefits. To pay income tax had been bad enough: she acquiesced only to the fact of the government's power to seize her property, and she had in some years been able to keep her earnings below taxable limits. But recently she had found her royalties subject to taxation and her status classified as "self-employed"; and to submit further to participation in an unfunded Ponzi scheme, by which the government could preempt her earnings and spend it for her own good—ultimately, she was sure, bankrupting the nation—was just too much. The National Economic Council was a nonprofit organization; by law, it could choose not to bring its employees under Social Security coverage. For reasons Rose could never fathom, the Council chose otherwise; and rather than submit her tiny monthly check to an immoral deduction, she ceased her work on the *Review of Books*. In the

years following, she would take some comfort in a mock-conspiracy with
the handyman who worked about her place not to deduct Social Security
taxes from his wages; and she would intermittently fight off solicitations
from the Social Security Administration to accept a number and enroll
for a retirement income. In this, her honor was at stake as much as in her
refusal to accept a wartime ration book. To the end of her days she remained without a number and without its benefits.

> The Internal Revenue Collector sent me a bill, including fine, for
> my not having paid the Self-Employment tax one year (no space
> for including it, no mention of it, having been on my tax form).
> I sent a check. At intervals since then, various Authorities have
> been trying to force a Social Security number on me. They tele-
> phone and tell me I MUST have one; since I have none, they are
> giving me one. I tell them I won't have it. I get forms, my humble
> request to be entitled to Social Security Benefits; with command,
> Sign here and return to—I put them in the wastebasket. I get orders
> to appear at such an hour, such a date, at such an office, with all
> records and receipts to show cause—I reply that it is not conve-
> nient for me to appear—etc., etc. I even get an order to appear and
> support with documents my claim for refund of the tax-and-fine
> that I paid; I return this, writing across it, I have made no such
> claim. The telephone rings, and I am informed that I am being
> given the necessary Social Security number; I say that I have none
> and shall NOT have one; I will have nothing to do with that Ponzi
> fraud because it is treason; it will wreck this country as it wrecked
> Germany. I won't have it; you can't make me.[13]

The income tax was another matter. Her royalties were being taxed
now, and although she was writing little, she was fond of claiming that
she had ceased writing to avoid the ignominy of paying taxes to an immoral government. A solution emerged in the person of young Roger
MacBride, recently a graduate of Harvard Law. They were informally
grandmother and grandson by now; she had arranged for him to visit
Herbert Hoover; and having taken her principles to college with him and
found much there in the climate of liberal opinion to test and confirm
them, he was ideally suited to be her aide and adviser. When she found
that she could simply give her manuscripts to him—and let him worry
about the taxes—she was delighted. Shortly he would become her agent,
formally her attorney, and ultimately her heir; implicit was the understanding that she could, in the last resort, depend on him as age descended on her.[14]

Age was descending rapidly now on Mama Bess, well into her ninth
decade, and the old concern brought Rose back for extended visits to the
old home town in the 1950s. Her renown remained of a different order
than her mother's, as Mansfield remembered the free spirit from the old
days and found her still hard to admit easily to their hearts. Rose, in her

turn, was not above posturing a bit for local benefit, raising her out-spoken anticommunism into a little drama in which she feared personal assassination: she would not sit with her back to a door in the local restaurants, said she would not do so anywhere. For her mother Rose was properly solicitous, but apparently no more so than she would have per-mitted for herself. A curious and revealing anecdote survives from this period, when Rose and Mama Bess and friends went out to dinner. Her mother slipped on the restaurant steps and fell down; Rose stood by, conspicuously not helping her as she struggled to her feet, embarrassed and apologetic. But when Rose arrived for her visit late in 1956, she found her mother delirious with what had not yet been diagnosed as diabetes. The nearest adequate medical treatment was in Springfield, sixty miles distant. A brief hospital stay restored Mama Bess's health for a time; but once she returned home it was clear that she could not be left alone, and Rose set about mastering the task of cooking for a diabetic. These were, she wrote, "the most exhausting and harrowing weeks of my life." She left no record of what was doubtless a concern: that she might have to remain in attendance on a permanent basis. It was a concern that would be soon obviated, however. In February there was a relapse. Mama Bess lingered in her bed at Rocky Ridge Farm until February 10, just past her birthday. She was ninety years old, and Rose had just turned seventy.[15]

ℳOTHER REMEMBERED

19

It would be a white house, she said, all built from our farm.

ama Bess was buried next to Almanzo in the bleak little Mansfield cemetery. Rocky Ridge farmhouse was still and empty now. The surrounding fields and woods, painfully added in past years to the original acreage, had long since passed to new ownership, and under the terms of Mama Bess's life-lease the house now passed as well—perhaps Mama Bess's last attempt to provide that no other Corinne Murray would, under Rose's sponsorship, succeed to possession. The homesteading saga that had begun with the wandering Charles Ingalls had at last run its course. Or almost, as Rose would add its last efflorescence in an indulgent expansion of her house on the Danbury acreage.

The strain of her mother's illness and death had exhausted Rose; and it was clear to her mother's friends as she moved among the accumulation of Mama Bess's lifetime at Rocky Ridge Farm that she could not wait to get away. Once the funeral was over and as she attended to the details of her mother's estate, she summoned two friends to keep her company. One was Elsie Jackson. Theirs was a correspondence that had continued since Rose had left Albania; Jackson had lately left England to live in Canada with her children, and she had become Rose's frequent companion in recent years. Rose gave over temporary residence in her Danbury home to Elsie's newly married daughter as a honeymoon gift. The other companion was the recently widowed Al Morgan, long a handyman at Rose's home. The threesome set off for a tour of the Southwest before returning to Danbury for the summer. Rose noticed a peculiar symptom of her debilitation: seldom much of a meat-eater, she now developed a lust for steaks, three and four times a day. She thought it the wisdom of her body to restore the vigor of her spirit.[1]

Among the adjustments she now had to make was to an income larger than she had ever known, but the adjustment involved complex emotional as well as financial settlements. One of the things Rose had done in Mansfield during her mother's last illness was to make her own will. Her old friend N. J. Craig drew up a simple document, in which Rose named Roger MacBride as her heir and specifically made no provision for her mother, "as I know that she has means ample for her support

and welfare." The provision and the language were probably legal for-
malities; but they carried their own irony, for the means were ample as a
result of Rose's work, of course. On Mama Bess's death, Rose had found a
last letter, dated some five years earlier:

> Rose Dearest,
>   When you read this I will be gone and you will have inherited
> all I have.
>   Please give to the Laura Ingalls Wilder Library in Mansfield all
> that is left in my private library after you have taken from it what
> you want for yourself. This includes the framed testimonials from
> Chicago, California, and the Pacific Northwest.
>   My jewelry is unique and should not be carelessly scattered.
> Do with it as you wish but preserve it in some way if you can.
>   We were proud of my Havalind china but loved best the English
> made blue willow ware. Do as you please with all the china, but I
> wish you might use it. . . .
>   My love will be with you always
>   Mama Bess
>   (Laura Ingalls Wilder)

The first sentence gives Rose her due, of course, but the parenthetical
addition of the authorial name stands as Mama Bess's last assertion of her
independent status as a writer. And Rose would find that Mama Bess's
will also took back just as it gave. The copyright and income from her
books were assigned to Rose during her life, but were to revert afterward
to the Laura Ingalls Wilder Library of Mansfield.[2]

The royalties from her mother's books were almost as much yearly
as Rose had made in her one great coup in selling *Free Land,* and Mama
Bess had accumulated substantial savings as well. Rose had always spent
her money as fast as she had earned it and often faster, and in her first
flush of this new prosperity she embarked on a further expansion of her
Danbury home, adding a huge brick-floored kitchen, a sun-porch, and a
guest bedroom and bath. The yard was graded and filled, and in the
midst of a chaos of dirt and lumber and disconnected utilities she and
Elsie Jackson camped through the Connecticut autumn. She fell victim to
the imported Hong Kong flu twice, she claimed; and her one surviving
dog, now thirteen years old, died slowly over a period in which it could
only sleep in her arms. "I have been a wreck this whole year," she wrote,
"and so has my house, which has been being remodeled forever. It should
have been finished last year; now I am hoping that it may be done before
this century ends." She yearned for sunshine, and between bouts with
the flu she and Elsie Jackson, with Roger MacBride in attendance as chauffeur, made a trip to the Grand Canyon and through the Southwest again.
Even as she perfected her Connecticut home, Rose was beginning to
think of living in other climes. But the transformation of her Danbury
home was so complete, particularly the enormous brick-floored kitchen,

that it caught the professional attention of Eileen Tighe of *Woman's Day*. The magazine featured Rose's account of the remodeling and captured her in place in her new surroundings in one of the rare photographs from her later years. Since middle age she had become sensitive about being photographed: this one caught her seemingly unawares, a distinctly aged woman with her hair in a dust-cap, her Maltese dogs at her feet.[3]

As Rose was adjusting to life without her mother, the people of her old home town were beginning to think of a suitable memorial to their most famous resident. Led by L. D. Lichty, a nonprofit organization was formed to repurchase the home and grounds and to convert them to a permanent museum. Rose was reluctant at first, asserting that her mother's books should be her memorial; but in time she approved of the project, largely as a means of ensuring the continued popularity of her mother's books and their dramatic message of courage and self-reliance. She came to an arrangement with the people from the old home town to contribute the money to reacquire the home and grounds, to make a substantial annual contribution from her new income toward its maintenance, and to finance in large measure the construction of a curator's home on the grounds of the museum. Mr. and Mrs. Lichty would become the curators. Mrs. Lichty sent her pictures of the house in progress at the framing stage, carpenters reassuringly at work under a contract promising to finish in one hundred days. Mrs. Lichty would later recall with some amazement Rose's detailed interest in the planning of the curator's home and her knowledge of home construction. It was, of course, not the first home Rose had built at Rocky Ridge.[4]

It was a curiously foreshortened, sunshine-and-shadow kind of life that she walked through in these days. Her future grew briefer daily, while the past expanded behind her in a personal panorama in which she could rummage for details of present interest. Not surprisingly, some of her more extravagant stories emerged in this period, as her penchant for posing and role-playing engaged the pliable past. The plane flight with Lincoln Beachey remains one of these, although the flier was more likely Art Smith. A claim to a marriage proposal from King Zog was probably an irresistible expansion of her romantic dalliance with one of his ministers. Her claim to have interviewed Mussolini finds no specific support in her papers, nor does her story of having met Stalin in Tiflis—although she did pass through Rome in 1921, and she did interview many minor Communist functionaries in Soviet Georgia. Her account of a visit by Leon Trotsky to her Danbury home seems to be pure fantasy, doubtless a narrative improvisation grounded in her fascination with the internecine struggles of world Communism. She was a compelling storyteller to the end.[5]

She literally had no demands to worry her anymore: her energies could be directed freely toward memorializing a version of the past embodied in her mother's books and projecting a national future that would in time reestablish itself on the principles of that honored past. If there were problems they were no longer personal ones: she was financially secure, she had become all that she would ever become, and she was, after so many self-consciously painful years, finally at ease with her own limitations. Which meant that the nagging inner voice that had regularly measured her failures against her aspirations had not only fallen silent but could not even be revived. Two years after Mama Bess's death, Rose opened her journal for another of her periodic surveys of her inner life—and found that she no longer had anything to say: "March 3, 1959. I am incapable of continuing the conversations with myself that fill this book so far. Don't know why. Just don't do them any more."

These were years, of course, when she could expect other deaths to rain down around her as well. But the first, curiously, was the one most remote, one that had been the first in her lifetime. For only when the terms of Mama Bess's will were executed, providing for care for the family plots in the De Smet cemetery, did Rose discover the death of her younger brother in his infancy on the old homestead claim. Mama Bess had kept her silence on this loss all during Rose's life—even, it seems, when Rose had lost her own son in 1909. It might have been the deepest thing they had in common; instead, their common response had been to bury the pain among those memories not to be raised again.[6]

Garet Garrett had finally married, late in life, and had been dead since 1954. And then George Bye, after twenty-five years of good service and good friendship, had died in the same year as her mother. Charles Clark, who had squired John Turner through Europe, died young of cancer in 1961, leaving a widow grateful enough to Rose for financing that trip that she funded a scholarship to the Freedom School. "In my eighth decade," Rose wrote her, "I feel all the time a sort of heaviness at my heart, so many of those I cared for are gone. I did not realize what a difference it made when they were *there*, even though I didn't see or hear from them." Dorothy Thompson, depressed by the death of her third husband, the alcoholism and marital problems of the son Rose had tended in 1932, and her own failing health, had retired and announced an intention to write her memoirs. Rose renewed their lapsed correspondence to return, for sake of the memoirs, years of Dorothy's letters she had saved, and there was a brief renewal, in letters only, of the old friendship over memories of their walking trip through the valley of the Loire. "I wish our friendship were revived," Rose wrote, "but how can it be, after so many years. We aren't what we used to be. . . . All lives are tragic. I WISH yours had not been, and we know that that is wishing that you had not lived, so I take it back quickly and so do you." And again, to news of another misfortune:

I am so sorry. How futile, but what can I say. All my own grief,
tragedies, suddenly new again with news of yours. O Dorothy,
you were to have none, they never should have happened to you.

Do you remember, once you said to me you couldn't live if...and
I said, "Oh, yes you will," because I had, and I knew you well
enough to know you would. And when the dreaded did happen,
you did. We survive, Dorothy, you and I and our like. In spite of
hell and high water, we are the survivors. Whatever the purpose
of the whole thing—of human life—is, the first essential is survival, and we survive; the gates of hell do not prevail against us.
It's American. . . .

Rose continued the letter with pages of reminiscence, a strategy itself
reminiscent of the letters she had written Dorothy from Albania to lighten
Dorothy's grief at the collapse of her first marriage. Within two months of
this letter, in January of 1961, Dorothy Thompson died while vacationing
in Portugal. The event passed unnoted in Rose's diaries and letters. As
did Hoover's death in 1964.[7]

Also unnoted, perhaps unknown, was the death of Guy Moyston in
the spring of 1962. His obituary appeared in the *New York Times*, although
possibly Rose did not see it; her paper had usually been the *Herald Tribune*,
which had carried Dorothy Thompson's column, and in later years she
took only the Sunday papers. Berta Hader clipped the notice of Moyston's
death, but Rose had been estranged for years from the Haders and the
circle that had continued to gather at their handcrafted home in Nyack.
"Guiltless 'innocents', artists and fringe intellectuals," she termed them
to Dorothy in her last letter, "so in the 1930s their handiwork was a nest of
comrades dearly beloved, and no place for me." Had she forgotten that it
was the Haders who had moved her from New York into her Danbury
home in 1938? In the interval, they had dropped from her ken, as had
Mary Margaret McBride, except for the occasional Christmas card. And
for years, Rose had whetted her wits against those of Isabel Paterson in
nearby Stamford, but that friendship had ended in an obscure quarrel
regarding Stalin, and Paterson had moved to New Jersey. Isaac Don and
Ruth Levine had relocated to Maryland, still affectionate toward Rose but
with feelings strained over her defense of Merwin K. Hart. Helen Boylston, no radical, still lived and worked nearby in Weston, but that old
friendship had cooled as well.[8]

Such matters had receded to a place where, in an important sense,
she could no longer reach them. As had earlier memories, she discovered
on receiving a letter from a woman once her sister-in-law, announcing
the death of Gillette Lane a decade earlier. "Emotional effect of the news
is peculiar," Rose wrote to the recently widowed Joan Clark. "I haven't
thought of Gillette Lane for at least thirty years and can't even remember
what he looked like. I keep thinking that I could find out what I feel if only
I had time." Perhaps what she could not recover, perhaps what she had

never known, was how she had marked this man in their years together. Gillette Lane had married twice again, the final time for the last twenty-four years of his life; and yet his widow would testify that Rose had been "his first and greatest love."[9]

||

In these years she came to rely more and more on Roger MacBride. It was a connection both practical and emotional: he had learned much from her that had fed his natural interests in political theory and she had always needed surrogate children at hand; and as a practicing attorney he was in a position now to offer pragmatic advice in the more complex engagement with the world that her new income made possible. She had made him her heir in 1956; upon the death of George Bye in 1957, MacBride became her agent; and more and more he began to act as her financial advisor. And when he married, his bride, Susan Ford, became immediately a granddaughter upon whom Rose could lavish advice and good wishes. Her income was sufficient to permit generous gifts to them, a car one year for Susan, and yearly cash gifts to each just under the taxable limit; and while her letters to Roger MacBride continued to be long on matters of political theory and the management of her financial affairs, her letters to Susan MacBride became volumes on household management, gardening, and cookery. Through experience, Rose had become a no-till gardener, letting her tomatoes and corn fight for life with the surrounding weeds; and she passed on her famous recipe for chicken pie, specifying, of course, that it begin with a thoroughly free American chicken. "Note: Exceptional flavor depends upon obtaining a local hen, raised on farm, grown up running in meadows, chasing grasshoppers, dust-bathing in sunshine." Although the MacBrides would later divorce, Susan Ford continued to remember her adoptive grandmother for her kind and thoughtful interest in carrying a young life forward. Rose had long held a somber view of marriage and particularly of romantic love, but she had also recognized it as an inevitable stage of growth and she would be tenderly supportive of young people passing through it.[10]

Roger MacBride would become in the years that followed something of an agent provocateur for an American revolution on Rose's principles. They had become his too, of course, and both took seriously the idea that American political thought had lost its way since the founding of the nation, with the corollary that the way could be found again if clear-thinking people would take exemplary stands. In 1960, MacBride moved his law practice to Vermont; and shortly afterward he was elected to the State House of Representatives. Once in place, he had the opportunity to play the political wise-fool, offering legislation to disengage the state from a host of enterprises that would substantially reduce the role of government and the state budget as well. There was a predictable reaction from liberals and assorted interest groups and considerable press attention. Rose enjoyed the whole spectacle vicariously, seeing in Mac-Bride's principled but essentially forlorn efforts a reaffirmation of her earlier stands against rationing, zoning, and social security. "He introduced all those budget-cutting bills," she announced gleefully to Jasper Crane, ". . . to reduce State income taxes, with profit of $1 million to the State treasury."

> And, Machiavellian, he put them all into one package-bill, so that at the hearing ALL those whose subsidy-graft was threatened appeared and ALL viciously attacked him, personally. There he stood, alone, friendless, unsupported, attacked from all sides with increasing fury, but there he *stood*. . . . Roger's purpose was to show his fellow legislators that the opposition to the bills was from porkers only trying to keep their noses in the tax-filled trough; and in that he succeeded perfectly.

It was, both Rose and MacBride recognized, essentially a moral gesture, a place to begin what might eventually be a real grass-roots movement back to limited government. MacBride carried his efforts so far as to mount a primary campaign for the governor's nomination before moving on to other things, having made the necessary stand.[11]

The larger backdrop to this parochial effort was the first flush of an emergent national conservative movement in the candidacy of Barry Goldwater in the 1964 presidential election. Rose had seen little in national politics since 1936 to permit her any enthusiasm. Eisenhower had broken the Democratic grip, but he had squandered his accomplishment as a national war-hero in running little more than a caretaker government. In the great national contention between Kennedy and Nixon, she could generate only contempt for what she saw as the empty elegance of the Kennedy charm; Nixon she thought the lesser of two evils, but with a typically revolutionary movement of thought she believed that a Kennedy win might bring the country to a saving crisis sooner. However, faced with such a poor choice (there had been, since 1936, only the Democratic New Deal and the Republican Me-Too), she had not voted in 1960. And the Kennedy assassination—surely a Communist plot—had left her unmoved: "It's interesting that Americans DON'T 'accept assassination' as normal," she wrote to Joan Clark, invoking the long historical perspective that grew out of her Albanian experience and that had let her contemplate seriously Roosevelt's assassination:

> . . . we don't accept war, either. There's an almost indefinable attitude here, which has nothing to do with reason and little even with experience, and is wholly unique; unique in the world and in

history. WHY don't we accept assassination? when it's more usual
here than anywhere else? . . . Yet you'd think from the outcry that
nobody ever had been assassinated, until our martyred president
who died for us and the Free World.[12]

But the emerging Goldwater movement gave her a flicker of hope.
Rose had long since given up on the terms *liberal* and *conservative* in her
own discourse: *liberal*, for her, still carried its nineteenth-century, laissez-
faire significance, a meaning now displaced by Democratic New Deal
liberalism; while *conservative* suggested an uncritical attachment to tradition that was the antithesis of her own habit of thought. ("My own view is
that 99 99/100ths of tradition is all wrong.") She had adopted the terms
individualist and *collectivist* as the polar coordinates of her thinking. As
she surveyed the conservative spokesmen of the day, those appearing in
William F. Buckley's *National Review,* she acknowledged a certain common interest in limiting government; but she was put off by the air of
silver-spoon privilege and unearned complacency, and she suspected
them all of sharing Edmund Burke's "reactionary" "assumption that a
commonwealth is a mystic Being, that Governments are ordained by
God." "Irrelevant as this is, I ask, Is Bill Buckley sacrificing his butler and
his speed boat?" Her trust was, as always, in the natural self-reliance
(and mistrust of government) of "all the innocent damnfool 'little people'
who know no better and can't believe evil . . . and can't understand why
everything costs so much, or why the harder they work and the more
they earn the less they have. So damnfool patiently holding the world
together. . . ." In this gloomy scene, Goldwater emerged as the first
candidate since Hoover that Rose could respect.[13]

The MacBrides worked hard for Goldwater, although both Roger
and Rose thought Goldwater a philosophically weak candidate, however
sound his instincts, and his campaign poorly run. In the end, she was not
surprised at his defeat. One other political figure did catch her eye and
her imagination that year, though. It was, of course, Ronald Reagan—
who would later admit that his favorite television program was "Little
House on the Prairie."[14]

As the MacBrides settled into a clearly domestic situation in Vermont, Rose began to lay plans reminiscent of her efforts to establish a
second home for herself with Rexh Meta. She had always had a hankering
for an expansive style in living accommodations, as evidenced by growth
of her Danbury home beyond all measure of the needs of a woman living
alone. In a revealing moment she had drawn the comparison between the
private homes of moderately prosperous rural Americans and the country houses of England and the châteaux of France; the very naming of
Rocky Ridge Farm had been an expression of her mother's aspirations
toward gentility that had left a mark on Rose. So that when Roger Mac-
Bride purchased some twelve hundred acres in rural Vermont with a

large house, woods, lakes, and trout streams, all bearing the name of Deer Park, she could not help crowing to Jasper Crane and Dorothy Thompson in proprietary pleasure. To Dorothy she had written:

> I have (I don't legally own, but complications are too many to bother with) 1200 acres at Halifax Center, Vermont, where I think I'll live when this town gets unbearably crowded. . . . I would love to live alone in the middle of 1200 acres. And maybe be snowed-in for Christmas. Which sounds so misanthropic, when in fact I am anything but. It's only that I keep me so busy and interested, and like space and silence to be busy in.

There is, in this little boast, perhaps some late claim to having arrived at an equality with Dorothy in this achievement, at least: the implied comparison is with the famous Twin Farms estate in Vermont kept by Dorothy and Sinclair Lewis in their heyday, and still in Dorothy's possession. Rose's attachment to this new estate would be by the addition to MacBride's Vermont home of living quarters for herself and a library for the six thousand or so books she had accumulated over the years. For this niche in a new home she supplied money, planning, and elaborate specifications for the construction, particularly of the bookshelves. The understanding was clear that should advancing age leave her unable to care for herself, her home would be with the MacBrides. Roger MacBride by this time found himself in a curious but inevitable brotherhood with Rexh Meta, for Rose had turned over to him the problem of transmitting clandestine funds to Rexh's family through third parties in Italy, a responsibility MacBride would continue to honor indefinitely. Word reached them that Rexh had been released from prison and was living quietly, his family still suffering as political lepers under the Hoxha regime. "Nothing is more important to me," Rose declared of the remittances MacBride was able to get through. She pressed for news of Rexh's children and, now, in this lost family of hers, grandchildren as well.[15]

She was able in these years to see further evidence of her influence and further hope for the future in other lives she had touched. Economists Orval Watts and Hans Sennholz in her own country and Jean-Pierre Hamilius of Luxembourg had taken light from her flame; she was particularly proud that Sennholz had in a few years transformed himself from a German soldier in an American POW camp, seeing Arkansas through barbed wire, into a prosperous American and college professor; and that Hamilius might carry the American Revolution back to the Old World. Both of these European intellectuals, as well as the American Watts, came to visit, and carried on a flourishing correspondence with her. Watts taught and wrote from Pepperdine College in California, while Sennholz was hopeful of organizing a graduate program in free-market economics in New York City, and later carried on his teaching at Grove City College in Pennsylvania. Rose wrote to Hoover and to Jasper Crane in attempts to forward their interests.

But perhaps the most striking testimony to her influence came with the establishment of the Freedom School in Colorado. Newspaperman Robert LeFevre had found confirmation and clarification of his political views in his reading of *The Discovery of Freedom*, and as he sought his own way to spread his ideas he founded a small, log-cabin summer school for the teaching of the principles of liberty and individualism in the mountains between Denver and Colorado Springs. LeFevre was a charismatic figure; he, his wife, and a small volunteer staff ran the school on a shoestring. Students, especially young people, were solicited nationwide; LeFevre was the principle teacher, although guest lecturers were frequent. The aim, of course, was to seed the nation with a cadre of dedicated, well-schooled individualists. LeFevre and Rose had common friends in Orval Watts, Leonard Read of the Foundation for Economic Education, and Merwin K. Hart of the National Economic Council. The two fell inevitably into a correspondence, profoundly theoretical, about the nature of freedom and its implications for political order; and when she and Elsie Jackson had a chance to visit the school during their trip through the Southwest in September of 1958, Rose was entranced with what she found: a small band of dedicated people working long hours gaily and gallantly for a cause they accepted without question. It was, Rose saw, just the obverse of a Communist cell—hard-core individualists.

> I like the Freedom School because it is real Hard Core devotion. And probably a little because it is repeating the socialist tactic that I saw in the 1890s that put the New Deal into Washington by the 1930s. And, too, because it is grass-roots, and little, and poor, and squeezing every penny's worth of value out of every dollar. As well as every minute's worth out of every hour.

LeFevre remembered her as shy and reserved at first: until she knew her ground, always she preferred the safety of letters to direct discourse. She was prevailed upon to meet with a class, which she did with great reluctance, but finally with great success as she took the occasion to present herself as a case study in conversion from her early socialism, complete with anecdotes from her travels. She also found the school about to go under financially, with a fifteen-hundred-dollar mortgage payment due and no funds to pay it: not yet having gained tax-exempt status, the school had lost many promised contributions. Rose had just sixteen hundred dollars in her checking account; she wrote the check, and the school was saved.[16]

It was a gesture that later would be repaid symbolically. The school thrived briskly in the next several years; in time, visiting lecturers would include such notables as Milton Friedman, Ludwig von Mises, and Frank Chodorov. In 1962, the school having expanded its buildings to include a new central lodge, Rose was honored at a ceremony in which the lodge was dedicated in her name. She spent the month previous to the event in Florida, ostensibly working on the perennial revision of *The Discovery of Freedom*. But the trip was for a personal indulgence as well. She had avoided photographs for years, no doubt because she had become self-conscious about the erosion of age upon her features. Now she submitted to a face-lift, and to cosmetic surgery on her hands as well—which, she said, she had to look at on the typewriter much more than she observed her face in the mirror. It was this new face that she took to the ceremony in Colorado and permitted to be photographed.[17]

IV

She no longer had to write to eke out a living, but her writing career was not over. Two books were yet to be done, each a labor more of love than of necessity, each growing in its own way out of her earliest days in Dakota Territory. There, in De Smet, working between her grandmother and her blind Aunt Mary while Mama Bess sewed buttonholes at the dressmaker's shop to finance their flight from that drought-stricken land, Rose had learned her knitting, her crocheting, her embroidery, and quilting. Her own domestic impulses and household economy were closely bound up with the need to keep her hands busy; time could be doubly used if the hands worked while the eyes read and the brain thought. It had been entirely natural during the war to sit with the Dorcas Society in Danbury, piecing coverlets for soldiers in the hospitals. In her European travels she had taken a lively interest always in native homecrafts, and she had been surprised to find in a Zagreb museum rudimentary crochet work on display as American lace. Her series of needlework articles for *Woman's Day* had paid the bills at a time when she could write nothing else, and as early as 1942 there had been plans for a book collecting these. Not until 1963 did such a book finally take shape as the *Woman's Day Book of American Needlework*.[18]

Few people would think of making a book on needlework a political treatise. Yet to identify the craft as American was to set it apart from its European origins, and this was a fundamentally political distinction for Rose. She could not resist the opportunity to enliven her account of the needlework forms themselves with an account of the nation's origins, and to link the various needlecrafts with the daily struggle of the European immigrants:

In a wilderness thousands of miles from home, depending only on themselves for their very lives, these poor immigrants learned the inescapable fact that a person is the only source of the only energy that preserves human life on this planet. With their minds and hands they made houses, they produced food, they wove cloth and built towns, and each ceased to think of himself as a bit of a class in a nation. They knew that each one was creating the neighborhood, the town, the colony.

It was a populist truth emerging from the experience of ordinary people, not from the inherited hierarchies of the European tradition: "It was not in the arts and writing that expressed the Old World's concept of the nature of man, and it was not in the colonies' social order of authority above, obedience below. But it was in the first American needlework." The argument becomes, then, simply a matter interpreting the forms American needlework had taken:

> The first thing that American needlework tells you is that Americans live in the only classless society. This republic is the only country that has no peasant needlework. Everywhere else, peasant women work their crude, naive, gay patterns, suited to their humble class and frugal lives, while ladies work their rich and formal designs proper to higher birth and breeding.
>
> American needlework is not peasant's work or aristocrat's. It is not crude and it is not formal. It is needlework expressing a new and unique spirit, more American than American sculpture, painting, literature or classical music.

On this premise, then, the various forms of American needlework are read as an expressive history of the free and innovative spirit of the most humble and voiceless of Americans, the women in their domestic sphere. And in this history Rose could read little exemplary dramas to engage her readers' imaginations, a strategy she had taken to many times before in her ill-fated history of Missouri and more recently in *The Discovery of Freedom*. The increasingly hasty stitches in a sampler tell a tale of a bored little girl, its triumphant finish her ascent to matrimony. From a quilt she learns that the daughter of Jefferson Davis stood firm for the Union. The whole enterprise became for her a chance to celebrate American history through a reading of its humblest folk art.[19]

V

Another project had landed in her lap when the Lichtys, on a trip east, stopped in Danbury with a collection of her mother's manuscripts that had been left at Rocky Ridge Farm. Among these were "The First Three Years and a Year of Grace," which Rose seems to have put aside without purpose, and Mama Bess's journal of their trip from De Smet to Mansfield in 1894. The manuscripts of the published work she returned to the Lichtys for use in the museum, cautioning them with the old fiction that they were early drafts not representing her mother's final intentions. "After more or less cutting it up and pinning it together again, my mother made a typed copy from it which she sent to her agent in New York, who sent it to the publishers, and that was the end of that." The journal of that exodus from Dakota, however, Rose kept by her. The ghost of Mama Bess was not yet laid.[20]

The Little House books would preserve a version of her mother's life from childhood through marriage; it was, essentially, a frontier romance that delivered young lovers into a green and fecund world and stood, in its implicit values, as an archetypal American story. "The First Three Years and a Year of Grace" was essentially an antiromantic, realistic assessment of the years that followed the wedding, adult fare of an order that Rose had done in *Free Land*, but uneasily poised between a grim fatalism and a prosing optimism. It had been Mama Bess's effort to enter the realm of adult fiction, and it would have taken Rose's best energies in her best years to wrench it into a work to harmonize with her mother's other books. But her mother's journal posed fewer problems and a real opportunity. The narrative itself neatly bridged the gap between the "Little Gray Home in the West" that ends the children's books and the substantial achievement of Rocky Ridge Farm that had crowned Mama Bess's dreams. With prologue and epilogue Rose could knit the segments together, leaving the readers of the Little House books with a satisfying romantic vision of Laura as young matron about to ascend to a kind of domestic apotheosis with the founding of Rocky Ridge Farm.

I have suggested earlier some of the kinds of repression Rose had to achieve to write this account of her mother's life in the years of her own suffering childhood. It was, in fact, a resurrection of her mother for a final tribute, a last gesture by the worshipful little girl who had always tried but could never please. The final vision poses them both forever in a climactic moment, beneath the great white-oak tree as the new house is planned:

> My mother stood under it in her brown-sprigged white lawn dress, her long braid hanging down her back. Below the curled bangs her eyes were as purple-blue as the violets. It would be a white house, she said, all built from our farm. Everything we needed to build it was on the land: good oak beams and boards, stones for the foundation and the fireplace. The house would have large windows looking west across the brook, over the gentle little valley and up the wooded hills that hid the town, to the sunset colors in the sky. There would be a nice big porch to the north, cool on hot summer afternoons. The kitchen would be big enough to hold a wood stove for winter and one of the new kerosene stoves that wouldn't heat up the place worse in summer. Every window would be screened

with mosquito netting. There would be a well, with a pump, just outside the kitchen door; no more lugging water from the spring. And in the parlor there would be a bookcase, no, *two* bookcases, big bookcases full of books, and a hanging lamp to read them by, in winter evenings by the fireplace.

When the mortgage is paid, in only a few more years, she said, and when the orchard is in bearing, if prices are good then, we will fence the whole place with wire and build the barn bigger; we will have more stock by then. And after that we can begin to build the house.

She woke from the dream with a start and a Goodness! it's chore-time! I'd better take the milk pail to my father, she said, and feed the hens before they went to roost; don't forget to fill their water-pans, and bring in the eggs; be careful not to break one. Oh, now that we had the cow, we'd have a treat for Sunday supper, French toast with that wild honey, to surprise my father. How wonderful it was to have a cow again.

While I scattered corn for the hens, fetched water from the spring to fill their pans, and hunted for eggs that the broody hens hid in the haymow, in the straw stack, and even in the wild grasses, I heard her whistling in the cabin, getting supper.[21]

VI

The conversion of Rocky Ridge Farm to a memorial museum was well under way; and the publication of *On the Way Home* had solidified her mother's image within the larger story that books and museum together were to tell over and over again to faithful readers and to curious visitors who might be enticed into becoming faithful readers. The sales of the books themselves continued strong; but Rose also took an ongoing interest in the conventional avenues of promotion. She had never been satisfied with the publishers' promotion of anything she had written; she had herself worked early and hard at promoting patent medicine, newspaper subscriptions, and land sales, and she had a correspondingly keen sense of what ought to be done. In 1963, she noticed that Harper and Row had technically violated the contracts covering her mother's books by failing to place certain specified advertisements. Through Roger MacBride, now her agent and attorney, she threatened to void the contracts and take the books to another publisher. It was a tactic, of course, to insist on her due; an amicable agreement was reinstituted, and sales increased correspondingly. But she kept her eye on the problem: a few years later, when the *New York Herald-Tribune* ceased publication, she requested that the advertising money that would have gone to the *Herald-Tribune* be reallocated to advertising in midwestern newspapers. "My whole audience and my mother's is in the mid-west—the Mississippi Valley," she argued.

> All the monuments to my mother's books, from Wisconsin to south-
> ern Kansas, are in that region. Still I have letters from would-be
> buyers of her books, reporting that bookshops and librarians report
> that they are out of print, so asking me desperately *where* they can
> get copies. I feel (unhappily) that the publishers should not leave it
> to me to write letters telling people that the books are available.
> Isn't that the publisher's job?[22]

Monuments to her mother's books were, in fact, developing across
the region. The books would always stand on their literary merits with
readers who had never known the locales; but their autobiographical
presumption tended to promote literary pilgrimages, and among local
citizens this presumption encouraged their reading as plausible local history. The step into local boosterism was inevitable, as sites developed
toward shrines of various kinds near Lake Pepin in Wisconsin, near Independence in Kansas, at Plum Creek near Walnut Grove, Minnesota (this
one complete, for a while, with a grave of Jack the bulldog), and at
De Smet, South Dakota. There was even a movement to call for a com-
memorative stamp honoring the hundredth anniversary of Mama Bess's
birth, which Rose sanctioned and encouraged. With the later advent of
the popular television series, something of a Laura Ingalls Wilder industry would be born, with local pageants and celebrations for the benefit of
thousands of tourists who had never read the books themselves.

Rose would not live to see all of these enlarged developments prop-
agating outward from Rocky Ridge Farm, but no doubt she would have
been satisfied: here was the large commercial success she had dreamed
of early in her career as a writer. But even in the early years of these
memorials the problematical relationship between history and fiction
would emerge in some vexing inquiries, as curious readers began ferret-
ing out the truths behind the Little House books. Premonitory of the
course of events that would eventually lead even to this biography was
the inquiry raised in a 1964 article for elementary teachers by Louise H.
Mortenson, who had found census evidence that Laura Ingalls Wilder
could have been not five, but only three years old, in *Little House in the
Big Woods*—and thus could not have written literally from memory. "As
an artist working with her materials," Mortenson wrote, "Mrs. Wilder
knew she could achieve a more artistic effect by altering the true facts
occasionally."

On seeing this article in print, Rose rushed to put her finger in the
dike. She acknowledged the factual discrepancy but laid it off on the publisher's interference. She insisted that her mother did remember events
from age three—which may well have been the case. Her mother may
have omitted some periods, Rose conceded, but she wrote the literal
truth. "This is important only because it has been charged that my
mother's books are fiction. They are the truth, and only the truth; every

detail in them is written as my mother remembered it. . . . she added nothing and 'fictionized' nothing that she wrote."[23]

Mortenson was apparently satisfied with this explanation; but a similar problem arose in the next year when a junior high school student who had become fascinated by the Little House books began preparing a booklet on the Ingalls family. William T. Anderson would become the most diligent of inquirers into the background of the Little House books; and when copy for his booklet suggested that the Ingalls had had neighbors in their first winter in De Smet, Rose insisted on their absolute solitude. "This is a formal protest against your proposal to publish a statement that my mother was a liar," she wrote. "You will please correct your proposed publication to accord with my mother's published statement in her books." As he adjusted his copy to her wishes, she grew conciliatory, reading him a lecture on weighing probability and assessing the credibility of witnesses. "If my mother's books are not absolutely accurate, she will be discredited as a person and as a writer, since a great part of the value of her books is that they are *true* stories.'" Long past acknowledgment now were those letters in which Rose had fought out this issue with Mama Bess, insisting on levitating her mother's mere remembered fact with the force and grace and artifice of fiction.[24]

$\mathcal{A}$ VISIT TO VIETNAM

"Because freedom is right and right is everlasting."

She had been more than a quarter of a century in her Danbury home, and she had now made all of it that her imagination and money could produce. She had endured on principle the isolation of the Connecticut winters, and she had developed a circle of everyday acquaintances through the Dorcas Society and the King Street Christian Church; there was no real reason why she might not expect to live out her days in the place her industry had carved out for herself. The restlessness, finally, was constitutional, although the winters were getting harder to bear and the stairs to her bedroom and study harder to climb as she drew nearer her ninth decade. Since her stay in McAllen, Texas, in 1942, during the ill-fated trip with Norma Lee Browning and her husband, Rose had recalled fondly the temperate winters of the Rio Grande Valley. Early in 1965 she returned for a visit. The McAllen she remembered she found "gone forever; a young metropolis where it used to be"; but after looking around for a while, she bought a small home in Harlingen, at 435 Woodland Drive.[1]

Since her earliest days as a world traveler she had wanted to have many homes in many places; and only financial exigency had ever persuaded her to give up her San Francisco apartment while in New York City, her Paris apartment on her return to the States, her Albanian home on her return to Rocky Ridge. In fact, the home at Rocky Ridge was the only one she had let go willingly. Now, in 1965, she was preparing to transfer her thousands of books to the quarters prepared for her with the MacBrides in Vermont; she was waiting to take possession of her new home in Texas; and she was turning her Danbury home over to Joseph and Mildred Kamp. The Kamps had become close friends in the years since Joseph Kamp had served his prison term as a matter of conscience. Rose had even built on to her home a studio to provide working space for Kamp and storage for his voluminous files; and now the Kamps agreed to occupy her Danbury home as more or less permanent caretakers. Into this chaotic situation came a call from Eileen Tighe, editor of *Woman's Day*. Would Rose like to go to Vietnam to write an article for the magazine?[2]

In 1965, the war in Vietnam had not yet become the fatal issue that would divide the nation in later years; indeed, most Americans were barely aware of it. Probably the decision of the Defense Department to sponsor visits by magazine writers, whose stories from special perspectives might supplement the daily reports by accredited news organizations, was essentially a public relations effort as the first questions about the nation's commitment began to arise. Apparently, selected magazines were simply asked to nominate appropriate staff members. Eileen Tighe no doubt had people on her staff who would have qualified; but she had known Rose for many years and knew something of her experience as a foreign traveler. That Rose was now seventy-eight years old did cross Tighe's mind, but it did not seem to be an issue until the Pentagon made it one.

For Rose, it was an assignment she had been prepared for since she had first gone to Europe as a correspondent for Fremont Older. In some measure, it would redeem her failure to press on to the Orient in 1923, when her energies had failed and she had turned back in Baghdad. It would also afford her an opportunity to confront directly the advance of world Communism, which she had seen creeping across the map since her days in the Caucasus. And, of course, she could report her findings to the kind of audience she wanted most to reach, the thousands of ordinary women who held American society together, to whom she had lately spoken of the ideological implications of their needlework and to whom she could now reveal the broader issues that threatened the domestic tranquility of their homes. She began at once to prepare herself by reading all she could about the history of the Vietnamese people and the origins of the current conflict. She had long studied the history of the Communist movement through the First, Second, and Third Internationale. It would have come as no surprise to her to discover Ho Chi Minh's history of association with the Party in France, and his tactics in taking power after the fall of Dien Bien Phu was a classic case of intimidation and subversion. At some point in this assignment she prepared a manuscript entitled "The Background of Vietnam." Essentially, it was history both of the emergence of human freedom, as in *The Discovery of Freedom*, and of the growth of world Communism. "This is the question in Vietnam," she wrote. "Shall the Third Internationale destroy the whole world, as Lenin organized it to do and his disciples are trying to do? Look at the globe and see how much they have taken in half a century." She had the outlines of her story in mind before she left Danbury; all she needed were the local details. The result would be one last professional assignment, one final brief moment in the spotlight, an epitome of her career and the beliefs that had grown from it.

"I'm doing an article for WD," she wrote hastily to Roger MacBride on June 19. She would send him the manuscript when it was done. "Then take it to Eileen, and STRESS that YOU are producing these articles, you own them, you sell them; I am in Vietnam getting data for *you*. She sent me $1,000. expense money, in MY name. Take care that her records don't implicate me as earning anything." Rose left shortly for Washington for a Pentagon briefing, where worried officials raised objections to a woman of her age undertaking such an assignment and attempted to cancel the trip for this representative from *Woman's Day.* "Things were bad enough without having little old ladies from America mowed down or blown up on the streets of Saigon," the magazine paraphrased the official concern. The record is silent on Rose's comments: they could only have been brisk and to the point, a speech she had been giving in various versions to representatives of the state for many years. Tighe reported only Rose's summary conclusion: "Age is indefensible." With reassurances from the magazine, the objection was dropped. Rose left Washington the next day, spent several days in San Francisco, and then took the long flight to Saigon, arriving at the Caravelle Hotel on July 1 after a layover in Honolulu. In a striking coincidence, in the hotel lounge she encountered the son of Isaac Don Levine. As a boy he had carried packages for her as she shopped in Danbury, serving as her *kvass*, she said. Now he was a public relations officer with the U.S. Information Agency, assigned to Vietnam. The Caravelle Hotel was a center for newsmen, many of whom affected safari jackets as a kind of uniform and an equally uniform professional toughness. Rose made a vivid impression, Levine recalled, provoking some chagrin and even outrage that somebody's grandmother had arrived as their professional peer. War was a man's job, many felt; and this little old lady could only be in the way.[3]

Her stay in Vietnam lasted until July 29. Saigon was her base, but she spent time as well in Qui Nhon, flying in and out over the sea because the Viet Cong held the surrounding hills and would fire on low-flying planes. She visited also the city of Can Tho in the Mekong Delta. From instinct, principle, or habit, she had little to do with government officials and military briefings; she found her way rather to the several civilian volunteer groups in Vietnam: the United States Operations Mission, Foster Parents, and the International Volunteer Services. These were, of course, familiar reincarnations of the Red Cross and Near East Relief missions she had known years ago. In these latter-day groups, she again found women in responsible jobs who would talk to her without condescension about their efforts to help the thousands of refugees displaced by the Viet Cong forces infiltrating from the north. By the time she returned with her notes and impressions, she had the details she needed for the story she intended to tell.

The manuscript was completed shortly after her return. It was a story that almost completely avoided the easy appeal to American patriotism for support of military action so far from home. Rather, it became a story of the Vietnamese people in their centuries-old effort to throw off a series of foreign oppressors, of which imported Communism was just the most recent. Thus this story became, for Rose, merely one more episode in the difficult contention between emerging human freedom and the reactionary forces it had always to stand against. With the instincts of a fiction writer, she elicited her readers' sympathy for a beautiful country and a beautiful people. "No land on earth is more beautiful than Vietnam," she began, her prose still crisp and sure. "The central mountain peaks climb blue beyond blue above dense forests and cleared slopes where hamlets cluster in villages and streams run swiftly. Below them, the South China Sea thrusts deep harbors between jungle covered mountains reflected, dark green, in the clear water." And the people she found equally beautiful, especially the women.

> There is something in these people that isn't explained, something that does not give up, that is not conquered.
>
> The women, maybe? We know that even in places where women are downtrodden, nothing is ever done without us. And Viet women have never been downtrodden. Foremost among Vietnam's heroes are the two sisters who led the first revolt against the Chinese 1,900 years ago. They freed the Viets and reigned as queens for a time; when the Chinese defeated them in battle they killed themselves. The next rebel leader was a woman, too. In Vietnam now there are businesswomen, women attorneys, writers, doctors, soldiers, army officers.
>
> They are said to be the most beautiful women in the world. In Paris, in Budapest, in Istanbul, even in San Francisco in the old days I have not seen as many such beautiful women as I saw in Saigon. They are not tall but perfectly proportioned, slenderly rounded, with slender hands and feet, bare feet on wooden sandals. Their smooth skin is not cream-yellow as Chinese skin is, not tanned-brown as Polynesian; it is golden, truly golden as the ring on your finger. You must see it to believe it. Their long hair is dense black, their eyes dark under straight upper lids, their lips remind you of a Greek statue's.

In contrast to these beautiful people in their beautiful land, she set the Viet Cong and their atrocities against the civilian population, simple people trying to grow food and educate their children. At their side are the American relief workers, not so much lifting these people up as making it possible for them to lift themselves. In their future, of course, lies their natural evolution toward freedom—or their submergence under the Communist terror. The American interest is touched lightly but deftly: "Filipinos checked it in their islands; it is halted in Malaya, Burma, Laos, Cambodia, waiting. If it takes strategic Vietnam, then to be 'liberated' are the Philippines, Australia, Hawaii. Hawaii?" The article moves by a kind of free association from subject to subject, a conversational reminiscence heavy on detail, light on doctrine, until the last few paragraphs, when she concedes that she has seen little of the military problem. Until she comes upon a resettlement project, from which twelve hundred mountain refugees have just been retaken by the Viet Cong and marched back to the mountains. There is nothing to be done. She meets a South Vietnamese Major in the local security force, whose unexpected outburst, "suddenly, as if a control broke," simply concludes her account. "Communism is *wrong*!" he said. "So it is short term, it rises up swiftly as a quick flame, it is gone soon. As Hitler flared up and is gone. We stay; we survive. Because freedom is right and right is everlasting."[4]

||

The major's words sounded the prophetic note that had been hers since "Credo." Once she had returned to Danbury, the local newspaper sent a reporter around to interview her about her experiences. Again she was in the public eye with an opportunity to state her views, and clearly she was prepared to make the most of the occasion:

> Mrs. Lane received her visitor in the attractive white and gold living room of her pleasant, remodeled farmhouse home. Her blue dress a bright color accent in the room, her white hair piled high and her two lively, silky haired white Maltese dogs, "Pepe" and "Pepe's Brother," all seemed somehow part of the decor.
>
> Matter of factly, Mrs. Lane revealed that she is closing her gracious New England home on Oct. 1 when she plans to leave Danbury at least temporarily to make her home in Texas.
>
> Her splendid library of some 10,000 volumes which fill the wall space of one room and overflow into others, will be moved to Halifax, Vt., to be housed in a private library which Mrs. Lane is having built.

Out of such gentility, her library now expanded by simple assertion, came a kind of authority, and further authority came from a brief rehearsal of her career as writer and world traveler. Vietnam received less attention in this interview than did the history of Communism and its tactics for seizing power, of which the recent events in Vietnam were illustrative:

> "It takes only a minority to accomplish all of this," Mrs. Lane pointed out. She showed how the "war of liberation" tactic would be applied here in an attempted take-over of the United States. She estimated that there are probably 1,000 communists in Connecticut.
>
> "Imagine," she said, "if 1,000 communists suddenly came out to murder every influential person in Danbury—the mayor, the priests and ministers, teachers, and editor of the News-Times. Suppose they came into Danbury at midnight, what would they do? They would burn the city hall and the churches. And in the

morning they'd be gone. This is what has been going on all over Viet Nam for eight years.

"They control the roads also. Suppose that on Rt. 6 a gang of 20 set up a road block, stopped a truck and killed the driver. The next day they stopped two trucks coming the other way and killed both drivers. How long would you be finding drivers to take out trucks on that road?"

And in this interview she was willing to make the national interest in the Vietnamese struggle against communism quite explicit: "If South Vietnam goes, then all Southeast Asia will go communist. And then will come Australia, the Philippines and Hawaii. . . . And that means the United States! And we'll have to fight the same thing all over again in Hawaii. The question is, do we want them on our soil?" These were dark days, as they had been for more than thirty years. But she was willing to take the long view, as had the Vietnamese major. "The United States will pull through but I don't pretend to be sanguine about it."

> She listed some liabilities: "the United States federal government is eating up the states, which is fatal; we're in debt beyond all possibility of paying up; our money is being debauched and we're going to have a crash in comparison with which the one in the 1930s will seem like a Sunday school picnic."
>
> Despite this dark picture, she said, "The country will pull through. I may not be here to see it but we'll come through. We're that kind of people."5

Ahead, of course, were the wrenching years of war protests and peace marches. Not long after her story had appeared in *Woman's Day,* Rose heard from Susan MacBride of a letter from an American soldier describing widespread disaffection for the war among the troops. Susan had written a reply, and she contemplated publishing it as a public letter. Rose doubted that the disaffection was widespread and counseled against a public reply:

> What good could it do? It could only encourage the enemy's hopes of victory, thereby prolong the fighting and kill more Americans and others.
>
> I met about a dozen American privates here and there in Viet Nam, as well as many officers of all ranks, and I did not meet *one* who had any tinge of the feeling your friend expressed in writing to you. EACH one thought well of the Viet soldiers, several were enthusiastic about their good qualities. They all wanted to stay there and win; the privates all expressed fear that "they" would compromise again as in Korea, and some were sore about the lack of all-out support from Washington. . . . I remember one youngster who asked if he could share my table in the Caravelle dining room. . . . he wondered what a woman's magazine wanted war-reporting for, I said, Well, you know all the mothers and wives and

sweethearts are wanting you men to come home, and he burst out, almost shouting, "We don't WANT to go home!" He tried to stop the words in his mouth, and then he almost wept—tears in his eyes, he said of course, my god, what else did they want night and day but to be home again…What he meant was, those Viet Cong, ma'am, they ain't *human*. And they's not a decent human being who'd *think* of quitting and leaving the Vietnamese to go on fighting 'em without help—He went into superlative praise of those darn little fighting men. And he emphasized that what he and every guy he knew was scared would happen—that Washington would sell 'em out, the Vietnamese, the way "they" sold out in Korea. All they wanted was to *finish* the job and get home, but not go home first.[6]

III

She would be spared the final failure of national policy and the humiliating loss of Vietnam to the Communists. Indeed, as much as she was committed to the uniqueness of the American political experiment and to the aspirations, as she read them, of the Vietnamese, she had always another fallback position if she invoked the infinite temporal perspective of the Wandering Jew. In fact, the recesses of time her imagination would probe provided a deeper perspective even than that Christian myth. In her ongoing attempt to trace the emergence of the idea of freedom for the revision of her book, she had regressed as far as the Code of Hammurabi and to the even remoter evolution of the outer brain; the future opened up beyond any easy belief in a Second Coming into an infinite future of civilizations rising and falling as each imperfectly realized ideal freedom or fell to reactionary regimes.[7]

    She had, in fact, once charted all of the partial, aborted, or failed revolutions worldwide since the eighteenth century. Thus she could, in the near term, continue to prophesy another age of revolution once the reactionary present had run its course, "that the twentieth century would end as the eighteenth century did . . . in a great liberal movement, this time world-wide." But it might be as imperfect a revolution as had been the Judaic or the Moslem insights into individual moral responsibility. Her admiration for both of these civilizations, central to *The Discovery of Freedom*, had been tempered by her observations of modern Zionism and the spectacle of the implacably bitter displaced Palestinians. Feelings injured by Catherine Brody and the Levines still rankled in regard to the first of these; the Jews ("the first—and still most rabid racists"), she argued, had been annealed by years of persecution into instinctive collectivists; and she had little sympathy for the claims of European Jews for a homeland in the Middle East. Moslem civilization at its finest, she believed, was simply individual moral behavior because "Mohammed forbade *orga-nization* per se"; she had seen powerful examples of spontaneous Moslem humanity to the suffering Armenians in 1923. But the philosophical insight into individual responsibility had been lost "in the fatalism of their 'intellectuals.' "[8]

And so might the incomplete American Revolution be lost in the poisonous inheritance of the New Deal, much as she loved her country. Her logic could lead her to the ultimate withdrawal and exile, as she wrote to Jasper Crane, who had praised "the beauties of our country." "I do not go into rhapsodies about 'my country,'" she responded:

> This whole world is almost unbearably beautiful. Why should I love Oak Creek Canyon or California's beaches . . . any more than the Bocca di Cattaro or Delphi or the Bosphorus? Because *I*, me, the Great RWL, was born in Dakota Territory? The logic seems weak, somehow, don't you feel?
>
> My attachment to these USA is wholly, entirely, absolutely to The Revolution, the real world revolution, which men began here and which has—so to speak—a foothold on earth here. If reactionaries succeed in destroying the revolutionary structure of social and political human life here, I care no more about this continent than about any other. If I lived long enough I would find and join the revival of the Revolution wherever it might be in Africa or Asia or Europe, the Arctic or Antarctic. And let this country go with all the other regimes that collectivism has wrecked and eliminated since history began. So much for patriotism, mine.[9]

This is truly a vision of the Wandering Jew, awaiting not the Second Coming but the discovery of the community of free men in which he will find his true nature. It might be the United States, or Vietnam, or some obscure enclave beyond the horizon of time and history, some undiscovered country from whose bourn the weary traveler would not return.

$\mathscr{L}$AST JOURNEY

I am going far away, a great distance.

On October 1, 1965, Rose turned her Danbury home over to the care of the Kamps, and with some local friends she made an automobile trip to the Grand Canyon. "Has been a happy trip," she noted in her diary. Her friends went on without her as she flew to her new home in Harlingen. After a few days, she flew to Houston to pick up her dogs, dispatched from Danbury by the Kamps; on the twenty-sixth, household goods from Danbury arrived. Her books had been sent to Vermont, where Roger MacBride was struggling to find bookshelves to her specifications. Without giving up her anchors in two other residences, she was again installed in a new home. "Weather here remains heavenly, days soft and sunny, evenings of this southern moonlight, thick as cream," she reported to the MacBrides.[1]

She quickly made a new circle of acquaintances, slipping readily into the middle-class round of visits, parties, and telephone conversations that she understood so well. She carried with her a certain local fame as the author of that recent article about Vietnam. And someone, an enthusiastic reader, was writing for background information about herself. In the long perspective she had disciplined herself to hold, her personal role was insignificant, as she wrote to Roger MacBride:

> Oh, it is so disheartening—all these readers who enjoy your writing and think you are wonderful and want to write a thesis about you. You might mention, or not as you like, that I answer no gushing inquiries about RWL, her life and times. I do not write about Vietnam to get anyone interested in *me*.
>
> One very nice thing did happen today. A woman called up to thank me; she said she read the piece with a map and "the World Book"—whatever that is—and she understands what is happening in Viet Nam, and why, and for that she wanted to thank me.
>
> Otherwise, it is wonderful to be back in the USA after three decades of Connecticut. I was asked to a fish fry last night—al fresco, candles in moonlight, heavenly food, and good solid sense talked all evening, about Viet Nam and States' rights, Presidents Truman, Kennedy, and Johnson and how they encourage the wreckage of this country. I have had six invitations to Thanksgiving dinner, "just the family, nothing special but we'd love to have you."

And so it would go, week in and week out. With a new house and new grounds to turn her attention to, she was content. She bought the vacant lot behind her house, which gave her frontage on both roads and a space almost as large as her Danbury lot for her dogs to roam. She soon had a Mexican gardener at work, custom ironwork ordered for her veranda, and rose-motif porcelain knobs installed throughout her cupboards and drawers.[2]

||

She spent September and October of 1966 with the MacBrides in Vermont, indulgently accepting the glories of a New England fall without the penalty of a winter there. She liked the new wing the MacBrides had built for her and her books, but she found living twelve miles from town on rural roads less entrancing than she had imagined, and she was concerned for Susan's winter isolation there. Also visiting with the Mac-Brides were three young women from Vietnam, one of them another instance of how Rose's impulsive affections would involve her in unforeseen obligations. While in Vietnam, she had come to know the sister of her interpreter, who had been awarded a scholarship to Southern Illinois University by a missionary group. Rose found Nguyen thi Hong Phan a charming young woman; she also found that Phan would have to forego her scholarship because she lacked travel funds to come to the States. Rose wrote the check and thought that she had simply solved the problem. Almost a year later she heard from a young faculty family at Southern Illinois that Phan was nearly destitute: the scholarship turned out to be for her tuition only, and although she was working part-time, she simply needed more money. Rose recognized her own extended responsibility and underwrote Phan's support, invited her to Harlingen for her college vacations, and thus accepted another informal granddaughter into the family she had been collecting through the years.[3]

For life in lotos-land could not dull her insistent concern for those few she had taken into her circle of affection. She had carefully watched the MacBride's marriage, mindful of the disillusion and damage she had found in her own. Susan MacBride earlier had miscarried in a difficult first pregnancy, and Rose had seen symptoms of emotional strain in the months that followed. In this case, too, she had memories too painful to express; but she felt obliged to intercede as she had some years earlier on behalf of Joan Clark. For Susan now faced serious surgery of a different origin; and Rose feared that her husband did not properly understand the cumulative effects of past trauma and the anticipation of more to come. It was a daring but heartfelt letter she wrote to Roger MacBride, urging him to put off a trip to Harlingen for Susan's sake:

You seem to me not—naturally—to understand the effects of such a catastrophe on a woman's whole nervous organism; it is a phys-ical-nerve-mental disaster from which it takes a long time to recover. I know this from experience. . . . Susie's self-control has been stu-pendous; I have often seen that, too; but it has been at a high cost in reserve strength.

Though I have not said this to her, of course, as I haven't to you, her acceptance of your supreme superiority as her law seems to me excessive. She will do what you want her to do if she can—if she possibly can, for some reason I don't know. She actually is not only a good common-sensical person; she has also a lot of wisdom. I doubt very much that she, herself, truly honestly wants to take on the extra load of a trip from there to here and back before that operation. I believe that she knows her need to be quiet, to rest, to relax and gather strength, and if she were alone that is what she would do. But she needs you, your love and approval, literally more than her life; she will do what you want her to do at any cost. . . . What I wish she could have is this next month at home, relaxing, resting, and completely unreasonably coddled and pam-pered and spoiled and praised and most blatantly loved by her husband. If she doesn't come back to us out of the ether, at least we will not have to reproach ourselves for tiring her out in these next few weeks. If this is an unpardonable invasion of privacy, please try to understand what drives me to it.[4]

Norma Lee Browning would also continue to receive ministrations by mail. Browning had gone on to a successful career as a journalist for the *Chicago Tribune*, and she was also doing well as a free-lance writer, spe-cializing in collaborative biographies of such figures as Joseph Maddy, of Michigan's famed Interlochen music camp, and insurance executive W. Clement Stone. Her career had been in certain ways like Rose's own, and Rose applauded each effort as it appeared; although, silently recalling her own career as ghostwriter, she did have qualms about Browning edging into this kind of work. "It's all to the good to LEARN to keep out of these ghosting and collaborating jobs," she wrote. "You are much too good EVER to have got into anything of that kind." In recent years, Browning had become the resident Hollywood columnist for the *Tribune*; at the moment, she found herself financially overextended in buying a home in Bel-Air. Rose made her a generous loan on a simple I.O.U., with no specified terms of repayment. "I shall put it in my safe-deposit box here, where executors will find it if I die before you find it convenient to repay the loan. It has no legal power, as I understand it; but it will serve as a memo." The letter that enclosed the check, however, was heavy with advice regarding finances, taxes, property values and property inspections.[5]

And then there was Jasper Crane, with whom she had corresponded through twenty years and hundreds of pages of letters. Crane had suf-

fered a stroke; he was ill and depressed at the state of the nation in the
1960s. Rose sought to cheer him as she had Dorothy Thompson and Fremont Older, with a combined recital of the simple pleasures of her daily
life and an optimistic assessment of the far horizon of future history.
"Now, dear Mr. Crane, don't be anxious about this country," she wrote,

> all sensible persons know that the politicians are running it straight
> into the worst times yet, but the youngsters are going to pull it
> through—the youngsters and the millions of simple decent people
> that nowadays are never heard from. These fifty states are NOT
> that feverish little eastern littoral, full of eggheads full of reaction-
> ary European notions. . . . You and I know that the truth prevails,
> always, in time. As Paine wrote: "An army of principles will march
> on the horizon of the world and it will conquer."
>   . . . Confusion is the beginning of greater wisdom (or less igno-
> rance, if you want to put it that way). Destruction is the essential
> obverse of construction. The new building begins in the destruc-
> tion of the old one. Human *life* as such is indestructible while this
> planet lasts; and it is indubitably true in history that human knowl-
> edge increases in Time. It is impossible, in the nature of man, that
> the Revolution for human rights will not transform the whole hu-
> man world on this earth, in time.
>   So don't be distressed—not really—by the day's news of the
> year's losses. Or by not being at the office and doing more than
> you are doing. You have done far more than your share, already.
> You and I must leave the tasks to the young ones—as they must,
> someday. A real world Revolution is not won in a couple of cen-
> turies, maybe not in millennium or two. . . . I myself have done
> almost nothing at all for the Revolution but the little I've done can
> never be lost. You who have done so much should be wholly con-
> tented, and glad, serene and untroubled no matter what immedi-
> ate transitory occurrences may be.[6]

III

This was, of course, her reflexive leap to the perspective of the Wandering Jew. But it was also, she recognized, necessarily a leap out of herself
and the narrowing possibilities she had forced herself to accept, year by
year, since the Depression had foreclosed the vague and grandiose dreams
of her youth. The personal life was yet occasionally a problem, and the
horizon of each day was sometimes more than she could cope with, let
alone the rising novelties the Wandering Jew might face year by year.
"For most of my life," she wrote to one correspondent, "it seemed ideal
to be that mythical Wanderer."

> Imagine having been thirty-five years old—the perfect age; vig-
> orously young yet somewhat recovering from being a total fool—

since the year One, when Rome's Golden Age was beginning and the Hellenic not yet wholly ended. Imagine being able to *remember* 1900 years, to be able to speak all languages, to know 19 centuries of history, and to anticipate seeing all the rest of human history to the final destruction of this planet.

Only lately I've decided against that youthful ambition. Here I'm not yet ninety, and far from knowing all languages, I don't even know my own. Words I've relied on all my life are quicksand under my feet. Just think of "square," for example. And hep, hip, hippie change so rapidly that they escape a grasp. As for understanding people—Once I thought I had begun to, but now I give up.[7]

A few years earlier she had complained, "I do not belong in this century; something went wrong with my shipment out of the everywhere into the here; I was addressed either to the 18th or maybe to the 38th century. I have a constantly flabbergasted feeling, of seeing a whole world that nobody else sees." Now she clearly felt her grasp on life slipping. If she had ever approached feeling wholly adequate, it was in her command of the language, and it was becoming foreign day by day. "You cannot have any adequate idea of the difficulties of living 80 years," she wrote to the MacBrides; "the whole vocabulary changes, and I can't understand the *words* used. Dictionaries are no help at all. . . . It is literally horrible—a horror felt—to be unable to speak or to write your own language." It was one thing to console Jasper Crane for the destruction time wrought as it brought forward a finer future, but another to accept the loss of so much she valued in her own personal past. "What happens is that generations go by like waves in a sea," she wrote to Norma Lee Browning.

and one after another they change everything—*everything*. Even the language. And survivors from earlier times become quaint survivals, out of step, out of key, out of context—OUT. . . .

People do not survive by merit, nor by being right, nor by talent or intelligence or diligence; they survive by being in the present fashion—a present which is rapidly past. What do you know about Art Young or Robert Minor, Floyd Dell, Ruth Comfort Mitchell, anybody whom everybody knew forty years ago?

And in a way unknown before, she found herself now looking back for comfort rather than ahead. Young William T. Anderson had collected a bundle of her books and old magazine stories, which he sent her for autographing: the occasion gave her an enjoyable opportunity to read much she had long forgotten, and to return them with comments and corrections. A San Francisco bookseller searched out for her titles from days before the world had been spoiled, for which Rose sent her thanks. One of them had been an autobiography, *The Gift of Life*, by William E. Woodward, in which he recalled meeting the pregnant Dorothy Thompson in California just before she had left to visit Rose in Missouri; Rose had known both Woodward and his wife in New York and Paris. "Nothing could please me more than having these books," Rose wrote. "In my ninth decade it's a crown of something—not sorrow—to remember—not happier—days but days irrevocably *gone.*" It was "the simple, clean, decently dignified world that used to be commonplace," she wrote to the MacBrides:

> And since 1914, in spite of all I *know,* an irrational RWL has been waiting, simply sitting still and waiting, for this impossible inter- lude to end and normal living to be resumed. I wait for the natural to return; for newspapers to report news with care for accuracy and grammar; for schools to teach and pupils to study; for faces to be sane and intelligent and even humorous; for American artists and writers and poets to be exuberant and optimistic and gay and VERY hardworking to create beauty and express truth; for poetry to be IMPORTANT again, and a new poem—beautiful or witty—to be a sensation from Maine to Baja California, a new painting to be intelligible as a matter of course, and discussed everywhere with intelligence, a new writer to be hailed with joy and hope; and everyone poor and busy and whistling and singing at work—at work 12 hours a day, seven days a week, a good day's work for a good dollar and devil take the hindmost, Hurrah! I wait for satisfy- ing food to be a square meal, and a man who gives everyone a square deal to be a square fellow, all wool and a yard wide. . . .
>
> It is all gone with the music of Vienna and the gaiety of San Francisco. But I see everything still against that background, and really I see nothing really funny anywhere. The Beatnik beard and the mini skirt and the topless waitress, they ARE funny, I know they are funny but they only make me tired, I don't laugh.[8]

IV

Yet there remained the consolations and distractions, very real and much valued, of the passing days. Her first Thanksgiving in her new commu- nity, with its six invitations to family dinner, was followed quickly with her first birthday in her new home, which in turn began the Christmas season with its distinctive local festivities. By her second Christmas in Harlingen she felt herself to be in full participation. The local decorations delighted her, she crowed to Norma Lee Browning: "Woodland Drive is a hairpin with both ends on Fifth Street. . . . we lined it on both sides with candles on standards, 10 feet apart; big red ribbons under the candles' chins. The effect is stupendous; you can't believe it till you see it." And when in the next Christmas season she turned eighty-one, she was feted: "I received masses of flowers, THREE birthday cakes, loads of presents, scads of telephone calls, and a surprise party—of ALL the Woodland Drive neighbors, with a fourth cake covered with pink and white whipped-cream roses." At Christmas, Phan came with another young Vietnamese woman to visit; and with the arrival of spring, Rose reciprocated her neighbors' good wishes with a garden party. "The party here was yesterday and a remarkable perfection," she reported to Norma Lee Browning:

> The gardens are impossibly beautiful, all busting out in a special blooming for the occasion; the weather was beyond belief—precisely heavenly temperature, huge white clouds in fathomless blue kindly shading the velvet smooth lawns, gentle breeze doing nothing but carrying perfumes from flowers to flowers—fantastic. . . . About 100 Valley ladies in gorgeous hairdos and attire wandered in [the] near, middle, and far distance or sat in groups on the lawns and in the walled garden by the waterfall, composing a landscape by a French painter for the Salon. I wore a blue-lined chiffon-print (or airplane) dress with double ruffles down the front and at wrists of long sleeves, simple low neckline, matching blue shoes and emerald ring matching green in the print (print green leaves, lighter and darker blue and pink flowers). A neighbor made this dress for me.

These were the gardens that had been destroyed by Hurricane Beulah the previous autumn, an event that let Rose practice her survival skills as she sat huddled with her dogs, reading by candlelight, while the eye of the storm passed over. "We were in the Eye for 70 minutes," she wrote with some excitement to her bookseller, "175 mph winds before and after the Eye. Trees laid down east to west, picked up and laid down west to east. I wouldn't have missed it for a pretty, as we Ozarkians say."[9]

V

Despite her many physical complaints through the years, Rose had not been dangerously ill since her bout with malaria in Constantinople. Now, however, she began to suspect that she was developing diabetes. It might be the last gift from Mama Bess. Her suspicion of doctors, however, was constitutional and deep-laid; and as she contemplated her own faltering body, the miracles of modern medicine struck her rather as perverse and obscene, particularly organ transplants and animal experiments. Her vivid imagination and her curious learning combined in a disquieting vision, as she wrote to Roger MacBride:

> Doctors are the most fiendish of the fiendish human race. Now they are skinning dogs alive at Harvard; they have succeeded in keeping a half-skinned dog alive for 22 days, and continue eagerly to beat the record if possible. . . . Doctors in Alexandria, 1st to 4th centuries, were vivisecting criminals and slaves in large numbers, day and night, and their screams were constant in the whole medical department (section of the city) of the famous University. But

now they first cut the vocal cords so that their victims are mute. I would not permit a doctor in my house; much less my insides.

I know you promised never to deliver me to any doctor but would it protect you from possibly damaging criticism if we added to my will a provision that if I die in any hospital all my property goes to a Home for Homeless Dogs, to be hugely paid for when brought to the Home?[10]

With such fears, she sought instead a self-testing kit for diabetes from Norma Lee Browning's husband. The results seemed to confirm her suspicions, so she prescribed her own diet—a radical change from a lifetime of eating what and when she pleased. With her usual thoroughness and curiosity about new topics, she began to study the nutritional theories of Adele Davis, hopeful of curing herself of her self-diagnosed disease, and perhaps curing Browning's husband as well. "Oh, well, all I care about is NOT falling into 'the doctor's care.' So long as I can stay awake or wake up or be waked up from sleeping, I'm not worrying. I'll keep on dieting; I'd just as soon; I'm not suffering any. I like milk and cheese and eggs."[11]

VI

What she had in mind was another trip to Europe. And perhaps beyond. Places she had not seen for forty years, and places yet unseen. Another young man was at hand now, calling her Grandma: Don Giffen, the son of one of her neighbors, who would act as her courier and chauffeur. "I shall wander around the British Isles for a while," she wrote to Norma Lee Browning:

> . . . would like to see Scotland and Ireland—in a hired car. Have bought a Volvo sedan, shall take delivery in Goteborg, I don't know when—any time I want to leave Britain. After that, no plans. I'd like to see the Etruscan country again, more thoroughly than before, and the Greek—Aegean—islands, and Iraq—Babylon, Ur—if not TOO dangerously unsafe. And maybe Samoa and Australia....

Another letter expands the itinerary: "After Sweden, I'd like to drive up the Rhine and down the Danube, with sidetrips through France to the Riviera and back through Luxembourg and Switzerland . . . and Cairo and Istanbul and the Fertile Crescent." "If I could possibly live elsewhere as cheaply as in the USA," she concluded, "I'd never come back."[12]

These plans began to take shape in the summer of 1968, just after the garden party that had marked her as a settled resident at 435 Woodland Drive. Phan was visiting with her again, studying Spanish and painting as Rose went through the inevitable round of immunizations. "I have been far under the worst weather possible," she wrote to Aubrey

Sherwood in De Smet, "submerged by smallpox, typhoid, cholera, yellow fever, plague, anthrax and assorted other 'shots'—as they are well-named. I liked this country much better when it wasn't so darned *healthy*. My arms, both of them, have been unusable and are still swollen and screaming." She had written him for the names of some cheap hotels his daughter had come upon in Europe. Norma Lee Browning was now at work on a book about the psychic Peter Hurkos, to whom she gave Rose's signature for a psychic "reading." Browning did not know of the planned trip, and Rose was impressed with the reading, however ominous the signs.

> He said I am old—75 or so—but healthy, walk briskly, am highly educated, intelligent, talk very little (!), never forget anything ("This is a person I do not want against me."); that I am going far away, a great distance ("You can't swim it.") and there will be an accident "where there is winter, deep snow," not [a] bad accident "but car slides on road, turns over in ditch, comes to barn."[13]

Despite such warnings, she went forward with her plans, which involved considerations apart from her itinerary. She prepared a final letter of instructions for Roger MacBride in case she died abroad, and she took Susan MacBride aside for a long talk about the future. "She told me she was going to die soon," Susan recalled, "and to LISTEN to her. She said there were going to be some hard times globally and then some very good times. . . . She urged me to be my own person, to have more fun, and to have more self-confidence, and complimented me on various strengths. While she loved us both, she had never understood how Roger and I had been able to stay married." At about this time, one of her dogs died in great pain, and the grief reduced her as thoroughly as had the loss of the original Mr. Bunting. "Please don't write me about it," she asked Norma Lee Browning. She made arrangements with Don Giffen's parents to take charge of her other dog.[14]

She scheduled herself to sail from New York on November 9. "I am not flying again across oceans," she declared. "I enjoy ships more than planes, I like to see the sea, and I don't like the biological mix-up that comes from whisking around the planet faster than time. Also I see no point in 'saving time.' For what? . . . I see no way to accumulate time; I myself always steadily spend 24 hours a day, no matter where I am or what I do." In October they left Harlingen in Don Giffen's car for a leisurely trip to Danbury, where she would rest a week or so before embarkation. They detoured through Florida to Key West and then began a gradual progress northward. The MacBrides had recently relocated from Vermont to a country home near Charlottesville, Virginia, and Rose and her driver stopped for a visit to admire the new home she would share with them. The next stop was a nostalgic visit with Floyd Dell in Washington, D.C.[15]

October was edging into November when they arrived at her home in Danbury, to be greeted by Joseph Kamp. In the interval, Mildred Kamp had died, and Joseph Kamp was living alone in great disorder in Rose's once immaculate house. On the twenty-ninth, Rose baked a supply of bread for the several days they would be spending with Kamp before her ship sailed, and that night she climbed the stairs to her bedroom in apparent good health. Sometime in the dark hours just before dawn, her heart stopped, and the journey was over.[16]

VII

The MacBrides were summoned to take charge. Roger MacBride found himself slipping into spasms of weeping, and many of the details of the succeeding days were handled by Susan. Rose had left instructions. "You know that I want the cheapest, quickest possible disposal of my body," she had written before leaving Harlingen, "without ceremony and if legally possible without embalming. Certainly without displaying to observers, a la American. And no gravestone. I hope to die and be sunk at sea. Or cremated and ashes dropped overboard."[17]

The MacBrides found that they could not be as indifferent to her passing as she had been herself. There was no funeral display in the American style, but there were individual memorial services in Danbury, Harlingen, and Mansfield. A Mansfield minister who had attended a costume party at Rocky Ridge Farm in the 1930s—perhaps it was the Halloween party for John Turner—paid a moving tribute, Roger MacBride reported to Norma Lee Browning. And although Rose had hoped to be buried at sea, he brought her ashes back to Mansfield and laid them beside the graves of Almanzo and Mama Bess.

There remained only to carry out Rose's few remaining instructions. She had left various small gifts to friends and neighbors, her remaining dog to Mrs. Giffen, and instructions for continuing annual gifts of silver place-settings that she had started as birthday gifts for several young women in Danbury. She specified continued friendship from the MacBrides for Phan, who "needs *alert* friends." She hoped that Kamp could have her Danbury home for life, and she ordered debts to her estate canceled. And to Blanche Coday Anderson, "my oldest friend" from the school days in Mansfield, she left a small annuity to ease her life in a Springfield nursing home. MacBride sent her as well a small piece of jewelry as a remembrance of Rose. Her note of acknowledgment, recalling the schoolgirl Rose Wilder's embarrassment by poverty and longing to fit in, reached for feeling she could find no words to express.

In the end, MacBride found that he could not leave the grave unmarked, and he decided to place a simple stone with an inscription.

"Could you suggest any line or lines—perhaps from one of her books—which you think are particularly appropriate?" he queried Browning. He recalled, finally, a passage Rose had taught him from Thomas Paine, and it was engraved in capitals on the plain granite stone:

> AN ARMY OF PRINCIPLES
> WILL PENETRATE WHERE
> AN ARMY OF SOLDIERS
> CANNOT. NEITHER THE
> CHANNEL NOR THE RHINE
> WILL ARREST ITS PROGRESS.
> IT WILL MARCH ON THE
> HORIZON OF THE WORLD
> AND IT WILL CONQUER.

Certainly Rose would not have denied the truth of the passage, and she had declined the chance to choose her own last remarks. Except, perhaps, years before, when her imagination had seized upon the inscription to the grave of an ancient Greek seafarer halted on his own last journey:

> A ship-wrecked sailor, buried on this coast,
> Bids you set sail.
> Full many a gallant ship, when we were lost,
> Weathered the gale.[19]

EPILOGUE
DAUGHTER AND MOTHER

She says she wants prestige rather than money.

Her death sent the few obituary writers who took notice back to their files to discover the publicity she had achieved in earlier years. She was identified by her opposition to the New Deal, and the stories of her self-sufficiency during rationing and of her encounter with the FBI formed the substance of the obituaries. The only significant appraisal of her career as a writer both of fiction and of political theory appeared in the *Kansas City Star,* which featured a fair-minded but finally unsympathetic account by Virginia Scott Miner, a reviewer who had done her homework. And then the name of Rose Wilder Lane slipped quietly toward oblivion. To seek her direct mark today is to find little more than the quiet persistence of the Freedom School, which was flooded out of its Colorado site and has since been reestablished in South Carolina. Less direct, perhaps, has been the emergence of the Libertarian political party, for whom *The Discovery of Freedom* has been a handbook, and which has fielded a candidate for president in each election since 1972. In 1976, the candidate was Roger MacBride. His campaign drew some significant media attention, and in one important interview he gave full credit to the woman who had been his mentor since childhood.[1]

Meanwhile, the reputation of Laura Ingalls Wilder has continued to flourish. Roger MacBride found the manuscript of "The First Three Years and a Year of Grace," which Harper and Row issued in 1971 as *The First Four Years,* a capstone volume to the Little House books; three years later MacBride made up another volume from Mama Bess's letters to Almanzo recounting her 1915 trip to San Francisco, *West from Home.* All books continued a steady sale, and the television series "Little House on the Prairie" both drew on the reading audience and enlarged it, while also creating a whole new class of enthusiasts whose knowledge consisted solely of stories concocted by television scriptwriters. In one episode, the child Rose was born to Almanzo and Laura, which gave Roger MacBride the curious experience of seeing his adoptive grandmother as a babe in arms. As a spin-off, *Let the Hurricane Roar* was dramatized on television as *Young Pioneers,* and the book was reissued under that title with the names of the hero and heroine changed to conform to the television adaptation. Traffic at the shrines increased apace, particularly in De Smet and at

Rocky Ridge Farm. Some sort of intersection of the political and the fictional occurred when President Ronald Reagan confessed that his favorite television program was "Little House on the Prairie."[2]

At about this time, I entered the story, drawn by the special power of the Little House books and curious about their origins. At least three people had preceded me into the shadowy background where Rose had so determinedly placed herself. Rosa Ann Moore had looked into some of the problems the manuscripts presented and had developed a tentative description of the mother-daughter collaboration. William T. Anderson was diligently pursuing the most minute details in the lives of the Wilders and was one of the energizing figures in developing the shrines in De Smet; his study of the manuscripts is the closest yet done, but its notion of Mama Bess's apprenticeship to her daughter seems to presume an achieved skill and control as author that again puts Rose in the background. Donald Zochert wrote a popular biography of Laura Ingalls Wilder, blending some original historical research with an uncritical identification of the Laura of the books with Mrs. A. J. Wilder, although he guessed privately at more than he could prove regarding Rose's hand in the books.[3] Hanging over all of these efforts was the spell of the mythical Laura Ingalls Wilder, frontier heroine and untutored genius of the Ozarks, which prevented an adequate assessment of the daughter's hand in the mother's work. Rose had created an almost impenetrable shield.

Even today Rose is regarded with some suspicion in Mansfield, where people tend to be protective of her mother's reputation. Just as she had been a discordant element in the carefully marked respectability of her mother's home, where her cosmopolitan experiences and outspoken character made her an easy target for the vague gossip she regularly shrugged off, even today there are hints of visits by "men" and "wild parties" when "she had those women living with her." And in her relationship with her mother, Mansfield duly remembers the occasional tense standoff: there was "blood-love" between them, one woman conceded, but they lived better in separate houses.[4] Any acknowledgment of the mother-daughter relationship as writers casts Rose in the role of borrowing from her mother's work. To insist on a clear reading of the complicated facts of the case requires the dismantling of an established myth, always a painful process. This biography, I am sure, will disappoint some lovers of the fictional Laura and the Little House books—so carefully has Rose hidden herself behind her mother's image.

||

"She says she wants prestige rather than money," Rose had noted as their project began.[5] What Rose wanted was less clear, but in effect Mama Bess collected both prestige and money, while Rose collected neither.

The great watershed in Rose's life came at the point when she had purchased her freedom by ghosting her mother's books—only to accept in another sphere the obligation to put self aside for the larger ideological vision she had discovered. And this transition was coincidental with her own progress—or decline—from her best creative work, well recognized, to obscure polemics. I once spoke with a Freudian psychiatrist, a specialist in treating writer's block, who believed that the decline of the creative power proceeded in step with the triumph of the superego. We do not have to accept the theory to suspect that the certitude of Rose's later life was purchased at the expense of certain ranges of her imagination.

Such a strenuous self-abnegation seems curiously the obverse of the radical individualism she embraced in theory, and it suggests a complicated connection between them. She seemed to be close on the track of this connection once as she argued political theory with Garet Garrett, trying to account for the crippling "need of man to belong to something beyond himself." "It is simply infantile . . . ," she asserted:

> newborn children . . . actually depend for their lives on a Power outside themselves; they ARE dependent; they *need*—let's say for short—love. A very large number of human infants don't get it. And they keep on wanting it for a long time after they no longer need it actually, sometimes all their lives. . . . When a shallow frivolous Clare Booth Luce joins the Catholic church, she wants Mama to love her, as Mama didn't when she was born.[6]

Rose was, I believe, striking close to a truth about her own experience here, describing the complex drama by which she had shed the claim of any clinging bond—only to submerge herself again in web upon web of surrogate obligations as she assimilated her mother's story to the larger history that so consumed her. And to carry this analysis one step further, it is possible to discover in that assimilation a covert rebellion, as, in a revealing symmetry, her fictional appropriation of her mother's life reversed that earlier childhood appropriation of her own life by her mother. In the arena of writing, Rose could reduce Mama Bess to dependency, and the fictional Laura Ingalls, ideological heroine of an exemplary American tale, became in a very real sense the daughter of Rose Wilder Lane.

So that despite the postured self-abnegation, she has left a trail for the biographer to follow; and it has been my happy task to set the record straight. Historical accuracy aside, I believe that the effort responds really to the natural force of her character: for although her stance toward her mother and toward her ideology alike demanded a diminished self in service of a greater truth, her typical mode was an expression of self that would not be forgotten—in conversation and argument, in every domestic art of her home, and above all in the dance and display of her letters. Already in her own time there were those who recognized that hers was a voice to be preserved. "Someday," Adelaide Neall exclaimed to George

Bye, "someone is going to publish a volume of Rose's letters—and that will be something!" These daily productions of her typewriter were for her a major indulgence, reflective of her best self, and their muscular thought and rippling wit so pleased the recipients that many thought to save them. Clarence Day hoped once to make a book of their exchanges; and Rose herself, obscurely recognizing the expense of talent she lavished on them, made carbon copies of much of her correspondence during the middle years of her career. She could give up Guy Moyston, but she could not come to discard the hundreds of letters she had written him; she even offered them at one time to George Bye to read as they considered making some kind of book of her letters to Bye.[7] And then there were the years of private journals and diaries, in which she recorded a self she showed to no one. It was, in short, a life preparing its own records, driven by a sense of its own significance. Writers truly reluctant to face posthumous scrutiny are careful to destroy such evidence, or to forbid its publication, as did Willa Cather. Rose left it all to the care of Roger MacBride, bound to her by admiration since childhood; and he took the next step of collecting her scattered correspondence where he could. The diarist, I believe, and certainly the writer of a daily journal, write both to themselves and to some ideal reader willing to accept, understand, justify, and explain. It takes no small courage—and no small vanity—to leave one's heart exposed to posterity. The gesture imposes no small obligation on the distant volunteer who undertakes to open that heart to the world.

What I hope I have revealed is a heart alive with desire, yet so inscribed with the copybook maxim from her school days that it became the determining condition of her life. *Sweet are the uses of adversity.* "I am a—maybe fanatic—believer in the uses of adversity," she wrote to Jasper Crane.[8] Combined with her reading of the story of the Wandering Jew, it says most of what can be said about her life; for what greater adversity than the curse laid upon that mythical wanderer, and what sweeter use made of it than the vision that filled Rose's mind as she stood in his shoes? Heart's desire will always meet adversity, of course, and to desire infinitely is, finally, to ensure defeat—but also to savor the unexpected pleasure as desire accommodates defeat and finds new ground to grow in.

    The theme runs through her mother's fiction and through her own; and its implications are made explicit in *The Discovery of Freedom.* The country had been eager for the gentled truths of a child's world; and it had responded well to the grown-up version Rose had provided in her fiction. But this was largely, perhaps, a sentimental attachment to values that in practice many were willing to sacrifice to the exigencies of the Depression and the ensuing war. For the hard truths of political life that Rose tried to offer them they were less eager. In *The Discovery of Freedom*, Rose had tried to ground the new world in values of the old; but the obvious response to her argument is that the complex interdependencies of an industrial democracy demanded substantial modifications of the radical freedom of the early pioneer. Or so a twentieth-century liberal would have said to her. Her response could only have been some spirited denunciation of the most recent regression toward serfdom.

Some might speak here of a failure of maturity—personal, historical, artistic, and political. But the error would be in attaching the metaphor of growth to a national vision too persistent to be outgrown. Like youth itself, it is a strength as well as a liability. The virtue of this vision lies in its romantic readiness for challenge, a perennially youthful optimism that is particularly American. Henry James's representative American, appropriately named Christopher Newman, speaks of his countrymen as possessed of "old heads and young hearts."[9] The resilience and hope that defy experience and refuse the consolation of defeat are a function, we might say, not of age but of heritage, a heritage that let Rose savor adversity for sake of the victory it permitted and that made the ambiguous ending of *Free Land* grimly true.

IV

It is but a step from optimism to prophecy; the step was reflex with Rose. In one of her most troubled hours she had written, "I think it will be a hundred years, or five hundred, before what America was will begin to stir again in history and to find its voices. . . . I am still au fond so American that I am an optimist believing in Life. Anyone who believes in Life must love and have faith in his murderer." The faith sustained her for thirty years, and grew stronger the darker the world seemed to grow. "Surely the darkest hour is not the time to be pessimistic about the dawn," she had written to Herbert Hoover.[10] But to prophesy is one thing; to become a prophet is to have prophecy confirmed by events. As the years went on and she settled in for her long struggle for the Revolution, Rose had looked forward quite specifically to the end of the twentieth century. In part she was reasoning hopefully by analogy with the end of the eighteenth century; in part she was, no doubt, shortening her horizon of prophecy as her own horizon drew near; but over and over, to Jasper Crane, Herbert Hoover, Roger MacBride, and others, she began to speak pointedly of the near-term future she would not live to see. She would put it clearly to Jasper Crane: "I am as certain as anyone can be of anything in the future that the twentieth century will end as the eighteenth did, with a great revival and resurgence of individualism."[11]

At this juncture, the biographer can only grow a little wistful, as he contemplates what Rose Wilder Lane did not live to see: the recent collapse of Communism as an ideology and a world power, and the resurgence of political liberty in eastern Europe—particularly the opening of Rose's beloved Albania to the West. There is a chapter yet to be written of what her response might have been to this vindication by history. Especially gratifying would have been the news of the safety of Rexh Meta's family, as Borë-Rose and her children emigrated to the United States under the sponsorship of Roger MacBride; and even though Rexh Meta and his wife did not outlive the darkness of their benighted country, his gifts to Rose, and hers to him, have marked his family to the third generation. "The longest lives are short," Rose had once written, referring to needlework but meaning much more; "our work lasts longer."[12]

$\mathscr{A}$PPENDIX
THE GHOST IN THE
LITTLE HOUSE BOOKS

> *Ghost:* One who secretly does artistic or literary work for
> another person, the latter taking the credit.
>
> The soul or spirit, as the principle of life.
> Oxford English Dictionary

have written and ghosted seventeen books," Rose noted in her journal
for January 24, 1933. How she arrived at the number is not clear; she
probably was counting some of her early newspaper ghosting as well
as her work for Frederick O'Brien and Lowell Thomas. And doubtless
her recent work for her mother as well, for she was in the midst of
revising the manuscript of *Farmer Boy* that had been rejected by Harper.
"There's a curious, half-angry reluctance in my writing for other people,"
she continued the next day, and her thoughts flowed quickly into a study
of the mutual resentment she and her mother struggled with in their
collaboration (see page 239 above). But despite the reluctance and resentment, some of her best work was achieved in this mode.

To appreciate Rose Wilder Lane's contribution to her mother's
books, one must simply read her mother's fair-copy manuscripts in comparison with the final published versions. What Rose accomplished was
nothing less than a line-by-line rewriting of labored and underdeveloped
narratives. Her mother would deliver her own best effort in full expectation that Rose would work her own magic on it; the manuscripts are
replete with parenthetical asides and relentlessly factual directives for
Rose's work. "The shumac (I don't know how it is spelled and my dictionary don't tell). . . ." "Ellen [the cow] was bred the first of September,
before the October blizzard. It takes 9 months. The calf would come the
last of May or first of June. We didn't get this straightened out in Hard
Winter." Facing her own limitations, Mama Bess acknowledged that
"without your fine touch, it would be a flop." But she tried to put the best
construction upon her problems: "You see, I know the music but I can't
think of the words" (see page 279 above). Rose, however, had not only to
find the words but to orchestrate the music as well.

From this manuscript Rose would retain the story line and many of the incidents, but sometimes little of her mother's original language, and that often retuned to render leaden lines more felicitous. She rearranged material freely to achieve foreshadowing and thematic clarity. She added much exposition, dialogue, and description, often inventing incidents as well. She suppressed much that was tedious or irrelevant or inconsistent. At some point, these myriad changes became formative and then transformational, and a struggling story came alive. Almost everything we admire about the Little House books—the pace and rhythm of the narrative line, the carefully nuanced flow of feeling, the muted drama of daily life—are created by what Mama Bess called Rose's "fine touch," as shining fiction is made from her mother's tangle of fact. Laura Ingalls Wilder remained a determined but amateurish writer to the end. *The First Four Years* represents a fair sample of her abilities, and even despite some editorial sprucing-up by Roger MacBride it requires all the levitation and momentum afforded by the earlier books to justify its existence between covers.

To give some sense of Rose's transformation of the manuscripts, I have selected a few passages from the manuscript and the published text of *Little Town on the Prairie* (New York: Harper, 1941; Newly Illustrated Uniform Edition, 1953) for comparison. The manuscript is in the Detroit Public Library. I have mentioned in chapter 11, note 6, how my interpretation of the manuscript evidence differs from those of Rosa Ann Moore and William T. Anderson.

———————————

Laura Ingalls Wilder:

Little Town on the Prairie
Chapter One

It was springtime and the Dakota prairie lay so warm and bright under the shining sun, it did not seem possible it ever was swept by the winds and snows of the long, hard winter just past.

Laura was glad to be on the homestead. She liked the spring wind and the sunshine. It seemed as though she could never get sunshine enough soaked into her bones.

Assessing the potential of the manuscript, Rose saw the need for a preliminary chapter to foreshadow Laura's introduction to town society and the world of work and to prepare the thematic conflict between home and society, country and town.

*Further needed was a retrospective summary of the previous book to justify
Laura's delight in springtime on the homestead. Three carefully worked pages
lead finally into a few lines from her mother's original version, and even these are
subtly revised.*

Rose Wilder Lane:

Little Town on the Prairie
Chapter 1: Surprise

One evening at supper, Pa asked, "How would you like to work in
town, Laura?"

Laura could not say a word. Neither could any of the others. They all
sat as if they were frozen. Grace's blue eyes stared over the rim of her tin
cup, Carrie's teeth stayed bitten into a slice of bread, and Mary's hand
held her fork stopped in the air. Ma let tea go pouring from the teapot's
spout into Pa's brimming cup. Just in time, she quickly set down the
teapot.

"What did you say, Charles?" she asked.

"I asked Laura how she'd like to take a job in town," Pa replied.

"A job? For a girl? In town?" Ma asked. "Why, what kind of a job—"
Then quickly she said, "No, Charles, I won't have Laura working out in a
hotel among all kinds of strangers."

"Who said such a thing?" Pa demanded. "No girl of ours'll do that,
not while I'm alive and kicking."

"Of course not," Ma apologized. "You took me so by surprise. What
other kind of work can there be? and Laura's not old enough to teach
school yet."

All in the minute before Pa began to explain, Laura thought of the
town, and of the homestead claim where they were all so happy now in
the springtime, and she did not want anything changed. She did not
want to work in town.

Chapter 2: Springtime on the Claim

After the October Blizzard last fall, they had all moved to town and
for a little while Laura had gone to school there. Then the storms had
stopped school, and all through that long winter the blizzards had
howled between the houses, shutting them off from each other so that

day after day and night after night not a voice could be heard and not a light could be seen through the whirling snow.

All winter long, they had been crowded in the little kitchen, cold and hungry and working hard in the dark and the cold to twist enough hay to keep the fire going and to grind wheat in the coffee mill for the day's bread.

All that long, long winter, the only hope had been that sometime winter must end, sometime blizzards must stop, the sun would shine warm again and they could all get away from the town and go back to the homestead claim.

Now it was springtime. The Dakota prairie lay so warm and bright under the shining sun that it did not seem possible that it had ever been swept by the winds and snows of that hard winter. How wonderful it was to be on the claim again! Laura wanted nothing more than just being outdoors. She felt she could never get enough sunshine soaked into her bones.

A similar crafting, both technical and thematic, can be seen at work in the chapter devoted to the Independence Day celebration.

Laura Ingalls Wilder:

Chapter Four: The Fourth of July

Laura was wakened in the morning by the "Boom! Boom! Boom! from the anvil at the blacksmith shop in town. It sounded like a great gun.

"Come girls!" Ma called. "Time to get up. Don't you hear the cannon?"

Breakfast was soon over, because everyone was in a hurry to go to the celebration.

While Laura and Carrie washed the dishes and Mary made the beds, Ma packed the picnic basket. "I wish" she said, "that I had some of our chickens from Plum Creek."

Rose Wilder Lane:

Chapter 8: Fourth of July

BOOM!

Laura was jerked out of sleep. The bedroom was dark. Carrie asked in a thin, scared whisper, "What was that?"

"Don't be scared," Laura answered. They listened. The window was hardly gray in the dark, but Laura could feel that the middle of the night was past.

BOOM! The air seemed to shake.

"Great guns!" Pa exclaimed sleepily.

"Why? Why?" Grace demanded. "Pa, Ma, why?"

Carrie asked, "Who is it? What are they shooting?"

"What time is it?" Ma wanted to know.

Through the partition Pa answered, "It's Fourth of July, Carrie." The air shook again. BOOM!

It was not great guns. It was gunpowder exploded under the black-smith's anvil, in town. The noise was like the noise of battles that Americans fought for independence. Fourth of July was the day when the first Americans declared that all men are born free and equal. BOOM!

"Come, girls, we might as well get up!" Ma called.

Pa sang, " 'Oh, say, can you see, by the dawn's early light?' "

"Charles!" Ma protested, but she was laughing, because it really was too dark to see.

"It's nothing to be solemn about!" Pa jumped out of bed. "Hurray! We're Americans!" He sang,

Hurray! Hurray! We'll sing the jubilee!

Hurray! Hurray! The flag that sets men free!

Even the sun, as it rose shining into the clearest of skies, seemed to know this day was the glorious Fourth. At breakfast, Ma said, "This would be a perfect day for a Fourth of July picnic."

"Maybe the town'll be far enough along to have one, come next July," said Pa.

"We couldn't hardly have a picnic this year, anyway," Ma admitted. "It wouldn't seem like a picnic, without fried chicken."

Once the Ingalls family reaches the Fourth of July celebration, the Laura Ingalls Wilder manuscript furnishes just a hint that Rose seized upon to raise Laura to her moment of political illumination.

Laura Ingalls Wilder:

. . . the speakers were coming onto the platform.

They were all strangers to Laura. She listened carefully while one read the Declaration of Independence. He was a tall man with a grand manner, and his voice boomed out strongly as he read—

"When in the course of human events [it] becomes necessary for one people to dissolve the political bands which have connected them with another"—

Then another speaker talked about "our glorious country" and how our ancestors fought, bled and died that we might be free as the Declaration said we should be. How they, a mere handful of ragged patriots, had beaten the whole British army and won our independence.

To be reminded of what Rose made of this passage, the reader may wish to return to chapter 16 above, or to read pages 72–77 of Little Town on the Prairie.

Finally, it is worth noting one of Rose's more significant editorial suppressions. Her mother's account, determinedly factual, reveals that Mary Ingalls went to college on a government subsidy. It was an inconvenient fact for a story that would stress the family's independence and Laura's self-sacrifice. The passage below was excised from the manuscript.

Laura Ingalls Wilder:

Chapter Six: Mary Goes to College

After thinking for so long, of sending Mary to college, the time had come at last when she was going.

Dakota Territory still had no school where the blind could be educated, but the territory would pay tuition, to the state of Iowa, for all Dakota blind children. And Mary could go to the Iowa College for the Blind at Vinton. Tuition included board and room and books.

With all this taken care of, there would be left the expense of the new clothes Mary must have and the railroad fare to Vinton. Mary must have some spending money. . . .

The suppression of this passage is of a piece with the incorporation into the story of an incident from the original Pioneer Girl *manuscript. There, Laura had found a copy of Sir Walter Scott's poems, hidden away by her mother as a Christmas present for her. In chapter 19 of* Little Town on the Prairie, *the book is a copy of Tennyson's poems, which gives Laura the opportunity to read, and be repelled by, "The Lotos Eaters":*

Even that poem was a disappointment, for in the land that seemed always to be afternoon the sailors turned out to be no good. They seemed to think they were entitled to live in that magic land and lie around complaining. When they thought about bestirring themselves, they only whined, "Why should we ever labor up the laboring wave?" Why, indeed! Laura thought indignantly. Wasn't that a sailor's job, to ever labor up the laboring wave? But no, they wanted dreamful ease. Laura slammed the book shut.

These are major instances of what occurred throughout in hundreds of minor ways as Rose wrought aesthetic and ideological order in her mother's manuscripts.

"This kind of work is called 'ghosting,' and no writer of my reputation ever does it," she had written to Rexh Meta, uneasy in conscience for a skill that had often paid her bills while it stood between her and work she deemed more serious, but that in this unique collaboration with her mother would produce work more fruitful than she could imagine. It is worth remembering, perhaps, that the word *ghost* also carries an older meaning—that of the spirit, the vital principle, which brings to the inert body the breath of life.

*N*OTES

Most of the letters, diaries, journals, and manuscripts cited are in the Laura Ingalls Wilder–Rose Wilder Lane Collection of the Herbert Hoover Presidential Library in West Branch, Iowa. The locations of other documents will be cited in the appropriate note, except as specified below:

Letters to and from George Bye: the James Oliver Brown Collection, Columbia University Library. Copies of much of his correspondence with Lane are also in the Hoover Library.

Letters to Floyd Dell: the Floyd Dell papers, Newberry Library.

Letters to Berta Hader: the Hader papers, University of Oregon Library.

Letters to Mary Paxton Keeley: Joint Collection, Western Historical Manuscript Collection and State Historical Society of Missouri Manuscripts, University of Missouri Library.

Letters to Fremont Older: the Fremont Older Collection, Bancroft Library, University of California–Berkeley.

Letters to Dorothy Thompson: the George Arents Library, Syracuse University. Carbon copies of many of these letters are in the Hoover Library.

Letters to the author remain in my possession.

When working with newspapers, I have had to rely on microfilm copies and clipping files. At times, I could not determine page numbers, but I have tried to make my references as complete as possible.

ABBREVIATIONS

JOB	James Oliver Brown
LIW	Laura Ingalls Wilder
RWL	Rose Wilder Lane
NECRB	*National Economic Council Review of Books*
SEP	*Saturday Evening Post*
SFB	*San Francisco Bulletin*
SFC&P	*San Francisco Call and Post*

Prologue: Mother and Daughter

1. Virginia Woolf, "The Art of Biography," *Atlantic Monthly* 163 (April 1939): 509.

2. RWL, "Who's Who—and Why," *SEP* 208 (July 6, 1935): 30. RWL to Roger MacBride, November 22, 1965.

3. By and large, the novels are historically and biographically accurate; the "fictionalizing" is a matter of selection and of dramatic re-creation within this larger framework. The account of the early years collapses time considerably and omits periods in Missouri and Iowa. The actual sequence has been retraced by Donald Zochert in *Laura* (Chicago: Regnery, 1976).

4. I have made this argument in more detail in "Closing the Circle: The American Optimism of Laura Ingalls Wilder," *Great Plains Quarterly* 4 (Spring 1984): 79–90. For a broader discussion of the problem, see Ray Allen Billington, *Westward Expansion: A*

History of the American Frontier, 4th ed. (New York: MacMillan, 1974), chap. 32; and Walter Prescott Webb, *The Great Plains* (Boston: Houghton Mifflin, 1936), 398–413.

5. The Wilders lasted longer than most who fled. "Between 1888 and 1892 half the population of western Kansas moved out and 30,000 left South Dakota" (Billington, *Westward Expansion,* 639).

6. LIW, *On the Banks of Plum Creek* (New York: Harper, 1937; Newly Illustrated Uniform Edition, 1953), 217. All quotations from the works of Laura Ingalls Wilder will be from this edition, with the exception of the posthumous *On the Way Home* and *West from Home.*

7. I use the term *myth* here to suggest a controlling communal vision, in some measure divinely sanctioned and prophetic, which broadly guides the choices both of a culture and of a personal history. History, shaped by empirical canons of truth, stands at the opposite pole from myth. Between them develop the fictions that comprise our literature, mainly the romance, tending toward myth, and the novel, staying closer to history. The conceptual framework here is adapted from several works by Northrop Frye, notably *The Anatomy of Criticism* (Princeton, N. J.: Princeton University Press, 1957) and *Fables of Identity* (New York: Harcourt Brace, 1961). The specific myth that I find at the heart of the Wilder books is most clearly described in its secular dimension by Henry Nash Smith in *Virgin Land: The American West as Symbol and Myth* (1950; reprint, New York: Vintage Books, 1957), especially book 3, "The Garden of the World." The religious dimension is examined in Robert N. Bellah, *The Broken Covenant: American Civil Religion in Time of Trial* (New York: Seabury Press, 1975).

8. The papers were in the possession of Rose Wilder Lane's heir, Roger MacBride. They were later donated to the Herbert Hoover Presidential Library in West Branch, Iowa, and have been open for research since 1983.

9. Annotation to a letter from RWL, January 19, 1948.

10. Unpublished journal, "My Albanian Garden," November 3, 1926.

11. RWL, "Credo," *SEP* 208 (March 7, 1936): 30.

12. Roger MacBride to William Holtz, May 21, 1991.

13. Journal, June 26, 1928.

14. Hans F. Sennholz to William Holtz, April 12, 1991.

15. Irene Lichty LeCount to William Holtz, February 24, 1986.

I. A Prairie Rose

1. LIW, *On the Way Home* (New York: Harper and Row, 1962), 1. Rose apparently received the manuscript from the Lichtys in 1960 or 1961.

2. For a summary of the economic problems, see R. Hal Williams, *Years of Decision: American Politics in the 1890s* (New York: John Wiley, 1978), chap. 4.

3. Billington, *Westward Expansion,* 69.

4. See a promotional pamphlet offering testimonials to the beauties of the region, apparently published by a railway company: *Among the Ozarks: The Land of the Big Red Apple* (Kansas City, Mo.: Hudson-Kimberley Publishing Company, 1892), Collection of the Missouri Historical Society, Columbia, Mo.

5. LIW, *On the Way Home,* 27.

6. RWL, "Who's Who—and Why," 30. Coxey's Army was nowhere near sixty thousand, but there were many such traveling bands of unemployed men, of which Coxey's was the most publicized.

7. LIW, *On the Way Home,* 69.

8. The passages quoted in this episode are from the epilogue to LIW, *On the Way Home,* 75, 81, 85, 93–94.

9. RWL to Fremont Older, August 7, 1931.

10. The unpublished novel, entitled "The First Three Years and a Year of Grace" in manuscript, had been conceived sometime prior to 1938, when a "framework" was mentioned (LIW to RWL, handwritten note on the back of a letter to LIW from Harper and Row, December 17, 1937). It would be published after the death of both mother and daughter as *The First Four Years* (New York: Harper and Row, 1971). Quotations here are from the published version.

11. As did *The De Smet Leader,* December 11, 1886: "At the home of Mr. and Mrs. J. L. [*sic*] Wilder, on Monday last, a daughter came." The item was copied in a letter from Aubrey Sherwood to RWL, July 12, 1968.

12. LIW, *The First Four Years,* 72. The literal veracity of this account is all the more likely for its not having been edited by Rose.

13. Diary of Grace Ingalls, March 5, 1888. A copy is in the Hoover Library. The diary is in the possession of William T. Anderson, who has reprinted it in *The Story of the Ingalls* (De Smet, S.D.: Laura Ingalls Wilder Memorial Society, 1971).

14. LIW, *On the Way Home,* 2–3.

15. Diary of Grace Ingalls, January 12, March 30, and October 1, 1887; March 5, 1888. William T. Anderson, "The Last Little House," *Laura Ingalls Wilder Lore* 4 (Fall–Winter 1978): 3–7; "Pa Ingalls Subject of 1898 Biography," *Laura Ingalls Wilder Lore* 6 (Fall–Winter 1980): 6.

16. The published version of the novel, edited for a reading audience of children, omits a description of the difficult labor.

17. LIW, *The First Four Years,* 104–6.

18. RWL, "I, Rose Wilder Lane . . . ," *Cosmopolitan* 79 (June 1926): 42.

19. LIW, *The First Four Years,* 133–34.

20. Rose wrote two substantially similar versions of this dream-vision; the one quoted here seems to be the earlier (untitled manuscript beginning "Before we went to Minnesota . . .").

21. Diary of Grace Ingalls, May 18, 1890. LIW, *The First Four Years,* 93–95.

22. The few facts have been collected by Mary Jo Dathe in *Spring Valley: The Laura Ingalls Wilder Connection* (Spring Valley, Minn.: Spring Valley Tribune, 1990), 1, 22, 23, 25.

23. LIW, *On the Way Home,* 3. Rose places it in De Smet in April, 1889; however, the original is marked "Spring Valley, Minnesota." Either memory played her false or she indulged in a little creative license for the sake of illustrating *On the Way Home.* I am indebted to William T. Anderson on this point.

24. Alene M. Warnock, *Laura Ingalls Wilder: The Westville Florida Years* (privately printed pamphlet, Glen Burnie, Md., 1979). The passage by LIW is from Stanley J. Kunitz and Howard Haycroft, eds., *The Junior Book of Authors,* 2d ed., rev. (New York: Wilson, 1951), 299. The style suggests that it was written by Rose.

25. RWL, "Innocence," *Harper's* 144 (April 1922): 577–84; reprinted in *O. Henry Memorial Award Prize Stories of 1922,* ed. Blanche Colton Williams (New York: Double-day, 1923), 23–35.

26. Warnock, *Westville Years,* 26.

27. LIW, *On the Way Home,* 105.

28. LIW, *On the Way Home,* 4. Records reveal the Wilders buying the property on November 14, 1892. I am indebted to William T. Anderson and Vivian Glover on this point.

29. RWL to Guy Moyston, July 25, 1925. RWL to Jasper Crane, December 13, 1961.

30. RWL, "Rose Wilder Lane, by Herself," *Sunset* 41 (November 1918): 26. She does not locate the incident specifically, but William T. Anderson's researches suggest that the locale was Spring Valley.

31. RWL to Priscilla Slocum, September 2, 1967.

32. RWL to Guy Moyston, June 14, 1925. RWL to Fremont Older, August 7, 1931.

33. The Wilders sold their De Smet property on May 25, 1894, for $350, netting a profit of $150. See note 28 above.

34. LIW, *On the Way Home*, 95. The description is very similar to one RWL had written in a journal addressed to Arthur Griggs, September 23–25, 1920.

35. LIW, *On the Way Home*, 97.

2. Old Home Town: Growing Up in Mansfield

1. Williams, *Years of Decision*, chap. 5.

2. RWL, *Old Home Town* (New York: Longmans, Green, 1935), 8–9.

3. Most of the following details of Rose's childhood in Mansfield come from reminiscences in a journal written as a continuous letter to Arthur Griggs when she traveled through Poland, September 23–25, 1920. The donkey-and-apple anecdote is from an unpublished manuscript ("The Value of Hard Work," 1935).

4. RWL, "I, Rose Wilder Lane . . . ," 42. The other details in this paragraph, including the comment on "mountain girls," are from Journal to Arthur Griggs, September 23–25, 1920.

5. RWL, *Old Home Town*, 3.

6. RWL to Mr. Cross, October 24, 1939.

7. Journal to Arthur Griggs, September 23–25, 1920.

8. RWL, "I, Rose Wilder Lane . . . ," 42.

9. RWL, "Who's Who—and Why," 30. RWL to Guy Moyston, July 11, 1925.

10. Journal to Arthur Griggs, September 23–25, 1920.

11. RWL, unpublished manuscript, "Grandpa's Fiddle." Diary, April 11, 1920.

12. Eventual freedom from that dream she connected with economic security (LIW to RWL, March 17, 1939).

13. Anita Clair Fellman has read much of this evidence in the light of a feminist theory of mother-daughter relationships in such a way as to connect the women's personal problems with their political positions. See her "Laura Ingalls Wilder and Rose Wilder Lane: The Politics of a Mother-Daughter Relationship," *Signs* 15 (Spring 1990): 535–61.

14. I have translated the German title of Miller's book, *Das Drama des begabten Kindes*; its English translation is suggestively retitled: *Prisoners of Childhood*, trans. Ruth Ward (New York: Basic Books, 1981). RWL to Guy Moyston, July 27, 1925.

15. RWL to Irene Lichty, August 30, 1963 (courtesy of Irene Lichty LeCount). Priscilla Howard to William T. Anderson, undated (courtesy of William T. Anderson).

16. Blanche Anderson to Roger MacBride, undated [1968]. RWL, "I, Rose Wilder Lane . . . ," 42. RWL, "If I Could Live My Life Over Again," *Cosmopolitan* 78 (March 1925): 32.

17. RWL to Irene Lichty, July 29, 1964 (courtesy of Irene Lichty LeCount). RWL to Joan Clark, February 7, 1963.

18. RWL to Joan Clark, February 7, 1963.

19. RWL to Jasper Crane, December 13, 1961. Rose also used the incident in *He Was a Man* (New York: Harper, 1925), 176.

20. *NECRB*, May 1947, 1.

21. The characterization of Rose as a dreamer was by Gorman ("Pete") Freeman, and has been passed on to me by William T. Anderson. The textbook was P. V. N. Myers, *A General History for College and High Schools* (Boston: Ginn and Company, 1899). Dated entries run from 1900 to 1902. The book is in the museum at Rocky Ridge Farm.

22. RWL to Jasper Crane, December 13, 1961; April 24, 1963.

23. RWL to Dorothy Thompson, March 8, 1930. According to Susan Hammaker,

Rose as a child once considered a career designing monograms (William T. Anderson to William Holtz, April 5, 1987).

24. RWL, *Old Home Town*, 23.

25. RWL to Norma Lee Browning, October 31, 1967.

26. The story of Eliza Jane is told by William T. Anderson in *A Wilder in the West* (De Smet, S.D.: Laura Ingalls Wilder Memorial Society, 1985).

27. Rose later recalled the five hundred dollars as a gift prior to her grandfather's death (RWL to Irene Lichty, August 30, 1963; courtesy of Irene Lichty LeCount). But William T. Anderson's research into the Wilder family history suggests that her memory was in error on this point and that the alternative reconstruction is more likely. The same letter specifies James Wilder's fortune as one hundred thousand dollars, which seems excessive. Rose was apt to exaggerate such matters; Anderson suggests a misplaced decimal point and a fortune of perhaps ten thousand dollars.

28. The story was repeated to me by William T. Anderson, who has visited the family. One version has Rose pregnant, which seems to sort ill with her continued presence in the Crowley school.

29. RWL to Jasper Crane, December 13, 1961. RWL to Norma Lee Browning, May 17, 1964, from which the quotation is taken. Rose endowed the hero of *He Was a Man* with her study techniques (219).

30. RWL, "World Travelogue," *SFC&P*, April 10, 1923. RWL, "Who's Who—and Why," 30. RWL to Fremont Older, November 16, 1928. William T. Anderson has reported to me that E. J. was presented a gold watch for her work on Debs's behalf.

31. Dorothy B. McNeely to William Holtz, April 14, 1981, quoting Rose's classmate Phila Bauer Egan. Mrs. McNeely was so kind as to interview Mrs. Egan for me.

32. Interviews: Daniel P. Bierman, March 28, 1989; Norma Lee Browning, April 8, 1980; Doris Lyman, April 4, 1989.

33. RWL, "If I Could Live My Life Over Again," 32.

34. RWL, *Old Home Town*, 24.

35. RWL to Irene Lichty, July 29, 1964 (courtesy of Irene Lichty LeCount).

3. Bachelor Girl, Married Woman

1. RWL to Roger MacBride, May 27, 1966.

2. RWL to Guy Moyston, August 25, 1924; July 11, 1925.

3. RWL, "Rose Lane Says," *Pittsburgh Courier*, April 3, 1943. RWL to Fremont Older, May 30, 1928. Nights at the Midland are described in *Faces at the Window*, published posthumously by the Laura Ingalls Wilder–Rose Wilder Lane Museum, Mansfield, Missouri, 1972; this little mystery story seems factual in its setting. See also RWL to Carl Brandt, undated, beginning "Oh, it isn't so serious. . . ." The Kansas City directory for 1906 lists Rose Wilder as a telegraph operator at the Midland Hotel.

4. RWL to Carl Brandt, undated, beginning "Oh, it isn't so serious. . . ." *NECRB*, November 1949, 1. RWL, "I, Rose Wilder Lane . . . ," 42. The story of the typewriting is recalled by Roger MacBride.

5. The motorcar story comes from an unpublished essay, "The Value of Hard Work" (1935). Julian Bucher sent a postcard to her in Mansfield from Kansas City, September 19, 1907; he is mentioned in one of the undated letters Rose wrote her mother in this period; in 1934 he visited the Wilders in Mansfield (*Mansfield Mirror*, September 6, 1934). Paul Cooley did not recall Bucher but he did remember Johnson (letter to William Holtz, May 29, 1980). The sexual reminiscence is from her unpublished journal, "My Albanian Garden," November 3, 1926; the lack of her mother's help is from a letter to Norma Lee Browning, October 31, 1967.

6. Unpublished journal, "My Albanian Garden," November 3, 1926.

7. *Kansas City Star,* August 18, p. 2; August 20, p. 1; October 14, p. 1. Vidkunn Ulriksson, *The Telegraphers: Their Craft and Their Unions* (Washington, D.C.: Public Affairs Press, 1953), chaps. 7–8. RWL, "Faces at the Window," 4. Postcard, L. D. Mathis to RWL, November 19, 1907. Addressed envelope among the general correspondence in the Hoover Library.

8. The card from Paul Cooley is in the LIW Museum in Mansfield. The April 1908 date is recalled in her diary entry of April 11, 1920.

9. Diary, April 11, 1920. Postcard, Julian Bucher to Rose Lane, September 3, 1907. Postcards, LIW to RWL, August 21, 30, 31, 1908. The inferences regarding the stock market wire and her meeting with Gillette Lane are from her novel *Diverging Roads* (New York: Century, 1919).

10. Eric Howard, "Famous Californians: Bessie Beattie," *SFC&P,* July 7, 1923. The address is from the San Francisco city directory. RWL to Evelyn Wells, May 14, 1935 (Fremont Older Collection). RWL to Dorothy Thompson, March 12, 1929.

11. Unpublished journal, "My Albanian Garden," November 3, 1926.

12. The account is drawn from a series of undated letters [1909–1914] from RWL to LIW.

13. RWL to Charles and Joan Clark, February 8, 1944. She mentions it also in a letter to Dorothy Thompson, March 8, 1930. See also her unpublished journal, "My Albanian Garden," November 3, 1926.

14. RWL to Guy Moyston, April 4, 1925. The *Kansas City Post* articles were among the clippings in her files; they run throughout May 1910; the excerpt is from May 20. A photograph in the Hoover Library reveals a connection with work for the *Kansas City Journal.*

15. Unpublished journal, "My Albanian Garden," November 3, 1926. The inferences about their itinerant life come from the undated [1909–1914] letters and a postcard that place them in Cincinnati and Louisville.

16. RWL to Clarence Day, May 26, 1928.

17. RWL to Clarence Day, May 26, 1928. RWL to LIW, undated [1911?], beginning "you'll be astonished. . . ."

18. RWL to LIW, undated [1911?], beginning "answers to poultry raisers. . . ." LIW to RWL, February 5, 1937.

19. RWL, "Rose Lane Says," *Pittsburgh Courier,* August 11, 1945. RWL to Guy Moyston, May 3, 1925. The manuscript of *The Emerald* is in the Hoover Library; it dates from 1911.

20. This hypothetical reconstruction from her novel can be grounded in occasional later references; e.g., *NECRB,* June 1948, 1–3.

21. RWL, *Diverging Roads,* 165, 178, 183–84. The book version adds the liberating experience of working among professional women; the serial version, which ran in *Sunset* from October 1918 through June 1919, ends with the suggestion that the heroine will marry her long-suffering childhood sweetheart.

22. Unpublished journal, "My Albanian Garden," November 3, 1926. RWL to Dorothy Thompson, undated [January 1927]; RWL, "I, Rose Wilder Lane . . . ," 42–43. RWL to Virginia Brastow, March 18, 1935, and June 22, 1936.

23. I assume that the poem is Rose's, but she sometimes copied out magazine verse that struck her as apropos.

24. RWL to Susie (Susan Hammaker; then Mrs. Roger MacBride), April 18, 1963. *NECRB,* June 1948, 3.

25. The fictional account of the end of the real estate sales in *Diverging Roads* is confirmed in several places in her letters; e.g., RWL to Evelyn Wells, May 14, 1935 (Fremont Older Collection).

26. RWL to LIW, undated [1914], beginning "Muvver Dear. . . ."

27. RWL to [Eliza Jane Wilder Thayer], undated [1914], beginning "Papa and Mama Bess. . . ."
28. RWL to LIW, undated [1914], beginning "I open this letter. . . ."
29. RWL to LIW, beginning "Muvver Dear. . . ."
30. RWL to LIW, beginning "I open this letter. . . ."
31. William T. Anderson, *Laura's Rose: The Story of Rose Wilder Lane* (Mansfield, Mo.: Laura Ingalls Wilder–Rose Wilder Lane Home Association, 1976), 16–17. Mr. Anderson reports to me that the incident comes to him from Rose's friend Roi Partridge.
32. RWL to LIW, beginning "Muvver Dear. . . ." Such an advertisement by Stine and Kendrick appeared in the *San Francisco Bulletin*, April 25, 1914, 20. RWL to Evelyn Wells, May 14, 1935 (Fremont Older Collection).
33. Unpublished journal, "My Albanian Garden," November 3, 1926.

4. Bulletin Days

1. RWL to Dorothy Thompson, January 21, [1928]; March 12, 1929. The outlines of Gillette Lane's career can be traced through the San Francisco city directory. Frances Lane Harris to Laura Ingalls Wilder Museum, August 6, 1974 (courtesy of Irene Lichty LeCount). RWL to Guy Moyston, May 2, 1925. To Bessie Beatty, at any rate, Rose's marriage during the early days on the *Bulletin* seemed unstrained, as the gossip on her page duly notes Rose's wedding anniversary (*SFB*, March 29, 1915).
2. RWL to Guy Moyston, February 19, 1925, citing George Brandes, *Main Currents in Nineteenth-Century Thought* (New York: MacMillan, 1906), 1:83.
3. RWL to Evelyn Wells, May 14, 1935 (Fremont Older Collection).
4. *SFB*, January 16, 1915.
5. RWL, "Not the Old Story," *SFB*, January 28, 1915, 11.
6. LIW, "Tuck 'em in Corner," *SFB*, March 17, 1915, 13; March 18, 1915, 13; March 19, 1915, 11; March 18, 1918, 13. These poems were probably from the little books Rose referred to in a letter from Maine in 1911 (see chap. 3 above). The illustrations to Rose's "The People in Our Apartment House," *SFB*, September 25–October 22, 1915, and "Bringing the Records to Berta," *SFB*, November 22–27, 1916, are by Berta Hoerner.
7. The account of Fremont Older and the *Bulletin* in this chapter is drawn from his autobiography, *My Own Story* (New York: MacMillan, 1926), the biography by Evelyn Wells, *Fremont Older* (New York: Appleton-Century, 1936), and the reminiscences of R. L. Duffus, *The Tower of Jewels* (New York: Norton, 1960). "A Jitney Romance" ran in the *Bulletin* from March 4 to April 13, 1915. The meeting with Older is described in the letter to Evelyn Wells cited in n. 3 above. Wells quotes the sections used here (272–73). Rose repeated essentially the same story in a letter to Dorothy Thompson of August 3, 1932.
8. Rose's claim to have flown with Beachey is recorded by Roger MacBride in his edition of LIW's letters regarding her San Francisco visit: *West from Home* (New York: Harper and Row, 1974), 4n. "'Art' Smith's Story" ran in the *Bulletin* May 19–June 21, 1915; it was reprinted as *The Story of Art Smith* (San Francisco: Bulletin, 1915).
9. MacBride, *West from Home*, 115–16.
10. RWL to Guy Moyston, April 8, 1925.
11. MacBride, *West from Home*, 33, 66–67, 74, 85–86, 115.
12. RWL to LIW, cited chap. 3, n. 12 above. Almanzo Wilder, "My Apple Orchard," *Missouri Ruralist*, June 1, 1912, 2. Almanzo Wilder had many skills, but writing was not one of them, as evidenced by the one letter to Rose that survives in his hand, January 15, 1939.
13. MacBride, *West from Home*, 33, 47–48, 66–67, 85, 115–16. RWL, "Ed Monroe, Manhunter," *SFB*, August 11–September 15, 1915. RWL, "Behind the Headlight," *SFB*, October 9–November 5, 1915. RWL, "The Big Break at Folsom," *SFB*, January 4–

February 1, 1917, followed by "Out of Prison," *SFB*, February 2–March 15, 1917. Rose identifies herself as the writer in a letter to Guy Moyston (January 14, 1924).

14. It is clear that Ford repudiated the book for its inaccuracies from the correspondence with the publisher in the Ford Archives, Greenfield Village, Dearborn, Michigan. (Douglas Bakken, Director, Ford Archives, to William Holtz, October 2, 1979.)

15. The letter is in the Chaplin archives at Vevey, Switzerland; it is quoted in part here as published by David Robinson, *Chaplin: His Life and Art* (New York: McGraw-Hill, 1985), 180–85. The suppressed book was eventually reprinted as *Charlie Chaplin's Own Story*, ed. Harry M. Geduld (Bloomington: Indiana University Press, 1985).

16. I have treated this episode more fully in "Jack London's First Biographer," *Western American Literature* 27 (May 1992): 21–36. Rose's "Life and Jack London" appeared in *Sunset*, October 1917–May 1918.

17. Charmian's relations with a series of London biographers are described in Richard W. Etulain, "The Lives of Jack London," *Western American Literature* 11 (Summer 1976): 149–64. RWL to Charmian London, May 1, 1917 (Huntington Library). RWL to Charmian London, May 22, 1917 (Utah State University Library). Charmian London to Charles K. Field, October 12, 1917 (Huntington Library).

18. Charmian London to RWL, September 19, 1917 (Huntington Library).

19. RWL to Charmian London, September 22, and December 7, 1917 (Utah State University Library). Eliza Shepard to RWL, October 13, 1917 (Huntington Library).

20. Charmian London to RWL, April 28, and May 6, 1918 (Utah State University Library).

21. RWL to Charmian London, May 31, 1917. Charmian London to RWL, June 2, 1917 (Utah State University Library). Charmian London to RWL, May 6, 1918 (Utah State University Library).

22. RWL to Charmian London, May 2, 1918 (Utah State University Library).

23. Charmian London to RWL, May 6, 1918 (Utah State University Library).

24. RWL to Charmian London, May 7, 1918 (Utah State University Library).

25. RWL to Guy Moyston, October 21, 1926.

26. RWL to Guy Moyston, December 4, 1925. "Rose Lane Says," *Pittsburgh Courier*, February 19, 1944.

27. RWL to LIW, undated [1914], beginning "I open this letter. . . ." RWL, "World Travelogue" *SFC&P*, April 10, 1923. RWL, unpublished manuscript, "The Value of Hard Work" (1935).

28. RWL, "Myself," *SFB*, pt. 7, June 4. RWL, "The City at Night," *SFB*, pt. 13, May 15.

29. RWL, "Credo," 5. RWL to Dorothy Thompson, August 3, 1932.

30. Rose mentions a talk to "the Jack London School of whatever it is" in a letter to Charmian London, June 7, 1917. Doubtless this was the left-wing socialist Jack London Institute that had christened their meeting place at 1256 Market Street the Jack London Memorial Hall—an appropriation of London's name that ignored his resignation from the Socialist Party because it would not support the war against Germany; see Joan London, *Jack London and His Times* (Seattle: University of Washington Press, 1939), 368–70, 376. The mention of the Finnish Singing Society comes from FBI files received under the Freedom of Information Act.

31. Unpublished journal, "My Albanian Garden," November 3, 1926. RWL to Guy Moyston, November 11, 1926.

32. The excerpt is from RWL to her agent, Carl Brandt, June 4, 1928; it has been reprinted as "Fattening Gertrude," *South Dakota Review* 26 (Summer 1988): 6–9.

33. RWL, "_____ and Peter," *SFB* August 23–October 11, 1917.

34. RWL, *Diverging Roads*, 183–84, 336. The serial version appeared in *Sunset*, October–December 1918. RWL to Carl Brandt, May 26, 1928.

35. RWL to Charmian London, September 22, 1917 (Utah State University Library). Dorothy Thompson to RWL, August 13, 1921. RWL to Guy Moyston, October 4 [1921]. Journal, October 17, 1927, and April 24, 1934.

36. RWL, "Soldiers of the Soil," *SFB*, February 23–June 3, 1916.

37. RWL, "The Building of Hetch-Hetchy," *SFB*, October 14–November 14, 1916.

38. RWL, "The City at Night," *SFB*, April 30–May 16, 1917.

39. Older, *My Own Story*, chaps. 31–32; *SFB*, January 25, 1917.

40. RWL, "Behind the Screens in Movie Land," *SFB*, October 25–December 12, 1917.

41. The story is told by Older himself in *My Own Story*, chap. 36; by Wells in *Fremont Older*, chaps. 21–22; and by Duffus in *The Tower of Jewels*, 238–50.

42. Journal, July 20, 1918.

43. Journal, July 22, 1918.

44. Journal entries for August 6–18, 1918. Brittany Journal, 1921.

45. Journal, September 27, 1918.

5. An Interlude and Herbert Hoover

1. *SFB*, February 21, 1918. Journal, September 27–28, 1918. *SFC&P*, October 11, 1918.

2. *Mansfield Mirror*, October 17, 1918.

3. RWL, "Rose Wilder Lane, by Herself," 26.

4. Personnel records furnished courtesy of American Red Cross.

5. RWL, "Drab Peace Spirit," *SFC&P*, November 12, 1918, 14.

6. RWL to Dorothy Thompson, November 18, 1960. RWL, "America Enters Jerusalem" (*Ladies' Home Journal* 36 [April 1919]: 7–8) and "Out of the East Christ Came" (*Good Housekeeping* 69 [November 1919]) are both written as eyewitness accounts of Red Cross overseas activities; but both seem clearly drawn from other published sources. From Frederick O'Brien's manuscript came "The Flowing Kava Bowl," *Asia* 19 (July 1919): 638–44; "My Darling Hope," *Asia* 19 (July 1919): 692–93; "The Passing of the Men of Ahao," *Asia* 19 (August 1919): 723–72; "O Lalala, the Gambler," *Century* 98 (August 1919): 446–54; "Atuona Goes to Church," *Asia* 19 (September 1919): 830–35. Elmer Hader, discharged from the Army Camouflage Corps and working in his own New York studio, furnished illustrations for these stories. "A Bit of Gray in a Blue Sky" (*Ladies' Home Journal* 36 [August 1919]) tells the story of Cher Ami.

7. RWL, "Strange as Foreign Places," *McCall's* 49 (September 1919). LIW, "Whom Will You Marry?" *McCall's* 49 (June 1919). RWL to LIW, April 11, 1919.

8. RWL, "Credo."

9. RWL, "World Travelogue," *SFC&P*, April 10, 1923. Lynne Stuart, Hader's heir, to Roger MacBride, February 17, 1981, in my possession. RWL to Frank Meyer, September 24, 1953. RWL to Guy Moyston, February 4, 1919, and April 8, 1925. RWL to Jasper Crane, August 25, 1955, and June 20, 1966.

10. Floyd Dell, *Homecoming* (New York: Holt, Rinehart, and Winston, 1933), chaps. 30–32 (especially 332–35). RWL to Guy Moyston, undated [summer 1924], beginning "There isn't any more I can say. . . ." Jane Burr was born Rosalind Mae Guggenheim, and carried her husbands' names of Punch and Winslow before adopting her pseudonym.

11. RWL to Carl Brandt, June 6, 1928. Lynne Stuart to William Holtz, August 5, 1981.

12. Floyd Dell to Joseph Freeman, November 24, 1951. RWL to Carl Brandt, undated [spring 1928], beginning "This morning. . . ." Annotation to a letter from RWL to Floyd Dell, January 19, 1948. Several manuscript fragments of *White Shadows in the South Seas* (New York: Century, 1919) are in the Hader papers at the University of Oregon Library. From them it is possible to infer an original manuscript, not from

Rose's typewriter, followed by a version bearing her handwritten notes and heavily edited (to the extent of rewriting sentences for cadence, moving material from page to page, and altering chapters). The published version was apparently the result of still further editing. She claimed to have fabricated from whole cloth one of the anecdotes in O'Brien's book—the story of "McHenry and His Dog" in chapter 3 (Journal to Arthur Griggs, 1920).

13. RWL to Jasper Crane, September 6, 1953.

14. Interview with RWL, *Westporter-Herald* (Westport, Connecticut), January 19, 1931. Doris Lyman located this interview for me.

15. RWL to Haders, undated (internal evidence dates it late summer 1919).

16. *Mansfield Mirror,* August 14, August 28, September 4, and September 25, 1919.

17. RWL to Berta and Elmer Hader, undated [summer 1919]. RWL to Guy Moyston, October 18, 1921. Genealogy file, folder marked "Rose Wilder Lane," Hoover Papers at the Hoover Library.

18. RWL to George Bye, February 20, 1937.

19. Guy Moyston to RWL, October 21, 1919, and March 10, 1920. Moyston obituary, *New York Times,* May 3, 1962.

20. Diary for 1920, March and April *passim* (quoted passage, March 29).

21. The details in these paragraphs are drawn from Rose's diaries for 1920–1921. Baghdad is mentioned as her eventual goal in the first installment of "Come with Me to Europe," *SFC&P,* February 21, 1921.

22. RWL, "Credo," 5. She identified Harold Rugg as one of her guides into leftist circles in a talk before the Danbury, Connecticut Lions' Club (*Danbury News-Times,* September 10, 1943).

23. Diary, April 26, 1920.

24. Rose had just published an article dramatizing the statistics of American infant mortality and deaths in childbirth: "Mother No. 22,999," *Good Housekeeping* 70 (March 1920).

6. "Come with Me to Europe"

1. RWL, "Come with Me to Europe," pt. 2, February 22, 1921.

2. RWL, "Come with Me to Europe," pt. 6, February 26, 1921.

3. Diary, May 18, 1920. RWL to Berta Hader, September 7, 1920. For Arthur Griggs, see the *New York Times* obituary, November 27, 1934. The outlines of the arrangement for the Bernhardt manuscript can be inferred from RWL to Bessie Beatty, June 16, 1920. The *demi-vierge* anecdote is from RWL to Norma Lee Browning, October 31, 1967.

4. RWL, "Come with Me to Europe," pts. 24–27, March 19–23, 1920.

5. Journal to Arthur Griggs, June 22–23, 1920. For the "ceaseless chatter," see chap. 13, n. 12. Diary, June 25, 1920.

6. RWL, "Come with Me to Europe," pts. 37–47, April 5–16, 1921. "The Insidious Enemy," *Good Housekeeping* 71 (December 1920).

7. RWL to LIW, June 27, 1920.

8. RWL, "Come with Me to Europe," pts. 49–63, April 18–May 3, 1921. Diary, July 7, 1920.

9. Diary, July 22, July 30, and August 29, 1920. RWL, "Come with Me to Europe," pt. 66, May 7, 1921.

10. Diary, September 4, 5, 8, 21, 1920. RWL to Berta Hader, September 7, 1920; September "sometime" [1920].

11. Journal to Arthur Griggs, September 23–25, 1920. RWL, "Come with Me to Europe," pts. 71–74, May 14, 16, 17, 1920. The episode on the train to Poland became the basis of an unpublished short story, "Desert Sands."

12. Journal to Arthur Griggs, September 23–25, 27–29, 1920.

13. RWL, "Come with Me to Europe," pts. 75–89, May 18–June 3, 1920.

14. Diary, October 8, 1920. RWL, "Come with Me to Europe," pt. 90, June 4, 1921.

15. Diary, October 24, November 7, and December 4–6, 18, 21, 28–29, 1920. Armen Ohanian, "The Dancer of Shamakha," trans. Rose Wilder Lane, *Asia* 22 (April–August 1922).

16. RWL to Berta Hader, November 30, 1920. RWL, "Come with Me to Europe," pts. 94–95, June 9–10, 1921.

17. RWL to Berta Hader, October 26, and November 30, 1920. Diary, October 28–29, and November 3, 1920.

18. RWL to Berta Hader, December 8, 1920.

19. RWL to Berta Hader, December 8, 1920. *Mansfield Mirror*, December 2, 1920. Diary, November 23, 1920.

20. Diary, December 29, 31, 1920. RWL, "Come with Me to Europe," pt. 98, June 14, 1921.

21. Diary, January 1–3, 1921. The friendship of the two women is traced in *Dorothy Thompson and Rose Wilder Lane: Forty Years of Friendship,* ed. William Holtz (Columbia: University of Missouri Press, 1991); see especially letters 48–49 of October 1960. RWL to Berta Hader, September 7, 1920. Journal to Arthur Griggs [September 1920].

22. Journal, January 20–22. Guy Moyston to Berta Hader, August 3, and December 5, 1920. RWL to Berta Hader, February 5, 1921.

23. Journal, undated entry preceding March 14, 1921.

24. Diary, February 6, 7, 1921. RWL, "Come with Me to Europe," pt. 100, June 16, 1921. Journal, February 1921.

25. Diary, February 8, 1921. RWL to Berta Hader, February 11, 1921.

26. Diary, February 9–26, 1921. RWL to Fremont Older, July 3, 1921.

27. RWL to Norma Lee Browning, May 17, 1964.

28. RWL, "Come with Me to Europe," pts. 111–20, June 24–July 11, 1921. According to the *Oxford English Dictionary,* the connection of *bogey man* with the Serb *bog* (God) is a false etymology. The term is Christian, not pagan.

29. Rose wrote of her first experience in Albania in *Peaks of Shala* (New York: Harper, 1923), printed with little change from her *SFC&P* serial entitled "The World's Strangest People" (July 18–September 15, 1921).

30. RWL to George Bye, October 19, 1936.

31. RWL to LIW, April 27, 1921.

32. Diary, May 5–7, 1921.

33. RWL to Berta Hader, May 18, 1921. Guy Moyston to Berta Hader, December 5, [1920]; February 7, [1921]. Moyston obituary, *New York Times,* May 3, 1962.

34. This manuscript is undated, but it seems clearly connected with her column in the *Red Cross Bulletin* for July 11, 1921, and was probably written sometime in June. She seems to have kept it as an experiment she might use in her fiction, even going over it with her editorial pencil.

35. I have treated this episode more fully in "Sherwood Anderson and Rose Wilder Lane: Source and Method in *Dark Laughter,*" *Journal of Modern Literature* 12 (March 1985): 131–52.

36. RWL to Fremont Older, July 3, 1921.

37. Journal to Arthur Griggs, September 23–25, 1920. For the publication of "Innocence," see chap. 1, n. 25 above.

38. Interview with Helen Boylston, May 20, 1980. Virginia Boyd, Helen Boylston's attorney, to William Holtz, February 20, 1980.

39. Diary, September 3–16, 1921. Journal, September 7, 16, 1921.

40. Brittany Journal, 1921. RWL to Guy Moyston, October 18, 1921. RWL, "Under the Spell of Brittany," *World Traveler* 16 (April 1924).

41. RWL to Guy Moyston, undated [December 1921].

42. RWL to Guy Moyston, undated [November–December, 1921]. Diary, December 1921.

7. The Road to Baghdad

1. Diary, January 1–21, 1922. RWL to Guy Moyston, January 18, 1922. RWL, "The Adventures of Rose Wilder Lane," *SFC&P*, June 29 and July 6–7, 1922.

2. Diary, January 5, 10, 13, 17, 1922. RWL to Guy Moyston, January 18, 1922. C. D. Morris to RWL, February 1, 1922.

3. Diary, January 22–February 6, 1922. RWL to Guy Moyston, January 29, 1922. RWL, "The Adventures of Rose Wilder Lane," *SFC&P*, July 10–12, 1922.

4. Diary, May 4–5, 1922. RWL, "The Adventures of Rose Wilder Lane," *SFC&P*, July 15, 1922. RWL to Guy Moyston, March 20, 1925. RWL to Norma Lee Browning, May 17, 1964.

5. RWL to Jasper Crane, November 4, 1962.

6. Diary, February 6–March 3, 1922. RWL to Guy Moyston, February 16, 1922. RWL, "A Day in Sarajevo," *World Traveler* 14 (December 1922). RWL, "Ragusa: The Sleeping Beauty" *World Traveler* 14 (October 1922).

7. RWL, "Unknown Albania," *World Traveler* 15 (March 1923). RWL, "The Adventures of Rose Wilder Lane," *SFC&P*, July 26–27, 1922. The note to herself is on a picture postcard dated March 5, 1922.

8. RWL to LIW, March 21, 1922. RWL, "The Adventures of Rose Wilder Lane," *SFC&P*, July 29–August 11, 1922. Rose's account of the skirmish is confirmed in its main details by that of the British minister: see J. Swire, *Albania: The Rise of a Kingdom* (New York: Arno Press, 1971), 392–94.

9. Diary, March 7–15, 1922. RWL to LIW, March 21, 1922. RWL to Guy Moyston, March 15, 1922. RWL, *Peaks of Shala*, 285–349.

10. RWL, "The Adventures of Rose Wilder Lane," *SFC&P*, August 19, 1922.

11. Diary, March 30, April 2, 1922. Undated picture postcard.

12. RWL's letter in *Harper's* 147 (November 1923): 870.

13. RWL, "Edelweiss on Chafa Shalit," *Harper's* 147 (November 1923): 764. Diary, April 20–27, 1922. RWL, "Adventures of Rose Wilder Lane," *SFC&P*, August 28, 1922.

14. RWL, "Budapest for a Bath," *World Traveler* 15 (May 1923). RWL, "The Adventures of Rose Wilder Lane," *SFC&P*, September 2–6, 1922. RWL to Norma Lee Browning, October 31, 1967.

15. Diary, May 5–26, 1922. RWL to Guy Moyston, March 20, 1925.

16. Diary, June 3–July 28, 1922. RWL, "Sadik Hassan of the Mati," *Junior Red Cross Bulletin*, December 1922, 53–54. RWL, "Unknown Albania." Journal, July 11, 1922. RWL to Guy Moyston, September 12, 1922.

17. Diary, August 10–September 4, 1922. Journal, July 20, 1933. RWL to Guy Moyston, September 12, 1922.

18. For a history of the Armenian problem, see Dickran H. Boyajian, *Armenia: The Case for a Forgotten Genocide* (Westwood, N.J.: Educational Bookcrafters, 1972), and Gerard Chalian and Yves Ternon, *The Armenians: From Genocide to Resistance*, trans. Tony Berrett (London: Zed Press, 1983).

19. Diary, September 7, 1922.

20. RWL, "World Travelogue," *SFC&P*, April 10, 18, 22–25, and June 25, 1923. RWL to Guy Moyston, April 1, [1925].

21. *NECRB*, August 1949, 1.

22. Diary, September 3–October 14, 1922. "World Travelogue," *SFC&P*, May 17, 1923.

23. Diary, September 27, and October 15, 1922.

24. RWL to Guy Moyston, February 18, 1924. RWL to Fremont Older, July 14, 1928. RWL, "Where the World Is Topsy-Turvy," *SFC&P,* August 20, 1923.

25. Diary, October 23, 1922. RWL to Guy Moyston, October 27, 1927.

26. Annette Marquis, "Two American Women in the Caucasus," *World Traveler* 16, pt. 1, February 1924; pt. 2, August 1924; pt. 3, September 1924; pt. 4, October 1924. RWL, "Peasant and Priest in Soviet Armenia," *Asia* 23 (July 1923): 494–97; "Christmas in Erivan," *Good Housekeeping* 79 (December 1924).

27. RWL, "Where the World Is Topsy-Turvy," *SFC&P,* May 31, June 11, and August 20, 1923.

28. Journal, 1929. RWL to Guy Moyston, October 27, 1927.

29. RWL to Clarence Day, June 19, 1926.

30. The original version of this anecdote is in an unpublished manuscript probably intended for the *World Traveler,* "Four Days in Azerbaijan." With some creative revision, it was later published as "A Little Flyer in Inflation," *Harper's* 167 (September 1933): 485–90.

31. Diary, December 5, 31, 1922.

32. Diary, January 6–20, 1923. RWL to Guy Moyston, January 29, 1923. RWL, "Where the World Is Topsy-Turvy," *SFC&P,* August 17, 1923.

33. RWL to Guy Moyston, January 29, 1923. RWL to George Bye, March 1, 1937. Diary, April 15, 30, and June 23, 1923.

34. RWL to Guy Moyston, January 29, 1923. Journal, undated entry [February?], 1923.

35. RWL to Jasper Crane, November 4, 1962.

36. RWL to Guy Moyston, February 10, 1927. Diary, June 23, 29, 1923. RWL, "Where the World Is Topsy-Turvy," *SFC&P,* September 8, 1923.

37. Diary, July–August 1923. RWL to Guy Moyston, June 5, 1925.

38. Journal, August 28, 1923. Diary, August 29, 1923.

39. Diary, September 1–4, 1923. Journal, September 1–3, 1923. RWL, "Egypt Smiles," *World Traveler* 16 (January 1924).

40. Diary, September 4–5, 1923. RWL to LIW, September 10, 1923. Journal, October 1923.

41. Diary, September 4–23, 1923. RWL, "Baalbeck: Built by Giants," *World Traveler* 16 (March 1924).

42. Rose's account of this trip is in "To Bagdad by Flivver," *World Traveler* 16 (August 1924) and in an undated letter [August 1924] to Guy Moyston. B. D. MacDonald wrote his own account in "The Elusive 'Air-Furrow' to Bagdad," *Asia* 24 (August 1924). See also Christina Phelps Grant, *The Syrian Desert: Caravans, Travel and Exploration* (New York: MacMillan, 1938), 270–93.

43. *NECRB,* September 1949, 1.

44. Diary, October 8–20, 1923. RWL, "In Xenobia's City," *World Traveler* 18 (August 1926). Journal, October 1923.

45. Journal, October 1923. RWL to Roger MacBride, February 10, 1968.

46. RWL to Guy Moyston, undated [late July 1924]. Diary, November 20–December 10, 1923.

47. Diary, December 18–22, 1923.

8. A Missouri Interlude

1. Diary, December 27, 1923. RWL, "Autumn," *Harper's* 149 (June 1924): 82–87.

2. RWL to Guy Moyston, January 14, 1924. Diary, January 10, 1924.

3. RWL to Guy Moyston, January 19, and February 9, 1924.

4. RWL to Guy Moyston, February 9, 1924; undated [August 1924], beginning "It's good to hear. . . ."

5. Diary, January 10, and February 2, 11, 1924. RWL to Guy Moyston, February 9, and March 3, 1924.

6. Diary, January 3, 8, February 5, 9, March 25, and June 29, 1924. RWL to Guy Moyston, January 26, 1924.

7. Diary, March 25, and June 20–24, 29, 1924. A series of undated letters to Moyston can be inferred to date from July and August of 1924; see especially the letter beginning "It's good to hear. . . ."

8. RWL to Guy Moyston, January 22, February 9, July 9, 10, and August 7, 25, 1924; undated [August 1924], beginning "There isn't any . . ."; undated [August 1924], beginning "Your reply. . . ."

9. RWL to Guy Moyston, undated [August 1924], beginning "and utterly comfy. . . ."

10. RWL to Guy Moyston, July 24, 1924; undated [August 1924], beginning "and utterly comfy . . ."; undated [August 1924], beginning "But how can I. . . ."

11. RWL to Guy Moyston, undated [July 1924], beginning "Wishing for something . . ."; undated [July 1924], beginning "And now another . . ."; undated [August 1924], beginning "Have you seen. . . ."

12. RWL to Guy Moyston, August 25, 1924, and undated [August 1924], beginning " 'Active Service' is a JOY. . . ." Diary, September 17, 22, 26, 27, 1924. Journal, October 1, 1924.

13. RWL to Guy Moyston, December 27, 1924. RWL to LIW, November 12, 23, 1924.

14. The *Missouri Ruralist* articles ran several times a year from 1911 until 1924. See also RWL to Guy Moyston, undated [August 1924], beginning "About the double by-line. . . ."

15. RWL to LIW, November 12, 23, 1924, and undated [November 1924], beginning "Check enclosed. . . ." Mama Bess's article, "My Ozark Kitchen," appeared in *Country Gentleman*, January 17, 1925, 19–20. A similar article, "The Farm Dining Room," appeared in the June 13, 1925, issue of the same journal (20–21), for the same $150 fee.

16. RWL to Guy Moyston, undated (inscription "24-12-24" apparently in Moyston's hand).

17. William T. Anderson, "Laura Ingalls Wilder and Rose Wilder Lane: The Continuing Collaboration," *South Dakota History* 16 (Summer 1986): 91–92. RWL to Guy Moyston, January 7, 12, 14, 1925.

18. RWL, "Hill-Billy Comes to Town," *Country Gentleman*, January 17, 1925. RWL to Guy Moyston, January 16, 20, 1925.

19. RWL to Guy Moyston, February 11, 25, and April 7, 1925.

20. RWL, "A Place in the Country," *Country Gentleman*, March 14, 1925.

21. RWL, "If I Could Live My Life Over Again." RWL to Guy Moyston, February 17, 25, 1925.

22. RWL to Guy Moyston, January 17, 1925 (one daytime letter, typed; one night letter in pencil).

23. RWL to Guy Moyston, January 17 (handwritten), and February 9, 1925. The sketch for the story is on a page with a thematic poem in the Manuscript Series (Poetry) in the Hoover Library. Rose's concern for Moyston's health is a running motif through her letters of this year.

24. RWL to Guy Moyston, April 25, May 2, July 27, and November 7, 1925.

25. RWL to Guy Moyston, April 19, May 30, and June 3, 1925. *He Was a Man* (New York: Harper, 1925) was published in England as *Gordon Blake*. See pp. 302, 353, 359.

26. RWL to Guy Moyston, February 17, 1925; undated [April 1925], beginning "I'm awfully lonesome. . . ." RWL to Fremont Older, November 25, 1926.

27. RWL to Guy Moyston, June 5, 14, and July 11, 1925.

28. RWL to Guy Moyston, July 18, 25, 27, 1925.

29. RWL to Guy Moyston, July 3, 25, August 12, and September 5, 1925.

30. RWL to Guy Moyston, July 27, August 2, 30, and December 1, 9, 1925. Margaret Sanger, *An Autobiography* (New York: Norton, 1938), 364. Emily Taft Douglas, *Margaret Sanger: Pioneer of the Future* (New York: Holt, Rinehart and Winston, 1970), 183–86. David M. Kennedy, *Birth Control in America: The Career of Margaret Sanger* (New Haven: Yale University Press, 1970), 183.

31. RWL to Guy Moyston, May 23, June 8, and July 25, 1925. Helen Boylston's diaries were published as "Coming of Age," *Atlantic Monthly* 136 (September–November 1925).

32. RWL to Guy Moyston, October 31, and November 8, 1925; January 17, 1927. RWL to Haders, November 25, 1925. Journal, 1925. Rose recalled the driving incident in letters to Frank Meyer (October 6, 1953) and Jasper Crane (July 20, 1959), misdating the event in both letters.

33. RWL to Guy Moyston, December 4, 12, 17, 1925.

34. Journal, "New Year's Resolutions for 1926," December 30, 1925. RWL to Guy Moyston, January 3, 7, 1926.

35. "Across the Editor's Desk," *Sunset* 47 (August 1925): 53. The editor has obviously cut up and rearranged passages from the original letter; I have reassembled them in what seems an appropriate order. RWL to Guy Moyston, September 5, 1925.

36. Diary, January 8–10, 13, February 12, 1926.

37. Diary, January 8, 1926. RWL to Guy Moyston, February 21, 1926.

38. RWL to Guy Moyston, undated [March 14, 1926], beginning "Please don't misunderstand. . . ." A draft of his reply, dated March 15, exists among Rose's letters to him; apparently it was mistakenly gathered into the batch of letters he subsequently returned to her. The notebook containing the definitions seems to be from 1924.

9. The Albanian Experiment

1. RWL to Guy Moyston, April 1, 10, 19, and May 1, 1926. Diary, April 6, and July 23, 1926.

2. RWL to Guy Moyston, April 10, 1926.

3. RWL, "I, Rose Wilder Lane . . . ," 42–43, 140.

4. Diary, April 7, 1926. RWL to Clarence Day, June 19, 1926.

5. RWL to Clarence Day, June 19, 1926. RWL to Guy Moyston, July 4, 1926. Diary, June 5–6, and July 1, 1926.

6. Diary, July 5–6, 26–27, 29, 1926. RWL to Guy Moyston, July 26, and August 1, 1926.

7. RWL, *The Discovery of Freedom* (New York: John Day, 1943), 48–51; quoted in *Travels with Zenobia: Paris to Albania by Model T Ford*, ed. William Holtz (Columbia: University of Missouri Press, 1983), 16–18. An early version of the story is in a letter to Guy Moyston (August 18, 1926).

8. RWL to Guy Moyston, July 12, 1926. Helen Boylston, "Still the Land of the Free," *Forum* 89 (March 1933): 310–17.

9. Boylston, "Still the Land of the Free," 310.

10. RWL to Guy Moyston, May 5, 1926.

11. Diary, August 15, 18, 20, 1926. RWL to Guy Moyston, July 4, and August 18, 1926.

12. Both versions of the journal are in the Hoover Library. The version for Mama Bess was probably a revision several months after arrival; it was read in Mansfield in the week of January 20, 1927, according to the *Mansfield Mirror* of that date.

13. Diary, October 11, 1926. RWL to LIW, September 25, 1926.

14. RWL to LIW, October 7, 1926. RWL to George Palmer, September 11, 1926.

15. RWL to W. H. Briggs, September 27, 1926 (Columbia University Library). RWL to Guy Moyston, October 21, and November 5, 11, 1926.

16. RWL to LIW, October 7, 1926. RWL to Guy Moyston, October 16, 1926. RWL to George Bye, January 31, 1937.

17. RWL to Guy Moyston, November 11, 1926.

18. Unpublished journal, "My Albanian Garden," November 1, 3, 8, 1926. Diary, February 23, 1927.

19. RWL to Fremont Older, November 25, 1926. RWL to Guy Moyston, November 9, 11, 1926.

20. Diary, November 24, and December 27, 1926; January 17, 1927. RWL to Guy Moyston, September [20?], October 7, 16, 21, and November 26, 1926.

21. Diary, November 23, 27, and December 23, 1926. RWL to Guy Moyston, December 28, 1926.

22. RWL to Guy Moyston, January 5, 27, 1927. Unpublished manuscript, "Notes for an Albanian Garden," February 1, 1927. RWL to Clarence Day, September 10, 1927.

23. "Notes for an Albanian Garden," January 13, 1927.

24. RWL, "Yarbwoman," Harper's 133 (July 1927): 210–21. RWL, "How I Wrote 'Yarbwoman,'" The Writer 40 (May 1928): 143–45. RWL to Clarence Day, September 3, 1927. Diary, February 2, 23, 14, April 7, and May 7, 25, 1927. Journal, June 5, 1927. RWL to Guy Moyston, March 5, 1927.

25. RWL to Guy Moyston, January 27, 1927.

26. RWL to Guy Moyston, March 7, and July 10, 1927. RWL to Dorothy Thompson, April 16, 1927.

27. Diary, July 3–8, 1927. RWL to Guy Moyston, July 10, 1927.

28. RWL to Almanzo Wilder, July 28, 1927; quoted in Holtz, Travels with Zenobia, 102–10.

29. Diary, July 30–August 25, 1927. RWL to Guy Moyston, September 2, 1927.

30. RWL to Guy Moyston, May 30, and September 6, 1927. RWL to Clarence Day, September 3, 1927. Diary, August 27, and October 14, 1927.

31. A description of her Albanian landlord's family to Moyston (March 5, 1927) reappears in an undated letter to Dorothy Thompson; a description of her auto trip and arrest in a July 10, 1927, letter to Moyston reappears in a letter of the same day to Clarence Day and in a letter of November 29, 1927, to Fremont Older; a description of the firing of their cook in a July 10 letter to Moyston reappears in an undated letter to Clarence Day.

32. RWL to Guy Moyston, March 5, July 10, September 6, October 7, and November 9, 1927. Journal, October 9, 1927. RWL to Clarence Day, October 23, 1927.

33. The passage from Lavengro is in an undated letter [March 1927] to Dorothy Thompson. The discussion with Older runs through her letters of January 13, February 23, 26, July 14, 19, October 10, and November 29, 1927; the quoted passages are from October 10 and November 29.

34. RWL to Dorothy Thompson, undated [March 1927]. Diary, December 15, 1927.

35. Diary, September 7, and December 10, 1927. RWL to Dorothy Thompson, January 10, 1928. RWL to Fremont Older, April 20, 1928. Journal, December 1927.

36. RWL to Dorothy Thompson, undated [January 1927]; January 10, 21, 1928.

37. Journal, September 7, 1921; February 1, and October 17, 22, 1927.

38. RWL to Mr. Hart, July 19, 1928. Journal, December 28, 1927. Diary, September 13, and December 31, 1927; 1928 memoranda page; January 12, 20, 1928.

39. Diary, January 23–February 16, 1928.

40. Diary, February 16–March 11, 1928. RWL to Guy Moyston, undated [February 27?], and March 6, 1928.

10. Experiment at Rocky Ridge

1. Journal, February 6, 1928. Diary, March 11–31, 1928. A copy of the party invitation was furnished me by one of the recipients, Carrie Rogers.

2. Diary, May 6, and June 5, 1928.

3. Diary, April 17, 1928.

4. Journal, April 23, June 24, and June 26, 1928. G. Jean-Aubry, *Joseph Conrad: Life and Letters*, 2 vols. (Garden City, N.Y.: Doubleday, Page, 1927). RWL to Clarence Day, April 7, and June 26, 1928.

5. RWL to Carl Brandt, April 24, and May 6, 1928; undated [May 1928]; May 26, 1928. Clarence Day to RWL, January 22, and May 26, 1928. Floyd Dell to RWL, undated [late 1928]. Diary, August 28, and November 22, 1928. RWL, "One Thing in Common," *Ladies' Home Journal* 45 (September 1928); "Long Skirts," *Ladies' Home Journal* 50 (April 1933); "Good Roads," *Country Gentleman*, October 1928; "Harvest," *Harper's* 58 (January 1929): 226–38.

6. Journal, December 3, 7, 1928. RWL to Carl Brandt, May 26, 1928. Diary, April 8, 1928. RWL to Clarence Day, May 26, 1928. Carl Brandt to RWL, undated [October 4, 1928], beginning "I'm not what is called. . . ."

7. RWL to Sherwood Anderson, May 11, 1928. Diary, May 31, and June 3, 1928. Garet Garrett, "Hoover of Iowa and California," *SEP* 200 (June 2, 1928): 18. RWL to Fremont Older, June 8, and November 16, 1928.

8. RWL to Fremont Older, April 20, 1928. Diary, July 25, 1928. RWL to Dorothy Thompson, July 11, and July 13, 1928 (the first letter was unsent, the second a more general warning); March 12, and December 29, 1929.

9. RWL to Fremont Older, June 27, 1928.

10. The discussion runs through her letters to Fremont Older of April 20, May 19, 30, June 8, 27, July 14, and November 16, 25, 1928. The quotations are from the letters of May 19 and November 16.

11. RWL to Fremont Older, May 19, and November 16, 1928. RWL to Dorothy Thompson, March 12, 1929. G. Jean Aubry, *Joseph Conrad* 1:186.

12. RWL to Carl Brandt, May 6 [1928]; undated [1928], beginning "I have just finished . . ." (not sent). RWL to Dorothy Thompson, July 11, 13, 1928.

13. RWL to Fremont Older, November 16, 1928.

14. Diary, May 16, 1928. RWL to Carl Brandt, May 26, 1928.

15. Diary, February 29, April 8, 17, May 29, June 9, 17, and July 13, 14, 1928. RWL to Clarence Day, April 7, 1928. RWL to Dorothy Thompson, July 13, 1928.

16. Diary, July 31, August 23–28, September 12, October 11, 30, and November 1, 12, 1928.

17. Diary, July 5–10, 1928. *Mansfield Mirror*, April 5, May 10, 17, 24, July 5, 12, 19, August 30, September 20, and October 18, 1928.

18. Diary, July 30, October 20, November 18, and December 5–31, 1928. Journal, 1928.

19. Diary, memoranda page for 1929.

20. Diary, January 10, and February 1, 11, 13, 17, 1929.

21. RWL to Fremont Older, January 3, 23, April 12, May 6, and July 19, 28, 1929.

22. RWL to Rexh Meta, February 16, and October 7, 1929.

23. Diary, May 20, 21, June 8, and August 26, 1929. RWL to Fremont Older, September 4, 1929.

24. Diary, March 14, April 24, May 6, June 19, and November 16, 1929. RWL to Fremont Older, May 8, 1929. Journal, May 28, and June 1, 1929. Reading notes, May 1929.

25. RWL to Mary Margaret [McBride], undated [1929], beginning "I am truly sorry. . . ." An exchange of letters, mostly undated, from the spring and summer of 1929 reveals McBride's high esteem for Rose's abilities and her gratitude for her help,

as does McBride's autobiographical *A Long Way from Missouri* (New York: Putnam's, 1959), 176–77. RWL to Fremont Older, April 12, 1929. Diary, March 11, May 30, and June 24, 1929. RWL to Heywood Hale Broun, July 8, 1929. RWL to Dorothy Thompson, undated [February 1929]. The story of Dreiser's plagiarism is told in Mark Schorer, *Sinclair Lewis: An American Life* (New York: McGraw-Hill, 1961), 562–63, and Robert Elias, *Theodore Dreiser: Apostle of Nature* (New York: Knopf, 1949), 250–51.

26. Journal, July 13, 1929.

27. Diary, October 23–November 7, 1929. *Mansfield Mirror,* November 7, 1929. In 1934, Rose entered the date of the Great Crash as October 23, apparently misremembering.

11. The Ghost Returns

1. Diary, November 7, 1929, January 13, 23, April 12, and August 5, 15, 1930. RWL to Rexh Meta, June 7, 1930. Journal, May 14, 1932.

2. Diary, December 1–24, and year-end memorandum, 1929. RWL to Dorothy Thompson, December 29, 1929. RWL to Fremont Older, January 3, [1930] (mistakenly dated as 1929).

3. Diary, October 22, 1929, January 19, February 24, March 8, April 6–9, and May 7, 1930. RWL to Dorothy Thompson, December 29, 1929; March 8, 1930. Dorothy Thompson to RWL, February 19, and March 1, 1930. RWL to Fremont Older, February 2, 25, and April 2, 17, 1930.

4. RWL to Fremont Older, April 17, 1930; the argument runs through her letters of January 3, February 2, 25, and April 2, 1930.

5. Diary, May 11, and June 7–9, 1930. Reading notes, 1930. RWL, "Reynard Runs," *North American Review* 130 (September 1930): 354–60. RWL to Dorothy Thompson, March 8, 1930.

6. LIW to Aunt Martha [Carpenter], June 22, 1925. Diary, May 7–17, July 16, 28, and August 6, 14. RWL to LIW, February 16, 1931. Rose's version of "Pioneer Girl" exists in a clean copy in a Brandt and Brandt folder and in an earlier draft heavily edited in Rose's hand; a draft of "When Grandma Was a Little Girl" survives, also edited in Rose's hand.

For my account of the collaboration of mother and daughter in the production of the books of Laura Ingalls Wilder, I am indebted to Rosa Ann Moore, "Laura Ingalls Wilder's Orange Notebooks and the Art of the Little House Books," *Children's Literature* 4 (1975): 105–19, and "Laura Ingalls Wilder and Rose Wilder Lane: The Chemistry of Collaboration," *Children's Literature in Education* 11 (Autumn 1980): 101–9. Moore's work has been carried forward by William T. Anderson in "The Literary Apprenticeship of Laura Ingalls Wilder," *South Dakota History* 13 (Winter 1983): 285–331, and "Laura Ingalls Wilder and Rose Wilder Lane: The Continuing Collaboration," *South Dakota History* 16 (Summer 1986): 89–143. Moore had only limited access to the Laura Ingalls Wilder manuscripts, however, and no access to Rose's diaries. Anderson's work is more thorough, but his two articles have been limited to the early manuscripts. My interpretation of the record differs significantly from these studies, which, I believe, minimize Rose's contribution to her mother's books and attribute an inordinate level of talent to her mother.

7. Diary, July 16, 28–29, 31, August 6, 14, 17, 27, and September 2, 1930.

8. Diary, September 2, 10, 14–15, 20, 27, 1930. Fremont Older to RWL, July 16, 1930.

9. RWL to Rexh Meta, September 17, 1930. Diary, October 1, 15, 1930.

10. RWL to LIW, undated [November 19, 1930], beginning "LHJ has turned down. . . ." Diary, October 17, 18, and November 2, 1930.

11. Diary, November 5–7, 1930. RWL to LIW, n. 10 above.

12. Diary, November 6, 1930; January 6, 16, 24, 27, 31, February 3, 26, March 2, 26,

April 4, 24, May 21, and June 12, 1931. RWL to Rexh Meta, March 23, 1931. Of the six or more manuscripts she worked over for Lowell Thomas, only four were published: *Rolling Stone: The Life and Adventures of Arthur Radclyffe Dugmore* (Garden City, N.Y.: Doubleday, Doran, 1931), *This Side of Hell: Dan Edwards, Adventurer* (Garden City, N.Y.: Doubleday, Doran, 1932), *Old Gimlet Eye: The Adventures of Smedley D. Butler, as Told to Lowell Thomas* (New York: Farrar and Rinehart, 1933), and *Born to Raise Hell: The Life Story of Tex O'Reilly, Soldier of Fortune, as Told to Lowell Thomas* (Garden City, N.Y.: Doubleday, Doran, 1936).

13. Marian Fiery to LIW, February 12, 1931. RWL to LIW, February 16, 1931. Diary, February 15, 1931.

14. Diary, March 13, 16, 26, 1931. Mary Margaret McBride to RWL, undated [1930], beginning "You've no idea. . . ." George Bye to RWL, March 19, and October 2, 1931. RWL to George Bye, September 25, and November 9, 1931.

15. Diary, April 24, and May 8–27, 1931; memorandum, end of May 1931. RWL to Marian Fiery, May 27, 1931.

16. Diary, February 20, June 6, 12, 19, 29, July 5, 18, August 15, and September 1, 4, 6, 10, 1931. Mary Margaret McBride to RWL, undated [early September 1931], beginning "Well, I said this time. . . ." RWL to Rexh Meta, March 23, and May 27, 1931. George Bye to RWL, May 4, 1931.

17. Diary, November 6–19, 1931. Fremont Older to RWL, January 18, 1932. George Bye to RWL, October 27, 1931. RWL to George Bye, December 26, 1931. Alexandra Tolstoi to RWL, December 13, 1931 (JOB Collection).

18. Diary, November 6–20, and December 1, 3, 1931. RWL to Rexh Meta, December 19, 1931. Journal, May 14, 1932.

19. Diary, November 26, and December 9–10, 1931. Marian Fiery to RWL, December 4 [1931]. Virginia Kirkus, "The Discovery of Laura Ingalls Wilder," *Hornbook Magazine* 29 (December 1953): 428.

20. Diary, December, 5, 14, 19, 21, and end-of-year memorandum, 1931. RWL to Rexh Meta, December 19, 1931. Rose's annual summary of her finances for 1927–1932 is in her journal for 1927.

21. Diary, January 7, 18, 20–22, 29, February 6, 10, 12, 29, March 6, 8, 16, 28, and April 7, 11, 22, 1932. RWL to George Bye, January 9, 1932.

22. Diary, April 7, 11, 22, 1931. "Old Maid," *SEP* 205 (July 23, 1932). The long excerpts are from her journal for 1932.

23. Diary, March 6, May 9–30, June 3, and August 12–15, 1931. RWL to Marian Fiery, undated [early November, 1931], beginning "Thank you so much. . . ." RWL to George Bye, May 8, 1932. Graeme Lorimer to George Bye, April 15, 1932.

24. RWL to George Bye, April 25, May 8, and July 30, 1932. George Bye to RWL, April 28, and August 9, 1932.

25. Diary, April 18, May 4, 9, 28, June 3, 10, 16, July 6, end-of-month memorandum, and August 1, 10, 12, 18, 28, 1932. Journal, June 2, 1932. Journal, 1927, summary of finances for 1927–1932.

26. Diary, August 6, and September 6, 22, 1932. Anderson, "The Continuing Collaboration," 104.

12. Courage

1. RWL to Clarence Day, June 6, 1928.

2. Dorothy Thompson to RWL, July 23 [1928]. RWL to Dorothy Thompson, August 14, 1928. Forster had actually written, "Curiosity is one of the lowest of the human faculties" (*Aspects of the Novel* [New York: Harcourt Brace, 1927], 131).

3. *Let the Hurricane Roar*, 121–22, 128–29. Journal, memoranda page for January 1931. RWL to Eleanor Hubbard Garst, *Better Homes and Gardens* 12 (December 1933): 19.

4. Undated postcard, RWL to LIW. RWL to Frank Meyer, June 6, 1955. Journal, April 1932. Reading notes for 1932.

5. Journal, December 23, 1932.

6. Diary, October 7, 1931.

7. Journal, June 5, 1932.

8. Diary, January 13, 19, 22, February 2, 5, 19, and March 2, 19, 1933. William T. Anderson describes the revision in detail in "Laura Ingalls Wilder and Rose Wilder Lane: The Continuing Collaboration," 133–39.

9. Journal, January 23, 29, 1933. Interview with Irene Lichty LeCount, October 3, 1981. Anderson,"The Continuing Collaboration," 109–10.

10. *"Let the Hurricane Roar,"* *SEP,* March 4, 1933, 22. Diary, June 23, 1933. Reading notes, January 11, 1933.

11. Diary, February 10, 1933. Journal, January 23, February 11, 13, 18, 20, 28, May 9, April 29, May 20, 23, 26, and June 25–26, 1933.

12. Journal, January 23, 1933.

13. Journal, April 5, 1933. RWL to George Bye, August 26, 1932. Catherine Brody to George Bye, September 2, 1932. RWL to Upton Sinclair, March 11, 1932 (Lilly Library, Indiana University). Dorothy Thompson to RWL, June 8, and July 28, 1932.

14. Journal, January 7, February 13, and May 3, 1933.

15. Journal, January 30, and July 9, 1933.

16. Journal, April 10, 1933. Diary, June 5, 1933.

17. Federal Income Tax Statement for 1932. Journal, May 14, 1932. Diary, March 4, and April 3, 1933. Journal, February 4–5, 1933. RWL to Mr. [Jasper] Spock, February 3, 1933. RWL to George Bye, March 20, and June 15, 1933.

18. Journal, June 2, 1932. Footnote to her journal entry for April, 1932. Journal, March 17, 1933.

19. RWL to Dorothy Thompson, August 3, 1932.

20. "Wheat and the Great American Desert," *SEP* 206 (September 23, 1933). Diary, July 24, August 9, 11, and September 24, 1933. Journal, June 28, July 16, and September 25, 1933. T. B. Costain to George Bye, June 30, 1933. RWL to George Bye, August 24, and September 3, 4, 1933. Catherine Brody to George Bye, August 29, 1933.

21. Diary, August 3, 1930; memoranda pages for March, and May 1, 1933. RWL to Virginia Brastow, December 16, 1933. RWL to Fremont Older, April 11, 1934. RWL to George Bye, January 28, 1934. RWL to Rexh Meta, January 5, 1935. Journal, April 8, and September 25, 1933.

22. Journal, September 26, 1933. RWL to Rexh Meta, January 6, 1935. RWL to Virginia Brastow, undated [late 1935, early 1936]. RWL to Joan Clark, April 4, 1961.

23. Diary, October 28–29, November 20 (memoranda page), and December 6, 1933. Journal, September 26, October 30, November 16, and December 16, 29, 1933. Journal, February 19, 1934. Dawn [Mundy?] to RWL, December 10, 1934. Interview with Al Turner, September 22, 1991.

24. Diary, memoranda page for December, 1933. Journal, final entry (undated) for 1933.

13. "Credo"

1. The details run continuously through Rose's diary for 1934; a sampling: January 18, February 15, March 9, 24, April 14, 30, May 9, 15, 31, June 7, and September 14, 20, 29. Journal, March 21, 1934.

2. Journal, February 14, 16, 1934.

3. Diary, February 1, March 5, 10, 17, May 19, 22, June 10–25, and September 7, 1934. RWL to Fremont Older, April 11, 1934. Journal, February 26, and March 20, 1934. R. B. Selvidge to LIW, July 5, 1933. Helen M. McFarland to LIW, June 19, 1933. Grant

Foreman to RWL, March 26, 27, 1933. Donald Zochert, *Laura* (Chicago: Regnery, 1976), 37. Zochert has written me that the story of the trip to look for the homesite came from a Mansfield resident.

4. Diary, June 24, July 4–8, 17, 21, 25, August 27, November 5, 30, and December 13 (end-of-year memorandum), 1934. RWL to Talbot Mundy, March 19, 1929 (Lilly Library, Indiana University). Talbot Mundy to RWL, April 24, June 12, 25, and July 2, 1934. RWL to George Bye, June 23, and August 17, 1934. Talbot Mundy, *Tros of Samothrace* (New York: Appleton-Century, 1934).

5. Diary, October 11, 29–30, and November 3, 26, 1934. Journal, February 15, 1934.

6. Diary, December 30, and end-of-year memoranda, 1934; January 6, 1935. RWL to Fremont Older, January 21, 1935.

7. Diary, January 11, 16, 28, 30, 1935. Corinne Murray to RWL, October 24, 1935. The anecdote regarding Catherine Brody was related to me by Irene Lichty LeCount of Mansfield. Interview with Al Turner, September 22, 1991.

8. Unpublished manuscript, "The Value of Hard Work."

9. RWL, Preface to *Old Home Town*, 23–24. See also RWL, "I Live in a Small Town," *Pictorial Review* 31 (February 1930). I have here adapted portions of an earlier article: William Holtz, "Rose Wilder Lane's *Old Home Town*," *Studies in Short Fiction* 26 (Fall 1989): 479–87.

10. Diary, March 29, April 29, and July 21, 1935.

11. Diary, February 1–2, 26, March 8, 15, 21, May 13, 18, and year-end memoranda page, 1935. George Bye to RWL, April 26, 1935. RWL to Fremont Older, January 21, 1935.

12. RWL to an unnamed correspondent, May 25–27, 1935; written perhaps to Talbot Mundy, the letter was not sent.

13. Journal, August 30, 1931. Diary, July 21, 1935.

14. RWL to George Bye, May 2, 1935. Diary, September 1, 19, and October 11, 1935. *Mansfield Mirror*, September 5, 1935.

15. Robert McBride to RWL, February 20, and March 4, 1936. RWL to George Bye, February 25, June 28, and July 3, 1936. RWL to Tom Davin, July 28, 1936. Bye apparently offered the manuscript to Longmans, Green, but despite encouraging efforts from her editor there, she did not bring the book into a form Longmans could accept. RWL to George Bye, September 1, and October 19, 1936.

16. Diary, March 29, 1936.

17. Diary, November 6, 1934; July 24–August 9, 1935. *Mansfield Mirror*, August 1, 1935. Aside from the visit of Catherine Brody, the visit to Talbot Mundy, and a meeting with the poet John G. Niehardt at the Old English Inn at Lake Taneycomo, Rose had talked to no one at her own level since December of 1932 (Diary, April 13, 1935).

18. RWL to Virginia Brastow, March 8, 1935. RWL to Jasper Crane, January 30, 1957; September 1, 1961. Garet Garrett, "Saving Agriculture," *SEP* 208 (October 19, 1935); "Managed Agriculture" (November 2, 1935); "Plowing Up Freedom" (November 16, 1935).

19. RWL, "Who's Who—and Why," 30. Diary, August 22, and September 1, 1935. RWL to George Bye, January 11, 14, 20, 28, and May 2, 1936. Unsigned copy of a letter from a *Saturday Evening Post* editor to RWL.

20. RWL, "Credo," 5, 6, 30, 35. RWL to Guy Moyston, April 1 [1925]. The peasant she refers to was probably the Ivan in whose home she and Peggy Marquis visited and stayed the night: see Annette Marquis, "Two American Women in the Caucasus," *World Traveler* 16 (September 1924). Rose was visiting at Rocky Ridge Farm when John Reed helped form the Communist Labor Party in Chicago in September 1919 (Robert A. Rosenstone, *Romantic Revolutionary: A Biography of John Reed* [New York: Knopf, 1975], 354–55). She just might, though, have been at a meeting in his

presence in New York City earlier or later than that date. She knew Floyd Dell and others of the Croton-on-Hudson circle of which Reed was a part.

21. Diary, April 11, 1936. RWL to George Bye, March 6, August 8, and November 1, 1936. George Bye to George Horace Lorimer, March 16, 1936. Herbert Hoover to RWL, April 16, 1936.

22. The note from LIW is part of the manuscript of *On the Banks of Plum Creek*, in the Joint Collection, Western Historical Manuscript Collection, State Historical Society of Missouri, Columbia, Missouri. Diary, May 10, and July 15, 1936. RWL to LIW, September 21, 1936. LIW to George Bye, September 24, 1936.

23. Diary, July 15, 1936. Journal, August 10, 1940. LIW to RWL, June 25, 1936 (manuscript of *On the Banks of Plum Creek*; see n. 22 above). Both Mary Paxton Keeley (May 25, 1979) and Mrs. Ruth Freeman (October 3, 1981) have mentioned to me that Rose's mother disapproved of the Turner boys. Interview with Al Turner, September 22, 1991.

24. Diary, April 27, and May 7, 9, 1936. RWL to George Bye, July 23, and August 3, 9, 1936.

25. RWL to George Bye, April 1, August 3, 9, and October 13, 19, 1936. RWL to Mary Paxton Keeley, July 1, 12, 1936.

26. Norma Lee Browning, "'Little House' in Danbury," *Laura Ingalls Wilder Lore* 12 (December 1986): 8. At about this time, Rose did write an essay, never published, on the problems of high school teaching, referring quite specifically to the Turner boys ("What Has Happened to Education?").

27. RWL, "The Song without Words," *Ladies' Home Journal* 54 (March 1937). RWL to George Bye, October 19, 1936.

14. Between Two Worlds

1. RWL to Evelyn Wells, April 16, 1936 (Fremont Older Collection). RWL to Graeme Lorimer, October 23, 1937 (Historical Society of Pennsylvania).

2. RWL to George Bye, November 5, 1936, in which she copied portions of a letter to Garrett.

3. RWL to Virginia Brastow, September 22, 1935. Garret's undated letters to Rose can be dated approximately by internal references. The ones quoted begin "What I mean is . . ." and "All that is the matter. . . ." Rose's undated letter is a fragment beginning "Americans know no more. . . ." The April letter is dated April 7, 1937. Diary, April 21, 1937.

4. Diary, April 3, and June 11, 1937. RWL to George Bye, February 26, 1937.

5. RWL to George Bye, March 1, 1937. LIW and Almanzo Wilder to RWL, February 5, March 12, 20, 25, and April 14, 1937. The questionnaire is undated but clearly connected with this series of letters.

6. RWL to George Bye, November 5, 1936.

7. RWL to Frank Meyer, July 6, 1955. In two decades, the story gained some dramatically inaccurate statistics regarding the vote figures for Landon and Browder in the local elections, so the 632 petitioners may be an exaggeration as well (*Columbia [Missouri] Daily Tribune*, November 5, 1936, 5). But whatever the truth of the anecdote, its relevance is emotional rather than factual, an index of her sense of isolation.

8. Diary, April 15, 1937. RWL to George Bye, January 22, 31, 1937.

9. Diary, April 3, 1937. Ralph D. Morrison (New Mexico Military Institute) to RWL, December 11, 29, 1936; February 6, 1937; Col. D. C. Pearson (New Mexico Military Institute) to RWL, March 27, 1937. RWL to George Bye, May 20, and June 13, 1937. Interview with Al Turner, September 22, 1991. Obituary, Dr. Charles Clark, *Washington Sunday Star*, July 24, 1960.

10. Diary, April 14, 1937. RWL to George Bye, May 30, 1937. Journal, August 10, 1940.

11. LIW and Almanzo Wilder to RWL, February 5, March 12, 20, 23, 25, and April 14, 1937.

12. RWL, preface to *Free Land*. LIW to RWL, March 12, 1937.

13. RWL to LIW, October 11, 1937.

14. The manuscript of the Detroit talk, in LIW's hand, is in the Hoover Library. RWL to LIW, undated [November 1937], beginning "I'm so glad. . . ."

15. The relocation can be inferred from details in letters from LIW to RWL (March 12, 20, 23, 1937). The threat to burn the books is mentioned in a letter from Rose (December 19, 1937).

16. Undated letter cited in n. 14 above.

17. RWL to Mary Paxton Keeley, September 7, 1937.

18. John Turner to RWL, November 2, and December 13, 14, 1937, as well as several undated letters from Paris.

19. Rexh Meta to RWL, February 13, March 5, April 10, August 14, 23, October 27, November 2, 8, and December 9, 1937.

20. Adelaide Neall to George Bye, September 17, 1937. George Bye to Adelaide Neall, October 25, 1937. Bye Agency statement of income, December 9, 1937. RWL to LIW, December 19, 1937. The visit to Garrett can be inferred from one of his undated letters.

21. LIW to Berta Hader, September 11, 1937.

22. Ida Louise Raymond to LIW, December 18, 1937; LIW's note to Rose is on the back. RWL to LIW, December 20, 1937. The problematical nature of *The First Four Years* was first noted by Rosa Ann Moore in "Laura Ingalls Wilder's Orange Notebooks and the Art of the Little House Books."

23. RWL to LIW, December 19, 1937, and January 21, 1938. LIW to RWL, undated [January 1938], headed "Plum Creek" and beginning "There is only a little . . ."; January 25, 26, 28, and February 19, 1938; undated [February 1938], beginning "Laura was impatient. . . ."

15. *Free Land*, New Homes, Lost Sons

1. An account of the meeting of the South Dakota Society of New York is in a clipping from the De Smet newspaper. The clipping itself is not dated, but it dates the meeting as March 12, 1938. Rose followed the book's popularity in the *New York Herald Tribune*'s Sunday Book Section, where it remained on the best-seller list through July 31, 1938. The editorial by Ralph Thompson recommending a Pulitzer appeared in the May 4, 1938, *New York Times*. The prize in fiction for 1939 would, however, go to Marjorie Kinnan Rawlings's *The Yearling*.

2. *Free Land* (New York: Longmans, Green, 1938), 331.

3. Fred T. Marsh, review of *Free Land*, *New York Times Book Review*, May 15, 1938; reply by RWL, June 5, 1938. Readers in De Smet apparently thought Rose had exaggerated the pioneers' difficulty, giving her hero more trials singly than any one settler could have experienced (Aubrey Sherwood to William Holtz, September 2, 1980).

4. *Free Land*, 6, 330–32.

5. *Free Land*, 7, 29.

6. Burton Rascoe, "We, the People," *Newsweek* 11 (May 9, 1938): 30 (Copyright 1938, Newsweek, Inc. All rights reserved. Reprinted by permission).

7. RWL to Burton Rascoe, May 9, 1938 (University of Pennsylvania Library).

8. RWL to Adelaide Neall, July 23, 1937.

9. Diary, February 5, 6, 10–12, and April 12, 14, 1938. Interview with Ruth Levine, April 12, 1991. Journal, August 10, 1940. RWL to Mary Paxton Keeley, January 25, and April 19, 1938. Rose Wilder Lane, "My House in the Country," *Woman's Day*, May 1941. Norma Lee Browning, "Some Scattered Memories of Rose Wilder Lane," *Laura Ingalls Wilder Lore* 12 (December 1986): 7.

10. Diary, August 2–16, 1938.

11. Diary, May 4, 1939; *Time* 33 (June 12, 1939): 47–51.

12. RWL to William Allen White, February 1, 1938 (Library of Congress). RWL to George Bye, March 29, 1939.

13. RWL, "The American Revolution, 1939," *SEP* 211 (January 7, 1939): 50. Herbert Hoover to RWL, January 5, 1939. RWL to Herbert Hoover, January 11, 1939.

14. RWL's articles in support of the Ludlow Amendment include "Who Shall Say When We Shall Go to War?" *Good Housekeeping* 108 (March 1939): 169–70; "Why I Am for the People's Vote on War," *Liberty,* April 1, 1939, 11–12; "War: What Women in America Can Do to Prevent It," *Woman's Day,* April 1989, 4; "We Who Have Sons," *Woman's Day,* December 1939. Herbert Hoover to RWL, January 5, 1939. RWL to Herbert Hoover, April 13, 1939. RWL to Mary Paxton Keeley, September 19, 1939. LIW to RWL, April 2, 1939. *New York Times,* May 11, 1939.

15. John Turner to RWL, August 27, and December 2, 1939; undated, beginning "I don't suppose . . ." [fall 1938] and "Please don't be alarmed . . ." [December 1938]; telegram, September 8, 1938. LIW to RWL, January 10, 1939. RWL to George Bye, November 1, 1938.

16. "Come into My Kitchen," *Woman's Day* (June 4, 1939): 49. *New York Times* (December 15, 1939). Alice Lambertson to William Holtz, June 30, 1987. Browning, "'Little House' in Danbury," 8–10.

17. Norma Lee Browning to William Holtz, June 2, 1991. Diary, January 13, and August 11–September 1, 1939. Journal, June–July, 1939. RWL to George Bye, June 27, 1939. RWL to Mary Paxton Keeley, June 17, 1939. RWL, "Minnesota Farm Boy," *Woman's Day* (July 1940). Adelaide Neall to George Bye, September 20, 1939. The manuscript of "The Forgotten Man" and the notes regarding McCrary's life are in the Hoover Library.

18. Diary, September 5, 6, October 18, 24, 31, November 4, and December 26, 1939.

19. Diary, November 12, 1939. LIW to RWL, May 23, 24, and June 1, 3, 1939.

20. LIW to RWL, January 27, and March 17, 1939. A statement of income from George Bye reveals royalties to LIW of $2,251.41 for 1939.

21. LIW to George Bye, September 12, 1939.

22. RWL, "American Jews," *American Mercury* 45 (December 1938): 501–2. For Josef Bard, see chap. 10; RWL to Carl Brandt, May 26, 1928.

23. The Krivitsky articles ran in the *SEP* on April 15, 22, 29, June 17, August 5, September 30, and November 4, 1939; June 1, 1940. See also Isaac Don Levine, *Eyewitness to History* (New York: Hawthorn Books, 1973), chap. 9; Paul Wohl, "Walter Krivitsky," *Commonweal* 33 (February 14, 1941): 462–68; *New Masses,* May 9, 1939, p. 3, May 16, pp. 20–21, and May 30, p. 19; *Daily Worker,* May 11, 1939, 2. RWL to Dorothy Thompson, June 1, 1939. I have treated this affair more fully in *Dorothy Thompson and Rose Wilder Lane,* 149–64.

24. Rexh Meta to RWL, February 28, March 8, May 9, August 12, and November 20, 1938; May 20, and September 12, 1939; May 4, 1940.

25. Journal, August 10, 1940. RWL to Charles Clark, August 11, 1943. Norma Lee Browning to William Holtz, September 6, 1989.

26. The letter is undated, but John Turner remembers its occasion. Much of my material here is drawn from an interview, with John Turner, May 20, 1991.

16. War and *The Discovery of Freedom*

1. Diary, August 18, 25, 1939. Journal, May 10, 1939.

2. Journal, May 11, 1940. Interview with Ruth Levine, April 12, 1991.

3. Journal, May 19, 23, and June 15, 1940. RWL to Mary Paxton Keeley, January 12, 1940. The poem, "Coronation" by Martha Keller, was copied into the back page of her diary for 1940.

4. Journal, May 9, 1940.

5. Diary, March 7, 9–11, and April 23, 1940. LIW to George Bye, May 7, and June 21, 1940. The manuscript of "The Hard Winter" is in the Detroit Public Library.

6. RWL to George Bye, June 5, 1940. RWL to Mary Paxton Keeley, January 22, 1940. Journal, September 17, 1940.

7. Diary, September 19, 1939. Journal, August 10–12, and September 17, 1940.

8. Interviews with Ruth Levine (April 4, 1980) and Norma Lee Browning (April 8, 1980). Norma Lee Browning, "Some Scattered Memories of Rose Wilder Lane," 7. Journal, August 12, 14, and September 20, 1940.

9. RWL to Adelaide Neall, October 4, 1940 (Historical Society of Pennsylvania). George Bye to RWL, October 22, 1940. Interviews with Daniel Bierman (March 28, 1989) and Doris Lyman (April 4, 1989). Ernestine Evans to Berta Hader, August 3, 1953. Jane Burr to Floyd Dell, November 9, 1949.

10. RWL to George Bye, January 15, and June 30, 1941. George Bye to Norma Lee Browning, December 6, 1940. LIW to George Bye, July 3, 1941. A note on one of the penciled manuscripts indicates that Rose sent it to a typing service to be transcribed, yielding a typescript which she revised into a finished version.

11. LIW, *Little Town on the Prairie* (New York: Harper, 1941; Newly Illustrated Uniform Edition, 1953), 73–77. The manuscript that makes this comparison possible, and that reveals Rose's hand in almost every page of the published version, is in the Pomona (California) Public Library. A photocopy of this manuscript is also in the Detroit Public Library. For a more detailed demonstration of Rose's hand in the manuscript, see Appendix: The Ghost in the Little House Books.

12. RWL to George Bye, June 25, 1941. RWL to Herbert Hoover, January 26, 1943. *The Discovery of Freedom* remains in print in an edition by the Arno Press (1972) and is listed in the catalog of Laissez Faire Books, sponsored by the Libertarian Review Foundation.

13. RWL to George Bye, June 25, and December 19, 26, 1941; January 2, 1942; undated [March 1942], beginning "My angel agent. . . ." Diary, January 1–4, 1942.

14. Diary, April 10, 12, 15, 1942. RWL to Mary Paxton Keeley, July 19, and August 23, 1942.

15. RWL to George Bye, January 3, February 28, March 17, 18, 23, and November 19, 1942. RWL to Mary Paxton Keeley, January 11, July 19, August 23, September 22, and October 30, 1942. RWL to Dorothy Thompson, May 20, 1943.

16. RWL, *The Discovery of Freedom: Man's Struggle Against Authority* (New York: John Day, 1943; reprint, New York: Arno Press, 1971), vii, xii, xv, 3, 262.

17. Joseph Mau, *Book Week*, April 11, 1943, 4. Bernard De Voto, *Weekly Book Review,* March 14, 1943, 4. Albert Jay Nock, quoted in Roger MacBride's introduction to a 1971 edition of *Discovery of Freedom;* I have not been able to trace the original publication. RWL to Herbert Hoover, September 5, 1942 (with his attached note); February 6, 23, 1943. Herbert Hoover to John Walsh, February 27, 1943 (Hoover Library).

17. Patriotic Subversion

1. RWL to Mary Paxton Keeley, January 26, 1943. George Bye to Norma Lee Browning, January 13, 1943. RWL to Jasper Crane, May 5, 1951.

2. LIW to George Bye, May 14, 1943.

3. RWL to Herbert Hoover, October 5, 1942. Rose Wilder Lane, "West from Danbury," *The Connecticut Nutmeg* (New Canaan, Connecticut), June 23, 1938, 1. RWL to Dorothy Thompson, May 20, 1943.

4. Her column in the *Pittsburgh Courier* ran from January 9, 1943 to September 8, 1945; the remarks on rationing are from January 9, 1943; on race, February 13, 20, 27, 1943; on publisher Robert Vann, October 30, 1943.

5. RWL to Jasper Crane, March 21, 1965. RWL to Mary Paxton Keeley, January 26, and February 2, 1943; February 4, 1945.

6. She appeared on the NBC program "Wake Up America" on April 4, 1943. The reference to German children, as her pamphlet makes clear, assumes a defeated Germany being reeducated by American conquerors. Her many scattered remarks on Social Security are epitomized in letters to Jasper Crane, January 1, 1955, and May 9, 1958.

7. The details of this episode come from the FBI file on Rose Wilder Lane, obtained under the Freedom of Information Act. *What Is This—the Gestapo?* (New York: National Economic Council, 1943). The story received two columns, with Rose's picture, in the *Washington Post,* August 10, 1943, and shorter notices in many other papers, as well as several editorials. Her letter to J. Edgar Hoover is dated September 9, 1943. Her talk to the Lions' Club was reported in the *Danbury News-Times,* September 10, 1943.

8. Diary, April 7, 1943. RWL to Jasper Crane, February 21, 1962. Attorneys Pullman and Comley to George Bye, December 6, 1943. Jasper Spock (for George Bye) to RWL, November 22, 1943. Receipt to RWL from George Bye, November 18, 1943. Sinclair Lewis's special interest in *Let the Hurricane Roar* is described in William Holtz, "Sinclair Lewis, Rose Wilder Lane, and the Midwestern Short Novel," *Studies in Short Fiction* 24 (Winter 1987): 41–48.

The newspaper article, by Helen Worden, was printed in the *New York World-Telegram* for April 3, 1944; it was picked up and condensed on the front page of the *Los Angeles Times* of April 4. The clipping was forwarded to the FBI director on April 22, but on this occasion the Bureau took no action.

9. "Mrs. Lane's Sitdown Strike," *New Republic* 110 (April 24, 1944): 553.

10. RWL to Herbert Hoover, August 12, 1945. *Danbury News-Times,* July 25, and August 6, 1945; April 26, 1946.

11. RWL to Jasper Crane, May 29, 1951.

12. RWL to Mary Paxton Keeley, March 23, 1945. RWL, "Force Won't Keep the Peace," *Woman's Day* (February 1945): 29.

13. The story, by Charles Cotthart, made the news wires again; I quote here from a clipping from the *Kansas City Star,* October 25, 1946.

14. RWL to Mary Paxton Keeley, June 27, 1945. RWL to Herbert Hoover, May 30, and June 12, 27, 1945; October 18, and November 8, 1946.

15. Interview with Roger MacBride, May 7, 1979.

18. Cold War Warrior

1. RWL to Jasper Crane, July 31, 1963. She edited the *National Economic Council Review of Books* (*NECRB*) from October 1945 until November 1950. Her remarks on the nihilism of modern literature are from the July 1950 issue. Roger MacBride has shared his reminiscences with me in a letter of May 21, 1991.

2. Her correspondence with Jasper Crane has been edited by Roger MacBride as *The Lady and the Tycoon* (Caldwell, Idaho: Caxton, 1973).

3. *NECRB,* July, November, and December 1946; March and November 1948; February, June, and July 1950.

4. Seymour Martin Lipset and Earl Raab, *The Politics of Unreason: Right-Wing Extremism in America, 1790–1977,* 2d ed. (Chicago: University of Chicago Press, 1977), 461.

5. *NECRB,* August–September 1947. (The letter, from Texas Technical College, September 11, 1947, ended up in Rose's FBI file.) RWL to Herbert Hoover, March 5, 1948. Herbert Hoover to Donald Tressider, October 15, 1947 (Hoover Library, PPI files).

6. Rose mentions the Dorcas Society a number of times in her letters to Jasper Crane; the quotation is from November 4, 1962. Just as she seemed little interested in

the excesses of Senator McCarthy, so had she shown no interest in the anti-Semitic sentiments of Father Coughlin in the 1930s. Nor would the vague conspiratorial theories of the John Birch Society attract her.

7. Joseph P. Kamp, *We Must Abolish the United States* (New York: Hallmark, 1950); the title comes from an address by Mortimer J. Adler (p. 39). *NECRB*, October 1950. RWL to Jasper Crane, September 5, 1963. Kamp had been called before congressional committees at least twice before; a fair sample of his style can be found in his testimony in the proceedings of the House Committee to Investigate Campaign Expenditures (78th Congress), September 20, and October 6, 1945. My preliminary inquiries revealed a fifteen-hundred-page FBI file on the Constitutional Education League.

8. Merwin K. Hart, "Is Christianity to Die?" *Economic Council Newsletter,* no. 229 (December 15, 1949); Isaac Don Levine, "The Strange Case of Merwin K. Hart," *Plain Talk* 4 (February 1950): 1–9; Hart, "The Smear by *Plain Talk,*" *Economic Council Newsletter,* no. 229 (February 15, 1950). *NECRB*, January 1948; March 1950. RWL to Dorothy Thompson, September 25, 1960. RWL to Jasper Crane, October 18, 1963. Interview with Ruth Levine, April 4, 1980. The episode epitomizes the rancor of Right and Left in these years. A long fragment of a letter by Rose at this time recounts evidence of a spy from the Anti-Defamation League planted in the offices of the National Economic Council, stealing and photographing documents for Walter Winchell.

9. Journal, January 17, 1949. RWL to Jasper Crane, June 9, 1946; December 5, 1955. By 1955, Rose's memory had transferred the guard's saving call from the pastor to herself.

10. RWL to Jasper Crane, September 9, 1947; December 1, 1954; July 31, 1946. Jasper Crane to RWL, July 15, 1946. Her views on Ayn Rand are in letters to Crane of April 12, 1961, and March 13, 1963. The correspondence with Felix Morley is in his papers, collected in the Hoover Library. The notes and drafts toward a revision of *The Discovery of Freedom* filled a suitcase in Roger MacBride's possession; they have since been catalogued by the Hoover Library.

11. Irene Lichty LeCount mentioned the royalty checks as matters of local gossip. For approximate income, see chap. 19, n. 3. *Mansfield Mirror,* May 2, 1957.

12. LIW to George Bye, July 16, 1949. Ernestine Evans to Berta Hader, August 3, 1953. The scholars who first wrote of the collaboration between mother and daughter were Rosa Ann Moore and William T. Anderson, whose contributions to my own work have been noted earlier.

13. RWL to Jasper Crane, December 11, 1954, and May 9, 1958.

14. RWL to Jasper Crane, July 27, 1962. RWL to Herbert Hoover, February 27, 1954. Interview with Roger MacBride, May 7, 1979.

15. William T. Anderson and Irene Lichty LeCount have both reported to me about Rose's Mansfield visits in these years. RWL to Jasper Crane, January 5, 1957.

19. Mother Remembered

1. William T. Anderson reports this impression among those who helped Rose close Rocky Ridge Farm. He had also reported to me his conversations with Al Morgan. RWL to Charles and Joan Clark, December 26, 1957; August 26, 1960.

2. LIW to RWL, July 30, 1952. *Mansfield Mirror,* May 2, 1957.

3. RWL to Joan and Charles Clark, December 26, 1957, and January 5, 1960. RWL to Jasper Crane, July 10, 1959. George Bye's records show earnings for the LIW account of over twenty-six thousand dollars for 1957 (letter to Marian, January 17, 1958, George Bye file, JOB Collection). The estate of LIW came to over eighty-eight thousand dollars. "Come into My Kitchen," *Woman's Day* (October 1960): 60–61, 98, 99.

4. *Mansfield Mirror,* May 2, 1957. Roger MacBride to RWL, November 22, 1963; RWL

to Roger MacBride, August 4, 1968. Federal Income Tax Statement for 1967. RWL to Susie [MacBride], May 26, 1963. Interview with Irene Lichty LeCount, October 3, 1981.

5. The story regarding Stalin comes from a letter from RWL to Robert LeFevre, August 2, 1957. The other tales come from Roger MacBride.

6. RWL to Aubrey Sherwood, October 23, 1958. The death of her brother is mentioned in the manuscript of "The First Three Years and a Year of Grace," but Rose apparently had not yet read it.

7. RWL to Joan Clark, February 28, 1961. RWL to Dorothy Thompson, September 4, 25, October 19, and November 18, 1960. Dorothy Thompson to RWL, September 21, undated [early October], and December 8, 1960.

8. Obituary for John Guy Moyston, *New York Times*, May 3, 1962; a clipping is in the Hader Papers. RWL to Dorothy Thompson, November 18, 1960. RWL to Robert LeFevre, August 2, 1957. RWL to Norma Lee Browning, June 19, 1965. Interview with Ruth Levine, April 4, 1980.

9. RWL to Joan Clark, December 10, 1961. Frances Lane Harris to Laura Ingalls Wilder Museum, August 6, 1974 (courtesy of Irene Lichty LeCount).

10. In her determination to avoid all possible taxable income, she simply gave her work to MacBride; the income was then his to pay taxes on. These matters run throughout the correspondence in these years (e.g., RWL to Susie [MacBride], April 18, 1963; RWL to Roger MacBride, June 19, and November 8, 1965). The chicken pie recipe has been printed as a pamphlet by the Laura Ingalls Wilder–Rose Wilder Lane Home Association. I have profited by conversations with Susan Ford Hammaker.

11. RWL to Jasper Crane, September 10, and December 28, 1960; April 24, October 25, and December 4, 1963; November 20, 1964; November 18, 1966.

12. RWL to Merwin K. Hart, November 10, 1960. RWL to Jasper Crane, February 14, 1961; December 4, 1963. RWL to Joan Clark, August 20, 1960; February 28, 1961; December 29, 1963. RWL to Irene Lichty LeCount, January 11, 1963.

13. RWL to Joan Clark, July 11, 1958; March 11, 1960; February 28, 1961. RWL to Jasper Crane, September 2, 10, and December 29, 1960; October 25, and December 4, 1963; November 18, 20, 1964.

14. RWL to Roger MacBride, October 29, 1964. RWL to Jasper Crane, November 20, 1964. Roger MacBride to RWL, November 22, 1963. *Newsweek*, July 20, 1980, 26.

15. RWL to Roger MacBride, November 22, 1965. Roger MacBride to RWL, December 9, 1965. RWL to Dorothy Thompson, November 18, 1960. Roger MacBride to RWL, July 1, 1965. RWL to Roger MacBride, October 29, 1967.

16. There are files of correspondence with Lefevre, Watts, and Sennholz in the Hoover Library; her regard for Sennholz and Hamilius is expressed in letters to Jasper Crane: October 3, 1954; July 20, 1955; October 8, 1957; August 23 and September 10, 1960. Hans Sennholtz to William Holtz, April 12, 1991. On the Freedom School, see RWL to Joan and Charles Clark, September 24, 1958; RWL to Jasper Crane, September 28, 1958, and July 2, 1962; *Colorado Springs Gazette-Telegraph*, August 4, 1962; and LeFevre's foreword to the Arno Press edition of *The Discovery of Freedom* (New York, 1972). Carl Watner, *Robert LeFevre: "Truth Is Not a Half-way Place"* (Gramling, S.C.: The Voluntaryist, 1988), 137, 159, 188, 197–99.

17. *Colorado Springs Gazette-Telegraph*, August 4, 1962. Carl Watner, *Robert LeFevre*, 199, 208. Interview with Norma Lee Browning, April 8, 1980.

18. RWL, *Woman's Day Book of American Needlework* (New York: Simon and Schuster, 1963), 78, 144, 145, 164, 165.

19. RWL, *American Needlework*, 10, 11, 14, 99, 100.

20. Interview with Irene Lichty LeCount, October 3, 1981. RWL to Irene Lichty, August 15, 1963.

21. LIW, *On the Way Home*, 97, 101.

22. Roger MacBride to Ursula Nordstrom, November 11, 1963. Roger MacBride to RWL, undated [October–November 1964]. RWL to Roger MacBride, October 29, 1967.

23. Louise H. Mortenson, "Idea Inventory," *Elementary English* 41 (April 1964): 428–29. Mortenson quotes a RWL letter to her of December 31, 1963.

24. RWL to William T. Anderson, June 17, June 30, and July 13, 1966 (courtesy of William T. Anderson). The booklet became his *The Story of the Ingalls*.

20. A Visit to Vietnam

1. RWL to Charles and Joan Clark, January 3, 1951. RWL to Norma Lee Browning, December 7, 1961. RWL to Jasper Crane, February 5, 1965.

2. RWL to Roger MacBride, June 19, and November 8, 1965. RWL to Mrs. Jahnke, April 19, 1966.

3. Unpublished manuscript, "The Background of Vietnam," 16. "Our Correspondent in Saigon," *Woman's Day*, December 1965, 3. Hotel bills and airline itineraries in the Hoover Library date her stay in Vietnam. RWL to Jasper Crane, June 27, and July 13, 1965. Interview with Don Levine, January 12, 1981.

4. Although she had spent July in Vietnam, the article was entitled "August in Vietnam" and appeared in the December 1965 issue of *Woman's Day* (33, 93, 94).

5. "Rose Wilder Lane Tells about Vietnam," *Danbury News-Times*, September 21, 1965.

6. RWL to Susan MacBride, March 20, 1966.

7. Diary, January 28, 1964.

8. RWL to Jasper Crane, October 7, 1956; the idea is repeated in a letter to Merwin K. Hart, January 4, 1961. RWL to Susan MacBride, January 28, 1965.

9. RWL to Jasper Crane, February 14, 1961.

21. Last Journey

1. Diary, October 1, 19, 20, 25, 26, 1965. RWL to Roger MacBride, November 8, 22, 1965. Roger MacBride to RWL, December 9, 1965.

2. RWL to Roger MacBride, November 22, 1965. RWL to Norma Lee Browning, December 7, 1967.

3. RWL to Jasper Crane, November 18, 1966. RWL to Norma Lee Browning, December 7, 1967.

4. RWL to Roger MacBride, March 18, 1967.

5. RWL to Norma Lee Browning, June 12, 1963, and December 7, 1967.

6. RWL to Jasper Crane, April 19, 1966.

7. RWL to Priscilla Slocum, September 2, 1967.

8. RWL to Susan MacBride, May 26, 1963. RWL to Roger MacBride, April 28, 1967, and March 5, 1968. RWL to Priscilla Slocum, September 2, 1967. Undated note [March 1991], William T. Anderson to William Holtz. RWL to Norma Lee Browning, December 7, 1967. William E. Woodward, *The Gift of Life: An Autobiography* (New York: Dutton, 1947), 343.

9. RWL to Norma Lee Browning, December 7, 1967; April 22, 1968. RWL to Roger MacBride, October 14, 1967. Postcard, RWL to Priscilla Slocum, September 30, 1967.

10. RWL to Roger MacBride, March 5, 1968.

11. RWL to Norma Lee Browning, April 22, 1968. RWL to Russell Ogg, May 20, 1968.

12. RWL to Norma Lee Browning, July 29, and August 4, 1968.

13. RWL to Aubrey Sherwood, August 31, 1968. RWL to Susan MacBride, October 10, 1968.

14. Susan Ford Hammaker to William Holtz, October 7, 1990. Undated postcard [September 1968], RWL to Norma Lee Browning.

15. RWL to Norma Lee Browning, August 4, 1968. A postcard now in the Laura Ingalls Wilder Museum in De Smet, addressed to Roger MacBride and dated October 25, 1968, refers to the visit to Dell.

16. Roger MacBride to William Holtz, January 14, 1991.

17. RWL to Roger MacBride, marked "Codicil," August 25, 1968.

18. RWL to Roger MacBride, August 25, 1968, marked "Codicil." Interview with Mary Cappiello, September 20, 1983. Blanche Anderson to Roger MacBride, undated [1968].

19. Roger MacBride to Norma Lee Browning, December 4, 1968. The quotation from Thomas Paine is slightly altered from its original wording in the closing lines to his pamphlet *Agrarian Justice* (1796); Rose had alluded to it in a letter to Jasper Crane of April 19, 1966. For the Greek-island tombstone inscription, see chap. 15, n. 3.

Epilogue: Daughter and Mother

1. Obituaries were carried in the *Danbury News-Times*, October 31, 1968, and the *New York Times*, November 1, 1968. The memorial review by Virginia Scott Miner appeared in the *Kansas City Star*, November 12, 1968. Current information about the Freedom School comes from a letter, Carl Watner to William Holtz, February 25, 1991. Andrew Ward, "The Libertarian Party," *Atlantic* 238 (November 1976).

2. *Newsweek*, July 21, 1980, 26.

3. I have cited Moore's and Anderson's work in chap. 11, n. 6. Donald Zochert, *Laura* (Chicago: Regnery, 1976). Zochert mentioned to Irene Lichty LeCount his suspicion of Rose's heavy hand in her mother's books.

4. The comment was reported to me by William T. Anderson (March 1991).

5. Diary, July 31, 1930.

6. RWL to Garet Garrett, July 8, 1953.

7. Adelaide Neall to George Bye, February 22, 1938. RWL to Clarence Day, April 7, 1928. RWL to George Bye, October 26, 1936.

8. RWL to Jasper Crane, April 20, 1959.

9. The substance of these two paragraphs comes from William Holtz, "Closing the Circle: The American Optimism of Laura Ingalls Wilder," *Great Plains Quarterly* 4 (Spring 1984): 79–90. Henry James, *The American* (1887; reprint New York: Signet, 1963), 87.

10. RWL to George Bye, November 5, 1936. RWL to Herbert Hoover, October 5, 1942.

11. RWL to Jasper Crane, September 9, 1947. She recurs to the idea in later letters: to Crane, October 7, 1956; to Hoover August 30, 1960; and to Frank Meyer, October 23, 1953.

12. RWL, *Woman's Day Book of American Needlework*, 170.

INDEX

Keeley, Mary Paxton, 272, 276, 284, 287, 302,
  308, 309, 316, 323
Krivitsky, Walter, 295–96

LaCava, Madeline, 321
Lane, Claire Gillette: marries Rose Wilder,
  50; life with RWL, 50–59 *passim*, 60, 64,
  65; divorce, 71; remarries, 91; death, 342;
  love for RWL, 343; mentioned, 73, 78, 80,
  113, 153, 249
Lane, Rose Wilder: Albania, love for, 122,
  124, 131, 156, 170, 174, 175, 271, 277, 296;
  alienation, 269–70, 304–5, 364–65, 366–67;
  appearance, 1, 8, 44, 141, 145, 265, 340;
  borrowing money, 65, 134, 176, 196, 252,
  253, 266, 288, 301; characterizes self as a
  girl, 61; cheerfulness, 96, 173–74, 180–81,
  291, 341, 347; dogs, love for, 197, 240–41,
  322, 324, 339; domestic impulses, 151–52,
  186–87, 343, 348; dream-vision, 23, 107;
  eccentricity in later years, 305; education,
  25, 30–33, 36–38, 42–44; ill health, 99, 117,
  124, 125–26, 194, 195, 199, 247–48, 249, 257,
  313, 323, 368; intellectual development,
  47, 72–74; introspective life, 105–6, 111,
  114–15, 125, 140, 151, 171–73, 183–84, 187,
  241, 252, 301, 324, 341; as Lady Bountiful,
  289, 314; Mansfield gossip regarding, 151,
  199–200, 241, 336–37, 374; metaphysical
  angst, 133, 147, 191–92, 229–30, 257–58; as
  "mother" to three sons, 265–66; mystical
  moment in Tiflis, 130, 153, 179, 258, 281;
  parents, relations with, 9, 21, 33–34, 155,
  221, 237–39, 335; as raconteur, 8, 9, 10, 340;
  romances, 42–44, 47–48, 77–78, 96–110 *passim*, 144–49, 151–52, 160, 185
—Opinions on: Americans, 98, 130; coddling of children, 302; Communists and
  Communism, 87, 222, 261, 263, 270, 295,
  308, 309, 318, 325–26, 330, 355, 357–60; compulsory military training, 321–22; conservative movement, 345; curiosity, 234; the
  Depression, 217–18, 222, 229, 230–31, 262,
  273, 365, 377; education, 265–66; Europe,
  modernization of, 165; the fall of Paris,
  300; the gold standard, 29–30; happiness,
  162; Herbert Hoover, 193–94, 246; houses,
  246, 272, 283–84; individualism, 9; Islam,
  147; Jews, 189, 294, 300, 330–32, 360; life as
  struggle, 233–35; love, 160; marriage, 44–
  45, 52, 55–57, 60, 73, 76–78, 182–83, 190,
  343, 363, 370; ordinary people, 234, 236, 314,
  345; personal credo, 84; personal freedom,
  9; political and economic principles, 10–
  11, 197, 246–47, 261, 267–68, 287–88, 294–
  96, 315–21, 326–36, 346–47, 355–56, 360–61;
  political assassination, 170, 271, 344–45;

political terminology, 345; presidents,
  344; propriety, 146; rationing in wartime,
  315–16, 322; religion, 26, 327; Roosevelt,
  Franklin D., 246, 257; racial issues, 315;
  smoking, 72; Social Security, 316–18; future of U.S., 192, 194, 236, 308–9; values of
  parents' generation, 255–57; Vietnamese
  women, 357; World War II, 299–300
—As writer: awards won, 113, 176; book reviewer, 326, 329; contemporary obscurity,
  1, 11; decline, 285, 291, 301, 303; dedication,
  230; defines great writer, 180; describes
  own mediocrity, 180; draws on parents'
  lives, 269, 313; ghostwriter, 8, 66, 85–86,
  88, 96, 102, 145, 148, 200, 224, 226, 230, 302,
  313, 375, 379–85, 395*n12*; hack writer, 66,
  111, 150; income from writing, 150, 177,
  188, 229, 268–69, 278, 313, 319; letter writer,
  10, 38, 178, 188, 191, 219–20, 221, 225, 326,
  375–76; plans ten-volume novel, 240; pro-
  motes ideas through mother's books, 306–
  7, 351–53
—Works: "The American Revolution, 1939,"
  286–87; "August in Vietnam," 356–58;
  Cindy, 188, 189, 200; "Credo" (*Give Me
  Liberty*), 258, 282, 286, 288, 310; *The Discovery of Freedom*, 310–13, 315, 326, 334, 348,
  349, 373, 375, 377; *Diverging Roads*, 54–55,
  61, 76–77, 83, 157, 166; *Free Land*, 269, 272–
  73, 278, 280–85, 288, 291, 296, 303, 313, 335,
  350, 377; *Henry Ford's Own Story*, 64, 66–
  67; *He Was a Man*, 145, 153, 154; *Hill-Billy*,
  150, 154, 159, 170; *Let the Hurricane Roar*,
  232, 235, 236, 238–39, 240, 241, 245, 247, 253,
  260, 269, 270, 272, 281, 305, 313, 319, 323, 373;
  "Life and Jack London," 68–71; *The Making of Herbert Hoover*, 88, 90–91, 99; *Old
  Home Town*, 39–40, 238, 254–57; *On the Way
  Home* (prologue and epilogue), 12–13,
  13–28 *passim*, 350–51; *Peaks of Shala*, 110,
  115, 132; *The Story of Art Smith*, 64, 66–67;
  *Woman's Day Book of American Needle-
  work*, 348–49

Life
—1886–1905: birthplace, 4; birth, 8, 18; leaves
  DeSmet, South Dakota for Mansfield,
  Missouri, 14–15; childhood in DeSmet,
  17–22, 24–27; possibly starts fire in kitchen,
  21; in Spring Valley, Minnesota, 22–23; in
  Florida, 23–24; return to DeSmet, 24;
  education in DeSmet, 25; winter evenings in cabin, 27, 31–32; childhood in
  Mansfield, 29–42; education in Mansfield, 30–32, 36–38; "Fiskoopo" language,
  31; explores cave, 31; childhood poverty,
  32–33, 35; spell-downs, 33; game called
  "Truth," 35–36; goes to Crowley, Loui-

Roosevelt, Eleanor, 261, 270, 285
Roosevelt, Franklin D., 246, 257, 261, 263, 268, 270, 271, 287–88
Rugg, Harold, 92
Russian Revolution, 73, 80, 87, 158, 226, 308, 325

Salt mines. *See* Wiliczka, Poland
Saluba, 139
San Francisco International Exposition, 63–64
Second Coming, 360–62
Sennholz, Hans F., 10, 346–47
Sherwood, Aubry, 369–70
Shipwreck in Europe (Bard), 189
Sinclair, Upton, 91, 241–42
Smith, Art, 66–67, 340
Spookendyke, 30–31
Spring Valley, Minnesota: Wilders in, 25–26; RWL visits, 235; mentioned, 6, 41
Stalin, Joseph, 340
Stellman, Louis J., 50, 91, 200
Stevens, Doris, 88, 90, 111, 116
Stock Market Crash, 202, 217, 218, 278
Story of Art Smith, The (RWL), 64, 66–67
Story Teller's Story, A (Sherwood Anderson), 189
Strunsky, Anna, 72, 110, 113
Strunsky, Rose, 72, 110
Sue, Eugene, 26, 38

Tarshis, Lorie, 329
Telegraph Hill, 76, 77, 80, 152, 157, 158
Thayer, Eliza Jane Wilder, 41, 42
These Happy Golden Years (LIW), 6, 313, 334
Thirer, Marjorie, 98–99, 100, 102, 103,
Thomas, Lowell, 223–24, 225, 229, 302, 303, 379
Thompson, Dorothy: meets RWL, 104; walks Loire Valley with RWL, 104–5; attends Bal Bullier Mardis Gras, 107; requests advice on marriage, 114; meets RWL in Vienna and Budapest, 118; admired by RWL, 153; meets RWL in Paris, 163; failure of marriage, 180; consoled by RWL, 182–83; plans marriage to Sinclair Lewis, 183–83; RWL worries over Thompson's marriage, 190; Thompson and Josef Bard compared, 193; plagiarized by Dreiser, 200; Thompson and Lewis visited by RWL, 218; visits RWL at Rocky Ridge Farm, 219; Thompson child cared for by RWL, 223; Catherine Brody's book recommended by Thompson, 242; quarrel with Isaac Don Levine, 295–96; advocates youth camps, 302; European perspective, 314; announces memoirs, 341;

death, 342; mentioned, 60, 73, 78, 106, 111, 177, 178, 192, 234, 241, 246, 281, 285, 303, 308, 318, 332, 346, 366
Tighe, Eileen, 302, 340, 354, 355
Tolstoi, Alexandra, 132, 226
Turner, Al: comes to Rocky Ridge Farm, 253–54; sent to Europe by RWL, 272; attends University of Missouri, 276; later career, 276; mentioned, 259, 264, 372
Turner, John: arrives Rocky Ridge Farm, 248–49; life supervised by RWL, 251–52; attends New Mexico Military Institute, 271; sent to Europe by RWL, 272; travels England and Germany, 276; studies at Sorbonne, 288; at loose ends 291–92; breaks with RWL, 297–98; later career, 298; mentioned, 254, 255, 259, 264, 266, 284, 303, 304, 322, 324, 371

Vienna: conditions after World War I, 97–98, 118
Vietnam, chap. 20 *passim*

Wandering Jew: symbolic significance for RWL, 192; mentioned, 26, 38, 46, 51, 84, 146, 154, 157, 179, 191, 233, 240, 258, 263, 360, 361, 365–66, 376
Warsaw: conditions after World War I, 101
Watts, Orval, 346–47
Week of the Demi-Vierges, 95
West from Home (LIW), 373
"What Is This—the Gestapo?" 317–18
White Shadows on the South Seas: RWL works on, 88; as best-seller, 103; mentioned, 116, 220, 223, 323. *See also* O'Brien, Frederick
Wilder, Almanzo James: first homestead, 4, 6; parents, 5; Tree Claim, 6; courtship of LIW, 6; death, 11, 335; diphtheria and paralysis, 19; as drayman, 35; name from Crusaders, 136; learns to drive, 154; as source for *Farmer Boy*, 238; as source for *Free Land*, 272–73; life of disappointments, 281; burial, 338; as writer, 393*n*12; mentioned, 23, 65, 83
Wilder, Angeline, 41
Wilder, Eliza Jane. *See* Thayer, Eliza Jane Wilder
Wilder, James, 41, 391*n*27
Wilder, Laura Ingalls: fame, 1, 2, 334, 335, 373–74; memorabilia, 2; life briefly, 3; parents, 5; marriage, 6; last illness and death, 12, 337; lap desk, 14; hundred-dollar bill, 14, 16, 27; buys Rocky Ridge Farm, 15; birth of daughter, Rose, 18; diphtheria, 19; fire in house, 20; death of second child, 20–21; in Florida, 24; sewing but-

tonholes, 24, 26; plans home at Rocky
Ridge Farm, 27–28; characterized by
RWL, 28, 235, 239, 243–45, 350–51; charac-
terized, 34; recurring dream, 34, 293;
cooks for road builders, 35; called "Mama
Bess," 41; visits RWL in Kansas City, 48;
early aspirations as author, 53, 57; visits
RWL in San Francisco, 64–65; letters
home from San Francisco, 65; writes
McCall's article, 85–86; early children's
poems, 86; hosts party for RWL, 104; on
RWL's absences, 145; writes *Country
Gentleman* articles, 148; hates *He Was a
Man*, 153; visits San Francisco with RWL
and Helen Boylston, 157; attitude toward
money, 155, 243–44; reads RWL travel letter to club, 166; invests in stock market,
169; calls RWL home from Albania, 184;
hosts party for RWL, 186; writes "Pioneer
Girl" manuscript, 220, 253, 263, 384; rebuffs
Catherine Brody, 254; income from books,
263–64, 292, 334, 413*n3*; anger at Corinne
Murray, 264, 265; on the Depression, 273;
Book Week speech, 273–74; proposes collaboration with Berta Hader, 278; self-
esteem as writer, 279; on Ludlow Amendment, 287–88; late prosperity, 292–93;
grateful to RWL, 293; corresponds with
George Bye, 293; pretense of independent authorship, 306; sells Rocky Ridge
Farm, 324, 334; donates manuscripts, 334;
assigns 10 percent of royalties to RWL,
334; manuscripts studied by scholars, 334;
alone at Rocky Ridge Farm, 335; death and
burial, 337–38; movement for memorial,
340; subsequent memorials, 352; mentioned, 2, 4, 8, 33, 83
—Works: *By the Shores of Silver Lake*, 269,
272, 279, 285, 292; *Farmer Boy*, 5, 228, 238–
39, 240, 245; *First Four Years*, 6, 7, 12, 18,
21, 278–79, 313, 314, 349–50, 373, 380; *Little
House in the Big Woods*, 2, 5, 227, 228–29,
238, 239, 274, 352; *Little House on the Prairie*,
253, 273; *Little Town on the Prairie*, 6, 306–7,
334, 380–84; *The Long Winter*, 231, 279, 294,
301–2, 306, 334; *On the Banks of Plum Creek*,
5, 7, 264, 273; *On the Way Home*, 12, 31, 351;
These Happy Golden Years, 6, 313, 334; *West
from Home*, 373
Wiliczka, Poland, 101
Wollenberg, Lucille ("Dee"), 92, 294, 303
Woman's Day Book of American Needlework
(RWL), 348–49
Woolf, Virginia, 1, 10, 188

Yusuf, Elez, 120

Zenobia (Ford Model T), 163–64, 166–67,
174, 177
Zochert, Donald, 374
Zogu, Ahmet, 120–21, 169, 197, 233